3/08

$29.99
B/LINCOLN
Miller, William Lee
President Lincoln : the
duty of a statesman

President Lincoln

President Lincoln

THE DUTY OF A STATESMAN

William Lee Miller

Alfred A. Knopf · New York · 2008

THIS IS A BORZOI BOOK
PUBLISHED BY ALFRED A. KNOPF

Copyright © 2008 by William Lee Miller
All rights reserved. Published in the United States by Alfred A. Knopf,
a division of Random House, Inc., New York,
and in Canada by Random House of Canada Limited, Toronto.
www.aaknopf.com

Knopf, Borzoi Books, and the colophon are
registered trademarks of Random House, Inc.

Library of Congress Cataloging-in-Publication Data
Miller, William Lee.
President Lincoln : the duty of a statesman / by William Lee Miller.—1st ed.
p.   cm.
Includes bibliographical references and index.
ISBN 978-1-4000-4103-9
1. Lincoln, Abraham, 1809–1865.   2. Lincoln, Abraham, 1809–1865—Military leadership.
3. Lincoln, Abraham, 1809–1865—Ethics.   4. Political leadership—United States—
Case studies.   5. Command of troops—Case studies.   6. Presidents—United
States—Biography.   7. United States—Politics and government—1861–1865.
8. United States—History—Civil War, 1861–1865.   9. United States—History—
Civil War, 1861–1865—Moral and ethical aspects.   I. Title.
E457.2.M645 2008
973.7092—dc22   2007015677
[B]

Manufactured in the United States of America
First Edition

For Linda

Double strength this time
for reasons she knows

CONTENTS

Contents

ABOUT THIS BOOK

Statecraft at the highest level is a most exacting human activity, one that presents distinctive moral dilemmas. This book examines the moral performance of Abraham Lincoln in the office of president of the United States. It is therefore indirectly a book about statesmanship and moral choice in the American presidency, through an examination of the conduct of the most remarkable occupant of that office. I wrote an earlier book, *Lincoln's Virtues: An Ethical Biography,* which dealt primarily with Lincoln before he became president. Of course a wit said the next book should be *Lincoln's Vices.* I offer this instead.

There has come to be a huge contradiction in American culture between the stereotyped disdain for "politics" and "politicians" on the one side and the celebration, on the other, of Abraham Lincoln. One intention of this book is to correct the stereotype by examining this exemplary figure. The pages that follow tell episodes in President Lincoln's story, selectively, in a rough chronological order, dealing with themes as appropriate along the way.

In the immense popular legend and endless outpouring of books about Lincoln, his life story and his personality sometimes seem to displace the role and the accomplishments that made his life story worth telling and his personality worth examining. So let us restate the obvious: he earned his place in the pages of history and in the memory of the world by his deeds and words, by the quality of his life as a national leader, between March 4, 1861, and April 14, 1865, while serving in the office of president of the United States.

PART ONE

Honest Abe Among the Rulers

A T NOON on March 4, 1861, the moral situation of Abraham Lincoln of Illinois was abruptly transformed. That morning, arising in the Willard Hotel at 14th Street and Pennsylvania Avenue in downtown Washington, he had been a private citizen, making choices of right and wrong, better and worse, good and evil, as human beings do, in his own right, for himself, by his own lights, as an individual moral agent. That afternoon, standing on the steps of the East Portico of the Capitol, before thirty thousand of his fellow citizens, he became an oath-bound head of state.

Although he had, in the previous two years, rather rapidly ascended from provincial obscurity to a certain national notice, and although he had in the morning the pendulant importance of a president-elect, he was as yet, so far as the law was concerned, one citizen alongside other citizens. At noon on that day he was transformed by the constitutional alchemy into something else—the "executive" of the federal government of the United States, the position that the framers in Philadelphia seventy-four years before had decided to call by the word "president." There immediately settled upon his elongated frame an awesome new battery of powers and an immense new layer of responsibility, obligating, constraining, and empowering him.

In that moment he was lifted to a dizzying new eminence. Before many days had passed the sometime backwoods rail-splitter would find himself sending greetings to his "great and good friend" Her Majesty Doña Isabel II, Queen of Spain; and to his "great and good friend" Her Majesty Victoria, Queen of the United Kingdom of England and Ireland; and to his "great and good friend" His Royal Majesty Francis Joseph I, Emperor of Austria, none of whom, of course, he had ever met.

Perhaps you had not thought of Abraham Lincoln of Little Pigeon Creek, Indiana, addressing as his great and good friend "His Imperial

Majesty Napoleon III, Emperor of the French," or "His Majesty Alexander II, Emperor and Autocrat of all the Russias," or "His Majesty Leopold, King of the Belgians." But he did. In the years to come there would be many such messages. They would be drafted, to be sure, in the State Department with Secretary of State Seward's name below that of the president, and they would be composed in diplomatic formulae of the utmost insincerity, compared to which U.S. senators calling each other "distinguished" is a beacon of truthfulness. But they would be signed by "your good friend" Abraham Lincoln, and sent to royal highnesses and imperial majesties and grand dukes and princes and queens and kings and an occasional president and at least one tycoon and one viceroy. The messages would express the president's alleged delight with the marriage of a royal niece or the safe delivery of a prince, his supposedly deep sympathy at the melancholy tidings of the decease of a late majesty or the passing of a well-beloved royal cousin, his putative best wishes that a reign might be happy and prosperous. Abraham Lincoln was now a member of this exclusive worldwide circle; he had become, in the pompous formality of international diplomacy, the quite unlikely equal and "friend" of these august personages around the world because, like them, he was now a head of state.

One can imagine that the lofty figures in high politics in Europe and around the world would find this new American leader a puzzle. He had no family heritage, no education, no languages, no exposure to the great world outside his own country, and he did not know that he should not wear black gloves to the opera. He was not accustomed to ordering people about. He did not insist on deference and did not receive much. He had never been in command of anything except a straggling company of volunteers in the state militia when he was twenty-three, who, it was reported, when he issued his first command told him to go to hell. His only service in national government had been one short and not impressive term as a congressman eleven years earlier. He had not been the "executive" of anything more than a two-man law firm; he had never in his life fired or dismissed anyone. One knew, because his party's campaign had insisted upon it, that he had once upon a time split some rails, but rail splitting was scarcely a qualification for the role into which he entered in March 1861. He memorized and recited reams of poetry, mostly of a wistful-melancholy sort, which might make one wonder about his grip on practicality. He was reportedly a constant teller of humorous stories, and a man in whom humor was neither incidental nor decorative but integral, in a way that perhaps an emperor might believe should be left to the jester. Would he, on coming into ultimate responsibility, like Shakespeare's Prince Hal, turn on his own inner Falstaff and say, *I know thee not, old man?* Or would he keep on telling jokes?

The characteristics that would lead his stepmother and his law partner and his friends to call him an unusually good, kind, conscientious man might have added to the world rulers' bewilderment, had they known about them. His friends had given him the sobriquet Honest Abe, which might indicate a handicap at the highest level of politics, where a certain amount of patriotic lying is usually thought to be required. Those in Illinois who knew him before he became president said he was an unusually generous human being. He was reported to have more sympathy with the suffering of his fellow creatures than was really advantageous in a ruler—not only for lost cats, mired-down hogs, birds fallen out of the nest, but also for his fellow human beings. Stories were told of his springing to the defense of an old Indian who wandered into camp during the Black Hawk War and whom his company wanted to shoot. But a national leader must deal in the hundreds and the thousands and in the realities of the world as it is.

The great mentors of statecraft would say that there are many human beings who may be filled to the brim with *personal* moral graces but who in spite of that—actually they might say *because* of that—would not make great statesmen. Great command may require actions that would be morally objectionable if done in a personal capacity and foreclose many acts that are possible in a private capacity.

A great captain, a ruler, a prince (so the mentors of rulers would say) needs to command and instill respect. It would be written that "one ought to be both feared and loved, but as it is difficult for the two to go together, it is much safer to be feared than loved."

But this new American leader was showing a quite perverse disinclination to make himself feared. He did not mark down the names of those who had not supported him, or nurse grudges, or hold resentments, or retaliate against "enemies"—indeed, he tried not to have enemies, not to "plant thorns." He had gracefully waited his turn in the competition with two others for the nomination for U.S. congressman from his district, and he had gone out of his way to tell his followers not to blame one rival for a whispering campaign against him. Although he had twice been defeated for the post he really wanted—senator from Illinois—and although those two contests left scars and resentments among his supporters, despite his deep disappointment, they did not leave scars and resentments in him; he would work amiably and productively with men who had blocked him. He had turned around and invited his four chief rivals for his party's nomination to serve with him in his cabinet. The question might have been asked about him, Is he too lacking in the assertion of will and the ruthlessness that the exercise of great power is said to require to serve as a commander and a head of state in a giant war? Should not tenderheartedness be reserved to those who do not propose to exercise ultimate authority? Magnanimity, in Aristotle, is a virtue of the high-souled aristocrat, a noble condescending from his secure aboveness to exhibit his liberality; this man seemed to have presumed to exercise magnanimity without having an ounce of noble blood.

A great commander is not supposed to be amiably self-deprecating, continually using the word "humble" to describe himself and his background, and insisting that others could do the work of commanding as well as, or better than, he. (One was not sure that this man really believed that, but he said it more than once.) He did not seem unduly pious, and rumor had it that in his youth he had produced a critical paper about religion so scandalous that his friends burned it—but one might occasionally suspect there was a hint, in his deeds and his words, of the utterly impractical parts of that religion common to most of the new great and good friends on both sides of the Atlantic, the religion that was invoked in the closing lines of those formulaic international communications with his sudden new friends. This was the religion into which those royal nieces had been brought by sacred baptism, and by which those archduchesses had entered into holy matrimony, and in which the sadly departed majesties had been buried. But surely those ceremonial exercises were all the religion one needed as a practitioner of statecraft at the highest level, along with, of course, God's support for one's own side in any warfare. Other elements, about blessed meekness and blessed peacemaking and loving neighbors and other-cheek-turning and extra-mile-walking, and particularly about forgiveness and judging not that one be not judged—surely those should be confined to the monastery or at most to private life.

If his new "friends" or their advisers had read again the central chapters of Machiavelli's *The Prince,* and if they had then learned more about this new American leader, they would surely have said: *This man will never do.*

CHAPTER ONE

A Solemn Oath Registered in Heaven

TWO PRESIDENTS

LATE IN THE MORNING of Inauguration Day in 1861, the fifteenth president of the United States, James Buchanan, in the last hours of his presidency, was signing bills that Congress had passed in its usual last-minute flurry when his secretary of war, Joseph Holt, came to him with a spectacularly ill-timed message. Major Robert Anderson, the Union army commander at the imperiled Fort Sumter in the harbor of Charleston, South Carolina, had suddenly expressed doubts that he could retain possession of the fort. His supplies would soon be exhausted, but providing sufficient reinforcements would require no fewer than twenty thousand "good and well disciplined men." Buchanan and Holt knew that no such force was available. Fort Sumter would therefore no doubt have to be surrendered, and that key symbol of Union resolve would be lost. The surrender, however, would now be the deed not of the Buchanan presidency but of the next.

His successor, waiting in the Willard Hotel, did not appear to have been as well prepared as President Buchanan had been for the demands of statecraft at the highest level. Buchanan had already been a member of the Pennsylvania state legislature when this new man had been a barefoot lad making his way with his sister through the Kentucky woods to a one-room schoolhouse. Buchanan had been an important member of Congress and chairman of the Judiciary Committee when young Lincoln, by his own later description, had been a "strange, penniless, uneducated, friendless boy working on a raft for ten dollars a month." When out in a frontier village of three hundred souls young Lincoln made his first venture into politics, and on the second try managed to be elected to the lower house of the legislature of his prairie state, and borrowed sixty dollars to buy a new suit in which he made his way to Vandalia, Illinois—Buchanan was making his way to the court in St. Petersburg as minister of the United States to Russia, where he would negotiate an important commercial treaty. While Lincoln served in the lower house of a distant western state legislature, Buchanan was an important U.S. senator. When Lincoln, in his third try, obtained the Whig nomination to a congressional seat, and finally appeared briefly in national politics for his one term in Congress, and had as a freshman member rather presumptuously attacked President James K. Polk about the Mexican War, Buchanan had been serving as secretary of state in the cabinet of the president that young congressman Lincoln was attacking. Buchanan had in 1848 been a serious candidate for his party's nomination for president of the United States, while Congressman Lincoln, even though an early supporter of the winning candidate Zachary Taylor, was unable to get any satisfactory appointment from the Taylor administration and had to subside into comparative obscurity.

When in 1853 the Democrats came back into power, the eminent party statesman James Buchanan was given the most important diplomatic post, minister to Great Britain, and in 1856 his impressive public career reached its climax as he was nominated and elected president of the United States. Buchanan was, by measure of offices previously held, one of the best-qualified men ever to be elected president. The Illinois lawyer, meanwhile, had for eleven years never held political office again after his one term in Congress. If the measure be a formal one of offices held, then on the day the executive authority in the U.S. government passed from James Buchanan to Abraham Lincoln, it passed from one of the most experienced hands in American political history to one of the least experienced.

But simply holding lesser offices is not all one needs in order to prepare for supreme national leadership. A fool or knave can rise through many eminent positions and still be a fool or knave. A thoughtful person can gain wisdom from the daily round of ordinary life; a superficial person can learn little from commanding armies or being king. It depends upon what happens in the depths of one's mind and inner being while one fills those roles, whether high or low. Had all those places he had filled left a deposit of profound understanding in James Buchanan?

PRESIDENT BUCHANAN on entering the White House four years earlier had asserted in his inaugural address, on March 4, 1857:

> What a happy conception then was it for Congress to apply this simple rule—that the will of the majority shall govern—to the settlement of the

question of domestic slavery in the Territories! . . . A difference of opinion has arisen . . . This is, happily, a matter of but little practical importance . . . it . . . legitimately belongs to the Supreme Court . . . To their decision, in common with all good citizens, I shall cheerfully submit.

Cheerful submission had not been the prevailing response to the Dred Scott decision, which held that slavery could not be prohibited in the territories and that the black man had no rights that the white man need respect. Then, with the worst economic panic in twenty years in 1857, and the worst corruption of any administration thus far in American history, and the worst split in a major party when the Douglas Democrats opposed a president of their own party over a proslavery constitution for Kansas, President Buchanan's four years had not been a happy time.

ON THIS INAUGURATION DAY the unusually tall president-elect unfolded himself and unfolded his manuscript, adjusted his glasses, and either did or did not look around for a place to put his hat, and Senator Stephen A. Douglas either did or did not take and hold the hat during Lincoln's address.

We may picture James Buchanan, at that moment still President Buchanan, sitting behind him, listening, perhaps tilting his large head to the side as he was wont to do, to the man who would shortly become his successor. Buchanan might already have begun to formulate the defensive claim with which he would occupy the rest of his life: that what this man was saying was not really all that different from what he had already himself maintained.

Buchanan had said these things especially in his last annual message, read to the opening of Congress on the previous December 3, after the Election Day victory of the Republicans in November. And then after South Carolina had passed its ordinance of secession on December 20, and other cotton states had followed suit, he had continued his argument in messages to Congress on January 8 and 28. Whereas Lincoln was now saying, "The Union of these states is perpetual . . . no government proper ever had provision in its organic law for its own termination," he, Buchanan, the supposedly discredited president now on the way out, had said in almost the same language, "The Union of these states was designed to be perpetual . . . Its framers never intended the absurdity of providing for its own destruction." Where Lincoln was now saying, "No state upon its own mere motion can lawfully get out of the Union," he, Buchanan, had already said that "no state has a right upon its own act to secede from the Union." He, Buchanan, had contributed to the argument a metaphor better than any literary touch in these pages of Lincoln's address, when he had written back in December that an assertion that the federal government is a mere voluntary association, to be dissolved at pleasure, would make it "a rope of sand."

In this newcomer's careful statements of what he would do, and refrain from doing, as president, Buchanan again might have heard an echo of his own position. Lincoln said, "I shall take care that the laws . . . shall be faithfully executed," a passage, as both presidents and many in the audience would know, taken directly from a clause in the Constitution. Buchanan, for his part, had said, "My province is to execute the laws." If Lincoln now said that the power confided in him would be used "to hold, occupy, and possess the property belonging to the government," Buchanan had said, "It is my duty at all times to defend and protect the public property." And if Buchanan had added "as far as this may be practicable," then he might notice that Lincoln too had said "so far as practicable." And the gentle pleas and firm cautions, the appeals to patience and to time, and the reassurances that the federal government would not be the aggressor—all these that the vast listening crowd heard from the president-elect—all had parallels, in Buchanan's mind, in his own messages. Buchanan had said—as Lincoln now said—that Lincoln's election as president had been in "strict conformity to the Constitution" and provided no just cause for revolution. In his retirement in Pennsylvania, as a mammoth civil war unfolded, Buchanan would spend his last days writing a defense of his presidency, and part of his defense would be that he and the man chosen to succeed him had, on these points, no serious differences.

To OTHERS IN THE AUDIENCE on March 4, 1861, the suggestion that there was an overlapping between the ideas of the two presidents would seem preposterous. The young assistant that Lincoln had brought with him from Illinois—John G. Nicolay, who at that moment was the new president's entire staff—would write, many years later, of that annual message composed by President Buchanan and presented to Congress the previous December: "As a specimen of absurdity, stupidity, and willful wrongheadedness, this message is not equaled in American political literature."

Before he rejected secession, in terms that might be compared to Lincoln's, Buchanan had already vitiated the effect of doing so by blaming the entire crisis on "the long continued and intemperate interference of the Northern people with the question of slavery in the Southern states." And if this president had thus identified the cause of the current troubles, he had also therefore the solution to them: all the antislavery agitation should stop. "All for which the slave states have ever contended," Buchanan maintained, "is to be let alone and permitted to manage their domestic institutions in their own way."

The new president had never said, and would never say, anything like Buchanan's inflammatory condemnation of the antislavery movement. On the contrary, he had a long record of opposition to slavery: his record, and his party's position, were the reasons the seven slave states had rebelled. Now that he was about to become president, he gave an inaugural address, it is true, that would be a severe disappointment to abolitionists. He was undertaking an overwhelming new obligation: he was sworn to preserve the Union. His preoccupation had to be keeping as much of the Union behind him as he could, including the eight slave states that had not joined the rebellion, and conservative Northerners.

So Lincoln in his address would start right off affirming his obligation to enforce the Fugitive Slave Law, even reading it and insisting it would be as enforced as any other part of the Constitution. He would not only reiterate his pledge, the Republican Party's pledge, not to interfere with slavery in the slave states, he would even include a last-minute insertion acquiescing in a proposed irrevocable amendment that prohibited that interference forever, which had just at four that morning passed in the Senate. Lincoln said he had not read this proposed amendment, and he said also that he understood that it represented no change from the prevailing constitutional situation; nevertheless this casual half endorsement was another shock to the antislavery forces. Frederick Douglass's response to the whole address would be deep disappointment. He had had hopes for Lincoln, but he wrote in his monthly magazine that Lincoln's address showed him to be no better than Buchanan. But Lincoln was decisively better than Buchanan, for all the concessions he had to make in his address. He made no analysis of the causes or the cure of the current troubles that remotely resembled that of Buchanan. He certainly did not blame the crisis on the abolitionists. And he put down an antislavery marker in just one sentence.

One section of our country believes slavery is right and ought to be extended, while the other believes it is wrong, and ought not to be extended. This is the only substantial dispute.

That was Lincoln's only mention of the moral wrong of slavery in this address—but it was enough to make clear a profound difference from his predecessor and to be a harbinger.

Lincoln's endorsements of the constitutional provisions about slavery were concessions out of reluctant obligation and the political necessity of his new position and the perilous moment; Buchanan's on the other hand sprang from his own manifest conviction.

The passages in Buchanan's messages that insisted (as Lincoln would) on the perpetuity of the Union and the illegitimacy of secession (making the Union a mere rope of sand) were further vitiated by the practical non-applications that followed them. Even though he said a state had no right to secede, the Union, said Buchanan, had no right to "coerce" a state to remain in the Union. A president could not act; he would have to refer an incipient rebellion to Congress—but then it appeared that Congress could not act either. It had no power, said President Buchanan, to make use of military might to "coerce a state by force or arms to remain in the Union." William Seward gave what would become a famous witty summary of the position Buchanan had put forth: "[He] shows conclusively that it is the duty of the president to execute the laws—unless somebody opposes him; and that no state has a right to go out of the Union—unless it wants to."

Lincoln's rigorous argument against secession was certainly not under-cut by any such sudden attacks of impotence. His defense of the integrity of the Union was not put forward as an abstract exercise in constitutional explication without regard to practice, but was the philosophical ground for action. Although his address was as conciliatory as his conviction allowed, and a reasoned effort at persuasion with his "dissatisfied country-men," it was nevertheless implicitly clear that, should they persist, force would be used to prevent their seceding, and that the oath-bound presi-dent would be the one to use it. Lincoln's concept of his presidential office did not begin with the modifier "mere." It began instead with his sworn duty to "take care" that the laws be faithfully executed in the states—in *all* the states, as he would emphasize—and with the obligation to preserve the government to which he would swear in the oath.

Where Buchanan had sought avoidance and found restriction and therefore excuse, this new president would accept responsibility and find necessity and therefore empowerment.

WHEN AFTER THE INAUGURAL EVENTS President Lincoln and Citizen Buchanan, their extremely limited association about to draw to a close, were escorted to the president's room in the Capitol, they had an exchange overheard by the young Illinoisan who was to join Nicolay on Lincoln's staff, John Hay. "The courteous old gentleman took the new President aside for some parting words into the corner where I was standing," Hay would write. "I waited with boyish wonder and credulity to see what momentous counsels were to come from that gray and weatherbeaten head. Every word must have its value at such an instant."

And so what in this pivotal moment in American history did John Hay hear the outgoing president tell his successor? "The ex-President said: 'I think you will find the water of the right-hand well at the White-House better than that at the left,' and went on with many intimate details of the kitchen and pantry."

As the two presidents ended their brief time together, Buchanan wished the new president happiness:

> [W]hile the battery on the brow of the hill thundered its salute, citizen Buchanan and President Lincoln returned to their carriage, and the military procession escorted them from the Capitol to the Executive Mansion on the threshold of which Mr. Buchanan warmly shook the hand of his successor, with cordial good wishes for his personal happiness and the national place and prosperity.

Citizen Buchanan, instead of spending the evening drinking Madeira and enjoying his freedom, was distressed enough by that undigested last-minute letter from Major Anderson to gather members of his not-quite-out-of-office cabinet that evening, and again the next morning at the War Department, to go over a presentation of the matter to the new president. Their deliberations would be set forth in a letter signed and delivered by Secretary of War Joseph Holt, who would stay on briefly into the new administration.

Finally, at midday on March 5, Buchanan, the only bachelor so far to have served as the nation's president, made his way alone back to his home in Pennsylvania.

PILED HIGH WITH DIFFICULTY

IF THE NEW MAN had no long list of offices held, he certainly did have a virtuous regard for his responsibilities. And no American president, before or since, would face the exacting responsibilities that now confronted Lincoln. His election in November had been the trip wire for catastrophe.

South Carolina's convention, on December 20, with impudent promptness and without a dissenting vote, had passed an ordinance of secession, declared itself an independent republic, and celebrated with fireworks in Charleston. Now the long-threatened act of a state seceding from the Union was actually to be put to the test.

A split screen showing the events that followed in the six weeks before Lincoln took the train for Washington would display scenes from three locations: in Springfield, Lincoln coping with office-seekers, reporters, and visiting politicians, shaping his cabinet, and writing letters to Republicans in Congress saying, "Let there be no compromise on the question of extending slavery"; in Washington, congressmen and senators scrambling to make some kind of Union-saving compromise, forming committees; in the Deep South, swift takeovers of federal forts, arsenals, customhouses, and U.S. mints. Then in January, one after another, conventions in the other deepest Southern cotton states voted to secede: Mississippi on January 9, Florida on January 10, Alabama on January 11, Georgia on January 19, Louisiana on January 26.

On January 27 Lincoln requested "utmost privacy" and no more visitors before his departure on February 11. He locked himself "in a room upstairs over a store across the street from the State House" and in "the unromantic surroundings of a dingy and neglected back room," with the short list of readings he had asked for, composed the draft of the first words he would speak to the whole nation, his First Inaugural Address. Lincoln wrote out his reasons why this Union was perpetual—from the nature of government everywhere and from the particular history of this nation. He stated, in a ringing paragraph, the conclusion applicable to the events that were taking place as he wrote: "It follows from these views that no state, upon its own motion, can lawfully get out of the Union—that resolves and ordinances to that effect are legally nothing." (Seward in Washington would persuade him to change that last word to the more lawyerly word "void.")

On February 2, as Texas was becoming the seventh state to proclaim its withdrawal from the Union, Lincoln was writing to a journalist that he had "the document already blocked out," but that given "rapidly changing scenes" he would now hold it and revise it nearer delivery time. When we look at what Lincoln was writing alongside what the rebels were proclaiming, we find a radical contrast. The passionate secessionist statements were filled with fury; Lincoln's address was, for the most part, a carefully reasoned effort at persuasion. The overwhelming preoccupations of the secessionist declarations were slavery and race, and the alleged mistreatment of the South by the North; Lincoln's argument dealt with the nature of government and the perpetuity of the Union.

Mississippi's declaration of the "Immediate Causes which Induce and Justify the Secession" certainly made clear what the coming war would really be about:

> Our position is thoroughly identified with the institution of slavery—the greatest material interest of the world. Its labor supplies the product which constitutes by far the largest and most important portions of commerce of the earth. These products are peculiar to the climate verging on the tropical regions, and by an imperious law of nature, none but the black race can bear exposure to the tropical sun . . . A blow at slavery is a blow at commerce and civilization . . . There was no choice left us but submission to the mandates of abolition, or a dissolution of the Union . . . Utter subjugation awaits us in the Union, if we should consent longer to remain in it. It is not a matter of choice, but of necessity. We must either submit to degradation, and to the loss of property worth four billions of money, or we must secede from the Union.

The proclamation by the Texas convention was quite explicitly racist:

> We hold as undeniable truths that the governments of the various States, and of the confederacy itself, were established exclusively by the white race . . . That the African race had no agency in their establishment; that they were rightfully held and regarded as an inferior and dependent race . . . That in this free government all white men are and of right ought to be entitled to equal civil and political rights; that the servitude of the African race, as existing in these States, is mutually beneficial to both bond and free, and is abundantly authorized and justified by the experience of mankind, and the revealed will of the Almighty Creator, as recognized by all Christian nations.

While these and the other five first rebel states were making similar proclamations, Lincoln was writing a rigorous argument against what they were doing. His draft dealt not with slavery or race but with secession and union. He argued that the acts of violence taken, in the name of these legally nonexistent entities, against the installations and activities of the United States—the taking over of forts, mints, and armories; the interference with the mail; the firing on the *Star of the West,* sent to Fort Sumter with provisions; the threats to both Sumter and Fort Pickens—were, "according to circumstances," either "insurrectionary or treasonable." At the end of his draft he made clear that the choice of war or peace was in the hands of the rebels: "With you, not with me, rests the solemn issue: Shall it be peace or the sword?"

Perhaps more concretely shocking to the sensibilities of Unionists than the formal votes to secede had been those seizures of federal facilities that had preceded them, in a rapid series of snatchings in nine days, possibly by conspiratorial design. On January 3, 1861, Fort Pulaski in Georgia. Then the federal barracks in Baton Rouge; Forts Jackson and St. Philip in Louisiana; Fort Morgan in Alabama; and on January 12 the federal navy yard and Fort Barrancas in Pensacola, seized by Florida and Alabama troops. More seizures followed in February—nineteen federal army posts in Texas were taken in one fell swoop before the Texas ordinance of secession. Arsenals, post offices, customhouses, and hospitals were taken over. So was the U.S. mint in New Orleans. Lincoln himself would later make this summary: "[W]ithin these states, all the Forts, Arsenals, Dock-yards, Custom-houses, and the like, including the movable and stationary property in, and about them, had been seized, and were held in open hostility to this Government."* The authority of the U.S. government in the seven seceded states was forced altogether out to the edges and reduced essentially to two places, hanging by a thread: Fort Pickens in Pensacola Bay and Fort Sumter in Charleston Harbor.

Here is a sample of a rebel takeover of a federal facility. At "10 1/2 a.m. o'clock" on December 30—just ten days after South Carolina's secession fireworks, before any other state seceded, and weeks before the Confederate government was formed—a Colonel John Cunningham in the South Carolina infantry sent this message to Captain F. C. Humphreys, the military storekeeper for ordinance at the U.S. Arsenal in Charleston:

> SIR: I herewith demand an immediate surrender of the U.S. Arsenal at this place and under your charge, and a delivery to me of the keys and contents of the arsenals, magazines, &c. I am already proceeding to occupy it with a strong armed detachment of troops. I make the demand in the name of the State of South Carolina, and by virtue of an order from its governor, a copy of which is inclosed.

*Message to the special session of Congress, July 4, 1861.

Captain Humphreys was forced by his circumstance to make the following reply.

> SIR: I am constrained to comply with your demand for the surrender of this arsenal, from the fact that I have no force for its defense. I do so, however, solemnly protesting against the illegality of this measure in the name of my Government. I also demand, as a right, that I be allowed to salute my flag, before lowering it, with one gun for each state now in the Union (32).

It is significant that Captain Humphreys specified the number of guns, for the number of states, in the salute to his flag. There had been thirty-three states in the Union when December began. Each state now in the Union; no salute for South Carolina.*

THE BETTER ANGELS OF OUR NATURE

As LINCOLN GAVE his address on March 4, the outgoing president would know, but the incoming president would not yet know, that even Fort Sumter, that most potent remaining symbol of the Union's integrity, was now in peril.

Senator Seward—as he still was on that day in March 1861, Senator William H. Seward of New York, on the Senate Committee on Arrangements, sitting on the platform—must have been another who listened to the newcomer's inaugural address with a maelstrom of emotions. On the one hand, he was incomparably more experienced and well prepared than this man, and but for the accidents of "availability," he would himself be delivering this address. On the other hand, he still at that point assumed, as much of the political world assumed, that he would nevertheless be the dominant figure, the prime minister, in this first Republican administration. Much that had happened in his relationship to the president-elect might seem to confirm that expectation. While Lincoln had been out in Springfield coping with office-seekers and reporters and writing his speech, Seward had been in Washington, in the Senate, playing the central

---

*There would be thirty-four girls in white dresses in the inaugural parade on March 4 because the supposedly seceded states were all included and Kansas had been admitted on January 29, 1861.

role in crafting the Republican Party response as the string of Deep South states claimed to take themselves out of the Union. Seward, once a prime spokesman for antislavery reformers, now became a prime conciliator, writing letters to keep Lincoln informed. When Lincoln began appointing his cabinet, his first offer was to Seward, proposing to make him secretary of state, and after a brief consideration, Seward accepted. Secretaries of state had often been key figures in government, sometimes as important as their presidents. So it seemed to many—including Seward himself—it would be now.

When Lincoln named the rest of his cabinet, however, it was by no means the cabinet Seward would have chosen, and in particular it included one of his rivals for the nomination, the Radical Republican leader Salmon Chase of Ohio. Seward, perhaps assuming that his importance gave him leverage, just two days before the inauguration sent Lincoln a brief note asking "leave to withdraw" from his acceptance of the office of secretary of state. The reports that Seward was unhappy with the appointment of Chase swirled through the capital city, and presumably Seward expected Lincoln to drop Chase in order to keep his indispensable self in the administration. But Lincoln did not do this. He was already showing small signs that perhaps he would not be as dependent on Seward as many, including Seward, expected. He had long since shown that he had the elementary political skill to measure power relations. On inauguration morning itself, while the procession was forming, Lincoln remarked to Nicolay, "I can't let Seward take the first trick," and handed him a note to Seward asking him to withdraw his withdrawal. "The public interest, I think, demands that you should; and my personal feelings are deeply inlisted in the same direction." Perhaps Seward had this note in his pocket as he listened to the inaugural address. After the ceremony the two men would confer, and Seward would stay.

As he listened to the address, Seward no doubt could hear many effects of his own suggestions. When President-elect Lincoln had arrived at the train station in Washington at six in the morning on February 23, after an embarrassing but perhaps necessary secret trip from Philadelphia through strife-torn Baltimore under dark of night, Seward had had breakfast with him at the hotel and taken him to dinner at his house in the evening. During that day Lincoln gave Seward one of the dozen copies printed in Springfield of the draft of his inaugural address, and Seward came to the hotel the evening of the next day, Sunday, February 24, with extensive proposed changes. Lincoln adopted many of them, the most important a revised ending that would one day carve itself into the national memory.

There cannot be much doubt that, at least with respect to that ending, Seward's proposals led to a distinct improvement. In Lincoln's original paragraph, the string of italicized contrasts between *you* and *me* went on too long and made the contrast too insistent. Seward, in line with his general purpose to make the address more conciliatory to the South, scribbled some words for two proposed alternative endings.

Working in the Willard Hotel under the intense pressures of the last week before he became president, Lincoln took one set of phrases Seward had written on the back of page four of his worked-over copy and transformed them by the alchemy of his editing from dross to gold. Seward had proposed starting the final paragraph by saying, "I close." Lincoln gave it emotional power by making it, "I am loath to close." Seward had dashed off an unedited longer sentence, "We are not we must not be aliens or enemies but countrymen and brethren." Lincoln broke that into two short sentences with punch: "We are not enemies, but friends. We must not be enemies." Lincoln did the same with Seward's effort to say that passion has strained but must not break our bonds of affection. Lincoln cut it, shortened it, picked up Seward's last words and dropped the others, added a few words of his own—and made it sing. Lincoln had picked up a phrase, and a metaphor, that Seward had written about "mystic chords," and other phrases that Seward wrote but marked out: "touched as they surely" and "better angel." Lincoln made the angels plural and made the mystic chords into mystic chords of memory, and he put together a beautiful flowing last sentence that was not there in Seward's notes. As Joshua Shenk has observed, Lincoln made one key change that was not only rhetorical but also substantive. Seward had had mystic chords breathed upon by "the guardian angel of the nation," a phrase of banal familiarity. He had written but marked out, above the line, the alternative, "better angel." Lincoln took that better angel—one angel contrasted to another—made him plural, and moved him from floating vaguely over "the nation" to engaging in struggle within ourselves—"the better angels of our nature"—a different idea altogether. The paragraph that Lincoln wrought out of Seward's proposal was not simply a rhetorical, literary, and political improvement, although it was all of those; it also gave a first glimpse of a profound moral imagination. It became something new, an echo of Seward's words in a higher register. One may imagine Seward, sitting on the platform, listening with some mixture of pride, envy, regret, and astonishment as he hears the man who is going to be president in his stead speak some words that are partly his and yet altogether this other man's.

> I am loath to close. We are not enemies, but friends. We must not be ene-
> mies. Though passion may have strained, it must not break our bonds of
> affection. The mystic chords of memory, stretching from every battle-
> field, and patriot grave, to every living heart and hearthstone, all over this
> broad land, will yet swell the chorus of the Union, when again touched,
> as surely they will be, by the better angels of our nature.

HE'S ALL RIGHT

THE REACTION TO Lincoln's address corresponded generally, although not entirely, to the nation's sectional, partisan, and ideological divisions: secessionists were outraged and contemptuous; Democrats were mixed; abolitionists were deeply disappointed; Republicans were mostly impressed.

Frederick Douglass would write sadly that it was "little better than our worst fears." The next four years would be a political education not only for Abraham Lincoln but also for Frederick Douglass.

Scholars at a later time, with the advantage (or perhaps disadvantage) of having seen Lincoln's first draft, would have a line of commentary that faulted the address in a way listeners at the time were not equipped to do, claiming it lost altitude from what he had written in Springfield. The distinguished twentieth-century historian David Potter goes through the four areas in which the limited federal government of the time would make its power felt within the states, providing this striking summary of how, in the address as he gave it, Lincoln drew back from each of them:

> This, then, was the much vaunted "firm" policy of Lincoln. He would
> assert the Federal authority vigorously—but he would not exercise it. He
> would enforce the laws—where an enforcement mechanism existed. He
> would deliver the mails—unless repelled. He would collect the duties—
> offshore. He would hold the forts—at least the ones which Buchanan had
> held, and which seemed capable of holding themselves.

Reading that paragraph, one may get a reminiscent whiff of that witty summary, quoted above, that Seward made of Buchanan's position. But on consideration one sees that Lincoln's position, for all the restraint, differed at its core; where Buchanan was making close distinctions in order to avoid responsibility, Lincoln was making close distinctions in order to exercise it.

Harry Jaffa, after quoting that stark paragraph from Potter, gives part of the answer to it:

> This commentary certainly highlights the genuine ambiguity in Lincoln's text. But it hardly suggests the practical wisdom in that ambiguity. Of course Lincoln would not, because he could not, enforce the laws where no enforcement mechanism existed . . . When we remember how militarily weak the Union government was at that moment, Lincoln's speech, notwithstanding its ambiguities, is remarkably bold. He makes no concession, either theoretical or practical, to the idea of any constitutional right of secession.

He not only makes no concession; he makes a thorough and fundamental argument rejecting any such claimed right, either in governments in general or in the United States in particular. But that is not the most important immediate point; as we have seen, even Buchanan rejected secession theoretically. The immediate question was: What is this new president going to do? And on that point he was indeed very careful—as he should have been—but still quite different from Buchanan.

Having an inadequate military force—only about seventeen thousand troops scattered in western posts—was not the primary justification for what critics call the ambiguity in Lincoln's address. Even if he had had a much larger army, it would still not have been wise to deliver the address as he had written it in Springfield. Historian David Herbert Donald asserts:

> That draft . . . was a no-nonsense document; it declared that the Union was indestructible, that secession was illegal, and that he intended to enforce the laws. "All the power at my disposal will be used to reclaim the public property and places which have fallen," he pledged, "to hold, occupy and possess these, and all other property and places belonging to the government, and to collect the duties on imports."

Donald says that the address as delivered was "an imperfectly blended mixture of opposites." Donald quotes the ending challenge to the South: "Shall it be peace or a sword?" and calls the Springfield draft "warlike." In his collection of newspaper comments on the address, Donald highlights, by placing it at the end, the "most thoughtful" verdict of the *Providence Daily Post:* "There is some plain talk in the address: But . . . it is immediately followed by obscurely stated qualifications."

But are we to judge Lincoln's revisions to the Springfield draft a mistake? Or the resulting address unwisely marked down from what he had written in Springfield? Rather, one could argue that Lincoln, in the changes he kept making in the printed draft, on the train and in the Willard, was beginning to learn what it is to be a statesman.

Worthy statesmen regularly combine ingredients—they state things plainly, then follow with qualifications, sometimes even "obscurely stated" qualifications, more often silences. Clarity and consistency are virtues in most human settings but may not be in relations among giant collectives in conflict. Lincoln recognized this and swiftly saw what the situation required. He made a rigorous statement of the enduring underlying principle (the unbroken Union) but then made expedient, implicitly temporary concessions. Much was left unsaid because explicit statement would itself have become a political act that would affect how others respond.

Lincoln had written in Springfield, in a paragraph intended to be reassuring: "The government will not assail you, unless you first assail it." But in his revision, at Seward's suggestion, he struck out "unless you first assail it," so that there was no mention of the Union doing any assailing, even as a rejoinder to a rebel act. The flat promise that there would be no initial Union assault was left unqualified. (But in the silence after that sentence, surely one could hear the echo of the clause that had been there.)

The epitome of the issue would be Lincoln's having written in Springfield that he would "use all the power . . . to reclaim . . . the usurped federal installations." That "reclaim" was consistent with his fundamental insistence that the Union was unbroken—but would it have been wise to say it? To say it—and not do it? Or to say it—and try to do it? To mount a military effort ("all the power . . . will be used") to recapture the forts, mints, arsenals all across the Deep South that the seceded states had taken? That would have been impossible in the first place and undesirable in the second—impossible because he did not have the force, undesirable because overt military action would have been seen to be the "coercion" that multitudes of border state citizens and Democrats would condemn. So he had to take out that "reclaim," even though the logic underlying it was the backbone of the address. His friend Orville Browning was surely right to have argued that the announced intention to reclaim the federal installations should be dropped. It "will be construed as a threat or menace," Browning wrote, "and will be irritating even in the border states. On principle the passage is right as it stands. The fallen places ought to be reclaimed. But cannot that be accomplished as well or better without announcing your purpose in your inaugural?" Again, the studied silence. Lincoln would do the same in the future, with respect, for example, to Kentucky's claimed "neutrality," when he did not believe there was any such thing as "neutrality" but did not say so.

The situation at the time he gave the address was this: eight slave states still had not joined the Confederacy.* The rebel tide had rolled across the Deep South, the cotton South, and then stalled. Opinion was volatile in the North. The moment was fraught with peril, with shifting passions. Lincoln was a new man, mostly unknown, representing a party that had never held national office. He therefore reshaped the Springfield draft, adding the promises of restraint alongside its fundamental firmness.

These political considerations, together with his sense of constitutional propriety, shaped also—we may surmise—those reassurances about slavery, offensive to Douglass and the abolitionists, with which he started his address. In the long run, and in his heart, he agreed with those critics, but he could not shape his stated policy at this moment to please them.

Citizens—including scholars—of a later time have the advantage (and, again, disadvantage) of knowing that although there would be a terribly destructive war, the outcome would be that the Union was preserved. They therefore can ignore the frightful contingency of the situation as Lincoln faced it: he did not know what the ultimate outcomes would be, what the shape of the contending forces would be.

The *New York Times* reported two exchanges with the Democratic leader Senator Stephen Douglas, in response to Lincoln's address:

> Mr. Douglas said, "He does not mean coercion; he says nothing about retaking the forts, or Federal property—he's all right." Subsequently, to another querist, Douglas said: "Well, I hardly know what he means. Every point in the address is susceptible of a double construction; but I think he does not mean coercion."

That partially positive response, mixed with a dollop of doubt, is about what a budding statesman in Lincoln's extremely perilous position would

---

*Virginia, North Carolina, Tennessee, and Arkansas would later join the Confederacy, and Kentucky, Maryland, Missouri, and Delaware would be kept out of it.

want from the leader of the Union-supporting Democrats, Stephen Douglas. That the Mississippi press should say Lincoln's inaugural was a declaration of war was inevitable; that Frederick Douglass would be outraged was regrettable; but had Stephen Douglas been hostile, it would have been a disaster.

Six weeks later, on the very day that the news came into Washington that the rebels had fired upon and "reduced" Fort Sumter—thereby initiating "coercion" from their side—Senator Douglas visited the president in the executive mansion and gave him his full support.

SOLEMN OATH

When he finished reading his address, there arose on the platform a withered figure, a "gnarled corpse," who tottered forward accompanied by a clerk holding a large Bible. This was Chief Justice Roger Taney. Taney had been attorney general of the United States before young Lincoln had held any public office at all; he had now served for a quarter of a century. Perhaps this ceremony had become for Taney a little humdrum; he was administering the presidential oath for the seventh time and was about to serve under a tenth president.* But there was nothing humdrum about it for the other participant in this little ceremony. Taking a "solemn" oath, "registered in Heaven," transformed his moral situation.

Lincoln had in anticipation of this day repeatedly emphasized what taking this oath would mean—to newspapermen when he was president-elect out in Springfield, to his friend Senator Orville Browning on the way to Washington, and particularly to the representatives of the so-called peace conference—the "old men's conference"—chaired by ex-president John Tyler. This group had come to him in the Willard Hotel to implore him to yield to the "just demands" of the South so that there would not be "national bankruptcy" in which "grass shall grow in the streets of our commercial cities." Lincoln had at first been mollifying toward this group, but when their persistence led them to ask whether his reply meant he would yield to the demands of the South, he invoked, with strong words, the oath

---

*Jackson had already taken his two oaths before Taney was appointed, and Taney missed the two vice presidents who inherited the office, Tyler and Fillmore. The *New York Times* dispatch to the Associated Press said that this was the *eighth* time for Taney, but they counted Fillmore, which they should not have. Fillmore was sworn in by Chief Judge of the U.S. Circuit Court William Cranch in the Hall of the House on July 10, 1850, the day after President Zachary Taylor died.

he would take and said that the Constitution must be obeyed, "let grass grow where it may."

Throughout his address he underlined the moral significance of the oath he would shortly take. In his very first sentence—the first words he would speak formally to the whole people—he said, "In compliance with a custom as old as the government itself, I appear before you . . . to take, in your presence, the oath prescribed by the Constitution." As he turned from his preliminary reassurances to the South—the part that most offended Frederick Douglass—to his main argument, he referred again to the oath he would take: "I take the official oath today, with no mental reservations, and no purpose to construe the Constitution or laws, by any hypercritical rules." At the end of the address he included a most dramatic reiteration of the importance of taking that oath—the contrast not only between his own previous and present situations but also between his moral situation and that of the "dissatisfied countrymen" to whom he was appealing. "You have no oath registered in Heaven to destroy the government, while I shall have the most solemn one to 'preserve, protect, and defend' it." That is: You are still in a realm of calculation and choice; I will be in the different moral realm of necessity. You can act differently; I cannot. The moral claim upon me is categorical; on you, hypothetical; for me, imperative, for you, discretionary. I will take a most solemn oath—you will have no such oath. My oath will be "registered in Heaven"—you have no such heavenly registration for any purpose of yours. I cannot alter my course of action—you are not prevented from altering yours.

With the clerk holding the Bible, the chief justice, in a voice that could scarcely be heard, administered, and the tall president-elect, in a more audible voice, swore the oath prescribed by the Constitution: "I, Abraham Lincoln, do solemnly swear that I will faithfully execute the office of President of the United States, and will, to the best of my ability, preserve, protect, and defend the Constitution of the United States." The echo of that oath would sound across the thirty thousand citizens standing in front of the East Portico and then, as we may say, across the ages.

That tableau made quite a tidy capsule of American history: Taney, who had been the author of the Dred Scott decision, denying that black persons had any rights, administered the oath to Lincoln, who would be the author of the Emancipation Proclamation.

The event certainly had different meanings to the two participants. Taney thought that the oath he was administering to Lincoln prohibited this executive from "coercing" states to remain in the Union; Lincoln thought that the oath administered to him by Taney *required* him to do so.

Were there not many other oath-takers on the scene on that March day? Yes, the platform behind Lincoln was loaded with them: senators, congressmen, judges, cabinet officials, governors. The Constitution specified that all officials both of the United States and of the states "shall be bound by oath or affirmation to support this constitution." But the president's moral situation is nevertheless unique: in his case, the words of his oath are specified. Where these others are sworn to support the Constitution, the president swears, more fundamentally, to defend it, to preserve it, to protect it. These other officials are numerous and have particular functions within the constitutional structure; the president is a single individual; in the oath, and also in the provision that "he [the president] shall take care that the laws be faithfully executed," he is given a general and a personal responsibility that goes beyond particular functions. The personal aspect is underscored by the interesting concession that the framers inserted in the very wording of the oath: "to the best of my ability." There is a human being in this office.

For most presidents most of the time, taking the oath, although no doubt a solemn moment, is rather remote in its application. But in Lincoln's case taking that solemn oath had existential immediacy. The constitutional union he was swearing to preserve (to the best of his ability) was at that very moment in desperate need of preservation.*

Before three months passed, there would come another exchange between the ceremonial pair, Taney and Lincoln, featuring both the oath and that "take care" clause. The chief justice would challenge the president's suspension of the writ of habeas corpus in Maryland, as it teetered on the brink of secession, turning that phrase back against this new president. One who has sworn to "take care that the laws be faithfully executed," Taney wrote, should not himself violate those laws. The new president would respond, not right away and not directly—actually he would ignore Taney's order—but in a passage in the message he would send to the July 4 special session of Congress. He would answer Taney, without naming him, with this oft-quoted counterchallenge: "Are all the

---

*Did not Jefferson Davis down in Montgomery also take an oath? Yes, but Davis had long before sworn oaths to the Constitution of the United States, when he had been secretary of war and a senator. Oath number two presumably does not have the moral dignity of oath number one, which it flatly contradicts—unless there has been some radical moral detour justifying such a betrayal.

laws but one to go unexecuted, and the government itself go to pieces, lest that one be violated?"*

He said more. He made a significant reference to his oath—a more potent reference as he first wrote it than in the official version he sent over to Congress and deposited in the collections we can read today. He first wrote this key passage—a novice president responding to the direct challenge of a venerable chief justice—in the first person. But then he appears to have been sobered by the formality of the occasion. He was writing his first formal message as president of the United States (the inaugural he had written as a private citizen) and he was addressing, as the Constitution says he may do, a special session of Congress that he had summoned, as the Constitution says he may also do. He would not be speaking his words himself; they would be read to the assembled congressmen by a clerk. He therefore hid his original first-person passages behind the curtain of the third person and the passive voice. One reads that "the Executive" does this and "the Executive" and sometimes "the present incumbent" does that. The sentence about the oath was recast in the form of a question and now read: "Would not the official oath be broken [not saying by whom] if the government was overthrown, when it was believed [not saying who did the believing] that disregarding the single law would tend to preserve it?" But the sentence had been much stronger as he had originally composed it, not as a question but as an assertion, and in the first person. In that form it epitomized the plenary Lincolnian justification for a long string of actions he was going to take in the years to come:

> I should consider my official oath broken, if I should allow the government to be overthrown, when I might think the disregarding of a single law would tend to preserve it.†

The distinguished twentieth-century constitutional lawyer Edward Corwin writes that this reference by Lincoln to the oath is the "outstanding precedent . . . for treating the oath as a source of power" and that Lincoln

---

*Lincoln then went on to say: "But it was not believed that this question was presented. It was not believed that any law was violated." In the draft he had made clear who it was who was doing this not believing: "In my opinion I violated no law." An editor might have said, *Why did you not say that in the first place?*

†*CW*, 4:430n. The draft versions and changes in the July 4 Message are given in the notes to the message.

"permanently recruited power for the presidency . . . recruited it, that is, from the presidential oath." But is it not a rather curious foreshortening of the meaning of an oath to treat it as a "source of power"? Is not Corwin's choice of the word "recruited" rather odd in this connection? An oath is not a distribution of power but a solemn engagement of the self. If there is any "recruiting," then the moral agent is recruited, and seriously engaged, to conduct himself in a specified way.*

HE HAS SO FAR DONE HIS DUTY

IN THE EXCRUCIATING SIX WEEKS that followed, Lincoln made history-defining decisions in fulfillment of his oath. He wrote out a summary in his message to the special session of Congress that he called for July 4. The last long paragraph bristles with the accents of duty and of moral necessity:

> It was with deepest regret that the Executive found the duty of employing the war power, in defense of the government, forced upon him. He could but perform this duty, or surrender the existence of the government.

A victory by the rebels would not be merely some graceful severing of ties. It would be the "surrender [of] the existence of the government." That was what he had a sworn duty to oppose.

Lincoln as an emerging politician had shown himself to be, in most circumstances, one who compromised, sought limited ends, and adapted to differing claims, differing possibilities. He did not continually invoke absolute moral claims or his own stern duty, as many moral reformers and abolitionists would do, without regard to consequences. But he was also one who recognized a point at which compromise was no longer morally permissible; he had shown already in the previous winter that he could draw the line, and he held to it with "a chain of steel." He resisted any compromise that gave new territory to slavery, and he would not mute the moral condemnation of slavery. This moment required him to say that "no com-

---

*"The oath clause does seem to place the president in a special position of responsibility regarding the Constitution. No other official is required to swear that he or she 'will to the best of my Ability, preserve, protect and defend the Constitution of the United States.' But this language does not purport to grant any additional powers. Rather, it is an injunction to use whatever powers the president does have as needed to achieve certain ends." Daniel Farber, *Lincoln's Constitution* (Chicago: University of Chicago Press, 2003), p. 128.

promise, by public servants could, in this case, be a cure," because it would be a precedent that destroyed the essence of popular government. "As a private citizen," Lincoln asserted, "the Executive could not have consented that these institutions shall perish; much less could he, in betrayal of so vast, and so sacred a trust, as these free people had confided to him."

These free people had confided in him a trust that was "vast"—a word Lincoln used often to indicate the reach that his moral imagination discerned. At the end of his first annual message to Congress, in December 1861, he would write, "The struggle of today is not altogether for today—it is for a vast future also." The decisions now taken have an immense extension in time. And at the particularly personal end of his first message as president, he used that word to indicate the magnitude of the trust the American people had given him, as president at this moment. It was also "so sacred" a trust. Lincoln's use of religious and semireligious terms was chaste and sparing but also powerful when he did it. In this case he deepened, made more serious, surrounded with an aura, the "sacred" trust the people had placed in him.

In the draft for his inaugural address he had written in the last paragraph, in a sentence that he cut, "You can forbear the assault upon [the government]; I can not shrink from the defense of it." Now in this climactic personal statement about those tremendous decisions of the first months of his presidency, he used similar words. "He felt he had no moral right to shrink," he wrote, "nor even to count the chances of his own life, in what might follow." Scholars have noted that Lincoln had a distinct inclination to make rhetorical references to his own death—an inclination that for us, knowing what would come, takes on poignancy. "In full view of his great responsibility, he has, so far, done what he has deemed his duty," he said to Congress. "You will now, according to your own judgment, perform yours."

In the four years that followed, Lincoln often distinguished what he did as an oath-bound president from what he might have done in his personal capacity. Doing so no doubt expressed his genuine sense of constitutional rectitude. At the same time, Lincoln being Lincoln, his making of that distinction could serve a political purpose. In the fall of 1861, when he had to outrage many opponents of slavery by rescinding the military emancipation proclaimed by General John C. Frémont, he wrote a letter—to Orville Browning on September 22, 1861—explaining his action, noting not only that he believed Congress could pass such an emancipation law but that he might himself vote for it if he were in Congress, thus keeping clear his personal opposition to slavery. But then he insisted that a president sworn to uphold the Constitution could not just take over "the permanent legislative functions of the government" by an act like Frémont's.

A PRETTY MESS YOU'VE GOT ME INTO

LINCOLN WAS FILLING a role that demanded all his powers, serving ends in which he deeply believed, accomplishing something worthy of the world's esteem, as he had said at age twenty-three was his ambition. But he certainly did not treat this high position as any personal triumph. He did not glory in it, swagger, or insist on preferment, let alone domination. He would treat his formal eminence instead with that humor that was often the carrier of his wisdom.

John Hay told this story:

At a dark period of the war a gentleman of some local prominence came to Washington, so as to obtain the assistance of Lincoln for some purpose. He brought a good deal of evidence to prove that he was the man who originated his nomination and therefore his holding the high office. This man of prominence came up to Lincoln in the "vestibule" of the White House and walked with him over to the War Department, talking to him steadily. When Lincoln went into the War Department the man waited patiently for him; and when Lincoln emerged, he walked back to the White House with him, citing further facts and arguments about his role in getting Lincoln the office.

At the door the President turned, and, "with that smile which was half sadness and half fun," he said: "So you think you made me President?"

"Yes, Mr. President, under Providence, I think I did."

"Well," said Lincoln, opening the door and going in, "it's a pretty mess you've got me into. But I forgive you."

CHAPTER TWO

Act Well Your Part, There All the Honor Lies

DISTINGUISHED PRESIDENTS—ON THE WHOLE

ABRAHAM LINCOLN WAS the sixteenth man to take the oath prescribed in the Constitution for the president of the United States. He had said in his inaugural that the fifteen men who had "in succession administered the executive branch" before this day had been "greatly distinguished" and had done their work "generally with great success." In his draft he had written "on the whole with great success," but he changed the wording slightly perhaps because "on the whole" might hint at faintness of praise.

Had they in fact been greatly distinguished? The first six presidents, counting that "first son of the Republic" John Quincy Adams among them, had been great men, pitched up to greatness by the events of the Revolution and the Founding. They represented an astonishing cluster of great men in one or two generations who, even after more than two centuries of national life, still compose a significant cadre of the nation's most luminous persons. But their greatness had not necessarily been concentrated in their presidencies.

Then there had come the large figure of Andrew Jackson. Lincoln had made his first political choice to join the party that was opposed to President Jackson. But now in his new role he did endorse, selectively, Jackson's Union-supporting backbone and executive force. Out in Springfield he had asked his law partner, William Herndon, for only three works to refer to as he wrote his inaugural address, and one of those had been President Jackson's strong defense of national integrity during the nullification crisis of 1832. In a stark moment of these first days he would refer to Jackson, along with Washington, as a model of presidential steadfastness. "There is no Washington in that—no Jackson in that," he would say to the delegation from Baltimore that would "have me break my oath and surrender the government."

31

Had the eight presidents since Jackson been "greatly distinguished"? Had they been "on the whole" successful? None had served more than one term—four of them less than one term, the two Whig generals Harrison and Taylor dying in office and their two accidental successors not being nominated when the term was up. President Polk, whom some would name as the best of the group, had been attacked with particular vigor by Congressman Lincoln for his role in initiating and trying to justify the Mexican War.

Five of these eight, as it happened, were still alive as the sixteenth took his oath; none of the five had supported his election. In addition to Presidents Buchanan, sitting behind him at his inauguration, and Pierce, in grumpy retirement in New Hampshire, there was Millard Fillmore, the nation's second accidental president, who after failing election on the nativist American Party line in 1856 had faded back into suitable obscurity in Buffalo. There was President John Tyler, the first vice president to succeed to the office, whom John Quincy Adams referred to disdainfully as "His Accidency." Tyler had just chaired that "old men's" peace conference that had met with President-elect Lincoln in the Willard Hotel, and he would now return to Virginia to support the rebellion. (His son, president of the College of William and Mary, would make a whole career of attacking Lincoln.) And there was President Martin Van Buren, the "little magician" from Kinderhook who, having been the Free-Soil candidate in 1848, had taken his magic back to Kinderhook. Lincoln had done his first full-fledged campaigning in a presidential election arguing against Van Buren—or, as Lincoln's fellow Whigs called him in 1840, blaming him for the Panic of 1837, "Martin Van Ruin." Lincoln had then campaigned against him again when Van Buren turned up in a quite different guise in 1848, as the rather surprising candidate of the Free-Soil Party; Lincoln tried to keep antislavery Whigs in line against the newly put-together Free-Soilers. Van Buren in the election just past had supported the "fusion" in New York, the effort by the other parties to combine to stop Lincoln and throw the election into the House. But before many months of civil war would pass, Van Buren would in his last days swing around to support President Lincoln.

All of the previous presidents except the two Adamses—we can now include the entire fifteen back to Washington—had been to some extent politically beholden to the slave states of the South. The two Adamses both believed, with reason, that had it not been for the three-fifths clause awarding an unjust bonus to the slave states in the electoral college, they would have been reelected.

If one counted commanding armies in battle, as Zachary Taylor had done in the Mexican War, as a high formal qualification for the presidency, then all of these previous presidents would also have formal qualifications for the office superior to Lincoln's. Even the dark horse Franklin Pierce and the accident Millard Fillmore had served longer stints in Congress than Lincoln's two years.

The immediate political impact of the presidential election of 1860 had not been that this relatively unknown westerner had won but that the Republican Party had won—a new party, winning for the first time, in only its second try, a party whose most salient position was opposition to the extension of slavery, a party that was totally shut out in the South. The party's nominee would be the first president in American history who had been elected with no support from the slaveholding South whose last name was not Adams.

Lincoln had not been one of those politicians, to become more common in the following century as presidential power and visibility would grow, who all his life had secretly pictured himself presiding grandly in the executive mansion. He was ambitious, but his ambition was not exactly focused on serving as president. Lincoln's own experience had been in legislatures, and his proven abilities were as the maker of clearly argued speeches and as a political organizer. Until the presidential taste came into his mouth a little in 1859, what he most wanted was to be a senator; he had tried very hard in 1855 to persuade the Illinois legislature to choose him, then had distinguished himself as the Republican candidate running (and losing) against the great Senator Douglas in 1858.

The office of president did not necessarily have the political centrality that it would acquire in the future days of the United States as a giant international power. If you were to name the presidents of Lincoln's adult lifetime—and set aside Jackson, to whom he was opposed—then you would not find much to inspire a young person's emulation: Van Buren, Harrison, Tyler, Polk, Taylor, Fillmore, Pierce, Buchanan. But the list of eminent members of the Senate in Lincoln's shaping years makes a sharp contrast: Daniel Webster, Henry Clay, John C. Calhoun, the Great Triumvirate, served all through those years. In his own generation both his Democratic rival Senator Douglas and his Republican rival Senator William Seward outshone the presidents of their time. There was no one like the presidents of the following century—the two Roosevelts, Wilson, Kennedy, Eisenhower, Reagan—who would give to that office a glow that stirred the hopes of ambitious youthful patriots.

Lincoln was not a man who brought an established reputation to the presidency, as Washington and the others of the first six had done, and as

Andrew Jackson had done—and in the future as Ulysses S. Grant and Dwight Eisenhower would do. Lincoln's was not a name that would have lived in historical memory had he not served as president. In the immediate politics of the time it was much more important that his *party* had won the election than that this particular individual had done so.

THE SPACIOUS MORAL OUTLINE
OF THE AMERICAN PRESIDENCY

WHAT IS IT that the framers expected the president to *be* and to *do*? To tell the truth, the great framers in their miraculous summer in Philadelphia did not think particularly clearly about the "executive" they were creating. They knew there were supposed to be three branches of the government— Montesquieu had said so, and the state governments set up since 1774 had moved in that direction—but their experience with "executive" was mostly negative. Legislatures were what the framers knew, and legislatures were what they celebrated and examined in the most detail; the legislature, in which popularly elected representatives engaged in mutual deliberation, was at the heart of the republican form of government that they were seeking to plant here on a new continent.

Most of them had served in the Continental Congress that had been the whole government for seven years under the Articles of Confederation and for six years before that, beginning with the First Continental Congress. For all those years that congress, in which Madison, Hamilton, James Wilson, and many other framers had served, was all the government the newly born nation had had. James Madison, the greatest among the makers of the Constitution, admitted in a letter to George Washington in the spring before the Philadelphia summer that he had not given the executive much thought.

For the legislature, the framers had many positive models and much experience themselves: there across the water was the "mother of parliaments" in the British government that many of them still regarded, despite independence, as the best in the world; at home the separation from the mother country had allowed the colonial legislatures almost a de facto rule. For the executive, they had mostly negative models. They had had a stomach full of kings. They did not want any equivalent of those royal governors imposing their will on the people from outside their control. On the other hand, they had learned that a congress has a hard time with some government functions.

Discussion of the executive wove through the summer days in Philadelphia intermittently, coming to a clinching point only toward the end, in August. The framers spent much more time on the composition of Congress and its powers, and on the relationship of the large states to the small states, than they did on the nature and powers of the executive, and that concentration of time and philosophy showed in the great document they produced: the article dealing with Congress comes first, and it is much longer and more carefully detailed than the shorter second one, which deals with the executive and is something of a hodgepodge.

What was the executive to be like in this *republican* government? The positive model was sitting in front of them presiding as they deliberated in Philadelphia, a presider, a *president*—George Washington.

This topic would in the unfolding history of this new country most often be discussed, understandably, in the language of power: What powers did the framers grant to the president? But one might also present it in the language of duty: What are the responsibilities, the duties, of this official? That was certainly the way the sixteenth president would read it.

The oath that the framers composed for this officeholder, with its string of three conservative verbs, suggests that his primary duty is to keep the polity as it had been and hand it on intact to his successor. He does not swear to *obey* the Constitution (although presumably he does) but rather—potentially the much bigger project—to preserve, protect, and defend it. And then there are those most heavily fraught duties: he is made commander in chief of the armed services. And "executive power"—whatever we may discern that to be—is "vested" in him.

Unlike past proponents of republicanism, James Madison had concentrated, in two preparatory memoranda, on the vices of republics: Where did they go wrong? And he had developed the realistic view of human nature that would run all the way through the Constitution the framers produced in Philadelphia: checking, balancing, hedging power. "All men having power should be distrusted to a certain degree," Madison would say, typically, on July 11 in the convention. The framers would apply that understanding to the division of powers *within* the national government, in a way that revolutionaries in Europe, who wanted a glorious centralized national government, would not dream of. The executive branch was shaped, in part, to be a hedge on the legislative branch—and vice versa.

The new Americans had learned that they wanted a government that, while it was hedged and balanced, at the same time could govern. There was one delegate to the Philadelphia convention, not a conscientious participant for the most part but a sporadic presence, who did care, supremely, about the executive. And he would play a decisive role in shaping the American constitutional conception of the presidency, not so much by what he said in Philadelphia as by what he wrote later in New York. This was Alexander Hamilton, and in his New York writing in Federalist 70, and in the Federalist Papers following it, Hamilton argued strongly for "unity" in the executive, for "a single executive and a numerous legislature." It is desirable to have unity and not "plurality" in the executive, in order that there be "energy" and "dispatch" in government action.

And the circumstances in which decision, energy, and dispatch in a single executive are most urgently needed are occasions like those Hamilton described, and sometimes Madison too, in other Federalist Papers: national emergencies, insurrections, wars. Republics had not been immune to wars, nor would this one be. "Have republics in practice been less addicted to war than monarchies?" Hamilton asks in Federalist 6. "Are not the former administered by men as well as the latter? . . . Are not popular assemblies frequently subject to the impulses of rage, resentment, jealousy, avarice, and other irregular and violent propensities?" And self-interest, magnified in groups as Madison explained; and rebellion and insurrections grounded in these passions? All this is still going to be present in republics, including this American republic. "We, as well as the other inhabitants of the globe are yet remote from the happy empire of perfect wisdom and perfect virtue."

A national emergency, to which this American republic would not be exempt, would be exactly the occasion when the vigorous government, and therefore the strength particularly in the executive that Hamilton and others recommended, would be most certainly required. It is to be doubted that Hamilton or Madison had in mind as the executive to fill that role, when the time came, a gawky self-educated rail-splitter from the untamed woods of the remote interior of the continent.

NO EXPERIMENT SO RASH

WHATEVER EXACTLY the American "president" was supposed to be and to do, there were in 1860–61 many highly placed people who believed that the man chosen in 1860 did not measure up. During the 1860 campaign the British ambassador to the United States, Lord Lyons, had described Lincoln as "a rough farmer—who began life as a farm labourer—and got on by a talent for stump speaking." In April just after Lincoln took office Lord Lyons would write to Lord John Russell, the British foreign secretary, that the new American president seemed to have "a comprehensive ignorance of everything but Illinois village politics."

When Senator Charles Sumner, chairman of the Senate Committee on

Foreign Relations and the most learned and well traveled of American political leaders, made a courtesy call at the Willard Hotel in the week before Lincoln's inauguration, he had been astounded when the president-elect, admiring his height, had proposed that they stand back to back to see who was taller. The humorless Sumner declined, reportedly saying stuffily that it was time to unite our fronts against the enemy and not our backs. For his part Lincoln is said to have remarked about Sumner that although he did not know much about bishops, Sumner fit his idea of what a bishop might be like.

Struggling in the first days to comprehend this odd figure who had become president, Sumner "could not get rid of his misgivings as to how this seemingly untutored child of nature would master the tremendous task before him."

Charles Francis Adams, who also questioned whether this uneducated westerner was at all prepared for this office, had superlative credentials for measuring presidential preparation: he was the grandson of one well-prepared president and the son of an even more well-prepared president. After the whole story was over, when Lincoln was a dead hero and Adams had served in London as his ambassador, Adams would still say, remembering no doubt in 1873 his judgment in 1861: "I must . . . affirm, without hesitation that, in the history of our government down to this hour, no experiment so rash has ever been made as that of elevating to the head of affairs a man with so little previous preparation for his task as Mr. Lincoln."

ACT WELL YOUR PART

But was Lincoln as unprepared as he appeared to Adams? He had not held any particularly elevated offices, and he did not have any advanced learning, and he had not come from a distinguished family, and he did not present a handsome appearance, and he had not had any giant national experience, and he had not done any heroic deeds, and he had not even received the votes of a majority of his countrymen, and almost nobody in Buchanan's strife-torn Washington knew this man, but he would nevertheless bring to the office more than contemporary observers could have imagined.

Nine months into his term the new president, whose letters would prove to be full of perhaps surprisingly explicit moral sagacity, would give some advice to General David Hunter that could have been directed to his own lowly status and alleged lack of preparation for the highest office, and taken as an indication of Lincoln's own moral self-shaping.

Hunter, a man whom Lincoln knew, had been sending him a "flood of grumbling" letters and had complained about being in command of "only 3000." Lincoln, preparing his response, first insisted that he was Hunter's friend and therefore could "dare to make a suggestion." Then he told Hunter—in a December 31, 1861, letter—that his grumbling about the smallness of his role was the best way to ruin himself. Lincoln in aid of his point then called up from his memory of English poetry a line from Alexander Pope's *Essay on Man*: "Act well your part, there all the honor lies."

One cannot help being a little impressed that this prairie politician, now suddenly thrust into the most crushing burden of the presidency, with all that he had going on around him, with no staff remotely comparable to those of later presidents, should—surely out of his own memory—come up with this exactly apropos line from the canon of English poetry. The full couplet from which the line comes goes like this:

> *Honor and shame from no condition rise;*
> *Act well your part, there all the honor lies.*

Honor does not arise simply from the condition of filling one of those high places, as his new "friends" did, nor from holding the presidential office, as Buchanan had done, as Pierce had done, as old Tyler had done, and Millard Fillmore, and the rest of them; and shame does not arise from any condition of provincial lowliness. It all depends, in Pope's little nugget of moral wisdom, on how one acts one's part, whatever that part may be.

In his letter to Hunter, after quoting the line from Pope, Lincoln wrote his own admonition: "He who does *something* at the head of one regiment will eclipse him who does *nothing* at the head of a hundred." That adds something to the garden-tending quietude perhaps implicit in Pope's couplet: *eclipsing*. The head of one regiment doing *something* outdoing the head of a larger one doing *nothing*. And Lincoln, although a quite conscientious person, had also been, like Hunter, ambitious; he would act his part well—but at the same time he sought a larger part in which to do that acting. Although the taste for the presidency came late, he had wanted intensely to be a senator in 1855 and 1858, and he had chosen politics, and sought office, rather early and persistently. He had been a resident of New Salem for only six months when at twenty-three he first ran for office.

Lincoln succinctly put these mingled motives together all the way back in his rather touching first effort at political self-presentation. Coming before the people of Sangamon County in a published statement on March 9, 1832, when he was twenty-three years old, he had said: "I have no other [ambition] so great as that of being truly esteemed of my fellow men, by rendering myself worthy of their esteem."

This thread of aspiration to do something, for his country and the world, that would be worthy of esteem—and, as he said in later statements, that would make his name worthy of being remembered—would run all the way through his life. Early in life he recognized his superiority in intellect and other ways. From that recognition, and from an imagination stimulated by the printed page, he conceived a high ambition for himself: he should leave a mark upon the earth. He did, in his imaginings, link the fame to which he aspired to some accomplishment for the public good, to something "worthy" of "public esteem," to "something that would redound to the interest of his fellow man," even to something that would elevate "the oppressed of my species," but still the praiseworthy accomplishments were to be linked to his name. He was not proposing to be an anonymous benefactor of mankind operating behind the scenes.

His friend Joshua Speed would write to Lincoln's partner and biographer William Herndon that in 1841, when Lincoln had a deep depression, he had said to Speed

> that he had done nothing to make any human being remember that he had lived—and that to connect his name with the events transpiring in his day & generation and so impress himself upon them as to link his name with something that would redound to the interest of his fellow man was what he desired to live for.

And twenty years later, at the time of the Emancipation Proclamation, according to Speed: "He reminded me of the conversation—and said with earnest emphasis—I believe that in this measure (meaning his proclamation) my fondest hopes will be realized."

WHO IS THIS FELLOW? HE IS SMARTER THAN HE LOOKS

THE DISTINGUISHED TWENTIETH-CENTURY HISTORIAN David Potter writes in some exasperation about the distorting power of the Lincoln myth as he tries to bring the reader to see Lincoln as he came into the presidency—to see how limited he was. Potter draws a rather deflationary picture: "Despite the stature which Abraham Lincoln afterward assumed, he was, until he entered the White House, simply a lawyer from Springfield, Illinois—a man of great undeveloped capacities and narrowly limited background. He was far more fit to become than to be President." Given the power of the Lincoln legend, we all need reminders that this man was an actual human being with human limitations. But Potter's deflationary description of the prepresidential Lincoln overdoes it.

Abraham Lincoln was an unusually able person, set down by an inscrutable Providence rather incongruously in an ungainly body and in an obscure, uneducated family in the remote Hoosier woods of a new nation across the Atlantic from the great centers of Western civilization. Lincoln's excellent mind therefore came before the world in multiple disguises. After he left home—where his peers had recognized his intellectual superiority— the larger world was repeatedly misled by the externals: his looks, his accent, his ill-fitting clothes, his lack of education and social polish, his jokes, his provincial origins, his undistinguished family. Again and again, when he would move into a larger world and would have the occasion to make a presentation, there would be a note of surprise in those he encountered: this young man is smarter than he looks. The upstaging of his intellectual ability by his other characteristics and identities would continue on into his candidacy, in which his having split rails was used to political advantage, and on into his presidency, during which only some in the inner core really comprehended the president's intellectual powers. Some observers were prevented by snobbery or egotism from grasping Lincoln's significant intellect: Salmon Chase, Wendell Phillips, Charles Francis Adams. In Adams's case distance had something to do with it; he was in London throughout Lincoln's presidency and dealt with the administration through his old family friend Seward, whom he much admired and to whom he gave credit for the Lincoln administration's accomplishments.

The eminent scholar of international relations Hans Morgenthau, after a career in Europe and the United States that spanned most of the twentieth century, may have startled some of his students with his choice toward the end of his life of an exemplary statesman: not Bismarck or any other European possibility, and not Thucydides or any other classical figure, but Abraham Lincoln. In a study that he was working on in his last years, he made this assertion: "His [Lincoln's] sheer brainpower must have exceeded that of all other presidents, Jefferson included."*

---

*The full paragraph from Morgenthau said: "Lincoln's political philosophy is not the result of theoretical reflection and study nor even of experience, but of innate qualities of character and mind. The qualities of his mind are as extraordinary as the quality of his character. His sheer brainpower must have exceeded that of all other presidents, Jefferson included. The manifestations are the more astounding, as Lincoln's mind was virtually untrained, his sporadic formal elementary schooling having amounted altogether to about one year. That

One may say that such intellectual ability is a gift, like any other inborn ability or talent, and therefore does not occasion distinctly *moral* approbation. A quality that is a sheer gift, like beauty, strength, or brains, may occasion other kinds of praise, but morality has to do with choice and the character that is built out of choices made in freedom. But a moral question does then immediately arise: What does this person, this moral agent, choose to do with this gift? Young Lincoln, when he discovered that his mind was superior to that of his father and others around him in his youth, made two choices: first, to educate himself, to develop his abilities in a remarkable series of projects in self-education; and second, to apply his abilities to politics, to public life.

The decisive point about Lincoln's preparation did not have to do with his résumé but with his mind—not with externals but with internals, not with positions held but with moral and intellectual habits inculcated. Lincoln had been teaching himself how to think, and how to conduct himself on the basis of what he thought, all his life, one might say, but with a particular intensity and definition since 1854. "He who thinks well serves God in his inmost court," as Thomas Traherne wrote. Lincoln's disciplining of his intelligence had not been carried on in isolation, or addressed to abstract topics, but was carried on in the midst of, and in relationship to, deep and continuous involvement in public life. He had been for almost thirty years an active participant in Illinois politics, and he had been for almost twenty-five years a lawyer crisscrossing that state's Eighth Judicial Circuit. He had had continuous exchanges with voters, editors, legislators, judges, lawyers, farmers, and mechanics.

The appraisals at the time, and even the immense myth that would grow around him after he became a martyr, would not include sufficiently the central role of his unusually able mind. Lincoln was not exactly untutored; on the contrary, he had been tutored to an unusual degree, in that he had repeatedly and quite consciously tutored himself. His powers and clarity of mind were both illustrated and reinforced by his reading Euclid in his early thirties and by his successful practice of law. It is not surprising that in his youthful addresses he appealed to reason—cold, calculating reason. His intellectual power, his self-discipline, and his ambition are all illustrated by his lifelong series of projects in self-education. He learned to read some-

---

extraordinary intelligence revealed itself in a philosophic understanding of public issues, in a judicious concern with politically relevant detail, in a mastery of political manipulation, in military judgment." Hans Morgenthau, "The Mind of Abraham Lincoln," in Kenneth W. Thompson, ed., *Essays on Lincoln's Faith and Politics* (Lanham, Md.: University Press of America, 1983), p. 59.

how, even though neither his stepmother nor his father were readers, and then read "everything he could get his hands on." He famously managed to obtain, and mastered, a book on grammar and could quote it in his adulthood. He taught himself enough geometry to be a surveyor. He found a copy of Blackstone and made himself a lawyer. As president of the United States, although he would make self-deprecatory gestures of deference to West Point professionals, he was not in fact intimidated by the arcana or mystique of military strategy. He did what he had done on other subjects all his life: he obtained the books and taught himself. He would then produce letters to his generals that showed his characteristic grasp simultaneously of the large purpose, the core strategy, and particular detail.

He was not exactly a "child of nature" either. To be sure, he had (as was now widely advertised) split some rails, and wielded an ax, and farmed some farms, and taken rafts on rivers, and lived in the woods by streams. But when he had a choice, what he did was read. And head for the state capital, leaving "nature" behind.

Lincoln discovered that he had an exceptional memory; his longtime friend Joshua Speed wrote in another letter to William Herndon an account of Lincoln's appraisal of his own mind that would often thereafter be quoted: "I once remarked to him that his mind was a wonder to me; that impressions were easily made upon it and never effaced. 'No,' said he, 'you are mistaken; I am slow to learn, and slow to forget that which I have learned. My mind is like a piece of steel—very hard to scratch anything on it, and almost impossible thereafter to rub it out.' "

REPUBLICAN ADVOCATE: EQUAL CHANCE

WHEN ONE EXAMINES the suitability of some person for high office, one asks not only about abilities but also about beliefs and, as we now say, "values." Is this person (to borrow from Lincoln) facing Zionward? One would not want in office someone, however able, who was facing the wrong direction.

By the criteria of mainstream Republicans in 1860, Lincoln was fully qualified by his beliefs—indeed, his effective presentation of the moral-political argument for the Republican position was the only basis for his nomination. He had energetically and sometimes eloquently presented that argument in 175 speeches between 1854 and 1860, most of them in Illinois but more recently in other states as well. He had come to be nationally known in 1858 by debating the great Democratic leader Stephen

Douglas to a draw. Lincoln himself saw to the publication of that debate. In 1860 he impressed the "mental culture" of New York City with his speech at Cooper Union, which was widely circulated as a pamphlet. Almost uniquely in American history it was his rigorous presentation of a policy position, a party position, a moral position, that brought him the nomination and hence election to the office of president.

When he came back into public life in 1854, contesting the ground with a noted senator from his state, he constantly invoked the Declaration of Independence. In his first great speech, at the state fair in Springfield and in Peoria in the fall of 1854,* he spoke with his characteristic extravagance on this topic:

> Our republican robe is soiled, and railed in the dust. Let us repurify it. Let us turn and wash it white in the spirit, if not of the blood, of the Revolution. Let us turn slavery from its claims of "moral right," back upon its existing legal rights, and its arguments of "necessity." Let us return it to the position our fathers gave it; and there let it rest in peace. Let us re-adopt the Declaration of Independence, and with it, the practices, and policy, which harmonize with it. Let north and south—let all Americans— let all lovers of liberty every where—join in the great and good work. If we do this, we shall not only have saved the Union; but we shall have so saved it, as to make, and to keep it, forever worthy of the saving. We shall have so saved it, that the succeeding millions of free happy people, the globe over, shall rise up, and call us blessed, to the latest generations.

His prepared speeches were loaded with such impassioned invocations of the Declaration's assertion of human equality. His spontaneous outbursts were even more impassioned. In Lewistown, Illinois, on August 17, 1858, just before the famous series of debates with Senator Douglas, he made unusually clear the link of God as creator to the American belief in equality:

> This [the second paragraph of the Declaration] was [the Founders'] majestic interpretation of the Universe. This was their lofty, and wise, and noble understanding of the justice of the Creator to His creatures.

---

*Lincoln gave portions and versions of this speech in several Illinois cities and towns in the fall of 1854. The Springfield State Fair was a major instance; the finished version he gave in Peoria on October 16. *CW*, 2:247–82.

Yes, gentlemen, to all His creatures, to the whole great family of man. In their enlightened belief, nothing stamped with the Divine image and likeness was sent into the world to be trodden on, and degraded, and imbruted by its fellows.

In Trenton, on his way to Washington to take up his duties as president, he referred—on February 21, 1861—to Americans as the Almighty's "almost chosen people." And then in Independence Hall in Philadelphia, where the Declaration had been adopted, he was moved, on the next day, in a "wholly unprepared speech," to fervent personal testimony:

> I can say in return, sir, that all the political sentiments I entertain have been drawn, so far as I have been able to draw them, from the sentiments which originated, and were given to the world from this hall in which we stand. I have never had a feeling politically that did not spring from the sentiments embodied in the Declaration of Independence . . . I have often inquired of myself, what great principle or idea it was that kept this Confederacy so long together. It was not the mere matter of the separation of the colonies from the mother land; but something in that Declaration giving liberty, not alone to the people of this country, but hope to the world for all future time. (Great applause.) It was that which gave promise that in due time the weights should be lifted from the shoulders of all men, and that all should have an equal chance. (Cheers.) This is the sentiment embodied in that Declaration of Independence.

Rather abruptly, it happened. He was suddenly lifted up past Stephen Douglas, up above William Seward, up beyond all the more familiar and presumably more deserving political eminences, into the nation's highest office, the place that his hero Henry Clay had sought all his life and never attained.

HE ALONE CAN DO GOOD
WHO KNOWS WHAT THINGS ARE LIKE

IF THE FIRST POINT (for an 1861 Republican) was established—that the new president believed in, and could write good speeches about, the moral significance of the American Union—the later points were not: Could he fill the practical requirements of the office? Could he apply the principles in his speeches to the complexities of particular situations?

Fulfilling his duties as the executive and the commander required qualities beyond any he had exhibited before. Could he find in himself the requisite practical wisdom for his new station? Did he have prudence, the virtue that used to be the "mother" of all other virtues? One cannot use the word to convey its older meaning effectively now, because its connotations have drastically shrunk and shriveled, but it was once the name of a quality that was most desirable and worthy of praise—particularly, we may say, in a statesman.

A modern interpretation of the classical virtue of prudence describes an essential quality:

> He alone can do good who knows what things are like and what their situation is. The pre-eminence of prudence means that so-called "good intention" and so-called "meaning well" by no means suffice. Realization of the good presupposes that our actions are appropriate to the real situation . . . We therefore take this concrete reality seriously, with clear-eyed objectivity.

It is true that Lincoln did make some large errors, as well as of course small ones. Along with most leaders in the North, in secession winter, he overestimated unionism and underestimated the intensity of secessionist conviction in the South.* He certainly made misjudgments, as we will see, about the colonization proposal—both about its practicality in general and about its acceptance by black Americans in particular. But in the large, and after he came into his own, he would have an unusually clear-eyed understanding of objective situations.

The modern interpreter of the virtue of prudence wrote: "It is necessary for the prudent man to know both the universal principles of reason and the singulars with which ethical action is concerned." Lincoln would know well the "universal principles of reason"—that is, the moral principles, which Lincoln had articulated repeatedly in the six years before he became president. But could he then shape their application?

We may make use of comments about another, later president, who, in the view of some, did not acquire that virtue, Woodrow Wilson. A shrewd English observer, the great economic thinker John Maynard Keynes, would note the disappointment that many in Europe felt with Wilson, another speech-maker much given to stating large moral ideals. These

---

*John Nicolay would not think the estimate of Southern unionism was wrong, because in his view secession was more a plot or coup or conspiracy brought off by a rabid few leaders. Nicolay, *The Outbreak of Rebellion* (New York: Da Capo Press, 1995).

Europeans, encountering him in the aftermath of the Great War, had very high hopes aroused by the distinction and moral elevation of Wilson's speeches. But they were to be disappointed, in a way that one might also have worried that this earlier moralist-president might have disappointed his supporters. Keynes wrote about Wilson:

> The President's programme for the world, as set forth in his speeches and his notes, had displayed a spirit and a purpose so admirable that the last desire of his sympathizers was to criticize details—details, they felt, were quite rightly not filled in at present but would be in due course . . . But in fact the President had thought out nothing; when it came to practice, his ideas were nebulous and incomplete. He had no plan, no scheme, no constructive ideas whatever for clothing with the flesh of life the commandments he had thundered from the White House. He could have preached a Sermon on any of them, or have addressed a stately prayer to the Almighty for their fulfillment, but he could not frame their concrete application to the actual state of Europe.

Lincoln had already established that he could present his own less Presbyterian equivalents to Wilson's thundering sermons and stately prayers; he too could give voice to large moral ideals, featuring in his case in particular the Declaration of Independence and, now, the case for the Union. But could he connect those world-encircling moral ideas to a decision about a beleaguered fort in Charleston Harbor? The equivalent of the "actual state of Europe" to which Lincoln had to apply his great principles of union and of popular government was the last-ditch situation at Fort Sumter, against a background of four months of falling forts and mints and arsenals, and a foreground of burgeoning Confederate presumption.

Could he discern objectively, not deceiving himself with wishes, the actual shape of the concrete reality in which he would make decisions? Could he connect the great moral principles to which he had given voice to the severely limiting realities of the actual complicated world he faced? Having made that discernment and that connection, could he *decide*? Or would he, like Buchanan, postpone, procrastinate, and waver? Having decided, could he persuade others? Could he lead? Having decided and persuaded, could he hold to his course through vicissitudes? But could he then change—admit mistakes, alter course—when circumstances would warrant?

Lincoln had some attributes that the public world did not yet know about that were even more valuable than world travel, high office, and "preparation": he had intellectual and moral self-confidence; he had deep conscientiousness, a powerful desire to achieve something worthy, a romantic idea of his country, and an unusual sympathy for creatures in distress. He had a willingness to admit what he did not know and a feel for the way large bodies of human beings were going to respond. A James Buchanan could be "prepared" by holding a long string of high offices at home and abroad, yet end up no wiser than he began; a Lincoln could be "prepared" by traveling in just one Illinois judicial district and just one Illinois congressional district, thinking all the time.

THE ESTABLISHMENT OF INTELLECTUAL RANK

WE HAVE TWO superb face-to-face and day-to-day witnesses to Lincoln's gradual self-formation as a statesman, his secretaries John Nicolay and John Hay. They were living there in the executive mansion itself, seeing Lincoln through the day most days, and sometimes evenings as well. What they would write in their big biography about those times has a distinct authority. They would have occasion far in the future to write a history of his life, and to include in their account the tentative sense of these first days:

> [I]t must be remembered . . . that during the month of March, 1861, Lincoln did not know the men who composed his Cabinet. Neither, on the other hand, did they know him. He recognized them as governors, senators, and statesmen, while they yet looked at him as a simple frontier lawyer at most, and a rival to whom chance had transferred the honor they felt to be due to themselves.

Nicolay and Hay then wrote striking sentences about the first groping toward understanding and eminence:

> The recognition and the establishment of intellectual rank is difficult and slow. Perhaps the first real question of the Lincoln Cabinet was, "Who is the greatest man?" It is pretty safe to assert that no one—not even he himself—believed it was Abraham Lincoln.

CHAPTER THREE

On Mastering the Situation

The Drama of Sumter

THE FIRST THING THAT WAS HANDED TO ME

THIS PRESIDENT HAD absolutely no honeymoon. Lincoln had no calm first days in which he could settle into the presidential office, find his way around the executive mansion, become accustomed to being called "president,"* get to know the recent rivals who had now abruptly become subordinates, learn more about how the federal government worked, and think his way toward what he wanted to do by careful steps. He was slapped in the face the first business minute of his presidency by the necessity of decision, and decision of the utmost gravity.

He anticipated that the burden of responsibility would be so heavy that he had said, in remarks at the train station as he left Springfield for the long trip to the capital, that he would have "a task before me greater than that which rested on Washington," and few either then or later have disputed that estimate. But although he expected the burden to be immense, he surely had not expected its whole weight to come crashing down upon him instantly.

Abraham Lincoln achieved a new level of poetic eloquence with the mystic chords and better angels in his last paragraph on March 4—but he would need something beyond eloquence on March 5. He had made a good speech on Monday—but no speech would solve his quandary on Tuesday. Fulfilling his duties as the executive and the commander would now require of him qualities beyond any he had exhibited before—and right away.

---

*As late as March 31 John Nicolay, writing to his girlfriend Therena back in Illinois, would refer to "the president" and then add in parentheses: "[I]t still seems queer to speak of Mr. Lincoln in that way, although I am becoming used to it." Note headed July 3, 1861, in John Nicolay file, *AL Papers*.

Lincoln would himself underline how abrupt it was, both in private and in a formal public report four months later. On the evening of July 3, as Congress was assembling, the president had a conversation with his friend Orville Browning, who had just been chosen to be senator from Illinois. "The first thing that was handed to me after I entered this room, when I came from the Inauguration," Lincoln told Browning, "was the letter from Maj. Anderson saying that their provisions would be exhausted before an expedition could be sent to their relief." And in his message read to Congress when it convened on July 4, he would take the trouble to insert a parenthetical reference to the firstness of it: "On the 5th of March (the present incumbent's first full day in office)," he wrote, "a letter from Major Anderson . . . written on February 28th and received at the War Department on the 4th of March, was, by that Department, placed in his hands." Along with Anderson's letter, he said, there were papers from the nine officers who shared command at Sumter, all of them concurring in Anderson's opinion that reinforcement could not be accomplished before their provisions ran out. This president thus had a mammoth and pivotal decision thrust upon him—immediately. He learned from Major Anderson's letter those shocking new items that Buchanan and Holt had learned the day before: that the shortness of supplies for Fort Sumter meant that they could not hold out more than six weeks without new provisions, and that the Confederates had so ringed the fort with threatening military batteries and fortifications as to make it now impossible to relieve his little garrison with anything less than a force of "twenty thousand good and well disciplined men."

The limitations of the available force were made clearer still when a month later the adjutant general gave him the particulars of the distribution: Department of the East, 3,894; Department of the West, 3,584; Department of Texas, 2,258; Department of New Mexico, 2,624; Department of Utah, 685; Department of the Pacific, 3,382; Miscellaneous, 686; grand total officers and men, 17,113. That was the U.S. Army when the Civil War began.

Grant would write in his memoirs that "the northern press" reported that Buchanan's secretary of war John Floyd, before he resigned, had "scattered the little army the country had so that the most of it could be picked up in detail when secession occurred." After scattering the army, Floyd resigned and became a Confederate general.

. . .

MAJOR ANDERSON and his engineer John G. Foster and the other officers in Fort Sumter plainly expected the facts they presented would evoke an order from the authorities in Washington that they evacuate the fort. So, manifestly, did the outgoing administration. The covering letter from Joseph Holt, Floyd's successor as secretary of war, was largely intended to absolve the previous administration from any blame for the evacuation that now, obviously, had to be ordered. Holt said, defensively, that these new communications from Anderson and his garrison at Sumter were "of a most important and unexpected character," as he put it in his first paragraph, and "[take] the Department by surprise," as he said in his last one. "His [Anderson's] previous correspondence contained no such intimation." Holt cited the exchange of letters with Anderson, underlining Anderson's having said on December 31 that "still we are safe" and "we can command this Harbor as long as our government wishes to keep it." And again, on the sixth of January, Anderson had written (said Holt), "My position will . . . enable me to hold this post against any force which can be brought against me." Holt quoted his own message to Anderson of January 16:

> Your late despatches . . . have relieved the Government of the apprehensions previously entertained for your safety. In consequence, it is not its purpose, at present, to reenforce you . . . Whenever in your judgment, additional supplies or reinforcements are necessary for your safety . . . you will at once communicate the fact to this Department.

But Anderson had made no such communication. He had on the contrary discouraged any attempt to relieve the fort. Holt's letter, an exercise in self-justification by the Buchanan administration, insisted that they had been ready to act if Anderson had indicated the need. They had in fact had a small expedition in preparation for possible use—but nothing like what Anderson was now saying would be needed.

If the new messages from Fort Sumter were a surprise and a shock to the outgoing president and his secretary of war, how much more of a surprise and a shock must they have been to the new president, not yet even seated at his desk?

Lincoln lived a thousand years between March 5 and April 14, 1861. In his conversation with Browning on July 3 he made a personal comment, a version of which both Browning and Nicolay got down on paper. Nicolay reports his having said: "Browning, of all the trials I have had since I came here, none begins to compare with those I had between the Inauguration and the fall of Fort Sumter. They were so great that could I have anticipated them I would not have believed it possible to survive them." Browning in his diary has Lincoln saying that "all the troubles and anxieties of his life had not equaled those which intervened between [the inauguration] and the fall of Sumter."

Lincoln not only had no honeymoon; he had no fresh beginning. Not only was he thrust immediately into the necessity of decision-making, he was also pushed into a corner, and his range of decision was sharply skewed by the events of the previous four months that culminated in the papers now in his hand. When in later years we hold in our minds the figure of Lincoln as our world has come to see him—the brooding giant on a throne in the Lincoln Memorial, for example—we may imagine that when this giant came upon the scene, history stopped for a beat or two, drew a line, and took a tidy new start, beginning the world anew again, as it were. But that image is totally wrong. The day was already far gone when Lincoln became president; he entered not only in medias res but also at the end of long series of mounting crises that were just now reaching a crescendo.

Fort Sumter, which Lincoln now suddenly learned to be in peril, had acquired a particularly heavy symbolic significance to both sides, for reasons of geography and recent history. It was one of four military installations ringing the harbor of the primary city in the state that had more than any other nurtured and led the rebellion, which claimed after December 20, 1860, to be all by its miniature self an independent nation, the Republic of South Carolina.

Fort Sumter had been further singled out for unique symbolic visibility for both sides by the daring, secret, surprise move of the Union garrison from Fort Moultrie to Fort Sumter on the night of December 26, 1860. Major Robert Anderson, who commanded the garrison of a hundred men, perceived from daily observation of the rebels' drilling and military preparation and from what they plainly said that there would soon be an assault on his Union band in Fort Moultrie, the only remaining place the American flag was flying after all other federal installations in the state and the city and the harbor had been taken over. The secessionists in their excitement after passing the ordinance and celebrating with fireworks on December 20 told Anderson, "We have to have the forts." Fort Moultrie, on a finger of the mainland, was markedly vulnerable; Fort Sumter, on a rocky island in the middle of the harbor, was much more defensible. Anderson had asked for reinforcements, but the Buchanan administration had sent none. There was, however, a bold step Anderson could take on his own: a sudden nighttime transfer of his force in boats silently crossing the harbor, evading the secessionists' guard boats, landing the Union soldiers on Fort Sumter without being discovered. "By nine o'clock that night . . . the officers sat down to eat the supper in Sumter that had been cooked for them in Moultrie." News of this daring act thrilled supporters of the Union, stunned the South Carolina rebels, made Major Anderson a hero in the North, and loaded Fort Sumter with additional symbolic resonance. A president of the United States would not thereafter lightly order that this brave garrison should now withdraw from the position that had been gained with such courageous audacity.

Sumter's symbolic meaning was elevated still another notch by an effort in January to reinforce it. December had brought resignations and new appointments in the Buchanan administration, a stronger Union-supporting contingent (including Edwin Stanton as the new attorney general)—and a brief flurry of action supporting the Union. The administration sent a merchant steamer, the *Star of the West,* with supplies and 250 recruits to reinforce the garrison at Fort Sumter. Secretary of the Interior Jacob Thompson of Mississippi, another secessionist still in the cabinet, learned of the effort and notified his friends in Charleston. The South Carolina rebels, after Anderson's transfer of the garrison to Sumter on December 26, took over Fort Moultrie and the other military installations in the harbor, hoisted over these U.S. government installations a Palmetto flag, and began the buildup that Secretary Holt would later report to President Lincoln. When in the early morning of January 9 the *Star of the West* approached Charleston Harbor, a shell was fired across her bow; the captain hoisted a larger American flag, only to be greeted with further rebel fire. When the *Star of the West* was fired upon, it turned back to sea and headed home to New York. Many believed that the government should have responded to this event as a provocation that justified a counterattack, a cause of war. And it heightened yet again the symbolic significance of the fort that the ship had been attempting to supply.

When the firing on Sumter began on the night of April 12, it would be not the first or the second but the third time the American flag had been insulted (to use Anderson's word) in Charleston Harbor. On April 3 a schooner named *R. H. Shannon,* bound from Boston to Savannah with a cargo of ice, in trouble in the fog at sea, with a captain who apparently was not a close student of current events, would in all innocence try to put in at the nearest port, Charleston. Astonished at being fired upon, the captain would raise the American flag, and would be still more astonished to be fired upon again, and would swiftly scuttle back out into the Atlantic.

ALL THROUGH THE DAYS when he confronted the Sumter crisis Lincoln, the party politician, was coping with office-seekers. He "was besieged from morning till night in his ante-rooms, in his parlors, in his library, in his office, at his matins, at his breakfast, before and after dinner, and all night, until wearied and worn he goes to rest." Lincoln himself remarked that he thought that about thirty thousand people were seeking jobs in this new, first Republican administration. And then he added cheerfully that that still left about thirty million Americans who were not looking for a job.

LINCOLN HAD MADE CLEAR in his inaugural address the two large moral commitments that would govern his decision about Fort Sumter. They were in sharp conflict with each other, and they both had practical reinforcement. The first was the fundamental obligation underlying everything he did, to which he had solemnly sworn on the previous afternoon, to "preserve, protect, and defend" the constitutional union. In light of the other moral consideration, he had made an implicit qualification of the application of his oath to the preservation of federal facilities: in his draft for the inaugural he did not say that he would "reclaim" the fallen forts and arsenals, as he believed the Union had an abstract right to do; instead he said only, under the conditions that prevailed, that he would "hold, occupy and possess the property and places belonging to the Government." His implicit postponement of any attempt to recover the fallen forts and properties increased the imperative to hold on to those that remained in Union hands—Fort Pickens and above all Sumter.

There was, however, the second obligation that limited how he could do that holding—let alone reclaiming. Lincoln had made repeated specific promises not to initiate armed conflict. He had said to the "assailants of the Government" that "you can have no conflict without being yourselves the aggressors . . . [T]here needs to be no bloodshed or violence; and there shall be none, unless it be forced upon the national authority." He said that "there will be no invasion—no using of force against, or among the people anywhere." He had said, "The government will not assail *you.* "

This reiterated promise also provided reassurance to the population whose support Lincoln had to win or to hold—in particular the Upper South—that there would be no "coercion."

Between these contending claims, Lincoln had a precise, concrete decision to make under the pressure of time with the salt pork running out: Should he order Major Anderson and the beleaguered garrison at Sumter to withdraw?

THE NEW PRESIDENT ON HIS FIRST DAY SAYS NO

WHAT SHOULD A NEW president, only a few hours into his presidency, do with the astounding communication from Anderson and Holt and the others describing the desperate situation about Sumter? Obviously, he should call on the best available military advice. For Lincoln, this advice would be provided by General in Chief Winfield Scott.

Scott is one of the large figures of American military history, a hero from the War of 1812, general in chief of the army already in 1841, one of the two great victorious generals in the Mexican War, the hero of Chapultepec, an associate of every president from Thomas Jefferson to Lincoln himself, the first person since George Washington to be granted by Congress the pay, rank, and emoluments of a lieutenant general. And so should not this new and inexperienced president be guided by the experienced General Scott?

The whole bundle of information about Fort Sumter was presented to General Scott, who wrote his comment as an endorsement on the letter that Holt handed Lincoln on his first day. Most summaries of these events, including Lincoln's own in his July 4 Message to Congress, do not convey the degree to which General Scott's answer was couched in terms of a lament for missed opportunities. He started right off: "When Major Anderson first threw himself into Fort Sumter it would have been easy to reinforce him." But alas that chance was missed. The general went on to say that "Fort Moultrie has since been re-armed & greatly strengthened. The difficulty of reinforcing has now been increased 10 or 15 fold." The chance to save the fort had passed. "I see no alternative but a surrender, as . . . we cannot send the third of the men in several months necessary to give them relief."

General Scott also informed the new president about the danger to the other fort still in Union hands, Fort Pickens in Florida, and mentioned "some thing like a truce established between the President [Buchanan] & a number of principal seceders—which truce or informal understanding included Ft. Pickens." Lincoln was now learning about this truce, and perhaps even about the danger to Pickens, for the first time.

General Scott on that very first day of the Lincoln presidency returned the Sumter papers to the new president not through the War Department but through William Henry Seward—another sign of the important role that many expected Seward to fill.

Major Anderson and his nine officers clearly expected that the report they sent would bring from the new civilian authorities an order to evacuate the fort. Joseph Holt's cover letter, giving the interpretation of events favored by the Buchanan administration, clearly was written in the expectation that the new president would have to order an evacuation, and with the intention to make clear that it was not their fault.

General Winfield Scott, by all means the most important military authority, said there was now no alternative but surrender. William Henry Seward, by all means the most important political leader in the president's party, had been actively seeking the evacuation of Fort Sumter and had effectively promised the "commissioners," who had been sent by the Confederates to attempt a deal, that it would happen. In the evening of his first full day in office—very full indeed—Seward and Lincoln conferred at length, and one may surely infer that Seward told the president that he should tell Scott to order Anderson and his garrison to withdraw.

But President Lincoln, altogether new to the job, did not order the surrender of the fort.

The summary of these events that Lincoln would present to Congress on July 4 would contain a significant little alteration of what he first wrote. This little alteration obscures a large presidential decision. After noting that General Scott concurred with Major Anderson in the view that Sumter must be evacuated, Lincoln wrote in the draft of the next sentence, "At the request of the executive, however, he [meaning General Scott] took full time" and consulted with others and thought it over some more. It is that draft, we may surely conclude, that tells us what actually happened. Hastily editing this document in the pressure of events in late June, Lincoln struck out the phrase "at the request of the executive" and substituted the phrase "on reflection," which made it sound as though General Scott had initiated the reflecting that caused him to draw back and take "full time" and confer with others and consider the matter again. But it was not Scott's initiative that caused this drawing back and reconsidering; it was Lincoln's—"at the request of the executive." That this newly arrived amateur had turned aside a decision that had been virtually already made by all the old professionals was in itself an immense development. No plan to evacuate Sumter would be set in motion that day.

Instead of acquiescing in the order clearly indicated in the papers before him and given by the most eminent advice, Lincoln, before retiring after his first full day in the executive mansion, directed General Scott to study the Fort Sumter matter more fully and, in addition, to take the steps necessary to "hold, occupy, and possess" other places still in Union hands—which had to mean Fort Pickens in Florida.

IT WOULD BE OUR NATIONAL
DESTRUCTION CONSUMMATED

WHEN A WEEK LATER General Scott, supported by "other officers both of the army and of the navy," and in answer to written questions from this new president, "came reluctantly, but decidedly, to the same conclusion as before," Lincoln in response also came to the same conclusion as before. The aging, portly, but enormously respected Scott gave pungent detail about the dwindling supplies for the U.S. garrison in Sumter, the impossible odds they faced (fewer than one hundred men, surrounded by 3,500 South Carolina troops with guns and mortars of large caliber), and the utterly impossible requirements for a successful U.S. supply and reinforcement: "A fleet of war vessels and transports, 5,000 additional regular troops and 20,000 volunteers . . . to raise, organize and discipline such an army would require new acts of congress and from six to eight months."

So the conclusion was unavoidable. The garrison, even if it were not attacked, could not hold out for two months, and assembling a force sufficient to reinforce the fort would take at least six months; therefore what the president had to do was order the garrison to evacuate the fort. General Scott even went so far as to submit to the president an already drafted letter to be sent to Major Anderson, ordering him to evacuate the fort. Most of Lincoln's cabinet supported such a course; Secretary Seward was strongly in favor of it. The *New York Times* reported that the cabinet on March 11 met at eleven in the morning and decided to withdraw the troops from "Fort Sumpter." (The *Times* followed Lincoln's persistent misspelling.)

All it would have taken at that moment—one week into Lincoln's presidency—was his acceptance of that letter already composed by the most respected of military advisers; and when Anderson received the order and notified General P. G. T. Beauregard in Charleston Harbor that he was evacuating the fort, the chivalrous South Carolinians would have allowed the Union troops to have a little ceremony, lower the American flag, and withdraw with dignity.

Lincoln certainly could have had a strong political cover for doing that:

blame Buchanan. It is not unknown in the history of this republic for a president to cast blame backward toward his predecessor, especially if there has been a change of party with the change of presidents. No president ever had richer material for such a gambit than Abraham Lincoln. He could have said that the Buchanan administration had allowed the situation at Sumter to come to this desperate necessity. That interpretation would have had the most potent witness in General Scott, whose every comment had lamented the missed opportunities of the recent past that now created the necessity to surrender Sumter. And he would have had a supporter in Secretary Seward.

But Lincoln did not indicate that Buchanan had left him in this tight situation, true as that certainly was. Instead, he grappled with what to do about Sumter in the terms that the issue came to him.

Again Lincoln made a mammoth decision. He did not permit Scott's letter to Anderson to be sent. Moreover, he had his secretary John Nicolay put in writing the message he had given to his military chief orally on the first day: "I am directed by the President to say that he desires you to exercise all vigilance for the maintenance of all the places within the military department of the United States."

On March 13 Postmaster General Montgomery Blair, the one cabinet member who opposed giving up Sumter, introduced Lincoln to his brother-in-law Gustavus V. Fox. Fox, thirty-nine years old, was an energetic Annapolis graduate and naval officer who disagreed with Scott and the others and believed that relief could be provided to Fort Sumter, which was what Lincoln wanted to hear. Fox at first proposed a naval barrage to clear the way, to be followed by a nighttime supply, by means of small New York tugboats making their way to the fort under the cover of darkness. Army officers believed it would not work; navy men thought it might. There was an intense flow of discussions, suggestions, cabinet meetings, and military consultations about Fox's proposal. In the days that followed Lincoln sent three visitors, or scouts, down to Charleston, one of them Fox.

ON MARCH 28 Lincoln told Fox to make a list of the ships, men, and equipment he would need for his expedition. That evening the Lincoln administration held its first state dinner. The president seemed in good humor but drew the cabinet aside afterward to share a disturbing memorandum from General Scott, in which he now recommended, for the soothing of the South and the border states, abandoning not only Fort Sumter but also the other major southern fort still in Union hands, Fort Pickens in Pensacola. The cabinet, except perhaps for Seward, was stunned at this proposed double capitulation; Lincoln asked them to come the next day for a regular cabinet meeting.

After the cabinet meeting on March 29, Lincoln began to function actively in the quite extraordinary role that the Constitution-makers had specified for the elected head of the American federal government, "Commander-in-chief of the Army and Navy of the United States." Up to this point in those crowded days of huge decisions, his action had consisted of issuing some quite general instructions and then of responding, negatively, to the recommendations that the nation's military had given—three times—that he order the evacuation of the fort. Now Lincoln took the initiative to set in motion by his orders a large military undertaking. He wrote at the bottom of Captain Fox's specification of ships and men and supplies and equipment this presidential command to the secretary of war: "Sir, I desire that an expedition, to move by sea, be got ready to sail as early as the 6th of April next, the whole according to the memorandum attached, and that you cooperate with the Secretary of the Navy for that object." Lincoln said that this expedition was "intended to be ultimately used or not according to circumstances." Lincoln ordered Fox to go to New York to supervise preparations.

MEANWHILE, WHAT ABOUT that other fort, Fort Pickens in Florida? Lincoln's moral commitment in his inaugural, and his orders to Scott both orally on his first day and in writing a week later, specified holding all federal facilities still in the government's control, which included Pickens as well as Sumter. But the reinforcement of Fort Pickens, as we will see in the next chapter, had not happened. On this extremely busy day Seward, foiled in his effort to prevent a Sumter expedition, called on Lincoln with a proposed expedition to Fort Pickens, and Lincoln began the planning for that one also.

SO NOW, after twenty-five days as president, as segments of the Northern press and public became increasingly eager for action, Lincoln began to set in motion not one but two hugely significant military expeditions to vindicate the Union. Nicolay and Hay, living in the White House at the time, described the Friday night after these decisions:

That night Lincoln's eyes did not close in sleep. It was apparent that the time had come when he must meet the nation's crisis. His judgment alone must guide, his sole will determine, his own lips utter the word that should save or lose the most precious inheritance of humanity, the last hope of free government on earth. Only the imagination may picture that intense and weary vigil.

On the afternoon of April 4 Gustavus Fox met with President Lincoln and Navy Secretary Gideon Welles to clinch the arrangements for an expedition to Fort Sumter. When Fox stressed the need for a naval armament, Secretary Welles added the powerful war steamer *Powhatan*, with three hundred sailors, to the flotilla.

On that same day Lincoln wrote out a message to Major Anderson, telling him not as he had expected, and no doubt hoped, that he was ordered to evacuate, but instead to hold out if possible until the eleventh or twelfth, when a relief expedition would arrive. Lincoln sent this message to Anderson by mail on April 4 and repeated it by messenger on April 6.

Fox returned to New York and subsequently dispatched his flotilla. The plan was for the ships to rendezvous ten miles off Charleston Harbor on April 12.

WHY DID THIS NEW PRESIDENT, in his first hours in office, defy all the expert advice he had been given? Because he was not only commander of the military force but leader of the nation. Because he saw the issue in its largest dimension, that of the nation's survival. His explanation of this decision demonstrated his awareness of the huge political stakes, far beyond military considerations, that lay in these events. In his summary of events in his July 4 Message, Lincoln wrote, "In a purely military point of view this [the response to his questions by General Winfield Scott and his military advisers] reduced the duty of the administration to the mere matter of getting the garrison safely out of the Fort." But he saw the issue as vastly more than military.

Lincoln's statements of the nonmilitary consequences—the moral-political consequences, we may say—were couched in the most stark, conclusive language. "The executive believed," he wrote in his draft (he would change that to "it was believed"), "that to abandon that position would be utterly ruinous . . . that, in fact, it would be our national destruction consummated." His conclusion was unequivocal, a line in the sand: "This could not be allowed." He gave three reasons why a voluntary Union evacuation of Sumter, not seen to be done under necessity, would consummate our national destruction: it "would discourage friends of the Union, embolden its adversaries, and go far to insure the latter a recognition abroad."

He showed an independent grip on high purpose, and a strength of will, that he would have abundant occasion to display in the events that would now follow. He would even have occasion shortly to make reference to the great Democratic symbol of presidential strength Andrew Jackson. But Lincoln would exhibit something more. His hero was not Jackson but Henry Clay. He had given a eulogy when Clay died in 1852, and what we choose to praise in someone else can be revealing. Lincoln said that Clay had an "indomitable will" and, in addition, good judgment. Without good judgment, Lincoln said, an indomitable will can be "nothing better than useless obstinacy."

Lincoln would also show, as these crushing days wore on, an unusual element of strategic imagination. While he was repeatedly deciding not to abandon Sumter, he was also beginning to see a way to meet the demands of his situation.

GIVING BREAD TO HUNGRY MEN

AT SOME POINT in the last two weeks of March, amid the discussion with Fox about his expedition and the exchanges with Anderson and others about the rapidly diminishing supply of hard bread, flour, rice, and salt meat in the fort, Lincoln had a masterful idea. It would be a way to signify the Union's intention to "hold" and "possess" this most important government property and at the same time to keep his promise not to initiate conflict, not to be the aggressor. The strategy had two parts, inextricably connected: send provisions only, and notify the South Carolinians.

The first part of the idea was to separate food from armament. The garrison needed bread—so Washington would send bread only, no arms. Orville Browning would write in his diary that Lincoln had told him that he "himself conceived the idea" of sending supplies "without an attempt to reinforce."

Lincoln would emphasize, underline, and insist that the provisions that he proposed to send were food, not arms. He took the following steps:

- In the letter dated April 6, 1861, notifying Governor Francis Pickens of South Carolina, Lincoln (who wrote all these key messages himself) had his messenger Robert Chew say: "I am directed by the President of the United States to notify you to expect an attempt will be made to supply Fort-Sumpter with provisions only."*

- Lincoln had Fox instruct the first boat's pilot to deliver to any person opposing his entrance into Fort Sumter a further letter to be taken to Governor Pickens. This letter would emphasize the predicament in which he had placed the Confederates. It read: "The U.S. government has directed me [the pilot of the boat] to deliver a quantity of provisions to Major Anderson at Fort Sumpter ... Accordingly I send here with the first load. *If your batteries open fire it will be upon an unarmed boat, and unarmed men performing an act of duty and humanity.*" (This emphasis, making the point doubly clear, is in the original, from Lincoln's own hand.)
- In the draft of his July 4 Message to Congress, Lincoln, summarizing these events, wrote that "the giving of bread to the few brave but starving men of the garrison, was all which would be attempted." On second thought, editing his draft, he apparently decided that "starving" might be overdoing it, so he changed "but starving" to "and hungry."

Lincoln wanted the world to know that this expedition brought bread; firing on it would be "firing on bread."

To be sure, from a rebel's point of view, bread was as bad as arms; either or both would sustain, or would indicate an intention to sustain, the objectionable occupying garrison and the objectionable flag in Charleston Harbor. But the rest of the world—including much of the wavering Upper South—would surely accept the distinction. Lincoln had skillfully hit a symbolic point: sending bread to hungry men was not "aggression" or "coercion" or "invasion."

As the bread-bringing expedition was leaving for Fort Sumter, a new message came from Major Anderson, indicating that the men might indeed be hungry; supplies in Fort Sumter were even shorter than had been thought in Washington. Lincoln drafted in his own hand a letter for Secretary of War

---

*It is unfortunately the case that the governor of South Carolina and the fort in Florida had the same name. It is also unfortunately the case that this president misspelled the name of the fort about which he had his first great crisis, inserting a "p" where it was not needed. But sometimes that was corrected.

Simon Cameron to sign, telling Anderson once again to hold out, if he could, until the eleventh or twelfth, when the expedition should arrive. If the expedition should find "your flag flying," it will attempt to provision you and, "in case the effort is resisted, also to re-inforce you." But, Lincoln wrote, if a capitulation became necessary to save himself and his command, Anderson was authorized to make it.

THE OTHER ELEMENT of Lincoln's plan was to notify the Confederates. Fox had proposed to send the smaller boats with provisions to Sumter surreptitiously, at night. For Lincoln, however, it was of central importance that the effort be quite open, with the governor of South Carolina notified ahead of time.

On April 6 Lincoln sent a State Department clerk named Robert S. Chew as messenger to Charleston to obtain an audience with the governor. It is significant that Lincoln sent this notification to Governor Francis Pickens of South Carolina, a legitimate official, a governor of one of the states, and not to the "illegal organization, in the character of Confederate states," in Montgomery.

Chew set out for Charleston with a companion named Theodore Talbot, an army captain who had just made the trip the other way, bringing a message from Major Anderson. Captain Talbot was now turned around and sent back to Sumter with Lincoln's message to Anderson—hold out until the twelfth if you can—that had already been sent by mail. Talbot had the original, in Lincoln's own handwriting. The two messengers arrived in Charleston on April 8. Talbot, whom the rebels already had met, was permitted to see Governor Pickens and asked him to receive Robert Chew, an emissary from the president of the United States, and the governor agreed. Chew then read to him, and gave him a copy of, Lincoln's "provisions only" message. The governor invited into the room General Beauregard, in charge of the rebel forces in Charleston Harbor, and read him Lincoln's message: provisions only, no arms unless you fire. Beauregard refused to let Talbot carry the message to Anderson out at the fort, so Chew and Talbot returned together and, after delays, reached Washington and reported to Lincoln and the cabinet on an important date—April 12.

This open notification about the expedition was a masterstroke by Lincoln, part of the unified Sumter masterstroke. Even an expedition with provisions only, if delivered by night with stealth, would not have been interpreted by the world in the benign light that Lincoln wanted. But doing it openly, with notification, made the difference. It put the issue squarely to the rebels. A last-minute notice, a notice too late for action or forcing hasty decision, would have destroyed his purpose: to let the rebels—and the world—know what he was doing and to let them decide.

DID LINCOLN'S LETTER CONTAIN A THREAT?

IN FINDING THE WAY to fulfill his two obligations—to hold U.S. property while not initiating conflict—Lincoln "took pains," as he himself described his eventual decision, "not only to keep the latter promise good, but also to keep the case so free from the power of ingenious sophistry, as that the world should not be able to misunderstand it."

Notwithstanding his scrupulous care in this regard, there has been some "ingenious sophistry." Critics have made the morally tinged charge that Lincoln deviously tricked the rebels into firing the first shot so that they could be blamed therefore for beginning the war. Both Jefferson Davis and Alexander Stephens would write versions of that self-justifying Confederate position. The scholarly version of that view would be presented in an oft-quoted article by historian Charles Ramsdell in 1937.

Before he criticizes Lincoln's action, Ramsdell gives a summary that might be read as praise:

> The tables were now completely turned on the Southerners. Lincoln was well out of his dilemma when they, who had heretofore had the tactical advantage of being able to wait until Anderson must evacuate, were suddenly faced with a choice of two evils. They must either take the fort before relief could arrive, thus taking the apparent offensive which they had hoped to avoid, or they must stand by quietly and see the fort provisioned . . . This, then, was the dilemma which they faced as the result of Lincoln's astute strategy.

Being astute in the matter of strategy is a worthy attribute of a statesman. Ramsdell also wrote that "too little credit has been given to Abraham Lincoln's genius for political strategy." Ramsdell's praise of Lincoln (a prelude to damning him) extends to his writing: "Lincoln was a rare master of the written word . . . He had the skill of an artist in so phrasing a sentence that it conveyed precisely the meaning he wished it to convey." Not only that, he could make it have different meanings to different audiences. That was what he did, according to Ramsdell, with that message to Pickens (and Beauregard, and from them to Jefferson Davis and company in Montgomery).

The charge is that the letter contained a threat, or even a double threat, which the Confederates would discern but others would not. Here is what Lincoln wrote, composing it carefully himself, giving instructions to Robert Chew:

> Sir—you will proceed directly to Charleston, South Carolina; and if, on your arrival there, the flag of the United States shall be flying over Fort-Sumpter, and the Fort shall not have been attacked, you will procure an interview with Gov. Pickens, and read to him as follows:
>
> I am directed by the President of the United States to notify you to expect an attempt will be made to supply Fort-Sumpter with provisions only; and that, if such attempt be not resisted, no effort to throw in men, arms, or ammunition, will be made, without further notice, or in case of an attack upon the Fort.

The North, says Ramsdell, would read in the statement only that Lincoln was sending bread (to brave and hungry men), and that if the rebels attacked they would be firing upon bread. The Southerners, by contrast, would read in the last part of the message a double threat hidden in a nest of negatives.

The first threat: If the bread-bringers were fired upon, then there would be an attack with soldiers and guns, with the flotilla of ships that the Confederates knew had sailed from New York.* Ramsdell describes their situation:

> But to allow the provisioning meant not only an indefinite postponement to their possession of the fort which had become as much a symbol to them as it was to Lincoln; to permit it in the face of the threat of force, after all their preparations, would be to make a ridiculous and disgraceful retreat.

One may respond: Lincoln's statement was a promise, a statement of what he would not do, before it was any kind of a threat. The threat, which was secondary to the promise, was only implicit. We have noted already

---

*Ramsdell adds that they assumed in this decision that all of that preparation up in the Brooklyn Navy Yard—the Pickens as well as the Sumter expedition—was headed for Sumter.

that Lincoln had written in the draft of his inaugural, "The government will not assail you, unless you first assail it," and that Seward, aware from the Senate of the thinness of Southern skin, suggested dropping "unless you first assail it" because those who heard the highest decibels of implicit threats would have heard one there. But of course the Union, like any government, would respond to an attack.

Lincoln's statement was a double threat, according to Ramsdell, because a further threat was hidden in a negative, in the phrase "without further notice." Did that not mean that at some later time, after the Sumter garrison had been given its pork and beans, there might be, after a notice was sent, an attack after all? Ramsdell writes: "Nor could they be sure that, if they yielded now in the matter of 'provisions only,' they would not soon be served with the 'further notice' as a prelude to throwing in 'men, arms, and ammunition.' "

Surely it was evident that Lincoln could hardly have done that. If the rebels had allowed Sumter to be provisioned and Lincoln had then turned around and sent them a notice and attacked, Lincoln would have incurred a horrendous double odium. He would have been both the one who fired the "first shot" and the one who responded to restraint with aggression.

And—a point that runs through this event—being seen as the aggressor would have been much more damaging for Lincoln, and for the Union side, than for the rebels, because that sensitivity about "coercion" had been so thoroughly developed in the border states as well as the South. Had the Union taken overt action that appeared to be blatant aggression, then it surely would have lost not only the four states that ultimately did join the Confederacy but also Kentucky, Maryland, and Missouri, and as Lincoln said, that would have been the game.

IN YOUR HANDS AND NOT IN MINE

ONCE THE SHIPS of the Sumter expedition had set forth and the Confederate authorities had been notified that an attempt would be made, the burden of decision shifted to Montgomery and Charleston. Lincoln had managed to put before the assailants of the government, and before the world, an unmistakably plain acting-out of his inaugural pledge and claim: "You can forbear the assault upon it; I can not shrink from the defense of it. With you, and not with me, is the solemn question 'Shall it be peace, or a sword?' "

Now Davis and the Confederate leaders had to decide what they would do. The distinguished Lincoln scholar Richard Current, in his *Lincoln and the First Shot,* writes about the respective roles of Jefferson Davis and Lincoln:

> Biographers of Davis and historians of the Confederacy have evaded or obscured their hero's role in the Sumter affair. They have digressed to levy accusations or innuendoes at Lincoln. If they have any concern for historical objectivity, however, they should face frankly the question of Davis's responsibility for the coming of the war. Upon them, upon his partisans, should rest the burden of proof. It should not have to be borne forever, as it has for far too many years, by Lincoln's champions. After all, Lincoln did not order the guns to fire. Davis did.

That Davis and his advisers might have chosen differently is indicated by Robert Toombs, the eminent Georgia politician who had been named secretary of state in the new Confederate government in Montgomery. Toombs is quoted as having said, about attacking the fort, "[I]t is unnecessary, it puts us in the wrong, it is fatal!" Jefferson Davis and the others, one might say, should have listened to Toombs, but in any case they could have—they were free to make other choices than the one they made.

Lincoln had strong reason to expect that the rebels would not allow provisions to be supplied to the fort. One of the visitors he sent down there to Charleston in the anxious six weeks, his friend Stephen Hulbert (who had grown up in Charleston), came back with the report that the rebel fervor was so strong and unanimous that even an attempt to bring supplies would be resisted. But the choice would be the rebels'.

In a passage often quoted, historian James G. Randall writes:

> Of course Lincoln was aware that sending provisions to Sumter might provoke hostilities, but that is not to say that he desired hostilities. And to argue that Lincoln meant that the first shot would be fired by the other side if a first shot was fired is by no means the same as arguing that he deliberately maneuvered to have the shot fired.

The hundred men in the fort posed no threat to Charleston, but maybe the revolutionary fervor was puffed up to a point that letting the bread be provided was not an option.

Perhaps if the Montgomery authorities had ordered restraint, the Charleston hotheads would not have obeyed, and South Carolina would have acted on its own, rebels within a rebellion. And the new Confederacy would then have given an immediate example of the point that Lincoln had made in his inaugural. He had said that the principle of secession set a dangerous precedent that might one day turn around and bite the original secessionists.

Jefferson Davis and his advisers might have let stand the instructions they had given General Beauregard on April 8, after hearing word of the expedition: "Under no circumstances are you to allow provisions to be sent to Fort Sumter." That would have meant that the guns of Charleston Harbor would have waited until a vessel carrying the American flag had actually steamed into the harbor before opening fire. That would have meant, on the negative side, that they fit the picture that Lincoln kept drawing and underlining: "firing upon bread." But at least they would then have been firing in response to an overt act from the other side—the entrance of the provisioning boat into the harbor they claimed as their own. Obviously it is much easier to convince the world that the other side has committed "aggression" if there is an unmistakable overt act.

The Confederate authorities in Montgomery instead notified Beauregard that he should demand the evacuation of the fort and, if that should be refused, "reduce" the fort. Reduce it he did.

I HAVE THE HONOR TO BEGIN BOMBING YOU

THERE FOLLOWED A SEQUENCE of supremely proper messages back and forth between Beauregard and Anderson—the utter propriety perhaps increased by the fact that Anderson had been Beauregard's teacher at West Point, and that both were Southern gentlemen (Anderson from Kentucky). Anderson responded to Beauregard's courteous demand that he leave the fort with this doubly courteous response:

Fort Sumter, S. C., April 11, 1861.

General:

I have the honor to acknowledge the receipt of your communication demanding the evacuation of this fort, and to say, in reply thereto, that it is a demand with which I regret that my sense of honor, and of my obligations to my Government, prevent my compliance. Thanking you for the fair, manly, and courteous terms proposed, and for the high compliment paid me,

    I am, general, very respectfully, your obedient servant,

Robert Anderson,
Major, First Artillery, Commanding.

These messages would usually begin "I have the honor to receive your communication" and would then include regrets that the writer could not accept the proposal that he had had the honor to receive; they then would close with the routine but under the circumstances somewhat ironical claim to be "respectfully, your obedient servant." The point to which Major Anderson's honor would let him go was not quite far enough for Beauregard's honor to accept. The exchange concluded with this message from Beauregard's two aides-de-camp, which managed to invoke honor twice in just two sentences.

Fort Sumter, S. C., April 12, 1861—3.20 a. m.

Sir:

By authority of Brigadier-General Beauregard, commanding the
Provisional Forces of the Confederate States, we have the honor to
notify you that he will open the fire of his batteries on Fort Sumter in
one hour from this time.
We have the honor to be, very respectfully, your obedient servants.

The Confederate batteries then had the honor to open fire at four-thirty in the morning, and the batteries at Sumter had the honor to return fire beginning at daybreak. After thirty-six hours of an unequal exchange between the guns in the fort and those on shore, and a fire in the fort, there were more "I have the honor" messages, and the garrison capitulated, and Major Anderson accepted the offer of transportation out to the Union flotilla.

Headquarters, Fort Sumter, S. C.,
April 13, 1861—7.5 p. m.

General:

I have the honor to acknowledge the receipt of your communication of
this evening, and to express my gratification at its contents. Should it be
convenient, I would like to have the Catawba here at about nine o'clock
to-morrow morning.
With sentiments of the highest regard and esteem, I am, general,
very respectfully, your obedient servant

Robert Anderson

No one had been killed, but the American Civil War had begun.

THE CAUSE OF THE COUNTRY WAS ADVANCED

THERE WAS, in the narrowest sense of sheer physical power, no military stake to either side in holding or not holding Fort Sumter. The fort, even if resupplied with provisions for a time, even for that matter if supplied with more men and armaments, was no military threat to the now well-fortified Charleston Harbor, or to South Carolina, or to the Confederacy; the loss of this fort did not endanger the Union, physically speaking. But one cannot separate the apparatus of physical power from the attitudes of the human beings who apply it. The "symbolic" meaning, the effect, the shadow that the fort cast upon public attitudes—the indications of intent and purpose—was immense.

In Lincoln's July 4 Message to Congress he described the government's purpose as "to maintain visible possession" and the rebels' purpose as "to drive out the visible authority," and he said that these competing visibilities carried with them the fate of the Union:

> They knew that this Government desired to keep the garrison in the Fort, not to assail them, but merely to maintain visible possession, and thus to preserve the Union from actual, and immediate dissolution . . . and they assailed, and reduced the Fort, for precisely the reverse object— to drive out the visible authority of the Federal Union, and thus force it to immediate dissolution.

And the rebels did fire the first shot.

> [T]he assailants of the Government began the conflict of arms, without a gun in sight . . . save only the few in the Fort, sent to that harbor, years before, for their own protection.

They thereby began the war, which Lincoln's actions had risked, with the Union itself at stake.

> In this act, discarding all else, they have forced upon the country, the distinct issue: "Immediate dissolution, or blood."

Lincoln claimed success for his Sumter policy in two statements that are often quoted in the windup of discussions of these events. One statement came in a consoling letter to Gustavus Fox and the other in that talk with Orville Browning, recorded in Browning's diary. Ramsdell interprets Lincoln's claim of "success" to mean that he managed to start the war while making the rebels take the blame for it. But one may understand Lincoln in a slightly different way, to a quite different appraisal.

To Fox he wrote: "You and I both anticipated that the cause of the country would be advanced by making the attempt to provision Fort Sumpter, even if it should fail; and it is no small consolation now to feel that our anticipation is justified by the result." Ramsdell asks: "Was this statement merely intended to soothe a disappointed commander, or did it contain a hint that the real objective of the expedition was not at all the relief of Sumter?"

One may answer that the real objective of the expedition was the demonstration of Union resolve by the attempt to relieve Sumter—that objective was accomplished. Depending upon how the rebels responded, the situation contained the further possibility of a Union moral advantage, and they responded so that that possibility was also realized.

Browning got down on paper after he returned to his room what Lincoln had said of the Sumter expedition: "He himself conceived the idea, and proposed sending supplies, without an attempt to reinforce giving notice of the fact to Gov Pickens of S.C. The plan succeeded. They attacked Sumter—it fell, and thus, did more service than it otherwise could." Ramsdell treats this quotation from Browning's diary as conclusive: "It completes the evidence."

Ramsdell assumes that the usually shut-mouthed Lincoln, secretly proud of what he had brought off, had in this relaxed meeting with an old friend revealed his true purpose, unaware that Browning would write it down when he got back to his room. Perhaps that assumption has a modicum of truth. But again there were layers to Lincoln's success. The first was simply to move the dilemma from his own shoulders to theirs. Sumter being provisioned and continuing as a visible symbol of Union resolve, flying the American flag in the harbor of the fiercest rebels, would have been another kind of success. But the attack "without a gun in sight" did something else: it abruptly unified the North and generated a huge desire to put down this rebellion. We may take Lincoln's phrase and say that the "cause of the country" was advanced.

Nicolay and Hay did not stint in their praise for their chief in this first great encounter. They would write, looking back in 1888 to the moment he sent the Sumter expedition:

> When he finally gave the order that the fleet should sail he was master of the situation; master of his Cabinet; master of the moral attitude and

issues of the struggle; master of the public opinion which must arise out of the impending conflict; master if the rebels hesitated or repented, because they would thereby forfeit their prestige with the South; master if they persisted, for he would then command a united North.

They did persist, and he did command, for a time, a united North.

CHAPTER FOUR

On Not *Mastering the Situation*

The Comedy of the *Powhatan*

NOT ALL THE EARLY undertakings of the Lincoln administration showed such mastery: the story of the *Powhatan* shows something else. We tell it partly because it has not been often told; partly because it shows the president making a big mistake; and partly because it shows how he handled it and learned from it.

The USS *Powhatan* was a 2,415-ton side-wheel steamer built in the Norfolk Navy Yard in 1852, named for the famous Indian chief who had ruled the coastal area of Virginia at the time Jamestown was settled. (Americans had a certain romantic inclination to give their warships Indian names. At one point in the spring of 1861 the U.S. Navy had only three active warships in Atlantic waters, and their names were the *Pocahontas,* the *Pawnee,* and the *Powhatan.*) The *Powhatan,* which had been the flagship of Commodore Matthew Perry in Japan eight years earlier, carried the most powerful weapons and was the most formidable of the small American navy's warships available for duty on the East Coast.

In the first days of April, with the Sumter crisis looming, the *Powhatan* was ordered to proceed to two different destinations at the same time; was put under command of two different officers; and received three successive orders, each one contradicting the last, from three high officials in a row: President Lincoln himself, Navy Secretary Welles, and Secretary of State Seward. The expedition in which it took part was planned by Seward, a total amateur in the art of war, with the help of a captain of the army engineers who had been working on an aqueduct and the expansion of the Capitol building, and a lieutenant in the navy, with perhaps some contribution from the new president, even more of an amateur. The expedition was planned in such secrecy as not to be made known to the two relevant cabinet members, the secretaries of war and of the navy, and plans made by the latter for another expedition, with the president's approval, were to be wrecked by conflicting orders from the president himself.

WE ARE YET WITHOUT A POLICY

THE KEY TO UNDERSTANDING this astonishing episode is that Secretary of State William Henry Seward had his own policy for the looming crisis, and it seemed to him that Lincoln did not. We know that Seward thought Lincoln had no policy because he said so, in a presumptuous little paper he sent, altogether privately, to the president on an extremely busy presidential day, April 1, 1861: "We are at the end of a month's administration and yet without a policy either foreign or domestic." This memorandum urged the president to "[c]hange the question before the Public from one upon Slavery . . . for a question upon Union or Disunion . . . from what would be regarded as a Party question to one of Patriotism or Union." One way to do that was deliberately to get into a war with another nation, a suggestion that Lincoln in his response quietly ignored. But the primary way to shift the question, according to Seward, was for the government to give up Fort Sumter and make the reinforcement of Fort Pickens the symbol of Union resolve.

Seward's opposition to provisioning Sumter, his insistence that Union troops be withdrawn "forthwith," was grounded not only in his analysis of the situation but also in the personal stake he had acquired. Every anxious week since South Carolina seceded on December 20, while Lincoln had been out in Springfield, riding the train, speaking hither and yon, meeting people, and editing his upcoming inaugural address in the Willard Hotel, Seward had been in Washington, in the Senate, speaking and acting for the Republicans. Effectively leading the Republicans in Washington, Seward had repeatedly informed the Confederate government, through informal communications to three "commissioners," that Fort Sumter would be evacuated.

So when, after the March 29 cabinet meeting, Lincoln signed the order setting in motion Gustavus Fox's preparations for a Sumter expedition, it was a serious blow to Seward's credibility. Ever the energetic activist, he could at least take steps to set in motion the alternative he much preferred, an expedition to Pickens.

Lincoln immediately wrote his own little paper responding, gently enough, to Seward's "thoughts." He denied that the administration lacked a policy; it had the policy that he had stated in the inaugural address, with which Seward had agreed: "I said 'The power confided to me will be used to hold, occupy and possess the property and places belonging to the government, and to collect the duties, and imposts.' This had your distinct approval at the time." And when that inaugural statement was combined with the order Lincoln gave the first day to the general in chief of the army, it represented precisely the policy in Seward's present proposal—with just one exception:

> [The inaugural statement] taken in connection with the order I immedi- ately gave General Scott, directing him to employ every means in his power to strengthen and hold the forts, comprises the exact domestic policy you now urge, with the single exception, that it does not propose to abandon Fort Sumpter.

On the Sumter-Pickens matter, Lincoln did not agree with Seward's interpretation: "I do not perceive how the re-enforcement of Fort Sumpter would be done on a slavery, or party issue, while that of Fort Pickens would be on a more national, and patriotic one." In contrast to Seward, Lincoln saw reinforcing Sumter, with its particular geography and history and sym- bolic meaning, as vastly the more important. But he assumed that Pickens should and would be held as well.

In the shock of his first day in office, March 5, Lincoln had learned from a note from General Scott not only that Scott believed that Sumter would have to be surrendered but also that this other fort down in Pensacola Har- bor in Florida was in jeopardy as well. Lincoln had, in response on that first day, given Scott orally the order of which he now reminded Seward.

Five days into his presidency, on March 9, as we have seen, Lincoln had Nicolay put his order to General Scott in writing: "I am directed by the President to say that he desires you to exercise all vigilance for the mainte- nance of all the places within the military department of the United States," in which of course he included Fort Pickens.

Although location and history made Fort Pickens less of a symbol, it was, like Sumter, located on an island in a harbor surrounded by Confeder- ate installations. But by its location, it was easier to defend than Sumter. Not only that, the Buchanan administration, in its brief and evanescent fortnight of fortitude in January 1861, had actually sent reinforcements: two hundred men on the USS *Brooklyn*. But these troops never landed at the fort because of "some quasi-armistice of the late administration," as Lincoln would call it, by which it had been agreed that if the United States would not land the troops, the Confederate forces would not attack.

This new president, however, had ordered General Scott to have those troops land and reinforce Fort Pickens. But General Scott sent the orders by the long, slow sea route, so they did not even arrive in Pensacola until the Sumter crisis was almost over. In addition, Lincoln learned that the *Brooklyn* had moved away from Pensacola to Key West, and so he assumed that his order to land the troops had, as he put it, "fizzled out." (It turned out, however, that before the *Brooklyn* left Pensacola the two hundred troops had been transferred to another ship, the *Sabine,* where they sat afloat in the harbor all through the Sumter crisis.)

MEET CAPTAIN MEIGS, FORTHWITH

LINCOLN, assuming the order to reinforce Pickens had failed, was more than receptive to the idea of sending a new Pickens expedition. Seward had not only argued on behalf of such a mission but had also proposed specifics: "I would call in Captain M. C. Meigs forthwith. Aided by his counsel, I would at once, and at every cost, prepare for a war at Pensacola."

Right away, on another busy presidential day, March 29, Seward brought Captain Montgomery C. Meigs in person to the White House and introduced him to the president. One might not have thought of Meigs as the man to lead a naval expedition to Florida. He was an army man, a graduate of West Point, and he was a mere captain. Moreover, he was an army engineer. The omnipresent Seward, who knew everybody, knew him as the overseer of construction on the Capitol. But Seward knew also that Meigs had recently visited the federal posts in Florida, including Pensacola, so he knew the territory. And, Seward said—in implied, unkind, and invidious contrast to the old and overweight General in Chief Winfield Scott, and perhaps also to General Joseph Totten, the chief army engineer, another veteran of the War of 1812—the president "ought to see some of the younger officers, and not consult only with men who, if war broke out, could not mount a horse."

When Lincoln asked Meigs whether Fort Pickens could be held, army man Meigs replied, "Certainly, if the navy would do its duty." Lincoln then asked him—this man whom he had just met and talked with for the first time—whether he would go down to Florida and secure Pickens. Meigs modestly responded that he was only a captain and could not command the majors down there. Nicolay and Hay report in quotation marks what Seward then said: "Captain Meigs must be promoted." "But there is no vacancy," said Meigs, modestly. Seward airily dismissed that objection and told Lincoln that Meigs was the man to undertake this task, making the analogy to William Pitt, when he desired to conquer Canada, sending for a young man he had met in London society and telling him to take Quebec.

After questioning and listening to Meigs, Lincoln asked him to make a plan.

To carry out his plan—which, like the plan for Sumter, entailed running a ship past the hostile Confederate batteries—Meigs needed a naval officer with talent and daring. He knew just the man: a close friend of his, David D. Porter. Porter was the son of a naval hero from the War of 1812. He was only a lieutenant and had been unsatisfied with his opportunities in the navy when Seward—at Meigs's suggestion—selected him for the Pickens expedition.

Seward insisted that the Pickens expedition must be kept secret from the Navy and Army Departments, even from the secretaries of the navy and the army. The Navy Department, in particular, was pockmarked with rebel sympathizers who wouldn't keep secrets. Nevertheless, the audacious irregularity of this undertaking was breathtaking.

April 1 was the day Lincoln learned that troops had not been landed at Fort Pickens. Also on that day Seward, Meigs, and Porter came to the executive mansion and, in an office next to the president's, wrote orders for him to sign regarding the developing Pickens expedition. Meigs would say in his diary: "Hard at work all day making orders for the signature of the President" and, specifically, "I sent a despatch to commandant of the Brooklyn Navy Yard to get the *Powhatan* ready for sea with least possible delay. This was signed by the President." Porter was hard at work too, with Seward as the overarching authority for all that they were doing. In two of the most significant of the eight orders signed by Lincoln—the two orders to David D. Porter, one giving him command of the *Powhatan* and the other giving him instructions as to his course once he would arrive in Pensacola Harbor—the signature of the president was followed by another signature: "Recommended: Wm. H. Seward."

BEWILDERMENT AT THE WILLARD

THAT VERY EVENING, as Navy Secretary Gideon Welles sat at dinner in the Willard Hotel, the president's secretary John Nicolay appeared and laid upon his table a package from the president. It had to be important, Welles thought, for Lincoln to interrupt his dinner in this way, and to send the overworked Nicolay. On being opened, the hand-delivered package proved to hold some signed orders from the president dealing with naval assignments—Welles's own department. The most remarkable of these letters, signed by Lincoln, was addressed to Welles himself and instructed him to make several changes in naval assignments. Welles objected to them all but especially to the reassignment of Captain Silas Stringham, who was directed to proceed "with all possible despatch" to Pensacola to take command of the squadron stationed there. Stringham was a senior naval officer whom Welles had known for years and to whom he had himself already given another, and very important, assignment: heading up the bureau dealing with naval personnel, at the very heart of the Navy Department. Stringham, a knowledgeable navy man, was to be brought on to help the new civilian secretary. Why in the world would he be removed? And still worse, why would he be replaced by the man this order proposed, Samuel Barron, whose loyalty to the Union Welles had reason to doubt? (And before many weeks had passed, his doubt would be vindicated: Barron would join the Confederate navy.)

Welles, sitting at his dinner table in the Willard reading these documents, was stunned. "Without a moment's delay," Welles went to see the president at the executive mansion. He found him sitting at his desk alone, writing. Lincoln's response to the abrupt evening appearance of his bearded secretary of the navy is instructive. "[R]aising his head from the table at which he was writing," Lincoln is quoted by Welles as saying, "What have I done wrong?"

Welles showed him the most remarkable of the letters, the one ordering the various reassignments in navy personnel. The handwriting in the body of the letter was that of Montgomery Meigs. The postscript was in the handwriting of David D. Porter, the naval lieutenant who was the friend of Meigs. And here they were—Meigs and Porter, under the aegis of Seward, drafting a letter about navy personnel, without even informing, let alone consulting, the secretary of the navy. And the letters bore the signature of Abraham Lincoln.

Reading Welles's account, one imagines that the president was a little sheepish as he tried to explain to Welles what had happened. Seward had been there that day, Lincoln said, with "two or three young men," discussing a subject that was a Seward specialty—Lincoln still did not tell Welles that the subject was Fort Pickens—which he, Lincoln, had agreed to, and as it involved many details, he had left Seward to prepare the papers. Lincoln told Welles that he had signed these letters without reading them, "for he had not time, and if he could not trust the Secretary of State, he did not know whom he could trust." An embarrassed Lincoln told Welles that, despite his signature on the letters, Welles could disregard the orders they contained and not make the reassignments they specified. And Welles, although still astonished by the whole matter, retired, assuming everything had been straightened out.

BAFFLEMENT IN THE BROOKLYN NAVY YARD

IF NAVY SECRETARY WELLES was bewildered at the Willard Hotel in the nation's capital, Andrew H. Foote was baffled at the Brooklyn Navy Yard. Admiral Foote, the executive officer of the yard, had received a blizzard of contradictory orders having to do with the warship *Powhatan*. The first one was a brisk message from Secretary Welles, who, after the cabinet meeting on Friday, March 29—the one setting Gustavus Fox's Sumter project in motion—had ordered him to "[f]it out the *Powhatan* to go to sea at the earliest possible moment." Welles wanted this most important warship to be ready for the Sumter assignment.

But then, only twenty minutes after receiving the message from Welles, Admiral Foote received a telegram giving the same order about the *Powhatan,* in almost the same language, but this time with a different and astonishing signature:

Washington, April 1, 1861

Fit out the *Powhatan* to go to sea at the earliest possible moment
under sealed orders. Orders by a confidential messenger go forward
to-morrow.

Abraham Lincoln.

This development was puzzling, not only because of the redundancy but also because of the irregularity—the president issuing an order directly, without going through the Navy Department.

Although more than a little unsettled, Foote did issue the orders to prepare the *Powhatan,* which was no small matter. The ship had been undergoing extensive repairs. But under the imperative of these orders Foote set the yard to work nights as well as days to prepare the *Powhatan* to go to sea.

But then on the next day, April 2, there came a still more disturbing development. An energetic navy lieutenant named David D. Porter burst into Foote's presence brandishing another astonishing order from the president himself, every line of which was baffling:

Executive Mansion, April 1, 1861

Sir: You will fit out the *Powhatan* without delay. Lieutenant Porter will relieve Captain Mercer in command of her. She is bound on secret service, and you will under no circumstances communicate to the Navy Department the fact that she is fitting out.

Abraham Lincoln

Foote could scarcely believe that this document was authentic. It was highly irregular to replace a senior officer of much higher rank—a captain, Samuel Mercer—with a mere lieutenant, to bypass channels, and to ignore seniority.

And there was one more mystery: that extraordinary sentence saying, "She is bound on secret service, and you will under no circumstances communicate to the Navy Department the fact that she is fitting out." What could this mean? Not tell the Navy Department about one of its own ships? When the secretary of the navy had just given him orders about this same ship?

Porter, in recalling these events years later, said that it took three hours to persuade Foote that his orders really came from the president and were not a Southern forgery. Admiral Foote was further astonished that an army man, Montgomery Meigs, joined Porter in the argument, insisting that he too had orders directly from the president, and that in fact he was in charge of the expedition of which the *Powhatan* was to be a major part.

Foote was worried enough to send self-protecting messages to Welles. On April 5 he sent a telegram saying that he was executing the governmental orders he had received "from the naval officer as well as the army officer." Now it was Welles's turn to be baffled: What army officer? Foote received back a telegram from Welles with another brisk order: "Delay the *Powhatan* for further instructions."

Foote's multiple bafflements and cautions led him to send Welles's telegram to Meigs and Porter, who were staying at the Astor House in New York City. Porter sent a letter right back to Foote, written at eight in the evening, saying, "I am with Captain Meigs and we are telegraphing to Mr. Seward." (Again one may note who was regarded as the center of power in Washington.) In any case, he argued, he and Meigs had their orders directly from the president, and the orders of the commander in chief trumped those of a mere cabinet secretary.

Back in Washington, plans for the Sumter expedition were under way. When Gustavus Fox met with Lincoln and Welles to make the final arrangements, Welles proposed adding the powerful warship *Powhatan,* which he had had the foresight to order prepared for duty. And the *Powhatan* could carry the three hundred sailors Fox proposed. Fox eagerly accepted the offer of the ship. Secretary of the Navy Welles then sent elaborate orders to Captain Samuel Mercer, commander of the USS *Powhatan* and also commander of the entire Atlantic naval force, which consisted of the U.S. steamers (in addition to the *Powhatan*) *Pawnee, Pocahontas,* and *Harriet Lane.* The ships were ordered to assemble "off Charleston bar, ten miles distant from and due east of the light-house, on the morning of the 11th inst." They were to endeavor first to deliver "subsistence" to the garrison in Fort Sumter, and then if that was resisted, to "use [the] entire force to . . . place both the troops and supplies in Fort Sumter." Welles read to President Lincoln the instructions to Captain Mercer, and the president approved what Welles had read to him. This moment was to prove critical to what was to follow.

The next day Lincoln learned that no troops had been landed at Fort Pickens. The president now had Secretary Welles send a special messenger to Pensacola, across land this time, carrying the order, now through the proper navy channels, that the troops from the *Sabine* should be landed at Pickens. So now at last a strong effort by the government was under way to retain both of the forts still in Union hands. Welles retired to the Willard congratulating himself that the navy was doing its part.

But once again on April 6 Welles's evening in the Willard was to be interrupted, this time at a later hour. It was after eleven o'clock when Secretary Seward appeared at Welles's rooms, together with his assistant, his son Frederick. They had in hand the telegram from Captain Meigs in New York saying that his undertaking was being impeded by some new orders that had just come from the secretary of the navy. The Sewards showed Welles the telegram from Meigs, but Welles could not understand what it referred to. Seward explained that it had to do with the *Powhatan* and Porter's command. The *Powhatan?* Porter's command? What was this all about? Naval Officer Porter had no command—the secretary of the navy surely ought to know. And the *Powhatan,* said Welles, was the flagship of the Sumter expedition and had just been ordered to a gathering force off Charleston Harbor. Moreover, Meigs was an army officer, not a navy man.

The president had not yet gone to bed when in the middle of the night this crew of government dignitaries appeared at the executive mansion. "On seeing us," wrote Welles, "he was surprised, and his surprise was not diminished on learning our errand." Lincoln looked at Seward, looked at

Welles, read and reread Meigs's telegram, then asked Welles whether he might be in error. Welles insisted he was not and reminded him that he had read to Lincoln his orders to Captain Mercer, and that Lincoln had approved. Welles's telling of the story continues: "He [Lincoln] recollected the circumstance," Welles wrote, "but not the name of the officer or the vessel—said he had become confused with the names *Pocahontas* and *Powhatan*."* Too many ships had Indian names that began with the letter "P." Welles insisted even at this postmidnight hour on making a trip to the Navy Department next door to the White House to obtain a copy of the order to Mercer.

Welles's biographer John Niven imagines a little scene there in the president's office in the middle of the night as this ad hoc group of government figures waited for the agitated Secretary Welles to bustle over to the Navy Department to get the letter he had read to Lincoln just the day before: "Seward, tense and tired, but alert, lounging carelessly on a sofa; young Frederick Seward and Captain Stringham in the background; Lincoln, weary beyond belief, his table cluttered with documents, possibly annoyed by Welles's sudden departure for proof, yet anxious that there be harmonious relations among members of his cabinet." We may continue the imagining on our own: the stout, bewigged, bearded Welles, full of righteous indignation, sweeps triumphantly back into the room brandishing the letter he had sent to Captain Mercer and read to the president the previous day. He shows the letter, with grim satisfaction, to Lincoln and squints obliquely over his little glasses at Seward on the sofa. Lincoln, reading the orders to Mercer, now registers the name: Mercer. Yes. Now I remember signing something about a Mercer back on that Monday of many signings, and then Welles yesterday reading his letter to Mercer. Yes, Welles is right.

Lincoln now grasped what a huge error he had made by signing, without reading, the earlier orders that Meigs and Porter—under Seward's aegis—had concocted in his anteroom on April 1. How was Lincoln going to respond? Reprimands? Self-laceration? Avoidance—it is late; maybe we should sleep on it? What he did was to start right in that instant, in the tired middle of the night, to straighten it out. He turned to Seward and told him that the *Powhatan* must be restored to Mercer and to the expedition to relieve Fort Sumter; he had not meant to do anything to interfere with the

---

*This sentence appears in an article Welles wrote in *Galaxy* in a passage quoted in *N&H*, 4:5. The little touch about the confusing names does not appear in the book edition of Welles's diary.

Sumter expedition. It tells us something about Seward's conception of his role in relation to Lincoln at this point that even in this circumstance—the late hour, his own machinations exposed, and a clear statement by the president—he nevertheless gave an argument. He said it would be hard at this hour to get word through to the Brooklyn Navy Yard to Mercer and the *Powhatan*. And not only that, he tried to argue the merits. The Pickens expedition was the more important, he said, and it would be injured if the *Powhatan* were withdrawn from it. Lincoln—surely understandably—said he did not want to discuss the matter; Welles used the words "peremptory" and "imperative" to describe Lincoln's instructions to Seward. Abraham Lincoln, the amiable politician and lawyer from Illinois, had not had many occasions in his life to be "peremptory" and "imperative," but now he was learning.

For his part, Seward did send a telegram—but perhaps not right away. It did not arrive in Brooklyn until three the next afternoon.

APRIL 6, BACK IN BROOKLYN

When Seward's terse telegram, sent by the president's "imperative" order, to Porter—"Give the *Powhatan* to Mercer," signed just "Seward"—arrived at the Brooklyn Navy Yard, Commander Foote, no doubt baffled yet again by the conduct of these new civilian overlords, had a fast tug chartered and sent it after the *Powhatan*. When the tug overtook the *Powhatan* and Porter read the message signed just "Seward," he decided he should ignore it. If his original orders from the president trumped an order from the civilian head of his own Navy Department, they certainly did the same for the head of another department. The *Powhatan* steamed on toward Pensacola.

FRUSTRATION IN CHARLESTON HARBOR

The four ships, including the *Powhatan,* and three tugboats that were to take part in the Sumter expedition as planned by Fox and set in motion by Abraham Lincoln were to assemble in the early morning of April 11 in Charleston Harbor, ten miles east of the lighthouse. But as is so often the case in war, and perhaps peace as well, acts of God and acts of men intervened, preventing that from happening. Only the revenue cutter *Harriet Lane* came close to carrying out the plan. The chartered steamer *Baltic,* with Fox on board, ran into a tremendous gale and did not arrive until the early morning hours of April 12. The storm also scattered the three tugs that were to have attempted the delivery of supplies to Sumter. Fox thought he might be able to use the longboats on the *Powhatan* instead of the tugs—but where was the *Powhatan?*

In Fox's report we see the dark comedy of these naval captains, in the heavy sea off Charleston Harbor, discussing their wait for a ship, the *Powhatan,* which in fact was at that moment steaming south to Florida, and their obligation to an officer, Captain Mercer, who in fact at that moment was back in New York.

They were trying to carry out the plan designed by Gustavus Fox and ordered by President Lincoln.

Fox asked the commander of the *Pawnee* to join him in the attempt to send in provisions. The captain replied that his orders required him to remain ten miles east of the light and await the *Powhatan,* and stated that he was not going in there to inaugurate civil war. (But that was being done, at that moment, by others.)

Fox reported:

[H]eavy guns were heard and the smoke and shells from the batteries which had just opened fire upon Sumter were distinctly visible.

Neither the *Pawnee* nor *Harriet Lane* had boats or men to carry in supplies. Feeling sure that the *Powhatan* would arrive during the night, as she had sailed from New York two days before us, I stood out to the appointed rendezvous and made signals all night.

But of course no *Powhatan* appeared. Fox's report continues:

The morning of the 13th was thick and foggy, with a very heavy ground swell . . . An officer of very great zeal and fidelity, though suffering from seasickness . . . organized a boat's crew . . . notwithstanding the heavy sea, for the purpose of having at least one boat, in the absence of the *Powhatan*'s to reach Fort Sumter.

At 8 a.m. I took this boat, and . . . pulled in to the *Pawnee.* As we approached that vessel a great volume of black smoke issued from Fort Sumter, through which the flash of Major Anderson's guns still replied to the rebel fire. The quarters of the fort were on fire.

And now, at this late moment and in this unlikely place, Fox at last learned about the missing ship and the missing captain:

I now learned for the first time that [the captain of the *Pawnee*] had received a note from Captain Mercer, of the *Powhatan,* dated at New York the 6th, the day he sailed, stating that the *Powhatan* was detached by orders of "superior authority" from the duty to which she was assigned off Charleston, and had sailed for another destination.

This "superior authority" was the president of the United States, whose letters signed unwittingly on April 1 effectively undercut the plan he wittingly ordered four days later.

On the afternoon of this climactic day, the *Pocahontas* finally arrived. Now there were two U.S. Navy ships with Indian names beginning with "P" ten miles off Charleston Harbor—but neither one, alas, was the *Powhatan.* Reported Fox: "[A]t 2 p.m. the *Pocahontas* arrived, and at 2:30 the flag of Sumter was shot away and not again raised."

Captain Gillis of the *Pocahontas* wanted to render assistance to the gallant men in Sumter but discovered it was too late. Instead, he received the message from Anderson that they had decided to evacuate the fort and needed transportation:

> I . . . proceeded to Fort Sumter [Captain Gillis reported to Gideon Welles] to offer [the available ships] in person. Found the fort a complete wreck, the fire not yet all extinguished. Its shattered battlements, its tottering walls, presented the appearance of an old ruin . . .
>
> I remained at Fort Sumter till the little band of patriots had saluted their old flag . . . and marched out with their tattered ensign to the tune of our own Yankee Doodle.

One may wonder where on a rock in the harbor of Charleston, South Carolina, on April 14, 1861, the brave men of Anderson's garrison could find musicians to play "Yankee Doodle" as they marched out of Fort Sumter—and then one looks back to the makeup of the garrison and finds, yes, "8 musicians."

And so as it turned out, to the intense frustration of Gustavus Fox, the flotilla that President Lincoln had ordered him to put together was to play only one utterly tangential role in the Sumter battle: it provided transportation for Anderson and the garrison after they had been bombarded into submission.

ANTICLIMAX IN PENSACOLA

Gustavus Fox headed north to New York in frustration over his nonparticipation in the events at Fort Sumter; meanwhile, the *Powhatan* under Porter's command was heading south in the excitement of anticipated service at Fort Pickens.

Meigs, on the chartered passenger ship the *Atlantic*, accompanying the *Powhatan*, wrote, as Richard Current says, "exultingly but cryptically" to Secretary Seward: "[W]hen the arrow has sped from its bow it may glance aside, but who shall reclaim it before its flight is finished?" The president of the United States, at least, had not been able to reclaim this particular arrow.

But while Porter and Meigs and the *Powhatan* expedition were making their way to Pensacola, the Union messenger, sent on April 6—this time by the swifter overland route, this time with orders from the navy—was at last able to get an order from Washington through to the Union command on the *Sabine* in Pensacola Harbor. On April 12 the troops that had been there offshore all the time were landed in the fort, which probably was already sufficient reinforcement (more followed) to keep the fort in Union hands throughout the war.

The *Powhatan*, which finally arrived on April 18, was not at all necessary to that result.

UNHAPPINESS IN CIVIL WAR WASHINGTON

Gustavus Fox, meanwhile, said glumly to Anderson, as they traveled north from Sumter on the *Baltic* on April 14, that while Sumter's Captain Anderson would be a hero, he, Fox, would be the goat, a figure of ridicule. He was not pleased with the events in Charleston Harbor:

> I do not think I have deserved this treatment . . . Had the *Powhatan* arrived the 12th we should have had the men and provisions into Fort Sumter, as I had everything ready, boats, muffled oars, small packages of provisions, in fact everything but the 300 sailors [who were to have been on the *Powhatan*].

But on that afternoon of Sunday, April 14, while Fox and Major Anderson were steaming north from Sumter on the *Baltic* and Porter was steaming south on the *Powhatan*, the overwhelming news of the fall of Fort

Sumter swept the country and drove all these preliminary events out of everyone's mind.

Or almost everyone's mind. Gustavus Fox remembered. On April 19 he wrote a report in which he noted that a fierce storm on the night of April 11–12 had delayed the rendezvous of his flotilla. But his primary complaint had to do not with acts of God but with acts of man:

> I learned on the 13th instant that the *Powhatan* was withdrawn from duty off Charleston on the 7th instant [actually, the 6th], yet I was permitted to sail . . . without intimation that the main portion—the fighting portion—of our expedition was taken away.

His many later accomplishments notwithstanding, Assistant Secretary of the Navy Fox apparently still had, even as late as February 1865, a touch of heartburn when he remembered that episode of the *Powhatan* back at the start of the war. Or maybe he was just tidying the department's records. In any case, we find him writing this to Nicolay in the White House:

Washington, Feby 22 1865

Dear Sir:

Early in April 1861, the *U.S.S. Powhatan,* under the command of Lieut. D. D. Porter, was despatched from New York to Pensacola on confidential service. The orders were from the President direct and do not appear in the records of this Department. If there is a record of them in your office, will you be kind enough to furnish a copy for the files of this department?

> *Very respect &c*
> G.V. Fox

Nicolay had to answer that he could find no record of that episode from long ago here at the White House. In fact—we may imagine him responding—to tell the truth, we would rather not remember anything about it. Go see Quartermaster General Meigs. Maybe he knows where that order is.

RAPID SELF-EDUCATION IN THE HIGHEST OFFICE

NOW WE COME to the primary purpose for telling this complicated tale: to examine the response of the man putatively at the center, the president of the United States. Lincoln was learning two contradictory lessons about this great office he now held: it was very powerful, and then again maybe it wasn't.

How would the new president respond to a first-class screwup in his administration? In the first place, Lincoln took his full share of the blame—maybe even a little more than his full share. Welles, telling about that midnight visit to the White House, concluded with this report about the president: "He took upon himself the whole blame, said it was carelessness, heedlessness on his part, he ought to have been more careful and attentive." Then Welles—writing later, after having served throughout Lincoln's presidency—generalized: "President Lincoln never shunned any responsibility and often declared that he, and not his Cabinet, was in fault for errors imputed to them, when I sometimes thought otherwise."

On May 1 after this episode the president would write a consoling letter to the disgruntled Gustavus Fox:

> I sincerely regret that the failure of the late attempt to provision Fort-Sumpter should be a source of annoyance to you. The practicability of your plan was not, in fact, brought to a test. By reason of a gale . . . the tugs never reached the ground; while by an accident, for which you were in no wise responsible, and possibly I, to some extent, was, you were deprived of a war vessel with her men, which you deemed of great importance to the enterprize.

Second, he learned from it. Of course there would be in the immense complexity of the four years of war many mistakes and errors, but Lincoln himself appears not to have done anything quite like this again. He immediately promised Welles that nothing like what had just occurred—bypassing the Navy Department and keeping Welles in the dark—would ever happen again, and Welles later testified that it did not. "Never from that day, to the close of his life," Welles would write, "was there any similar interference with the administration of the Navy Department, nor was any step concerning it taken without first consulting me."

What Lincoln learned went well beyond noninterference with the chain of command in the navy. Not only would he not sign anything he did not understand, or something someone else had written, he himself would compose, in his own careful penmanship, the key presidential and administration orders and public documents, including many signed by others.

Third, as damaging as this episode was, Lincoln blamed no one, repri-manded no one, and fired no one. The staff and the subordinates of those who hold high office are supposed to protect, build up, and help their chief. As Justice Louis Brandeis said one day to his clerk Dean Acheson, after the latter had made an unfortunate mistake, "Your role, young man, is to correct my errors, not to introduce new ones of your own." Kings in the past, and American presidents in the future, would insist that those under them serve and protect them, in order to preserve the awe or respect in which they are held and thus protect the power of the state. Lincoln, in these first weeks at least, had no such support. On the contrary, one could say he was unmercifully manipulated by his subordinates. All of the principals in this bizarre episode, however—an able group despite this incident—went on to perform prominent roles in the war effort, with Lin-coln's help and support, and he and the nation benefited from their abilities.

One may measure what the president might have done by noticing how his wounded cabinet members felt about it.

The secretary of the navy, Gideon Welles, and the secretary of war, Simon Cameron, just six weeks into their new jobs, were incensed at the utter irregularity of that expedition that had been kept secret from them and at the role of men nominally under their authority. According to Welles, Cameron thought that Seward, trying to run the War Department, had caused Captain Meigs to desert, that Meigs was absent without leave and expending military appropriations without authority from the secre-tary of war, and that he—Cameron—would have Meigs arrested and tried by court-martial.

Did the president share in this indignation? No, Lincoln not only held no grudge against Meigs but that very summer went out of his way, over-coming Secretary Cameron's resistance, to obtain for him an enormously important post: quartermaster general. Meigs went on to become an important figure in the Civil War, calculating accurate estimates of Confed-erate armies when General George McClellan was giving inflated estimates and then organizing extraordinary feats in transporting Union armies. He would be present at Lincoln's deathbed and would serve on as quartermas-ter general for decades after the war.

Welles had complaints about Porter of the navy like those of Cameron about Meigs of the army. "Although Lieutenant Porter had gone with the *Powhatan* to Pensacola, there was no order or record in the Navy Depart-ment. He was absent without leave; the last sailing orders to the *Powhatan* were [sent by Welles himself] to Mercer. The whole proceeding was irregular and could admit of no justification without impeaching the integrity or ability of the Secretaries of War and the Navy." And Andrew H. Foote, who had been tugged one way and then another by the telegrams to the Brooklyn Navy Yard, when he learned the whole story said to Porter: "You ought to have been tried and shot."

But Porter was not tried, not shot, not reprimanded, and like Meigs he went on to a distinguished career. He stayed for six weeks in Pensacola but later played a major role in the battle for New Orleans, at Vicksburg, and at Fort Fisher. His career was given a huge boost by President Lincoln in the late summer of 1862, when Lincoln was looking for a commander of the Mississippi squadron who would cooperate with the army and had some dash. Welles gave Porter a desk assignment, but Porter went to see the president to try to get assigned to active service. Lincoln had not seen him since the *Powhatan* caper and might have been expected to have some resentment about it. But no—Lincoln questioned Porter about the operation on the Mississippi, and the battle for Vicksburg, and was impressed. A few weeks later Porter was promoted all the way to acting rear admiral, an enormous step, jumping over numerous officers with superior claims. He was a key figure cooperating with Grant in the capture of Vicksburg. Near the end of the war, in a conference made famous by a distinguished painting, the Union leaders conferring about the ending of the war are Lincoln, Grant, Sherman—and Rear Admiral David D. Porter. By that time, the April night four years before on which he had insisted on taking over the command of the *Powhatan* from Captain Mercer must have faded into a distant memory. Certainly it had for the president.

And what of Gustavus Fox—not a perpetrator but a victim? Far from being the butt of ridicule, despite the fizzling of his Sumter plan, he would go on to have a distinguished career in the Navy Department throughout the war. Much of the credit for the rapid improvisation of a Union navy, and for that navy's successes, belonged to Fox, who had had a prior career in the navy that Welles had not.

Nevertheless, Fox did not completely wipe from his mind his memory of those hours out there ten miles from Charleston Harbor waiting for the *Powhatan* to show up.

Sooner than one might suppose—May 1, only two weeks after Sumter's fall, while overwhelmed with other events—President Lincoln did find time to write a consoling letter to Gustavus Fox, making the important interpretation of the whole Fort Sumter event that we have quoted in the previous chapter.

President Lincoln, after saying the expedition's failure was not at all Fox's fault and was to some extent his, was careful to give the disgruntled Fox a solid personal endorsement: "For a daring and dangerous enterprise, of a similar character, you would, to-day, be the man, of all my acquaintances, whom I would select." And then Lincoln wrote a last paragraph that is often quoted as his appraisal of the entire Sumter undertaking. He joins Fox and himself, generously, in mutual anticipation of the effort ("you and I") and finds it to have been a success by the larger criterion of advancing "the cause of the country":

> You and I both anticipated that the cause of the country would be
> advanced by making the attempt to provision Fort Sumpter, even
> if it should fail; and it is no small consolation now to feel that our
> anticipation is justified by the result.

Very truly your friend,
A. LINCOLN

Finally, Seward. Another leader would have found Seward's conduct in this affair hard to forgive. It was the culmination, indeed, of a number of episodes that had occurred since Seward's bitter defeat by Lincoln in Chicago. But Lincoln, generous and clearheaded, realized that he needed Seward—needed him for his following, for his reputation, and, despite what Lincoln might have concluded from this episode, for his experience and advice. Before many more weeks were out, Seward would be writing to his wife, Frances, about Lincoln's executive skill. And by the time his four years were over, Seward would have become Lincoln's closest friend on the cabinet, and a great admirer.

The firing on Sumter, the evacuation of Sumter, and the president's call for troops—the beginning of the Civil War—so thoroughly changed the subject and the atmosphere as to sweep everything else aside and send an electric charge of Union sentiment throughout the North. So retrospectives on the *Powhatan* caper, and the recriminations it provoked, were altogether upstaged by vastly larger events. And President Lincoln, who would show a distinct ability to concentrate on what was essential, would put it aside entirely.

CHAPTER FIVE

Days of Choices

Two April Sundays

ALTOGETHER NEW to the highest level of national decision-making, indeed to executive responsibility of any kind; wearied by the pressure of reporters and visiting politicians in Springfield and by an exacting trip from Springfield to Washington; embarrassed by a dark-of-night skulking entrance into the capital city; exhausted by ten crowded preinauguration days in the Willard Hotel; stunned by an altogether unexpected bombshell of a message in the first minute of his presidency; harassed in every working hour, and some nonworking hours, by long lines of office-seekers outside his door, the novice president Abraham Lincoln gathered himself, in the days of March and the first weeks of April, to make the weightiest turning-point decisions in the history of the American republic since the Founding.

Sunday, April 14, 1861, was a day of enormous decisions. Sunday, April 21, was another.

I HAVE SAID WHAT I WOULD DO

WHEN ON THE MORNING of Saturday, April 13, news of the bombardment of Fort Sumter tapped in on the wire at the War Department, Lincoln had occasion to write a revealing paper announcing the shape of the new policy.

As it happened, a committee from the Virginia convention that was considering secession was scheduled to meet with him that day. The Virginians asked about the "policy which the federal executive is to pursue in regard to the Confederate states." Lincoln answered: *I have already told you what I will do.* As in his response to his secretary of state twelve days earlier, so now to this delegation of Virginians teetering on the brink of secession, he said: *Read my inaugural address.*

One can almost detect a little pout that the Virginians had not suffi-ciently consulted that address: "It is with deep regret, and with some mor-tification, I now learn, that there is great, and injurious uncertainty in the public mind as to what that policy is and what course I intend to pursue . . . I commend a careful consideration of the whole document . . . [I]t is now my purpose to pursue the course marked out in the inaugeral [*sic*] address." He quoted the inaugural paragraph about using his power only to "hold, occupy, and possess" federal property and places—that is, places already held—but he also made explicit his underlying position: "I scarcely need to say that I consider the Military posts and property situated within the states, which claim to have seceded, as yet belonging to the Gov-ernment of the United States, as much as they did before the supposed secession."

But the promises in his address were *conditional*, of course. The news of the bombardment of Sumter was sizzling through the telegraph wires. In the first paragraph of the statement to the Virginia committee, he wrote of "not having, as yet seen occasion to change." But in the second paragraph, almost as though the ground were shifting under his feet, he indicated a change caused by events:

> If, as now appears true, in pursuit of a purpose to drive the United States authority from those places an unprovoked assault has been made upon Fort Sumter, I shall hold myself at liberty to repossess, if I can, like places which had been seized before the Government devolved upon me.

The rebels, by their action, had released him from the self-limiting pledge in his inaugural address: he now was at liberty to repossess, if he could, all those forts and mints and arsenals the rebels had seized.

And then he made explicit his intention (quite in contrast to Buchanan) to repel the attack: "And in every event I shall, to the extent of my ability, repel force by force."

The precision with which he interpreted his inaugural promises is indi-cated by a little dialogue with himself, in his statement to the Virginians, about what he would do "in case it proves true that Fort Sumpter has been assaulted": "I shall perhaps cause the United States mails to be with-drawn . . . believing that the commencement of actual war against the gov-ernment justifies and possibly demands this." At the end of this statement, when he insisted that he was not repudiating but was reaffirming the whole of his inaugural address, he scrupulously added the words "except so far as what I now say of the mails may be regarded as a modification." He was being careful to keep intact the moral charter of his inaugural, altering it only as events warranted, carefully noting when and why he was doing so.

But the days when the U.S. mail would be delivered in the Deep South were over.

IN VIRTUE OF THE POWER VESTED IN ME

ON SUNDAY MORNING, April 14, the news came that after thirty-six hours of bombardment Major Anderson and his garrison had capitulated and were even then being evacuated. After attending the New York Avenue Presbyterian Church in the morning, Lincoln met at the executive mansion with the cabinet and his military advisers.

We may picture him there, still new by the calendar although suddenly matured by six weeks of impossibly concentrated history-turning decisions on every day of his presidential life, talking perhaps to advisers—to whom on Inauguration Day he had been a stranger—and then sitting down at his desk with his pen and writing out the proclamation that would summon the militia.

General Scott had mentioned in a memo on April 5 the 1795 Militia Act, which had been passed at the time of George Washington and the Whiskey Rebellion. Lincoln must now have had a copy of that act with him, because he found in it both his legal justification and his language. Lincoln took from that act the phrase describing the condition making his action necessary: the obstruction in seven states (which he named), by "combinations too powerful to be suppressed by the ordinary course of judicial proceedings," of one of the constitutionally specified, sworn duties of the president, that he "take care that the laws be faithfully executed." Execution of the laws was being obstructed not by the states as such—Lincoln did not recognize their supposed secession—but by these "combinations" *in* those states. And the Militia Act would provide the legal ground for the president to call the state militia into federal service.* Many of the actions Lincoln would now take would have no legislative sanction, but the first one did: calling into service "the militia of the several states of the Union, to

---

*Section 2 of the 1795 Militia Act: "That whenever the laws of the United States shall be opposed, or the execution thereof obstructed, in any state, by combinations too powerful to be suppressed by the ordinary course of judicial proceedings, or by the powers vested in the marshals by this act, it shall be lawful for the president of the United States to call forth the militia of such state, or of any other state or states, as may be necessary to suppress such combinations, and to cause the laws to be duly executed; and the use of militia so to be called forth may be continued, if necessary, until the expiration of thirty days after the commencement of the next session of Congress."

the aggregate number of seventy-five thousand." The Constitution gave the executive that power; the Militia Act specified the conditions.

His decisions of that April Sunday afternoon defined the crisis as an immense insurrection, called forth the military force to suppress it, and implicitly defined his own role of command. His secretaries made a point that the proclamation was "drafted by himself," copied on the spot by his secretary, concurred in by his cabinet, and signed "and sent to the State Department to be published in the next day's papers."

It would later be said that 75,000 soldiers were far too few, and indeed before three weeks had passed, the president would be issuing calls for an increase in the regular army and navy, and for subsequent increases that would dwarf this initial call. Who could have known, on that first afternoon, that before this terrible war was over 2.1 million men would have served in the U.S. armed services?

On the evening of this Sunday, April 14, Lincoln's old rival, the leading war Democrat Senator Stephen Douglas, came to the executive mansion and held a remarkable private interview that lasted almost two hours. He gave Lincoln his full support and said he should have called for 200,000 troops. Nicolay and Hay noted that 75,000 was already almost five times the then-existing force; that supplies and arms for a larger force were not available; that recent government loans had been discounted; and "that the loyal states had suffered the siege of Sumter and the firing on the *Star of the West* with dangerous indifference." The two secretaries then added this striking sentence: "Twenty-four hours later all this was measurably changed." By Monday evening they would know that for opinion in the North the firing on Fort Sumter would be like the breakup of a great dam, through which torrents of passion now cascaded.

OFTEN AT THE OUTBREAK of a long-anticipated war, the populace feels a profoundly perilous but nevertheless invigorating shot of clarified resolve, and offers up a "vast human sigh of relief."

There is also often, in countries well supplied with invidious national pride (as what country is not?), an eruption of stereotyped contempt for the enemy-to-be, a pseudo-confident boast, filled with national egotism and swagger and disdain, that one's own armies will quickly dispose of the despised other. Across the American South there would be much swaggering and invidious contrasting of the fighting capacity of the clerks and accountants of the moneygrubbing Yankee North with that of manly Southern farmers, hunters, and horsemen.

And how then was it, in this first moment of the American Civil War, in the executive mansion itself? "While discussing the proclamation, some of his advisers made a disparaging contrast of Southern enterprise and endurance with the Northern." Lincoln's secretaries surely were in the room and reported what they heard. They put Lincoln's response to "this indulgent self-deception" in quotation marks:

> We must not forget that the people of the seceded states, like those of the loyal ones, are American citizens, with essentially the same characteristics and powers. Exceptional advantages on one side are counterbalanced by exceptional advantages on the other. We must make up our minds that man for man the soldier from the South will be a match for the soldier of the North and *vice versa.*

In calm years later critics looking back would chastise Lincoln for setting the date when Congress would assemble in special session as late as ten weeks from the date shots were fired and the war begun. Could he not have called the people's representatives much sooner than July 4? Why did Lincoln allow so long a period in which he alone, or the executive branch alone, made the decisions?

There are reasonable answers to these not unreasonable questions. Elections for Congress were impending, and they were critical. The delicate issue of whether the border states would remain loyal, and which ones, was still unresolved, which would affect the composition of Congress. But the decisive consideration was a restriction built into the 1795 Militia Act: the law authorized the service of the militia only for thirty days after the start of the next congressional session—so the earlier Congress returned, the earlier the service of the thirty-day soldiers would have to end.

NOT GOOD DAYS FOR POETRY

ALMOST EVERY DAY during the avalanche of events in the April fortnight following the fall of Sumter, Lincoln heard good news and bad news. But the good news came from a remote and inaccessible distance, often only by rumor, while the bad news was at his doorstep, and unmistakable.

In the North—so it was reported—there was a tremendous outpouring of patriotism; of rallies, cheers, and parades; of support for the war; of volunteering far beyond the quotas for the states. Every governor of a free state sent an enthusiastically positive response to Lincoln's call for troops.

But in Washington that fervent activity in the North was mostly a distant report, while the threat to the nation's capital was real and immediate. The Founders in their wisdom had planted the nation's capital in the foggy bottom of a swamp in between two slave states; in April 1861 it surely must have seemed that they should have left it in Philadelphia. If slave state Maryland joined slave state Virginia in the rebellion, then Abraham and Mary Lincoln might soon be scurrying from the nation's capital the way James and Dolley Madison did when the British burned the White House in 1814. In a gush of initial enthusiasm the Confederate secretary of war had all but officially predicted that the Confederate flag would fly over the Capitol in Washington by May 1.

On April 17 Virginia made the not-so-secret secret decision to join the rebellion. Ex-governor Henry Wise, the rascal who more than two decades earlier had traded verbal blows with John Quincy Adams in the gag rule fight over antislavery petitions in the House of Representatives, and who more recently as governor of Virginia had signed the death warrant for John Brown when the old fanatic was hanged, now in his eagerness announced in the Virginia secession convention that the state's militia was already moving on Harpers Ferry and also on the Gosport Navy Yard in Norfolk, the nation's prime shipbuilding base. After Virginia's decision, occupants of the White House could look out the window and see a Confederate flag flying in Alexandria, across the Potomac.

On April 18 came the news that soldiers just up the river defending Harpers Ferry had to set the rifle works on fire, and that the attacking Virginia militia had taken over, saved some of the machinery, and shipped it to Richmond to make rifles to shoot Yankees. On April 19 still more shocking news arrived. A mob had attacked the first regiment to head for the nation's capital, the Sixth Massachusetts. Lincoln's call had come on Monday the fifteenth; Massachusetts governor John Andrew had been eager to respond, and so had many others in his state. A regiment was mustered on Boston Common on Tuesday the sixteenth, left by train amid cheers with their regimental flag on the seventeenth, and sped past cheering throngs in New England and New York to be greeted with enthusiasm in Philadelphia late on the eighteenth. Then the cheering stopped. In Baltimore on April 19 the regiment met not cheers but rocks and fury. They had to change not only trains but stations, and a mob of Baltimore "rowdies" attacked them as they moved through the city streets, and in the exchanges nine soldiers and twelve civilians were killed, the first casualties of the war. At midnight the mayor and the marshal and the police board, and maybe the wavering

Maryland governor, ordered the destruction of the railroad bridges on the only two lines that connected Washington with the North—so the nation's capital was completely cut off from any railroad connection to that North which (rumor reported) was trying eagerly to give support.

April 19 was not only the day of the Baltimore riot but also the day Lincoln issued a blockade of Southern ports, in response to Jefferson Davis's invitation to privateers to prey on Union ships. And it was the day that Lincoln learned that Harpers Ferry had been taken, that Gosport Navy Yard could not be saved, and that the Maryland authorities had burned the bridges, thereby cutting railroad connection to Washington.

At some time on this overwhelming day a young woman named Mary Rebecca Darby Smith, who as a friend of President Buchanan had attended the inauguration, managed to get in to see the new president. She got from him this inscription, revealing his state of mind with a somber wit:

White House, April 19, 1861.

Whoever in later-times shall see this, and look at the date, will readily excuse the writer for not having indulged in sentiment, or poetry. With all kind regards for Miss Smith.

A. Lincoln.

Nor would April 20 be a good day for sentiment or poetry. The *Pawnee,* which on its return from the futile wait ten miles off Fort Sumter had been sent out again to help save centrally important Gosport Navy Yard in Norfolk, now returned with the word that the yard, betrayed by subordinate officers, was lost. Meanwhile, Lincoln asked Governor Thomas H. Hicks of Maryland and Mayor George W. Brown of Baltimore—summoned them, really—to come by special train to talk about "preserving the peace in Maryland." Both men were implicated in the burning of the railroad bridges to stop Union troops from coming through, although the wavering Governor Hicks would finally be a Unionist. "Troops must be brought here," Lincoln told Mayor Brown when they conferred on Sunday, April 21. Brown brought with him a committee, including one ardent secessionist.

We can find the essence of the president's presentation to the mayor and his committee on Sunday in remarks he made on the next day, Monday, to another visitation from Baltimore, this one unofficial: a band of fifty religious folk brought together by the nascent interdenominational organization the YMCA, with a Baptist preacher as the spokesman. They made their way to Washington to urge the president to recognize the independence of the Southern states and send no more troops through Baltimore. Lincoln's response captured the quintessence of his understanding of his moral responsibility in this perilous moment. He began with a reprimand, which carried with it his view of the immediate rights and wrongs:

> You, gentlemen, come here to me and ask for peace on any terms, and yet have no word of condemnation for those who are making war on us. You express great horror of bloodshed, and yet would not lay a straw in the way of those who are organizing in Virginia and elsewhere to capture this city.

He indignantly rejected what they proposed he do, with a significant reference to his oath:

> The rebels attack Fort Sumter, and your citizens attack troops sent to the defense of the Government, and the lives and property in Washington, and yet you would have me break my oath and surrender the Government without a blow. There is no Washington in that—no Jackson in that—no spunk in that.

Other records of what he said—we do not have it in his hand—make this last phrase, instead of "no spunk," "no manhood and honor"; that is the way it is in *The Collected Works* and in Nicolay and Hay's account. But the *Baltimore Sun* for April 23, 1861, according to James G. Randall, reported instead the more interesting phrase, "no spunk in that." Lincoln's vigorous moral condemnation of their proposal was that they were asking him to break his oath, and there was no spunk/manhood/honor in doing that, no Washington, no Jackson. Such a betrayal of his oath would violate the standard set by the best past presidential conduct on such a matter.

Then, to this visitation of earnest Baltimoreans, he summarized the situation:

> I have no desire to invade the South; but I must have troops to defend this Capital. Geographically it lies surrounded by the soil of Maryland; and mathematically the necessity exists that they should come over her territory. Our men are not moles, and can't dig under the earth; they are

not birds, and can't fly through the air. There is no way but to march across, and that they must do.

Given that essential point, he would be flexible.

> But in doing this there is no need of collision. Keep your rowdies in Baltimore, and there will be no bloodshed. Go home and tell your people that if they will not attack us, we will not attack them; but if they do attack us, we will return it, and that severely.

Lincoln did not at that moment yet command any troops to respond with, "severely" or otherwise, but they were rapidly being gathered, so it was reported, up north.

He had occasion to state his distinction between "invading," on the one hand, and defending what he had to defend, on the other, when he responded two days later to a plaintive note from the distinguished and conservative Maryland senator Reverdy Johnson. Johnson had written of the fear in Maryland and Virginia that Lincoln was going to use the force being assembled for an "invasion" of the states. Lincoln replied to Senator Johnson:

> I *do* say the sole purpose of bringing troops *here* is to defend this capital.
>
> I *do* say I have no purpose to *invade* Virginia, with them or any other troops, as I understand the word *invasion*. But suppose Virginia sends her troops, or admits others through her borders, to assail this Capital, am I not to repel them, even to the crossing of the Potomac if I can?
>
> Suppose Virginia erects, or permits to be erected, batteries on the opposite shore, to bombard the city, are we to stand still and see it done? In a word, if Virginia strikes us, are we not to strike back, and as effectively as we can?

Johnson thanked Lincoln, and said he now understood and endorsed his position.

Lincoln no doubt had made the same points to Mayor Brown and his associates back on Sunday, April 21, in his insistence that he must have troops to defend the capital. And that geography dictated that the troops must come through Maryland. But beyond that he was flexible about how they made their way. "Troops must be brought here," he had written to

Brown and the governor. "But I make no point of bringing them through Baltimore." General Scott outlined three routes for troops, two of them— from Harrisburg and by way of Annapolis—that did not involve traversing Baltimore and tempting its rowdies.

Mayor Brown, in the meeting on Sunday morning, April 21, agreed to do all he could to keep the "rowdies" from attacking troops passing through Maryland outside the city, and he and the committee departed, and the president and the cabinet went on to other hugely important matters.

But then the mayor and his group astonished everyone by appearing again in midafternoon, with a telegram saying that there were three thousand Union troops just fourteen miles from Baltimore, at Cockeysville, nearing Baltimore by the Harrisburg route, and that the rowdies were aroused. Mayor Brown and his entourage now indignantly suggested that they had been deceived: while they were conferring with the president, the Union forces had taken advantage of their absence to sneak these Pennsylvania troops almost to Baltimore.

The cabinet and Scott were brought back, and discussion ensued, but the president made a firm decision, reported later by Mayor Brown himself: "The President, at once, in the most decided way urged the recall of the troops, saying that he had no idea they would be there today." Yet again he would take steps so that even "ingenious sophistry" could not misconstrue his action or intention. Lincoln said: "Lest there should be the slightest suspicion of bad faith on his part in summoning the mayor to Washington, and allowing troops to march on the city during his absence, he desired that the troops should . . . be sent back at once."

Desperate as he was and would become for troops to defend his capital, he did not want to seem to have tricked the Marylanders to get them there. He had Secretary of War Cameron order the troops back to York. He had General in Chief Winfield Scott order the Pennsylvania troops to take an ingenious alternative route, by way of steamers on the Chesapeake and Annapolis, that would become famous in Civil War history.

EXTRAORDINARY MEASURES

IN ADDITION TO COPING with not one but two visits by Mayor Brown and his crew, on Sunday, April 21, President Lincoln held an extraordinary meeting with his cabinet, about which we have two later testimonials from participants—one from the president himself, and one from Secretary Seward.

Lincoln had occasion, a little over a year later, in a special message to the House on May 26, 1862, to describe the war's beginnings:

> The insurrection which . . . aims at the overthrow of the federal Constitution and the Union, was clandestinely prepared during the winter of 1860 and 1861, and assumed an open organization in the form of a treasonable provisional government at Montgomery, in Alabama, on the 18th day of February, 1861. On the 12th day of April, 1861, the insurgents committed the flagrant act of civil war by the bombardment and capture of Fort Sumter, which cut off the hope of immediate conciliation.

President Lincoln then gave this account of the dire situation of the nation's capital during that first week of war:

> Immediately afterwards all the roads and avenues to this city were obstructed, and the capital was put into the condition of a siege. The mails in every direction were stopped, and the lines of telegraph cut off by the insurgents, and military and naval forces, which had been called out by the government for the defence of Washington, were prevented from reaching the city by organized and combined treasonable resistance in the State of Maryland. There was no adequate and effective organization for the public defence. Congress had indefinitely adjourned. There was no time to convene them.

Lincoln then described his own momentous decision, and the moral ground for it:

> It became necessary for me to choose whether, using only the existing means, agencies, and processes which Congress had provided, I should let the government fall at once into ruin, or whether, availing myself of the broader powers conferred by the Constitution in cases of insurrection, I would make an effort to save it with all its blessings for the present age and for posterity.

He had another pivotal decision to make. He and his colleagues were now about to take a series of actions for which there was no explicit legal ground. But he appealed to the "broader powers" available in the unique circumstance of an insurrection that threatened the very existence of the nation. Later presidents who would be tempted in times of crisis to take the broadest possible view of the Constitution would invoke Lincoln as a model, but none of them faced the mortal threat to the nation that Lincoln confronted. He faced "a clear, flagrant, and gigantic case of Rebellion," as he would put it later. He dealt with an "insurrection," one of the two terms the Constitution names—the other being "invasion"—in its only explicit recognition of emergency powers. These two terms appear in the clause permitting habeas corpus to be suspended when the "public safety" requires it. The Constitution, in this rather indirect way, does recognize emergency situations that require extraordinary action—but it defines them "in exceedingly narrow terms . . . There have been only two such emergencies since the Constitution was written, and none since 1865." The altogether extraordinary actions President Lincoln took had a unique justification.*

Lincoln described that cabinet meeting of Sunday, April 21, 1861, getting the day wrong: "I there upon summoned my constitutional advisers, the heads of all the departments, to meet on Sunday, 20th day of April, 1861, at the office of the Navy Department." And at that meeting the president, "with their concurrence," took a long series of actions—obtaining and arming ships, transporting troops and munitions of war, and empowering private individuals in New York to take action and spend money for the "military and naval measures necessary for the defense and support of the government." They should do this (another passage revealed the conditions that made necessary such extraordinary measures) "until communication by mails and telegraphs should be completely re-established between the cities of Washington and New York."

It was necessary to empower trustworthy private individuals to take action and spend public money for this further revealing reason:

> The several departments of the government at that time contained so large a number of disloyal persons that it would have been impossible to provide safely, through official agents only, for the performance of the duties thus confided to citizens favorably known for their ability, loyalty, and patriotism.

---

*"Makers of the modern 'imperial presidency' have drawn heavily on the example and immortal fame of Abraham Lincoln for vindication of their actions, conveniently ignoring the extent to which precedents taken for the Civil War are rendered invalid by its uniqueness. It is accordingly possible to conclude that Lincoln's use of executive power was wise and appropriate in its context, but not an unmixed blessing as a presidential tradition." Don E. Fehrenbacher, *Lincoln in Text and Context* (Stanford, Calif.: Stanford University Press, 1987), p.122.

On the day after this meeting in the Navy Department, Monday, April 22, there would come a dramatic illustration of this point as scores of government workers and officers in the armed services, including the commodore in charge of the Washington Navy Yard and much of his staff, resigned, left the city, and headed south.

Another passage from this Lincolnian message still further reveals the moment: "The several orders issued upon those occurrences were transmitted by private messengers, who pursued a circuitous way to the seaboard cities, inland, across the States of Pennsylvania and Ohio and the Northern lakes." That was the U.S. government, sending its orders to New York by way of secret couriers cutting across the inland states to circle in by the lakes.

Lincoln's conclusion about these measures is fundamental to his outlook: "I believe that by these and similar measures taken in that crisis, some of which were without any authority of law, the government was saved from overthrow." That fortnight in April 1861 was the moment when the U.S. government may have been in the greatest peril in the entire sweep of its history down to the present day.

Lincoln's extraordinary actions in confronting that peril are to be distinguished from those of later presidents who attempt to use him as vindication not only in that the crisis he faced was unique but also in that he never claimed to have a presidential authority going beyond that of Congress: everything he did was subject to congressional approval.*

In his message to the special session Lincoln would say of these and of actions that would follow that they were "ventured upon, under what appears to be a public demand, and public necessity, trusting, then as now, that Congress would ratify them." And Congress did.

---

*"Lincoln never claimed that he possessed full authority to act as he did. In fact, he admitted to exceeding the constitutional boundaries established for the President and thus needed the sanction of Congress . . . Lincoln therefore invoked each stage of the executive prerogative acting in the absence of law and sometimes against it; explaining to the legislature what he had done, and why; and requesting the legislative body to authorize his actions. The superior lawmaking body was Congress, not the President. Congress debated this request at length . . . Congress eventually passed legislation 'approving, legalizing, and making valid all the acts, proclamations, and orders of the President, etc. as if they had been issued and done under the previous express authority and direction of the Congress of the United States.' " Louis Fisher, *Presidential War Power* (Lawrence: University Press of Kansas, 1995), p. 48.

SEWARD COMPARES IMPORTANT MOMENTS

THE OTHER retrospective account of the events of April 21, 1861, comes from another key participant—Seward. In June 1864 Francis Carpenter was in the White House painting *First Reading of the Emancipation Proclamation of President Lincoln.* Seward came up to Carpenter at a reception and said he had told the president that Carpenter's picture made a false presumption: that the Emancipation Proclamation was the central act, and the end of slavery the central deed, of the administration. But, said Seward, that was not so. Carpenter reported Seward's words as follows:

> Slavery was killed years ago. Its death knell was tolled when Abraham Lincoln was elected President. The work of this Administration is the suppression of the Rebellion and the preservation of the Union . . . Slavery has been in fact but an incident in the history of the nation, inevitably bound to perish in the progress of intelligence. Future generations will scarcely credit the record that such an institution ever existed here; or existing, that it ever lived a day under such a government. But suppose, for one moment, the Republic destroyed. With it is bound up not alone the destiny of a race, but the best hopes of all mankind.

Seward had an occasion which, he said, could serve as a symbol for this deeper significance:

> Had you consulted me for a subject to paint, I should not have given you the Cabinet Council on Emancipation, but the meeting which took place when the news came of the attack upon Sumter, when the first measures were organized for the restoration of the national authority. That was the crisis in the history of this Administration—not the issue of the Emancipation Proclamation.

Neither Lincoln nor Carpenter would agree with Seward in his comparative depreciation of the Emancipation Proclamation, but all would agree that this earlier gathering had its central place too. By April 21 Seward was in accord with the cabinet decisions—or the presidential decisions—as he had not been on March 29.

Unless one is painting a distinct symbolic painting, one does not need to choose which is the single most important gathering in Civil War history; of course the events that the several meetings symbolize are closely intertwined. Seward was altogether too blithe about the ending of slavery, but it is nevertheless obvious that without the preservation of the United

States, the Emancipation Proclamation and the Thirteenth Amendment ending slavery would not have happened.

THE GREAT EXODUS

THE UNNERVING ISOLATION of the capital city had the perhaps salutary result of sorting the residents according to loyalty: Monday, April 22, was the day of the Great Exodus—the great exposure, resignation, and departure. Hundreds of government clerks, scores of army and navy officers, dozens of high officials, including justices of the Supreme Court, fled the capital of the government they had sworn to serve and joined with those who would overthrow it.

Robert E. Lee and Winfield Scott, both Virginians and outstanding military leaders, were offered high positions in both of the armies that were forming. Lee, whom Scott had selected in his mind as worthy of the highest command, was unofficially offered the command of the Union army; he conferred with Scott, then tendered his resignation to the U.S. Army. Even before that resignation had been accepted, without any discharge or permission, he was offered and accepted the chief command of the Virginia forces in rebellion against the United States. Meanwhile, a committee of Virginians visited Winfield Scott to offer him the command of the forces of his native state. One who was there making the offer was reported to have said: "General Scott received him kindly, listened patiently, and said to him 'I have served my country under the flag of the Union for more than fifty years, and as long as God permits me to live I will defend that flag with my sword, even if my own native state assails it." When a spokesman of the committee began to describe the rewards of wealth and honor that Virginia held out to him, Scott stopped him. "Go no farther. It is best that we part before you compel me to resent a mortal insult."

Of the 1,080 officers on duty in the U.S. Army when the war started, 313 resigned and, as Lincoln would put it, "proved false to the hand which had pampered them." There were significant defections in the civilian departments as well; of ninety employees in the War Department in 1860, thirty-four were gone, mostly to join the rebels, by the summer of 1861. For an executive in those first days the worst condition prevailed—not knowing whom one could and could not trust. One of Seward's motives in keeping Welles in the dark in the *Powhatan* fiasco was his not trusting the loyalty of Navy Department employees. Gideon Welles would write: "When I took charge of the Navy Department, I found great demoralization and defection among Naval officers. It was difficult to ascertain who among those that lingered about Washington could and who were not to be trusted."

There were nasty surprises. The commandant of the Washington Navy Yard, and the upper echelon of officers at Gospert, went over to the rebels. One of those who decamped, particularly astonishing and painful to Lincoln, was a Captain John B. Magruder of the First Artillery, assigned by General Scott to play a key role in the defense of Washington; only three days before (said Lincoln) he had given him the most earnest protestations of his loyalty.

In his special message to Congress on July 4 Lincoln made a claim about the split between the loyal and the disloyal in the armed services that is a little hard to believe but that certainly testifies to his democratic understanding. He was arguing that the "plain people" would understand and appreciate that the struggle then beginning was "a people's contest," and by way of illustration he said:

> It is worthy of note, that while in this, the government's hour of trial, large numbers of those in the Army and Navy, who have been favored with the offices, have resigned, and proved false to the hand which had pampered them, not one common soldier, or common sailor is known to have deserted his flag.
>
> The . . . most important fact of all, is the unanimous firmness of the common soldiers, and common sailors. To the last man, so far as known, they have successfully resisted the traitorous efforts of those, whose commands, but an hour before, they obeyed as absolute law. This is the patriotic instinct of the plain people. They understand, without an argument, that destroying the government, which was made by Washington, means no good to them.

THE ISOLATED CAPITAL

FOR FOUR DAYS, from April 21 to April 25, the capital was effectively cut off from the nation it ostensibly governed. The anxiety-ridden population of Washington received its impression of great events by means of rumor. John Hay wrote in his diary: "Any amount of feverish rumors filled the evening . . . [T]here was a Fort Monroe rumor and a 7th Regt. Rumor and an RI Rumor."

Troops from the North were indeed landing in Annapolis and, with Yankee ingenuity, fixing the railroad and making their way slowly toward

Washington, but the residents of the beleaguered city only half knew that this was so.

Surely if there is one bedrock duty of a chief executive, a head of state, it is to protect against the humiliation of having the seat of government captured. "Day after day prediction failed and hope was deferred; troops did not come, ships did not arrive, railroads remained broken, messengers failed to reach their destination." Lincoln's secretaries, attesting to his outward public calm, nevertheless give two famous glimpses of the tension of those days. One was Lincoln's remark to the Sixth Massachusetts, which had battered its way to Washington: "I don't believe there is any North. The Seventh [New York] Regiment is a myth. Rhode Island is not known in our geography any longer. *You* are the only Northern realities." The other was his plaintive exclamation as he stood alone looking out the window: "Why *don't* they come?"

Washington in those April days had something of the aspect of threatened and besieged cities in the fearsome conflicts of other years and other places: families packing belongings, women and children being sent to safer places; prices for essential goods skyrocketing; theaters closing. A pungent symbol of the peril of those days—startling indeed to those who live in the hugely powerful United States of later centuries—is General Scott's plan for the last-ditch defense of the government if the city were invaded. Perhaps Abraham and Mary would not be fleeing the city like James and Dolley Madison but rather would be holed up in a bunker. Scott had chosen the fine old Treasury Building at 15th and Pennsylvania as the citadel to be surrounded by sandbags, and stocked with pork and beans, with Lincoln and the cabinet in the basement and all available troops concentrated around Lafayette Square.

The available defenders, in these anxious April days, have been described as follows:

> [T]he national capital in the first anxious days after Sumter had for its protection one dilapidated fort twelve miles down the Potomac, six companies of regulars, about two hundred marines at the Navy Yard, two companies of dismounted cavalry, and the flatfooted, flatchested, untrustworthy, militia or uniformed volunteers of the district, numbering fifteen companies on April 15 and about twice that number a week later.

A kind of home guard was created from volunteers, given arms and put in the charge of two of the colorful characters then in the city who had had military experience: Cassius Clay of Kentucky, who made a "melodramatic" appearance in the president's reception room on April 22 with three pistols and an "Arkansas Toothpick" (a bowie knife), and Jim Lane, a notorious leader of the Kansas Radicals. In a surreal moment in the third week of April 1861, Lane's "Frontier Guard" not only drilled in the East Room of the White House but slept there.

AN ANTIWAR CONGRESSMAN
APPEALS TO THE WAR POWER

THE NEW PRESIDENT whose huge April decisions had brought this war footing to the capital was in his own original nature a quite unusually peaceful, uncontentious, unbelligerent man. He himself would remark on the incongruity of his being in this position—"a man who couldn't cut a chicken's head off—with blood running all around me."

When at twenty-three he spent six weeks as a volunteer in the state militia it was some combination of a needed job, a duty, and a lark. Although we are told he was in his secret heart rather proud of his brief and desultory but comradely participation in this most rudimentary exercise of his nation's armed forces, his public presentation of it was self-mockery.

Lincoln voted against the only war he had ever voted on. He voted against it—and spoke strongly against it, on the House floor as a congressman and in letters home. Back in 1847, when he was a newly elected congressman, he expressed a clear-cut position against President Polk's presidentially initiated war, and against such a war of choice as an instrument of state policy. He voted with the majority of Whigs to say that this war had been "unconstitutionally and unnecessarily" begun by the president.

To William Herndon, about the more general question of presidents initiating wars, he wrote:

Allow the President to invade a neighboring nation, whenever he shall deem it necessary to repel an invasion, and you allow him to do so, whenever he may choose to say he deems it necessary for such purpose—and you allow him to make war at pleasure . . .

This, our Convention understood to be the most oppressive of all Kingly oppressions; and they resolved to so frame the Constitution that no one man should hold the power of bringing this oppression upon us.

He wrote that resolutions endorsing Polk on the war "make the direct question of the justice of the war, and no man can be silent if he would." Lincoln was not silent; he gave his answer: it was an unjust war.

Thirteen years later the one-term antiwar congressman from the West would himself sit where Polk had sat, and he would make decisions that would shape a war dwarfing Polk's war, a war that would be more destructive by far than any other in American history for a century and a half.

But in Lincoln's view this war was vastly different, a war not of choice but of duty, a war not of conquest but of the most quintessential national self-defense. He faced not the opportunity to acquire California but the danger that he would lose the nation. An "attempt to divide and destroy the Union" was already under way when he took office. The functions of the government he had sworn to defend were already suspended in seven states. Federal forts, arsenals, dockyards, and customhouses had been seized and were being "held in open hostility to this Government"; for any nation in the world, the forceful seizure of only one of those forts or arsenals by a hostile military force would not only justify but require a forceful response: a war of necessity. He said that "[i]t was with deepest regret that the Executive found the duty of employing the war power, in defense of the government, forced upon him. He could but perform this duty, or surrender the existence of the government."

FORTUNATELY, in those days in April 1861, the defense of the government did not fall to the ragtag defenders who spent that night in the East Room. The next day, finally, the situation changed. "Those who were in the federal capital on that Thursday, April 25, will never, during their lives, forget the event." About noon on that day the Seventh New York, having made its way across Maryland with pluck and luck, with its band playing and its flag flying, marched down Pennsylvania Avenue to the White House. The question of which flag would fly over the Capitol on May 1 had been answered.

CHAPTER SIX

Realism Right at the Border

YOU MAY HOLD political sentiments that spring entirely from the Declaration of Independence, as Lincoln said he did when he spoke in Independence Hall in Philadelphia on the way to being sworn in as president of the United States. You may hold, as he said he did, that the sentiments embodied in the Declaration give promise to all the world that the weights should be lifted from the shoulders of all men, and that all should have an equal chance. You may testify, as he did in Trenton the day before he spoke in Independence Hall, that you hope to be a humble instrument in the hands of the Almighty and of his "almost chosen people" to advance that great objective. But when you arrive in Washington and actually become president, you find that you are a humble instrument, not to advance the great cause of the equality of all men but rather to keep the slave state Kentucky in the Union. Legend has Lincoln saying, "I hope to have God on our side, but I must have Kentucky."

Although you may have universal moral ideals as your original and fundamental purpose, what you find yourself dealing with, as an actual head of state in a crisis, are geopolitics, numbers, balances of forces: reading not the Declaration of Independence but a map. With Kentucky gone, the Confederate line would have moved north to the great natural barrier, the Ohio River. With Maryland gone, the nation's capital would have been surrounded, impossible to hold. With Missouri gone, the Father of Waters would never have flowed unvexed to the sea. If all three of these slave states on the border had joined their fellow slave states in the rebellion, the white population, and the available military manpower of the Confederacy, would have been increased by 45 percent, the manufacturing capacity by 80 percent.

"I think to lose Kentucky is nearly the same as to lose the whole game," Lincoln wrote to his friend Orville Browning on September 22, 1861.

"Kentucky gone, we cannot hold Missouri, nor as I think, Maryland. These all against us, and the job of our hands is too large for us. We would as well consent to separation at once, including the surrender of this capitol."

A prime requirement of worthy statecraft is to discern accurately the shape of the objective situation, and to act on that discernment and not on dreams, imaginings, or ideological prepossessions. "Morality" in statecraft does not lead one away from reality but requires one to attend to it. Lincoln, looking at the map and the numbers, would see a wide band of the United States in which slavery existed as a protected institution yet nevertheless was essential to Union victory over the slavery-based rebellion. This crucial stretch of territory began on the Atlantic with the little slave state of Delaware, stretched through Maryland into the mountains, continued through the western counties of Virginia, followed along the Ohio River through the elongated state of Kentucky to the Mississippi, and then crossed the Great River to the western state of Missouri. This great band of territory was essential not only for the balance of numbers and resources but for transport and access: the Ohio River, the Mississippi River, and the Baltimore and Ohio Railroad would be indispensable avenues for the Union army that was now being fumbled into existence.

Three of the states had active movements for secession, and all had an internal struggle between rebels and Unionists. These Upper South states had fewer slaves than their counterparts farther south, but they were still slave states, with all the implications for laws, institutions, politics, and local attitudes. There were about 420,000 slaves in the border states that never left the Union.* The key to a state's public opinion on secession was the proportion of slaves to the white population. The larger pattern had been, since the invention of the cotton gin in 1794 and the end of legal transatlantic slave trade in 1808, for the proportions of slaves to decline in the border states and to increase in the Deep South cotton states; there was a drainage southward, a selling down the river of slaves from the border states. "In the four Border States [that were kept in the Union] the proportion of slaves and slaveowners was less than half what it was in the eleven states that seceded." The correlation of the number of slaves in proportion to whites with opinions about secession applied both among states and within states. Each of these states had internal divisions—areas of concentrations of slavery and areas with few slaves.

---

*Abraham Lincoln would never be president of any but a slaveholding republic; the Thirteenth Amendment would take effect after he was dead.

The secession of Virginia, North Carolina, Tennessee, and Arkansas left four northernmost slave states still in the Union: Delaware had just 1,798 slaves—only 1.6 percent of the population. The percentages of slaves in the population of the other three states, although well below those in the cotton states, were significant: 9.7 percent in Missouri, 12.7 percent in Maryland, 19.5 percent in Kentucky. The historian William Freehling has remarked that "the war between the states" was also a war within states, especially border states. Keeping these turbulent places on the Union side required making most careful judgments about when to use and when to avoid military force. Sometimes the presence of Union troops and overt military action would solidify a dominant Union opinion (as in Maryland); in other cases such action might push a touchy, fragile public over into the arms of the secessionists (as it probably would have done in Kentucky). Lincoln had to summon not only a most exacting and well-timed combination of forbearance, tact, and the use of force but also the toleration (or embrace) of some quite irregular proceedings.

A DESPOT'S HEEL ON MARYLAND?

LINCOLN'S COMBINATION of firmness and flexibility was exhibited immediately in the first week, in his insistence that Union troops, unable to burrow or to fly, had to cross Maryland but did not need necessarily to pass through Baltimore. When old General Scott said, "Let them go around," Lincoln seized that idea, and finally troops did make their way by boat around the Eastern Shore peninsula, then up the Chesapeake Bay to Annapolis, south of Baltimore, and then by foot and railroad across land to Washington, leaving the Baltimore rowdies to simmer down.

Western Maryland was largely Unionist; secession support was concentrated in the tobacco country of the Eastern Shore and southern Maryland; Baltimore, the third largest city in the nation in 1860, held the balance. Baltimore was a great railroad city, not only the anchor of the Baltimore and Ohio Railroad but the site of great railroad shops and industries. It was not a slaveholding center: "In 1860, slaves accounted for only 1% of 212,418 Baltimoreans. Free blacks outnumbered enslaved blacks eleven to one, and foreign immigrants outnumbered blacks two to one." Baltimore was more of an East Coast industrial city than a Southern slaveholding center, and it had nativist-immigrant rumblings that were more characteristic of the former than the latter. The opposition to Yankee invaders came not only from secessionists but from nativists and Irish immigrants;

when the invasions ceased, Baltimore went back to trading with the North. Another contingent of Massachusetts troops under General Benjamin Butler, arriving by sea, occupied Annapolis, which was not only a landing point for troops getting to Washington without provoking Baltimore but also the state capital. The governor of Maryland, Thomas Hicks, unlike the governors of Kentucky and Missouri, was on balance, although a little shakily, a supporter of the Union. He called the legislature into session to consider the question of secession. Since the state capital, Annapolis, was occupied by Union troops and simmering Baltimore did not seem like a good alternative location, he summoned the legislature to assemble in a special session on April 26 out in safer western Maryland, at Frederick.

Certainly some secessionist noises accompanied the session. The forthright General Butler—soon to be called "The Beast," according to John Hay's diary—"sent an imploring request to the President to be allowed to bag the whole nest of traitorous Maryland legislators and bring them in triumph here." Lincoln, as is not surprising, did not adopt Butler's proposal, or any other proposal to intervene immediately, at this early stage, in the doings of the Maryland legislature. He wrote to General Scott:

> The question has been submitted to . . . me, whether it would not be justifiable, upon the ground of necessary defence, for you, as commander in Chief of the United States Army, to arrest, or disperse the members of that body. I think it would not be justifiable; nor, efficient for the desired object.
>
> First, they have a clearly legal right to assemble; and, we can not know in advance, that their action will not be lawful, and peaceful. And if we wait until they shall have acted, their arrest, or dispersion, will not lessen the effect of their action.
>
> Secondly, we can not permanently prevent their action. If we arrest them, we can not long hold them as prisoners; and when liberated, they will immediately reassemble, and take their action. And, precisely the same if we simply disperse them. They will immediately re-assemble in some other place.
>
> I therefore conclude that it is only left to the commanding General to watch and await their action.

Watchful waiting was the better course. But that was not the end of Lincoln's letter. He went on to say that if the action of the Maryland legislature turned out to be "to arm their people against the United States," then General Scott should consider himself instructed "to adopt the most prompt, and efficient means to counteract" that hostile move, even to the point of "the suspension of habeas corpus" and, in extreme necessity, "the bombardment of their cities."*

The bombardment of their cities? What did Lincoln have in mind? Until the last line this order was an epitome of Lincoln's policy: as much forbearance as could be to allow the putative adversary to fire the first shot if he would; forceful immediate ("prompt, and efficient") countermeasures if he did fire. But then "bombardment of their cities" (bombing Baltimore?) sounds like something Lincoln wrote in a careless moment.

Maryland's legislators had their meeting in Frederick, with General Scott watching and waiting, and the legislators did not do anything that triggered bombardment. "They called Benjamin Butler a Beast. They proclaimed Lincoln a despot. They termed federal coercion a monster. But they raised no army. They called no secession convention. They fired nothing but insults at Abraham Lincoln." And he did not fire even insults back at them.

They sent a committee to tell Lincoln that they would not make any immediate effort at resistance or secession and to ask that "the state . . . be spared the evils of a military occupation or a revengeful chastisement for former transgressions."

Lincoln did not know how the events in Maryland would play out, and he was a novice president in the early stages of learning how to conduct himself; he could not promise to spare them something that would look very much like a military occupation, but when the committee mentioned "revengeful chastisement," it touched on a theme on which he knew his mind: he was not going to engage in anything like "revengeful chastisement." He told the Maryland committee that the public interest, and not any spirit of revenge, would determine his measures.

THE STATE OF MARYLAND managed to extract from a poem written in response to these early Civil War excitements an astonishingly belligerent

---

*Mark E. Neely, Jr., has explained a garble in the last line of this order to Scott. In the text as we have it in *The Collected Works,* Lincoln seems to be treating the suspension of habeas corpus as more extreme than bombardment, but Neely, looking at the holograph original, shows that to have been the result of a hasty editing. See Neely, *The Fate of Liberty: Abraham Lincoln and Civil Liberties* (New York: Oxford University Press, 1991), p. 7.

anti-Union state song. The first stanza refers to "the despot's heel," the despot presumably being Lincoln, and includes the memorably gruesome phrase "patriotic gore" (which Edmund Wilson would lift to visibility as the title of his twentieth-century Civil War book).

> *The despot's heel is on thy shore,*
> *Maryland!*
> *His torch is at thy temple door,*
> *Maryland!*
> *Avenge the patriotic gore*
> *That flecked the streets of Baltimore*
> *And be the battle queen of yore,*
> *Maryland! My Maryland!*

Later stanzas call on Marylanders to "burst the tyrant's chain," and they claim of proud Maryland:

> *She is not dead, nor deaf, nor dumb—*
> *Huzza! She spurns the Northern scum!*

The poem was written in the excessive excitement following the Baltimore riots by a Marylander teaching in Louisiana. The subsequent Civil War politics of Maryland did not, generally speaking, follow the fervent exhortations in that song. Marylanders traded and had other dealings with the "Northern scum" more than with her proud sisters to the South.

Lincoln's actions needed firmness with forbearance. He authorized General Scott or his officers to suspend habeas corpus along the railroad line supplying troops from Philadelphia to Washington, an action that brought a counterorder from Chief Justice Taney and eventually a famous court case. Northern troops moved into the state, first to protect the passage of troops to Washington, then to fortify Baltimore itself.

After the Confederate victory at Bull Run, an invigorated secessionist impulse in Maryland would lead to the planning of another session of the Maryland legislature, scheduled to meet on September 17, again in Frederick, and it was rumored that the gathering's secret purpose was to vote secession. These rumors mentioned intelligence that the government had allegedly received, saying that the "secesh members of the Maryland legislature" intended to hold a "secret, extra, and illegal" session to vote secession and that simultaneously there would be a Confederate invasion of

Maryland and an insurrection in Baltimore. This time there was no "watch and wait" order from the commander in chief, and some secessionist legislators were arrested by Union army authorities.

Who set in motion this arrest of Maryland legislators? General George McClellan was certainly a central figure. In West Virginia in the summer he had provided the Union its badly needed first victories, and he had thereupon been brought east, loaded with prestige, to command the Army of the Potomac. On September 11 he sent to his nominal immediate civilian boss Secretary Cameron an already drafted order—all Cameron had to do was sign it—that instructed General John Dix to arrest six persons, named, who were known secessionists, including new Baltimore members of the legislature. Cameron did as he was asked.*

What was Lincoln's role in this second encounter with the Maryland legislature? Before the arrests, writing to General Banks on September 12, McClellan began: "Gen'l: After full consultation with the president, secretaries of state, war, etc., it has been decided to effect the operation prepared for the 17th." To include the president on a list, along with all these other civilians, and then add "etc." is a particularly nice Little Mac touch—an expression of vanity and disdain like others sprinkled throughout McClellan's papers. Neither of McClellan's later accounts makes any mention of Lincoln. McClellan in all his references to this episode unequivocally defended it in detail, which increases one's sense that he had the major role.

Although McClellan orchestrated the arrests, the ultimate responsibility for making them rested with the president of the United States. It helped, in defending the arrests, that the two key figures—General McClellan and General Dix, who carried out the arrests in Baltimore—were known to be Democrats and publicly claimed military necessity. Maryland's governor Thomas Hicks approved of the arrests.

The preponderance of Union sentiment in Maryland was showing itself

---

*War Department, Washington, September 11, 1861.
Maj. Gen. N. P. Banks, Commanding, near Darnestown, Md.

General:

The passage of any act of secession by the Legislature of Maryland must be prevented. If necessary all or any part of the members must be arrested. Exercise your own judgment as to the time and manner, but do the work effectively.
Very Respectfully, your obedient servant.

Simon Cameron
Secretary of War.

in elections, in enlistments in the two armies, and in the response of the public to events. The elections of November 1861 chose a new general assembly, eleven senators, various local officials, and a governor. The Union army was present in the state, sometimes at the polls, but, according to a key scholar, "the activities of the army were remarkably restrained and curiously dissociated from partisan politics." The army was unconcerned enough about the election to release a group of the "graduates of Fort McHenry" (as some of the arrested legislators called themselves) just before the election. Although Governor Hicks thought this was not a good idea, Union candidates carried the elections handily; the new governor was a patriotic Unionist, an ex-Whig brought back into politics after having retired.

Marylanders did not continue guerrilla resistance to Union troops, nor burn more bridges, nor rise up when General Lee's army marched into the state. They joined the Union army in twice as great numbers as the Confederate. Henceforth Maryland was securely in the Union, the "first of the redeemed," as Lincoln had predicted. Lincoln would be able to claim, in his 1861 annual message:

> Maryland was made to seem against the Union. Our soldiers were assaulted, bridges were burned, and railroads torn up, within her limits; and we were many days, at one time, without the ability to bring a single regiment over her soil to the capital. Now, her bridges and railroads are repaired and open to the government; she already gives seven regiments to the cause of the Union and none to the enemy; and her people, at a regular election, have sustained the Union, by a larger majority, and a larger aggregate vote than they ever before gave to any candidate, or any question.

Lincoln's forbearance in the first place and acquiescence in the arrests in the second helped to bring Maryland by the end of 1861 securely to the side of the Union, where the sympathies and connections of the larger number of her citizens, given time to think, would be found.

WHICH VIRGINIA, OR WHO SECEDES FROM WHOM?

THAT FIERCE MARYLAND POEM "Maryland, My Maryland" included among its fervent appeals:

> *Virginia should not call in vain,*
> *Maryland!*

She meets her sisters in the plain—
"Sic semper!" 'tis the proud refrain. *

But a Maryland novelist pointedly asked about these appeals to join Virginia: "Which Virginia?"

Lincoln, looking at the map and the numbers, would see the crucial importance not only of Maryland, Kentucky, and Missouri but also of the essential link provided by the trans-Allegheny section of Virginia, the mountainous region that joined Maryland to Kentucky, that pointed a dagger up the Ohio River, and that included crucial links in the Baltimore and Ohio Railroad. One way or another Lincoln knew the Union had to control western Virginia.

The state of Virginia, when Lincoln was inaugurated, covered an unwieldy expanse of territory, from the Chesapeake Bay and the Atlantic Ocean all the way over to the Ohio River, chopped in two by the Allegheny Mountains.[†] In the east it had a long history, an intimate association with the nation's beginnings, great plantations, lofty family pride, aristocratic pretension, property owners with enough property to vote, Episcopalians who used to be Anglicans, tobacco, cotton—and slavery. In the west it had mountains, valleys, a much shorter history, pioneers, evangelicals, hunters, miners, lumbermen, propertyless citizens who could not vote, and the beginnings of industry. East Virginia in 1860 had 472,494 slaves; West Virginia had only 18,571. The arrogance that slavery bred bisected the state. The eastern portion had wealth, history, population, and power and shaped state policy to its own advantage in tax policy, in the apportionment of legislative seats, and in "internal improvements." The mountain counties and beyond were treated not as an integral part of the state but as a province, and their residents perceived that they were disdained. Western Virginia felt itself under a "despot's heel," but the despot was not Lincoln or the Union or the North but Tidewater Virginia.

---

*Sic semper tyrannis—"thus always to tyrants"—was and is the Virginia state motto, and would be John Wilkes Booth's cry on the stage of Ford's Theater on April 14, 1865. At the dedication of a monument to Lincoln in Richmond in April 2003, a small airplane flew overhead throughout the ceremony towing a banner taunting the audience with that phrase.

†To be sure, colonial Virginia had been even larger, including all the territory that would become the state of Kentucky. At the dedication of that Lincoln memorial statue in Richmond in 2003, former Virginia governor Linwood Holton would say: "I dare suggest that the man we honor today was also a Virginian. He was born in one of our far western counties—some call it 'Kentucky.' "

The far northern and western counties of this huge old Virginia reached over and up into the Midwest. A sliver of a panhandle reached up between Ohio and Pennsylvania, farther north than Columbus, as far north as Pittsburgh. Wheeling, a river city far from any plantations, was only 60 miles from Pittsburgh but 330 miles from Richmond. When the news came on April 14 that Fort Sumter had fallen, and on April 15 that Lincoln had called for troops, while Virginia governor John Letcher way over in Richmond was indignantly refusing to send any troops to "subjugate the southern states," the "Virginians" in the counties farthest north and west were asking where they could sign up to do just that. They were responding as did their nearby neighbors in Ohio and Pennsylvania: they displayed the American flag, marched in parades, held mass meetings supporting the Union, and tried to volunteer to fight for the Union. Unable to fight for the Union under their own state's banner, northwestern Virginians enlisted in Ohio and Pennsylvania.

At the secret secession convention in Richmond on April 17, 1861, the overwhelming majority of the delegates from the Tidewater and the Piedmont—that is, from east of the mountains, old Virginia—voted in favor of secession, while the majority of the delegates from west of the mountains voted against secession. One western Virginia delegate offered a resolution that illustrated yet again Lincoln's description of the endlessly fissiparous effect of the principle of secession: "The right of revolution can be exercised as well by a portion of the citizens of a state against their state government, as it can be exercised by the people of the state against the federal government." In other words, the minute that secession was proposed, westerners immediately thought of a secession from that secession.

The Union's rescue of these western counties of Virginia would not have come about without military force. Major General George McClellan, with superior force and help from the locals who knew the territory, defeated rebels in two early battles in July, clearing northwestern Virginia of Confederate forces. Although the numbers involved in the western Virginia battles were small, they were the first victories the Union could celebrate, they made McClellan a hero, and they led to the political actions that created a new Union-supporting free state.

On June 20 a convention meeting in Wheeling called the Richmond traitors illegal, formed "the restored government of Virginia," declared all offices vacant, and then unanimously chose Francis Pierpont as governor of Virginia—restored Virginia. A rump legislature from the northwestern counties chose new U.S. senators from "restored" Virginia, replacing noted secessionists who had resigned from the Senate. After a brief bout of throat clearing and eye rolling, the U.S. Senate seated the new senators.

Lincoln felt that the U.S. government was bound to recognize and protect, as the government of Virginia, not the traitors in Richmond but these loyal citizens who had organized a loyal government in the counties over the mountains. When in July 1861 the newly elected governor wrote to President Lincoln asking for support, he received a positive response addressed to "Francis H. Pierpont, Governor of Virginia." (The governor in his letter to Lincoln spelled his last name "Peirpoint." Lincoln, responding, spelled it "Pierpoint.")

Lincoln instructed the secretary of war to provide arms for whatever troops the restored government could raise to support the Union. "This government is bound to recognize and protect those loyal citizens," Lincoln said (meaning Pierpont and his "restored" government), "as being Virginia." In the draft of his message he had made it even starker: "those citizens are Virginia."

Governor Letcher in Richmond had disdainfully rejected Lincoln's call for militia and had supported hostile military action against the U.S. government; Governor Pierpont in Wheeling was in full support of that government and by the end of 1861 had raised many more troops to fight for the Union than was the quota for the whole state.

For Lincoln's purposes, Union military control and a loyal government-in-exile was all that he needed. But the Virginia mountaineers had something more in mind. Union military control enabled a referendum on a new state to proceed; the new state was overwhelmingly supported by those who voted, who also elected delegates to a constitutional convention that produced a constitution for a new state now called West Virginia. (The proposed state's name in the earlier round had been "Kanawha.") This constitution was embraced by the people of the counties included, again by an overwhelming vote.

In order for a new state to be carved out of the territory of an existing state, there had to be, according to the U.S. Constitution, "consent of the legislature(s) of the state(s) involved." But how could the proud old state of Virginia consent to its own dismemberment? Again the question comes: "Which Virginia?" On May 13, 1862, the Restored Government of Virginia, meeting in Wheeling, gave its consent to the formation of the new state. This government, at that moment, exercised authority over only the four eastern Virginia counties where Union arms had prevailed, in addition to the counties over the mountains that would compose the new state. The bill admitting the newly constructed state then made its way through the U.S. Senate and the House under considerable hostile fire about its constitutional and legal propriety, but both houses of Congress did finally vote to admit the new state and sent the bill to Lincoln's desk in December 1862.

On December 23 Lincoln asked his cabinet about the statehood bill. With the secretary of the interior post vacant for the moment, the six other cabinet members were exactly divided. Seward, Chase, and Stanton favored it, but Welles, Blair, and Bates opposed it.

Attorney General Edward Bates stated the objection most pointedly: "We all know—everybody knows—that the [restored] government of Virginia . . . does not and never did, represent and govern more than a small fraction of the state . . . And the legislature which pretends to give the consent of Virginia to her own dismemberment is . . . composed chiefly if not entirely of men who represent those forty-eight counties which constitute the new state of West Virginia. Is that fair dealing? Is that honest legislation? It seems to me that it is a mere abuse, nothing less than an attempted secession, hardly veiled under the flimsy form of law."

Abraham Lincoln would find it awkward indeed to support anything that might be called "secession." But his answer to this charge, written out in his own statement after he had the cabinet contributions, would turn entirely on *who* had seceded and *why:* "It is said that the admission of West-Virginia is secession, and tolerated only because it is our secession. Well, if we call it by that name, there is still difference enough between secession against the Constitution, and secession in favor of the Constitution."

The irrepressible Henry Wise, ex-governor of old Virginia and now a not-very-competent Confederate general, scarcely a disinterested observer, had put the matter pungently. He had described the new state as the bastard child of a political rape. Lincoln's response to the statehood bill would come very close to saying: Yes, but it is *our* bastard child.

One of the worries about this bill was that it would set a precedent, leading to the chopping apart of other states. Lincoln answered this widespread anxiety in the way he would answer the worries about the suspension of habeas corpus—that the emetic one takes for the illness of wartime one surely would not keep taking in the health of peace: "The division of a State is dreaded as a precedent. But a measure made expedient by war, is not precedent for times of peace." But West Virginia statehood, unlike the temporary suspension of habeas corpus, was not an action that could be reversed or removed when the healthy condition of peace returned.

Later in the war, as the issue of reconstruction came to the fore, Lincoln would disagree with Charles Sumner and others who saw the rebel states now as conquered territory, to be dealt with however the conqueror decided; he would then be respectful of the antecedent states. But in this earlier moment he concentrated wholly on the war, and his arguments turned altogether on the contest at hand.

Although slaves were comparatively few in the western counties, those counties nevertheless did hold slaves. The endgame of making a new state would include a requirement by a Republican Congress of a swifter emancipation than the new state had initially proposed. Lincoln saw this as a huge moral and practical gain. It is to be noted that he is here taking for granted that slavery is the cause of the war: "Again, the admission of the new State, turns that much slave soil to free; and, thus, is a certain, and irrevocable encroachment upon the cause of the rebellion."

Lincoln's only alternatives in late December 1862 were to sign or to veto a statehood bill that had been shaped and voted on by the western Virginians and had then been passed by both houses of Congress. Having carried their project through to passage, the loyal West Virginians would regard a presidential veto as a slap in the face. Lincoln was in receipt of many communications telling him that opinion there had come to combine support for the Union with support for the new state. He said in his statement:

> Her brave and good men regard [West Virginia's] admission into the Union as a matter of life and death. They have been true to the Union under very severe trials. We have so acted as to justify their hopes; and we can not fully retain their confidence, and co-operation, if we seem to break faith with them.

Lincoln signed the bill, and West Virginia became a state.

OUR RATHER FAIR PROSPECT FOR KENTUCKY

GOVERNOR BERIAH MAGOFFIN OF KENTUCKY responded unfavorably to the president's April 15, 1861, call for militia: "Kentucky will furnish no troops for the wicked purpose of subduing her sister Southern states." Many Kentuckians, by contrast, regarded secession itself as the wicked purpose. And many Kentuckians agreed simultaneously with both of these views: wickedness in both directions. "A public meeting of leading citizens at Louisville first denounced secession," wrote Nicolay and Hay, "and then denounced the president for attempting to put down secession." Kentucky had more of this plague-on-both-your-houses attitude than any other state. And it had a tradition, of which it was proud, of standing between, conciliating, mediating. Henry Clay had been the "Great Compromiser"; John Crittenden, who right away on April 17 gave a let-us-mediate speech, was now his successor. Those familiar Civil War stories about brothers fighting against brothers and fathers with a son on each side come as often from Kentucky as from any other state. Kentucky had the largest proportion of slaves of any of the border states, nearly 20 percent of the population, which meant that Kentucky was well supplied not only with slave owners but also with the apparatus supporting slavery in the culture and institutions of the state.

Kentucky also had strong ties to the North—to the states just across the Ohio River—and traded with the North; it had a strong, if modulated, attachment to the Union. Both secessionists and Unionists, aware of Kentucky's volatile political mixture, would for strategic reasons support a position that others endorsed in its own right: "Neutrality!" On May 16 the lower house resolved that Kentucky "should take no part in the Civil War now being waged, except as mediator and friend to the belligerent parties, and that Kentucky should, during the contest, occupy the position of strict neutrality." Governor Magoffin, although at heart himself a secessionist, saw the way the Kentucky wind blew and issued a long gubernatorial proclamation of armed neutrality; he prohibited the movement of non-Kentucky armies on Kentucky soil. On May 24 the state senate also voted for a state policy of armed neutrality.

So Kentucky was—formally, officially, legally, by enactment, resolution, and proclamation—"neutral." That posed a problem, theoretical and practical, both for the rebels and for Lincoln, different problems, because of different theories, for each. As it turned out, the rebels (who should in theory have respected it) violated Kentucky's neutrality, and Lincoln (who in theory rejected it) prudently respected it. Jefferson Davis and the Confederates should have respected Kentucky's neutrality because they believed (or said they believed) in state sovereignty; Lincoln need not (theoretically) have respected it, because he didn't. But the conduct on the two sides did not accord with the theories.

When on September 3 the former Episcopal bishop, now Confederate general, Leonidas Polk, given authority by the Confederate command, ordered his troops into Kentucky and occupied the town of Columbus, he was hard put to justify the deed. He did not find time even to notify Governor Magoffin until six days later. Polk then wrote to the governor, in the apologetic tone of all dilatory correspondents: "I should have dispatched to you immediately, as the troops under my command took possession of this position, the very few words I addressed to the people here; but my duties since that time so preoccupied me, that I have but now the first leisure moment to communicate with you."

Of course he justified his action, violating Kentucky's neutrality, by an alleged necessity. These actions of "preemption," these first shots, are in wartime inevitably justified by reference to some less overt prior action by the enemy that is claimed to have made them necessary, claims that are rarely persuasive to disinterested parties. Polk was forthright at least to Governor Magoffin for the reason he violated Kentucky's neutrality:

> I had information on which I could rely that the Federal forces intended and were preparing to seize Columbus. I need not describe to you the danger resulting to Western Tennessee from such occupation. My responsibility could not permit me quietly to lose to the command intrusted to me so important a position.

He was referring to a small body of Union troops under Ulysses S. Grant that had occupied Belmont, Missouri, directly across from Columbus.

The chairman of a committee of the Kentucky Senate, enclosing a resolution of that body, put the case sharply to General Polk:

> [T]he people of Kentucky are profoundly astonished that such an act [military occupation] should have been committed by the Confederate States, and especially that they should have been the first . . . The people of Kentucky . . . with great unanimity determined upon a position of neutrality in the unhappy war now being waged . . . In obedience to the thrice repeated will of the people, as expressed at the polls and in their name, I ask you to withdraw your forces from the soil of Kentucky.

Polk in answer would give a ridiculous list of additional justifications for his action: that Kentucky had allowed the Union army to recruit in Kentucky; had allowed them to train in a Kentucky camp; had allowed Kentucky timber to be cut and used in ships that would attack the South; had allowed its congressmen to vote supplies to Union troops.

There were those in the Confederate camp who perceived the danger in Polk's action. Confederate secretary of war L. P. Walker wired a blunt order to Polk to withdraw the troops from Kentucky.

The Confederate governor of Tennessee Isham G. Harris, aware of the precarious state of opinion in his neighbor state, urged Jefferson Davis to order immediate withdrawal. Governor Harris received his answer not from President Davis but from Secretary Walker: "General Polk has been ordered to direct the prompt withdrawal of the forces under General Pillow from Kentucky. The movement was wholly unauthorized."

But wait. Had Secretary Walker's order to withdraw been obeyed? On the day previous to this exchange, Jefferson Davis had responded, with rare brevity, to the appeals and self-defenses by General Polk justifying the entry of troops into Kentucky: "General Polk: the necessity justifies the action."

Davis later wrote to Polk: "Governor Harris and others have represented to me that the occupation of Columbus and Hickman would work political detriment to our cause in Kentucky. It is true that the solution of the problem requires consideration of other than the military elements involved in it; but we cannot permit the indeterminate qualities, the political elements, to control our actions in cases of military necessity."

Polk, supported by Davis, did not withdraw Pillow's men from Kentucky soil. He said he would withdraw if the federal forces also withdrew. After the Confederates occupied Columbus, Union forces under Ulysses S. Grant occupied another strategic Kentucky town, Paducah. But the decisive point was that the Confederates had marched onto Kentucky soil first. The efforts by Governor Magoffin to get both sides to withdraw did not work. Kentucky had been tipped. On September 18 the legislature passed a resolution saying: "Kentucky has been invaded by forces of the so-called Confederate States, and the commanders . . . have insolently prescribed the conditions under which they would withdraw, thus insulting the dignity of the state by demanding terms to which Kentucky cannot listen without dishonor; therefore, be it resolved . . . that the invaders must be expelled." The ardent proponents of states' rights had managed to lose a state by violating what that state regarded as its rights; the Southerners with their strong sense of "honor" had made their fellow Southerners in Kentucky feel dishonored.

LINCOLN HAD no such theoretical constraints as the Confederates professed; he did not believe in state sovereignty, and he did not believe a state on its own hook could be "neutral." He had explained, both in his inaugural address and in his July 4 Message to Congress, the impossibility of state "sovereignty." He had in that message also explicitly repudiated any possibility of "neutrality" for a state.

But he nevertheless did recognize the importance of what Jefferson Davis had rather dismissively called "the indeterminate qualities, the political elements" in Kentucky attitudes. His implicit respect for Kentucky's "neutrality" was like his other prudent adaptations to real, if false, opinion: he knew how strongly public opinion in the crucial border states opposed anything that looked like "coercion," and so he avoided it even while he disagreed on the ultimate rights and wrongs and definitions. Lincoln avoided making declarations that would have upset the precarious balance in Kentucky. When immediately after the fall of Sumter Governor Magoffin issued his defiant refusal to furnish troops for Lincoln's "wicked purpose," Lincoln might have responded by throwing federal armies into the crucial state, or not yet having much by way of federal armies, he could have sent a shower of belligerent words to match Magoffin's defiant ones. But he did neither of those things. In fact on April 26, in an interview with a Kentucky Unionist named Garret Davis, an old friend, he gave assurance that he intended to order no movements of troops into or through Kentucky. When, however, the Confederacy, with Magoffin's connivance, began secretly to recruit in the state, Lincoln did mix a little use of potential force with his political shrewdness: he secretly began to furnish what came to be called "Lincoln guns" to a committee of Kentucky Unionists headed by a former naval officer and native Kentuckian, William "Bull" Nelson.

When Kentucky's legislature and governor officially enacted and proclaimed the state's "neutrality" in May, and prohibited federal troops from "trespassing" on Kentucky's "sovereign" soil, and thereby violated their oaths to support the Constitution, Lincoln again might have made his rejection of that idea explicit and insisted that Kentucky meet her responsibility as a state and furnish troops to the commander in chief, but again he didn't. He did set up a military department of Kentucky, but it included only the generally loyal section of the state, and—in another application of the "no obnoxious strangers" policy that he had announced in his inaugural—appointed as its head the Kentuckian who was the hero from Sumter, Major Robert Anderson.

Lincoln did feel he should refute the false doctrine of state "neutrality" in his message to Congress on July 4, but he did not name Kentucky or speak these words in direct response to Kentucky defiance, and when Governor Magoffin sent emissaries (one of them Senator Crittenden) to ask what he intended, he said he had no present intention to send troops into Kentucky and hoped he would not in the future, although he could not promise.

Lincoln's prudent circumspection in word and deed allowed Kentucky opinion to sort itself, after the initial shocks, and Union candidates won nine of ten congressional seats in a special election, and in another election in August the Union side won control of the state legislature by a wide margin. So the Union forces were in a strong position in Kentucky politics as the new legislature assembled.

COPING WITH FRÉMONT

THE SUCCESS of Lincoln's careful nurturing of Kentucky was now abruptly threatened by an event in a neighboring border state.

On August 30, 1861, John C. Frémont, commander of the West, with headquarters in St. Louis, declared martial law and on his own military authority proclaimed instant emancipation of the slaves of all disloyal Missouri persons. That lightning bolt suddenly made ending slavery the topic of the day and reverberated in radically contrasting ways in antislavery circles and in slaveholding Kentucky.

Frémont was the "Pathfinder," whose western explorations and exploits had brought him glittering celebrity. He had led expeditions to California and to map the Oregon Trail, the Oregon Territory, the Great Basin, and the Sierra Mountains. With the help of his wife, Jessie, he wrote accounts of these explorations that left his name scattered across the western landscape: Fremont Peak; Fremont Pass; Fremont, Nebraska; Fremont, California; Fremont, Michigan. His fame, his marriage, his powerful connections, and his political eminence had all elevated him above his modest abilities. Before 1861 he had certainly been a far better-known person than Abraham Lincoln. When President Lincoln dealt with Frémont, he was touching a tender spot in the psyche of the new Republican Party: Frémont had been the party's first presidential nominee, Lincoln's predecessor, in 1856. His name set off emotional vibrations in segments of the party—which now this proclamation revived and augmented. When Lincoln first came into office, he had had a certain what-to-do-with-him problem. Lincoln declined to give Frémont the cabinet post some had expected the most glamorous of Republicans to receive, and Seward rejected him as ambassador to France. But surely commander of the West would be just the place for him. He was strongly supported by the powerful Blair family and was appointed to the post with fanfare.

But he took his time making his way out to St. Louis and was not a success once he got there. There was scandal, disorganization, and failure to send support in a key battle. Ridiculously ambitious projects were never realized. Frémont would eventually lose the support of the Blairs, to the point that he had Frank Blair arrested and Blair in turn sued him. Meanwhile, on August 30, he issued this proclamation in an attempt to subdue by brute force the guerrilla forces of Missouri and to revive by antislavery radicalism the reputation of John C. Frémont. In the latter aim he met with some success; for the rest of the war his would be the first name put forward as an alternative to Lincoln by antislavery radicals, particularly in Missouri.

Letters back and forth between St. Louis and Washington were now followed by visitors each way, passing en route: Lincoln sent Postmaster General Blair and Quartermaster General Montgomery Meigs to St. Louis to report on and give advice to the command in the West, while Frémont sent his articulate wife to Washington to give unsought advice to the commander in chief.

The president learned about the extraordinary proclamation issued by his putative subordinate out in St. Louis not through channels, not directly from Frémont, but from the newspapers. Lincoln responded by sending a surprisingly gentle letter, strictly private and carried by a special messenger, quietly arguing against "two points in your proclamation" that "give me some anxiety." Both at the time and since, the emancipation feature has so usurped attention as to obscure the stunning additional point in Frémont's ukase, which Lincoln took up first: his proposal to shoot to death any men "caught with arms in their hands within these lines." Lincoln wrote that that would surely mean that "the Confederates would very certainly shoot our best man in their hands in retaliation; and so, man for man, indefinitely." So Lincoln *ordered* Frémont not to allow any man to be shot without first gaining Lincoln's consent.

On Frémont's proposed emancipation, on the other hand, Lincoln *requested* a modification by Frémont himself. ("Allow me . . . to ask, that you will, as of our own motion . . .") Lincoln asked Frémont to modify the proclamation to bring it into line with the Confiscation Act just passed by Congress, which provided for the confiscation only of property (slaves included) actually used in combat against the Union. The president of the United States, by no means sure that his general out in St. Louis was following national legislation closely, took the trouble to send Frémont a copy of the act.

Lincoln tried to get Frémont to see the larger picture as he had to see it as president: thus abruptly liberating slaves by proclamation "will alarm our Southern Union Friends, and turn them against us—perhaps ruin our rather fair prospect for Kentucky."

Instead of doing as Lincoln asked, Frémont wrote an argumentative letter insisting, about his emancipation order, "If I were to retract it of my own accord, it would imply that I thought myself wrong." He asked Lincoln, if he really disagreed, to "openly direct me to make the correction."

Up to this point the Lincoln-Frémont exchange had been private; by this move Frémont forced it into public view, casting himself as the opponent of slavery and leaving it to Lincoln to overrule him and incur the wrath not only of abolitionists but of many others in the North.

When Frémont began issuing personal deeds of manumission (he was now spending his time doing little else, they heard in the White House), it rang sudden loud bells in the North. But the bells that sounded celebration in the North rang with desperate alarm in Kentucky. Lincoln received torrents of mail and telegrams full of anger from his native state, telling him that if the Frémont proclamation prevailed, "Kentucky is gone over the mill dam," as one telegram briskly put it. Lincoln's old friend, once his closest friend, Joshua Speed, after sleepless nights, sent an anguished letter giving Lincoln potent comparisons: "You had as well attack the freedom of worship in the North or the right of a parent to teach his child to read—as to wage war in a slave state on such a principle." Perhaps the most effective of the arguments he received was the sheer practical one he got from the Sumter hero Robert Anderson, telling him that on hearing of Frémont's order a whole company of Kentuckians who had volunteered to fight for the Union "threw down their arms and disbanded." Lincoln himself would add, "I was so assured, as to think it probable, that the very arms we had furnished Kentucky would be turned against us."

When Lincoln publicly ordered Frémont to change the proclamation, the bell ringings and alarm soundings reversed themselves. Now there came new torrents of editorial and public outrage at Lincoln for quashing Frémont's order. A string of powerful newspapers hailed Frémont's action, then condemned Lincoln for undoing it; an abolitionist reported that public mention of Lincoln's name would now be greeted with groans. Lincoln's action was said to be a worse defeat for the Union than Bull Run. James Russell Lowell asked, "How many times are we to save Kentucky and lose our self-respect?" But Lincoln thought we could, with prudence and with time, save both. (Would Kentucky joining the Confederacy really boost the Union's self-respect?) Lincoln took comfort from the other side of the reversal of opinion: the rejoicing among Kentucky Unionists at his modifying of Frémont's order.

Frémont's decree had come at a dangerous moment, just when Kentucky's legislature had been meeting to consider disavowing "neutrality";

the legislature refused to do that unless Frémont's decree was modified; Lincoln ordered that it be modified, and Kentucky's legislature abandoned neutrality and called for forty thousand volunteers for the Union.

A scholar in a still useful book on the "Borderland," written more than three-quarters of a century ago, introduced his discussion of Frémont's proclamation by saying that "the cause of the Union [in Kentucky] was placed in serious jeopardy by the stupid and high-handed act of a federal general in a neighboring state." He followed his treatment of that topic with a paragraph beginning, "Fortunately for the national government, it did not have a monopoly of military commanders who were incapable of foreseeing the political consequences of their acts. The Confederates had Leonidas Polk." Polk as a bishop might have been expected to have political sense, this writer said, but Polk was not only an Episcopal priest and bishop but also a graduate of West Point, before he went into the ministry, and he was not alone in bearing responsibility for the Confederacy's Kentucky fiasco. Jefferson Davis, another graduate of West Point and a classmate of Polk, had countermanded the orders of his secretary of war, supported Polk, and declined to order him to withdraw. These two West Pointers could see that the line of bluffs at Columbus, the "Gibraltar of the West," was the only good point for many miles from which to command the Mississippi and hence a military objective of the highest priority. What they could not see, as Lincoln could, was that the "indeterminate qualities, the political elements" in the Kentucky struggle, were vastly more important than any military objective, however well situated it might be on the Mississippi River.

Moral criticism of Lincoln has regularly featured this countermanding of Frémont's emancipation order, as well as his later rejection of an emancipation order issued by General David Hunter. But these critics both at the time and later insufficiently appreciated Lincoln's actual situation. Preserving the United States was and had to be for Lincoln the first priority. The morality of statecraft entails layers of action and an awareness of sequences of consequences: the great promise of the Declaration to all the world would not be realized unless its bearer, the United States of America, was preserved, and the United States would not be preserved unless Kentucky was kept in the Union, and Kentucky would not be kept in the Union unless Frémont's order was quashed.

In his annual message in December 1861, Lincoln could claim that "Kentucky . . . for some time in doubt, is now decidedly, and, I think, unchangeably, ranged on the side of the Union."

BLEEDING MISSOURI

AFTER THE WAR a lad from Hannibal, Missouri, would make himself into a great literary figure, indeed the "Lincoln of our literature," producing among his short humorous pieces a self-mocking account of his own role in the war, "A Private History of a Campaign That Failed." Mark Twain's introductory jokes, before settling down to stories of youthful ineptitude in the Confederate militia, would deal with "leaning first this way, then that, then the other way" between supporting the Union or supporting the Confederacy—but being belligerently certain of the rightness of whichever side he fiercely defended this week and furious with exactly the position he had taken last week. That reciprocating intransigence would be something of a symbol of Missouri Civil War politics.

Missouri was, as a result of the famous 1820 Compromise, the only slave state that extended above the line, a salient of slavery surrounded on three sides by freedom and a border state that, like border states Maryland and Kentucky, the Union had to retain for geopolitical and military reasons. It was a western state with at least its quota of frontier violence; a state with a complex population; and the only state in the Union in which in the election of 1860 all *four* parties to the contest had a significant presence.* Because there was a strongly antislavery German population in St. Louis, Lincoln received fifteen thousand votes in Missouri, more than in all other slave states put together. And Missouri shared a long, easily crossed border with "Bleeding Kansas." Much of the notorious bleeding was caused by antislavery insurgents, called bushwhackers, from Missouri.

The Civil War had already begun on the Missouri-Kansas border, with barbarous guerrilla warfare, six years before Lincoln had any role except commentary. The passage of Stephen Douglas's Kansas-Nebraska Act in 1854, repealing the Missouri Compromise and opening Kansas to "popular sovereignty," had set off a fierce contest: Would Kansas be a slave state or free? Back in 1854, as a rising Illinois politician, Lincoln saw that the Kansas-Missouri border would become what would be called in the following century a proxy war: "each party WITHIN, having numerous and determined backers WITHOUT, is it not probable that the contest will come to blows and bloodshed? Could there be a more apt invention to bring about collision and violence, on the slavery question, than this Nebraska

---

*Republican (Lincoln); Northern Democratic (Douglas); Southern Democratic (Breckinridge); Constitutional Union (Bell).

project is?" He used a metaphor to illustrate the point: "if they had literally found a ring, and placed champions within it to fight out the controversy, the fight could be no more likely to come off, than it is."

And so it would be. New England sent antislavery champions to Kansas; Missourians sent border ruffians to beat them up. "While anti-slavery men were the first to organize migration as a means of continuing the contest over slavery, Missourians were first openly to invoke the use of force."

Many of the cast of characters in the guerrilla war in Civil War Missouri had been shaped by the prior battle over Kansas: Bleeding Kansas bled into Missouri. Leading Kansas antislavery activists had come to Kansas from other states after 1854 (Jim Lane, Charles R. "Doc" Jennison, Nathaniel Lyon) and often had then been further radicalized after they experienced the raids and massacres. Supporters of slavery came to Missouri and joined native Missourians in bushwhacking raids and retaliations into Kansas; they had a parallel radicalizing experience (William Quantrill, "Bloody Bill" Anderson, Frank and Jesse James).

It was a time and place of polarizing atrocities that increased in scope, sometimes with quasi-official endorsement by the embattled armies and governments, after the national war of the rebellion began.

WHEN WAR CAME, this already embattled state would be kept in the Union by a swift and unique series of irregularities that Lincoln would support at pivotal moments. The prime movers in these events were a short, intense, no-nonsense Connecticut Yankee named Nathaniel Lyon, who at the start of the war was only a captain in the Union army guarding the St. Louis arsenal, and Frank Blair, whose brother was postmaster general.

President Lincoln's call for the state militias at the war's beginning was disdainfully dismissed by Missouri's utterly secessionist governor, a former bushwhacker named Claiborne Fox Jackson. Instead he sent a letter to Jefferson Davis asking for Confederate help in capturing the federal arsenal in St. Louis—the largest arsenal in the slave states—and he created a "Camp Jackson" on the edge of St. Louis for drilling a militia that would surely support the South and be used to take the arsenal. Blair and Lyon began drilling irregular volunteer bands of Union-supporting Germans in St. Louis as a counterforce. Blair then used his Washington connections to have the Union commander in St. Louis, General W. S. Harney, suddenly summoned to Washington—a decision in which Lincoln concurred.

Although he was a loyal Unionist, Harney as an old-fashioned military man did not in these slippery first days clearly perceive what Governor Jackson was doing; if the governor had asked to be given control of the federal arsenal, General Harney might have yielded it.

With Harney deftly lifted out of the picture, there came a truly extraordinary, and pivotal, order from the president. The recipient of these instructions, Captain Nathaniel Lyon, was "commanding in the West" only because Harney was gone.

> Sir: The President of the United States directs that you enroll in the military service of the United States the loyal citizens of Saint Louis and vicinity, not exceeding, with those heretofore enlisted, ten thousand in number, for the purpose of maintaining the authority of the United States . . . and you will, if deemed necessary for that purpose by yourself and by [six loyal citizens including Blair] proclaim martial law in the city of Saint Louis.

This remarkable order to a mere infantry captain, signed by the secretary of war, has two "endorsements." One is "Approved, April 30, 1861 A. Lincoln." The other, signed by the initials "W. S.," for General in Chief Winfield Scott, speaks volumes: "It is revolutionary times, and therefore I do not object to the irregularity of this."

This irregular order was endorsed by Lincoln on April 30, just eight days after the cabinet meeting at the Navy Department at which a series of other "irregular" actions were taken. It was indeed, as General Scott said, "revolutionary times," and Lincoln took the actions that in his view the preservation of the United States required.

Lyon himself reconnoitered in Camp Jackson (as legend has it, disguised as a woman) and found weapons recently lifted from the arsenal at Baton Rouge. He surrounded the camp with his new troops and forced its surrender, then marched the captured militia through the streets and set off a skirmish with a mob.

General Harney returned, resumed his command, and made a truce with Governor Jackson and the ex-governor, now general, Sterling Price, an old army acquaintance. On May 12 Nathaniel Lyon, "Captain, Second Infantry, Commanding," sent to the army in Washington another in the series of remarkable messages that are sprinkled throughout the event, explaining "with great delicacy and hesitancy" that Harney's taking over would ruin the plans that Lyon had made to *anticipate* threatened actions against the U.S. government. Harney didn't get it; Harney trusted Price and others and was no anticipator.*

In Washington Lincoln had to decide whether to support the distinguished army man Harney or the upstart Captain Lyon. The contest had partisans in the innards of the cabinet: Attorney General Bates was for Harney, while Frank Blair's brother Montgomery was for Lyon. General Scott was an old army friend of Harney, an honorable professional. The gulf in rank was ridiculously large: Harney an experienced brigadier general, Lyon a mere captain. But Lincoln made a revealing, significant decision: he decided that Lyon was to be jumped all the way to brigadier general and, if necessary, given command.

Lincoln himself wrote Frank Blair telling him that the War Department was sending him an order to relieve General Harney. With his usual political tact, Lincoln explained that Blair should use or not use it at his discretion: "We had better have him a friend than an enemy." Blair did not present the order right away. But Harney, who had had and would have a distinguished career as a professional army man, was too trusting a soul for Missouri politics in 1861. Lincoln sent Harney a message through channels:

> The president observes with concern that, notwithstanding the pledge of the state *authorities* . . . loyal citizens in great numbers continue to be driven from their homes . . . The professions of loyalty by the state authorities of Missouri *are not to be relied upon.*

But Harney did rely upon them. He knew General Sterling Price as a distinguished veteran of the Mexican War and a sometime governor of the state: "My confidence in the honor and integrity of General Price, in the purity of his motives, and in his loyalty to the government remains unimpaired."

But General Price was one of those who was loyal to Missouri and to the United States only as long as it did not "coerce" Missouri. Later he would become a Confederate general. On May 29 Blair handed Harney the presidential order relieving him of command.

The state authorities now had to deal with Brigadier General (recently

---

*"It is with great delicacy and hesitancy I take the liberty to observe that the energetic and necessary measures of day before yesterday . . . require persevering and consistent exertion . . . and that the authority of General Harney under these circumstances embarrasses . . . the execution of the plans I had contemplated, and upon which the safety and welfare of the Government . . . so much depend." *OR*, ser. 1, vol. 3, p. 9.

Captain) Nathaniel Lyon and asked for a meeting. Blair and Lyon, Jackson and Price met for four hours, in a gathering famous in Missouri folklore. Would Lyon disband that (Lyon-commanded) Union home guard? Promise no more Union troops? Lyon said no. Would he disarm that rebel state guard? Allow federal troops to go anywhere in the state? Jackson said he should not. Legend reports that Lyon announced, "This is war!" Jackson and Price hastened back to the capital, Jefferson City, burning railroad bridges on the way. Lyon immediately took his battalions by steamship as fast as they could go to Jefferson City, took possession of the town, and raised the Union flag. Jackson and his government fled, taking with them the state seal so they could try to be official wherever they would end up. General Price gathered a state rebel force up the river at Booneville; Lyon reembarked with his troops and routed them on June 17, 1861, in an actual skirmish, the first battle of the Missouri Civil War. Governor Jackson fled still farther south, holding on to his seal.

And so how to restore a civic government? In the first days of the war Governor Jackson had called a state convention, expecting that it would vote for Missouri to secede and join the Confederacy. But although Union sentiment in the state was sharply divided and fractious, it came together to oppose the vote to secede. The convention then did something else: it provided for an emergency recall of itself. It was now reassembled, with a quorum, even though many members had joined the rebellion, and that quorum set up a provisional government, with the conservative (a "conditional Unionist") Hamilton Gamble as governor. That makeshift Union government remained in authority for the entire war.

ON THE ONE HAND, Missouri was thus secured to the Union fairly early and therefore was a kind of success. On the other hand, it was the scene of the worst guerrilla warfare of the war, of atrocities, and of violations of civil liberties, and therefore by another criterion it was a failure.

If you tell the Missouri Civil War story casting Lyon (the "savior of Missouri") and Blair as the heroes, then Lincoln must be something of a hero too, because he made pivotal decisions that made their coup d'état work; he backed Lyon and Blair at every decision point through the sequence of irregularities by which they kept the state in the Union.

But if you tell the story casting them not as heroes, then Missouri is by another measure a particularly egregious failure, and then does Lincoln bear some responsibility for the failure?

Here are two summaries of the situations in the three border states, both of which conclude with a negative judgment about Missouri.

The historian William Gienapp, using criteria for success going beyond simply keeping the state in the Union, and going beyond 1861, writes: "Lincoln's policies were fairly successful in Maryland, produced a mixed record in Kentucky, and were largely a failure in Missouri ... [Missouri] left a dark blot on his otherwise generally positive record of accomplishments in the border states."

Mark E. Neely, Jr., dealing with civil liberties, writes:

> When questioned about military repression in the border states, Republican contemporaries of Abraham Lincoln pointed with pride to the role of the administration's vigorous measure in saving Maryland for the Union. Even Democrats in the North frequently admitted the necessity of the early arrests in Maryland. Likewise, historians have long emphasized the crucial place of Kentucky on the Union map, and many of them have praised the administration for keeping that state in the Union by a shrewd mixture of tough policies and sympathetic treatment ... Nobody bragged about Missouri ... Civil War Missouri became a nightmare for American civil liberties.

Lincoln was implicated in the most dubious actions by a Union command, General Order No. 11, issued by General Thomas Ewing in Kansas City in August 1863. This order was issued in retaliation for the "Lawrence Massacre," a raid by proslavery Missouri bushwhackers who rode fifty miles into Kansas, arrived at dawn, and killed most of the male population, 185 men and boys, in the antislavery town. In the excited aftermath Ewing ordered the evacuation of four Missouri counties that bordered Kansas, on the theory that these civilians had furnished support for the raiders. Lincoln's endorsement came less than six weeks later in a letter to Ewing's superior in St. Louis, dealing with a number of items. Lincoln wrote: "With the matters of removing the inhabitants of certain counties *en masse;* and of removing certain individuals from time to time, who are supposed to be mischievous, I am not now interfering, but am leaving to your discretion."

Lincoln should have taken a moment to imagine what this "removing ... *en masse*" meant to the human beings to be removed—civilians living their lives in a (nominally) loyal state. Instead, he went along with the generals' contention that this order had legitimate military purposes—to forestall the Kansas vengeance and to end the insane border war in these counties.

This civilian removal was certainly not the only violation of human rights that occurred during this savage conflict in Missouri, but it was the most egregious and created long-lasting resentment. Those responsible for General Order No. 11 had the misfortune that in the affected area lived a talented American painter of realistic western scenes, a Missourian named George Caleb Bingham, who would turn his talents to attacking the order. He produced a large crowded canvas, called simply *General Order No. 11,* which showed devastation and misery in many forms: smoke from burning homes rising in the background, prostrate and begging and weeping figures in the foreground, loaded wagons, a swaggering General Ewing in the center.

Among the inhabitants removed en masse by General Order No. 11 was an eleven-year-old girl riding in an oxcart with her mother and five sisters away from her burning home. She would one day, in the curious circling of history, become the mother of a president of the United States.

When President Truman's mother visited him in the White House, he played a little joke on her, which we learn about in the memoirs of their fellow Missourian Clark Clifford, who was present when it happened. "Tonight, Mother," said the president, "we are going to give you a special treat, a chance to sleep in the most famous room in the White House, the Lincoln Room, and in the very bed in which Abraham Lincoln slept."

There was quiet in the group for a moment, Clark Clifford reported. Then Mrs. Truman spoke not to her son but to his wife. "Bess, if you'll get my bags packed, I'll be going back home this evening." The president and the others burst out laughing, and eventually his mother understood that it was a joke and joined in. But initially it had been a serious matter. She was not going to spend the night in the bedroom of the man who bore ultimate responsibility for General Order No. 11.

BY WAY OF MITIGATING the blame on Lincoln personally for this nightmare and dark blot, we may suggest these considerations about the sadly "guerrilla-ridden and war-smitten state" of Missouri, as Lincoln's secretaries would call it:

- The five-year Kansas-Missouri border war that preceded the Civil War in Missouri, before Lincoln or the Lincoln administration had any role, created terrible patterns of conduct, brutal memories, fierce resentments, and guerrilla warriors on both sides. This conduct continued right through the war and even beyond.

- Missouri had a wider range of opinion on slavery and Union than any other state, with a concentrated and radical antislavery German population in St. Louis, fierce defenders of slavery along the river that went back to the French, and conservative Unionists in the towns and rural areas. Missouri had, for example, two different kinds of Unionists who hated each other.
- Missouri had a toxic mixture of frontier violence with slave state violence.
- Missouri was a long way from Washington. Lincoln was dependent for information and help upon the Blair family, and the Blair family was inclined to simplifications and sharp swings of opinion.

That Missouri was secured for the Union by a virtual coup d'état was more a reflection than a cause of the state's distinct extremism in politics and war. Lincoln was faced not with a tabula rasa on which to play out graceful alternatives but with fierce realities and narrow choices. Lincoln's overwhelming priority—a sacred trust—was the maintenance of the Union, and to that end the securing of Missouri within the Union.

And the fact that it was more or less secured in the early going meant that for an overwhelmed war president it could thereafter be not a prime focus of attention but only an intermittent "torment"—his very own word about it.

Broad historical treatments of the American Civil War often cease dealing with the impossible complexities of the border states once they were more or less securely attached to the Union. But to put it mildly, the difficulties did not stop. This broad area, and Missouri in particular, would be the scene of continuing battles and of the worst guerrilla activity throughout the war.

LINCOLN, operating at the moral as well as the geographical border, had condoned if not instituted the arrest and imprisonment of state legislators as they were about to legislate, and of police commissioners, a police chief, and a mayor; had suspended habeas corpus and declined to honor an order by the chief justice of the United States; had sent troops to occupy a state not in rebellion and to provide the presence of force as voters went to the polls; had recognized as a governor a man appointed by delegates from less than a quarter of the counties of a state; had acquiesced in the division of an existing state on the thinnest of rationalizations; had surreptitiously sent arms to sympathetic civilians in a state that was not in rebellion; had insisted that a general's order emancipating slaves be canceled, thereby infuriating his antislavery supporters; had acquiesced in the mustering of civilians directly into the federals' service, skipping the state militia; had jumped a captain all the way to brigadier general, ahead of a lifetime army man; and had condoned making war on an elected governor, driving him into exile. These and like acts to come would set terrible precedents for later chief executives, but they could be defended in their own time and place not only by the necessity but by the *unique* necessity of civil war, in which the physical and moral essence of the nation was at risk—uniquely at risk. These actions were made necessary by a profound and original irregularity: that the rebels sought to overthrow by force of arms the government that Lincoln was sworn to defend.

He did defend it. Maryland, Kentucky, and Missouri were kept in the Union, and the western counties of Virginia were added to it. After four years of the mighty scourge of war, the Union would indeed be preserved.

CHAPTER SEVEN

The Moral Meaning
of the Union and the War

WHEN THE FRAMERS of the Constitution in Philadelphia wrote their sentence providing that the president may convene the houses of Congress, they said that he may do so "on extraordinary occasions." President Lincoln in the spring of 1861 dealt with the most extraordinary occasion in the history of the republic. In the proclamation that he wrote in the dramatic moment after the fall of Sumter, issued on Monday, April 15, 1861, in addition to calling out the militia, he summoned Congress to meet July 4.

The framers of the Constitution also provided that the president "shall from time to time give Congress information of the state of the Union"; the custom had developed that he do so at the start of each session of Congress. And so this new president, with all that was going on around him, managed to find the time—and, harder still, to clear his brain—to compose a most extraordinary message to this extraordinary session on this extraordinary occasion of rebellion and war. He covered the business of the hour, reporting to Congress on what he had done, asking for their retroactive endorsement, and making new requests. But he went much beyond that. He used this message to address the fundamental moral meaning of the war.

He first tried out his ideas on his two young assistants. John Hay in his diary for May 7 quoted Lincoln as saying: "I consider the central idea pervading this struggle is the necessity that is upon us, of proving that popular government is not an absurdity. We must settle this question now, whether in a free government the minority have the right to break up the government if they choose." John Nicolay wrote, in a memorandum dated the same day: "he [Lincoln] remarked that the real question involved in [the existing contest] . . . was whether a free and representative government had the right and power to protect and maintain itself. Admit the right of a minority to secede at will, and the occasion for such secession would almost as likely be any other as the slavery question." Both Hay and Nicolay made clear that the little seminar in which the president made these remarks was part of his preparation to write the message to the special session. Hay wrote: "He is engaged in constant thought upon his Message: It will be an exhaustive review of the questions of the hour & of the future." Nicolay, in a parenthesis, had Lincoln say of the idea he floated that "he should think further about it, while writing his message."

The July 4 Message to the special session that came out of these scribblings was Lincoln's first big production written as president of the United States. His First Inaugural Address had been the work of a president-elect when the nation was in an unresolved, anxious time. But the July 4 Message was written and edited—somehow—in the executive mansion by the president himself, in the midst of daily crises, after war had begun.

Although Seward again made an editorial reading of the draft and persuaded Lincoln to change a word here and there, his influence was slighter than it had been on the inaugural address. From the middle of June the president concentrated on writing his message. Nicolay reported that Lincoln "has refused to receive any calls whatever, either of friendship or business, except from members of the cabinet, or high officers."

Unlike the inaugural address, the message to the special session was never presented by Lincoln to any public audience. At that time it was not the practice of presidents to present their messages in person to Congress; their words were read to Congress by clerks. Lincoln did review it at noon on July 3 with the cabinet, but only one person ever heard Lincoln actually read the message—the new senator from Illinois, Lincoln's old friend Orville Browning. On the evening of July 3, the night before the special session began, Browning called at the executive mansion, and in the course of the visit Lincoln read the message to him. Lincoln scholar James G. Randall regrets that the message, read in a "perfunctory manner" to Congress and upstaged by the live address by the new Speaker of the House, received "inadequate notice." "Not the large public, not the assembled Congress, the press and galleries, but one lone Senator, heard Lincoln's oral delivery."

Lincoln produced, as Douglas Wilson has shown, multiple drafts of this carefully composed production. As we noted on an earlier page, in first writing the heavily fraught passage answering Chief Justice Taney about habeas corpus—about his being charged with failing to "take care" that the laws be faithfully executed—Lincoln resorted to, or burst into, the first person: "I felt it my duty," "my verbal request," "I should consider my official oath broken." This first-person passage has an immediacy and a force that contrast with the sometimes awkward formality of the other passages, and of later versions in which these deeds and duties are attributed to "the present incumbent" or "the administration" or most often to "the executive." Perhaps it was necessary, given what was deemed appropriate in a presidential message, to shield the actor behind those impersonal descriptions, but one wishes the message could have been written in the first person, as he had first drafted that sensitive part of it.

He summarized for Congress what "the executive" had done in response to the rebellion and the firing on Fort Sumter: relying on the war power, he had issued a call to states for 75,000 militia; he had proclaimed the blockade of Southern ports (that is, "proceedings in the nature of blockade"); he had made a new call for volunteers on May 3, quickly following on the earlier one of April 15, now to serve not for three months as in the first call but for three years.

He had done these things, in the necessity of the case, without congressional approval, but he fully recognized the authority of Congress. He now asked Congress for retroactive sanction for what he had already done, and he made new requests: at least 400,000 men and $400 million. Congress—in which Southern withdrawals had left large Republican majorities—not only granted these presidential requests but also raised them, to 500,000 men and $500 million.

Lincoln could have stopped after the first half of this address, having reported to Congress what had happened and what he had done, and having made his requests. But now, gathering as we may suppose all his powers, he proceeded, as James Randall would put it, to "an exalted commentary on fundamentals."

This exalted commentary was Lincoln's first presidential statement of what was at stake in the war.

OUR NATIONAL DESTRUCTION CONSUMMATED

To UNDERSTAND LINCOLN in this crisis, we must understand what the attempted secession meant to him: not the mere withdrawal of some states, leaving the others undamaged and the Union intact, but the *dissolution* of the Union, the *destruction* of free government—both words that he used more than once. The choice that he faced, as he stated it in the core of this address, was to "perform this duty [of calling on the war power], or surrender . . . the government." He said the issue was whether "discontented individuals" can "break up their government, and thus practically put an end to free government on earth."

To have acquiesced would have been "our national destruction consummated." In the references to himself ("the executive") in the penultimate paragraph, he asserted that the alternative to his performing his duty would have been to "surrender the existence of the government."

This interpretation of the rebellion as a mortal threat to the United States of America itself would reappear in Lincoln's utterances throughout the war. Even in the Second Inaugural, as he is graciously avoiding triumphalism and vindictiveness and evenhandedly insisting—perhaps more generously than the facts would justify—that in these first days "both parties deprecated war" and "all sought to avert it," the way he described what the insurgents sought to do would still be stark: "insurgent agents were in the city seeking to destroy it [the Union] without war"; "one of [the two parties, both deprecating war] would make war, rather than let the nation survive; and the other would accept war rather than let it perish." In both clauses the effect of the success of the rebellion—whether in war or by negotiation—would be deadly.

When one looks through all of Lincoln's presidential utterances about the effect of a successful slave state rebellion, one is impressed, first, with how many different terms he used, and second, with how stark and how dire, they are. Lincoln used the following verbs, nouns, and phrases: "surrender"; "destruction"; "immediate dissolution"; "our national destruction consummated"; "go to pieces"; "broken up"; "fall into ruin"; "the early destruction of our national Union"; "abandon"; "overthrow"; "not survive"; "perish." And when one asks what entity it is that would be destroyed, dissolved, broken up, and overthrown, the answer is, variously and interchangeably, the Union, the government, the nation.

So this was Lincoln's view: the success of the rebellion would mean that the United States of America would not be just diminished or damaged; it would be destroyed.

Statesmen speaking of reasons-of-state and national interests sometimes seek to intensify a particular national concern by describing it as a *vital* national interest; on examination these matters rarely turn out to be literally vital—a matter of a nation's persisting or ceasing to be. For Lincoln, the issue for the United States in the Civil War was indeed vital. Lincoln finished his summary of events by saying that the "assailants of the Government" had by their act at Fort Sumter "forced upon the country this distinct issue, 'Immediate dissolution or blood.' "

THE WHOLE FAMILY OF MAN

AND TO WHOM did that matter? Perhaps the congressmen, assembling in their special session, would not have attended closely enough to the drone of the clerk's voice to hear what a grand leap the president now made, but surely Senator Browning, hearing Lincoln himself read it the night before in the executive mansion, must have sat up a little straighter at this point.

In the first substantive philosophical paragraph of his presidency, Lincoln took the issue all the way to its worldwide and historic significance: "And this issue embraces more than the fate of these United States. It presents to the whole family of man, the question, whether a constitutional republic, or a democracy—a government of the people, by the same people—can, or cannot, maintain its territorial integrity, against its own domestic foes." Can "discontented individuals, too few in numbers to control administration . . . break up their government, and thus practically put an end to free government upon the earth"?

In November 1863, at the dedication of a cemetery in Gettysburg, he would put the point more succinctly and gracefully, asking for a high resolve "that government of the people, by the people, and for the people shall not perish from the earth."

From the start, Lincoln saw a sweeping, drastic, universal consequence to this assault upon government in the United States. This American case presented the universal issue: Was there, in all republics, this inherent and fatal weakness? Could such a government be maintained against a "formidable" attempt to overthrow it from within? Could it demonstrate to all the world that such a government could have the strength to prevent a successful appeal from ballots back to bullets? Put negatively, defending such a government against *destruction*, for the whole family of man and for the "vast future also," was the moral purpose of Lincoln's war.

Not only Confederates at the time and neo-Confederates later but also—at least momentarily—some Northern antagonists would not quite see why the success of the secessionists would mean the destruction of the Union. There were antislavery folk who in the purity of their disgust with slavery would say, "Let the erring sisters go; depart in peace." But not Lincoln.

Republican government—democracy, we say now—requires a tacit understanding between majorities and minorities. Majorities rightly prevail, but they respect the liberty of minorities to agitate to try to replace them; minorities have the right to express and organize in behalf of their view, but when the votes are counted, they must acquiesce. That did not happen in this case, and the implication was immense.

1. Bullets would have replaced ballots, as those who lost an election, instead of accepting the result, revolted and resorted to force.
2. If successful, this act would introduce a principle of continual disintegration that no government could sustain.
3. And that would demonstrate to all the world that republican government, popular government, had a fatal weakness.

The American Civil War is such a mammoth event, and its roots run so deep and its coming had such a long prelude, that we may obscure the point that the overt rebellion came in response to the results of an election. But Lincoln, the man chosen to be the national executive in that election, did not forget that point. And he saw the significance on the world stage:

Our popular government has often been called an experiment. Two points in it, our people have already settled, the successful establishing and the successful administering of it. One still remains—its successful maintenance against a formidable [internal] attempt to overthrow it. It is now for them to demonstrate to the world, that those who can fairly carry an election, can also suppress a rebellion—that ballots are the rightful, and peaceful, successors of bullets; and that when ballots have fairly, and constitutionally, decided, there can be no successful appeal, back to bullets; that there can be no successful appeal, except to ballots themselves, at succeeding elections.

Lincoln pointed out the choice that the Confederate constitution makers themselves had to face, as to whether to incorporate this essence of anarchy into the government they were setting up:

The seceders insist that our Constitution admits of secession. They have assumed to make a National Constitution of their own, in which, of necessity, they have either discarded, or retained, the right of secession, as they insist, it exists in ours. If they have discarded it, they thereby admit that, on principle, it ought not to be in ours. If they have retained it, by their own construction of ours they show that to be consistent they must secede from one another, whenever they shall find it the easiest way of settling their debts, or effecting any other selfish, or unjust object. The principle itself is one of disintegration, and upon which no government can possibly endure.

One of the key items in the American Constitution that was not changed by Montgomery seceders was the provision that their constitution shall be "the Supreme law of the land," binding on the states. These seceders thus turned right around and denied the right of secession in the governing instrument of the body they set up. In addition to this general, supreme denial, they took many provisions en bloc from the U.S. Constitution that represented a specific and practical denial of the "sovereignty" of states: under the Confederate constitution, no state could, for example, enter into an alliance on its own, or make a treaty, or coin money. The provisions of the Confederate constitution, wrote John Nicolay many years later, represented "a sweeping practical negation of the whole heretical dogma of state supremacy upon which they had built their revolt."

Writings about republics—popular government—in the history of the West had often concluded, both from reasoning about how they would work (or wouldn't work) and from historical examples of collapsed fractious city-state republics, that they could not last. In the very first argument he made in the July 4 Message, after his summary of recent events, Lincoln carried the issue all the way to "the whole family of man." What the success of the American rebellion would show to the whole family of man was that republican government had a fatal weakness.

STATE SOVEREIGNTY: A SUGARCOATING FOR TREASON

THE JUSTIFICATIONS for secession were of two sorts, often mingled but logically distinct:

1. It was a legitimate act under the U.S. Constitution.
2. It was a revolutionary act, like that of the American and the French revolutionaries, throwing off an oppressive regime.

Lincoln's arguments were directed almost entirely to the first, and indeed he insisted that only that justification could have persuaded such of the Southern population as was persuaded (not, he believed, a majority in most states) to support secession. But he responded at least implicitly to the second, revolutionary justification also when the dispute was lifted up to the ultimate moral qualities of the contending societies.

The leaders of the rebellion, wrote Lincoln, knew they could never raise significant support for their treason by obviously violating the law. The good people in their section were "possessed of as much moral sense, as much of devotion to law and order, and as much pride in, and reverence for, the history, and government, of their common country, as any other civilized, and patriotic people." So these Confederate leaders "sugar-coated" their treason with the "ingenious sophism" that "any state of the Union may, consistently with the National Constitution, and therefore lawfully and peacefully, withdraw from the Union, without the consent of the Union or of any other state." With this sophism they had been "debauching" and "drugging the public mind of their section for thirty years." By this debauching, drugging, and sugarcoating, "they have brought many good men to a willingness to take up arms against the government the day after some assemblage of men have enacted the farcical pretense of taking their state out of the Union, who could not be brought to such a thing before."

WHENCE THIS MAGICAL
OMNIPOTENCE OF STATES' RIGHTS?

"THIS SOPHISM derives much—perhaps the whole—of its currency, from the assumption, that there is some omnipotent, and sacred supremacy, pertaining to a *State* of our Federal Union." Lincoln made his argument against the assumption that the states had some "omnipotent and sacred supremacy" again, as in the inaugural especially, from America's short history. He now made the argument, also from the Constitution, from political philosophy, from logic and common sense, and from moral idealism.

The largest part of his argument was historical and constitutional. Lincoln argued that there was and had been no such thing as an independent and freestanding "State" in the brief history of this nation. He produced several summary statements of the history on this point: "Having never been States, either in substance, or in name, *outside* of the Union, whence this magical omnipotence of 'States rights,' asserting a claim of power to lawfully destroy the Union itself?" Whatever standing the American states had, they had *only* as creatures of the Union: "The states have their *status in* the Union, and they have no other *legal status.*" He said, in another brief summary of the history, that the states had achieved their existence and their liberty only through the Union: "The Union, and not themselves separately, procured their independence and their liberty. By conquest, or purchase, the Union gave each of them whatever of independence, and liberty, it has." And he said then this key summary sentence: "The Union is older than any of the states, and, in fact, created them as states."

Lincoln, the lawyer, made a variety of other arguments, with varying ingenuity and persuasive power, including a particularly odd one that would have required the departing states whose land had been purchased with federal money to pay a refund to the United States.

A WICKED EXERCISE OF PHYSICAL POWER

IF THE ARGUMENT for secession as a legal act within the Constitution was just a sugarcoating for treason, the other, revolutionary argument remained. If the states pretended to break from the Union, Lincoln said, "[t]hey can do so only against the law, and by Revolution."

There were two revolutions they could appeal to: (1) the American Revolution; or (2) a universal right of revolution. The American Revolution of course figured constantly in the Confederacy's self-presentation. Jefferson Davis would say in his inaugural address that the Confederacy "merely asserted a right which the Declaration of Independence in 1776 had defined as inalienable," and paradoxically he said in the same speech that "it is by abuse of language that [the seceding states'] act has been denominated a revolution."

Others went ahead and embraced the argument of revolution, singing a "Southern Marseillaise" and accepting the designation of Henry Wise of Virginia as the "Danton" of secession. If the rebels claimed to have an abstract, universal right of revolution, they might also have claimed support from the great revolutions of the eighteenth and nineteenth centuries. In the heady year of 1848, when a revolutionary fervor had swept Europe and large numbers of refugees fled to the land of democratic revolution across the Atlantic, a congressman said on the floor of the House:

> Any people anywhere, being inclined and having the power, have the right to rise up, and shake off the existing government, and form a new one that suits them better. This is a most valuable,—a most sacred right— a right, which we hope and believe, is to liberate the world.

The congressman who said this, in the course of a condemnation of President Polk's conduct of the war with Mexico, was the Whig from the Seventh District of Illinois, Abraham Lincoln.

Thirteen years later his view of "revolution" had become more discriminate. In 1848 it had been implicit in the celebration of "revolution" that the revolutions in question were moving in the direction of democracy and human rights; Lincoln's reference to a right to revolution that would "liberate the world" indicates that assumption. Now he confronted a so-called revolution that was no world liberator but rather the opposite, a retrograde step away from human rights. In the argument of his inaugural, Lincoln made a concession, in passing, to a right of revolution, but only when it met a moral test.

> If, by the mere force of numbers, a majority should deprive a minority of any clearly written constitutional right, it might, in a moral point of view, justify revolution—certainly would, if such right were a vital one. But such is not our case.

In the case he faced in 1861, the rebels had no morally justifiable cause for mounting a revolution against the American government, either in the procedural treatment of the "dissatisfied countrymen" or in their moral substance of the alternative society they proposed.

As to their treatment, he had argued in the inaugural:

> Is it true . . . that any right, plainly written in the Constitution, has been denied? I think not . . . Think, if you can, of a single instance in which a plainly written provision of the Constitution has ever been denied.

All that had happened to the secessionists was that they had lost an election; no vital right had been infringed. Even the fugitive slave provisions, obnoxious though they were to many in the North, had been enforced as well as might be. The secessionists had all the freedoms of the American Constitution to argue and to attempt in the next election to win.

THE MORAL CONTRAST BETWEEN THE UNITED STATES AND THE CONFEDERACY

THE OTHER POSSIBLE moral justification for secession as a revolution would be that the social order that the secessionists proposed would be radically superior to the social order they challenged.

Toward the end of the July 4 Message, as in the inaugural, Lincoln celebrated the American republic and set it in contrast to the alternative proposed by the rebels. The rebellion if successful would destroy the

American Union, he said, and that destruction would mean the end of what this Union has meant and will mean for the history of liberty in the world:

> It may be affirmed, without extravagance, that the free institutions we enjoy, have developed the powers, and improved the condition of our whole people, beyond any example in the world . . .
>
> Whoever, in any section, proposes to abandon such a government, would do well to consider, in deference to what principle it is, that he does it—what better he is likely to get in its stead—whether the substitute will give, or be intended to give, so much of good to the people.

What kind of a social order was it that the Confederacy proposed to replace the Union?

> There are some foreshadowings on this subject. Our adversaries have adopted some Declarations of Independence; in which, unlike the good old one, penned by Jefferson, they omit the words "all men are created equal." Why? They have adopted a temporary national constitution, in the preamble of which, unlike our good old one, signed by Washington, they omit "We, the People," and substitute "We, the deputies of the sovereign and independent States." Why? Why this deliberate pressing out of view, the rights of men, and the authority of the people?

What the Confederacy offered was not an alternative version of the American experiment but a betrayal and violation of it.

THIS IS A PEOPLE'S CONTEST

A COMMON MODERN VIEW of the American Civil War discovers moral meaning in it only with the Emancipation Proclamation. Before that proclamation was set forth, on January 1, 1863, in this view, because Lincoln's express purpose was "only" to restore the Union, the project had no particular moral elevation but was only a realistic power-political undertaking. Lincoln's famous letter to Horace Greeley would be presented, with a certain deflationary relish, as though it gave evidence for such a view. Lincoln wrote to Greeley in August 1862:

> My paramount object in this struggle is to save the Union, and is not either to save or to destroy slavery. If I could save the Union without free-

ing any slave I would do it, and if I could save it by freeing all the slaves I would do it; and if I could save it by freeing some and leaving others alone I would also do that. What I do about slavery, and the colored race, I do because I believe it helps to save the Union; and what I forbear, I forbear because I do not believe it would help to save the Union.

Lincoln's stated desire that the war be limited—that it not "degenerate," as he put it in his first annual message, "into a violent and remorseless revolutionary struggle"—might be cited as further evidence of his merely state-preserving purposes. His countermanding of the efforts to free slaves in the districts under their military command by Generals Frémont and Hunter might be further evidence. At its furthest reduction this view would hold that during the first year and a half of the war Lincoln and the Americans had been engaged only in a power-political struggle, like those that appear throughout human history. The foreign secretary of the nation whose appraisal was the most important, Lord John Russell of Great Britain, described the American Civil War dismissively as much like the struggles that had gone on repeatedly in European history in which two states contended, "the one for empire and the other for power."

But there are two deep errors in this view. In the first place, vindicating the Union was for Lincoln no mere power-political struggle but an undertaking with vast and universal moral significance—showing that free, popular, constitutional government could maintain itself, a project that, as Lincoln on one occasion said, goes down about as deep as anything.*

In the second place, the moral principles that Lincoln understood to define that Union placed slavery under condemnation from the start.

As to the first point, Lincoln certainly did not regard the war, in 1861, as simply a realistic contest between two power units. And it was not slavery alone that made the Civil War for Lincoln a giant moral struggle; nor was it only after the Emancipation Proclamation that it became so for him. Nor did he present it as such only in the later great short utterance at the dedication of the cemetery in Gettysburg. A primary moral meaning of the war, for Lincoln, had been there from the start, as he set forth in his two

---

*"Let me say one thing more: I think you should admit that we already have an important principle to rally and unite the people in the fact that constitutional government is at stake. This is a fundamental idea, going down about as deep as any thing." "Reply to Emancipation Memorial Presented by Chicago Christians of All Denominations," September 13, 1862.

important compositions of 1861, the First Inaugural Address and the July 4 Message to the special session.

Lincoln's first statement of the meaning of the war, in the July 4 Message, anticipated the famous formulation at Gettysburg:

> It [the war] presents to the whole family of man, the question, whether a constitutional republic, or a democracy—a government of the people, by the same people—can, or cannot, maintain its territorial integrity, against its own domestic foes.

His later statement, toward the end of the message, had an economic and social dimension:

> This is essentially a People's contest. On the side of the Union, it is a struggle for maintaining in the world, that form, and substance of government, whose leading object is, to elevate the condition of men—to lift artificial weights from all shoulders—to clear the paths of laudable pursuit for all—to afford all, an unfettered start, and a fair chance, in the race of life.

Douglas Wilson has noted, in *Lincoln's Sword,* that Lincoln originally wrote "an *even* start" and then changed it (the one editorial change he made) to "an *unfettered* start"—surely a deliberate choice of a word in order "subtly to enhance the anti-slavery resonance." One can scarcely say that a "contest" so understood is lacking in moral reach.

This socially egalitarian understanding of the United States and of the stakes in the war would mark President Lincoln's statements all the way through the war. Speaking to an Ohio regiment in the dark days of mid-August 1864, for example, he would say:

> I wish it might be more generally and universally understood what the country is now engaged in. We have, as all will agree, a free Government, where every man has a right to be equal with every other man. In this great struggle, this form of Government and every form of human right is endangered if our enemies succeed. There is more involved in this contest than is realized by every one. There is involved in this struggle the question whether your children and my children shall enjoy the privileges we have enjoyed.

Four days later, to another Ohio regiment, he used himself as an example:

I happen temporarily to occupy this big White House. I am a living witness that any one of your children may look to come here as my father's child has. It is in order that each of you may have through this free government which we have enjoyed, an open field and a fair chance for your industry, enterprise and intelligence; that you may all have equal privileges in the race of life, with all its desirable human aspirations. It is for this the struggle should be maintained, that we may not lose our birthright—not only for one, but for two or three years. The nation is worth fighting for, to secure such an inestimable jewel.

As to the second point, Lincoln had an understanding of the Union's moral essence that excluded slavery.

President Lincoln understood it to be his oath-bound duty to preserve, protect, and defend the United States, whatever that might mean immediately about slavery. But it did *not* mean that slavery would be accepted as permanent and right. Lincoln had a six-year track record, after all, making clear his own position about slavery. Lincoln himself not only believed it to be wrong—if slavery is not wrong, nothing is wrong—and a monstrous injustice, but a wrong and an injustice as measured specifically by the moral foundation of the United States, the Declaration of Independence, with its affirmation that all men are created equal.

Much of the Northern public, and English and other opinion abroad, did not yet perceive that Lincoln's war purpose from the start included an implicit moral condemnation of slavery. But one audience did perceive it: the firebrands of South Carolina and the defenders of slavery across the Deep South. When he was elected—they revolted.

Lincoln had made *almost* no mention of slavery in his inaugural, but the one mention he did make said everything. He used a formula that he had used before, one that avoided moralizing by simply describing the disagreement—but that still put down the marker: "One section of our country believes slavery is right and ought to be extended, while the other believes it is wrong, and ought not to be extended. This is the only substantial dispute." It was a substantial dispute in which his own position was made clear—slavery was wrong.

Lincoln had made the egalitarian premise of the Declaration of Independence, specifically including black persons, the centerpiece of his six-year argument with Stephen Douglas, and that premise was for him part of the core meaning of the constitutional union. When he made large statements of inclusive national ideals, like the one quoted above about lifting weights from all shoulders, he was implicitly including black persons.

Those shoulders from which weights would be lifted—*all* shoulders—would for Lincoln include, though he would not make it explicit perhaps even to himself and certainly not to his listeners, the shoulders of black men.

The next sentences in this paragraph in the message to the special session indicate again, in a backhanded way, that the eventual end of slavery was part of the meaning of Lincoln's concept of the Union. "Yielding to partial, and temporary departures, from necessity," wrote President Lincoln to Congress, "this [the unfettered fair start for all] is the leading object of the government for whose existence we contend." What can he have meant by that preliminary concession about temporary partial yieldings to necessity except slavery? He meant that we must accept slavery in the states where it exists, but only by necessity and only temporarily, and not on principle and not forever.

The moral purpose of Lincoln's war at the beginning was not yet explicitly to generate "a new birth of freedom"; it was rather to preserve, maintain, defend, and prevent the destruction of the old—but the old in *Lincoln's* terms. The "old" government that the Union fought to maintain had for Lincoln an ideal and an aspirational content from which a new birth of freedom would one day spring.

CHAPTER EIGHT

Bull Run and Other Defeats

Lincoln's Resolve

THE BITTERNESS OF DEFEAT

ON THE EVENING of July 21, 1861, President Lincoln for the first time confronted the grim news of battlefield defeat. Nicolay would write, many years later, that the defeat was "inexpressibly bitter" because it was not only the first experience of defeat but the first "recognition of even the possibility of defeat." Moreover, the defeat represented an excruciatingly painful reversal of expectations.

A dispatch in the *New York World* by "Our Own Correspondent" (almost certainly young John Hay himself, writing anonymously, perhaps in the executive mansion itself) had described the electric anticipation when on July 16 General Irvin McDowell's 34,000 Union troops tromped across the Potomac bridges and headed out toward Beauregard's Confederate army of 24,000, encamped twenty-five miles to the west at Manassas Junction:

> The solemn midnight March of the grand army across the Potomac roused an intensity of feeling and expectancy . . . The marching regiments . . . were cheered on their departure with a lusty enthusiasm and hopefulness unprecedented in the annals. It was believed that the federal forces had started on a march to be crowned with brilliant victories; that the enemy would be routed . . . their cannon captured, and intrenchments demolished. Under the bold leadership of our officers, the thunder of our batteries, and the heroic courage of our infantry columns, we were to march victoriously to Richmond. This was to break the bone of the Rebellion, to end the war, to restore again our nationality.

None of this happened. "Our nationality" was not restored; to the contrary, the rebels were emboldened and almost had their own nationality created in the eyes of the world. The war was not ended but would stretch on through the weeks and months and years to a "magnitude" and a "duration" that neither side anticipated. The "grand army" would not march victoriously into Richmond; it would not make its way even to Manassas Junction. The "marching regiments" with "heroic courage" who had set forth across the bridges to the "lusty enthusiasm" of the populace on July 16 would come tumbling and scrambling and fleeing back into Washington, to the city's dismay, on the evening of July 21. By the description not only of journalistic observers but also of their own commander, they had become "a confused mob, entirely demoralized."

Messages from the front coming into the telegraph office first aroused, then punctured, expectations of victory; during that one day they executed a complete and abrupt turnaround, from apparent triumph to undeniable defeat.

When President Lincoln returned from church that Sunday morning, he went promptly over to the telegraph office to read the dispatches on the fighting that was going on some thirty miles to the west. A wire from "near Fairfax" at 1:10 p.m. made its positive point by indirection: "Firing more in the distance and greatly slackened. No guns at Centreville since last dispatch. 10 mins interval still fainter and less guns. You can draw your own inference." The inference to be drawn was that the Union forces were about to achieve a great victory. Lincoln was reading these wires as they came in every fifteen minutes or so and talking to visitors who returned early from the front. At 3:00 p.m. the succinct dispatch said simply: "Firing ceased 10 minutes since." Lincoln ate a late lunch at 3:30 p.m., and when he returned, a wire sent at 5:20 p.m. had good news: "I am en route to Washington with details of great battle. We have carried the day—Rebels accepted battle in their strength but are totally routed."

Lincoln went out for a Sunday drive, thinking the battle was won, but while he was gone the reports reversed themselves. Indeed, a dispatch from General McDowell, who was in charge of the attack, sent at 5:45 p.m. from Centreville, rather turned around within the one message:

> We passed Bull Run. Engaged the enemy, who, it seems, had just been re-enforced by General Johnston. We drove them for several hours, and finally routed them.
>
> They rallied and repulsed us, but only to give us again the victory, which seemed complete.

If Lincoln stopped reading at that point, he might have felt that, although it would be hard-won and fragile, the Union was winning a victory. But McDowell's dispatch went on:

But our men, exhausted with fatigue and thirst and confused by firing into each other, were attacked by the enemy's reserves, and driven from the position we had gained, overlooking Manassas. After this the men could not be rallied, but slowly left the field.

McDowell's next wire, from Fairfax Court House rather than Centreville (that is, five miles back toward Washington), must have been still more dismaying to the readers in the telegraph office:

The men having thrown away their haversacks in the battle and left them behind, they are without food; have eaten nothing since breakfast. We are without artillery ammunition. The larger part of the men are a confused mob, entirely demoralized. It was the opinion of all the commanders that no stand could be made this side of the Potomac. We will, however, make the attempt at Fairfax Court-House. From a prisoner we learn that 20,000 from Johnston joined last night, and they march on us to-night.

The Johnston in this and the earlier message was the Confederate general Joseph Johnston, whose ten thousand troops in the Shenandoah Valley were supposed to have been kept out of the fight by a Union force under sixty-nine-year-old Robert Patterson. But Johnston feinted Patterson out of the battle altogether, and Johnston's troops, showing up late in the day, spooked the exhausted Union soldiers. The failure of Patterson to tie down Johnston's force would be one of the explanations, Patterson one of the culprits, when the time came for explaining the Union defeat at Bull Run.

A distraught Seward brought the miserable story to the White House at six o'clock, while Lincoln was still on his drive. When at 6:30 p.m. Lincoln returned, it was his secretaries (they tell us) who broke the bad news to their president. "He listened in silence, without the slightest change of . . . expression, and walked away to army headquarters." The telegram that made the point plain came from a captain of engineers:

General McDowell's army in full retreat through Centreville. The day is lost. Save Washington and the remnants of this army. All available troops ought to be thrown forward in one body. General McDowell is doing all he can to cover the retreat . . . The routed troops will not reform.

General in Chief Winfield Scott, who did not quite believe "the bad news from McDowell's army," nevertheless sent wires to the commanders in Baltimore and Alexandria to be alert against uprisings.

THE NIGHT THAT FOLLOWED was bad, and the day after was worse—
Black Monday, soaked in rain. "There was never such a day here before,"
wrote "our special correspondent" to the *New York World* from a rain-
drenched Washington, and

> it is to be hoped there never will be another. With the ushering in of day-
> light there came pouring into the city crowds of soldiers, some with mus-
> kets, some without muskets, some with knapsacks, some without
> knapsack, or canteen, or belt, or anything but their soiled and dirty uni-
> form, burned faces and eyes, that looked as [if] they had had not sleep for
> days, to indicate that they were soldiers.

The report represents an immediate and on-the-spot description of
Lincoln's first encounter with modern warfare in the large:

> One by one came wagons filled with the dead and wounded. Most horri-
> ble were the sights presented to view, and never to be forgotten by those
> who witnessed them. The bodies of the dead were piled on top of one
> another; the pallid faces and blood-stained garments telling a fearfully
> mute but sad story of the horrors of war. And the appearance of the
> wounded, bereft of arms, of legs, eyes put out, flesh wounds in the face
> and body, and uniforms crimsoned with blood, proclaimed with equal
> force the savage horrors of human battling with weapons of war.

ALL GREEN ALIKE

THE NOVICE in the executive mansion bore the ultimate responsibility
for this debacle. It was his decision, or his endorsement of the collective
decision, to make the attack at Bull Run in the first place, at least to make it
as soon as it was made. One can surely argue that on this occasion he
should have taken General in Chief Winfield Scott's advice, reinforced by
McDowell. Scott had originally proposed as the Union's overarching military strategy the squeezing envelope around the South that would be
derided as the "Anaconda" plan. But Northern impatience seemed to
mock and reject anything as slow and long-term—and tender on the
South—as that. The militias that had been pouring into Washington now
made an army bigger than any American army had ever been, 34,000

troops encamped in Alexandria. And there was General Beauregard from Fort Sumter, now with 24,000 Confederate troops, sitting out there at a key railroad junction just twenty-five miles from Washington. They were a threat to the nation's capital. Moreover, capturing Manassas would open the road to the new Confederate capital, Richmond. Lincoln had asked General McDowell for a plan of attack, and on June 29 at the executive mansion his cabinet and military advisers considered the plan that the general proposed. McDowell wanted to postpone its commencement because his troops were green, and because he did not want to fight the war "piecemeal." As to the greenness, Lincoln is reported to have told McDowell, "You are green, it is true, but they are green also; you are all green alike."

The president and the general who would command on the Union side were also green. Historian James Rawley describes the situation: "A Commander-in-Chief, innocent of military affairs, a General-in-Chief, archaic in knowledge of his staff, and a field commander, inexperienced in handling large bodies of troops, launched a great offensive to end the war in one mighty swoop."

As to the widespread and reciprocal greenness, the two sets of troops had this significant difference: Captain of Engineers D. P. Woodbury noted that the green Confederates were fighting on the defensive while the green Yankees had to mount an offensive attack. In his July 30 report Woodbury gave this diagnosis of the Union army's disintegration:

> An old soldier feels safe in the ranks, unsafe out of the ranks, and the greater the danger the more pertinaciously he clings to his place. The volunteer of three months never attains this instinct of discipline. Under danger, and even under mere excitement, he flies away from his ranks, and looks for safety in dispersion. At 4 o'clock in the afternoon of the 21st there were more than twelve thousand volunteers on the battle-field of Bull Run who had entirely lost their regimental organizations. They could no longer be handled as troops, for the officers and men were not together. Men and officers mingled together promiscuously ... We cannot suppose that the troops of the enemy had attained a higher degree of discipline than our own, but they acted on the defensive, and were not equally exposed to disorganization.

On the Union side there was another wrinkle: the ninety-day enlistment of the first set of volunteers. One finds in General McDowell's official report of the battle, looking back on August 4 at the whole event, this stunning passage:

> On the eve of the battle the Fourth Pennsylvania Regiment of Volunteers and the battery of Volunteer Artillery of the Eighth New York Militia, whose term of service expired, insisted on their discharge. I wrote to the regiment as pressing a request as I could pen, and the honorable Secretary of War, who was at the time on the ground, tried to induce the battery to remain at least five days, but in vain. They insisted on their discharge that night. It was granted; and the next morning, when the Army moved forward into battle, these troops moved to the rear to the sound of the enemy's cannon.
>
> In the next few days, day by day I should have lost ten thousand of the best armed, drilled, officered, and disciplined troops in the Army. In other words, every day which added to the strength of the enemy made us weaker.

The effect was not only the melting away of those who left but also the fading away in battle of those who stayed, whose term was almost up and whose reluctance to be shot understandably increased as it approached. These men were not easy to command. Another telegram from McDowell, this one on the morning of July 22 from Fairfax Court House, described the situation:

> Many of the volunteers did not wait for authority to proceed to the Potomac, but left on their own decision. They are now pouring through this place in a state of utter disorganization. They could not be prepared for action by to-morrow morning even were they willing. I learn from prisoners that we are to be pressed here to-night and to-morrow morning, as the enemy's force is very large and they are elated. I think we heard cannon on our rear guard. I think now, as all of my commanders thought at Centreville, there is no alternative but to fall back to the Potomac, and I shall proceed to do so with as much regularity as possible.

As we have seen, Lincoln had made the decision on April 14, announced on April 15, to call for 75,000 volunteers to the state militias for the ninety-day enlistment that the law provided. Presumably he and General Scott and whoever else participated in that decision expected then that ninety days would be enough to put down the rebellion. Just forty-eight hours later, on April 17, it was clear that Virginia would join the rebellion, and he and they might have made a different estimate both of the number and of the time it would take.

But as we noted in Chapter 5, the ninety days was not a number he pulled out of the air; it was specified in the 1795 Militia Act, shaped in response to President Washington's coping with the Whiskey Rebellion. Ninety days, which the law specified, had been enough to cope with a "rebellion" of Pennsylvania farmers over whiskey, but as Bull Run showed, it would not be enough to put down this rebellion of more than a third of a nation over slavery. Lincoln had already on May 3, without a specific statutory basis, authorized an increase of 22,714 in the regular army and of 18,000 in the navy. And he had asked Congress in its special session—meeting from July 4 until August 8, with Bull Run on July 21 a sharp chop in the middle—to authorize 400,000 volunteers for three years. Congress, which retroactively endorsed all those extraordinary actions of the president except the suspension of habeas corpus, and granted all his wartime requests, raised the number to 500,000, "the largest citizens' army yet known to history." Congress approved the Army Bill on July 18; Lincoln signed it on Black Monday, July 22. The earlier acceptance of the law's mere ninety days, like the decision to ask for only 75,000 men, had been based on the estimate in that first brief moment, which was quickly revised and by July 22 altogether exploded.

After the June 29 consultation, Lincoln had ordered McDowell to attack at Bull Run on July 9. There were delays. When the troops finally started the march on July 16, there were more delays; the men were not trained for cross-country marching, and stopped to pick blackberries, and got very tired. For all that, when the battle came, they did not do as badly as would be reported in the initial shock of defeat.

They had the bad luck that the battle came on a Sunday, which meant that senators and congressmen and journalists and ladies in their summer dresses were free to come to see it. These observers were all green too; they did not yet know that war was not a spectator sport, and when the retreat began, they mingled with it and caused a traffic jam on their hurried way back to Washington. And what these spectators saw, and reported to the world, was not the fighting but the fleeing—notoriously the correspondent for the *Times* of London, William Russell, who acquired from his coverage the nickname "Bull Run."

Lincoln had shown in the struggle for Kentucky that he could perceive and evaluate the political elements, in comparison to the military, more shrewdly than the West Pointers Davis and Polk. But in this case perhaps the sheer military considerations that Scott was telling him about deserved particular attention: these men were not trained. McDowell was to write: "I wanted very much a little time. All of us wanted it. We did not have a bit of it."

The strong political reasons for making an early attack had to do with Northern opinion, which was still mostly unified since the shock of the fall of Sumter. That would not last, and the momentum would diminish. And the pressure to act was intense. In the middle of May the Confederate capital had moved from remote Montgomery to nearby Richmond, which if you were a congressman, a senator, or an eastern seaboard journalist looked like easy prey now that all those volunteers had swarmed into the militias: "Forward to Richmond!"

On June 26 Horace Greeley's widely read newspaper, the *New York Tribune*, essential to the Republican cause, carried this proclamation at the top of its editorial page:

THE NATION'S WAR CRY
Forward to Richmond. Forward to Richmond!

The rebel Congress had scheduled its first Richmond session for July 20; the *Tribune* seized on that for a deadline:

The Rebel Congress must not be allowed to meet there the 20th of July.
BY THAT DATE THE PLACE MUST BE HELD BY THE NATIONAL ARMY

The *Tribune* kept carrying this war cry on its editorial page every day, and other papers picked up versions of it. "On to Richmond" passed into Civil War folklore.*

When on July 21 the Union army not only did not go "on to Richmond" but fell back from Bull Run, retreated from Fairfax Court House, and came tumbling back into Washington, the response included shock, dismay, despair, and blame. Edwin Stanton wrote to his former chief Buchanan about the "imbecility" of the Lincoln administration.

---

*The public assumed that the slogan had been written by Greeley, the *Tribune*'s editor and the best-known newspaperman in the land. But in fact the actual words had been written by the paper's Washington correspondent, a man named Fitz-Henry Warren, although of course Greeley endorsed them. On June 28 Lincoln reportedly called Warren to the White House and told him that what he was calling for would indeed happen—which, if true, meant that Lincoln had already made up his mind before the June 29 gathering with his cabinet and advisers. Harry J. Maihafer, *War of Words: Abraham Lincoln and the Civil War Press* (Washington, D.C.: Brassey's, 2001), p. 42.

In an overwrought letter Greeley patronized Lincoln, exalted his own importance, indirectly accused Lincoln (said Nicolay and Hay) "of criminal indifference," and proposed that the Union "make peace with the Rebels." Lincoln did not reply to Greeley's letter.

Walt Whitman wrote of these days:

> [I]t is certain that the talk among certain of the magnates and officers and clerks and officials everywhere, for twenty-four hours in and around Washington after Bull Run, was loud and undisguised for yielding out and out, and substituting the southern rule, and Lincoln promptly abdicating and departing . . . One of our returning colonels express'd in public that night, amid a swarm of officers and gentlemen in a crowded room, the opinion that it was useless to fight, that the southerners had made their title clear, and that the best course for the national government to pursue was to desist from any further attempt at stopping them, and admit them again to the lead, on the best terms they were willing to grant. Not a voice was rais'd against this judgment, amid that large crowd of officers and gentlemen.

Lincoln was only four and a half months into his role as president when, on the night of July 21, it fell to him to cope with this wholly unexpected, humiliating, and devastating defeat.

Up to that point Lincoln's life had been a series of steep ascensions to new plateaus, developing himself anew repeatedly. He had known defeat, but only personal and party defeat; he had known sorrow, but only personal sorrow. What he dealt with now was too vast (to borrow his own phrase) for the sorrows and defeats of merely personal life. This was the night when the civilian politician became fully a war leader—a leader of a nation at war, a commander of immense and embattled armies (as they would become) in war.

Lincoln's transformation had had anticipations in those overwhelmingly concentrated days of high policy decision about Fort Sumter and Pickens and the calling out of the militia; he had had a taste of battle in the Baltimore riots; he had had to make decisions about remote events through the fog of distance and war in Missouri. But this was the moment when the full weight of decisions he made came home to his doorstep.

The report in the *New York World* said:

> All the forenoon fugitive soldiers have come straggling into the city. They were like lost sheep without a shepherd. Notices at length appeared at

the different hotels, calling upon members of the various regiments to assemble at such and such a place, at an appointed hour, the object being to discover how many and who were missing. Meantime the returned soldiers clustered about the hotels, and some in their weariness lay down on doorsteps, or any place they could find where the rain did not touch them.

A NIGHT LIKE THIS CAN NEVER AGAIN RETURN

WHEN THE PRESIDENT learned that Bull Run was a horrendous defeat, at about six-thirty on the evening of July 21, he walked immediately to the War Department to read the confirming telegram. He conferred with General Scott and with several eyewitnesses to the battle. And so began a sleepless night. At two in the early morning of July 22 a wire from the War Department summoned General McClellan, the hero of the battles in West Virginia, to "come hither without delay" to organize a new army, now composed of three-year regiments. Lincoln and Scott worked through the night, and Lincoln probably began that night to compose a list of steps to be taken that would be given the date July 23.

That memorandum, written in pencil in his own hand, with a couple of additions on July 27, shows by its tone and its content Lincoln's response to the defeat. It reflected a civilian's inexperience with military matters, no doubt, but at the same time it also showed resolve, and the beginnings of a conceptual grasp on the scope of the war.

July 23. 1861.

1. Let the plan for making the Blockade effective be pushed forward with all possible despatch.
2. Let the volunteer forces at Fort-Monroe & vicinity—under Genl. Butler—be constantly drilled, disciplined, and instructed without more for the present.
3. Let Baltimore be held, as now, with a gentle, but firm, and certain hand.
4. Let the force now under Patterson, or Banks, be strengthened, and made secure in it's possition.
5. Let the forces in Western Virginia act, till further orders, according to instructions, or orders from Gen. McClellan.
6. [Let] Gen. Fremont push forward his organization, and operations in

the West as rapidly as possible, giving rather special attention to Missouri.

7. Let the forces late before Manassas, except the three months men, be reorganized as rapidly as possible, in their camps here and about Arlington.

8. Let the three months forces, who decline to enter the longer service, be discharged as rapidly as circumstances will permit.

9. Let the new volunteer forces be brought forward as fast as possible; and especially into the camps on the two sides of the river here.

Years later a Republican functionary would report that on Black Monday, July 22, when he visited Lincoln's office, Lincoln burst out: "John, if hell is not any more than this, it has no terror for me." Throughout the war there would be reports of Lincoln's privately anguished responses. But on Black Monday he also took action. He signed the bill for the enlistment of 500,000 men. Three days later he signed another bill for an additional half million. He tightened the blockade of Southern ports and strengthened forces in the Shenandoah Valley and at Fort Monroe in Virginia. He rapidly gathered forces in Washington. Most important, he began training and restoring morale in the army that McDowell had led at Bull Run. For that purpose the hero of the West Virginia battles, George McClellan, arrived in Washington on July 26. On July 27 the president would add these items to his memorandum.

When the foregoing shall have been substantially attended to—

1. Let Manassas junction, (or some point on one or other of the railroads near it;); and Strasburg, be seized, and permanently held, with an open line from Washington to Manassas; and and [*sic*] open line from Harper's Ferry to Strasburg—the military men to find the way of doing these.

2. This done, a joint movement from Cairo on Memphis; and from Cincinnati on East Tennessee.

Walt Whitman would write, in *Specimen Days*, about Lincoln's response to Bull Run:

[W]hatever returns . . . a night like that can never again return. The president, recovering himself, begins that very night—sternly, rapidly sets about the task of re-organizing his forces, and placing himself in positions for future and superior work. If there were nothing else of Abraham Lincoln for history to stamp him with, it is enough to send him with his wreath to the memory of all future time, that he endured that hour, that day, bitterer than gall—indeed a crucifixion day—that it did not conquer him—that he unflinchingly stemm'd it, and resolv'd to lift himself and the Union out of it.

THE LAST BREATH OF THE UNION— THREE OR FOUR TIMES

THIS FIRST DEFEAT was by no means the last or the worst that the Union forces would suffer; it was not even the last or the worst they would suffer on this very spot. A year and a month later there would be a second battle at Bull Run, and another precipitous retreat by a Union army, and the casualties would be much worse. (Union casualties at First Bull Run were 2,950; at Second Bull Run, 13,830.) And there would be other and much worse defeats, and bloody battles in which it would be hard to say who won, and battles that counted as victories but had Union army casualty lists much longer than those of Bull Run. But Bull Run would be the first, the harbinger, the announcement, the alarm.

Whitman would conclude his paragraph on Bull Run with a parenthetical observation: "The fact is, the hour was one of the three or four of those crises we had then and afterward, during the fluctuations of four years, when human eyes appear'd at least just as likely to see the last breath of the Union as to see it continue."

In October 1861 Union arms would see defeat in General McClellan's northern Virginia operation—a botched effort on the Potomac—at a place called Ball's Bluff. This would be a smaller affair than Bull Run, with fewer casualties, but one death would hit Lincoln personally. Edward Baker, his friendly rival from the Seventh Congressional District in Illinois, the friend for whom he named his second boy, Eddie, who had moved to Oregon and become a senator, and who had introduced him on Inauguration Day, had been shot dead. To this day he is the only sitting U.S. senator to be killed in action in the armed services.

Lincoln had already had the shock of another personal loss in the earliest days of the war, on May 24, in a Union army movement to secure Alexandria. His young friend E. E. Ellsworth was waylaid and shot while on a sudden quixotic venture: he was removing the rebel flag from the top of the Principal Hotel, where it had been flaunting its treason within sight of the nation's capital. The hotel owner shot Ellsworth as he came down the stairs with the flag, and was in turn shot dead. Lincoln wrote the first of his eloquent and sensitive letters of condolence to Ellsworth's parents.

The deaths of Ellsworth and Baker would be harbingers for him personally of the casualty lists to come, which would reach a dimension that in those first months neither he nor anyone else could have anticipated. And Lincoln, the unmilitary western politician rather abruptly put in this office, would become the commander in chief who issued the calls for volunteers, eventually instituted a draft, sent men into battle, appointed and dismissed their generals, and again and again in the telegraph office read the reports of defeat and the counting of the dead.

The history of the war would be the experience of Bull Run multiplied and repeated, of high hope followed by devastating disappointment; of dark days followed by reviving hope; of repeated expectation of an ending that did not come; of repeated, staggering increases in destructiveness.

Lincoln's firm response to this first and shocking defeat at Bull Run revealed to the world, and possibly to himself, the resolution that he would need and would draw upon during four years of lost lives, lost battles, sometime opposition, and lack of courage from the public, even from his own generals.

After the reverses of 1861, the late winter and spring of 1862 would revive hope. There would be victories, particularly in the West—Forts Henry and Donelson on the rivers, captured by a new general named Grant—and in Missouri and along the Atlantic coast. Union hopes were so high that in April the new secretary of war ceased recruiting. But in that same month, after exactly a year of war, a western battle once again redefined the war's magnitude. As the reports came in from the battle called Shiloh in the North and Pittsburg Landing in the South, the nation began to comprehend some of the scale to which this war would extend. Within the battle itself fortunes had been reversed. It had been a near defeat, which a recovery by U. S. Grant would turn into victory. It nonetheless represented a leap in deadliness for both sides, a first glimpse of the scale of what was coming, 13,047 Union dead.

And then the failure of the Army of the Potomac before Richmond would bring another reversal, another dark day. In March the huge army drilled and named by McClellan had made a grand display of its departure from the Washington area, vastly more impressive than the tromp across the bridges on the way to First Bull Run. Taking the army of 112,000 and all its horses and guns and equipment in four hundred boats of every description down the Potomac to the bay, and along the bay down to Fort Monroe, was said by an English observer to be "the stride of a giant." But thereafter McClellan's progress up the peninsula toward Richmond would be the waddle of a dwarf. As it came up the peninsula, the army would be defeated and turned back by the new Confederate commander, Robert E. Lee, in a series of battles that came to be called the Seven Days. Northern morale plummeted. Lincoln realized that recruiting had to be renewed but feared the effect of a presidential call. So he maneuvered to have Northern governors urge him to call for more volunteers. In a letter to Seward on June 28, 1862, intended to be shown to Union governors, he presented his view of the current state of the war and included one of the great Lincolnian sentences. It is remarkable alike for its moral rigor, its literary grace, and its lawyerly covering of all contingencies: "I expect to maintain this contest until successful, or 'till I die, or am conquered, or my term expires, or Congress or the country forsakes me."

The mythic picture of Lincoln as a giant of brooding kindliness, of charity for all and malice toward none, turns out, on investigation, to be truer than many myths about great persons. But it is only half of the more complex and remarkable truth. Lincoln was indeed a man of extraordinary generosity. But at the same time he displayed a formidable resolve, including a willingness to employ the relentless use of force. He was a statesman managing the immense coercive machinery of a nation-state fighting for its life in a profoundly destructive war. He discovered or developed in himself the strength of will and tenacity required for executive leadership and high command in his own non-Napoleonic way.

It is true that in those first April days, and later too, he found in the Constitution—or really in the logic of the situation—the necessity to exercise powers beyond those that had been exercised by any other president or that were explicitly provided in law. And to be sure, his enemies would call Lincoln a tyrant, and in after years scholars would debate whether to attach to him the word "dictator" (a debate that has now happily subsided). But if one reads through his letters and messages and examines the reports of his conduct, one finds that Lincoln's resolution and strength of will did not spring from, or lead to, mindless stubbornness or egotistical willfulness. Lincoln's high resolve arose, rather, from the response of a rigorously dutiful intellect to a moral imperative that he found in the objective situation. A strong resolve was of great importance, but only as it rested on the stability of truth.

CHAPTER NINE

On Holding McClellan's Horse

ABRAHAM LINCOLN, the humorous citizen from the raucous back-woods politics and argumentative civil law courts of the "least milita-rized of Western societies," suddenly in 1861 had thrust into his large hands the management of a giant modern war. That meant, among a great many other things, that he had the exacting duty of coping with an out-burst of generals.

The United States had come out of a republican tradition that was explicitly opposed to standing armies. No general in the most recent Ameri-can war, the Mexican War, had commanded a force even as big as McDow-ell's green troops that crossed the Potomac bridges headed for Bull Run. The United States had trained few military leaders; when civil war came, nearly a third, including some of the ablest, joined the rebellion.

Among the experienced military leaders who remained, as we have seen, was the great old figure Winfield Scott. There then came onto the scene a brilliant well-trained younger man, a protégé of Scott, George McClellan. McClellan floated into the capital on the afternoon of July 26, 1861, accompanied by glowing reports of his career, his talents, and his victories in western Virginia.

But McClellan proved to be a master not of battle but of delay. He would proceed to test Lincoln's forbearance by the longest series of snubs, slights, slurs, affronts, demands, complaints, missed opportunities, and failures to follow orders by any supposed subordinate during the whole of his presidency. Lincoln patiently put up with a great deal from the young general in the effort to extract victories in the field. But those victories never seemed to happen; trying to get George McClellan to lead men into battle proved to be like pushing a noodle.

Lincoln had a crushing awareness, as McClellan did not seem to, of the enormous public stake in achieving victories sooner rather than later. The pent-up yearning for results brought forth what must have been the largest collection of imaginatively pointed tropes, right up to the borderline of sarcasm, that Lincoln ever uttered about any person. The pressure of Lincoln's controlled exasperation with this extremely difficult young general would have its outlet in the steady whistle of escaping wit.

McCLELLAN AND LINCOLN

LINCOLN AND McCLELLAN both came rather suddenly into great power in 1861, and neither man had much preparation for the immense responsibility that fell to him. McClellan's task, although much more narrowly focused than Lincoln's, nevertheless resembled and overlapped with it. He would be the shaper as well as the first and longest-serving commander of the Army of the Potomac, and for a time of all the Union armies. He and Lincoln had a great deal to do with each other—more, we may guess, than either of them wanted, at least fifty-seven meetings in the six months McClellan was in Washington. And then—to look ahead—McClellan would be nominated in 1864 by the Democrats to run against Lincoln for president. In August of that year both men thought that on March 4, 1865, McClellan would succeed Lincoln as president.

George McClellan was an able man, intelligent, much better educated and more widely traveled than Lincoln; by reputation at least he was a good organizer and administrator. He was young, only thirty-four when the war started. (He would not yet be forty when, after the election of 1864, his career on the national stage would be over.) He came from a cultured doctor's family in the upper reaches of Philadelphia society, went to a good private school, and had been a success at everything he had done: he was second in his class at West Point, did honorable service in the Mexican War, was singled out to study European armies and the Crimean War, was given plum army assignments, and then, after resigning his commission, became one of the highest-paid railroad executives in the country. (In 1858 he had loaned his private railroad car to Senator Douglas in his Illinois Senate campaign against Lincoln.) When war broke out, the three most populous states, New York, Pennsylvania, Ohio, sought him out as commander of their militias. While commanding Ohio's troops he had won victories in western Virginia, the only victories at first the North could celebrate. McClellan, summoned in a 2:00 a.m. telegram in the bad hours after Bull Run, was an obvious choice to play a central role in the rapidly expanding U.S. Army.

And McClellan began right away to do what was needed: to make an army out of the dispirited troops after Bull Run. He cleaned out the loiterers on Washington streets and brought them back into the army. He gave the army a name—the Army of the Potomac—and began to give it spirit, morale, pride. He became proud of the men, and they became proud of him.

McClellan and Lincoln would respond quite differently to a sudden ascension to prominence and power. The higher McClellan rose, the more it went to his head; the higher Lincoln rose, the weightier he felt his duty to be.

McClellan's ascent was more abrupt, and the deference given him more unalloyed. The day after his arrival in Washington in late July 1861, he wrote to his wife: "I almost think that if I were to win some small success now I could become dictator or anything else that might please me." At a state dinner in those heady first days, the British ambassador Lord Lyons said to a French dignitary who had been speaking to McClellan, "You are aware that you are talking with the next President of the United States?" When the remark was repeated to McClellan, he smiled.

He wrote to his wife: "Who would have thought when we were married, that I should so soon be called upon to save my country?" That he was called upon to save the country, or had already saved it, would be a recurrent theme for the next year and a half.*

Lincoln wrote, "I shall do nothing in malice," and he pretty nearly succeeded; McClellan's letters to his wife express his disdain for everyone in a position over him and for every rival to him, starting right away with his benefactor and superior General in Chief Winfield Scott.

The seventy-five-year-old Scott, who had been an American war hero before George McClellan was born, had been McClellan's sponsor; he had been the chief guest at McClellan's wedding to Mary Ellen in Calvary Church in New York in May 1860, and had been the key figure in his rise since the war started. And yet no sooner had McClellan taken his command in Washington than he began to snub Scott and write contemptuous remarks about him. Scott was a "perfect imbecile" who "understands nothing, appreciates nothing, and is ever in my way"; "the great obstacle . . . either a traitor or incompetent"; "the most dangerous antagonist I have."

*McClellan would serve as governor of New Jersey in 1877–80, an important post perhaps but something of a comedown from Savior of the Nation. He would continue to live in New York, going to Trenton only one day a week. Saving the nation took full time; governing New Jersey took only Tuesdays.

General Scott, loaded not only with honors but also with years and pounds and infirmities, felt himself repeatedly undercut by his "ambitious junior," who was swirling around the capital casting up plans and demands and phony threats without consulting "the nominal General-in-Chief of the Army."

Commander in Chief Lincoln had to deal with the wounded ego of General Scott on the one side and the inflated ego of General McClellan on the other. On October 31, 1861, Scott wrote to Secretary of War Cameron resigning his command, indirectly addressing the president, "who has treated me with distinguished kindness and courtesy," and on November 1 he retired. He was replaced as general in chief not by Henry Halleck, whom Scott wanted, but by George McClellan, who would combine that overall job with continuing to command the Army of the Potomac. When Lincoln asked whether combining the two jobs might be a "vast labor," McClellan coolly answered, "I can do it all."

George McClellan had won his victory over General Scott. But he had not won any victory over General Beauregard, or General Johnston, or any general on the other side in the war.

McClellan's pattern with Scott would be the pattern with other authorities and rivals: Stanton, when he became secretary of war ("the most unmitigated scoundrel");* Halleck, when he became general in chief ("the most stupid idiot I ever heard of"); and Irwin McDowell, when he became a rival general ("a scoundrel a liar & a fool who in seeking to injure me has killed himself"). One could decorate the page with McClellan's epithets for all the cabinet, both individually and collectively.

In September 1862, after he had been restored to the command of his army, he wrote to his wife about his enemies, meaning not Robert E. Lee and the rebel army but Stanton and Halleck: "It is something of a triumph that my enemies have been put down so completely." Two days earlier he seemed to consider any victory over the Confederate army a secondary matter, a possible addition to his victory over his primary enemies: "my enemies are crushed, silent & disarmed—if I defeat the rebels I shall be master of the situation."

---

*McClellan did not hold back on Stanton. In a letter to his wife he went on to say that "had he lived in the time of the Saviour, Judas Iscariot would have remained a respected member of the fraternity of the Apostles, & that the magnificent treachery & rascality of E. M. Stanton would have caused Judas to have raised his arms in holy horror & unaffected wonder." Stephen W. Sears, ed., *The Civil War Papers of George B. McClellan: Selected Correspondence, 1860–1865* (New York: Da Capo Press, 1992), p. 354.

One would be hard put to name any comparable words and acts in Lincoln's career. In the 1850s, as a rising Republican, he did feel a personal competition with Senator Stephen Douglas, mainly as a result of contesting views of public policy but with a flavoring of personal rivalry as well. Most of that sort of thing, mild as it was, was put aside in his presidency—except for some wry remarks that fall well short of being mean-spirited.

Shortly after McClellan was made general in chief, succeeding Scott, Lincoln, Seward, and Hay (according to Hay's diary) went to McClellan's house; a servant said the general was attending a wedding and would return soon. After the three had waited about an hour, McClellan did return, and "without paying any particular attention to the porter who told him the President was waiting to see him, went up stairs, passing the door of the room where the President and Secretary of State were seated. They waited about half-an-hour and sent once more a servant to tell the general they were there, and the answer ['cooly' scratched out] came that the general had gone to bed."

John Hay's diary entry concluded: "Coming home I spoke to the President about the matter but he seemed not to have noticed it specially, saying it was better at this time not to be making points of etiquette and personal dignity." In another of these episodes that point was explicit: Lincoln waited with a general and the governor of Ohio for McClellan to keep a stated appointment—and waited and waited and finally said, "Never mind. I will hold McClellan's horse if he will just bring us successes."

The root of Lincoln's conduct was not solely his modesty and lack of ego; it was also—or rather primarily—his concentration on the immense national purpose of which he was the instrument. What Lincoln dealt with was too vast for mere personal pride. If McClellan will bring us victories, he might have said, then I will overlook repeated snubs and hold a dozen horses. Deference to me is not the point; victory is the point; a preserved and reborn United States of America is the point.

PHANTOM ARMIES

VANITY, rudeness, and malice were not, however, McClellan's most distinctive vices as a commander; many other leaders are guilty of those vices. It was Lincoln, unusually free of all three, rather than McClellan, who was the exception on those counts among human beings who have been pushed up to vertiginous levels of power.

McClellan had another pair of vices that, linked together, were more decisively crippling to him as a leader. His readings of the reality he faced were sharply skewed, and he balked at the risk of making decisions.

The most distinctive of McClellan's deficiencies was his everlasting self-deception about the size of the armies he faced. After the war, with Confederate records available, scholars could settle the matter: he *always* said the army he faced was larger than it really was, and he *always* underestimated his own force in comparison to it.

This central delusion started right away, upon his arrival in Washington in the summer of 1861. In a letter he ostensibly addressed to General Scott (he actually sent it by messenger to President Lincoln, instructing him to read it "attentively"), he insisted that Washington was in "imminent danger." He said that he had "information from various sources" that the Confederate army out at Manassas had 100,000 men threatening the capital, and that if he were General Beauregard, he would attack the Union forces. On September 13, in a letter to Secretary of War Cameron, he wrote that "the enemy probably have 170,000!" In fact, the peak strength of the Confederate field army facing Washington in these months was less than 45,000.

Through that winter of 1861–62 the newly named Army of the Potomac, encamped around Washington, grew to be the biggest and best-equipped army in American history to that point. When the Peninsula Campaign began in March 1862, and the army and McClellan began their slow movement toward Richmond, his overestimates of the Confederate armies went with him all the way, until, as he approached Richmond, he believed them to number 200,000; in fact, they never numbered more than 85,000.

Parallel to this inflation of the opposing force was a deflation of his own. "With the figures for his own forces McClellan could also do amazing things; here his forte was subtraction." "The normal sick, the normal absent on leave or without leave, and the normal number in the Guard House—every military command has men so classified every day, cannot help it and expects it. But McClellan subtracted all the ineffectives." This mathematical wizardry meant that McClellan *always* needed reinforcements.

This trait of McClellan's was an ongoing stimulus to Lincoln's powers of satirical imagination: "Sending men to that army is like shoveling fleas across a barnyard; not half of them get there." "The president told me," wrote Orville Browning in his diary for July 25, 1862, "that if by magic he could reinforce McClellan with 100,000 men today he would be in ecstasy over it, thank him for it, and tell him he would go to Richmond tomorrow, but that when tomorrow came he would telegraph that he had certain information that the enemy had 400,000 men, and that he could not advance without reinforcements."

LINCOLN TRIES TO MAKE SOMETHING HAPPEN

AT THEIR FIRST MEETING on July 27, 1861, Lincoln asked McClellan for a war plan, and just a week later the general provided one—a plan to end all plans, a plan to end the war in a swoop: 273,000 men under his command, 100,000 in reserve, "such an overwhelming strength, as will convince all our antagonists . . . of the utter impossibility of resistance." McClellan wrote to his wife, "I shall carry this thing on 'en grand' and crush the rebels in one campaign."

So McClellan set about drilling and reviewing and parading his impressive army, living at 15th and H, riding about on his horse Daniel Webster, and dining out in Washington. All through the good fighting days of autumn Lincoln and Washington and the North waited for McClellan to attack and win victories, but it did not happen. The conscientiously self-educating president, during the winter of quietude on the Potomac, began to read some military strategy for himself. When, in late December, George McClellan came down with typhoid fever, it meant that both the commander of the biggest army in the East and the general of all the Union armies were out of commission.

On January 10, therefore, President Lincoln called a council of war, mingling generals and cabinet members. In this setting Lincoln made, according to General McDowell, another of his canonical wry remarks about McClellan, saying that if McClellan was not going to use the Army of the Potomac, he, Lincoln, would like to borrow it.

McClellan, when he learned they were having meetings without him, recovered quickly and attended the second such meeting, with three generals and three cabinet members, on January 13—but he maintained a sullen silence about his plans.

Lincoln, in his frustration with the dilatory McClellan and in his eagerness to make something happen, issued to General McClellan two quite dubious orders. On January 27, 1862, Lincoln issued his General Order No. 1, ordering a "general movement of the land and naval forces . . . against the insurgent forces" on February 22—an abrupt and bizarre order commanding the whole sweep of the Union force to march forward at once on the same day. And then in another special order, on January 31, he specifically ordered General McClellan to execute his, Lincoln's, proposed plan of attack on the supply lines of the rebel army out at Manassas Junction.

These orders did seem to have the intended effect: McClellan came forth with his own plan. He proposed to take the army around by the Chesapeake Bay to the east of Richmond and to come up on the rebel capital by way of the rivers and railroads on the peninsula between the York and the James Rivers.

McClellan did not think his president—this amateur, this civilian—should speak of "my" plan for the attack in contrast to his own professional one, but Lincoln did and posed a clearheaded set of questions about the differences between the two "plans."* At another odd meeting—a gathering of the twelve division generals—the vote was eight to four in favor of McClellan's plan. Lincoln, saying that of course he was not a military man, acquiesced. McClellan, pleased, wrote to his wife that Lincoln was his friend.

Lincoln had acquiesced without being persuaded, so this major campaign, which would be called the Peninsula Campaign and absorb immense energy and attention, went forward without the commander in chief really believing in it. One distinguished military historian says that Lincoln should not have given his grudging approval; that this was the point at which he should have replaced McClellan.

On March 11, 1862, in preparation for McClellan's departure for the peninsula, Lincoln did remove McClellan from the post of general in chief, leaving him with only the Army of the Potomac under his command. He appointed no one to the vacated post, and instead Lincoln and Stanton, working together in close collaboration, took on the overall command of all the armies for four months, until Henry Halleck was appointed to the general in chief post in July.

Doubtless McClellan forged a remarkable bond with his army—"my" army, he would call it. Some of the forging was manipulated. Bruce Catton gives a description: "A Massachusetts officer noted that when the army

---

*"1st. Does not your plan involve a greatly larger expenditure of *time,* and *money* than mine? 2nd. Wherein is a victory more certain by your plan than mine? 3rd. Wherein is a victory more valuable by your plan than mine? 4th. In fact, would it not be less valuable, in this, that it would break no great line of the enemie's communications, while mine would? 5th. In case of disaster, would not a safe retreat be more difficult by your plan than by mine?" Lincoln to McClellan, February 3, 1862.

took to the road McClellan would remain in camp until the entire column had been formed. Then he would ride to the head of the column, preceded by a staff officer who went galloping along the line crying, 'McClellan's coming; Boys! McClellan's coming! Three cheers for McClellan!' ... Loyalty to McClellan was built up in the army as deliberately as loyalty to a leader in a political organization ... it came from the top, actively generated by the officers." Nevertheless we may infer that some of it was real, and so also was McClellan's love (his word) for this army he had made. McClellan's claim that he took care "to gain success with the least possible loss" no doubt was one element both in the attachment of the men to him and in his own reluctance to commit to the risk of battle.

When after spending its first six months in parades and reviews around Washington the army prepared to leave for this Peninsula Campaign, its commander addressed it with an exclamation point—"Soldiers of the Army of the Potomac!" In that address the general said, "The patience you have shown, and your confidence in your General, are worth a dozen victories," to which Lincoln would surely have responded: *No, they are not.**

In early March, just before a spectacular departure for the peninsula, McClellan finally did what Lincoln had been urging him to do all winter and in Special Order No. 1 on January 31 had ordered him to do: McClellan moved upon the rebel army in Manassas and Centreville. In fact, he marched his whole army in battle formation, flags flying, out to the rebel fortifications—but the rebel army had withdrawn, moved south of the Rappahannock. And they had left for McClellan two further embarrassments: clear evidence that their numbers had been much smaller than he had been claiming, and some "guns" threatening Washington that turned out to be logs painted black—the famous "Quaker guns" about which McClellan would be mocked. Nevertheless McClellan would soon be presenting this march on Manassas—a "promenade," a modern writer calls it—as a notable victory.

Something similar would happen in the first encounter on the penin-

---

*"[E]ver bear in mind, that my fate is linked to yours ... I am to watch over you as a parent over his children; and you know that your General loves you from the depths of his heart. It shall be my care, as it has ever been, to gain success with the least possible loss, but I know that, if it is necessary, you will willingly follow me to our graves, for our righteous cause ...We will share all these together, and when this sad war is over we will all return to our homes, and feel that we can ask no higher honor than the proud consciousness that we belonged to the ARMY OF THE POTOMAC." Sears, *Papers of McClellan,* p. 211.

sula at Yorktown. The Confederate general John B. Magruder, who had talent as a stage manager, directed his mere eleven thousand troops to hurry from place to place, making a show now here, now there, barking orders to nonexistent battalions in the empty woods. So McClellan concluded that the opposing force was huge—which was what he was always inclined to think anyway and one may say what he *wanted* to believe. Military experts, and the intelligent nonexpert Lincoln, believed he should have attacked, and analysis afterward suggests that, having in fact much larger numbers, he could have prevailed had he done so—another in the long list of McClellan's missed opportunities.*

What McClellan did instead was to lay down a siege. "He liked siege warfare, with its slowness, its engineering problems, and its small loss of life," T. Harry Williams observes. He had studied the siege of Sevastopol; his West Point education and his military and civilian life featured engineering. But the slowly passing days of the siege of Yorktown gave the rebels time to make reinforcements and fortifications to defend Richmond. When McClellan finally did march on Yorktown, the rebel armies had already withdrawn back up the peninsula—this was an "open" siege, with a back door—and once again when the Army of the Potomac marched into an enemy camp, it was deserted, and once again he would nevertheless regard it as a victory.

As the army made its dwarf-size steps toward Richmond, McClellan did not attack, but Confederate general Joe Johnston did, and boldly. In a battle twelve miles from Richmond, McClellan for the first time commanded forces in a battle with significant casualties, and he was unnerved by it. Lincoln would be haunted by the killed and wounded also, and for that as well as other reasons he constantly pressed McClellan to bring the war to the soonest possible victorious conclusion; he was aware of the human cost of every delay. In one message to McClellan Lincoln deplored the "indefinite procrastination" that he perceived in a McClellan proposal. Such postponement of action meant more killed not only in other Union armies but also, because more men died of disease than of bullets, in the Army of the Potomac as well. McClellan would be taking his army into unhealthy swamps that he had not calculated on as he approached Richmond and as he retired to Harrison's Landing.

---

*"Joe Johnston, after an inspection of Magruder's lines, would write to Lee, 'No one but McClellan could have hesitated to attack.' In military history it would be difficult to find a more crushing indictment than that." Kenneth P. Williams, *Lincoln Finds a General: A Military Study of the Civil War*, 5 vols. (New York: Macmillan, 1949), 1:166.

Each time McClellan drew near to a decisive military engagement, he had a sudden attack that Lincoln—in perhaps his master trope for McClellan—would describe as "the slows." Surely there was something rooted in McClellan's psyche that made all those phantom armies spring up before him and get bigger when the time approached for him to commit to battle: some combination of human attachment to his army; perfectionism about this work of art, his army; fear of defeat that would stain his vanity; and temperamental avoidance of risk.

Among McClellan's many excuses was the weather. Nicolay and Hay write, "It is characteristic of him that he always regarded bad weather as exclusively injurious to him and never to the other side." And they then record another of Lincoln's steadily flowing McClellan-inspired jests: "The President . . . said of him that he seemed to think that, in defiance of scripture, Heaven sent its rain only on the just and not on the unjust."

One can count in Lincoln's *Collected Works* forty-five messages, long and short, that Lincoln sent McClellan in the nearly five months of the Peninsula Campaign. These messages make an extraordinary record of thorough, clearly reasoned, incredibly patient, and persistent argument trying to bring McClellan to act, to move, to fight. In the first major communication with the general after his removal to Fort Monroe, Lincoln reminded him that he, Lincoln, had not believed that it was necessary to move all that way when the rebel army had been all winter just twenty-five miles away in Manassas. On April 9, 1862, Lincoln wrote to McClellan:

> And, once more let me tell you, it is indispensable to you that you strike a blow. I am powerless to help this. You will do me the justice to remember I always insisted, that going down the Bay in search of a field, instead of fighting at or near Manassas, was only shifting and not surmounting a difficulty—that we would find the same enemy, and the same, or equal, intrenchments, at either place. The country will not fail to note—is now noting—that the present hesitation to move upon an intrenched enemy, is but the story of Manassas repeated.

Lincoln grasped, as McClellan did not seem to grasp at all, the importance of *time*. A military authority in later years would praise the three lines in which the "unexperienced lawyer" Lincoln summed up the situation—at the outset of the siege of Yorktown—which the professional soldier was constitutionally incapable of realizing. Lincoln wrote to McClellan: "By delay the enemy will relatively gain upon you—that is, he will gain faster, by fortifications and re-inforcements, than you can by re-inforcement."

Lincoln ended that letter with four words in italics that, preceded by a reassurance, summarized the whole correspondence: "I beg to assure you that I have never written you, or spoken to you, in greater kindness of feeling than now, nor with a fuller purpose to sustain you, so far as in my most anxious judgment, I consistently can. *But you must act.*"

AFTER MIDNIGHT ON JUNE 28 an exhausted, demoralized, overwrought, and resentful McClellan poured out the first of two insulting messages he wrote to Lincoln in the summer of 1862. His army had been defeated, with many casualties, at the battle called Gaines' Mill, in which Robert E. Lee's boldness and McClellan's loss of nerve had saved Richmond. McClellan's long telegram to Stanton (obviously to Lincoln as well) explicitly said not only that he was not responsible for the defeat and that it was *their* fault but also that this "sacrifice" had been deliberate.

> [O]ur men . . . were overwhelmed by vastly superior numbers . . . The loss on both sides is terrible . . . Had I 20,000 or even 10,000 fresh troops to use to-morrow I could take Richmond, but I have not a man in reserve . . . If we have lost the day we have yet preserved our honor, and no one need blush for the Army of the Potomac . . . You must send me very large re-enforcements, and send them at once . . .
>
> As it is, the Government must not and cannot hold me responsible for the result.
>
> I have seen too many dead and wounded comrades to feel otherwise than that the Government has not sustained this army. If you do not do so now the game is lost.
>
> If I save this army now, I tell you plainly that I owe no thanks to you or to any other persons in Washington.
>
> You have done your best to sacrifice this army.

These last two sentences accusing Stanton (and "any other persons in Washington"—that is, Lincoln) of having "done your best" to see this Union army defeated—in effect, of committing treason—so shocked the head of the War Department's Telegraph Office that he had the deciphered telegram recopied without them, so Lincoln and Stanton did not see the very worst passage. But the rest is bad enough, plain enough: his men had been "needlessly" sacrificed by "the government," upon whom all blame for the defeat rests.

Lincoln calmly responded by trying to bring McClellan to see the situation more objectively. "Save your army at all events," said Lincoln, starting off with the most basic point. And then he tried to show the solipsistic young general that there were other fronts. "If you had a drawn battle, or a repulse, it is the price we pay for the enemy not being in Washington . . . it is the nature of the case, and neither you or the government that is to blame."

TELLING THE PRESIDENT WHAT
THE WAR'S PURPOSE SHOULD BE

McCLELLAN'S withdrawal from the line before Richmond is often said to mark the end of the first phase of the American Civil War; Lincoln in response made immensely consequential decisions that, as we will see, changed the war.

When the president came down to Harrison's Landing on the James River for an examination of the army, McClellan handed him a letter that presumed to tell him what the purpose of the war should be. "The time has come," McClellan wrote, "when the Government must determine upon a civil and military policy, covering the whole ground of our national trouble."

McClellan's letter raised the larger matters that were now coming to the fore. McClellan was a Democrat, and throughout his service in the army he kept up a correspondence with leading Democrats in New York. He was also soft on slavery, and hostile to abolitionists and Radical Republicans. Although some Republicans had eagerly supported him when he first came on the scene, that support had long since turned sour.

For months the dispute about McClellan's conduct had had a partisan cast. He may not have realized how much Lincoln was his defender in an administration in which most were antagonistic.

He had expressed his views on slavery and the war in western Virginia and, in muted terms, about respecting "property," but at that point, in the first summer of the war, he would have had wide support. In this letter to Lincoln a year later, he made a much more extended and explicit statement:

This . . . War . . . should be conducted upon the highest principles known to Christian civilization. It should not be a War looking to the subjugation of the people of any state . . . Neither confiscation of property, political executions of persons, territorial organization of States or forcible abolition of slavery should be contemplated for a moment.

Military power should not be allowed to interfere with the relation of servitude . . . A declaration of radical views, especially upon slavery, will rapidly disintegrate our present armies.

The letter was so much a political statement that it would be reprinted and used in 1864 as a campaign document in McClellan's presidential campaign.

Lincoln read the letter on the spot, made no comment, thanked McClellan, put it in his pocket, and never mentioned it again. And back in Washington he made some decisions that were altogether at odds with McClellan's recommendations, as we shall see.

McCLELLAN LETS POPE GET OUT
OF HIS SCRAPE BY HIMSELF

LINCOLN COULD OVERLOOK snubs to himself. He could respond with patient reasoning to the insulting charge in McClellan's postmidnight June 28 telegram (called the Savage Station telegram because of the place of its sending). He could quietly pocket McClellan's presumptuous letter from Harrison's Landing on July 7. But then came an episode to which his pardon would *not* extend, in which he would explicitly describe McClellan's conduct as "unpardonable," and which would evoke his wrath. This would be McClellan's failure to send support to General John Pope's army, which Robert E. Lee decisively defeated, in the Second Battle of Bull Run in northern Virginia, at the very end of August 1862. Lincoln suspected McClellan of deliberately declining to support Pope.

While McClellan had been going through his long buildup to bad news before Richmond in the East, there had been some good news in the West, a series of Union victories that made February through May 1862 the first positive period for the harried Union president. When in the summer it appeared that McClellan would not ride triumphantly into Richmond after all, and the able new Confederate commander Robert E. Lee threatened Washington, Lincoln brought one of the victorious generals from the West, John Pope, to head an Army of Virginia, newly created by amalgamating old units, including many of the troops that had been commanded by McClellan.

To McClellan's dismay, units from the Army of the Potomac were transferred to Pope's command. The new general in chief Halleck (who, to be sure, McClellan also soon detested) ordered McClellan, the favorite general of conservatives and Democrats, his Peninsula Campaign now defunct, to bring what remained of his army as rapidly as he could to northern Virginia, to help to protect Pope.

Lincoln perceived that McClellan, as usual dilatory, in this case had his slowness increased by his contempt for his fellow Union army general. McClellan's modern biographer writes that "had General McClellan willed it, 25,000 reinforcements would have been at General Pope's call in time for ... the second and decisive day of the Second Battle of Bull Run." When Lincoln in the telegraph office wired McClellan for news of the battle, McClellan responded with a statement of his preferred course of action that included this phrase, understandably infuriating to Lincoln: "to leave Pope to get out of his own scrape, and devote ourselves to securing Washington." A newsman in the telegraph office wrote that he had never seen Lincoln so "wrathful," and that evening Lincoln told John Hay that "it really seemed to him that McC. wanted Pope defeated."

AN EXCESS OF MAGNANIMITY?

LINCOLN'S SECRETARIES, who rarely hint at a fault in the great man they served, would produce, about his dealing with McClellan, this near criticism, grounded to be sure in a virtue: "Mr. Lincoln certainly had the defects of his great qualities. His unbounded magnanimity made him sometimes incapable even of just resentments. General McClellan's worst offenses had been committed against the president in person. The insulting dispatch from Savage's Station and the letter from Harrison Landing, in which he took the president to task for the whole course of his ... administration, would probably have been pardoned by no ruler that ever lived."

There would be more to the story after that summer of 1862; Lincoln's dealings with McClellan were not yet over. In the rush of severely exacting circumstances in the first week of September 1862, Lincoln, much against his inclination, returned the command of the now combined armies to McClellan.

After Second Bull Run, Lee's army threatened Washington: Halleck (exhausted) and Lincoln on September 1 put McClellan, the builder of the fortifications and the shaper of defenses, in charge simply of the defense of the capital. When word came from Pope reporting "unsoldierly and dan-

gerous conduct" in the upper ranks of the Army of the Potomac, a demoralization caused by resentment over the change in high command, Lincoln
told McClellan that he should tell his subordinates to give Pope full support, and ostensibly McClellan did that, wiring his closest associate Fitz
John Porter "for my sake and that . . . of the old Army of the Potomac" to
give Pope "the fullest and most cordial co-operation . . . the same support
they ever have to me." But the touches of implicit egotism chipping away at
the telegram's explicit message took over in a last sentence, undercutting
his earlier dutiful words. "I am in the charge of the defenses of Washington," McClellan wired to his old comrades, "and am doing all I can do to
render your retreat safe should that become necessary." This told them that
as the army fell back to Washington, it would come once again under his
command, and that was indeed what happened.*

On September 2 Lincoln and Halleck appeared at McClellan's house
during his breakfast and asked him to take command of the combination of
the Army of the Potomac with the army that Pope had commanded. Lincoln did so with great misgivings, and intended it to be temporary and for
the defense of the city only, as he told his dismayed cabinet at a meeting
later that day. Gideon Welles wrote in his diary, "There was a more . . .
desponding feeling than I have ever witnessed . . . the President was greatly
distressed." Welles reported the president's explanation of his action:
"McClellan knows this whole ground; his specialty is to defend; he is a
good engineer, all admit; there is no better organizer; he can be trusted to
act on the defensive; but he is troubled with the 'slows' and good for nothing for an onward movement."

But Robert E. Lee did not know he was supposed to attack Washington
so that McClellan could show his defensive skills. Instead he boldly led his
army across the Potomac into Maryland—to rouse Maryland's slumbering
rebel spirit, to forage in the North, and to win the war.

So now the Union armies needed to be led in the field in pursuit of Lee.
Who could command? Lincoln and Halleck tried to persuade Burnside,
but he declined. Lincoln left open the possibility that Halleck himself
might do it, but the man they called "Old Brains" was not going to leave his
desk. That left McClellan, who in any case was already commanding.
While Lincoln would be entrusting this task to McClellan with the deepest

---

*Fitz John Porter would be court-martialed for his failure to support Pope in the battle at the
end of August, just before these September events. When the court-martial came to Lincoln, he declined to pardon Porter.

misgivings, McClellan would be writing to his wife, "Again I have been called upon to save my country."

When McClellan and his armies pursued Lee into Maryland, Providence tried to give McClellan a unique personal boost, and it still did not move him to action. The tale of the "lost order" is one of those episodes that seems to have spilled into history from fiction. A Union army corporal from Indiana discovered in a field near Frederick an envelope containing three cigars, and wrapped around the cigars was a paper with official writing on it, and at the end of the writing was this heart-stopping signature: "By command of Robert E. Lee." So Order No. 191, giving the disposition of Confederate forces before Harpers Ferry, was passed up through ranks, authenticated, and put in General McClellan's hands. McClellan, who had been welcomed on that very morning to the Maryland town of Frederick with cheers, flowers, flags, and kisses, sent an unusually ebullient telegram to Lincoln gloating that "I have all the plans of the rebels and will catch them."

For McClellan to take advantage of the order, however, he would have had to order immediate exertion—which was not his way. Kenneth Williams remarks: "[I]t is to be hoped that some capable smokers derived more good out of the three cigars than McClellan was to get out of the order in which they were wrapped."

On September 17 the two armies near Antietam Creek in Maryland produced the bloodiest single day in American history. Because the Union army at the end of the day possessed the field and stopped Robert E. Lee's advance into Maryland and Pennsylvania, it was deemed a Union strategic victory, but it was a heavily qualified victory, deeply disappointing to Lincoln because of what might have been.

McClellan thought Lee had 120,000 men, three times more than he in fact had, and he kept troops in reserve that, had he used them, would have provided a decisive result: "the practical annihilation of Lee's army." On the morning after the terrible battle, on September 18, McClellan declined to attack: "The fault was in the man. There was force enough at his command either day [September 17 or 18] had he seen fit to use it."

Lee, who had taken McClellan's measure, kept his battered army in place on the eighteenth, and only after dark withdrew back across the Potomac into Virginia. From Lincoln's point of view, it was another opportunity missed. McClellan claimed that he had saved Maryland and Pennsylvania and that, as he wired Halleck, "[w]e may safely claim a complete victory." To his wife he wired that "our victory [is] complete." But the destruction of Lee's army, which was Lincoln's objective and should have been McClellan's, was not accomplished.

It is often said that McClellan, ironically, made more likely the very outcomes that he did not want. He did not want the war to deal with slavery, and if he had had the characteristics of Robert E. Lee and had used this great army to trounce the rebels early, then the abolition of slavery might have been postponed.

The battle of Antietam had ironies in the opposite direction. General McClellan thought that he had "defeated Lee so utterly and saved the North so completely" that now his enemies Stanton and Halleck would be replaced, and that he would be honored as a general who could win and be restored to the position of general in chief in place of Halleck. He expected the vindication to begin with a meeting of Northern governors in Altoona. However, the governors called for the removal not of Halleck or of Stanton—but of McClellan.

He found that the great victory he had won, which Lincoln did not regard as a victory, would nevertheless be used by Lincoln as the occasion for an immense development in policy, which he, McClellan, abominated: the preliminary emancipation proclamation, issued September 22.

McClellan considered making a public criticism of the president's proclamation "inaugurating servile war and emancipating slaves," but his fellow generals and political friends talked him out of it. Instead he issued a general order stating that "firm steady and honest support of the Authority of the Government . . . is the highest duty of an American soldier, and that discussions of public matters within the ranks should not be carried to a point that impairs discipline and efficiency." It was, actually, quite a sound statement, but still the question arose: Why was it necessary to issue it? And it did say that "the remedy for political error if any are committed is to be found only in the action of the people at the polls," which is where McClellan himself would before long seek to remedy Lincoln's errors.

"After the battle of Antietam," Lincoln would tell Hay, "I went up to the field to try to get him [McClellan] to move." This was the first week in October. He encountered yet again what his secretaries called McClellan's "amiable inertia." The widely disseminated photographs of General McClellan and Lincoln in camp come from this visit. Lincoln wrote to his wife a subtle jibe at McClellan that she surely would pick up: "We are about to be photographed," he wrote; that is, "[i]f we can sit still long enough. I feel Gen. M. should have no problem." Sitting still was what Gen. M. was best at.

A more famous instance of Lincoln's wryness about McClellan came on an early morning walk with a friend on October 3, 1862, when Lincoln visited McClellan and his armies in Maryland after Antietam. From a hilltop he and his friends saw the vast army camp spread before them. Gesturing, Lincoln asked:

"Did you know what this is?"

"It is the Army of the Potomac," replied the astonished friend.

"So it is called," said Lincoln. "But that is a mistake. It is only McClellan's bodyguard."

In his summary two years later Lincoln told Hay: "I came back [from that October visit] thinking he would move at once. But when I got home he began to argue why he ought not to move. I peremptorily ordered him to advance." That order was issued by Halleck on October 6. But McClellan had long since demonstrated that he regarded presidential orders simply as topics for discussion. "The dispatch opened a thirty-day war of words between McClellan and [his superiors in] Washington. Unwilling either to obey the order . . . or resign in protest," writes his biographer, Stephen W. Sears, "McClellan generated one excuse after another . . . [W]hile Lincoln and Halleck pressed him almost daily to march, he was playing host to his wife and his year-old daughter and his mother-in-law in a farmhouse near his camp."

On October 13 Lincoln tried reason again, in a blunt letter to McClellan: "Are you not over-cautious when you assume that you can not do what the enemy is constantly doing? Should you not claim to be at least his equal in prowess, and act upon the claim?" Lincoln, now a good deal more confident in his understanding of these matters than he had been at the start of their relationship in July 1861, quoted from his reading in military strategy the maxim "to operate on your enemy's communication without exposing your own," and wrote: "You seem to act as if this applies against you, but can not apply in your favor. Change positions with the enemy, and think you not he would break your communication with Richmond within the next twenty four hours?"

Reversing positions is a necessary, self-correcting exercise not only in moral reasoning but also in military strategy. Lincoln described, with clarity and economy, the ways the opposing armies might get to Richmond. The route the enemy must take, wrote this self-taught student of Euclid, was the arc of circle, while the route McClellan *could* take was the chord:

"Why can you not reach [Richmond] before him, unless you admit that he is more than your equal on a march?" Lincoln again stated the necessity to defeat the rebel army and not to postpone, avoid acting, or procrastinate: "We should not operate as to merely drive him away. As we must beat him somewhere, or fail finally, we can do it, if at all, easier near to us, than far away. If we cannot beat the enemy where he is now, we never can."

He closed this notable letter with another insistence that Union troops could match the rebels: "It is all easy if our troops march as well as the enemy; and it is unmanly to say they can not do it."

BUT STILL the great army stayed in camp, and its commander sent justifying messages insisting on his lack of shoes, guns, knapsacks—and horses.

McClellan sent to General in Chief Halleck an extract from a cavalry officer noting that out of 267 horses, 128 "are positively and absolutely unable to leave the camp . . . The horses . . . are absolutely broken down from fatigue and want of flesh."

A telegram in response came immediately, sent not to the cavalry officer but to General McClellan, and coming not from Halleck but from the president of the United States: "I have just read your dispatch about sore tongued and fatigued horses. Will you pardon me for asking what the horses of your army have done since the battle of Antietam that fatigue anything. A. Lincoln"*

This famous telegram set off a three-day telegraphic dustup on the great subject of McClellan's horses. Already at six on the same day an indignant McClellan fired back a detailed defense, having the honor to specify all the arduous work his army's horses had done—foraging, scouting, picketing, expeditions of two hundred miles, seventy miles, laborious service back on the Peninsula—and ending with the proud claim that no horses had worked harder. President Lincoln responded not only by suggesting that if the army moved maybe the horses would not have to do so much "foraging," but also by perhaps inadvertently stepping right on McClellan's toes

---

*Mark E. Neely, Jr., describes this message as "one of the few ill-tempered and mean-spirited letters of his [Lincoln's] life," in *The Last Best Hope of Earth: Abraham Lincoln and the Promise of America* (Cambridge, Mass.: Harvard University Press, 1993), p. 71. It might more accurately be described as sarcasm provoked by extreme frustration, with still a faint trace of wryly exasperated humor in it. But a reader seeing the context can make his own evaluation.

by mentioning Jeb Stuart's horses: "Stuart's cavalry outmarched ours," wired Lincoln, "having certainly done more marked service on the Peninsula and everywhere since."

That blew all of McClellan's whistles. Those spectacular raids by the bold rebel cavalry commander Jeb Stuart, more than once riding clear around McClellan's army, obviously were an acute embarrassment. McClellan wired back to Lincoln at nine that same evening a sputtering insistence that someone was giving the president an erroneous impression. McClellan responded as though there were some kind of Olympic contest between the cavalries and Stuart had cheated:

> Stuart . . . received a relay of fresh horses when he crossed the river . . . had extra lead horses to take the places of those that gave out on the road . . . stole some 1,000 horses in Pennsylvania . . . Notwithstanding all this, he dropped a great many broken-down horses along the road. [The Union cavalry] made . . . the entire trip without a change of horses.
>
> After this statement of facts . . . I feel confident you will concur with me that our cavalry is equally as efficient as that of the rebels.

Lincoln's point had not been to denigrate the Union cavalry as less "efficient" than the Confederates' but to ask that it be *used*. Jeb Stuart *acted;* McClellan didn't.*

In his next message—now on October 27—Lincoln gave a hint of an apology, explaining the reasons "something of impatience" may have been forced into his messages by the almost hopeless prospect McClellan kept presenting:

> To be told after more than five weeks total inaction of the Army, and during which period we had sent to that Army every fresh horse we possibly could . . . that the cavalry horses were too much fatigued to move, presented a very cheerless, almost hopeless, prospect . . . ; and it may have forced something of impatience into my dispatches. If not . . . rested then, when could they ever be?

---

*When on October 13 McClellan had to report that Stuart had again circled his army, Halleck wired another entry in the anthology of Lincolnian wrynesses about Little Mac: "The President . . . directs me to suggest that, if the enemy had more occupation south of the river his cavalry would not be so likely to make raids north of it."

When could they ever be? Once more has a sharp sense of the different meaning to each of them of *time*. Lincoln had said to McClellan in his strong letter of October 13, about one of McClellan's perfectionist projects, that although he would "certainly be pleased for you to have the advantage of the Railroad from Harper's Ferry [*sic*] to Winchester, but it wastes all the remainder of autumn to give it to you; and, in fact ignores the question of *time*, which can not, and must not be ignored."

McClellan's main army sat on the north bank of the Potomac from September 18 until October 26. Lincoln was then startled to receive, at three o'clock in the afternoon of the same day as he sent his "something of impatience" telegram, a message requesting that a draft be ordered to fill McClellan's depleted regiments, which message included the quite disheartening phrase "before taking them [these regiments] again into action."

Just twenty-five minutes later, Lincoln fired a telegram back, asking for a "distinct answer" to this question: "Is it your purpose not to go into action again until the men now being drafted in the States are incorporated into the old regiments?" McClellan, embarrassed, scrambled to answer and blamed a subordinate.

Finally he did start to bring his army across the Potomac, slowly. Lincoln in his summary to Hay would remember the precise count: "It was 19 days before he put a man over the river. It was 9 days longer before he got his army across and then he stopped again, delaying on little pretexts of wanting this and that."

Lincoln had defended the general against the charges of the Radical Republicans, but at this point, looking back, he said, "I began to fear he was playing false—that he did not want to hurt the enemy." And so again he made a trial: "I saw how he could intercept the enemy on the way to Richmond. I determined to make that the test. If he let them get away I would remove him. He did so & I relieved him."

He relieved him not before but immediately *after* the fall elections on November 5, so that Lincoln's dismissal of this heavily politicized figure would not affect the outcome. Lincoln told Halleck to replace McClellan with Burnside, and George McClellan's military career was over.

In the days after he relieved McClellan, in November 1862, Lincoln told Francis Blair that he had "tried long enough to bore with an augur that would not take hold."

And he also said about him, as Nicolay wrote to his girlfriend, "He is an excellent engineer, but he seems to have a special talent for the stationary engine."

A PARADOXICAL NECESSITY

IN 1862 AMERICANS would have been astonished to know that in the twenty-first century a political writer would assert that in his dealings with generals, in comparison with more recent presidents, Lincoln was "an exceptionally unforgiving boss." Unforgiving? Lincoln? In relation to McClellan? Most of his cabinet and much of Congress and the public thought the opposite.

Were his dealings with McClellan an instance of Lincoln carrying his "unbounded magnanimity" too far? Radical Republicans thought so; according to Hay, mail from the public said so; Stanton surely thought so— in the end almost the whole cabinet thought so. When Lincoln came to the cabinet meeting on September 2 to tell them that he had restored McClellan to command, Stanton had been ready with a petition, signed by a majority of the cabinet, voicing strong opposition to entrusting the army to McClellan.

So we come to the question: Why did Lincoln not dismiss McClellan until almost a year and a half of war had been endured?

His restraint was not solely or primarily due to his magnanimity, although at a personal level it was that. Overlooking slights and not holding grudges were virtues of Lincoln's that helped him to focus on larger public purposes. Lincoln had two justifications for his incredibly patient, perhaps even perversely patient, support for George McClellan and specifically for returning him to command in September 1862. The first was the paucity of alternatives. When questioned by Senator Ben Wade, Lincoln responded as follows: "Well . . . put yourself in my place for a moment. If I relieve McClellan whom shall I put in command?" "Why," said Wade, "anybody." "Wade," replied Mr. Lincoln, with weary resignation, "*anybody* will do for you, but not for me. I must have *somebody.*"

Is it really true that he had nobody else? The American Civil War was a wholly new experience, much larger than the Mexican War or any other American war, and many reputations would be established in the event. Lincoln himself surely did find and elevate new people: Montgomery Meigs in the *Powhatan* affair, for one of many examples.

But a defender of Lincoln might say that the command of a giant army is a particularly demanding job, different from lesser jobs. The scantiness of the alternatives available to Lincoln is suggested by the performance of those whom he would appoint to replace McClellan. Burnside protested that he was not competent to lead such an army and in the battle of Fredericksburg would give devastating proof that he was right. The egregious "Fighting Joe" Hooker would withdraw from fighting at Chancellorsville in such a way as to rouse in some a desire to get McClellan *back*. John Pope was now blamed, whether justly or not, for the defeat at Second Bull Run. George Meade would lead the army to victory in the crucial battle at Gettysburg, but then while others were rejoicing in the victory, Lincoln was dismayed that Meade allowed Lee's army to get back over the Potomac.

So we come to Lincoln's second reason: McClellan was an unusually able military leader in certain regards—in shaping an army and giving it morale. This second reason had a twist in its tail that linked it back to the first. Bruce Catton formulates the large point: "[T]he most compelling reason for removing General McClellan from command of the Army of the Potomac was precisely the reason that made his removal impossible. The gravest charge against him was at the same time his greatest asset . . . McClellan had turned the Army of the Potomac into his own personal instrument . . . the Army actually would not fight for anyone else."

And it did fight bravely, however poorly it was commanded, on September 17 at Antietam, and that heavily qualified victory was, just barely, a vindication of Lincoln's decision. The victory, such as it was, punctured any reviving European inclination to recognize the Confederacy, and it served Lincoln as the occasion for his most important initiative, the Emancipation Proclamation. The realistic politician Abraham Lincoln said to John Hay, when he returned McClellan to the command of the Army of the Potomac, "We must use what tools we have."

CHAPTER TEN

The Trent *and a Decent Respect*
for the Opinions of Mankind

I~N~ N~OVEMBER~ 1861 the larger world abruptly intruded into the American Civil War and required from the American president a brief foray into that utterly realistic and putatively amoral arena, politics among nations: realpolitik, national interest, reasons of state, balances of power. Allegedly there is no intrusion of moral ideals into this realm.

Lincoln, from the start of the rebellion, had had to watch out of the corner of an eye the reaction of nations abroad, Britain and France particularly. Rebel leaders had hopes that the old nations of Europe would recognize the Confederacy as an independent nation—which would have been devastating to the Union cause. Even the Declaration of Neutrality by his great good friend Queen Victoria back in May had been worrisome. But what came to be known as the *Trent* affair threatened, for a brief moment, a far more catastrophic result: not merely recognition of the Confederacy but Great Britain at war with the Union, which, as Lincoln quickly perceived, was one more war than it could handle. He expressed his policy with unvarnished clarity: one war at a time.

The episode featured contrapuntal outbursts of passionate nationalism, first on the part of the Americans, then on the part of the British. Fortunately, communication was slow enough that these two outbursts did not coincide.

The circumstances were these. A swashbuckling captain, Charles Wilkes, of an American warship, the *San Jacinto,* had learned in Havana that two Confederate emissaries and their secretaries had booked passage on the British mail steamer *Trent* to take them to the Danish island of St. Thomas, where they were to make connections for Europe. Wilkes on his own initiative sailed ahead, laid ambush in the Bahama Channel, and on November 8 intercepted the *Trent.* He sent a team of marines to board the

mail packet and to extract the Confederate emissaries; he then took them to
Fort Monroe, arriving on November 15. The news of the seizure was
immediately trumpeted across the North and brought an eruption of jubilant chauvinism. The Northern public was starved for something to cheer.
Throughout 1861, since the war began in April, most of the big public
news had been bad—the rout at Bull Run, the botch at Ball's Bluff, the
killing of Lyon and the loss at Wilson's Creek in Missouri—and then
George McClellan, with his huge Army of the Potomac, seemed to do more
parading than fighting. Suddenly there came this satisfying stroke of forthright, overt action, Captain Wilkes reaching out and snatching these emissaries of treason.

The identities of the two added to the satisfaction. James Mason of
Virginia and John Slidell of Louisiana had been among the most objectionable of articulate proslavery, prosecession senators in the turmoil of the
1850s: "Probably no two men in the entire South were more obnoxious to
those of the Union side," wrote Charles Francis Adams, Jr., "than Mason
and Slidell." That it was their mission that was thwarted intensified Northern glee. They had been on their way to Europe, Mason to England, Slidell
to France, to seek support for the Confederacy. That they had been
snatched from a British vessel may have added juice to the American jubilation in the first unthinking moment: although England was the mother
country and perhaps the nation's first friend, she might also be said to have
been the first enemy, against whom the Americans had fought two wars and
almost fought another in 1841, the country whose Tory classes looked
down at the vulgar American democracy and whose *Times* of London
thundered in favor of the Confederacy. Furthermore, particularly since
their own abolition of slavery in the West Indies in 1833, British opinion
had been laced with lofty disapproval of the slaveholding republic across
the seas. And at the same time—such condescension notwithstanding—
since the Civil War broke out, the British in the large had not sprung to the
support of the Union, in its battle with real slaveholders.

But the great point was, here at last was action, a victory for the Union
over traitors. Captain Charles Wilkes was an instant hero: editorials in the
Northern press praised him, and Massachusetts governor Andrew gave a
public dinner in his honor in Boston. Within Lincoln's own cabinet, Secretary of the Navy Welles wrote him a letter of approval, and when Congress
convened in early December, the House of Representatives voted to give
him a gold medal. The celebration of Wilkes's deed was extravagant, bipartisan, and ubiquitous and included astonishing statements of approval

made by leading lawyers, editorialists, and intellectuals—and alleged experts in international law.*

Fortunately at that time, in 1861, communication across the Atlantic was blessedly slow. The transatlantic cable had not yet been laid, and the ships that carried messages crossed the great ocean at a stately pace. Captain Wilkes had struck his daring blow for the Republic on November 8. He had brought his prisoners to Fort Monroe, as noted, on November 15, whereupon, as the telegraph did stretch across the American North and the unbuttoned press of that day flung itself upon the story, a tumult of American jubilation erupted. The joy continued, with an important sobering interruption, until the end of the affair on December 26. But the British did not know, at the start of this period, either about the seizure or about the American rejoicing; they learned about it all on November 27 with the arrival of some passengers who had been on the *Trent* and had transferred at St. Thomas to a ship that went on to dock in Southampton. The British then promptly began their own firestorm, not of glee but of fury.

As they saw it, a ship of a neutral power, pursuing a lawful, innocent, and peaceful voyage from one neutral port to another, with Her Majesty's mails on board, had been forcibly stopped by shots across the bow from an American man-of-war and had been boarded by "a large armed guard of marines" (there are two insults already—the shots and the boarding), and four passengers (Mason and Slidell and their secretaries), who had been traveling "under the protection of the British flag," were forcibly removed. This was "an affront to the British flag and a violation of international law." All segments of British opinion, including those that supported the Union, exploded in indignation; editorials in papers of all stripes condemned the insult. The prime minister, Lord Palmerston, said to the cabinet, "You may stand for this but damned if I will!" The ministry ordered eight thousand troops to prepare for transfer to Canada with a supply of munitions. It was even rumored that as one regiment embarked, its band played "Dixie."

Now comes another contribution by the blessed slowness of communication: Americans in their turn did not learn about the British uproar until a ship called the *Hansa* arrived in New York on December 12. For almost a

---

*Charles Francis Adams's son, also named Charles Francis Adams, would produce an article that included pages and pages of quotations from American literati that, after the affair was over, must have been intensely embarrassing to those who uttered them. At one celebratory dinner "the speakers . . . seemed to vie with each other in establishing a record from which thereafter it would be impossible to escape." Adams, "The *Trent* Affair," *American Historical Review* 17, no. 3 (1912), p. 546.

full month—from November 15 until December 12—Americans had been able to revel, if they wanted to, in Wilkes's deed without the unpleasant distraction of the British fury. Before December 12 a little moral imagination might have suggested the meaning that the event was likely to have in Great Britain; after that date no imagination was required—the newspapers performed that service. The British were irate, and now at last the Americans knew it.

At the center of the American government as it confronted this outburst from across the seas (and at the same time the sharply contrasting eruption at home, not yet contained) was a new president who had never once been outside his native country, who spoke no foreign language, who had no personal friend abroad, and who had no experience in world politics. All the key participants in the *Trent* affair—the British ambassador Lord Lyons, the British foreign secretary Lord John Russell, the American secretary of state William Seward, the chairman of the Senate Foreign Relations Committee Charles Sumner, the American ambassador to London Charles Francis Adams—had at one time or another expressed severe reservations about this man's capacity to cope with world politics at its highest level. Seward, who had far more experience abroad and in world politics than most American politicians, had explained at the outset of the Lincoln administration that because of "the utter absence of any acquaintance with the subject in the chief [executive], his [Seward's] would be the guiding hand in Union diplomacy."

ALTHOUGH HE DID indeed cede much of the foreign relations of the administration to Seward, Lincoln had already, well before the *Trent* affair, made pivotal interventions. He had quietly ignored the cockamamie notion in Seward's April Fool's Day memorandum that the way to bring peace to the United States was to bring war to the world: to unite North and South in battle against a foreign power. The shared nationalism, so Seward thought, would override the ideologies of the sections, and South Carolina would be the belligerent companion of Massachusetts in the war against—somebody.

One did not need to have long years of experience in the highest levels of diplomacy to recognize that that was not a good idea. As his opposition as a congressman to Polk's Mexican War had demonstrated, Lincoln did not believe in American presidents deliberately provoking wars or to warmaking on trumped-up charges. And now as president himself he had considerations not only of principle but of elementary prudence: the likelier scenario in early April 1861 was not that South Carolina firebrands would wheel around and join Massachusetts abolitionists in fighting an American war against another country—Great Britain? Russia? Spain? France?*— but that some of these nations would give recognition and aid to the Confederacy. For Washington to provoke a war with any of them, thinking that Montgomery (or soon Richmond) would join in that war, would surely be folly of the highest order.

Between April 12 and April 15 Sumter was attacked and "reduced," and Lincoln called out the militia; on April 17 Jefferson Davis endorsed privateering on Union shipping; on April 19 Lincoln, in response, ordered a blockade of Confederate ports. The problem about a blockade was that it is an act of war between sovereign states, which if effective is, in international law, to be recognized by other states. But Lincoln and the Union did not grant that the Confederacy was a state. So there was an ambiguity, a problem. On May 13 the British government promulgated Queen Victoria's proclamation that her government would be "neutral" in this American fracas, and France soon followed her example. If Kentucky's "neutrality" was one kind of problem, Great Britain's "neutrality" was another. It meant at least that they gave the Confederacy the status of a "belligerent power." It was dangerous ground.

On May 21 Seward completed a draft of a dispatch of instructions to the American ambassador Charles Francis Adams, who had just arrived in London to take up his post. Seward's draft, responding to the British Declaration of Neutrality, was laced with truculent injections and signs of annoyance at what the British had done. Seward read the draft to the president, who, for all his alleged inexperience, managed to detect some things in it that shouldn't be said. Lincoln kept a copy and read it over. So here was the "rough farmer," the "child of nature" with his "comprehensive ignorance" and his "utter absence of any acquaintance with the subject," sitting there reading and editing this key document, his first intervention in world affairs. He made several small changes, all in the direction of making it less truculent and aggrieved. He spotted the most belligerent of Seward's

---

*"I would demand explanations from Spain and France, categorically, at once. I would seek explanations from Great Britain and Russia, and send agents into Canada, Mexico, and Central America, to rouse a vigorous continental spirit of independence on this continent against European intervention. And if satisfactory explanations are not received from Spain and France, would convene Congress and declare war against them." Seward's April 1 "considerations," *CW,* 4:317–18n.

flourishes, the rhetorically high-charged claim that "British recognition" of the pretended new state "would be British intervention to create within our own territory a hostile state by overthrowing this republic itself." And Seward had finished with a drumbeat echo of the Declaration of Independence: "When this act of intervention is distinctly performed, we from that hour shall cease to be friends and become once more, as we have twice before been forced to be, enemies of Great Britain." Lincoln said, Leave that out.

Lincoln also said to drop two long rhetorical paragraphs, a peroration with memories of the prose and events of 1776, with which Seward had ended the dispatch. As rousing as that prose might be to an American, an English reader, particularly a responsible official in the British government, would have found it rousing in a different way: 1776, and Jefferson's ringing apostrophes, would represent not inspiration but menace. "We see how," Seward had written, "upon the result of the debate we are now engaged, a war may ensue between the United States and one, two, or even more European nations"—again he grandly multiplied prospective imaginary wars. "[I]f it comes it will be fully seen that it results from the action of Great Britain, not our own, that Great Britain had decided to fraternize with our domestic enemy." Seward then made explicit the echoes he heard from the War for Independence: "A war not unlike it between the same parties occurred at the close of the last century. Europe atoned by forty years of suffering for the error that Great Britain committed in provoking that contest." If "that nation shall now repeat the same great error," there will be social convulsions, but afterward it will not be the United States "that will come out of them with its precious constitution altered or its honestly obtained dominion in any degree altered." If you were a British diplomat trained to detect implicit meanings, you would have detected Seward's hint of a threat: *go to war with us, and we will take over Canada.* Seward finished with more trumpet-sounding American pride and another echo of Jefferson. Jefferson had referred to the "last stab of agonized affection" for "our unfeeling brethren." Seward's version spoke of Britain now losing "forever . . . the sympathies and the affections of the only nation on whose sympathies and affections she has a natural claim."

Lincoln said, *Cut all that out.*

And then Lincoln adopted a better idea. Although technically this dispatch consisted of instructions to Ambassador Adams, Seward had also directed that a copy be delivered to the British Foreign Office, without elaboration. (Seward plainly had not been composing these sentences just for Adams's edification; his implied readers throughout were the British leaders.) Lincoln countermanded that instruction. After striking the last long paragraph, he substituted this sentence, which plainly is addressed just to the American ambassador: "This paper is for your own guidance, and not to be read or shown to any one." That solved it all. If the British Foreign Office had been presented with Seward's unqualified paper in its original form, without comment, they would have been required to take the kind of dark counterthreatening posture that diplomats representing the pride and interest of a nation must take. But Lincoln scotched that.

The situation was exacerbated by the memory of the performance of the garrulous Seward in the period leading up to the war. In the spring of 1860 he had made rather a practice of dropping anti-British remarks, and these of course came to be known in England. He had responded aggressively to signs of English acceptance of, or favor toward, the Confederacy. The Confederate government, now moved to Richmond, had in May sent as head of a delegation to London the hottest of fire-eaters, William L. Yancey, not—one would have thought—a very good choice for a sensitive diplomatic post. Seward was understandably upset when Lord Russell granted Yancey and his crew two meetings: from the American Union's point of view those men were insurgents, traitors, being granted an audience with the foreign secretary of an allegedly friendly nation. And then came the queen's Declaration of Neutrality. So Seward was irritated as he composed the electric dispatch to Adams that Lincoln quietly unplugged.

Lincoln's revision of his instruction left the skillful Adams room to be diplomatic in the way he conveyed to the British government American unhappiness about any British palaver with the American rebels. Although Lincoln may not have fully appreciated how good an ambassador Charles Francis Adams was, and although Adams certainly did not appreciate how good a president Lincoln was, the Union's relationship to Great Britain seems nevertheless to have been handled rather well, both in London and in Washington, given the disasters that might have happened.

Lord Russell indicated that there would be no more meetings with Yancey. Throughout the rest of 1861 relations between the Americans and the British simmered, until they came to a sudden boil in November, when the Confederacy named new and eminent emissaries to Britain and France, Senators Mason and Slidell, and when Captain Wilkes of the American navy, famous already for Antarctic expeditions, undertook his act of freelance derring-do.

. . .

In late November and the first days of December 1861, the president of the United States, in addition to handling a great many other activities, was preparing his first annual message to Congress, the constitutionally mandated report on the "State of the Union," to be intoned by a clerk over the heads of congressmen on December 3. In contrast to the message to the special session in July, which had been a powerful moral argument on central matters, this was one of those more characteristic lists for the governmental laundry. He folded in material from each department and proposed a new one, a Department of Agriculture. He said there was no reason to withhold recognition of two new black nations, Haiti and Liberia—an unthinkable position for any earlier American administration. If one wanted to know the U.S. government's revenue from all sources for the fiscal year ending June 30, 1861, down to the penny, in words and in numbers, it was here ($9,049,296.40). The war, military affairs, and foreign relations of course were not omitted. There is an early mention of the effort by the "disloyal portion" of the country to invoke foreign intervention, and even a reference to one incident the previous June involving Great Britain and the blockade. And yet in all these pages there was no mention whatever of the *Trent,* of the alleged hero Captain Wilkes, or of the capture of Mason and Slidell—the incident that was throbbing in the daily news exactly at the moment this message was being prepared and presented. That was a significant presidential silence.

To be sure, there had been from the start of this episode, for those Americans who would stop cheering for a moment and think, questions about proper national conduct. Captain Wilkes had defended his action with the novel theory that Mason and Slidell were the "embodiment of dispatches." Since a nation at war could stop the ship of a neutral on the high seas in order to seize enemy dispatches, his action could be justified on the ground that Mason and Slidell were themselves, in person, as it were, human enemy dispatches. But under that same international law, what Wilkes then should have done was to bring the ship into port so a prize court could judge the action. Wilkes had not done that. He had seized the two by force and sent the *Trent* on its way to St. Thomas, leaving the crew and outraged passengers to take a ship there to tell their tale in London.

Although much theorizing justifying Wilkes in international law blossomed in American centers in November and December 1861, some Americans from the outset did not think the seizure was such a good idea. Senator Sumner heard from his British friends—liberals, friends of the United States, opponents of secession and slavery—that all England was outraged and that the cabinet had met twice to contemplate war and that those eight thousand British troops were being sent to Canada. When he showed his correspondence to Lincoln, the troubled president told him "there will be no war unless England is bent on having one." The admiring Nicolay and Hay would write: "The President's usual cool judgment at once recognized the dangers and complications that might grow out of the occurrence." And they quote "a well-known writer" who recorded what Lincoln said "in a confidential interview" on the very day he heard the news: "I fear the traitors will prove to be white elephants."

One did not have to be an expert in international law to grasp the moral and practical shape of this incident. As Charles Francis Adams's son would write fifty years later, "The United States did not have, and never had, in reality, a justifying leg to stand upon." If an American would do the elementary moral exercise of reversing positions, of putting himself in the other's situation, he might come across a memory. Suppose a British man-of-war fired a shot across the bow of a merchant ship flying the American flag on the high seas, then sent a body of armed men onto the totally civilian ship, and suppose these armed intruders then demanded a list of those on board—wait, wasn't that exactly what happened not so long ago? Americans objected so strongly when the British navy at war with France did that in their "impressment" of sailors that it became a cause of the War of 1812. On the issue of freedom of the seas, the two nations seemed to have suddenly switched their positions.* And that opened an opportunity. That "well-known writer," whom Nicolay and Hay quote, reported that, after the remark about white elephants, Lincoln continued:

> We must stick to American principles concerning the rights of neutrals. We fought Great Britain for insisting, by theory and practice, on the right to do precisely what Captain Wilkes has done. If Great Britain shall now protest against the act, and demand their release, we must give them up, apologize for the act as a violation of our doctrines, and thus forever bind her over to keep the peace in relation to neutrals, and so acknowledge that she has been wrong for sixty years.

*Charles Francis Adams, Jr., in his article published more than a half century after the event, notes the irony that if there were *any* nation under whose interpretation of international law Wilkes's action back then might have been justified, it was that of Great Britain. "If it was the law and practice in Great Britain then, it was the law and practice nowhere else; least of all the United States."

If Lincoln did say that, on the very first day of the incident, then he surely did move swiftly to the heart of the matter.

Lincoln himself drafted a proposed American reply (never sent) to a dispatch from Lord Russell in which he pointed out that the American government "intended no affront to the British flag, or to the British nation," and that Wilkes had acted without the authority of his government. But, he wrote, since the act had been done, it was necessary to consider that the United States, like Great Britain, had "a people justly jealous of their rights." He proposed "such friendly arbitration as is usual among nations." Or if it could be established that the United States should make reparation, then "the determination thus made shall be the law for all future analogous cases, between Great Britain and the United States."

One may note in passing, about the moral dilemmas of American presidents, that this executive of an abruptly enlarged governmental apparatus was repeatedly put in this position: a (nominal) subordinate takes an action that the president neither ordered, nor had been told about, nor would have approved had he been told. Often indeed he might definitely have disapproved of the action. But he then nevertheless has to cope with a fait accompli for which he has a nominal responsibility and which has political consequences. In the present case—Charles Wilkes having taken his excessively bold action and a large segment of the American public having responded with an enthusiastic whoop—Lincoln would have to steer away from war with England without completely puncturing the balloon of his own public's proud thrill. The categorical requirement of his policy in this *Trent* episode was that it not end in war. Lincoln had an alternative formulation of his elementary judgment of prudence: his chief thought, he said, was to avoid the folly of having "two wars on his hands at a time."

Fortunately there was prudence also on the other side of the Atlantic, particularly in the person of Queen Victoria's husband, Prince Albert, who, though ill, in the last public act of his life, acting as confidential adviser and private secretary to the queen, cooled down the British cabinet's heated dispatch, which had been a virtual ultimatum and a demand for reparations. Prince Albert's changes make the dispatch rather an expression of Her Majesty's hope that she would be informed that the American captain had acted on his own, not under instruction from his government, and that the American government would spontaneously offer redress. (Perhaps it was Prince Albert who really *was* Lincoln's "great and good friend.")

On both sides the hot blood roused by the first outburst would have to be cooled and kept from further inflammation by the other side. Charles Sumner, who conferred often with the president during this affair, showed him letters from his friends, the great English reformers John Bright and Richard Cobden, who urged that the United States make "a courageous stroke, not of arms, but of moral action, in order to avert a war."

Britain asked that Mason and Slidell be released into British custody, with a suitable apology, and indicated that if this were not done within seven days, Lord Lyons and his delegation should withdraw from Washington. Although this last was not put exactly in the formidable shape of an "ultimatum," with all the somber attention-grabbing, mind-concentrating meaning that form of address has in world politics, and although the seven-day period was not to start until Lord Lyons actually presented his note to Seward (and Lord Lyons postponed presenting it), American decision-making nevertheless still had a certain clock-ticking urgency. And those eight thousand British troops were still headed for Canada.

At a four-hour cabinet discussion on Christmas Day, with Senator Sumner in attendance, Seward, now switching over to his diplomatic posture, argued for the release of the prisoners, and Sumner read letters from Cobden and Bright. Afterward Lincoln proposed to Seward that Seward draft a dispatch proposing the release of the prisoners while he, Lincoln, would write one opposing it, proposing arbitration. This last was evidently a ploy. Lincoln had already written the draft reply to Lord Russell insisting that Wilkes's act was not that of the government and that no affront to the British flag was intended—but nevertheless proposing "friendly arbitration." He wrote no new paper. The next day there was no Lincoln proposal; only Seward's was discussed.

Seward's dispatch was a bit of a tour de force. Captain Wilkes had gone wrong, he said, not in stopping and boarding the ship or extracting the Confederate emissaries—they were indeed contraband of war and capturing them had been legal—but rather in not then taking the ship to an American port where a prize court could have made the judgment. Wilkes's error was that he had done what the British had done in their impressments at the time of the War of 1812. So in pressing for Mason and Slidell's release, the British were now implicitly endorsing American principles, and the United States, in releasing them, was following "an old, honored, and cherished American cause." Whatever they thought of Seward's way of reaching the result, the cabinet did adopt his dispatch, and the message went out that Mason and Slidell would now be "cheerfully" released.

On New Year's Day a tugboat from Boston brought Mason and Slidell from Fort Warren to a British sloop anchored in Provincetown, and the *Trent* affair was over. Audiences in London theaters cheered when the announcement was made. Great Britain was happy to accept the release of the men as the equivalent of an apology. There would be no war.

Although avoiding war was mandatory, it was also quite important to let the air out of the balloon of truculent American jubilation *slowly*—not to puncture it abruptly. American pride could be assuaged by showing that even as we yielded, we achieved something at the same time—we brought Great Britain over to our view on freedom of the seas.

Seward was proud of his dispatch. Charles Sumner, who thought Seward's moral reasoning and knowledge of international law were defective, was even prouder of the address, well attended and adorned with learned quotations, that he gave in the Senate correcting Seward. Sumner agreed of course that the men had to be released, but for more fundamental moral reasons than Seward had stated.

In 1912 Charles Francis Adams, Jr., produced the article we have already referred to. With the convenient perspective of five decades and a radically altered world, Adams would find the heroes in the *Trent* affair to be not Seward, not Lincoln (scarcely mentioned), but rather an oddly assorted pair: the conservative postmaster general Montgomery Blair and the Radical chairman of the Senate Foreign Relations Committee Charles Sumner (and, subtly included, the father of the writer of the article, "Mr. Adams," the American ambassador in London). These two men wanted to do what the younger Adams, with the perfectionism of hindsight and insulated distance, thought should have been done. Mason and Slidell should have been released, not for Seward's complicated pseudo-English reasons but for American reasons: *We don't do that sort of thing. We have always believed in the freedom of the seas, the rights of neutrals, and we still do.* Blair (Adams wrote) saw immediately that Wilkes's action was indefensible and proposed that he be ordered to take Mason and Slidell back on the *San Jacinto* and deliver them to England. Adams was retrospectively thrilled by the effect he thought that such an act would have had: "What a magnificent move . . . how effectually a checkmate would have been administered to the game of both the Confederates and their European sympathizers!" Bullying Britain suddenly undercut in midfury! Maverick commanders like Wilkes rebuked! American principles of freedom of the seas categorically affirmed and dramatically practiced! Outrageous British naval treatment of neutrals unequivocally rejected!

Perhaps it was magnificent, abstractly considered, for the purpose of an article written fifty years later. But for a president in office at the time, it would have been the opposite. The point about morals in high politics presents itself again and again: being "right" in the abstract can be only one consideration; timing is everything; context is everything. Of course what Wilkes did was both wrong and a blunder. Of course Mason and Slidell would have to be turned over. But to have slapped Wilkes in the face and abruptly punctured American glee, letting down the public ecstasy with a tremendous deflationary bump, in order to chortle at British discomfiture at your having done already what they were just rousing the indignant demand that you do—that would have been not magnificent but disastrous. For an American president the state of American public opinion is a fact not to be ignored.

Lincoln's quieter, slower, less dramatic course was much wiser. Historian James Randall in the middle of the next century would give this summary:

> Though Lincoln's part in the episode was not publicized, it was of decisive importance. It is now possible to see the president's contribution in his restraint, his avoidance of any outward expression of truculence, his early softening of the state department's attitude toward Britain, his deference toward Seward and Sumner, his withholding of his own paper prepared for the occasion, his readiness to arbitrate, his golden silence in addressing Congress, his shrewdness in recognizing that war must be averted, and his clear perception that a point could be clinched for America's true position at the same time that full satisfaction was given to a friendly country.

THE HAPPY RESULT of the *Trent* affair as it actually did play out was not only that war was avoided and American principles about ships at sea affirmed but also that relationships between Britain and the United States were momentarily improved. But only momentarily.

Lincoln would soon have other occasions in which he would need wisdom and restraint to restrict the number of wars he was engaging in to the manageable number he had specified.

There would continue to be, at a lower temperature, simmering disagreements with the British and the French. Nicolay and Hay wrote that "the original mistake of the French and the British governments" was in "putting upon equal terms a great and friendly power and the insurgent organization of a portion of its citizens." One result was the building and fitting out in British ports of Confederate raiders like the *Alabama*. Constructed in the Liverpool shipyards of a Confederate-sympathizing member of Parliament, its orders were "to sink, burn, or destroy everything which flew the ensign of the so-called United States of America." The *Alabama* proceeded to do that for almost two years, capturing or burning more than two dozen American ships, until she herself was sunk by an American ship in 1864. "The vessel was English, the armament was English, almost all the crew was English"; but she did the destructive deeds of the American insurgency. American ambassador Adams steadily, patiently, firmly protested to the English government. Nicolay and Hay would write: "In reviewing this long correspondence, one would hesitate to say that the British government was actuated by feelings positively unfriendly to the United States. It is easier to conclude that not being sure which side would win and being entirely indifferent to the contest between the federal government and the rebellion, it stood simply on the letter of the English law."

Lincoln was acutely aware of the importance of that "not being sure which side would win." He wanted to *make* them sure, and soon.

War rumblings would arise in 1864–65 over the toleration of Confederate nests in British-controlled Canada, out of which came terrorist raids, political interventions in midwestern elections, and notorious acts of rebel daring: the capture and sinking of a ship on Lake Erie; an attempt to free rebel prisoners in the Union prison Johnson Island; the derailing of a train in upstate New York; an attempt to burn thirty-two buildings, including ten hotels and Barnum's Museum, in New York City.

Late in 1864 there was a raid from a Canadian base on St. Albans, Vermont, in which the town was plundered, banks robbed, horses stolen, and one citizen killed. When a posse captured the raiders, a British major demanded that they be turned over to Canadian authorities. And a Canadian magistrate, instead of extraditing them, outraged American opinion by releasing them.

So there was belligerent talk, even of war. General John A. Dix, commanding in New York, on his own angry initiative ordered all commanders to shoot such invaders, to pursue raiders over the border into Canada, and "under no circumstances" to turn over captured raiders to British authorities in Canada. The British could not take lightly that infringement on British sovereignty.

But Lincoln the next day revoked Dix's order. Here was another example of the maverick subordinate. This time it could be solved. The Canadian prime minister, appreciating Lincoln's quick revocation of Dix's order, took steps to rearrest the fugitives, recompense St. Albans, and patrol the border. Lincoln for his part then set aside a proposal that passports be required to enter the United States from Canada.

France offered additional chances to multiply wars. Lincoln's allegedly good friend the Emperor Napoleon III granted interviews to the Confederate emissary John Slidell (momentarily elevated to fame by the *Trent* affair), told Slidell of his sympathy with the South, and proposed that France too get into the business of building Confederate ships. In 1864 Napoleon intervened in Mexico and set up a puppet regime. Lincoln privately deplored the setting up of an imperial, nonrepublican regime in the Western Hemisphere, but in his public statements he assured the French government that the United States had no intention to intervene and was not hostile either to France or to its puppet. Now it was the American turn to be strictly neutral. This president did *not* do what many Radicals in Congress and loud voices in the press insisted he ought to do: he did *not* invoke the Monroe Doctrine. This was another extra war he was not going to encourage.

Lincoln was in foreign affairs what admirers would one day praise him for in military affairs: one who without experience and without technical knowledge nevertheless "grasped the main facts and gave them their proper value." He not only listened to and learned from but also managed Seward, Sumner, and even Adams.

He was also the key agent making strong currents that moved much deeper than the episodes on the surface: bringing the rulers and peoples of the world to see who would win the war and what the war was about. The victories he was constantly pushing for finally demonstrated that the U.S. government would prevail in the end, so realistic power-balancing governments of the world would begin to tilt accordingly.

Meanwhile, he had generated another force that went beyond all that; in the Emancipation Proclamation and steps he took after it, he redefined for the world the moral meaning of the one war in which he was engaged.

THE AMERICAN CIVIL WAR had an enormous presence in British public opinion. Aristocrats, Tories, the British upper classes, and the thundering *Times* tended to favor those gentlemen in the South who wanted to separate from the vulgar democracy and crass Yankee materialism in the North.

A distinguished modern American historian would write: "[I]t remains one of the unsolved mysteries of nineteenth century history that the most anti-slavery nation on earth, Great Britain, harbored so much sentimental identification with the Confederacy."

That identification was, however, far from universal; radical and liberal opinion in the middle and working classes of England included a considerable support for the Union. Lincoln saw that this support could be encouraged by American action—which he vigorously set out to provide.

Lincoln had a realistic awareness of the economic context of slavery that not every opponent of slavery, distant from the institution, would display. In one potent argument indicating the spread of general complicity in it, he observed "how unhesitatingly we all use cotton and sugar, and share the profits in dealing in them."

As the war, and the blockade, moved into late 1862, that unhesitating use of cotton, and sharing in profits, had international consequences. King Cotton, American slavery's biggest crop, was made into clothing in Lancashire in England. When the American Civil War broke out and Lincoln ordered the blockade of Southern ports, it shut off the supply of raw cotton to the English mills. They had sufficient goods to last the duration of the short war that was then generally expected, but by October 1861 the mills began to cut back or close, and workers were put on short hours or thrown out of work. Soup kitchens sprang up. "Outdoor relief." The dole. Pawnshops. Unemployed young men roamed the streets. "The American Civil War was becoming a matter of dire concern," Bruce Catton writes, "to hundreds of thousands of men and women who had barely heard of Abraham Lincoln or Jefferson Davis and did not know Alabama from Michigan."

At the time the cotton famine was at its worst, in September and October 1862, the political leaders of Great Britain would have their severest temptation to intervene in the American war. McClellan's huge and well-drilled Army of the Potomac had accomplished nothing. The Union armies had managed to be defeated twice now at Bull Run. Robert E. Lee was poised to take the offensive, striking north. The great British liberal W. E. Gladstone, chancellor of the exchequer, in a speech in Newcastle October 7 said:

Jefferson Davis and other leaders of the South have made an army; they are making, it appears, a navy; and they have made what is more than either—they have made a nation . . . We may anticipate with certainty the success of the Southern States so far as regards their separation from the North.

The British cabinet considered making a formal proposal to mediate the American war, an intervention that would have ripped the Union and implicitly granted the rebels all that they wanted.

But in these same months came a tremendous contending influence on British opinion: the preliminary emancipation proclamation on September 22 and the final Emancipation Proclamation on New Year's Day of 1863. The London *Times* would sneer that Lincoln had freed the slaves where he had no power but kept slaves in bondage where he did have power; but for broad segments of English opinion the proclamation clinched the identification of the South with slavery, the North with freedom, and the American war with the universal struggle for justice.

A series of "remarkable meetings" were held in "York, Bolton, Halifax, Sheffield, Birmingham, Leicester, Preston, Coventry, Manchester, and at the Great Exeter Hall in London." James Randall calls them "spontaneous gatherings"; David Herbert Donald writes that "Lincoln himself began a campaign to win popular support in Great Britain, where, with some hidden subvention from American funds, numerous public meetings were held."

In Manchester and in London great meetings were held on the evening of December 31, 1862, in anticipation of Lincoln's signing of the Emancipation Proclamation the next day. The meetings affirmed central Lincolnian points: the unique place of the United States in the history of liberty and equality ("a singular, happy abode for the working millions"); the one huge wrong, human slavery, that alone marred that distinct place ("the slavery and degradation of men guilty only of a colored skin or an African parentage"); and the significance of the Union effort, and Lincoln's deeds, in overcoming that one huge wrong ("we have discerned . . . that the victory of the free North . . . will strike off the fetters of the slave.")

These British meetings addressed him; Lincoln could then write a response.

I know and deeply deplore the sufferings which the workingmen at Manchester and in all Europe are called to endure in this crisis.

It has been often . . . represented that the attempt to overthrow this government, which was built upon the foundation of human rights, and to substitute for it one which should rest exclusively on the basis of human slavery, was likely to obtain the favor of Europe.

Through the actions of our disloyal citizens the workingmen of Europe have been subjected to a severe trial, for the purpose of forcing their sanction to that attempt . . .

Under these circumstances, I cannot but regard your decisive utterance . . . as an instance of sublime Christian heroism which has not been surpassed in any age or in any country.

To tell the truth, the great meetings in Manchester and the other cities were more the doing of middle-class reformers than of actual textile mill workers ("workingmen and others," the Manchester statement said significantly). And the opinions of actual working-class families about the American war were varied. And to be sure, the Confederacy did not deliberately cause the cotton famine in order to bring Europe to its side. Nevertheless, many textile mill working-class families in the English Midlands, offered the chance to blame their economic distress on the Union's refusal to let the cotton South go, would, to their own perceived disadvantage, support Lincoln in a war against human slavery.

Lincoln said this was a "reinspiring assurance of . . . the ultimate and universal triumph of justice, humanity, and freedom."

To "the workingmen of London," Lincoln anticipated Gettysburg: "It seems to have devolved [upon the American people] to test whether a government, established on the principles of human freedom, can be maintained against an effort to build one upon the exclusive foundation of human bondage."

Rebel intellectuals and English sympathizers liked to compare the Confederacy to Greece and Rome. Lincoln cut that connection: the Confederacy alone was uniquely, exclusively, originally founded on slavery, promoting slavery.

Lincoln did not often use the word "Christian" as a moral modifier, but it came to his pen in the winter and spring of 1863 when he addressed Englishmen. Apparently he felt that when he was addressing Europe, he should invoke her ancient religious identity as a moral norm. The previous summer when a disgruntled McClellan had insisted that the war be conducted "upon the highest principles known to Christian civilization," he had meant a gentlemanly limited war that protected property (including slavery). When Lincoln used the word "Christian" in his praise for the workingmen's "sublime Christian heroism," he meant self-sacrifice for righteous principle—against the evil of slavery. When he wrote of "the family of Christian and civilized nations" and "all Christian and civilized men everywhere," he meant nations, and human beings, who treat all men with charity as children of God—rejecting the monstrous injustice of slavery.

These last two phrases appear in a curious little document that Lincoln wrote in the spring of 1863. One day in April Lincoln sent for Senator

Sumner and showed him a proposed resolution, written in his own hand on the back of a page of executive mansion stationery, which he said might be adopted by public meetings in England. There is no record of this actually happening—an English public gathering adopting this resolution ghostwritten for them by an American president—but it is interesting to see what he tried to get them to say.* Lincoln would be particularly intent to plant firmly in British opinion the understanding of the Confederacy as a uniquely obnoxious government in the "Christian" West. Whereas some nations in the past had tolerated slavery, the Confederacy proposed now to construct a new nation "upon the basis of, and with the primary, and fundamental object to maintain, enlarge, and perpetuate human slavery." The proposal Lincoln drafted resolved then that no such state "should ever be recognized by, or admitted into, the family of Christian and civilized nations and that all Christian and civilized men everywhere should . . . resist to the utmost such recognition or admission."

The English friend to whom Sumner sent this proposal—sent the actual paper itself with Lincoln's signature—was the great liberal parliamentary leader John Bright, who was a strong supporter of the American Union. At the time of the *Trent* affair Bright had given a speech in Rochdale that helped to dampen the fire of British outrage. During the cotton famine in December 1862 Bright gave an address in Birmingham about American politics that included a quotation from a source that Lincoln knew well, Thomas Gray's "Elegy Written in a Country Churchyard." The quatrain from which Bright borrowed, assuming his hearers would recognize it, deals with vicious acts that, along with glorious accomplishments, the poor folk in this cemetery were prevented from achieving by "chill penury." By being born poor they missed their chance to "wade through slaughter to a throne, and shut the gates of mercy on mankind." Bright changed the word "slaughter" to the word "slavery" and applied the lines to the project of the Confederacy. Abraham Lincoln found it to be something he wanted to preserve and wrote it out in his own hand: "I can not believe that civilization, in its journey with the sun, will sink into endless night, to gratify the ambition of the leaders of this revolt, who seek to wade through slavery to a throne, and shut the gate of mercy on mankind."

---

*If any English public gathering *had* adopted the ghostwritten resolution, Lincoln would surely have produced a response fully endorsing everything they had said. Then we would have had a nice parallel to that wonderful moment back in 1789 when James Madison wrote the House's response to President Washington's inaugural—which Madison himself had drafted—and then drafted Washington's reply to the response he had written for the House.

CHAPTER ELEVEN

Too Vast for Malicious Dealing

NOT MANY HEADS OF STATE with Lincoln's power of appointment would maintain in the two most eminent positions in their nation's military, as Lincoln did throughout most of 1862, two men who were capable of calling him a "gorilla." General McClellan had already, in letters to his wife back in 1861 when he first arrived in town, called the president an "idiot" (August 16) and a "well-meaning baboon" (October 11); then in a letter on November 17 he referred to Lincoln as "the *original* gorilla" and again as "the gorilla," putting these terms in quotation marks to indicate he was borrowing them from his new friend, the attorney general left over from the Buchanan administration, Edwin Stanton. For a brief time in late 1861 these two Democrats collaborated, and part of their collaboration was their shared disdain for the Republican president. When McClellan wrote to his wife, on October 31, 1861, that he was "concealed" in order to dodge all enemies in the shape of browsing presidents, it was in Stanton's house that he was hiding.

If Lincoln had been a holder of grudges, Edwin Stanton would have been a prime candidate for a Lincoln grudge. Back in 1855 Lincoln the provincial lawyer had been royally snubbed in a national law case about reapers in Cincinnati, and Stanton had been a full participant in the snubbing.

Stanton's anti-Lincoln sins were then compounded when Lincoln, unlikely as it would have seemed to anyone in the Cincinnati courtroom in 1855, had been nominated by the new Republican Party and elected president of the United States in 1860, and Stanton, as one of the few in Buchanan's Washington who had ever met this westerner, had made no secret that he thought him a "low, cunning clown." In the first months of the Lincoln administration Stanton, writing to fellow Democrats, applied to the new president a term of abuse widely used in nineteenth-century

American politics: "imbecility." And then he met fellow Democrat George McClellan and joined him in comparing the president to primates.

Nevertheless, when in mid-January 1862 Lincoln was able to move the feckless Simon Cameron out of the War Department and appoint him minister to Russia, he reached out and appointed the able, experienced, and strongly Union-supporting Democrat Edwin Stanton to the centrally important position of secretary of war, which turned out to be a superb appointment.

Stanton's opinion of Lincoln soon changed radically, and his opinion of McClellan changed radically too. And Stanton was soon at the top of McClellan's enemies list. Stanton took the telegraph office away from McClellan's headquarters and located it in the War Department, and on examining the files he gave voice to an opinion about McClellan's dilatory parading around in Washington that was destined to be repeated often in histories of the war: "While men are striving nobly in the West, the champagne and oysters on the Potomac must be stopped."

Stanton's biographers would say about Lincoln and Stanton: "[B]ecause Lincoln was a great man, Stanton reached in his service a plane far higher than his more prosaic spirit could have touched." McClellan's biographers would say nothing of the kind.

In his valedictory outburst in late October 1862, McClellan would revert to his prime epithet, and he would significantly include "socially" in the list of his superiorities: "[T]he good of the country requires me to submit to all this ['mean and dirty' dispatches, 'wretched innuendo'] from men whom I know to be greatly my inferiors socially, intellectually, and morally! There never was a truer epithet applied to a certain individual than that of the 'Gorilla.' "

Stanton's contrasting valedictory to Lincoln would come on April 14, 1865: "Now he belongs to the ages."

LINCOLN TAKES DEFINITIVE STEPS

IF YOU HAD KNOWN LINCOLN in Illinois before he became president, you would not have been surprised that in the presidency he would be capable of overlooking slights to himself and would be forbearing and generous. What you could not have known—what Lincoln himself did not know— was whether he could, at the same time, command armies and make the demanding decisions of a nation at war. He had been an active politician, a writer of excellent speeches, and a political organizer, and in those roles he had been an unusually kind and forgiving person. But did he have, to use the phrase of a future secretary of state, Dean Acheson, "the stuff of command"?

The stuff of command, especially in a giant deadly conflict, would not seem ordinarily to combine very well with the stuff of forbearance and generosity. Executive skill and vigor, like a surgeon's skill, would appear to require a certain withdrawal of empathy. The resolution necessary to great statesmanship would appear to invite, if not even to require, a certain ruthlessness with those whose wills and whose complex humanity complicate, impede, and even defy one's vigorously pursued purpose.

A moral agent who has as his gigantic central duty the preservation of a nation (as Lincoln suddenly would) would have to use the ultimate resort, violent coercion—physical force, armies, navies, artillery, bombardment, killing an opposing force. This nation-state, like all others, would have a "monopoly of legitimate violence" and would use that means to defend itself at the decision of a political leader, with all the moral hazards that entails. Would the amiable politician from the plains be able to do that well?

Lincoln showed that he could make shrewd decisions about the use of force right away in the first days of his presidency, but the necessity of making more decisions kept coming.

Every day of Lincoln's presidency was fraught with wartime decision, but some moments were even heavier than others: April 1861, and the aftermath of Bull Run in July, as we have seen. In July 1862 President Lincoln would face another particularly heavy moment. He had to make huge decisions that altered the character of the war.

When General McClellan did not go "on to Richmond" and Union hopes slumped, Lincoln had to confront the fact that this rebellion against the United States was not going to be suppressed by the limited means with which the Union at first had conducted the war.

On July 7–10, 1862, Lincoln visited McClellan at his peninsula headquarters and, as we have seen, did not respond to this general's presumptuous letter proposing a limited war that did not touch slavery. On July 12, in a famous carriage ride, Lincoln revealed to two cabinet members his intention to issue a proclamation that would free slaves in territory still in rebellion. At a cabinet meeting on July 21 the president, according to Secretary Chase's diary, revealed that he "had been profoundly concerned at the present state of affairs, and had determined to take some definitive steps in respect to military action and slavery." It is significant that the first whisper of the Emancipation Proclamation and the military steps to a wider war were decided upon together. The "definitive steps" about slavery would come to include the preliminary emancipation proclamation, a draft of which he would read to the cabinet on the next day, July 22.

Still on July 21, though, he would propose the "definitive steps" with respect to "military action." He read to the cabinet an order which "contemplated authority to Commanders to subsist their troops in the hostile territory," and this proposed order, according to Chase, was, after discussion, unanimously approved.

The first item in Lincoln's executive order specified that military commanders in nine rebel states, starting with Virginia, should "[i]n an orderly manner, seize and use any property, real or personal, which may be necessary or convenient for their several commands for supplies or for other military purposes."

He did specify also the limiting restraints: "While property may be destroyed for proper military objects, none shall be destroyed in wantonness or malice."

But the harder war, the warfare that included appropriation and destruction of enemy property that began in 1862 and would lead to wider destruction in 1863 and 1864, and to Sherman's march across the Deep South and Sheridan's 1864 campaign in the Shenandoah Valley, had one of its beginnings in the decisions of a determined president in the summer of 1862.

Lincoln had already in June brought east the aggressive and ambitious General John Pope, a victor in an important battle in the West, and given him command of a newly assembled Union army. Pope issued a series of orders authorizing his army to live off the land and to punish civilians who supported guerrillas.

McClellan was outraged by all of Pope's orders (and implicitly by Lincoln's as well) and insisted that for any property *his* army had to take, there would be *receipts*. He told his wife that he would issue an order that would give "directly the reverse instructions" to his army and "take the highest Christian ground." In the order itself he would insist, with all the invidious implication of saying so, that the war "should be conducted up on the highest principles known to Christian civilization."

An explicitly "moral" twenty-first-century critic of Lincoln's conduct of the war, Harry Stout of Yale, laments the disappearance, with McClellan's departure, of those high Christian principles, and says this about Lincoln's presumably less "Christian" decisions at this moment in 1862: "When forced to choose between principled war and victory, Lincoln chose victory." One may suggest that this formulation is doubly perverse. In the first place it implies that Lincoln, seeking mere victory, threw over all moral restraints in the conduct of the war, which is false. Lincoln continued to observe and to help his armies to observe, even in the passions of warfare, the moral restraints of what he would call "civilized belligerents," as we will see in Chapter 18.

But in the second place that formulation is perverse because it discounts (as mere "victory" devoid of "principle") Lincoln's overriding duty, to preserve the Union—implying no moral weight whatever for that vast and sacred trust, that huge good (keeping in being the United States and hence its contribution to the world the possibility of republican government). He had to prevent huge evils (the "destruction," the "overthrow," of the United States and the coming into being of a new slave empire). "Victory" for Lincoln was not an amoral objective in the realm only of power but a stringent personal obligation entailing a huge historic good for the whole human family. Lincoln would be a principled warrior for a principled victory.

It is to be remembered that McClellan's war "conducted upon the highest principles known to Christian civilization" included among its principles a repudiation of all confiscation of property—including property in slaves. "Forcible abolition of slavery," wrote McClellan, should not be "contemplated for a moment." And on Lincoln's side the new orders included the taking of property—and the freeing of that peculiar form of property, millions of human beings held in bondage. The "harder" war and emancipation were bound together.

FACING THE ARITHMETIC

FOR ALL HIS KINDLINESS and magnanimity, this president was proving himself capable of facing the realities of a giant war.

The battle of Fredericksburg in December 1862 was one of the most appalling defeats of a Union army in the entire war. Ambrose Burnside sent the Army of the Potomac in a series of frontal attacks on entrenched Confederate positions on the heights behind the town that resulted in staggering Union casualties particularly as compared with Confederate casualties.* The president, like everyone else in the federal establishment, was of course dismayed, but one of his secretaries, William O. Stoddard, reported

---

*Estimated Union casualties were 18,000; Confederates, 4,500.

that at the same time Lincoln also made this bluntly realistic assessment—notable for his recognition of the *arithmetic* and of the toll that *disease* took as men dawdled in camps:

> If the same battle were to be fought over again, every day, through a week of days, with the same relative results, the army under Lee would be wiped out to its last man, the Army of the Potomac would still be a mighty host, the war would be over, the Confederacy gone, and peace would be won at a smaller cost of life than it will be if the week of lost battles must be dragged out through yet another year of camps and marches, and of deaths in hospitals rather than upon the field. No general yet found can face the arithmetic, but the end of the war will be at hand when he shall be discovered.

Lincoln himself was able to "face the arithmetic" in the stern calculations of a major war. He was able to make decisions, even going against the grain of advice, as he did on his first day in office and throughout the demanding period up to the fall of Sumter, and then in the radically altered context after the fall of Sumter, giving shape to the clarified public will, doing what needed to be done to save the capital city and build the armed services. He would begin to show his resilience after the stunning, altogether unexpected debacle at Bull Run. Lincoln would come to have, in his own way, the steadfast strength of will to direct collective action. He could discern the contours of a situation; there are paragraphs in his letters to generals that show a most extraordinary grasp of detail. At the same time he could relate political to military requirements, and both to moral purpose; he could bring others to his will by persuasion perhaps more than some great statesmen but by command as well. And he could persist, remaining steadfast in pursuit of his purpose, as he would have the most wrenching occasions to demonstrate.

MAJOR KEY AND THE PURPOSE OF THE WAR

THAT THE TENDERHEARTED Lincoln was capable of making hard decisions could be seen not only in the large matters but in lesser matters involving one person only: for example, the case of Major John Key. Among the many individual cases that came to Lincoln's attention, this one was unusual in that it arose from Lincoln's own initiative and in that it set Lincoln's sympathy for the bereaved directly against high policy.

Lincoln learned, in late September 1862, that Major John J. Key, the brother of an important aide to McClellan, when asked by a fellow officer the baffling question of why the Army of the Potomac had not pursued and destroyed the rebel army after Antietam, had replied: "That is not the game. The object is that neither army shall get much advantage of the other; that both shall be kept in the field till they are exhausted, when we will make a compromise and save slavery."*

Lincoln called in and cross-examined Major Key and also Major Levi Turner, to whom the comments had been made. Receiving confirmation, he dismissed Key from the Union army: "In my view it is wholly inadmissible for any gentleman holding a military commission from the United States to utter such sentiments."

Key had friends. General Halleck supported him. Major Turner insisted he had never heard Key say anything disloyal. Key himself protested that he was altogether loyal to the Union. And then came an event that might have been expected to clinch his reinstatement with a tenderhearted president: on November 11, 1862, in the battle near Perryville, Kentucky, Major Key's eighteen-year-old son, James (or Joseph) Key, of the 50th Ohio Volunteers, was wounded, then died of his wounds. So Major Key was now a bereaved parent, the father of a soldier who had died fighting for the Union. Major Key now asked Lincoln for reinstatement.

Lincoln wrote this response on November 24, 1862:

A bundle of letters including one from yourself, was . . . handed me by Gen. Halleck . . . I sincerely sympathise with you in the death of your brave and noble son.

In regard to my dismissal of yourself . . . , it seems to me you misunderstand me. I did not charge . . . you with disloyalty. I had been brought to fear that there was a class of officers in the army . . . , who were playing a game to not beat the enemy when they could, on some peculiar notion as to the proper way of saving the Union; and when you were proved to me, in your own presence, to have avowed yourself in favor of that "game," and did not attempt to controvert the proof, I dismissed you as an example and a warning . . .

I bear you no ill will; and I regret that I could not have the example without wounding you personally. But can I now, in view of the public interest, restore you to the service, by which the army would understand

*A document in Lincoln's handwriting, together with the editors' note, in *CW,* 5:442–43, tells the story of the dismissal of Major Key.

that I . . . approve that game myself? If there was any doubt of your having made the avowal, the case would be different. But when it was proved to me, in your presence, you did not deny . . . it, but confirmed it in my mind, by attempting to sustain the position by argument.

I am really sorry for the pain the case gives you, but I do not see how, consistently with duty, I can change it. Yours, &c.

A. LINCOLN

When Lincoln told John Hay about his dismissal of McClellan, he followed immediately with a reference to the Key case: "I dismissed Major Key for his silly treasonable talk because I feared it was staff talk and I wanted an example"—staff talk in the circles around McClellan about holding back so as to save slavery.

THE GENEROSITY OF A STATESMAN

SO PERHAPS THE QUESTION about the original kindly Lincoln would now reverse itself.

Might it then be that the Illinois politician who taught himself to make the mammoth decisions he made, who broadened the war, faced the arithmetic of army deaths, and gathered his strength to fire silly-talking majors and dismiss generals, would no longer be the generous man he had been? The answer to that question came very soon and kept coming. The golden thread of magnanimity and generosity that would wind its way through his presidency had already been apparent in his choice of the three strongest candidates opposing him for the Republican nomination—four if you count Cameron—for the most important positions in his cabinet. To be sure, there were political considerations in doing so; he needed Seward and Chase in particular, and Bates too, to help consolidate behind the administration the diverse elements of the still-new Republican Party. All presidents have considerations of these kinds, but, still, other presidents have not appointed *all* of their top defeated rivals to the top cabinet posts.

Even in the immediate crushing pressure of the Sumter crisis, little indications of this great quality of this president had appeared. Four days into his presidency, in the midst of the crunch of decisions about Fort Sumter, President Lincoln took time to write a careful letter of explanation to a perhaps disappointed candidate for a cabinet position. He put into insistent words what would *not* guide him in his administration. Caleb Smith was named secretary of the interior almost certainly because he came from Indiana and thereby provided a needed geographical spread, and also perhaps because he had made a well-timed seconding speech for Lincoln in Chicago. But another Hoosier might have received that appointment, the rising Republican congressman Schuyler Colfax. Significantly Lincoln, soon after taking office in 1861, went out of his way to write to Colfax to explain why he had appointed Caleb Smith and to insist that Colfax's own support for Douglas for the Illinois Senate seat in 1858 had nothing to do with the matter ("Indeed, I should have decided as I did, easier than I did, had that matter never existed"). He concluded with the characteristic Lincolnian plea: "I now have to beg that you will not do me the injustice to suppose, for a moment, that I remembered anything against you in malice."

QUARREL NOT AT ALL

PRESIDENT LINCOLN'S charity and nonvindictiveness were explicit and reasoned. Although something in the given nature of a boy who told his classmates not to put hot coals on the backs of turtles no doubt made its contribution, this quality was a reflection not merely of an original disposition but of thought.

Both in public speeches and in private letters, both in informal comment and in formal orders, he made explicit reference to avoiding malice and to not seeking revenge and to not planting thorns often enough to indicate that it was a developed and settled conviction.

Among the many instances of Lincoln's explicit rejection of political resentments was his prudent response, recorded in Hay's diary, to the glee of Welles and Fox at the defeat of two men they regarded as enemies of the Navy Department. "You have more of that feeling of personal resentment than I," Hay quotes Lincoln as saying. "Perhaps I have too little of it, but I never thought it paid. A man has not the time to spend half his life in quarrels. If a man ceases to attack me, I never remember the past against him."

The full text of a letter of Lincoln's about avoiding quarrels was not discovered until 1947, when his papers were opened, although Nicolay and Hay had published part of it. In his diary for October 23, 1863, John Hay attached a copy of this letter, together with the remark that it contained "rather the mildest cussing on record." The person so mildly cussed was James Madison Cutts, who had connections both to Stephen Douglas and to Dolley Madison. "The poor devil seems heartbroken," wrote Hay. "He can scarcely stare one in the face."

Cutts's connections, and his sins, were as follows. Douglas's first wife died in 1853, and in 1856 he married a grandniece of Dolley Madison named Adele Cutts. She had a brother named James Madison Cutts, who served as Douglas's secretary through the 1860 campaign (thus campaigning, obviously, against Lincoln). When war came, Cutts enlisted at first as a private but then presented Lincoln a letter of recommendation from Douglas, and in May 1861 the president appointed him a captain. On the staff of General Burnside, he came to be charged with two rather disparate offenses: he was caught in a hotel hallway standing on a suitcase peering over the transom at a woman dressing (offense number one) and (offense two) he fiercely attacked Burnside, his commanding officer, in letters that he sent to the president, and quarreled with his fellow officers. This rather oddly assorted pair of offenses led a court-martial to find him guilty of conduct unbecoming an officer and a gentleman and to dismiss him from the army.

The case came to the commander in chief. The transom offense evoked from Lincoln not just one but two puns—that Cutts might be elevated to the "peerage" and that his title might be "Count Piper" (pronounced "Peeper"; Lincoln's pun and allusion were probably suggested by the name of the Swedish minister Edward Count Piper). Lincoln upheld the findings of the court-martial but reduced the penalty to a reprimand, and wrote to young Cutts this letter:

Executive Mansion
Washington Oct 26, 1863

Capt. James M. Cutts,

Although what I am now to say is to be, in form, a reprimand, it is not intended to add a pang to what you have already suffered on the subject to which it relates.

Part of the point of a reprimand is to add such a pang, but apparently not at the hands of Abraham Lincoln.

You have too much of life yet before you, and have shown too much of promise as an officer, for your future to be lightly surrendered.

The transom-peeping offense the no-pang president sets aside without much fuss.

> You are convicted of two offenses. One of them, not of great enormity, and yet greatly to be avoided, I feel sure you are in no danger of repeating.

Cutts's contentious behavior, his attacks on and quarrels with his fellow officers and even his commanding general, on the other hand, provoked Lincoln to interesting moral instruction.

> The other [offense] you are not so well assured against. The advice of a father to his son, "Beware of entrance to a quarrel, but being in, bear it that the opposed may beware of thee" is good, but not the best.

That was Lincoln's equivalent of "Ye have heard of old time." Now comes the "But I say unto you."

> Quarrel not at all. No man resolved to make the most of himself, can spare time for personal contention. Still less can he afford to take all the consequences, including the vitiating of his temper and the loss of self-control.

Maintaining self-control was of central importance to Lincoln; it was one of the reasons he did not drink. Now comes the further specific injunction:

> Yield larger things to which you can show no more than equal right; and yield lesser ones, though clearly your own.

Interpreting Lincoln, we might say: We overestimate our own interest, and we underestimate our adversary's, so that the advice to yield on all small matters, and on all matters that even to our distorting eyes seem equally balanced, is a moral corrective. Here is a lawyer, and a politician, and a war leader in the midst of tremendous battles giving this surprising advice: quarrel not at all.

NOT ALTOGETHER FREE OF RIDICULE:
I AM USED TO IT

WE MAY SURMISE that a key reason that President Lincoln was able to combine tenacious resolve with remarkable generosity was that the "clear-eyed objectivity" with which he saw the world extended also to himself.

Lincoln's resolution and strength of will did not spring from, or lead to, mindless stubbornness or egotistical willfulness. A strong will, as most human beings have occasion to know, is not necessarily a blessing in a person with a great deal of power. Often it is heavily interwoven with egotism and self-absorption. Often those dirges sung by leaders in high places about how "tough" their decisions have to be, and how strong they have to be to make those "tough" decisions, involve a good deal of self-sympathizing. Lincoln was not like that. Let us say he was able to be detached. His self, his ego, did not get in the way of his decisions.

As a sample of both his ability to forgive and his objectivity about himself, we may tell the story of his dealing with a Shakespearean actor named James H. Hackett. It is not an episode in which any great public issue was involved, but it is quite revealing about the central figure.*

In Washington Abraham Lincoln, for the first time in his life, had a chance to see Shakespeare performed on the stage. An actor he saw, James H. Hackett, famous for his Falstaff, pleased that the president of the United States had "favored" him by a "spontaneous" visit to see his "personation" of Falstaff in *Henry IV*, sent Lincoln a book he had written, *Notes and Comments upon Certain Plays and Actors of Shakespeare*, in which Hackett made some points about "that renowned character." That was in March 1863. It took the busy president some months to thank Hackett for the gift, but when he did, perhaps by way of additional apology for the long delay, or perhaps because he was pleased to be dealing with someone other than an impertinent general, on a topic other than the war, he threw in some comments:

> For one of my age, I have seen very little of the drama. The first presentation of Falstaff I ever saw was yours here, last winter or spring. Perhaps the best compliment I can pay is to say, as I truly can, I am very anxious to see it again.

Then Lincoln indulged in a personal comment about his relationship to Shakespeare: "Some of Shakspeare's plays I have never read; while

---

*The James Hackett story can be found in two letters Lincoln wrote to him: the letter of August 17, 1863, *CW*, 6:392–93, and Lincoln's great response—"I am used to it"—written on November 2, 1863, *CW*, 6:558–59. See the notes to both letters.

others I have gone over perhaps as frequently as any unprofessional reader." He listed the plays he had read most often and liked especially, particularly *Macbeth*, and he ventured the opinion that in *Hamlet* the soliloquy beginning "O, my offense is rank" is superior to the one preferred by "you gentlemen of the profession" that begins "To be or not to be." "But pardon this small attempt at criticism," Lincoln wrote. And he said that he would like to hear Hackett recite the opening speech in *Richard III* (which Lincoln himself had in his memory and would recite on the *River Queen* near the end of the war).

Hackett, who clearly was an energetic self-promoter, made the bad mistake of having this private letter from the president of the United States printed as a broadside. He gave it the heading "A Letter from President Lincoln to Mr. Hackett" and added, obviously with a guilty conscience, "Printed not for publication but for private distribution only, and its convenient perusal by personal friends." But of course it fell into the hands of hostile journalists and editorial writers, and of course they proceeded to write scornful lines about the pretentions of this uneducated president now setting himself up as a literary critic. The *New York Herald,* the influential and often anti-Lincoln paper of James Gordon Bennett, ran an extended piece of patronizing, sustained, and heavy-handed sarcasm, which said in part:

> Mr. Lincoln's genius is wonderfully versatile. No department of human knowledge seems to be unexplored by him. He is equally at home whether discussing divinity with political preachers, debating plans of campaigns with military heroes, illustrating the Pope's bull against the comet to a pleasure party from Chicago, arguing questions of constitutional law with Vallandigham sympathizers, regulating political parties in Missouri, defending his policy before party conventions . . .
>
> It only remained for him to cap the climax of popular astonishment and admiration by showing himself to be a dramatic critic of the first order, and the greatest and most profound of the army of Shakesperean commentators. And this he has now done.

The *Herald*'s piece kept going a good deal longer than the basic sneer would support:

> If Mr. Lincoln had time to dilate upon the subject of his letter and to analyze the plays and passages to which he particularly refers, we would have

an article on Shakespeare which would doubtless have consigned to merited dust and oblivion the thousands of tomes that have been printed on the subject, and would have been accepted as the standard authority henceforth.

And still that was not the end of it.

Hackett was embarrassed, as well he should have been, and wrote Lincoln something of an apology. Lincoln in his response (this time marked "private") wrote:

> Give yourself no uneasiness . . . on the subject mentioned in that of the 22nd.
>
> My note to you, I certainly did not expect to see in print; yet I have not been much shocked by the newspaper comments upon it. Those comments constitute a fair specimen of what has occurred to me through life.

And then Lincoln produced this sentence—or two sentences:

> I have endured a great deal of ridicule without much malice; and have received a great deal of kindness, not quite free from ridicule.
>
> I am used to it.

This letter has been admired on literary grounds for the balanced key sentence,* but the still more striking feature of Lincoln's response is its extraordinary moral and human balance.

In the first place, he surely had reasons for resentment against the eagerly self-promoting Hackett for exploiting a private letter for his self-promotion and thereby subjecting Lincoln to a barrage of sarcasm. But Lincoln said, "Give yourself no uneasiness . . . I have not been much shocked . . . I am used to it." Hackett's name can be added to the long list of those against whom Lincoln had a legitimate grievance that he nevertheless set aside.

But in the second place, the content of his dismissal is remarkable in its utterly detached acceptance, without complaint, of his situation in the world. Lincoln could not help but know that he presented the world with a

---

*David Herbert Donald writes that it is "one of [Lincoln's] most perfectly balanced sentences." Donald, *Lincoln* (New York: Simon & Schuster, 1995), p. 569.

figure that was easy to laugh at, to mock—his height, his physical appearance more generally, his rustic origins and speech, his own jokes and homely stories. Not many great commanders would calmly refer to the "ridicule" directed at himself and accept it—*I am used to it.*

PURPOSIVE STATECRAFT AND CHARITY FOR ALL

TOWARD THE END of that month of huge decisions, on July 28, 1862, Lincoln wrote a letter to a Louisiana Unionist with closing paragraphs that neatly juxtaposed two great aspects of his presidency. The Louisiana Unionist, named Cuthbert Bullitt, had complained that the Union effort in that state was disturbing slavery. At the end of his unsympathetic response Lincoln wrote two passages that are often quoted—but separately, to make different points. The first part, with its colorful sarcasm about "elder-stalk squirts, charged with rose water," appears when one wants to illustrate Lincoln's steadfast prosecution of the war. The second part, one of the great Lincoln statements, is quoted when one wants to emphasize Lincoln's self-restraining benevolence. But these two are not only parts of one letter; they stand near each other, a great disavowal of malice following almost directly upon a particularly vigorous statement of wartime resolve.

As he often did in argument, Lincoln made use, in place of flat assertions, of a series of rhetorical questions that bring the reader into his situation:

> What would you do in my position? Would you drop the war where it is? Or, would you prosecute it in future, with elder-stalk squirts, charged with rose water? Would you deal lighter blows rather than heavier ones? Would you give up the contest, leaving any available means unapplied?

Then Lincoln abruptly stopped himself. Perhaps he saw the danger that his slightly sarcastic and assertively belligerent sequence of rhetorical questions might push him into bullying, swaggering, and hard-line ill will. To impose one's will on other, resistant human wills by physical coercion—the exercise of power—is morally precarious, actually for both parties, but notoriously for the powerful. And so Lincoln, apparently sensing the danger in himself, drew back and disavowed boasting, and then added a direct personal statement about his mood, his limitations, his duty.

I am in no boastful mood. I shall not do more than I can, and I shall do all I can to save the government, which is my sworn duty as well as my personal inclination.

And then he completed the abrupt turn from the necessity of heavy blows and strong means to a profound and self-restraining disavowal of all malevolence:

I shall do nothing in malice. What I deal with is too vast for malicious dealing.

This last is one of Lincoln's great sentences, scratched out in a letter in the midst of heavy business. It adds something even to the Second Inaugural: the "vast" reach of the decisions Lincoln makes, which have consequences for millions living then and will reach far into "a vast future also." And the conclusion to be drawn from this vast reach of presidential decision is to leave aside all the hostile attitudes that conflicts engender, all merely personal animosities, all ill will.

In another letter, also dealing with complaining slaveholding Unionists in Louisiana, sent two days before the no-rose-water and no-malicious-dealing letter, Lincoln had closed with two similar elements, differently described and in the reverse order, with a somewhat oddly joined pair of references: Christian forgiveness and card playing.

I am a patient man—always willing to forgive on the Christian terms of repentance; and also to give ample time for repentance. Still I must save this government if possible. What I cannot do, of course I will not do; but it may as well be understood, once for all, that I shall not surrender this game leaving any available card unplayed.

Historian Mark Neely, looking late in the twentieth century at Lincoln as commander, remarks: "Lincoln had demonstrated from the start a quality not easily squared with his kind and forgiving nature—he possessed an instinct for the jugular."

The closest observer, William Seward, after he got over his mistaken assumption that he would be prime minister, gradually came to appreciate these two qualities in his president. In early June 1861 Seward wrote to his wife, Frances, that "[e]xecutive skill and vigor are rare qualities. The President is the best of us." In mid-May had already written: "It is due to the President to say, that his magnanimity is almost superhuman."

Not many great commanders and heads of state who held in their hands the power to turn the wheel of history would exercise that power with the grace and humane consideration that Lincoln did.

On the other hand, not many tenderhearted human beings, who have shown unusual sympathy with those in trouble or oppressed, would in the event prove to be decisive, steadfast, resilient, resolute commanders of armies in battle and masters of power-wielding statecraft.

At the primary level these qualities seem to stand in sharp contrast as "not easily squared": profound charity and relentless coercive action. But at a deeper level, in Lincoln, they had ultimately a common root. Both qualities arose from a moral imagination that saw the immense impact on human life of these decisions and events. The same awareness of "the vast and long-enduring consequences, for weal, or for woe, which are to result from the struggle" that made malicious dealing repugnant also made it imperative that every card be played to preserve the United States.

And to overcome her one great wrong.

PART TWO

Lincoln's Nation Among the Nations

A S A NEW HEAD OF STATE Lincoln confronted an uncommonly vexing conundrum, one more intricate than even the various troubles that bedeviled the kings, tycoons, princes, queens, grand dukes, emperors, autocrats, and viceroys whose company he had suddenly, with the utmost superficiality, joined. It was more intricate because the new nation of which he was now the "executive" had a radical moral contradiction at its core.

To be sure, the lands ruled by their various majesties had their full supply of entrenched evils, and their national hypocrisies. But except perhaps in some revolutionary spasms of their own, most other peoples on the globe did not claim to be beginning the world anew.

Or to be reaching for their moral essence all the way to creation. Or to be founded on self-evident truth. Or to have captured ideals that applied to the whole family of man.

Or to have been founded yesterday. Whereas other nations knew they had grown out of history, these Americans thought they had sprung into being in Philadelphia.

Other peoples measured their years by the century or even by the millennium; these Americans measured their years by the score.

Whereas other societies saw their origins stretching back through the mists of time to some ancient mythic beginning, the Americans found their beginning in the springtime of the Enlightenment.

The Americans presented their country as a nation founded not on blood or sacred soil or ancestral religion or ancient tribal myth—or on conquest—but on universal moral ideas. And they believed their nation to have been created not by force or by accident or by mindless tradition but by "deliberation and choice."

The great Founders some four-score years before Abraham Lincoln took office had explicitly grounded their claim to liberty in a universal moral order, explicitly tied to equality, extended explicitly to all men.

And yet at the same time they held 567,000 persons in bondage. Samuel Johnson in London scored a direct hit: "How is it that we hear the loudest yelps for liberty from the drivers of Negroes?"

The Americans' great seal claimed that their new nation was a Novus Ordo Seclorum—a New Order for the Ages. But their society included a particularly noxious Old Order of the Ages.

The Founding generation left a conflicted double legacy: universal ideals of liberty and equality—and an institution that radically contradicted those ideals.

The great orator Patrick Henry said, "Give me liberty or give me death"—and owned slaves. The father of his country George Washington owned 277 slaves, and the author of the Declaration, which said "all men are created equal," owned almost as many.

The Americans' much revered Constitution, in which We the People would "establish justice" and "secure the blessings of liberty to ourselves and our posterity," contorted itself with embarrassed circumlocutions to deny any such blessings and establish no such justice for the one-sixth of the population whom the framers could not bring themselves to name.

Article I, section 9, with averted eyes, referred to "such persons as any of the states now existing shall think proper to admit" and to the "migration or importation" of these unmentionable persons. That migration or importation was "not to be prohibited by the Congress prior to the year one thousand eight hundred and eight."

That meant that for the first twenty years of its existence the new nation conceived in liberty would continue to participate in the "migration" of Africans across the Atlantic from an old world into slavery in the new.

In Article IV, section 2, the framers shamefacedly referred to a person "held to service or labor in one state, under the laws thereof," who escapes into another state; this person shall not, "in consequence of any law or regulation" in this second state, "be discharged from his service or labor, but shall be [now one heard the whiplash of servitude in the charter of liberty] delivered up on claim to the party to whom such service or labor may be due."

States have rights but no right not to *deliver up* those persons "held to service or labor" under another state's laws.

In Article I, section 2, the framers managed to make the unnamed persons both a fraction and a residual category: "Representatives . . . shall be apportioned among the several states which may be included within this union according to their respective numbers, which shall be determined by adding to the whole number of free persons, including those bound to service for a term of years, and excluding Indians not taxed, three fifths of all other Persons." "Free persons"—and then "other persons."

This three-fifths ratio augmented the power of slave states by twenty-five to forty votes not only in passing legislation in the House but also in electing presidents in the electoral college.

So the great experiment in liberty protected slavery.

In the last half of the eighteenth century the Americans carried on, with pamphlets, speeches, sermons, and books, one of the most informed discussions of the meaning of liberty in the annals of mankind. When it was over, they held twice as many slaves as they had when the great seminar on liberty had begun.

In 1861, as Lincoln took office, American slavery was a huge, entrenched, enormously powerful, fiercely defended, and increasingly profitable institution. The half-million slaves present at the nation's beginning had grown now to four million, or one eighth of the nation's population. Slavery was not only an enormous economic force in itself but had fundamental ties to other industries—cotton, sugar, rice, tobacco, indigo—and the whole economy, indirectly.

Slavery had become the foundation of a distinctive social order, a way of life, in a region that was almost half of the nation. When Great Britain ended slavery by a vote of Parliament in 1833, it had two huge advantages over its American cousins across the water: the slaves to be freed were in safely distant lands in the West Indies, and the power to take action to free them was concentrated in one central national government. In the United States, slavery and the slaves and the slaveholders were present within the political order, and the right to deal with the issue was dispersed to the states, where the slaveholders held immense power.

The economic power of slavery was one immense barrier to its ending; the constraint of the Constitution as almost universally understood was another. In the inaugural Lincoln had said—what the Republican Party said, what almost everybody said, even including originally the abolitionists— that the federal government had no power over slavery in the states.

It had been thought at America's beginning that under the contagion of liberty slavery would gradually end, but by Lincoln's time, historian Peter Kolchin writes, "expectations that the peculiar institution would wither away had themselves largely withered away."

Eight of Lincoln's fifteen predecessors, five of the first seven presidents, had themselves been slaveholders. For fifty of the seventy-two years since the first president was inaugurated, the American head of state had been a slaveholder.

The oath of office had been administered to Lincoln by the onetime slaveholder Roger Taney, who had been appointed by the slaveholder Andrew Jackson to succeed the slaveholding John Marshall.

And slavery had the power not only of economic interest and of formal and political advantage but also of a deep racial consciousness and racial fear.

Because the "property" in this case consisted of millions of grossly mistreated human beings, there were unique elements of *fear,* not only in the South but in the North, about what liberation would mean. And the original universal ideals ironically had a double effect: they placed slavery potentially under moral condemnation but perversely they could make the racism it rested on worse. In order to affirm Liberty and Equality, much of the white population under conditions of slavery made a categorical exclusion of black persons.

In the House of Representatives on February 1, 1836, a notorious South Carolina congressman named James Henry Hammond had concluded: "I feel firmly convinced that, under any circumstances, and by any means, emancipation, gradual or immediate, is impossible . . . slavery can never be abolished."

CHAPTER TWELVE

I Felt It My Duty to Refuse

P RESIDENT LINCOLN would find in the same paragraph of the Constitution that made him commander in chief this rather surprisingly
unqualified, unchecked, quite explicit grant: "he shall have the Power to
grant Reprieves and Pardons for Offenses against the United States."

As we will see in Chapters 16 and 17, Lincoln in his use of the pardon
power was usually merciful to individuals caught up in something beyond
their control in which they ran afoul of legal judgments—to farm boys who
fell asleep on sentry duty, to Union soldiers who left camp to make sure
their girlfriends had not taken up with rivals, to ordinary citizens on the
Confederate side because of where they lived, to German speakers who did
not understand what they had been told. His generosity in the use of that
power would come to be much praised and would eventually be part of his
legend.

But not everyone praised it. Critics would insist that tender mercy was
not what a statesman ought to exercise, and not what justice and the
national interest required.

One charge was that Lincoln was too easily swayed by the entreaties of
large numbers of citizens, of eminent figures, of friends of the accused and
friends of his own. General Sherman, one of the persistent critics, complained that Lincoln found it hard to hang spies "when a troop of friends
follow the sentences . . . with earnest appeals."

Another charge was that he was a politician too responsive to appeals
by politicians. It is true that when you read through the cases of Union soldiers found guilty by courts-martial, you discover that when a congressman asked for a pardon for some "boy," he almost invariably got it.

But the most common complaint by Lincoln's critics was that he was
too easily moved by a personal, emotional appeal, particularly from
women. His own attorney general, Edward Bates, according to Francis

Carpenter, said that Lincoln was almost an ideal man, lacking only one thing:

> I have sometimes told him . . . that he was unfit to be entrusted with the pardoning power. Why, if a man comes to him with a touching story his judgment is almost certain to be affected by it. Should the applicant be a woman, a wife, a mother, or a sister,—in nine cases out of ten, her tears, if nothing else, are sure to prevail.

The pardon clerk working in the Justice Department under the attorney general made the same point:

> My chief, Attorney Bates, soon discovered that my most important duty was to keep all but the most deserving cases from coming before the kind Mr. Lincoln at all, since there was nothing harder for him to do than to put aside a prisoner's application and he could not resist it when it was urged by a pleading wife and a weeping child.

In the first winter of Lincoln's presidency, 1861–62, there would come to his desk an appeal for mitigation of punishment that would seem to be just the sort of case that the tenderhearted Lincoln would find impossible to resist. The accused was still a relatively young man, a "respectable Presbyterian" we are told, from a "respectable sea-going family" in Portland, Maine. In the Docket of Pardon Cases in the National Archives we read: "Clemency invoked by Rev. J. W. Chickering, Portland Maine, who says the accused was once a boy in his Secondary School and his parents are members of his [the Reverend Mr. Chickering's] church." The accused also had a young and pretty wife, and we may surely infer that there was weeping. The *Elmira Daily Advertiser* reported that when the accused had been sentenced to death and was then recommitted to the notorious New York City prison, the Tombs, "he was met by his wife. An affecting interview took place." If a presumably hard-bitten reporter found a meeting between the condemned husband and his wife affecting, surely this unusually compassionate president would be deeply moved.

They had a young son: so a mother and a child were appealing for the life of the father. At the climax of the case a powerful advocate from New York, a woman named Rhoda White, the wife of a Republican judge, a friend of Horace Greeley, an active advocate who had written Lincoln before, would join in the appeal. There would be a veritable phalanx of quite possibly weeping women.

The accused's neighbors in Portland would submit two petitions for clemency. One of these petitions said that the undersigned were "deeply moved by a painful sympathy for the aged and venerated mother of the convict, for his wife and only child."

Indeed, "a troop of friends" would make "earnest appeals." Lincoln would write that he had received petitions for clemency from "a large number of respectable citizens." And afterward he wrote that there would be more, including a petition from eleven thousand New Yorkers.

As to politicians, the governor of New York would make an appeal, and a protest meeting would be held in New York City the day before the execution. And all that the earnest and presumably touching appeals sought was not a complete pardon but only a commutation of the death sentence to "imprisonment for life." Rhoda White would write: "His wife, an interesting woman of twenty two and his aged Mother are here, and through me implore you to commute the punishment."

So what did the tenderhearted president do? He turned them all down.

It is instructive to notice how Lincoln phrased his decision: "I have felt it to be my duty to refuse." This was a duty, a moral imperative, not the outcome of a calculation of contending considerations.

And what was the moral necessity that derailed Lincoln's mercy? The records of the Circuit Court of the United States for the Southern District of New York in the Second Circuit, with flowering verbosity and magnificent redundancy, summarize the case in these words:

> On the Eighth day of August in the year of our Lord one thousand eight hundred and sixty with force and arms in the River Congo on the Coast of Africa, out of the jurisdiction of any particular state of the United States of America, in waters within the admiralty and maritime jurisdiction of this court, the said Nathaniel Gordon, then and there being master of a certain vessel being a ship called the Erie . . . did piratically and feloniously forcibly confine and detain eight hundred negroes . . . in and on board of said vessel, being a ship called the Erie, with the intent of him the said Nathaniel Gordon to make slaves of the aforsaid eight hundred negroes.

Nathaniel Gordon, in other words, was a slave trader. He was the captain of the full-rigged five-hundred-ton ship *Erie,* which had been sighted in August 1860 at the mouth of the Congo River by the USS *Mohican* and signaled to show its colors. The *Erie* raised an American flag and shortened sail.

The *Mohican,* part of the African Squadron, had the assignment of apprehending violators of the American laws against the slave trade. The boarding party from the *Mohican* discovered 897 Africans tightly packed together below deck of the *Erie,* and it arrested Captain Gordon and other officers. The Africans were released to an American agent in Monrovia, Liberia, after 37 had died en route; Gordon and the others were sent to New York for trial.

A reader today might assume that no president would extend clemency to a slave trader. But in the context of the time, that was by no means clear. American history up to that point had a deep ambivalence not only about slavery but even about the slave trade.

It is true that most of the Founders condemned slavery. It is also true that the Philadelphia framers tied their prose in knots to avoid using the actual words "slave" and "slavery" in the Constitution. They made this gesture, said Madison, to avoid admitting in this fundamental document that there could be "property in man." Lincoln had put it this way, in his first great speech in Peoria in the autumn of 1854:

> Thus, the thing is hid away, in the constitution, just as an afflicted man hides away a wen or a cancer, which he dares not cut out at once, lest he bleed to death; with the promise, nevertheless, that the cutting may begin at the end of a given time . . . They hedged and hemmed it in to the narrowest limits of necessity.

It is true that fervor of the Revolution led to the abolishing of slavery in the Northern states—all the original thirteen colonies had had at least some slaves—which was no small accomplishment.

It was true that, as Lincoln had said in his summary of events in his 1854 speech, "[i]n 1794, they prohibited an out-going slave-trade—that is, the taking of slaves FROM the United States to sell." And that was, indeed, "the first action against the trade by any nation."

It was further true, as Lincoln said that "[i]n 1807, in apparent hot haste, they passed the law, nearly a year in advance to take effect the first day of 1808—the very first day the constitution would permit—prohibiting the African slave trade by heavy pecuniary and corporal penalties."

It is yet again true, as Lincoln the antislavery politician would say in his last item: "In 1820, finding these provisions ineffectual, they declared the trade piracy, and annexed to it, the extreme penalty of death." In another place in his 1854 speech, twisting the ironies in the South's position, he said: "In 1820 [the South] joined the north, almost unanimously, in declaring the African slave trade piracy, and in annexing to it the punishment of death." And that almost unanimous act was said by scholars to be the most severe slave-trade act of any nation.

But this sequence of actions against slavery and the slave trade was only the more benign thread in the early American story on slavery. Lincoln in Peoria (and for the next six years) had been doing what we all do—selecting the parts of our country's past that vindicate our current position: he was arguing against Senator Douglas's willingness to allow slavery to enlarge into new territory, and against Douglas's don't-care shoulder-shrugging about the moral chasm between slavery and freedom. He was maintaining that the attitude of the Founders and shapers of the nation toward slavery had been "hostility to the principle, and toleration, only by necessity."

But that was one part of the story. There was another, darker part. If slavery had been to the framers, as Lincoln had said, a "wen or a cancer" to be hidden away, then it was a cancer that had grown. As scholar Peter Kolchin writes: "Indeed, for all the talk of natural rights, manumission, and abolishing imports from Africa, the slave population of the new nation in 1810 was more than twice what it had been in 1770." And by 1860 that number had tripled. Lincoln's America had four million slaves. The cancer was not hidden and had not been cut away.

Looked at from this darker side, the framers of the American Constitution, those demigods in Philadelphia, had not really distinguished themselves on the subject of slavery. They did not fight as hard on issues of slavery as Madison and Jefferson had done in Virginia on religious liberty, or as Madison and James Wilson would do in that convention on small state–large state matters, or indeed as the whole people of the British colonies in America would do on the touchy issue of taxation without representation—which makes us "slaves."

On the substantive issues in Philadelphia the antislavery majority would push, but not too hard, and when (as Madison reported to Jefferson) "S. Carolina and Georgia were inflexible on the point of slaves," they made compromises with the existing reality of slavery, cloaked in euphemism. Don Fehrenbacher describes the result: "It is as though the Framers were half-consciously trying to frame two constitutions, one for their own time and the other for the ages, with slavery viewed bifocally—that is plainly visible at their feet, but disappearing as they lifted their eyes."

One of the stark realities at their feet was the transatlantic slave trade, the terrible traffic that showed the monstrous institution at its worst. In Philadelphia in 1787 the framers wanted to allow Congress to prohibit the slave trade starting in 1800, but General Charles Pinckney of South Carolina proposed to move that date back to 1808. This would mean twenty more years (1788–1808) of legal slave trading. James Madison protested: "Twenty years will produce all the mischief . . . So long a term will be more dishonorable than to say nothing." But an offstage bargain had been made, and the revised provision passed. This meant that for the first twenty years of its history the new nation born in freedom would have not only a large, growing institution of human slavery but a flourishing and altogether legal transatlantic slave trade. (As Lincoln had noted, up until 1808 the Constitution of this land of the free had *forbidden* the ending of the slave trade.) During the years 1800 through 1808—the period of time added that August afternoon in Philadelphia—South Carolina imported some forty thousand new African slaves into the United States.

The American outlawing of the slave trade, when it finally occurred, did not mean that American participation promptly stopped. On the contrary, in the long years of its illegal but real continuation many successful and profitable voyages were made without interference. Those few slavers who were caught were often acquitted or given pardons. And none at all were hanged. There would be dismissals of charges, ineffectual prosecutions, deadlocked juries, acquittals, forfeitings of bail, escapes, nominal fines, short jail sentences, and full pardons.

Why did the new United States have the deep ambivalence that this record reflects? Again, a quotation from Don Fehrenbacher neatly summarizes the situation: "At the Constitutional Convention and for the first half century of the nation's life slavery was an *interest* (concentrated, persistent, practical, and testily defensive) while anti-slavery was only a *sentiment* (diffuse, sporadic, moralistic, and tentative)."

That "interest" was by no means concentrated in the South alone. New York City's business with the slave South was so brisk that when secession came there was a considerable movement to have New York City secede also. And when one turns to the slave trade, one discovers that the role of the North was not peripheral but central. Thomas Jefferson, in explaining why the tortured passage condemning slavery (blaming American slavery on the king of England) had been dropped from the Declaration of Independence, wrote not only that South Carolina and Georgia objected but also that "our northern brethren . . . felt a little tender"—a wonderful phrase—for "though their people had very few slaves themselves, yet they had been pretty considerable carriers of slaves to others."

They kept on being carriers of slaves to others. During the century in which the United States had participated in the entirely legal transatlantic slave trade, the center for building slave-trading ships had been not Charleston, South Carolina, or Norfolk, Virginia, but New York City. And the ports from which the trade was carried on were not as much Savannah and New Orleans as Boston and Newport, Rhode Island, and the old Puritan settlement of Salem. And Portland, Maine.

And now we come to the key truth: slave trading, although full of risk, was obscenely profitable. Ron Soodalter writes:

> It has been estimated that during the mid-1800's, when Nathaniel Gordon was pursuing his career, a slave purchased in Africa for approximately $40 worth of trade goods would bring a price ranging from $400 to $1,200 . . . Even after factoring in the cost of outfitting the ship, paying—and paying off—all the people involved in the voyage, and the inevitable loss of "inventory" a successful slaving expedition realized a profit many times . . . the initial investment . . . A single successful trip could more than compensate for three or four previous failures, and make the fortunes of investors and captain.

Heinrich Heine in his poem "The Slave Ship" has the slaver say:

> *I got them by barter, and gave in exchange*
> *Glass beads, steel goods, and some brandy*
> *I shall make at least eight hundred per cent,*
> *With but half of them living and handy.*

This last line suggests one of the risks, and the horrors: the terrible mortality, not alone from disease, storm, and starvation: "In 1781, running short of water, the captain of the *Zong* ordered 132 Africans thrown overboard, because his insurance covered death from drowning but not from starvation."

When Congress enacted the law ostensibly ending American participation in the slave trade, on January 1, 1808, that trade did not immediately come to an end. All of those ships, outfitted in New York, sailing from Boston, Newport, and Salem, did not stop engaging in this lucrative trade. The American market was still there—expanding, in fact, with the purchase of Louisiana, with sixteen sugar plantations, in 1803, and with the expansion of the cotton kingdom in the gulf states after the invention of the cotton gin. And the American market was not the largest: more of the illicit slave trade by American carriers after 1808 supplied the slave markets of Brazil and Cuba. The prohibition of the international slave trade by American laws in 1808—and before and after, at the federal level and the state level—had this difference from Prohibition and the drug laws: the markets to which the illegal traders brought their goods (slavery in the American states, in Brazil, Cuba, and Jamaica) were themselves altogether legal.

The story of the American struggle with the nefarious trade in slaves is a tale of the passage of rigorous laws, followed by nonexistent or ineffectual enforcement; of stirring condemnation, followed by quiet acceptance. The act of 1820 itself, making slave trading a capital crime, had to make a revealing distinction: between the "negro or mulatto" whom you could be put to death for "seizing" with intent to make him a slave, and the "negro or mulatto . . . held to service or labour by the laws of either of the states" who had already been "seized."*

Among the moral anomalies accompanying American slavery were condemnations of the transatlantic slave *trade* by many who defended slavery. Henry Wise, a leading Virginia politician throughout the prewar period—an energetic defender of slavery on the House floor and governor of the state just before the war—would in one interlude in his career, as American minister to Brazil in the middle 1840s, become a most articulate *opponent* of the slave trade. He collaborated in that undertaking, to one's total surprise, with the ambassador from the Great Britain that he had repeatedly attacked when he was a House member.

A skeptic may point out that a Virginian (in contrast to a slaveholder from Alabama or Louisiana) could have a self-interested reason for opposing the international trade: Virginia had a surplus of slaves to sell southward, so the international trade represented the state's competition. Nevertheless, one would not want to discount a certain amount of displaced moral revulsion even in the states whose social order still rested on the results of the trade. Perhaps if you were foreclosed from making moral judgment on the institution itself by your own involvement with it, you could compensate by being particularly fierce against the trade from which it had sprung.

---

*"If any citizen of the United States . . . or any person whatever . . . of the crew of any ship owned . . . or navigated in behalf of . . . any citizen of the United States, shall . . . seize any negro or mulatto not held to service or labour by the laws of either of the states . . . of the United States, with intent to make such negro or mulatto a slave . . . such citizen or person shall be adjudged a pirate and . . . shall suffer death." Warren S. Howard, *American Slavers and the Federal Law* (Berkeley: University of California Press, 1963), p. 26.

That trade—particularly the Middle Passage—had a blatant inhumanity that perhaps could be shielded in the settled world of the slave society. After the Mexican War, as the tensions over slavery sharpened and swaggering invocations of Southern "honor" grew, and the "right" to spread the institution to new territory was adamantly insisted upon—how then could the defenders of slavery condemn the slave trade? Part of the argument that slavery was a positive good was that it was good for the African, bringing him the benefits and comforts of "Christian" civilization. So could the traders buying slaves on the West African coast to transport them to a new land with all those benefits have been doing anything evil?

There even came to be in the 1850s a body of opinion in the South proposing the reopening of the Atlantic slave trade. The Constitution of the Confederate States of America of February 1861 did have a clause forbidding the international slave trade, but firebrand opposition to that clause was strong. And the states' rights interpretation of it was so complete as to make it altogether possible, according to W. E. B. DuBois, that under a successful Confederate States of America individual states would have reopened the African slave trade.

Enforcement of the laws against the slave trade that Lincoln had summarized in his Peoria speech would have required appropriations from a Southern-dominated Congress and executive action by administrations that for the most part had strong political ties to the slave states. Conviction of those apprehended would require proof that the accused was an American or that the vessel was American-owned. The law required that the slave trader be arrested by American officers; capture by the much more diligent British did not count. Only seafarers could be charged, not the owners gathering in the profits back on dry land. And then if a trial were held, prosecution and conviction were doubtful.

Between 1820 and 1854, when American slave trading was a crime punishable by hanging, few Americans had been caught; fewer had been convicted, and none had been executed. In 1854 one James Smith, master of the brig *Julia Moulton,* into which had been packed 664 Africans ("lying on their right sides, to be sure, so their heart action would be as easy as possible"), was apprehended. He tried to shuffle his citizenship to indicate he was not an American citizen and to claim that his vessel also was not of American ownership, but he was brought to trial, prosecuted, and found guilty by a jury after only an hour's deliberation. He was the first American to be convicted as a slave-trading pirate and therefore was subject to execution by hanging. But Smith was unworried, not without reason. His skilled lawyer (later to defend Jefferson Davis) made no effort to present Smith as an innocent led astray but assiduously worked the technicalities and got a mistrial, and eventually a plea-bargain, that brought Smith's punishment all the way down from hanging to two years in jail and a fine of $1,000. Smith served his term and applied to President Buchanan for a remission of the fine; in May 1857 President Buchanan granted, to the first man ever convicted of being a slave-trading pirate under American law, a full pardon. The *New York Tribune* commented acidly that presumably President Buchanan "thinks it a pity . . . now that the slave trade is so brisk, that Captain Smith should not have an opportunity to re-engage in his favorite employment."

Given this history, it is not surprising that Nathaniel Gordon and his seagoing family and his friends in the busy port of Portland, Maine, did not expect that he would ever face the hangman, or perhaps any severe punishment at all.

He had had brushes with these laws before, to no serious damage. In 1838 his father, also named Nathaniel Gordon, master of the brig *Dunlap* of Portland, had been charged with importing a Negro slave. Ten years later, in 1848, in the streets of Rio a ship named the *Juliet* was rumored to be a slaver; it was boarded, searched, then reluctantly let go when the boarding party could find nothing decisive, and it was later rumored to have returned, now under Brazilian management, carrying a cargo of slaves. The registry of the *Juliet,* before this sleight of hand, had been Portland, Maine, and the captain, Nathaniel Gordon the son.

Three years later Gordon turned up in Rio again, commanding a ship called the *Camargo,* also suspected of being a slaver. When Brazilian authorities arrested members of the crew, the American consul talked with two of them and learned the story of the earlier ship, the *Juliet.* Evading the African Squadron, the ship had gone all the way around to the east coast of Africa (a rare trip in the transatlantic slave trade), had taken on board five hundred Africans, had made the long voyage back to Brazil, had landed the Africans and the crew in another secluded spot, and then—this was the particularly striking point—was deliberately set on fire and burned. The profits from one successful voyage so far outweighed the value of the ship that it might be prudent (especially, one might surmise, in the case of a vessel already suspect like the *Juliet*) to destroy the evidence.

None of these brushes with the law led to any conviction of either of the Nathaniel Gordons.

. . .

SO WHEN IN AUGUST 1860 this Captain Nathaniel Gordon was arrested in the mouth of the Congo River, now on his ship the *Erie,* with a cargo of 897 Negroes, he certainly would not have feared—the 1820 law notwithstanding—for his life.

But Gordon this time had the bad luck that the American nation had elected its first full-fledged antislavery administration. So the newly appointed district attorney who would prosecute him, a man named E. Delafield Smith, a rising young New York Republican, would have an ardor that had not marked previous prosecutions.

When the first trial, in June 1861, ended in a hung jury—seven to convict, five to acquit—District Attorney Smith did not give up or plea-bargain but filed for a new trial, and he found witnesses who had not testified in the first trial. And this time he sequestered the jury, so they could not be bribed.

Of course Gordon had shrewd lawyers, and of course they tried all the dodges and technicalities that had worked in other cases. Gordon's lawyers claimed that the *Erie* (rather suddenly, like the *Juliet*) had ceased being an American vessel because it had been sold to foreigners. They made the particularly ingenious argument that Gordon *himself* might not be an American because his mother sometimes accompanied his father, the earlier Nathaniel, on his voyages, and this Nathaniel might have been born at sea. They argued that the crime had been committed so far into the mouth of the Congo as to have been in *Portuguese* water, therefore outside American jurisdiction.

Finally, it was common for a slave ship captain when caught suddenly to claim irresponsibility: No, no, I am not in command of this ship; I am just a passenger. The commander is that Spaniard over there. And that was what Nathaniel Gordon's lawyers did: he was no longer in charge of the *Erie,* they said, once some Spaniards came aboard.

The judge dismissed the first three of these arguments, and witnesses contradicted the fourth.

District Attorney Smith's witnesses at the second trial, who had been sailors on the *Erie,* testified that they had had a confrontation with Gordon about the purpose of the voyage. As sometimes happened, the whole crew had not been fully informed at the outset. The *Erie* had been detained by a wary U.S. consul in Havana, but Gordon had given a sworn affidavit that his ship was chartered for a legal voyage to the coast of Africa. (Trade with the African coast in many other items of course was fully legitimate, offering further opportunities for subterfuge.) But when the Africans were taken aboard in the Congo and members of the crew challenged Gordon, he offered them each a dollar a head (so the witnesses now testified) for every African landed in Cuba.

Republican district attorney Smith presented a particularly pungent episode, one of those lightning-flash glimpses of the horrors of the slave trade. While the crew from the capturing ship, the *Mohican,* was sailing the *Erie* to Monrovia, they brought the Africans on deck for water, then found they had been so tightly packed that they could not get them back in place. Gordon himself showed them "the manner of doing it, which was by spreading the limbs of the creatures apart and sitting them so close together that even a foot could not be put upon the deck."

The jury this time deliberated for only twenty minutes and returned with a verdict of guilty. The judge, William D. Shipman, having heard his first slave-trade case, gave a stern condemnation of the "wickedness" of the slave trade, sentenced Gordon to be hanged February 7, 1862, and told him that "you are soon to pass into the presence of the God of the black man as well as the white man."

Gordon and his lawyer, however, still did not think he would have any such confrontation just yet. They had a fallback plan: that power to pardon that the framers had bestowed upon the nation's chief executive.

So Gordon's counsel, a former judge named Gilbert Dean, hurried to Washington and presented all his arguments to the president of the United States.

What arguments for mitigation of Gordon's punishment would be made, by Gilbert Dean and Rhoda White and others?

First, that the law under which Gordon had been found guilty had never been enforced before, so it ought not to be enforced now. Nobody had been hanged; few had been punished at all. Gilbert Dean wrote to Lincoln: "For more than forty years the statute under which he has been convicted has been a dead letter." The placard posted around New York had the same metaphor: "Captain Nathaniel Gordon is under sentence of execution for a crime that has been virtually a dead letter for forty years. Shall this young man be made a victim of fanaticism?"

In one of his arguments Dean made affirmations of the value of human life that have a deeply ironic ring when you remember Gordon's crime. The issue was a technical one, that the court had taken greater care with property cases than with this one. At the end of a paragraph deploring the allegedly greater technical care taken for titles to property than for Gordon's possible execution, Dean wrote, without evident consciousness of the irony, that "human life is of less consequence than Bales of Cotton or Boxes of Dry Goods"—the human life being that of Nathaniel Gordon, not the 897 Africans packed in the hold of the *Erie* exactly like bales of cotton or boxes of dry goods.

One of Dean's more ingenious arguments was built on a judicial interpretation of the 1820 statute that went like this: "that a person having no interest in, or power over the negroes, so as to impress on them the character of slaves and only employed in their *transportation* is not guilty of the capital offense." In other words, they were already slaves in Africa when I picked them up; somebody else sold them in Brazil, Cuba, or South Carolina; I'm just in the *transportation* business.

Some of the arguments took account of the surrounding scene of civil war. Dean noted: "While the prison doors are opening to Convicted Pirates and acknowledged Traitors, the Gallows is being erected for Gordon, and why? Is the moral crime of which he is guilty greater than those of you are releasing?"

Rhoda White expressed the view of Gordon's supporters that the rules had abruptly changed when she said (with some truth), "Mr. Gordon was engaged in the slave trade at a time when many *then* in power upheld it, and engaged in it." And then she added, with emphasis: *"Not since the war began."* (To be sure, Gordon had been arrested in August 1860 and so had not been in a position to engage in the trade since the war began.)

One last argument on behalf of Gordon is particularly revealing and has a kind of parallel in reverse to arguments made by the antislavery politician Abraham Lincoln out in Illinois in the 1850s. Gilbert Dean, discussing why the statute had been for forty years a dead letter, explained it thus: "because the moral sense of the community revolted at the penalty of death imposed on an act when done between Africa and Cuba, which the law sanctioned between Maryland and Carolina." Dean's most pungent sentence: "It was, nay it is, lawful to carry a child born in Virginia to Louisiana and there to sell him into perpetual slavery . . . is it an offense then deserving death to bring a barbarian from Africa to the same place?"

So the Gordon case came to President Lincoln, one of his first major pardon cases.

As a rising Illinois politician, Lincoln had made arguments that *assumed* that his hearers shared his own moral revulsion at the slave trade.

In a remarkable series of paragraphs in his first great speech, in the fall of 1854, he drove home the point that his hearers, including those who owned slaves, could not really deny the humanity of the slave. One way that appears is in their attitude toward a slave trader. Lincoln presented as disdainful a picture of a human being—sneaking, crawling, snaky, untouchable, a native tyrant—as one is likely to find anywhere in the generally temperate Lincoln:

> [Y]ou have amongst you, a sneaking individual, of the class of native tyrants, known as the "SLAVE-DEALER." He watches your necessities, and crawls up to buy your slave, at a speculating price. If you cannot help it, you sell to him; but if you can help it, you drive him from your door. You despise him utterly. You do not recognize him as a friend, or even as an honest man. Your children must not play with his; they may rollick freely with the little negroes, but not with the "slave-dealers" children.
>
> If you are obliged to deal with him, you try to get through the job without so much as touching him. It is common with you to join hands with the men you meet; but with the slave dealer you avoid the ceremony—instinctively shrinking from the snaky contact. If he grows rich and retires from business, you still remember him, and still keep up the ban of non-intercourse upon him and his family. Now why is this? You do not so treat the man who deals in corn, cattle or tobacco.

And as to the moral abomination of the *transatlantic* slave trade, he asked: Why did you join, in 1820, almost unanimously, in making the African slave trade punishable by hanging? You never thought of hanging men for catching and selling wild horses.

He made the same comparison that Gilbert Dean would make, between the domestic and the international trade, but came to a contrasting moral conclusion. Dean said: Since it resembles the domestic slave trade, the transatlantic trade is not so bad as to be punishable by death. Lincoln the antislavery politician had said: Since the domestic trade resembles the abominable international trade, do not *expand* this abomination into new territory.

One place Lincoln made this comparison was in his satire on Stephen Douglas's use of the word "sacred" in the phrase "*sacred* right of self-government"—meaning the right to take slaves into the territories.

> If it is a *sacred* right for the people of Nebraska to take and hold slaves there [he said, with heavy sarcasm] it is equally their *sacred* right to buy

them where they can buy them cheapest; and that will be on the coast of Africa; provided you will consent not to hang them for going there to buy them. You must remove this restriction too, from the *sacred* right of self-government. I am aware that you say that taking slaves from the states to Nebraska, does not make slaves of free men; but the African slave-trader can say just so much. He does not catch free negroes and bring them here. He finds them already slaves in the hands of their black captors, and he honestly buys them at the rate of about a red cotton handkerchief a head. This is very cheap, and it is a great abridgement of the *sacred* right of self-government to hang men for engaging in this profitable trade!

The heavy sarcasm from Lincoln the rising politician assumed that his audience knew that the transatlantic slave trade was a moral abomination—and he tried to bring them to see the parallel wickedness in extending the slave trade to new territories.

So now the politician who had made those arguments was president of the United States and had before him a real live transatlantic slave trader.

There were petitions, arguments, and pleas for mercy of the sort to which Lincoln was usually quite responsive. All anyone was asking for at this point was commutation of the death sentence to life imprisonment.

Lincoln cast his decision in the plainest moral terms: "I have felt it to be my duty to refuse."

He refused any mitigation of the death penalty for this blatant captain and owner of a slave trader.

No mercy this time.

Well, almost no mercy.

He did make one little concession. He knew that Gordon never imagined that he actually would be executed. And there was that word "reprieve" in the Constitution. He asked Attorney General Bates whether he could grant a "respite of his sentence without relieving him altogether of the death penalty." Bates answered yes. That power to grant a "reprieve" does not "annul" the sentence; it only "prolongs the time." So three days before the scheduled hanging Lincoln issued a formal "stay of execution" full of whereases, one of which was: "whereas, it has seemed to me probable that the unsuccessful application made for the commutation of his sentence may have prevented the said Nathaniel Gordon from making the necessary preparation for the awful change that awaits him," now, therefore, I President Lincoln, grant him a respite until February 21.

The "said Nathaniel Gordon" was given an extra two weeks, to prepare for the awful change that awaited him.

But still Gordon and his lawyers were not ready to make preparation for that awful change. Gordon's energetic counsel tried the Supreme Court, tried again at the circuit court with another technical argument, tried again to persuade President Lincoln by bringing not only Gordon's wife but also his mother and Rhoda White and the petition now from *eleven thousand* New Yorkers. The governor of New York made yet another last-minute appeal to Lincoln, and attorney Gilbert Dean, trying everything, now argued: Don't desecrate the period of Washington's birthday with a hanging! Dean wrote: "Do not, I beseech you allow . . . the eve of the preparation for solemnizing the Anniversary of the 22 February to be marred by the creaking of the gallows—or saddened by the report of the dying groans and struggles of a human being sacrificed to appease the spasmodic virtue of men."

On February 20 a protest rally was held at the Merchant's Exchange, and an armed guard of eighty U.S. marshals surrounded the gallows at the Tombs, the city prison. The next day someone, perhaps his wife, smuggled Gordon some strychnine, which he secreted in a crack in a bench, but he succeeded only in making himself ill and accelerating his punishment. The authorities moved the execution from two o'clock up to noon. He was then placed "beneath the fatal beam" and hanged, the only slave trader ever executed under American law.

In granting the two weeks' respite, Lincoln had said that "it becomes my painful duty to admonish the prisoner that, relinquishing all expectation of pardon by human authority, he refer himself alone to the common God and Father of all men."

Surely it is significant that Lincoln, in stating his refusal to do anything more, referred to the common God of all men. In this case justice for the 897 Africans crammed into the slave deck of the *Erie,* and for the perhaps 500 Africans on the last voyage of the *Juliet,* and for the hundreds or perhaps thousands of Africans whom Gordon brought in chains across the Atlantic on the *Camargo* and how many other vessels, and for all the other damage that the nefarious trade did to the common life, outweighed the claim of even a limited mercy to this man.

LINCOLN WOULD MAKE two huge moral decisions about Americans in the slave trade: about a particular individual in the Gordon case, weighing mercy against this man's participation in this "inhuman traffic"; and about state policy, weighing American naval principles and national pride against the only effective way to stop that traffic.

This second hard choice presented itself because the British Royal Navy had become the only effective suppressor of the slave trade on the seas. Throughout those long years since 1808, during which the American slave trade persisted even though it was illegal, the American effort to suppress the trade had been hampered by an unwillingness of its enforcers to cooperate fully with the British. Great Britain, having once been the most extensive national participant in the transatlantic slave trade, had outlawed the trade in 1807, had ended slavery itself in 1833, and with the world's greatest navy had become the prime world enforcer of international efforts to suppress the trade. But although other nations cooperated with the Royal Navy in its role as constable of the seas, the idea of British ships stopping and boarding ships flying an American flag gave Americans heartburn; it represented a staggering violation of tender American feelings going back to 1812 and before, feelings that would be reaffirmed in the *Trent* affair. The Americans had signed a treaty of cooperation, the Webster-Ashburton Treaty of 1842, but it definitely did *not* give the British the right to stop and search American ships. So, ironically, flying an American flag became a certain protection for a slave ship, because it meant that the ship was vulnerable only to the thinly spread and rather halfhearted American patrol and could not be boarded by the effective enforcer, the Royal Navy. It will be remembered that when the *Mohican* approached the *Erie*, what Gordon did was to run up the American flag.

Even the execution of Nathaniel Gordon was not quite enough to frighten American citizens out of participation in the immensely lucrative transatlantic slave trade. That Gordon had been caught, they believed, was a fluke; that official attitudes had suddenly lined up so that he was executed was another fluke. None of the other men arrested on the *Erie* was executed; nor was anyone else. So if you had a ship and connections in the Congo, you could continue to make trips—because after the war started, you were not going to be caught.

At the outset of the Lincoln administration, scattered federal efforts to suppress the slave trade were consolidated under the secretary of the interior and his new assistant, George C. Whiting. In his first annual message President Lincoln said of the African slave trade: "It is a subject of gratulation that the efforts which have been made for the suppression of this inhuman traffic have been recently attended with unusual success." Whiting and

Interior Secretary Smith reported to Lincoln in their first account the capture of five slavers.

But Lincoln's "gratulation" was premature. Although his administration certainly had a stronger desire than any previous one to stop that inhuman traffic, it soon had fewer ships to do it with. The war would require all the ships in the U.S. Navy, including those from the African Squadron and the Cuban patrol. These vessels had been patrolling to catch slavers; now they would be patrolling to catch rebel blockade runners and bringing naval support to operations of the U.S. Army in a war at home. The *San Jacinto*, before Captain Wilkes took his colorful initiative with the *Trent*, had been patrolling African waters; Admiral Foote, before he served at the Brooklyn Navy Yard in the *Powhatan* affair, had been a commander in the African fleet. That had been back under Democratic administrations. Gordon himself had been caught, after all, by a warship, the *Mohican*, assigned to the African Squadron under the Buchanan administration. For all its general softness on slavery, that administration had at last in 1859 put together an African Squadron of eight ships and a Cuban patrol of four steamers to catch slavers. And so, ironically, there finally came this one little moment, 1860–61, when the American slave patrol did have some success; and now it was going to be interrupted by the first antislavery administration to come into office. Those five slavers whom the Lincoln administration had "gratulated" itself for catching were caught by a squad put in place by the Buchanan administration, and the necessities of war would mean that squad would now be broken up.

So Lincoln, just a few months after the *Trent* affair, faced an exacting test of his priorities: Would he, to suppress the slave trade, allow the Royal Navy to stop and board American ships? Spain, Portugal, and Brazil had granted the British navy the right to search and seize suspected slavers. Would only ships flying the American flag be exempt? Lincoln made the choice: he would indeed allow the British navy to search and seize American ships suspected of being slavers.

Lincoln quietly had Seward begin negotiations with Lord Lyons; they quietly agreed upon a treaty; Lincoln quietly asked the Senate (with the withdrawal of Southerners, now overwhelmingly Republican) to ratify the Seward-Lyons Treaty. It quietly ratified it, in executive session, behind closed doors. On July 11, 1862, Lincoln signed "a treaty between the United States and Great Britain for the suppression of the slave trade."

Giving the Royal Navy permission to seize and search ships flying the American flag was painful; but allowing the African slave trade to be carried on by those ships was worse. Lincoln could not allow the American flag to provide the one national identity that would protect a slaver against the one effective enforcer.

In a sop to national pride, the treaty's grant was reciprocal: each country's navy had the "right of visitation" on suspected slavers from the other. But the U.S. Navy, otherwise engaged, was in no position to do any visiting, and even if it had been, there were no longer British slavers to visit. The whole point was that the British navy would catch American slavers. Ships found to have evidence of slave trading were to be taken to special courts, with a British judge and an American judge, in Sierra Leone, the Cape of Good Hope, and New York.

The experience at the New York court was typical. "It was held in a rented room in the Union Building in New York, certainly one of the most modest courts on the North American continent. Judge Truman Smith had no clerk, and his furnishings were limited to a carpet, one table, a washstand, one lounge, a secretary, six chairs, and three volumes of the *United States Statutes at Large*. Yet this humble establishment was more than equal to the demands placed upon it, for not one case ever came before Judge Smith's court." Nor did any case come to any of the designated courts in other parts of the world.

American participation in the moral abomination of the transatlantic slave trade was really stopped not in Thomas Jefferson's administration in 1808, as intended by the Founders, but in 1862 during the presidency of Abraham Lincoln.

CHAPTER THIRTEEN

In Giving Freedom to the Slave, We Assure Freedom to the Free

MY STATION AND ITS DUTIES

WHEN ABRAHAM LINCOLN became president of the United States, as we have seen, his moral situation was radically redefined. He was no longer a private citizen advocating a position; he was now an oath-bound public servant with prescribed duties. He had sworn by a solemn oath "registered in Heaven" to "preserve, protect, and defend" the U.S. Constitution. "The Constitution" meant also, to him, the nation and its government. "I did understand," he would write, looking back after three years' service, "that my oath to preserve the Constitution . . . imposed upon me the duty of preserving, by every indispensable means, that government—that nation—of which the Constitution was the organic law. Was it possible to lose the nation, and yet preserve the Constitution?"* Lincoln had as his solemn obligation the preservation of the United States of America.

Moreover, this duty was for him real and immediate. Whereas for other presidents most of the time the sworn obligation to preserve the Union is a latent premise, for Lincoln it was an inescapable daily imperative: the union he had sworn to preserve was in mortal peril.

In his understanding, a victory by the rebels would not be merely some graceful severing of ties, the erring sisters curtsying and gently departing, while the Union, slightly diminished but otherwise unharmed, would go waltzing on as before. A rebel victory would be instead "the surrender of the existence of the government." When one looks through Lincoln's presidential utterances about the effect of a successful slave state rebellion, one is impressed to find, as we have seen in Chapter 7, how many different terms he used, and how stark, how dire, they are.

---

*In the important letter to A. G. Hodges, Esq., April 4, 1864.

And that newly acquired overriding duty recast his purpose with respect to slavery. Lincoln brought to the nation's highest office these two vigorously expressed moral convictions: a devotion to the American Union as the republican example to the world and a condemnation of American slavery as a "monstrous injustice" that violated that republican example. But now he had taken a solemn oath that placed him under formal obligation only to the first of these, not to the second. He had no parallel *official* duty—no "perfect" duty—to attack the evil of slavery. On the contrary, the Constitution he had sworn to uphold contained euphemistic recognitions of slavery and protections for it, and the Union he had sworn to defend had slavery as a legally recognized institution in fifteen states, eight of which, at the time he was inaugurated, had not seceded.

He was now the executive of that Union, enjoined to "take care" that the laws be faithfully executed. In his inaugural address Lincoln went so far as to read the constitutional provision about returning fugitive slaves (persons "held to service or labor") and to note that it is "as plainly written in the Constitution as any other" and that "all members of Congress swear to support the whole Constitution." And he had said that "all the protections which . . . can be given, will be cheerfully given to all the states . . . as cheerfully to one section as to another."

It had been almost universally believed that the Constitution that Lincoln had sworn to uphold left the matter of slavery entirely to the states—indeed left most matters to the states—but that slavery was the peculiarly sensitive point. That conviction ran so deep that even the Anti-Slavery Society in its founding document acknowledged it; the Republican Party platform recognized it; the cabinet members all affirmed it; and Lincoln in his inaugural reiterated it, compounding the obligation with an inaugural pledge. He quoted himself as having said, "I have no purpose, directly or indirectly, to interfere with slavery in the states where it exists. I believe I have no lawful right to do so, and I have no inclination to do so."

Gradual, compensated emancipation, voluntarily undertaken by the border states themselves, was a way Lincoln could start right away acting against the monstrous injustice of slavery without violating his pledge not to interfere with it in the states and while honoring his duty to preserve the Union—actually, he argued, while *serving* that overarching duty.

Such gradual emancipation would not be coercive federal interference or a moralistic imposition on the slave states, but would come "gently as the dews of heaven," with no reproaches, no one acting the Pharisee. Lincoln's persistent (but futile) efforts to persuade the border states to accept such a program, gradually to buy out the slaveholders, have a pleading quality. It is not true that Lincoln's efforts against slavery were postponed through the first year and a half of his presidency until the Emancipation Proclamation; actually, he started early. As early as November 1861 he proposed a scheme for compensated emancipation in Delaware; he presented the first national proposal for a voluntary gradual buyout of slaves to Congress on March 6, 1862, and he met with border state representatives to try to persuade them to accept it in March and in July 1862; and in his annual message in December 1862, even after the preliminary emancipation proclamation by the commander in chief in September, he made one last thorough and earnest appeal to the states to adopt compensated emancipation.

When Lincoln showed the abolitionist Wendell Phillips the message that he had sent to Congress on March 6—the first time any American president had proposed emancipating slaves—he told Phillips a story about an Irishman, under the restriction of Maine's prohibition law, who ordered a lemonade but hinted that he would not mind if "a drop of the creature" could be put into it "unbeknownst to me self." Lincoln "hated [slavery] and meant it should die" but had included that ingredient in the message "unbeknownst" to himself.

Lincoln needed to slip the brandy of emancipation into the lemonade of Union-saving for reasons both of his formal moral and legal obligation and of political reality.

Three groups understood from the start the tie between freeing slaves and saving the Union—the slaveholders who rebelled against it, the antislavery forces in the North who kept up the pressure for it, and the slaves who took it for granted by fleeing to Union lines. But the key to the politics Lincoln had to pursue was the huge group that did not make that link—indeed that rejected it and opposed it.

The body of opinion that supported the Union but did not support emancipation was very large, and essential to victory, not only in Kentucky, Missouri, and Maryland but also across the North. This was the body of opinion for which he would write a great public letter after the Emancipation Proclamation, his letter to James Conkling, read to an audience in Springfield: "You say you will not fight to free negroes. Some of them seem willing to fight for you; but no matter. Fight you, then, exclusively to save the Union." Efforts at freeing slaves, taking account of this crucial body of opinion, would have to be made with a justification other than simply that slavery was wrong. These people did not think it was wrong.

·   ·   ·

BUT THE PRESIDENT made clear from start to finish that preserving the Union was mandatory, and that he would use whatever means were required to do it. In his first annual message, on December 3, 1861, he said, "The Union must be preserved; and hence all indispensable means must be employed." In his March 6 message to Congress proposing gradual emancipation, he quoted that statement and then added a certain note of warning: "If . . . resistance continues, the war must also continue; and it is impossible to foresee all the incidents, which may attend." On April 25, 1862, General David Hunter, commanding the Union army's Department of the South, issued a declaration of martial law for his department, and then on May 9 declared that slavery and martial law were incompatible, and that "the persons . . . hitherto held as slaves" were now free. Lincoln countermanded the emancipation order but went on—in his proclamation issued May 19, 1862—to make a statement that went beyond anything he needed to have said, not being at all required by the business at hand:

> I further make known that whether it be competent for me, as Commander-in-Chief of the Army and the Navy, to declare the Slaves of any state or states, free, and whether at any time, in any case, it shall have become a necessity indispensable to the maintenance of the government, to exercise such supposed power, are questions which, under my responsibility, I reserve to myself, and which I can not feel justified in leaving to the decision of commanders in the field.

He did not say: *nobody* can free slaves within a state. For the first time he was saying only that Hunter, a commander in the field, was not the one to do it, if it should be done. It would be the commander in chief's decision, whether "it be competent" to declare slaves in the states free, and whether it had become necessary. Mark Neely writes, "Here is the first indication, public or private, that Lincoln thought slavery could be abolished under the powers of the commander in chief."

WHEN HE PUBLISHED in a rival newspaper a reply to an effusion in the *Tribune* by the mercurial newspaperman Horace Greeley, Lincoln included a new indication of what he believed he could do,* and would do. Readers of this letter in the luxury of later times often get it exactly wrong, noticing only that he said that if he could save the Union by keeping slavery he would do it; but that was not the news. They may fail to read his last sentence, "I have here stated my purpose according to my view of official duty; and I intend no modification of my oft-expressed personal wish that all men every where could be free." And they may not know that when he wrote this letter he had a draft of the Emancipation Proclamation in his desk. But most important, they miss the stunning importance in its time of this item among the alternatives: "If I could save [the Union] by freeing all the slaves I would do it."†

The churches, and the Protestant flavor of American culture after it had been marinated in the juice of revivals in the first half of the nineteenth century, were, as Lincoln biographer Richard Carwardine has made particularly clear, an essential constituency for Lincoln's fulfillment of his attack on slavery. When a delegation of antislavery "Chicago Christians of All Denominations" visited him on September 13, 1862, to present memorials condemning the evil institution of slavery and asking for national emancipation, Lincoln in response said he did not want to issue a document as inoperative as the pope's bull against the comet.

Then he added, just as though it were an aside, this enormously significant point:

> Understand, I raise no objections against it [an emancipation proclamation] on legal or constitutional grounds; for, as commander-in-chief of the army and navy, in time of war, I suppose I have a right to take any measure which may best subdue the enemy.

One can say that the war made possible the ending of slavery, but Lincoln would put it differently: the continued resistance of the rebels to the authority of the government made it necessary.

After the defeats and doldrums of 1861, and the Union successes particularly in the West in the first quarter of 1862, failure of the vaunted McClellan Penninsula Campaign to make progress that summer came as an

---

*Lincoln's famous letter to Greeley was published on August 22, 1862.

†Douglas Wilson and Allen Guelzo both praise the rigor of this letter. Wilson indicates that Lincoln had already written the body of it and just took the opportunity of Greeley's letter to issue it.

immense shock and disappointment. The border state representatives, at a meeting with the president, responded negatively to his proposal for compensated emancipation. The war was not going well for the Union, either in the West or in the East. In July 1862, as we have seen, the president made enormous decisions: he widened the rules for legitimate military objectives to include rebel property, which changed the character of the war; and he decided to declare slaves in rebel states free—which changed the character both of the war and of the nation that came out of it.

There was a bit of history about using the "war power" to free slaves. Old John Quincy Adams, when he was serving in Congress after having been president, shocked his fellow congressmen by twice maintaining that in a war Congress could free slaves. And on April 12, 1861—during Lincoln's first days as president—Adams's young friend Charles Sumner had told the new president about that idea.

One could certainly make a strong case that emancipation was "a fit and necessary war measure for suppressing said rebellion." But would a president who was less convinced of the monstrous injustice of slavery have accepted that case? This president believed that slavery was not only profoundly wrong but profoundly wrong specifically as measured by this nation's moral essence. These convictions about the deep wrongness and severe damage to the nation represented by human slavery would surely tilt his estimate of the military necessity that required the proclamation, and the positive results for the war that would follow from it.

Suppose the president had been William Seward, with his rather odd new theory that slavery was in principle already defeated when the Republicans won the election of 1860, so that no further measures were necessary.

Attorney General Bates, along with Blair the most conservative member of the cabinet, rather surprisingly did endorse the proclamation—but only with the repugnant and prohibitive requirement that the freed slaves be forcibly deported. Salmon Chase, the most radical member of the cabinet, favored a different way forward—an incremental approach allowing generals, like Hunter, to organize and arm slaves in their command. Bates, Cameron, and Chase were the three other men whom the Republicans might have nominated in 1860; it is to be doubted that any one of them would have made the jump that Lincoln did.

One's estimate both of the plight of the Union effort necessitating the Emancipation Proclamation and of the result that would actually follow from it was loaded with contingency and flavored with one's moral conviction. Another president might say that such a proclamation would cause revolt in the armies, damage enlistments, intensify Confederate resistance, dilute Union loyalty in the border states, and cause Republican losses in the elections in the fall of 1862.* All of these effects did, indeed, occur to some extent. Lincoln judged that in the longer run they would be overcome by the positive military, political, and diplomatic effects, and he proved to be right.

On the evening of the very day the Union armies won their unfulfilled victory at Antietam, on September 17, 1862, Lincoln at Soldiers' Home worked on the final draft of what would come to be called the preliminary emancipation proclamation. He continued to work on it Saturday and Sunday, September 20 and 21, and on Monday he held a cabinet meeting, for which we are presented with two quite contrasting versions of Lincoln's opening moments.

Twentieth-century Lincoln biographer William Barton wrote in 1925:

> Bishop Fowler in his noted lecture on Abraham Lincoln told his millions of interested hearers that Lincoln, before presenting to his Cabinet the Proclamation of Emancipation, read to them a chapter from the Bible. That is precisely what Lincoln would have done if he had been Bishop Fowler. What he actually did read was a chapter from [the humorist] Artemus Ward.

Chase in his diary said that Stanton did not think it was very funny, and one suspects that Chase didn't either.

But then Lincoln made a remark, surprising for him, that Bishop Fowler, presumably, and the sober Episcopalian Chase would have regarded as more suitable to the occasion. He told about the promise he had made to himself and—"hesitating a little"—his Maker, that when the rebels were driven from Maryland, he would issue the proclamation, which he proposed now to do. Antietam provided that moment. The substance was decided; he was submitting the document to the cabinet only for editorial and other minor improvements. The proclamation gave the rebel states one hundred days to stop rebelling; if they continued, on January 1 he

---

*"Looked at coldly, the timing of the [preliminary, September 22] Proclamation amounted to political suicide: Lincoln was putting the most highly charged issue of the war before the voters, and the voters into the hands of the opposition, without any time for the shock to wear off." Allen C. Guelzo, *Lincoln's Emancipation Proclamation: The End of Slavery in America* (New York: Simon & Schuster, 2004), p. 168.

would, by presidential order justified by his war power, free all the slaves in the areas still in rebellion.

Lincoln's two giant purposes had now come to coincide, and not just to coincide but also to be brought into a relationship in which his supreme duty required that he act in accord with his deepest moral conviction.

He now must free the slaves—in order to save the Union.

HERETOFORE, HENCEFORWARD, AND AFORESAID

WHEN A READER TODAY takes up a copy of the Emancipation Proclamation and begins to read, he may have a puzzled feeling that somehow he has got hold of the wrong piece of paper. Surely there must be some mistake. The proclamation is said to be "perhaps the greatest document of social reform in American history," and Lincoln is widely recognized as the greatest writer among American presidents, and an extraordinary writer by a much more exacting test than that one. But this document certainly is no Gettysburg Address. It begins with "Whereas" and proceeds to spell out a date in the wordy formal numberless way: "on the twenty-second day of September, in the year of our Lord one thousand eight hundred and sixty-two." It then includes two paragraphs pasted into the text from a printed document issued back on that date. And if one then looks back at that September 22 production—known to history as the preliminary emancipation proclamation—one finds that even more had been pasted in from two acts of Congress. Lincoln, so skillful with a pen, also made repeated use of scissors and paste.

Reading through this "final" proclamation—the one that rang all the bells on New Year's Day 1863 and was called by Frederick Douglass "the greatest event in our nation's history"—one finds it replete with lawyers' words like "thereof" and "hereby" and "wherein and whereof" and "hereafter, as heretofore" and "to wit." One verb is not allowed to serve when two or more can be summoned: "I do hereby proclaim and declare" and "I do hereby enjoin upon and order all persons . . . to observe, obey and enforce" That September 22 "preliminary" proclamation, issued, as we learn, "the full period of a hundred days" before this final proclamation, and a short "first draft" that Lincoln had presented to the cabinet back in July, prove also to be soaked in lawyers' language.*

*One can follow the complicated tale of the composing of these multiple versions in Douglas Wilson's *Lincoln's Sword* and the surrounding story—including the debated point about in what place or places Lincoln did his writing—in Guelzo's *Lincoln's Emancipation Proclamation.*

A modern reader therefore may understand why none other than Karl Marx, writing as a journalist in a Vienna periodical, had sneered that the proclamation had "all the mean pettifogging conditions which one lawyer puts to his opposing lawyer." The pettifogging is particularly thick in a paragraph, introduced by "to wit," that proceeds not only to list the states in rebellion in which the slaves were to be freed ("Arkansas, Texas . . . Mississippi, Alabama . . .") but also then to add in parentheses after some states a list of exceptions:

> Louisiana, (except the Parishes of St. Bernard, Plaquemines, Jefferson, St. Johns . . . St. Mary, St. Martin, and Orleans, including the City of New-Orleans) . . . Virginia, (except the fortyeight counties designated as West Virginia, and also the counties of Berkley, Accomac, Northampton, Elizabeth-City, York, Princess Ann, and Norfolk, including the cities of Norfolk & Portsmouth) . . .

And it then nails down, in a careful lawyer's way, the significance of these specified exceptions:

> and which excepted parts are, for the present, left precisely as if this proclamation were not issued.

So this great edict of freedom frees slaves in Baton Rouge—but not in New Orleans? Frees them in Richmond and Alexandria—but not in Norfolk? Proclaims that freedom shall reign up to the border of Berkley County, Virginia—but not across that border? In fact, the Emancipation Proclamation freed slaves only in rebel territories and not in any of those territories that were now held by the Union army.

A modern reader may be further puzzled because this proclamation really does not seem to do much proclaiming. Is Lincoln not supposed to be the Great Emancipator? Where in these paragraphs is any Great Emancipating? Where is the Lincoln of the rousing last passage of the Cooper Union address? Where is the Lincoln who started his rise in politics proclaiming that slavery was a "monstrous injustice" that he hated? Where is the Lincoln who had condemned slavery repeatedly as "evil," "an unqualified evil," a "vast moral evil," and "the sum of all villainies"? Where is the Lincoln who said slavery was a wrong that should be treated as a wrong? Where is the Lincoln who insisted, for six years, against Senator Stephen Douglas, that slavery violated this nation's foundation, found in the Declaration of Independence's assertion that all men are created equal? One can read almost all the way through this paper without finding any moral reason why slaves are to be declared free in those carefully delimited areas. This document is not making grand moral assertions; it is making close legal distinctions. There is (almost) no *moral* reason given why slaves are to be freed anywhere. The most widely quoted criticism of the proclamation, written by historian Richard Hofstadter well over half a century ago and repeated in absolutely every book on the topic since then, puts the two puzzlements a reader may feel—about the legalistic language and the lack of moral lift—into one pungently sarcastic phrase: the proclamation has all the moral grandeur of a bill of lading. And it is certainly true that "moral grandeur" is not to be found in this paper.

A reader who has worked his way through seven paragraphs of "herebys" and "aforesaids" and names of excepted counties may at last find a little spark in a paragraph near the end:

And upon this act, sincerely believed to be an act of justice, warranted by the Constitution, upon military necessity, I invoke the considerate judgment of mankind, and the gracious favor of Almighty God.

There at last lined up behind this proclamation are justice and Almighty God and the considerate judgment of mankind. (Historian Allen Guelzo says this last line provides a little link to the "decent opinions of mankind" in the Declaration.) But the reader may feel that this brief nod near the end is just what Franklin Roosevelt, in conversation with his speechwriter Sam Rosenman, once called the "God stuff" that is routinely required at the end of presidential utterances.

And then one finds that it was not even Lincoln's own God stuff. Lincoln did not write this paragraph. It had been Chase's suggestion. All Lincoln did was to strike out a clause of Chase's and insert the phrase "upon military necessity." Justice and Almighty God and the opinion of mankind were all very well as far as they went, but what Lincoln wanted everyone to be clear about was that this action was "warranted by the Constitution, *upon military necessity.*"

When Lincoln describes himself taking this action, he puts on the full dress uniform of his military identity in the present military emergency:

Now, therefore I, Abraham Lincoln, President of the United States, by virtue of the power in me vested as Commander-in-Chief, of the Army and Navy of the United States in time of actual armed rebellion against the authority and government of the United States . . .

And then gives the reason for the action he is taking:

as a fit and necessary war measure for suppressing said rebellion . . .

He did not free slaves because slavery was a great wrong, although he believed it to be a great wrong; he did not free slaves because slavery violated this nation's founding ideals, although he believed strongly that it did. He freed slaves "as a fit and necessary war measure for suppressing said rebellion." Such an act would weaken the Confederate states and bring freed slaves into the Union army.

The Emancipation Proclamation sounds like a legal document because it *is* a legal document. It does not have the lift of a moral argument because it is not making a moral argument. Lincoln was not making an argument at all; he was making *law*. He was not giving inspiration; he was giving an order.

The lawyer's prose was not a literary or moral failure but a necessity. The document was at its core an act of law in wartime—a military order—an order to military commanders to liberate slaves in conquered territory, in the teeth of strong resistance. The tedious specificity was central to Lincoln's justification: as military chief he could command, on his own authority, the freeing of slaves in states *in rebellion* as a necessary military measure. He could not do that in states and areas that were *not* in rebellion, which included areas captured by U.S. forces.

Douglas Wilson in *Lincoln's Sword* writes: "Abraham Lincoln's Emancipation Proclamation constituted a special problem in writing . . . It had to be emotionally chaste. It must avoid words and phrases that would appeal only to partisans and be land mines for others. Unlike almost any other kind of purposeful writing, it would be enhanced by its rhetorical barrenness." Paradoxically, Lincoln's role in ending slavery was a moral accomplishment that required that he not admit that it was a moral accomplishment.

To have asserted that the evil of the institution was the reason for the action would have not only lost the Union effort the support of that large portion of the country that did not believe it to be an evil, but also offended the constitutional sensibilities of much of the nation, including himself. He did not believe that presidents could simply assert as law their own moral convictions.

He would insist in a letter to a group of Kentucky leaders that he wrote at their request, on April 4, 1864—the letter to Albert Hodges and others—that he had *not* acted in that way. He began this letter with his most adamant presidential condemnation of slavery: "If slavery is not wrong, nothing is wrong"; "I am naturally anti-slavery . . . I cannot remember when I did not so think and feel." But he then would follow that vigorous assertion of his lifelong *personal* moral condemnation of this unmitigated evil with an avowal of his *presidential* restraint:

> I have never understood that the Presidency conferred upon me an unrestricted right to act officially upon this judgment and feeling [that slavery is wrong] . . . I understood . . . that in ordinary course of civil administration this oath even forbade me to practically indulge my primary abstract judgment on the moral question of slavery . . . I aver that, to this day, I have done no official act in mere deference to my abstract judgment and feeling on slavery.

He not only had not done such an act; he understood that his oath *forbade* him to do so.

But that oath required him to defend the United States, and when events made necessary extraordinary action in that defense, he chose emancipation by federal decree as an instrument. He might have chosen otherwise. Others would not have made that decision. But as a strong opponent of the monstrous institution, he made the huge moral and intellectual jump from the sort of antislavery efforts he had been proposing all the way to a national immediate emancipation with the force of the Union army behind it. It was one of the central moral decisions of American history.

This is not to say that Lincoln's appeal to military necessity was in any degree a mere cover for what he wanted to do independently; prevailing militarily over the rebellion was his prime duty, and this action was a strong instrument for that purpose. Lincoln calculated what it would mean to move the slave population from one side of the war to the other, doing the "arithmetic" as he often did, saying the effect could be measured as a physical force, as steam power can be measured.

Lincoln scholar Phillip Paludan has written, in a provocative and illuminating way, about Lincoln's two great achievements and identities—Savior of the Union and Great Emancipator—which, he wrote, have too often been divided.

Freeing the slaves and saving the Union were linked as one goal, not two optional goals. The Union that Lincoln wanted to save was not a Union where slavery was safe . . . Slave states understood this; that is why they seceded and why the Union needed saving.

These last two sentences are surely correct and important, but we might qualify the first one: "saving the Union" had to be, for the oath-bound office-holding president, something more than a "goal." It was now his supreme duty. "Freeing the slaves"—that is, opposing the evil institution of slavery—although indeed for him closely linked in aspiration to the moral essence of the Union that was to be saved, was not a mandatory formal obligation but a profound purpose springing from a deep moral conviction. Bringing these two moral claims into accord would be not the beginning but the triumph of his presidency.

FOREVER FREE

THERE HAD BEEN ONE moment in the preliminary document—repeated when Lincoln pasted it into the final version—when, for all the repetitive formality of the expression, a glint of moral profundity did peep out. It is a phrase that stood in the short draft back on July 22 at the very end, as a climax, but with a subtle defect: the former slaves, Lincoln wrote in that short first draft, "shall then, thenceforward, and forever, be free." Rewriting this for the preliminary proclamation, Lincoln saw that that little word "be" needed to be relocated. On September 22 the passage read: "All persons held as slaves . . . shall be then, thenceforward, and forever free." That lawyerly threefold coverage, including the first alliteration, lifts itself to the huge word "forever," which appears in the second alliteration that carries immense meaning—"forever free"—and gives this one phrase a sudden bell-ringing resonance.

The phrase remains in the final proclamation in the pasted-in quotation from the preliminary proclamation, but in the new text Lincoln made two changes, a positive shift in immediacy and a negative shift in permanence. Instead of writing that slaves "shall be" free, he wrote that they "*are,* and henceforward shall be free." But he dropped the word "forever," perhaps because it promised something he was not quite sure at that point he could deliver.

There was one other passage in the September 22 preliminary proclamation that rang some bells for a different reason. Immediately following "forever free," Lincoln had written: "The Executive Government of the United States will, during the term in office of the present incumbent, recognize such persons as being free, and will do no act or acts to repress such persons, or any of them, in any effort they may make for their actual freedom." Lincoln presumably had in mind, in writing this passage, the scandal of the Union army serving as a slave catcher, returning runaways to their "masters," an outrage now being corrected by the March 1862 act prohibiting the Union army from returning slaves who had escaped into Union lines, and by the Second Confiscation Act, portions of which he pasted into his proclamation.

There would be a particularly consequential editing of this passage. In the cabinet discussion Seward said, according to Chase's diary, that it might be better to leave out all reference to the act being sustained merely in the current president's incumbency, and that it might be better to say not only that the government "recognizes" but also that it will *maintain* the freedom of those herein declared forever free. Lincoln made the change, scratching out lines and entering words above, on the original copy. He added a specification of the role of the armed forces that magnified the unintended effect that the passage was now to have in some quarters. As edited it now read:

> The Executive Government of the United States, including the military and naval authority thereof, will recognize and maintain the freedom of such persons, and will do no act or acts to repress such persons, or any of them, in any efforts they may make for their actual freedom.

Eminences in England and France, looking at what these Americans were doing across the water—unsympathetic in the main to the Union, without close awareness of the fugitive slave controversy or the actual American conditions, from their own colonial experiences and ideologies inclined to fear mass insurrections—read something in that passage that Americans, by and large, did not. They seized on this particular passage with simulated fury to insist that Lincoln was proposing that slaves revolt and that the Union army support their insurrection. The army was not to "repress" but to "maintain" "any efforts" the slaves would make for their "actual freedom": Did that mean a Union-supported servile insurrection?

The most disgraceful of many fierce statements by English and French leaders, worse than most from the slave states themselves, appeared in the London *Times:* "He [Lincoln] will appeal to the black blood of the

African; he will whisper of the pleasures of spoil and of the gratification of yet fiercer instincts; and when blood begins to flow and shrieks come piercing through the darkness, Mr. Lincoln will wait till the rising flames tell that all is consummated, and then he will rub his hands and think that revenge is sweet."

John Hope Franklin, the distinguished twentieth-century African American historian, would remark: "Few Confederate editors exceeded the *London Times* in its denunciation of the proclamation as an atrocious measure, hardly worthy of a civilized nation."

Republicans had lost ground in the 1862 elections, although they retained their majorities, with reduced margins, in Congress. They lost the governor's seat in New York and lost also in Illinois, New Jersey, and Wisconsin; reaction against emancipation was presumed to be the cause.

Would the president sign the final proclamation on January 1? Losses in the election, congressional criticism, negative stirrings in the army, and disappointing responses from abroad caused some to fear or hope that he would not.

Black Americans, slave and free, awaited the day with tense anticipation. John Hope Franklin observed: "Wherever Negroes were on New Year's Eve, 1862, there was little time for sleeping!" And on New Year's Day, as the news spread across the country that Lincoln had signed the proclamation, there were rejoicings that the participants would never forget. As a valuable recent study put it:

> However deficient in majesty or grandeur, the president's words echoed across the land. Abolitionists, black and white, marked the occasion with solemn thanksgiving that the nation had recognized its moral responsibility, that the war against slavery had at last been joined, and that human bondage was on the road to extinction. But none could match the slaves' elation. With unrestrained—indeed, unrestrainable—joy, slaves celebrated the Day of Jubilee. Throughout the South—even in areas exempt from the proclamation—black people welcomed the dawn of a new era.

THE EDICT OF FREEDOM

THE GREAT POINT of the Emancipation Proclamation—the "Edict of Freedom," as Nicolay and Hay would call it—was that (with all its geographical and legal-temporal limitations) it was *national* law enforceable by the U.S. armed forces. It was not voluntary, it was not gradual, and it was not left to the states.

The great national moral task here begun was not only to free slaves but also to destroy the evil institution of slavery and to overcome the monstrous race-based social construction upon which it rested and which it fed. And that would not be done—would not be begun—by an emancipation controlled by the states. The sad history after Reconstruction of black codes, white supremacy, Jim Crow, and lynching—the "lost hundred years," as C. Vann Woodward would call the period from the last civil rights efforts after the Civil War to the civil rights revolution of the 1960s—would show all too plainly what state control of postslavery race relations would mean. Overcoming the "monstrous injustice" (Abraham Lincoln), the "one huge wrong" (Lyndon Johnson), that had been planted in the foundation of the American republic would require national government action.

The final proclamation, signed by Lincoln's hand on New Year's Day, had this hugely important departure from the preliminary one, and from Lincoln's previous efforts: the freedmen were to be received into the U.S. armed services. This was a pivotal, monumental decision whose effect led far beyond its immediate context: henceforth the United States (by the president's implicit definition) was to be a biracial—a multiracial—society. No one believed that after the freed slaves had faced rebel guns on the nation's behalf in the Union army they could be returned to slavery or invited to depart.

Critics would say that the Emancipation Proclamation freed no one—that it applied where the Union had no power and did not apply where it did. But it turned the Union armies into armies of liberation wherever they advanced. By its inescapable symbolism it encouraged acts of self-liberation even in areas where the Union army already had control and the proclamation technically did not apply. It meant a great deal more than it said. Its symbolic significance completely outran its technical application. Rarely in history can there have been a document whose moral reach so far exceeded its legal grasp.

The claim that the proclamation freed no one is mistaken in this further regard: it did free one person—Abraham Lincoln. With the proclamation his objectives—saving the Union and ending slavery—implicitly linked but in tension with each other from the start, came now to be explicitly joined. He no longer needed to disguise the strong stuff of emancipation in the club soda of backward-looking Union-saving. Just eighteen days after the signing he could describe the Confederacy's effort, to the workingmen of Manchester, England, as "an attempt to overthrow this government, which was built upon the foundation of human rights, and to substitute for it one which should rest exclusively on the basis of human slavery." At Gettysburg he could speak of a "new birth of freedom." He would be freed to make the decisions of the last two years of his presidency, to recruit black troops, and to defend their role in an eloquent public letter that would guarantee thereby a biracial America; to insist none would be returned to slavery; to seek, when it looked as though he might lose, in August 1864, to increase the number of blacks behind Union lines; to initiate what would become the Thirteenth Amendment and to twist arms to achieve its passage and end American slavery forever.

In the longer run his great obligations would come together in the reverse direction from the proclamation. Saving the Union, as it would prove—winning the war—would lead to freeing the slaves.

It would do more than free the persons then enslaved: it would free the persons who might tomorrow have become slaves; it would free nonslave Americans from the curse of slavery; it would free the nation from the terrible hypocrisy that Lincoln had identified—and hated—at the outset of his great career. It would end the *institution* of slavery in the land of the free.

WE CANNOT ESCAPE HISTORY

THE ELOQUENCE excluded from the Emancipation Proclamation had been supplied back on December 1 in the annual message, a month before the proclamation. Lincoln had then surprised many both by his most peculiar proposal and by his most eloquent appeal for the end of slavery.

One might have thought that the president's efforts at compensated state-controlled emancipation had ended when the border states rejected every effort he had made in that direction, and then when the preliminary emancipation proclamation on September 22 announced an immediate uncompensated Confederacy-wide freeing of slaves by presidential decree and military force, leaving behind, one would have thought, all efforts to persuade states voluntarily to accept a gradual plan.

But his annual message read to the Thirty-eighth Congress on December 1 included his most intricate scheme yet for compensated gradual state-run emancipation, including voluntary colonization. It seems a most peculiar effort. The president of the United States went to all the trouble himself to write out in detail an elaborate program, including the specific wording of three amendments to the Constitution, setting forth proposals that had already been multiply rejected. And then he accompanied this gargoyle with some of the most moving and eloquent prose he ever wrote—

that any president, any head of state, ever wrote. Since the Emancipation Proclamation has no lift to it, it has been tempting to borrow phrases from this eloquent ending of the message of December 1 and attach them to the content of the prosaic proclamation of January 1.

One could adduce these reasons for Lincoln's bizarre effort: first, since the Emancipation Proclamation would proclaim slaves free only in rebel territories, this proposal could be a parallel emancipation for border slave states still in the Union; and second, since the proclamation would be a war measure whose future legal standing was dubious, these amendments could settle the long future and be permanent constitutional law.

But it was not going to happen that way. The gist of Lincoln's proposal had already been rejected, more than once, by the key states—the slave states still in the Union. Slavery in the United States would in time be ended by amending the Constitution, and Lincoln would be the key figure in making it happen, but it would not be done by these amendments.*

The limitations of the proposal that it recommended would provide an ironical undertow to the moving appeal with which Lincoln ended his 1862 annual message one month before he issued the Emancipation Proclamation. After poignant appeals for collaboration ("We can succeed only by concert") and for realism ("It is not 'can any of us imagine better?' but 'can we all do better?' "), he pulled out all the stops on the organ and moved into one of the great passages in American political writing.

One may evoke two pictures: one of the harassed president at his desk somehow finding not only the time but the intellectual wattage to compose these paragraphs; the other of the clerk of the Senate, John Forney, reading them out across the assembled congressmen.

Forney must have been reading for more than an hour, through some quite forbidding material—data from the census as well as Lincoln's detailed proposals—because the message was 8,500 words long. Were the congressmen snoozing, bustling around, chatting, slipping in and out of the chamber? Did a couple of alert ones, noticing what was suddenly being intoned over them from the podium, look at each other in wild surmise?

They were the first to hear, if they did hear, some phrases that would ring forever thereafter in American memory.

---

*The three are labeled "articles" so they are sometimes regarded as parts of one amendment, but on the other hand Lincoln does introduce them as "amendments," plural.

The dogmas of the quiet past, are inadequate to the stormy present. The occasion is piled high with difficulty, and we must rise with the occasion. As our case is new, so we must think anew, and act anew. We must disenthrall our selves, and then we shall save our country.

Lincoln himself, rising to the occasion, was disenthralling himself exactly of the limitations this very message had displayed.

Fellow-citizens, we cannot escape history. We of this Congress and this administration, will be remembered in spite of ourselves. No personal significance, or insignificance, can spare one or another of us. The fiery trial through which we pass, will light us down, in honor or dishonor, to the latest generation. We say we are for the Union. The world will not forget that we say this. We know how to save the Union. The world knows we do know how to save it. We—even we here—hold the power, and bear the responsibility.

Here, because he was not issuing an order but attempting to inspire and persuade, he was able to include a surpassingly eloquent picture of the weight of the decision that rested on them all, and then, in one majestic flight, of the national accomplishment of which he was to be the leader. Giving freedom to the slave assured freedom to the free, the two tied together, both honorable, and joined together they will "nobly save" the best that this nation represents.

In giving freedom to the slave, we assure freedom to the free—honorable alike in what we give, and what we preserve. We shall nobly save, or meanly lose, the last best, hope of earth.

The national effort to accomplish that noble objective would be initiated not by the dubious effort that this magnificent ending accompanied but by the actions that the man who wrote it would begin to take a month later with the Emancipation Proclamation.

CHAPTER FOURTEEN

The Prompt Vindication of His Honor

IN THE SUMMER and fall of 1863 the president would be inundated with another barrage of petitions, telegrams, and personal appeals, this time asking for mercy in the case of Dr. David M. Wright, a well-respected physician and citizen and family man of Norfolk, Virginia, who had been found guilty of murder and sentenced to be hanged.

When back before the war in 1853 Dr. Wright and his family had moved from Edenton, North Carolina, to Norfolk, some leading citizens of Edenton had taken the trouble to send a testimonial, on blue paper, with rows of those flowery nineteenth-century signatures, commending Dr. Wright's worthiness: "He stands professionally among the first in the eastern part of North Carolina" and "His personal character is untarnished in any respect. We commend him to the citizens of Norfolk as an able physician, a gentleman in all aspects, and as possessing social qualities that will endear him to the community to which he goes." Unfortunately those endearing social qualities were thoroughly soaked in the presuppositions of a slaveholding, deeply racist society, and the respectable Dr. Wright was caught in a major clash of moral cultures.

On July 11, 1863, he was standing in the doorway of Foster and Moore, a store on Norfolk's Main Street, when a company of soldiers came marching by, two abreast, to the beating of a drum, on the sidewalk. There were several unsettling novelties in this scene for a "gentleman in all aspects" from Virginia and North Carolina.

In the first place, that they were marching on the sidewalk was, in Dr. Wright's opinion, a dubious novelty. Sidewalk etiquette—who steps aside for whom—was a point of no small importance in the caste society of the slave South.

In the second place, these were Union soldiers. The Norfolk area, Portsmouth, and the Gosport Navy Yard, the nation's prime naval base and a major shipbuilding facility, had first been seized by the Virginia secessionists in April 1861, even before Virginia technically had seceded from the Union: it was a major prize. Its capture included the taking of the *Merrimack,* which a year later, on March 9, 1862, refitted and renamed the *Virginia* by the rebels, would engage in the famous duel of ironclads with the Union's *Monitor.* But then in May, as the Army of the Potomac was advancing in force up the peninsula toward Richmond, the Confederate forces under Joseph E. Johnston withdrew from Norfolk and retreated back up the peninsula. President Lincoln himself had been present, visiting Fort Monroe with Chase and Stanton, and had given orders and had himself picked out a landing spot for the Union troops; Chase had the thrill of accompanying the troops as they received the surrender of Norfolk.

So now, a little over a year after that recovery, the area was a Union-held enclave within a Confederate state—indeed, the state in which the Confederate capital was now located and major battles of the war in the East were being fought. And there were soldiers dressed in blue uniforms marching down the streets—and sidewalks.

One more novelty, the most important. These were "colored" soldiers: Company B, First Regiment, U.S. Colored Volunteers.

At the start of the war in 1861, the Union armies of a deeply prejudiced nation had been all white, and black volunteers had been rejected. During 1862 the first sporadic organizing of African American units had begun, in Sea Island, in Louisiana, in Kansas, under the initiative of individual commanders in particular situations, still surrounded by doubts. One hugely significant provision of the Emancipation Proclamation of January 1, 1863, six months before these events in Norfolk, was the declaration that "such persons [the former slaves who are now to be forever free] will be received into the armed forces of the United States."

And the first six months of 1863 had seen the first systematic recruiting of free black men, freed slaves, and fugitives into new regiments in the Union army. At first, like all the other troops of the Union army, they were attached to particular states—the famous 54th Massachusetts is an example. But then in May 1863 the Lincoln administration regularized and systematized the recruiting and organizing of "colored" troops, establishing a "Bureau of Colored Troops" in Washington. The regiments into which African Americans would henceforth be organized would not be tied to any state. Black Americans would be mustered directly into the federal service uniquely under the authority of the United States, with a regimental name and number not from any one state but as part of the "U.S. Colored Troops"—as was the case with this company marching down the sidewalk of Main Street in Norfolk in July 1863.

The past six months had seen a revolutionary change in the relationship of the Union army to black men and the mounting of systematic efforts to fill the new "colored" regiments. Northern opposition was being diminished, even overcome, particularly as reports spread of the brave performance of the Negro troops under fire first in small encounters in Florida and the West, and then in battle in places called Port Hudson and Milliken's Bend in Louisiana. And just a week after this July 11 episode in Norfolk, on July 18, the 54th Massachusetts would cover itself with glory storming the rampart of Fort Wagner.

July 1863 was also the month of the dreadful draft riots in New York City, in which a mob, largely Irish, protesting the draft, burned a black orphanage, attacked the homes of abolitionists, and killed black men, women, and children, hanging many from lampposts—the worst riots in American history. But just eight months after that outrage, in March 1864, New Yorkers would cheer and celebrate the 20th U.S. Colored Troops as it marched through the city streets and was honored by leading citizens in a ceremony at Union Square. Attitudes toward black soldiers in the North, in the flux of war, were undergoing astonishingly rapid change.

But the South saw quite an opposite reaction. Fear. Fury. Fierce indignation. Murderous rage. To regard a black man in the uniform of the opposing armies as a legitimate enemy struck at the very foundation of the newly founded Confederacy. Its core was not only slavery but also a "cornerstone" belief in racial inequality and racial subordination that justified slavery. In the first days of the Confederacy, when hope and candor still reigned, that "cornerstone" was quite explicitly defended—as in a famous nation-defining speech by the vice president of the Confederacy, Alexander P. Stephens, in March 1861. Stephens had not only insisted on the inferiority of the Negro "race" and its necessary and perennial subordination to the superior white "race," but he had also (this part was unusual) specifically rejected the egalitarian generalities of Jefferson and other Founders: they were wrong. The Confederacy, by contrast, was now founded on the "truth" about racial inequalities and therefore slavery.

These were not, to be sure, merely dry points in social and political theory. They were passionately held attitudes inculcated in the citizenry of a slavery-based society. The responses of Confederate political leaders and generals to the Union army recruiting and arming black men had a passion, a touch even of fanaticism, that revealed how deeply that new development struck at their collective self-conception and their prejudices. Jefferson Davis had described the Emancipation Proclamation, and specifically its proposal to recruit and to arm black men ("human beings of an inferior race," in Davis's view), as an attempt to bring on "the most execrable massacre recorded in the history of guilty man." The Confederate Congress resolved that officers of units of Negroes "if captured be put to death or otherwise punished" at the discretion of a military court. Negro soldiers themselves were to be treated in accord with the laws of the state in which they were captured, which meant they would be returned to or (for free blacks) newly placed in slavery. Some Confederate officials and army officers, in rhetoric and in practice, went further. James Seddon, the Confederate secretary of war, said as widespread Union recruiting began that his War Department had "determined that Negroes captured would not be treated as prisoners of war," a determination that would stall prisoner exchanges almost to the end of the conflict. Seddon also said, "As to white officers serving with Negro troops, we ought never to be inconvenienced by such prisoners."

So on this summer day, in this slaveholding Southern city, a company of black Union soldiers marched to the beat of a drum up the sidewalk of Main Street. This must have been the first time such a sight was seen in Norfolk. The officer in charge of this company was a young white man from Vermont named Anson L. Sanborn, only twenty-one years old, a lieutenant. (The racial mores of the whole nation did mean that almost always as yet the officers of these "colored" units were white.) Something of a crowd assembled in the Norfolk streets, taunting and jeering at this deeply disturbing sight. From the doorway of Foster and Moore Dr. Wright called out a remark that included the word "cowardly." He would himself characterize his remark as "offensive."

Lieutenant Sanborn commanded his troops to halt. He sent one of his company in the direction of the provost marshal's office and gave the command to "order arms." Sanborn then moved around the troops toward Dr. Wright, making remarks of his own that included, apparently, the proposal that Dr. Wright was to be arrested. There was, one witness reported, "considerable excitement." As Sanborn was turning "as if to move away," Dr. Wright lifted a pistol he had been holding behind his back and shot Sanborn, wounding him in the hand and shoulder. As Sanborn "stooped down," Wright almost immediately fired a second shot from his five-chambered Colt revolver. This bullet entered Sanborn's body at the collarbone and did not come out, causing an internal wound that would shortly cause his death.

Still alive for the moment, Sanborn "rushed in on the Doctor" and "forced him back into the store." They tussled over the gun, with Wright holding it still from the butt and Sanborn from the barrel. Dr. Wright, arguing later that he had never meant to kill Sanborn, pointed out that if he had so intended, he could have fired again directly into Sanborn's body at that later moment in the melee.

Norfolk was under martial law, with other Union troops in the area, in particular a regiment of New York volunteers. Some of them too had been on Main Street and had seen these events. One witness at Dr. Wright's trial—a Union army colonel from the 155th New York Volunteers named Hugh C. Flood—reported that the "Negroes of the company" had set up a shout that he thought was "Let's kill him" (Wright) and charged into the store. Colonel Flood "rushed in with the foremost of them" and kept himself moving, as he put it, up to the lieutenant struggling with the doctor. Colonel Flood ordered the others back, appropriated the pistol, took the doctor by the arm, and told him he was a colonel in the U.S. service and that he, the doctor, was under arrest. Dr. Wright said, "Very well, sir, I am under arrest, and give myself up to your charge."

Lieutenant Sanborn, meanwhile, "slid along the counter and fell to the floor and the blood gushed out of his nose and nostrils." Then came the odd moment when Colonel Flood sent for a doctor—and then was reminded that the perpetrator himself was a doctor. When Colonel Flood proposed to take Dr. Wright, under arrest, to the provost marshal, Dr. Wright said, "Let me do something for this man—I want to do something for this man," meaning Sanborn, bleeding to death on the floor. In the trial Wright's counsel did not do much cross-examining—Wright's only real defense struck at more fundamental levels—but on this one point the counsel for the defense would ask the significance of Dr. Wright's saying, "Let me do something for this man." Colonel Flood answered: "I should judge that he wanted to do something to alleviate the lieutenant's pain." He had reverted to being a physician. And one may even read in Colonel Flood's testimony that as Dr. Wright was being led away, he reached out his hand toward Sanborn, dying on the floor.

ANOTHER UNION SOLDIER from the New York volunteers, testifying at the trial, when asked what he knew about the deceased, gave a memorably succinct summary of the short, happy life of Anson Sanborn: "I knew him as Lieut. Sanborn of Vermont; became acquainted with him in Portsmouth, Va., where he was recruiting colored troops. I saw him alive on the Eleventh inst. And afterwards on the same day, I saw him dead in the store of Foster and Moore, on Main Street, in this city." *I saw him alive . . . I saw him dead.*

Two interpretations of this episode were cast up by the warring cultures behind the warring armies. Confederate secretary of war James Seddon, no doubt reflecting the version of the story current in Richmond, said that one should have sympathetic understanding for the "natural indignation" that Wright felt at the "shameful spectacle" he was witnessing. Seddon had to mean the sight of black troops in Union army uniforms marching in formation down the streets of his Southern city—a city of which Dr. Wright was such a respectable and eminent and well-connected citizen. And what did he do out of his "natural indignation" at this "shameful spectacle"? The next phrase that Seddon used is truly wonderful, a revelation of a deep moral gulf: what Wright then did, said Seddon, was "a prompt vindication of his honor."*

Judge Advocate General Joseph Holt, on the other hand, in his summary of the case for President Lincoln, had rather a different phrase to describe the same event. It was, Holt said, an "unprovoked assassination."

The trial took place in Norfolk before one of those military commissions that were a new feature of the Civil War—a military court trying civilians in an area in which, presumably, the war had displaced the civil justice system. The fairness and legitimacy of these military commissions were an issue at the time and continued to be an issue before the Supreme Court and in historical writing—one of the issues about civil liberties in the Civil War. Wright's counsel did raise the question of proper jurisdiction, and Dr. Wright himself would refer to it. One may surely guess that Dr. Wright's fate would have been different had he had a civil trial with a jury of Norfolk citizens. The prosecution responded that this court "was sitting within a district congruent from rebel enemies [surrounded by seceded Virginia], held by military force, and utterly dependent upon the military power for each moment's enjoyment of security."

The court—the military commission—consisted of three Union army

---

*[H]onor was inseparable from hierarchy and entitlement, defense of family blood and community needs. All these exigencies required the rejection of the lowly, the alien, and the shamed." Bertram Wyatt-Brown, *Honor and Violence in the Old South* (New York: Oxford University Press, 1986), p. 4.

officers appointed by the commanding general of the Department of Virginia. The charge was that David M. Wright "did willfully, feloniously, and with malice aforethought kill and murder A. L. Sanborn, 2nd Lieut., Company B, 1st Regiment, U.S. Colored Troops, by shooting him to death with a pistol."

Wright pleaded not guilty.

Mark E. Neely, Jr., in the leading study of civil liberties during the Civil War, indicates that despite the denunciation of these military commissions by Democrats and some Republicans at the time and by some later scholars, such trials "definitely stood a step above no law at all [or the mere will of the commander]." Despite the allegations against them, "trials by military commission were marked by procedural regularity. The best proof of this is the existence of the records themselves," turning brown and bound in red ribbons in the National Archives. These trials were better on that score than ordinary trials below the appellate level, which had no record: "Trials by military commission were all recorded," and in a legible hand, preserved across the decades. The accused is present, allowed to confront his accusers and to question all witnesses, and to have the advice of counsel. In fact, the commission sitting for Dr. Wright's trial twice postponed its proceeding in order for him to retain adequate counsel. The lawyers retained were about as able and well connected as one could ask: L. H. Chandler, who had been U.S. attorney for the Eastern District of Virginia and a congressman-elect (from the shadow Union state of "restored Virginia"), and Samuel J. Bowden, a U.S. senator. They were supporters of the Union, well connected enough to be able to write letters to President Lincoln, to call on him, and to make a case to him for clemency for Dr. Wright.

If you read through the transcript of the trial, you will surely not conclude that it was arbitrary or unfair in its procedure—assuming you agree that under the circumstances a civilian might be tried by a court consisting of three army officers. Wright and his lawyers were given every courtesy and safeguard. Dr. Wright himself (and his wife, as one learns from a letter she wrote at a later point) wanted to emphasize that in fact he had no malice toward Sanborn and no premeditation of the act. "With malice aforethought?" They said no. Wright would insist that he had never known Sanborn before their encounter, and he described the event this way in his remarks to the court: "Suppose that two strangers meet at the corner of the street, bump heads, get into a difficulty and one of them is killed. This would be a parallel case." (But it would not be a parallel case. The "difficulty," needless to say, was not just a reciprocal head bumping.) So he had never met or heard of Sanborn until that fateful moment on a July after-noon. Premeditation? We may note, arguing a little across the years with the Wrights outside the record of the trial, that in her letter his wife says that her husband was asleep when the company marched past their house (on their way downtown) and that one of his grown daughters awakened him saying, "Look!" and that they looked out the window at the black men in Union army uniforms marching by. Better that he had stayed asleep! Mrs. Wright does not go on with the story, but what happened is plain enough. The good doctor, in some excitement, we may infer, headed quickly for Main Street, taking with him—fateful decision!—his loaded five-chambered Colt revolver.

Chandler and Bowden did not try to defend their client with respect to any of these features of the incident. Except for the one question about the doctor saying he wanted to do something for "this man" (Sanborn), elicit-ing the sympathetic response that the statement was not threatening but a doctor's desire to help, the lawyers declined to cross-examine Colonel Flood or the other witnesses. They had a different defense in mind. They would challenge the jurisdiction of the military commission; failing that, they would plead that Wright was temporarily insane.

A plea of temporary insanity was a new feature in American law, having been successfully used just four years before in a sensational trial of the famous Tammany politician and congressman Daniel Sickles. Sickles was a notorious philanderer, but when his wife took a lover, Congressman Sick-les shot him dead on a Washington street. The plea in this murder trial was that he had been driven "temporarily" insane by the outrage of this man being his wife's lover—and Sickles was acquitted. And his life had gone on. In fact, Sickles, the temporarily insane murderer of his wife's paramour, was now serving as a general in the Union army, a political general serving as a corps commander on the staff of "Fighting Joe" Hooker.

So: Dr. Wright was temporarily insane? Bowden and Chandler had material about his state of mind on the day of the shooting, and midway through the trial they made an effort to get some of it included, but the mil-itary commission did not let them introduce it. They asked for a half-hour recess to consult—and then Bowden and Chandler withdrew from the trial. They moved their attention to a perhaps more promising level at which to make their argument: an appeal to the president of the United States for a pardon.

Meanwhile, their client had to sail on through the choppy waters of the rest of the trial without counsel. He himself would use that metaphor, in a poetic and sympathetic moment in his closing remarks. "I feel like a man in a small boat on a tremendous sea at night," he would say, "with no friendly star to guide him." When he was offered the opportunity to speak before the court retired for decision, he hesitated; the court obliged him with a postponement, after which he spoke. A friendly star would have said, *No, no, don't.* But he did.

As he began to speak to the court, he said, "My friends have advised me not to make an address, and I fear that I am not able to explain myself as I would wish." But, unfortunately, he explained himself all too well. His own reasons for acting were deeply rooted in the ethos of the racist and slave-holding South, and in the end, as his rather rambling remarks proceeded and his passions mounted, he would plainly reveal that root.

He tried at the outset to echo some of the arguments his lawyers had made. He said that his making remarks did not imply that he accepted the jurisdiction of the court. He used the word "madman" four times in the early part of his remarks. He said that unless his act was done in self-defense, it would have been the act of a madman and asked rhetorically, "What motive appears in this case? What cause can be given for my act?" Unfortunately for his own case, before he was through, he would give an answer to his own question.

"I did not intend to say anything, Mr. President," he said in the midst of his ramble, addressing the president of the court, "but from the fullness of my heart I have spoken."

A friendly star, or a lawyer, would have guided him away from the revealing outburst that came suddenly in the midst of his remarks.

"May I be permitted to ask why that colored company was brought over from Portsmouth?"

"Was it not known that great feeling and fear would be excited in Norfolk?"

"Who in this city has forgotten the Southampton massacre?"

No Southerners in the room needed to have it explained that he was referring to the Nat Turner affair at Southampton, only thirty-two years in the past and less than one hundred miles from Norfolk, in which some fifty-five white persons had been killed. And why was he calling up that event in this context? The answer came in Dr. Wright's worst sentence: "Who does not know that these creatures, the Negroes, when restraint is removed, become unmanageable savages?"

That sentence was heard now in the court by the Union army officers who composed the court, then would be read into the record by the commanding general who appointed the commission, and then would from there be read by Judge Advocate General Joseph Holt in Washington when he prepared his recommendation to the president. And then it was there on the page for the president himself to read when he considered a pardon.

Dr. Wright, the fullness of his heart having broken through the wary constraints of the earlier part of his remarks, now spilled out the feelings that did indeed motivate him and was carried away into his own explanation of the whole event.

> It seems to me that there was a purpose in bringing this colored company into this city. It was not enough to march them through the streets. More than that was to be accomplished. Difficulty was to be provoked and the sidewalks were appropriated and old men and women were driven from the sidewalks into the streets and into the stores.
>
> The Lieutenant of that company hearing some one of the remarks that were of course made chose to appropriate it to himself and thus his end was accomplished, and he said to himself "Now I'll have recruits in abundance. I'll march this old secesh [slang for secessionist] through the streets and will have an abundance of recruits." What else could have been the motive of the Lieutenant?

Dr. Wright implicitly granted that he himself made one of the remarks that were "of course" made—what else could one expect?—and he later granted that the remark was "offensive." But he implicitly suggested that it was not necessarily directed at Sanborn, or at Sanborn exclusively— perhaps at the whole company and its sidewalk marching?—because he indicated that Sanborn chose to take it as addressed to him personally. And then Wright, bordering on sarcasm, suggested that Sanborn's response to this offensive remark was not itself tame and gentle: "You cannot believe that he appropriated to himself an offensive remark . . . and then came round as peaceful as a dove and merely said 'consider yourself under arrest.' "

No, Sanborn's response to Wright's offensive remark, including the proposal to arrest him, presumably was not made in the accents of the harmless dove. And now Dr. Wright uttered another passage—a rhetorical question, followed by bedrock personal resolution—that reveals again, as in the "unmanageable savages" passage, the depth of the moral gulf between the nation's institutions and the ethos that had shaped him: "And is it to be supposed that a citizen of Norfolk, himself an owner of slaves, not knowing but what some one of my slaves was in that company, would submit to be arrested by Negroes, and marched off to the guard house? No, sir, I would not submit to that."

Passion mounting, he shifted from the third person "citizen-of-Norfolk-himself" to the first person "my slaves—I would not submit." And he pictured the stark humiliation of the prospect that provoked his act: to be arrested by Negroes. To be marched through the streets to the guardhouse by three Negroes, among whom there might even be his own former slaves. No, it was an indignity too deep to be borne. In a sentence that echoes all that code of a Southern gentleman's "honor," he insisted that he would not submit to it. And so, having all too conveniently brought with him his loaded five-chambered revolver, he raised it and promptly vindicated his honor. Twice. And an hour later Lieutenant Sanborn lay dead in his own blood on the floor of Foster and Moore's store.

AS HE WOUND DOWN his remarks to the military commission, Dr. Wright seems to have cooled, to have remembered (too late) the cautions of his friends and lawyers, and to have regretted what he had said.

"Mr. President, I did not intend when I arose to make any remarks except to thank the Court for giving me a day to prepare an address. I meant to have left my case just where it was left by my counsel, and I should be glad not to have what I have said made any part of the proceedings of this Court."

But of course it was made a part of the proceedings and was referred to in two key papers as the case worked its way upward through the system. In the trial itself, before the military commission in Norfolk, the judge advocate (the prosecutor, in effect) noted that "there is . . . in the statement of the accused a motive apparent, and the court cannot mistake the nature of the emotion, the passion excited in his mind, he a slaveholder and secessionist, by the sight of colored troops in the service of the Union."

And after the three members of the military commission had unanimously found Wright guilty of murder and sentenced him to hang, and the general commanding the Union army in the district had concurred in the verdict, and the papers in this capital case had been sent to Washington for consideration by the president, Judge Advocate General Joseph Holt in his presentation to Lincoln also referred to Wright's remarks:

He [Wright] then proceeds to intimate what his motive really was, and finds it in his determination not to be arrested and marched off under a guard of "Negroes"—an indignity which he represents as having been

threatened by the deceased . . . and which he asserts he "would not submit to." He further alleges a provocation for his act in the presence of the
colored troops, whom he deems to have been brought into Norfolk to
provoke and insult the inhabitants.

So now the case came to Lincoln himself. The system of trials by military commissions during the Civil War did provide, in addition to a certain
level of procedural protection, the possibility of "mercy as well as military
justice." Capital cases were always referred to the president; there were
good records for him to examine, and "their quantity was limited enough
to allow Lincoln to examine a substantial percentage of the cases." Not surprisingly, in a majority of cases Lincoln did accept the recommendation of
his judge advocate general, Joseph Holt. "But when Lincoln defied Holt's
advice, it was most often to indulge mercy." And when, in accord with
Holt's recommendation, he went against the commanding general's position, it was also most often to mitigate punishment.

In the midst of all his other duties, Lincoln surely did give serious consideration to this case coming up from Norfolk in August 1863. Before the
final decision down at Fort Monroe, he had already received a letter
addressed to "his excellency A. Lincoln, President of the United States,
from Attorney Lemuel J. Bowden." Bowden summarized the case, explained why he and his partner Chandler had withdrawn from it, insisted
that "the fact of Dr. Wright's being insane could have been established" if
they had been allowed to do it, and explained that "affidavits which are not
in the record well show such a state of mental unsoundness in the accused
as would make manifest the impropriety of holding him to criminal accountability for any act that he may have committed."

Sickles, seeing his wife's lover on the Washington street, went "temporarily" insane and shot him dead; he was acquitted and now commands
Union army corps. So—Dr. Wright? He went "temporarily" insane when
he saw "colored" Union army troops—should he not now be pardoned for
"any act that he may have committed"?

President Lincoln with his conscientiousness gave this argument more
attention than you may think it deserves. He granted an interview in the
executive mansion to Chandler and promised to give the case a full examination. He sent an order to "Major General Foster, or whoever may be in
command of the military department, with headquarters in Fort Monroe,
Virginia," that if Dr. Wright had been convicted, to stop the execution and
send Lincoln the papers.

So there was Lincoln in August 1863 reading through the material summarized above, including Dr. Wright's own self-damning testimony. He sent telegrams, as he had promised to do, to Chandler and Bowden that he had read the record and was ready to hear them, with what they called this "mass of testimony which has been taken to prove the insanity of Dr. Wright."

It would appear that Lincoln on reading through the papers and Holt's summary and recommendation rejected any other argument for a pardon for Wright; he would eventually write that he was "satisfied that no proper questions remained open" except the insanity question. The petitions that poured into the White House from multitudes of "respectable" citizens—including, it was pointed out, many "Union men"—testified to Wright's character and worthy personal qualities. But all of that would not expunge the deed and in fact might seem to stand in some tension with the argument that he was "insane." Wright himself in his remarks, and his wife in a plea she would later write to a woman friend of Mary Lincoln and some of the petitioners, made a considerable point that he had no "malice" and no "pre-meditation." He had never known, had never met or heard of Sanborn before that fateful afternoon; he had had no prior intentions to harm him, and in shooting him no intention to kill him.

But none of this, we may say, would serve to exculpate him or merit pardon. David Wright, an all too fully respectable Southern gentleman, had in him two elements of the ethos of the slaveholding South that, in the terrible chemistry of a passionate moment, led to his undoing and Sanborn's death: "racism," as it would come to be called, and the Southern code of "honor." He was sufficiently agitated by the sight of the "unmanageable savages" in Union army uniforms marching beneath his window to rush— we assume he rushed—down to Main Street with his five-chambered Colt revolver, loaded. Why do that? Not premeditation, exactly, but a fateful decision. He was then imbued with a deep racial feeling sufficient to call out "offensive" remarks, including the word "cowardly"—this gentleman and professional man—as the troops marched by on the sidewalk on Main Street. And then when the young Yankee lieutenant halted the troops and sent a ("colored") soldier to the provost marshal and came round to tell Wright, standing there in the doorway of Foster and Moore, that he was under arrest, an absolutely intolerable picture flashed into Wright's mind: being marched off to the guardhouse by some of these black men in uniform, maybe including his own former slaves. It would be an intolerable insult to his honor.* So he promptly lifted his pistol and shot Sanborn. And promptly shot him again.

Secretary Seddon's description of the deed, no doubt reflecting an interpretation in Confederate Richmond of these events in Union-controlled Norfolk, captured an ethos succinctly in a phrase, every word loaded: "A prompt vindication of his honor." If only Wright had been a little less prompt.

LINCOLN CONSIDERED only one possible basis of pardon, the claim that Wright in that moment was so mentally unsound as not to be accountable. He did not decide that claim on the basis of Chandler and Bowden's affidavits but sought independent expert testimony. Lincoln thought of calling on the head of the Government Asylum for the Insane to examine Wright, but Secretary of State William Seward—who back in his days as a lawyer had a worthy record of using the insanity plea in the defense of accused black men—proposed another "alienist," one John P. Gray of Utica, a leading specialist in mental health. Lincoln wrote to Dr. Gray engaging him to "serve the government for a month or less." He gave Dr. Gray a rather extraordinary assignment, going to much trouble, one might say, about one particular pardon case, in the midst of the events of the fall of 1863. He asked Dr. Gray to go to Fort Monroe and to "take in writing all evidence . . . on behalf of Dr. Wright and against him . . . directed to the question of Dr. Wright's sanity or insanity." Chandler and Bowden were notified. A judge advocate was appointed on the other side. Witnesses were called. If proper, said Lincoln to Dr. Gray, "examine Dr. Wright personally." It would be an extraordinary hearing on Dr. Wright's sanity, set up by the president of the United States.

So Dr. Gray went to Fort Monroe and conducted, at the behest of the president, this second, nonmilitary "trial" of Dr. Wright, directed exclusively to the question of his sanity. Dr. Gray, editor of the *American Journal of Insanity*, was now presiding. He called thirteen witnesses for Wright and thirteen for the prosecution, and interviewed Wright himself for two hours. He found no previous symptoms of insanity and no current symptoms. A

---

*Both Dr. Wright's responses throughout this episode and this statement of Secretary Seddon are precise illustrations of themes of Southern "honor" as examined by Bertram Wyatt-Brown: the sharp sense of insult when those who do not belong are in the wrong place, and the "necessity for valiant action" and "morally purifying violence." See Wyatt-Brown, *Honor and Violence.*

suddenly appearing insanity, Dr. Gray said, would not utterly disappear after one action. So he made his report, after his thorough hearing, to the conscientious president.

When one is reading through the papers on this case in the National Archives, almost 150 years after the fact, one is startled to come upon a single sheet of lined paper, brown and deteriorating around the edges, with quite neat handwriting filling the whole page and the signature at the bottom, "Abraham Lincoln": Lincoln's decision in this case—there it is—on the paper he wrote it on, in his own hand.

Dr. Gray had reported, and President Lincoln now gave his decision:

[B]eing satisfied that no proper question remained open except as to the insanity of the accused, I caused a very full examination to be made on that question, upon a great amount of evidence, including all offered by counsel of accused, by an expert of high reputation in that professional department, who thereupon reports to me, as his opinion, that the accused Dr. David M. Wright, was not insane prior to or on the 11th day of July, 1863, the date of the homicide of Lieutenant Sanborn; that he has not been insane since, and is not insane now (October 7, 1863).

Very thorough: Dr. Wright was sane before the deed, sane during it, sane after it, and he is sane now.

The ending of the story was not "prompt." There were multiple appeals, pressures, petitions. Once again, as with Nathaniel Gordon, Lincoln ordered the postponement of the scheduled execution for a week to provide Wright time for "his preparation." Although Dr. Wright had not been a church member, he had read prayers regularly to his family, and now in prison he was baptized and received into a church. Major General John G. Foster at Fort Monroe, who said that although it was his rule not to allow anyone to leave the department who was not willing to take the oath of allegiance, nevertheless, because Lincoln had postponed the execution, did pass on the request from Chandler that Mrs. Wright and a companion be allowed to visit Lincoln to plead in her husband's behalf. The president, notoriously susceptible to such pleas in general, especially from women, in this case said no: "It would be useless for Mrs. Dr. Wright to come here. The subject is a very painful one, but the case is settled."

An attempt to escape was made and thwarted. An attempted bribe was indignantly rejected. A proposal by the lawyers to exchange Dr. Wright for a specific prisoner held by the Confederates was denied. On the day of the execution hope remained for a pardon, but in this case no last-minute presidential telegram arrived. On October 23, 1863, Dr. Wright was hanged at Fort Monroe. His reported last words on the scaffold suggest that he still interpreted the event in entirely individualistic terms, as only between himself and this young white man, Anson Sanborn, whom he had never met before the terrible moment. "Gentlemen, the act which I committed was done without the slightest malice." But there are different sorts of "malice." And also of "honor."

CHAPTER FIFTEEN

And the Promise Being Made, Must Be Kept

THE STAMPEDE OF RUNAWAYS

BY ISSUING the Emancipation Proclamation, and particularly by recruiting black men into the Union army, Lincoln acquired a new duty, about which he would make his most rigorous presidential commitment to a particular group of human beings. No one was to be returned to slavery. *If such treachery, such a cruel breach of faith, is to be done, get someone else, not me, to do it.*

The response of the slave population to the war had been a giant engine of change. Four million human beings, spread from the Atlantic to Texas in a wide variety of settings, were not passive victims acted upon by others but were moral agents making decisions. If the slaves were not free legally, they were still free in the profounder sense that moral judgment implies: like prisoners and residents of tyrannies, within severe constraints and dangers, they still had choices.

Some slaves did work for the Confederate army, digging trenches, building breastworks, producing munitions at the Tredegar Iron Works, serving as body servants taking care of their masters in the army itself; a few were even allowed rifles and served as Confederate sharpshooters. A great many more did the work of keeping Confederate society going while the white men were off to war.

But the more significant choices made by slaves were the perilous decisions to defy the slave system and to attempt escape. American slaves, unlike those in Haiti who successfully revolted against their "masters," did not have a numerical advantage; any attempt at the massive "servile insurrection" that loomed large in some fevered white fears would have been an enormous disaster and was not really possible under American conditions of the greater presence and larger numbers of whites and slave owners.

(Jamaica had ten blacks for every one white; in the American South it was two whites to one black.) But once the war began, American slaves could and did engage in acts of noncooperation to such an extent that the great black scholar and writer W. E. B. DuBois could speak of a "general strike."

There does not appear to have been anything as organized as that term implies, but there was malingering, shirking, and defiance, with the white males gone and the grapevine carrying the word about the war. Although much of the white North would hold, for the first year and a half, that the war was only about the Union, not about slavery, those who had the greatest existential stake in the matter—the slaveholders and the slaves—perceived otherwise.

South Carolina's declaration of the causes for its secession, for example, with its many echoes of the Declaration of Independence, took for granted the defense of slavery as the war's purpose and the election of Lincoln as a precipitating cause of the war:

A geographical line has been drawn across the Union, and all the States north of that line have united in the election of a man to that high office of President of the United States, whose opinions and purposes are hostile to slavery. He is to be entrusted with the administration of the common Government, because he has declared that that "Government cannot endure permanently half slave, half free," and that the public mind must rest in the belief that slavery is in the course of ultimate extinction.

Charles Dew, a historian of Southern origins, examined the letters and speeches of the "commissioners" sent by the Deep South states to other slave states in 1860–61 to try to persuade them to join. What were they saying to each other, in private as it were, about the definition of the Confederacy? The answer to the question is blatant: the cause of their secession was the maintenance of slavery based on racism.

The commissioners said, for example, that the North has "chosen their leader [Abraham Lincoln] upon the single idea that the African is equal to the Anglo-Saxon, and with the purpose of placing our slaves on [a position of] equality with ourselves."

The Confederacy's rabid self-interpretation had the ironical result of persuading the slaves who overheard that this war was more exclusively and immediately about slavery, and that the newly elected Lincoln more immediately a liberator, than was in fact the case.

[M]ost slaves learned about the deepening sectional dispute from their owners' denunciation of the North and of the Republican party and its champions, the most threatening of whom was Abraham Lincoln. Indeed, the slaveholders' indiscriminate condemnations exaggerated the antislavery commitment of white Northerners, "Black Republicans," and Lincoln himself. Masters with no doubts about the abolitionist intentions of the North inadvertently persuaded their slaves of the ascendancy and pervasiveness of antislavery sentiment in the free states. The general politicization of Southern society thus reached deep into the slave community, imparting momentous significance to Lincoln's election.

The major action that slaves took was to run away and to present themselves to the Union army as it approached. W. E. B. DuBois, in 1933, correcting the then prevailing neglect of the role of the slaves, wrote:

The moment the Union army moved into slave territory, the Negro joined it . . . Every step the Northern armies took then meant fugitive slaves. They crossed the Potomac, and the slaves of northern Virginia began to pour into the army and into Washington. They captured Fortress Monroe, and slaves from Virginia and even North Carolina poured into the army. They captured Port Royal, and the masters ran away, leaving droves of black fugitives in the hands of the Northern army. They moved down the Mississippi Valley, and if the slaves did not rush to the army, the army marched to the slaves.

DuBois called this the "stampede of runaway slaves." Lincoln in his argument for compensated emancipation in border states would point out that the war had already freed many slaves. He would say that "the institution in your states will be extinguished by mere friction and abrasion—by the mere incidents of war." As the rebellion continued and more and more slaves fled, he would point out that "broken eggs cannot be mended." The eggs were the pieces of the institution of slavery that the stampede of runaways had already broken.

FUGITIVE MASTERS

WHEN RUNAWAY SLAVES presented themselves to the Union army, seeking asylum, the commanders in the field had decisions to make, as runaways often provided intelligence. Union soldiers made decisions about the treatment of runaways also. Racism led to some horror stories, but some Union soldiers increasingly perceived the evil of slavery and appreciated the role the runaways could play.

Commanders in the Union army held a spectrum of political opinions and racial attitudes. West Point conservatism and Lincoln's need to include prominent Democrats probably meant that the commanders were tilted against emancipation. McClellan, Burnside, Buell, and Halleck all returned fugitive slaves to "masters." It is reported that throughout McClellan's command of the Army of the Potomac the regimental bands were forbidden to play "John Brown's Body."

In the first months of the war General Ben Butler (in prior life a Tammany Democratic politician) managed to illustrate all by himself two contradictory military responses. When he first came into Maryland with the Third Brigade of the Massachusetts Voluntary Militia, in the exciting days of late April 1861, he reassured Governor Thomas Hicks not only that these Massachusetts troops would be "passing quickly through the state," "respecting private property," and "outraging the rights of none," but also that they would be available to put down any "negro" insurrection.

But almost exactly a month later, on May 23, when Butler was commanding at the little pocket of Union control in Virginia, Fort Monroe, and three runaway slaves presented themselves saying they would rather build fortifications for the Union than for the Confederacy, Butler had the inspired idea to claim them as "contraband of war." That concept spread. (There was, however, this little whiff of the old order: Butler gave the "masters" who claimed these fugitives a *receipt*.)

The West would provide similar contradictory responses by commanders. As we have seen, Frémont in Missouri in September 1861 tried to go all the way to military emancipation but was countermanded by Lincoln. But then on November 20 his successor Henry Halleck issued an oppressive order, Order No. 3, barring all fugitives from the Union lines and sending away those who had already made it.

To read Halleck's order is to sense the gulf of attitude in the North: "It has been represented that important information respecting the numbers and condition of our forces is conveyed to the enemy by means of fugitive slaves who are admitted within our lines. In order to remedy this evil it is directed that no such person be hereafter permitted to enter the lines . . . and that any now within such lines be immediately excluded therefrom." Others in the Union army, looking at the fugitives with different eyes, saw the matter more accurately: most fugitives were a source of intelligence not to the Confederate but to the Union forces.

A Vermont abolitionist named General John Phelps, commanding a camp north of New Orleans in May 1862, confronted swarms of black fugitives and organized them into companies. When he asked his commander in New Orleans for arms for them, that commander—the ubiquitous Benjamin Butler—told him he could not have guns but could put them to work with shovels and axes. Phelps refused, saying he was a general, not a slave driver. He tendered his resignation and spent the rest of the war in Vermont.

Union generals Phelps and David Hunter, who first recruited black troops, were declared outlaws, to be shot, by the Confederate government.

Lincoln revoked military emancipations issued not only by Frémont out in Missouri and then by Hunter on the Southern coast but also by his secretary of war, Simon Cameron. In his report of December 1861 Cameron recommended that slaves should be emancipated and armed as part of the war effort, and he sent a copy of the report to newspapers without informing Lincoln. The president promptly ordered the report recalled and the passage about freeing slaves expunged. Cameron's appointment had smacked of political necessity in the first place, and his conduct of the War Department did nothing to improve his already malodorous reputation.* Cameron was surely aware of the president's disapproval; his emancipation proposal in the report presumably was an attempt to engender some support for himself, like that which had burst forth from the antislavery world in response to Frémont's edict in Missouri. But Lincoln held that it would equally have brought forth a revolt on the border, and in places in the North, that the Union effort could not withstand.

David Hunter, a thoroughgoing abolitionist by personal conviction, came fresh from the Kansas border war to take command in March 1862 of the Department of the South, which nominally consisted of the entire states of Georgia, Florida, and South Carolina but practically consisted only of the coastal areas that the Union had recovered the previous November. Hunter was the friend whom Lincoln had enjoined to act well his part, and he apparently was determined to do so now in this arena by declaring martial law, freeing slaves, recruiting black soldiers, and ending the war at a stroke. On April 25, 1862, he issued a declaration of martial law for his department, and then on May 9 he declared that slavery and martial law were incompatible, and that "the persons . . . hitherto held as slaves" were now free.

---

*Cameron was the subject of one of American history's classic wisecracks. His rival, Pennsylvania Republican Thaddeus Stevens, said Cameron would steal anything except a red-hot stove. When Cameron protested, Congressman Stevens recanted with beautiful ambiguity: "I said that Secretary Cameron would steal anything but a red hot stove. I now withdraw that statement."

Hunter's action resembled that of Frémont and Cameron at least in this regard: he did not tell Lincoln beforehand. Salmon Chase urged Lincoln to approve Hunter's action. Lincoln's response made one essential point: "No commanding general shall do such a thing, on *my* responsibility, without consulting me." Lincoln countermanded Hunter's order.

But there was more. Hunter had found that the whites on the cotton plantations had fled en masse, leaving behind the huge population of slaves, which had outnumbered the whites five to one. There were able-bodied men among these suddenly masterless sometime slaves, and short of soldiers as he was, he recruited a regiment from the now free population, using methods that bordered on coercion. He dragooned five hundred of them, organized them into squads, and issued them weapons.

A conservative Kentucky congressman demanded an explanation from Cameron's successor Edwin Stanton, and Stanton sent the congressman's questions on to Hunter. Hunter, who seems to have had glimmers of a writerly ambition, seized on the opportunity, one might infer, with glee, and himself composed a response to the congressman's questions. When Secretary Stanton received and read Hunter's letter, he hurried it down to the House (according to Hunter's later account), where its reading by the clerk brought the gentle rain of laughter in the desert of congressional debate.

> I reply that no regiment of "fugitive slaves" has been ... organized in this department. There is, however, a fine regiment of persons whose late masters are "fugitive rebels"—men who everywhere fly before the appearance of the national flag ...
>
> It is the masters who have, in every instance, been the "fugitives," ... whom we have only partially been able to see ... dodging behind trees in the extreme distance. In the absence of any "fugitive master law," the deserted slaves would be wholly without remedy had not the crime of treason given them the right to pursue, capture, and bring back those persons of whose protection they have been thus suddenly bereft.

Hunter, pleased with himself, later said, "[T]he effect was magical. The Clerk could scarcely read it with decorum; nor could half his words be heard amidst the universal laughter."

To be sure, the laughter was not quite universal. A Kentucky colleague of the congressman who asked the original questions said: "The scene was one of which I think this House should forever be ashamed ... It was a scene ... disgraceful to the American Congress." Hunter certainly did not think it was a disgrace, however, and in Hunter's opinion, neither would Lincoln.

And although the president declared Hunter's emancipation edict "altogether void," he accompanied his declaration with his first statement that the president might under the war power do what Hunter had tried to do, which we quoted in Chapter 13. And Lincoln did not order Hunter to disband his nonfugitive nonslave regiment. Moreover, Lincoln sent no order directly to Hunter censuring him. As Hunter's edict had appeared in the "public prints," so did Lincoln's revocation. Hunter would say: "Lincoln repudiated in the newspapers my orders freeing slaves." Hunter believed Lincoln privately "rejoiced in my action."

Whether or not he rejoiced in Hunter's action, Lincoln did use it for polemical purposes, the way presidents do—*see how I am pressed by this other side.* In his presentation to border state representatives on July 12, he made reference to Hunter as an example of the pressures he was under from abolitionists.*

A MEETING AT THE WHITE HOUSE

The president, who had to cope with this extremely volatile situation, would suffer in after years from an acute version of the Mount Rushmore effect—or rather, in his case, the Lincoln Memorial effect. Simplified and exaggerated celebration would lead, on further knowledge, to simplified and exaggerated disillusionment. Lincoln would turn out to be not the brooding perfection of the memorial but an actual human being living in a particular time and place. His role in the world was not to be an unsullied moral hero but to be a shrewd, worthy, prudent politician.

Although Lincoln had strong and consistent convictions against slavery and a dedication to an inclusive but abstract principle of human equality, he had not in fact in his shaping years had many dealings with actual black persons. He had been born a poor white in a slave state; he spent his for-

---

*"I am pressed with a difficulty . . . which threatens division among those who, united are none too strong. An instance of it is known to you. Gen. Hunter is an honest man. He was, and I hope, still is, my friend. I valued him none the less for his agreeing with me in the general wish that all men everywhere, could be free. He proclaimed all men free within certain states, and I repudiated the proclamation . . . Yet in repudiating it, I gave dissatisfaction, if not offence, to many whose support the country could not afford to lose. And this is not the end of it. The pressure, in this direction, is still upon me, and is increasing. By conceding what I now ask, you can *relieve me, and much more, can relieve the country, in this important point.*"

mative years, from age eight to age twenty-one, in the all-white world of the southern Indiana woods, and his first days as an independent adult in the all-white village of New Salem. His life had been spent in a heavily prejudiced atmosphere; Indiana and Illinois were probably the most "racist" of free states. When Frederick Douglass praised Lincoln's freedom from prejudice, he would make a point of this geography—that Lincoln came from a state with severely restrictive racial laws.

Lincoln had had a few encounters with slavery—on a raft trip to New Orleans and a visit to the Kentucky home of his friend Joshua Speed—which would be much examined and sometimes made into myths in later years, and he had one encounter with a wandering black barber, a Haitian, whom he helped and befriended. In his growing law practice he defended slaves, in one case not only obtaining the freedom of a young slave woman named Nance but also providing "a mass of data supporting the principle of freedom," and in another case raising the money to purchase "freedom" for a young black man snared by New Orleans curfew laws. But in another case, embarrassing to his admirers in later years, he was associated in the attempt to recover a slave for an owner named Matson.

Shortly after he was elected, to the world's astonishment, as president of the United States he was asked by the editor of the *New York Times* whether he had been the speaker at a meeting held by Negroes to give an award to the great "attorney for the runaways" who had become the governor of Ohio, Salmon Chase. Lincoln sent the deflating answer: "I never was in a meeting of negroes in my life."

The great evil of Lincoln's lifetime was slavery. When in the next century, after the Second World War, the great evil would become racism, the Great Emancipator would be perceived to have warts. Taking a verbal beating from Senator Douglas in front of prejudiced white male Illinois voters in their 1858 debates because of his strong endorsement of equality, Lincoln in the southern Illinois town of Charleston explicitly disavowed social equality in words that a hundred years later would be repeatedly quoted against him. It would turn out that he had used the terms "Sambo" and "Cuffee"; that he had called Sojourner Truth "Aunty"; that he had attended minstrel shows; that he had probably told and laughed at some jokes that would not meet the standards of a later time.

Perhaps worst, he was a longtime supporter of the national movement to "colonize" American blacks in Africa or somewhere else outside the United States.

To modern ears that sounds morally repulsive; it is something of a test of historical imagination to think one's way back into the situation in which an honorable person might support such a movement. One can avoid the test by saying that no honorable person would do that, but in doing so one would be throwing overboard quite a list of presumably worthy Americans, including not only Lincoln's beau ideal Henry Clay but also Jefferson and Madison, multiple "eminent divines," and several leading abolitionists. The great antislavery novel *Uncle Tom's Cabin* ends with "a black's dream of freedom in Africa." Although the great majority of blacks rejected the colonizing project, some supported it, and their numbers grew after the Fugitive Slave Law of 1850 and increasing white racist restriction and attack. Even the great opponent of colonization Frederick Douglass, according to William Freehling, wavered for one brief despairing moment in January 1861. The motives for black colonizationists were despair about a racist America and hope for a black republic elsewhere. Were those radically different from Lincoln's motives? He did not know much about black life, but he did know white racism.

Lincoln had acquired his colonization convictions from his first political hero, Henry Clay; had spoken at colonization society meetings in Springfield; had defended colonization in his debates with Stephen Douglas; and as president would recommend it in his first two annual messages, endorse it in the preliminary (although not the final) emancipation proclamation, and go to some lengths actually to launch colonization projects—utterly futile as they would prove to be—near Haiti and in Panama.

In August 1862—significantly, after he had decided to issue the proclamation but before he had done so—he held a famous meeting in the White House with "a committee of colored men" to discuss the colonizing of American blacks in Central America. (Earlier it had been Liberia; later it would be an island in the Caribbean.) That five black men were invited to the White House by the president was altogether new, a crack in the racial caste system, but what Lincoln said once they got to the meeting did not do him credit. Lincoln's patronizing effort to persuade these "intelligent" blacks is said to have been the "nadir" of his presidency. One appalling argument was that it would be "extremely selfish" on the part of free black Americans not to want to help their more unfortunate brothers by leaving this country to build a colony elsewhere. Another was his suggestion that the white race, like the black, "suffers" from the presence of the other. Frederick Douglass was particularly offended by his implication that the presence of blacks in the country was the cause of the war ("But for your race among us there could not be war"), which he said was like a horse thief pleading the existence of the horse as the apology for his theft. In addition to the obtuse touches in Lincoln's presentation, as a multitude of commentators then and now have observed, the whole project was staggeringly impractical. In the first place, the overwhelming majority of blacks in this country did not want to embark on any such venture—to leave the country of their birth (as this group of five, as well as Frederick Douglass and many others soon told Lincoln). But in the second place, there was the sheer impossibility of the numbers.

In the several dubious efforts actually undertaken, the numbers were certainly small, measured against the natural increase each year of American blacks—not to mention the four million total. Lincoln, speaking to the five black visitors, indulged in a swift markdown of the number of families he sought for volunteers. One may be excused for remembering a joke he would tell on a later occasion. His April 1865 entrance into Richmond, with Confederate blockades of the river, kept being reduced to simpler transport: from the *River Queen* escorted by Admiral Porter's grand flotilla, to the *River Queen* without one ship and then another, to the admiral's barge pulled by a tug with a marine guard on board when the *River Queen* was blocked, to the barge without the tug but propelled by oarsmen, which barge then ran aground. Lincoln entered Richmond on foot. This devolution evoked from Lincoln a story about the applicant who came to him asking to be appointed an ambassador, and on being turned down asked to be appointed a postmaster, and on being turned down asked to be made a waiter, and finally, when that was rejected, said to Lincoln: Do you have an old pair of trousers I could have? We may turn this Lincoln story back against Lincoln's own self-reducing in his asking for families to go to the colonization project in Central America:

> The practical thing I want to ascertain is whether I can get a number of able-bodied men, with their wives and children, who are willing to go ... Could I get a hundred tolerably intelligent men, with their wives and children ... Can I have fifty? If I could have twenty-five able-bodied men, with a mixture of women and children ... I think I could make a successful commencement.

Lincoln may be vulnerable both on moral and on practical grounds for his long support of colonization, and he certainly is vulnerable for some of the arguments he made to the five black leaders, but it is unfair as well as anachronistic to apply to him terms used for abominations of a later century, "ethnic cleansing" and "apartheid." Lincoln's motive was not racial malice. The point was not the subordination or humiliation of a people but their rescue. Unlike some other advocates of colonization, he supported only a voluntary movement. The stated reason for it was the depth of what today we would call white racism, which indeed was a prime motive also for black nationalist supporters. Lincoln, speaking to the five black visitors, did give a thorough condemnation of the prevailing racial attitudes: "Your race are suffering, in my judgment, the greatest wrong inflicted on any people. But even when you cease to be slaves, you are yet far removed from being placed on an equality with the white race."

The colonization movement, certainly as Lincoln took part in it, was an *antislavery* movement, resisted by the fiercest defenders of slavery. We have the notes of one of his talks to the Springfield association, in which he gave a history of the efforts to end slavery, culminating in the colonization movement in the United States, with this overall theme: "All the while— conscience was at work." Colonization, which is sometimes treated in modern anti-Lincoln polemics as though it were Lincoln's own individual perversity, was in fact a movement supported by a distinguished list of American leaders.

Lincoln himself gave his explicit argument in his remarks to the five black leaders: white prejudice was so strong that blacks would never be accepted as equal, so a colony should be created in which they could be equal and free. But we may surely infer that his primary purpose was not to persuade blacks to leave but to persuade whites to accept emancipation. Colonization was an answer—symbolic at least—to the fears of whites about tides of freedmen overrunning the country and taking their jobs.

Much of Lincoln's presidential effort on behalf of colonization came in the second half of 1862, as he was taking the steps that led to the Emancipation Proclamation. After it was issued one might think—by the logic of his argument to the five black leaders—that his activity in behalf of colonization would increase. But it didn't. It stopped.

A scholarly examination looking not just at Lincoln's rhetoric but at his actions and their timing concludes that Lincoln, "always the careful politician," in his strategy would "propose colonization to sweeten the pill of emancipation for conservatives from the North and the border states . . . [A] clear picture emerges of Lincoln using the prospect of colonization to make emancipation more acceptable to conservatives and then abandoning all efforts at colonization once he made the determined step toward emancipation in the Final Emancipation Proclamation."

There is an immense contrast between what he said to the five black visitors in August 1862 and what he would say, as we will see, to Springfield Unionists in August 1863: two radically different pictures of the American future.

Something different already started to appear in a significant passage in Lincoln's 1862 annual message to Congress, a month before the proclamation. This message, read to Congress on December 1, 1862, includes—as we have seen—an elaborate last full argument for gradual compensated emancipation, with a proposal for colonization. But having laid out that proposal, Lincoln then took the argument in quite another direction:

> I cannot make it better known than it already is, that I strongly favor colonization. And yet I wish to say there is an objection urged against free colored persons remaining in the country, which is largely imaginary, if not sometimes malicious.

This sometimes malicious argument, now refuted by the president of the United States in an official document, is the argument that freed blacks would take white men's jobs. Lincoln's counterargument is accompanied by a sober warning about the seriousness of arguments made in these portentous times:

> If there ever could be a proper time for mere catch arguments, that time surely is not now. In times like the present, men should utter nothing for which they would not willingly be responsible through time and in eternity.

Emancipation was not going to increase the number of black laborers.

> Is it true, then, that colored people can displace any more white labor, by being free, than by remaining slaves? If they stay in their old places they jostle no white laborers; if they leave their old places, they leave them open to white laborers. Logically, there is neither more nor less of it. Emancipation, even without deportation, would probably enhance the wages of white labor, and, very surely, would not reduce them ... But is it dreaded that the freed people will swarm forth, and cover the whole land? Are they not already in the land? Will liberation make them any more numerous?

He is arguing now not for the separation of the races but for their shared life in this country.

SOME OF THEM SEEM WILLING TO FIGHT FOR YOU

THE FINAL Emancipation Proclamation included a harbinger of a wholly different conception: it invited black men into the Union armed services, which had to mean citizenship, their continuing presence, and a biracial America.

The recruiting and volunteering of black soldiers—free blacks, runaways, slaves, in the North, the South, the coast, Louisiana, the Mississippi Valley, finally even in Union slave state Kentucky—would be a tremendous story. "Despite the resistance of many whites," historian Joseph Glatthaar writes, "the recruitment of blacks into military service proceeded at an almost breathless pace."

By the end of the war there were 186,017 blacks in the U.S. armed services. The Bureau of Colored Troops "at one time had over 123,000 soldiers in uniform," Glatthaar notes—"a force larger than the field armies that either Lieutenant General Ulysses S. Grant or Major General William T. Sherman directly oversaw at the height of their campaigns in 1864 and 1865."

In 1863 black units fought bravely in battles at Port Hudson and Milliken's Bend and Fort Wagner, but although acceptance grew and converts were made, the resistance in segments of the Northern public was still strong. In July the New York City riots, provoked by the Conscription Act passed in March, were fiercely and terribly antiblack. Copperheads, opponents of the war and of the draft, trumpeted their attack on a war that was no longer fought simply for "the Union as it was."

Lincoln was given the opportunity to write a public letter in response to the prejudiced outcry against the Emancipation Proclamation and the recruitment of black soldiers when an old friend, James C. Conkling, invited him to speak to a large gathering in Springfield. He had been developing the device of the public letter; his letter to Horace Greeley in the fall of 1862, before the proclamation and preparing the public for it, had been a success, and the letter the following summer to a New York gathering about civil liberty had been another success. This letter to Conkling, dated August 26, 1863, would be the strongest of them all. It was written to be read aloud to a large gathering—in fact, Lincoln instructed Conkling to read it very slowly—but of course it was then to be read across the nation as it was published in the press.

After carefully explaining to these citizens who "maintain unconditional devotion to the Union" why the peace some thought possible wasn't, he took up the burning central complaint: "But, to be plain, you are dissatisfied with me about the negro. Quite likely there is a difference of opinion between you and myself upon that subject. I certainly wish that all men could be free, while I suppose you do not." He insisted, as he would throughout, that what he had done had not turned on this fundamental moral difference: "Yet I have neither adopted, nor proposed any measure, which is not consistent with even your view, provided you are for the Union." He stated their difference about the proclamation: "You dislike the emancipation proclamation; and, perhaps, would have it retracted. You say it is unconstitutional—I think differently. I think the constitution invests its commander-in-chief, with the law of war, in time of war."

And then he justified it, again, in the utterly practical terms that they all could share:

> The war has certainly progressed as favorably for us, since the issue of the proclamation as before . . . some of the commanders of our armies in the field who have given us our most important successes, believe the emancipation policy, and the use of colored troops, constitute the heaviest blow yet dealt to the rebellion; and that, at least one of those important successes, could not have been achieved when it was, but for the aid of black soldiers.

In the sentence about "the heaviest blow yet," Lincoln was borrowing exactly the words that U. S. Grant had used in a letter he had written to Lincoln on August 23. Lincoln added this passage after he had mailed the text by sending a telegram to Conkling, telling him where to insert it.

He made clear that the commander holding this view of the positive effect of black soldiers did not do so from ideological presumption:

> Among the commanders holding these views are some who have never had any affinity with what is called abolitionism, or with Republican party politics, but who hold them purely as military opinion.

Douglas Wilson, in his illuminating discussion in *Lincoln's Sword,* notes that throughout this quite direct and forceful letter Lincoln makes repeated use of aggressive rhetorical questions:

I thought that in your struggle for the Union, to whatever extent the negroes should cease helping the enemy, to that extent it weakened the enemy in his resistance to you. Do you think differently?

And then in crucial sentences he put the moral choice plainly:

You say you will not fight to free negroes. Some of them seem willing to fight for you; but no matter. Fight you, then, exclusively to save the Union.

The sentence "Some of them seem willing to fight for you; but no matter" was an inspired late editorial insertion. He had written the flat injunction: You won't fight for Negroes—fight then for the Union. But adding that Negroes meanwhile fight for you—followed by the quiet shrug "but no matter"—was a brilliant stroke, shaming the reader with the sharp contrast and then seeming to take the edge off with the shrug.

I thought that whatever negroes can be got to do as soldiers, leaves just so much less for white soldiers to do, in saving the Union. Does it appear otherwise to you? But negroes, like other people, act upon motives. Why should they do any thing for us, if we will do nothing for them? If they stake their lives for us, they must be prompted by the strongest motive— even the promise of freedom. And the promise being made, must be kept.

Promises are a problem to utilitarians and a chief argument for their opponents. We don't mean by a promise that we will do what we engage to do only if it appears that doing so will work to an overall balance of greater happiness. Promises (like oaths) are a binding of the self that cuts through that. A utilitarian ethic faces the future and is in a sense impersonal: anyone looking at the probable good and evil future consequences of this deed should act so as to produce the greater happiness (or, more broadly, the greater good). But a promise or an oath, by contrast, creates a claim from the past, a bond from some earlier time that does not depend on weighing and measuring consequences. It is particular to these moral agents; *I promised you*. Lincoln had a sacred trust from the whole people; the emancipation and recruitment had created a bond that he in particular had to keep. The moral rigor of that promise to the black soldier would run all the way through the rest of his presidency: to betray it would be treachery, "a cruel and an astounding breach of faith" deserving the "curses of Heaven."

That strong sentence "And the promise being made, must be kept" had been the last sentence of his draft. But he later decided to add a cautiously optimistic passage about the war. "The signs look better," he said, and produced the memorable sentence about the opening of the Mississippi by the capture of Vicksburg in July—"The Father of Waters flows unvexed to the sea." At the conclusion of a survey of hopeful signs, he summarized what victory would mean and then returned to a vivid picture of that soldier to whom the promise had been made:

> Peace does not appear so distant as it did. I hope it will come soon, and come to stay; and so come as to be worth the keeping in all future time. It will then have been proved that, among free men, there can be no successful appeal from the ballot to the bullet; and that they who take such appeal are sure to lose their case, and pay the cost. And then, there will be some black men who can remember that, with silent tongue, and clenched teeth, and steady eye, and well-poised bayonet, they have helped mankind on to this great consummation; while, I fear, there will be some white ones, unable to forget that, with malignant heart, and deceitful speech, they have strove to hinder it.

He took the trouble to fashion a graphic image of the black soldier who helped the great consummation (silent tongue, clenched teeth, steady eye, well-poised bayonet) and in contrast summoned two sharply negative characteristics of the white men who tried to hinder it (malignant heart, deceitful speech). It was surely a different picture from the one he painted just a year earlier to the five black visitors.

Lincoln the continual self-improver underwent marked changes in moral outlook at several points in his life. One may compare the mediocre partisan speech he gave for the Whig presidential candidate Winfield Scott in 1852 with his first great speech, which he gave in the fall of 1854 at the state fair in Springfield and then in Peoria. And one may compare what he said to the five visitors in August 1862 with his letter to Conkling in August 1863—a major jump in moral imagination.

Biographers in later years would say that he "grew," but his alteration was not like an acorn becoming an oak. It was like a human being making and remaking his understanding by deliberate and continual reflection. Lincoln had been educating himself all his life, and that very much included reeducation about the moral possibilities of American society. White prejudice, while strong, could be diminished by experience and by the growing appeal of the original egalitarian ideal. Insofar as colonization had been a ploy, a sop, a sugarcoating to emancipation, it had served its purpose; insofar as he had believed it to be a real possibility for the American future—he changed his mind.

HERE IS MY FRIEND DOUGLASS

WHILE HE WAS WORKING on his letter to Conkling, Lincoln had his first meeting with Frederick Douglass. His meetings with Douglass were, by Douglass's repeated testimony, the meetings of equals—more so, Douglass would say, than he felt with any other leader.

Douglass's appraisals of candidate Lincoln and President Lincoln's policies would go up and down, but his testimony about his respectful personal treatment by President Lincoln, once they first met on August 10, 1863, would be strong and unwavering. Douglass, urged to see the president to object to mistreatments of black soldiers in the Union army, had expected to wait half a day to see the swamped president. Douglass's own account helps to recapture some of the immense social distance imposed by the caste system of that time and place.

> I need not say that at the time I undertook this mission it required much more nerve than a similar one would require now. [This was published in 1881.] The distance then between the black and the white American citizen was immeasurable. I was an ex-slave, identified with a despised race, and yet I was to meet the most exalted person in this great republic . . . I could not know what kind of a reception would be accorded me. I might be told to go home and mind my business . . . or I might be refused an interview altogether.

Douglass was not only not refused an interview, and not kept waiting half a day, but was summoned to see the president within moments of his arrival, leaving others who were waiting to see the president sputtering.

And then of the moment of meeting with the president himself, Douglass would write:

> I entered the room with a moderate estimate of my own consequence, and yet there I was to talk with, and even to advise, the head man of a great nation . . . I was never more quickly or more completely put at ease in the presence of a great man than in that of Abraham Lincoln.

Commenting afterward on the meeting, Douglass would emphasize the personal respect Lincoln showed him, this treatment as an equal. "I have just come from President Lincoln. He treated me as a man; he did not let me feel for a moment that there was any difference in the color of our skins!"

For Lincoln's part, he would later say of Douglass himself that "considering the conditions from which Douglass rose, and the position to which he had attained, he was, in his [Lincoln's] judgment, one of the most meritorious men in America."

In the months after this meeting Douglass would be disappointed by Lincoln on some particulars, but the personal respect would remain.

Douglass wrote years later, "In all my interviews with Mr. Lincoln, I was impressed with his entire freedom from popular prejudice against the colored race. He was the first great man that I talked with in the United States freely, who in no single instance reminded me of the difference between himself and myself, of the difference of color, and I thought that all the more remarkable because he came from a state where there were black laws."

Benjamin Quarles, the twentieth-century African American historian whose excellent book *Lincoln and the Negro* serves as a considerable corrective to some more recent treatments, surveys President Lincoln's encounters with black persons. He formulated Lincoln's manner:

> He treated Negroes as they wanted to be treated—as human beings . . . Negro visitors to the White House were treated without false heartiness, but without any sign of disdain. Never condescending, Lincoln did not talk down to Negroes, nor did he spell out his thoughts in the one-syllable language of the first reader.

A speech that Frederick Douglass would give in the much different atmosphere of a later time—at the dedication of the freedmen's monument in Lincoln Park in 1876—would be quoted repeatedly in assessments of Lincoln's racial views in the twentieth century. Phrases from that 1876 speech, taken somewhat out of context, would be featured: "He was pre-eminently the white man's president" and "We [blacks] are at best only his step-children."

He would be quoted as having said that for Lincoln the black man was "only a stepbrother." But there surely were some moments at least when for President Lincoln, the commander in chief who had called them into battle, the black man in a Union army uniform was a brother indeed. And whatever the degree of his fraternal fellow feeling may have been, he came to have, as he saw it, a potent obligation both to liberated slaves and to black soldiers in the Union army. Some of the strongest examples in Lincoln's life of his invoking an ethic of unequivocal duty have to do with black Union soldiers.

Even in that speech there were other passages that qualified those stark assertions and showed some appreciation of Lincoln's actual political situation.* And Douglass showed more appreciation in earlier presentations. Michael Burlingame has unearthed two speeches that Douglass gave in 1865 that have been, in the recent atmosphere, neglected. One is a eulogy that Douglass delivered at Cooper Union on June 1, 1865, in which he included the assertion that Lincoln was "emphatically the black man's president," so that scholars and polemicists of the future are presented with the opportunity to use dueling Douglass quotations. Douglass said at Cooper Union that Lincoln was "the first [president] to show any respect for [blacks'] rights as men . . . He was the first American President who . . . rose above the prejudice of his time, and country."

CIVILIZED WARFARE PERMITS
NO DISTINCTION AS TO COLOR

DOUGLASS had come to talk to Lincoln about unequal treatment of black soldiers—they were paid at a lower rate than white soldiers, were more often assigned to fatigue duty than combat, and were rarely commissioned as officers. All were injustices that it would take time to correct, insofar as they were corrected. But the most serious problem was the treatment of black soldiers by Confederates after capture.

One practice was to reenslave or (in the case of those who had been free) to enslave them. But another widespread response was summary execution. Confederate secretary of war James Seddon said, as we have noted in Chapter 14: "We ought never to be inconvenienced by such prisoners . . . summary execution must therefore be inflicted on those taken." The numbers are not known because the Confederate refusal to acknowledge them

---

*Douglass said about Lincoln, in his 1876 speech, "Had he put the abolition of slavery before the salvation of the Union, he would have inevitably driven from him a powerful class of the American people and rendered resistance to rebellion impossible. Viewed from the genuine abolition ground, Mr. Lincoln seemed tardy, cold, dull, and indifferent; but measuring him by the sentiment of his country, a sentiment he was bound as a statesman to consult, he was swift, zealous, radical, and determined."

as legitimate prisoners of war meant that they did not keep adequate records.

Lincoln's response was notable both for its severity (unusual in this most unretaliatory of public men) and for its explicit emphasis on the racial aspect. He had the War Department draft what was explicitly called an order of retaliation and signed it on July 30, 1863. Four times in this short document he specifically rejected any distinction among Union soldiers as to "color":

1. Every government has the duty to protect its citizens "of whatever class, color, or condition."
2. The laws of civilized warfare "permit no distinction as to color."
3. "[T]o sell or enslave any captured person on account of his color . . . is a relapse into barbarism." (The head of the Confederate Bureau of War had said, "The enlistment of our slaves is a barbarity"—so there were sharply contrasting convictions about what was barbaric.)
4. "[I]f the enemy shall sell or enslave anyone because of his color, the offense shall be punished by retaliation upon the enemy's prisoners."

The specific order for that retaliation was stark: "It is therefore ordered that for every soldier of the United States killed in violation of the laws of war, a rebel soldier shall be executed."

It is to Lincoln's credit that in the depth of his original righteous indignation he signed this order, and it is also to his credit that in the event—in the scrupulous care of his later reflection—he never carried it out.

In the next year, April 1864, there came a terrible test. President Lincoln described the "rumor" of this event in an insertion in the speech he gave at the Baltimore Sanitary Fair on April 18, 1864, six days after it had happened: "the massacre, by the rebel forces, at Fort Pillow, in the west end of Tennessee, on the Mississippi River, of some three hundred colored soldiers and their white officers who had just been overpowered by their assailants."

Lincoln explicitly recognized a public anxiety about whether the government was doing its full duty to the black soldier. He fully acknowledged his own personal accountability, as the one who had initiated the use of black troops, now for their fate, "to the American people, to the Christian world, to history, and on my final account to God." He specifically stated the principle that had to be applied: "Having determined to use the Negro as a soldier, there is no way but to give him all the protection given to any other soldiers." He admitted, however, that it would be difficult to apply that principle, as events were to prove: "The difficulty is not in stating the principle, but in practically applying it." He insisted that the government was doing, or trying to do, its part: "It is a mistake to suppose the government is indifferent to this matter, or is not doing the best it can in regard to it." At the end of his remarks in Baltimore he said, twice, that if what was rumored had indeed happened at Fort Pillow, then "the retribution will surely come." "It will be a matter of grave consideration" exactly what form it will take, but retribution must come.

But before one reached that point, one must be sure one knew what truly happened. As in the cases of young soldiers condemned to be executed, and of Southern women wishing to pass through the Union lines, and of Indians in Minnesota whom many white residents wanted to execute en masse, and in many other cases, Lincoln wanted to make sure the particular facts in the individual case were correct before he made a judgment. Going clear back to the days of the fury against the abolitionists, and of his Lyceum Address, he knew how "passion" could swamp "reason," including the reason that patiently seeks out the facts. In Baltimore he said: "We do not to-day *know* that a colored soldier, or white officer commanding colored soldiers, has been massacred by the rebels when made a prisoner. We fear it, believe it, I may say, but we do not *know* it." And to take severe action on the basis of rumor, before one knew what had happened, could lead to a radically wrong act indeed: "To take the life of one of their prisoners, on the assumption that they murder ours, might be too serious, too cruel a mistake." It certainly would have been—and in the event, even when Fort Pillow was proved true, it was "too serious, too cruel" "to take the life of one of their prisoners."

"We are having the Fort Pillow affair thoroughly investigated," he said in Baltimore on April 18. By May 3 the investigation had reached a conclusion, and the president wrote to the cabinet:

> It is now quite certain that a large number of our colored soldiers, and their white officers, were, by the rebel forces, massacred after they had surrendered, at the recent capture of Fort Pillow . . . I will thank you to prepare, and give me in writing your opinion as to what course, the government should take.

What to do? In the two cabinet meetings at which the response to Fort Pillow was discussed—an ethics seminar in the highest reaches of American government—three members of the cabinet (Bates, Montgomery Blair, and the new appointee who was briefly secretary of the interior following Caleb Smith) were, in spite of that order of the president's the previous year, against any use of hostages for retaliation. There should be punishment only for the specific perpetrators of the terrible deeds.

Four members of the cabinet—Seward, Chase, Stanton, and Welles— were for selecting hostages from among Confederate prisoners of war. And apparently the president, also, believed that more was needed than the impotent outlawing of the specific individuals who perpetrated the massacre.

Chief among those perpetrators was the brilliant but notorious Nathan Bedford Forrest, an outstanding Confederate general who in his earlier life had been a slave trader and who in his future life would be a founder of the Ku Klux Klan. Forrest had explicitly said that "I regard captured negroes as I do other property, and not as captured soldiers," and that "no quarter" would be shown black troops. He is reported to have called out, riding among the wounded and the dead, that he knew some of them: "They've been in my nigger yard in Memphis." Other Confederate officers were reported to have shouted, "Kill the niggers." But the testimony about Fort Pillow also stated that some Confederate officers and men tried to *stop* the massacre. Carl Sandburg quotes one Confederate officer shouting this unlikely warning: "Boys, I will have you arrested if you don't stop killing them boys."

On December 8, 1863, before Fort Pillow, Lincoln had issued the Proclamation of Amnesty and Reconstruction, in which he had made one exception to the generous offer that was grounded in deeds rather than official positions. The amnesty did not extend to "all who engaged in any way in treating colored persons or white persons, in charge of such, otherwise than lawfully as prisoners of war."

On May 17 Lincoln drafted a letter to Secretary of War Stanton asking him to notify the insurgents, through channels, that the government had proof of the "massacre" (the word he used) "after [the soldiers of the United States] had ceased resistance, and asked quarter." He went on to say that the government had set apart by name a number of "insurgent" officers, held as prisoners of war, equivalent to the number of Union soldiers massacred at Fort Pillow. If the insurgents would give assurance, he wrote, "as nearly perfect as the case admits" by July 1 "that there shall be no similar massacre" and that no officer or soldier of the United States, "whether white or colored" (he specifically said), "shall be treated other than according to the laws of war," then the Confederate set-asides would be returned to the regular conditions of prisoners of war. The implied threat, of course, was that *if* there were another Fort Pillow, *if* black soldiers in the Union army were again slaughtered, enslaved, or otherwise mistreated, maybe even *if* the Confederates gave no assurance by July 1— then something else might happen.

Before he explained this implied threat, he specifically said (a continual Lincolnian doctrine) that governments should not act for "revenge" and that "blood cannot restore blood"—which is to say, presumably, that these hostages (all officers) were not to be executed for backward-looking reasons, in revenge by blood for Fort Pillow. But they were to be set aside, by name, and in the exact number of those killed at Fort Pillow. One might say that Lincoln was trying to devise a policy of what would in the next century be called deterrence—a way to stop an action by an opponent by an implicit threat.

But suppose the Confederate government gave no assurance by July 1? Worse—suppose there were indeed another Fort Pillow? What then? Would one in the moment of truth execute those hostages? Presumably in thinking this through to the moment of truth, Lincoln saw the difficulties, both moral and practical, for any such deed. These Confederate officers selected *by name* from one's prisoners of war were, in relation to Fort Pillow, innocent. If you answer that officers in the Confederate armed forces were not "innocent" in the law of war, as civilians are, one would have to say, still, that their noninnocence pertains only to their participation in an objective force that may justly and of necessity be resisted; when they are captured, and become prisoners of war, they are no longer part of that objective force and are protected by the law of war from having their lives used as pawns. Hostage killing is not something we should do. Gideon Welles said such a policy would be "barbarous." And here, as so often happens in life but particularly in war, the moral intersected with the practical: Could one imagine that if the Union executed Confederate prisoners of war the Confederacy would not reciprocate?

And that would set in motion a vicious and unending bloody circle of retaliation. To Attorney General Bates, it would be a compact for mutual slaughter, a cartel of blood and murder.

The Union threats of retaliation for the treatment of black soldiers may have had some effect. James McPherson writes that when Confederates put captured black soldiers to work on fortifications under enemy fire, Union generals put an equal number of captured Confederates to work under enemy fire—and the practice stopped. That "retaliation" had a kind of moral equilibrium that worked.

Black soldiers, understandably, used "Fort Pillow" as a battle cry and were reported to have killed captured Confederates. The discussion of the issue was then overwhelmed by the battle of the Wilderness. The only solution was to win the war, the passion for doing which was increased by this incident.

EQUALITY AND LIBERTY: A NEW BIRTH OF FREEDOM

LINCOLN GAVE what would prove to be his most enduring expression of his own (and, as he saw it, his country's) commitment to equality in his dedicatory remarks at the Gettysburg cemetery on November 19, 1863. The powerful opening sentence of this incantatory masterpiece (of only eleven sentences, 275 words) simply took the key point for granted, by sheer patriotic assertion, in an affecting summary of the nation's beginning: "Four score and seven years ago our fathers brought forth upon this continent, a new nation, conceived in Liberty, and dedicated to the proposition that all men are created equal."

Matthew Arnold is said to have stopped reading in literary disgust at the word "proposition." Nations aren't "dedicated" to "propositions." Perhaps he thought nations should be "dedicated" to kings and queens, to flags, to the ties of blood or soil or a long shared history, to something with more symbolic and evocative juice than a "proposition," to which one gives rational assent, not dedication. Lincoln, however, American to the core, understood his nation's distinctive self-definition, coming out of the springtime of the Enlightenment, in universal moral truths that we hold, in a creed. He had had the poetry in him to make it work: he wrote not of a moral ideal the nation sought, nor of a principle that it served, but of a proposition to which it was dedicated: all men, as Jefferson had written, created equal.

The significance of reasserting that Jeffersonian phrase in November 1863 was to say that, for all the temporary contradictions in practice, in America's original aspiration black persons are from the beginning and fundamentally equal to white ones.

Lincoln would then end his brief remarks, after eloquent recognition of the brave men who consecrated the battleground, with a call to a high resolve, "a new birth of freedom." A more inclusive freedom was to be born: a freedom linked to the equality to which the nation was dedicated.

THE FOLLOWING APRIL, in a much less elegant speech at the Baltimore fair—the same speech in which he inserted his remarks about Fort Pillow—Lincoln spelled out the most elementary requirement for a new birth of freedom. "The world has never had a good definition of the word liberty," he told the Baltimore fairgoers, grandly sweeping aside acres of past philosophical effort, "and the American people, just now, are much in want of one."

> We all declare for liberty; but in using the same word we do not all mean the same thing. With some the word liberty may mean for each man to do as he pleases with himself, and the product of his labor; while with others the same word may mean for some men to do as they please with other men, and the product of other men's labor.
>
> Here are two, not only different, but incompatable things, called by the same name—liberty. And it follows that each of the things is, by the respective parties, called by two different and incompatable names— liberty and tyranny.

Lincoln perceived the precarious one-sidedness in the profound value of "freedom": its close connection to power, both freedom and power meaning something like the ability to do as one wishes to do. So the question regularly arises about how doing as one pleases impinges on others. The correction is for a nation conceived in liberty also to be dedicated to the proposition that all men are created equal, so that there is a balancing that prevents one man's liberty from becoming another man's tyranny. Lincoln had a little fable:

> The shepherd drives the wolf from the sheep's throat, for which the sheep thanks the shepherd as a liberator, while the wolf denounces him for the same act as the destroyer of liberty, especially as the sheep was a black one. Plainly the sheep and the wolf are not agreed upon a definition of the word liberty; and precisely the same difference prevails to-day among us human creatures, even in the North, and all professing to love liberty. Hence we behold the processes by which thousands are daily passing from under the yoke of bondage, hailed by some as the advance of liberty, and bewailed by others as the destruction of all liberty.

Maryland, a Union state not covered by the Emancipation Proclamation, was just then moving to hold a convention at which it would be voted, on June 24, to amend the state constitution to end slavery. Lincoln referred to these positive developments in the ending of his little fable: "Recently, as it seems, the people of Maryland have been doing something to define liberty; and thanks to them that, in what they have done, the wolf's dictionary, has been repudiated." By tying it practically to equality, they had begun to define "a new birth of freedom."

CHAPTER SIXTEEN

The Benign Prerogative to Pardon Unfortunate Guilt

TO SOFTEN THE RIGOR OF THE GENERAL LAW

As the resounding chords of giant presidential choices over war and treason and slavery and disunion reverberated across the land, there would soon begin to be heard a counterpoint in another key, a sweet-sad little melody of grace notes in the higher moral registers. This sequence of presidential choices would deal one by one with the fate of individual human beings whose lives had been tossed about by some deed they had done, or were alleged to have done, in the terrible fog of war.

As we have seen in the cases of Nathaniel Gordon and David Wright, in the same paragraph of the Constitution (Article II, section 2, paragraph 1) that made the president commander in chief, the framers made this quite definite grant: "he shall have the Power to grant Reprieves and Pardons for Offenses against the United States." In those two cases he disappointed the supporters of the condemned men, but in many other cases he would extend a mercy that would become part of his legend.

One might be a little surprised that the celebrated framers of this new "republican" government should have included, among the few explicit powers they extended to the "executive," an absolute, unchecked, unreviewable, personal power to grant pardons, commutations, and reprieves. Many of the sources upon whom the American framers drew did *not* think a republic would, or should, give over to one individual the power to alter the results of the legal system. Pardons, to them, smacked of kings and priests, of favors, whims, and special dispensations.

One who favored pardons precisely because the practice had a royal loftiness was Blackstone, the great English codifier of the common law, much read in the American colonies, whom Lincoln himself read in order to make himself a lawyer.* In his famous *Commentaries on the Law of England,* in 1769, Blackstone was quite explicit that pardoning power belonged to kings. "This is indeed," he wrote, "one of the great advantages of monarchy in general, above any other form of government; that there is a magistrate, who has it in his power to extend mercy, whenever he thinks it is deserved: holding a court of equity in his own breast, to soften the rigour of the general law."

When Blackstone wrote of "holding a court of equity in his own breast," he was thinking of a royal breast, hedged with divinity, not the untutored breast of some total commoner of dubious family from a remote province, tossed up by an accident of popular election.

In fact, Blackstone specifically wrote, "In democracies this power of pardon can never subsist, for there nothing higher is acknowledged than the magistrate who administers the laws . . . [I]n monarchies the king acts in a superior sphere; and, though he regulates the whole government as the first mover, yet he does not appear in any of the disagreeable or invidious parts of it."

But these American "presidents," for whom nobody claimed any aboveness (at least after George Washington was gone), would come to be wholly engaged in the "disagreeable" and "invidious" parts of governing. Particularly the sixteenth president: Lincoln would certainly not in his own time be looked up to as "the fountain of nothing but bounty and grace," as Blackstone said was the case with graciously pardoning kings.

The Americans in their revolution were separating from and repudiating the kind of lofty royal superiority that Blackstone, writing in King George's England, was rhapsodizing about. The greatest pamphleteer of the American Revolution wrote that an honest man is worth all the crowned ruffians who ever lived. Benjamin Franklin, that original American, is said to have remarked that calling King George III of England "the Royal brute" was unfair to brutes.

The French Revolution, in its first spasm of enthusiasm, would sweep away all provision for pardoning. But the Americans did not do that. They were perhaps never as purist, tidy, or utopian as were the French revolutionaries and Continental philosophers, and by the time the Americans

---

*When a young schoolteacher who wanted to become a lawyer asked Lincoln for "the best mode of obtaining a thorough knowledge of the law," he answered that the mode is "simple, though laborious and tedious. It is only to get the books, and read and study them carefully. Begin with Blackstone's *Commentaries* . . . Read it carefully through—say, twice." Lincoln to John M. Brockman, September 25, 1860, *CW,* 4:121.

wrote their Constitution, they had had thirteen scrambling years of experience under the Articles of Confederation, which provided for no executive head. They were more realistic about human nature and the flaws in social systems; where the French constitution-makers provided for no process of amendment, the Americans had provided for amending their Constitution and started doing so right away. Perhaps the provision for pardons was a flavoring of their republican idealism with a dash of realism.

In any case, they included in their constitutional system an executive with the power to pardon. Hamilton produced in Federalist 74 this most central statement from an American Founder about the "benign prerogative" of the pardon power: "The criminal code of every country partakes so much of necessary severity that without an easy access to exceptions in favor of unfortunate guilt, justice would wear a countenance too sanguinary and cruel." Seventy-two years and fifteen presidents after Hamilton wrote his paragraphs, there would come to the executive office a man who, faced with the nation's greatest crisis, would repeatedly hold "a court of equity in his own breast, to soften the rigour of the general law."

There he sits, with the papers of a particular case and the fate and often the life of a convicted person resting on his decision. The pardoning power of presidents is a point in the formal system at which the particular characteristics of a single case on the one side and the moral understanding of a single individual on the other can determine the result—a point at which a president's moral understanding may be revealed with a rare clarity.

OFFENSES AGAINST THE UNITED STATES

"OFFENSES AGAINST THE UNITED STATES" included everything that federal law covered—and the coverage of federal law was just then undergoing a gigantic enlargement. You might think that a president in the midst of a great war should not have to decide whether Herman Kirchner, restaurant owner in Washington, should be excused from paying a fine of twenty dollars, imposed upon him for allegedly selling spirituous liquors to a soldier. (Kirchner claimed that all he did was to send brandy to a wounded soldier in a neighboring house.) Or whether John Knowles and his brother should be pardoned, as their mother pleaded, for their alleged crime of assault and battery upon a man whom they thought had insulted their sister. Lincoln, like other presidents, was confronted with petitions on behalf of those found guilty of counterfeiting and larceny and embezzlement and mail robbery and murder and rape and arson, whose cases for some jurisdictional or substantive reason fell under the federal rather than the state courts.

Often someone in the chain of authority would recommend clemency, which then Lincoln would endorse. Lincoln would often ask, in civilian cases, for the recommendation of his attorney general, Edward Bates or (at the end of his presidency) James Speed. Sometimes the recommendation made the case an easy one. In a civilian case in 1863, Jacob Varner of West Virginia was sentenced to three years' imprisonment for robbing the mails, but even members of the jury that found him guilty signed a petition explaining that Varner was an "ignorant man" who had been persuaded by "designing politicians" that he had an allegiance to the state superior to his duty to the U.S. mail. On June 1, 1863, Lincoln the humorist pungently explained his decision: "As the Judge, Jury, Marshall, District Attorney, and Postmaster General join in asking a pardon in this case, I have concluded to grant it."

Lincoln thus would find in these cases, as everywhere else, occasions for wit. Perhaps he should have restrained himself from responding—on May 27, 1863—when one Robert B. Nay came to the White House to discuss his pardon: "I will not say thee 'Nay.' "

In some of the requests for pardons, justice needed no great boost from mercy: President Lincoln would correct the operations of a lower body with a more careful reading of what was just. Thus, for example, on October 10, 1864, he would decide: "I do not think a man offering himself a volunteer when he could receive a bounty & being rejected for disability should afterwards be compelled to serve without bounty as a drafted man. Let this man be discharged."

Sometimes he could appeal to the elementary logic of a situation, and to elementary human nature, as moral reasoning to determine what was just, as in a case of alleged racketeers: surely, if you were going to commit fraud in a matter involving more than a million dollars, you would manage to extract for yourself more than a mere one hundred dollars.

Lincoln pardoned more than three hundred "nonmilitary" offenders, more than his two predecessors combined. That increase was a side effect of the war, but cases coming from the civilian courts were now to be radically surpassed and eclipsed, in number and in significance, by pardon cases that arose from the military justice system.

The largest single episode in which Lincoln called upon the pardon power did come from a military commission, but it did not arise from the war—that is, not from the American Civil War. We may cite this case, the sentencing of 303 Sioux (or Dakota) Indians in Minnesota in the fall of 1862, to examine and disagree with a misgiving that some had about Lincoln's mercy.

OUT OF SIGHT

LINCOLN WOULD acquire his reputation for a quite unusual tenderheartedness during his lifetime, and it would be expanded in the legend after his death. But a provocative qualification would come from an important source: his law partner and eventual biographer—and source for everyone else's Lincoln biography—William Herndon:

> Mr. Lincoln was tender hearted when in the presence of suffering or when it was enthusiastically or poetically described to him: he had great charity for the weaknesses of his fellow man: his nature was merciful and it sprang into manifestation quickly on the presentation of a proper subject under proper conditions: [but] he had no imagination to invoke, through the distances, suffering, nor fancy to paint it. The subject of mercy must be presented to him.

The time when Herndon knew Lincoln well was before he was president, before the hard choices and vast consequences of wartime. But his proposed qualification about Lincoln's tenderheartedness was picked up and made more stark by an early twentieth-century biographer, William Barton, who in general would be rather dismissive of Lincoln's larger generosities:

> Lincoln was a man of deep sympathy, but his sympathy had a certain well-defined limitation. He felt sympathy where he could see or visualize the personal sorrow that was caused by an act or condition. What was out of sight was more or less out of mind.

Neither Herndon nor Barton gives any example of suffering at a distance that Lincoln had insufficient imagination to grasp, but the distinguished twentieth-century Lincoln scholar Richard Current, who picked up this point with one hand after he had set it aside with the other, *does* give an example: Lincoln's "creative interest in new weapons." Current listed breech-loading rifles, a "coffee mill gun that was an ancestor of the machine gun," mortars, an explosive bullet, and incendiary shells.

But was that persistent interest a sign of Lincoln's failure to comprehend the distant suffering that those weapons would cause? It was the result, surely, of the intersection of his lifelong interest in mechanical devices with his determination to prosecute the war relentlessly to the earliest conclusion.

In the summer and fall of 1862 Lincoln decided on a case in which he did exactly what Herndon and Barton said he did *not* do. He used his imagination to invoke the suffering of those far away from him and different from him—out of sight: the Sioux warriors of Minnesota, many of whom at least were unjustly condemned.

These Minnesota Indians were remote from Lincoln and removed from his experience, but he also had a family history with other Indians that might have made another man bitter. His paternal grandfather, also named Abraham, had been killed by Indians, as the famous grandson himself would tell it, "not in battle, but by stealth, when he was laboring to open a farm in the forest" in Kentucky. That event was an important cause of the poverty of Thomas Lincoln, who "was but six years of age" when his father was killed. Thomas Lincoln, the youngest son, "even in childhood was a wandering laboring boy, and grew up litterally [*sic*] without education." That, and "the narrow circumstances of his mother," led to the upbringing in poverty of his son, Abraham.

Abraham Lincoln had, in addition to this potentially embittering family memory, the typical experience of a frontiersman. He joined the militia in 1832 when he was twenty-three to fight Indians (although he never actually fought any) in the Black Hawk War.

But Lincoln never shared the frontiersman's categorical hostility to Indians. He made his experience in the Black Hawk War into amiable, self-deprecating jokes. There is no record of his even engaging in a skirmish with the Black Hawk, let alone killing or wounding any, and his campaign biography in 1860 by William Dean Howells, which he approved, said that during the Black Hawk War he saved the life of an old Indian who had wandered into camp thinking he was protected by a safe conduct pass that he had from a white man. The men in Lincoln's company thought they would seize the opportunity to kill an Indian, but Lincoln stopped them. William G. Greene, Lincoln's helper in Denton Offutt's store and a fellow volunteer in the militia, independently told the same story. Another of Lincoln's men in the militia, Royal Clary, provided further details when he later recalled the incident to Herndon: "Lincoln jumped between our men & the Indian and said we must not shed his blood—that it must not be on our Skirts—some one thought Lincoln was a coward because he was not savage: he said if any one doubts my Courage Let him try it."

Thirty-one years later the sometime captain in the Black Hawk War would be president of the United States. His rare encounters with Indian affairs would show him to be, although radically ignorant and loaded with stereotypes, amiably disposed and sympathetic, not likely to produce any of the bloodthirsty comments about Indians that would come from many westerners, and from generals in his army.

A presidential audience he held on March 27, 1863, in the "big wig-wam" on Pennsylvania Avenue for a group of Indian chiefs, of which the Washington *Daily Morning Chronicle* the next day printed a report, is to be sure patronizing and, if you want to say so, using our late twentieth-century epithet, "racist," because he refers to "your race" and "our race." But may one not also say that it is well intentioned, as a great many treatments—*most* treatments—of Indians by white Americans, especially in those days, especially by westerners, were not? One might also see in it a piece of high unintentional comedy, quite politically incorrect no doubt.

The meeting was held in the East Room of the White House (also called the executive mansion in those days). There were present about fifteen Indian chiefs, from the Cheyenne, Kiowa, Arapahoe, Comanche, and Apache, and an assortment of "celebrated personages," including Secretaries Seward, Chase, and Welles. The chiefs were seated on the floor in a line, and the celebrated personages in a ring around them, which "notwithstanding the assiduous but polite efforts of Mr. Nicolay" did not provide everyone a good view, and according to the *Chronicle* there was a good deal of whispering and jostling in the "restless and eager crowd of visitors."

"Still," the *Chronicle*'s reporter said, "everything went off very well." He calmly describes the chiefs, though favorably, as "savages" with "cruel lines" in their faces:

> These Indians are fine-looking men. They have all the hard and cruel lines on their faces which we might expect in savages; but they are evidently men of intelligence and force of character. They were both dignified and cordial in their manner, and listened to everything with great interest.

Abraham Lincoln came into this scene in the East Room at eleven-thirty on a March morning. Commissioner William P. Dole introduced the chiefs, and the president shook hands with each of them, some of whom responded with "a sort of salaam or salutation by spreading out the hands," some with "the inevitable 'how' of the plains Indians."

The president told the interpreter to tell them that he was very glad to see them and that if they had anything to say, it would afford him great pleasure to hear them.

Lean Bear, a Cheyenne chief, spoke. Spotted Wolf, an Arapaho, spoke. Then President Lincoln began with a sort of geography lesson: "You have all spoken of the strange sights you see here, among your pale-faced brethren; the very great number of people that you see; the big wigwams; the difference between our people and your own. But you have seen but a small part of the pale-faced people. You may wonder when I tell you that there are people here in this wigwam, now looking at you who have come from other countries a great deal farther off than you have come.

"We pale-faced people think that this world is a great, round ball," he soberly explained to the chiefs. "One of our learned men will now explain to you our notions about this great ball, and show you where you live."

Professor Henry, according to the record of this event, then gave "a detailed and interesting explanation of the formation of the earth, showing how much of it was water and how much of it was land."

When the president came back on the program, he indicated that the pale-faced people had come "from all parts of the globe—here, and here, and here." And he also, helpfully, gave his explanation, two reasons, of why the pale-faced people are "more numerous and prosperous" than their red brethren: "Because they cultivate the earth, produce bread, and depend upon the products of the earth rather than wild game."

And the pale-faced ones were more numerous because "we are not, as a race, so much disposed to fight and kill one another as our red brethren." Mark E. Neely, Jr., David Herbert Donald, and David Nichols all note the irony of the president making this claim in the midst of an immense war that would in the end kill 620,000 of the pale-faced people.

Apparently the chiefs had asked for "advice about their life in this country." Twice in his short remarks the president was careful to say that he did not know what was best for the red brethren: "I really am not capable of advising you whether, in the providence of the great spirit, who is the father of us all, it is best for you to maintain the habits and the customs of your race, or adopt a new mode of life."

Lincoln knew, by March 1863, if he had not known it before, that some of the numerous and prosperous pale-faced people had made themselves more prosperous by the way they took land from, and exploited, their red brethren. He made a sort of preemptive half apology to the chiefs: "It is the object of this government to be on terms of peace with you, and with all our red brethren. We make treaties with you, and try to observe them; and if our children should sometimes behave badly, and violate their treaties, it is against our wish." Then he reminded them, just among us chiefs, how it is sometimes with the "children." "You know it is not always possible for any father to have his children do precisely as he wishes them to do."

The *Chronicle*'s report of the meeting ends, believe it or not, as follows: " 'Ugh,' 'Aha' sounded along the line as the interpreter proceeded, and their countenances gave evident tokens of satisfaction."

I COULD NOT AFFORD TO HANG MEN FOR VOTES

BUT LINCOLN had had a much more serious encounter with Indian affairs in the late summer and fall of 1862, some months before this gathering of the chiefs. The long, sad history of the treatment of the red brethren had been particularly long and sad in the state of Minnesota. The Episcopal bishop of the state, a man named Henry Whipple, had predicted in a letter to President Buchanan in 1860 that the corruption in the administration of Indian affairs in that state would lead to a Sioux uprising. "A nation which sowed robbery would reap a harvest of blood," Whipple warned.

When the Lincoln administration came to power, Whipple made an attempt to have the "Indian system" reformed. The core of the corruption was the use of the posts of Indian agents and traders entirely as political rewards; in a well-established tradition, the political appointees, who needed to have no knowledge of, or sympathy with, their Indian charges whatsoever, would make money from the post. In some cases they made themselves rich.

Whipple's hopes that the new Lincoln administration would reform this Indian system were doomed to disappointment. By the time Bishop Whipple made his appeal, Lincoln the politician had already made appointments of Indian administrators on the old basis of political reward. Lincoln's administration was clearly not going to be much better on this score than the previous Democratic administration.

Later in Lincoln's administration, after he had been educated both by Whipple's arguments and by harsh experience, Lincoln did, in his annual message of December 1862, call for reform of the Indian system. But his administration, which had other matters on its mind, did not accomplish that reform.

Antecedent to the corruption in the Indian administration had been the robbery of land and violation of treaties with respect to it; some of Lincoln's pale-faced "children" had behaved very badly indeed toward their red brethren. David A. Nichols's monograph *Lincoln and the Indians,* the leading treatment of the subject, gives pungent and shocking details and quotations. With respect to land, he quotes Senator William Pitt Fessenden of Maine, almost the only defender of Indian rights in Congress, as having said disapprovingly, of proposals for Indian "removal," that "all the rights and all the justice . . . are to be reserved for the whites and . . . Indians do not seem to have any rights in relation to the matter." As to treaties guaranteeing territory to tribes "forever," Nichols quotes Senator Fessenden as saying that "forever" really meant "until the white people want it." And with respect to the role of the traders and providers, Nichols quotes a supplier who was supposed to provide food for the Indians: "[S]o far as I am concerned, if they are hungry, let them eat grass or their own dung."

In 1862 the harvest of blood that Bishop Whipple had predicted arrived. Some young Sioux men, desperate, as we may say, raided a farm for eggs; in the resulting melee they killed five white settlers. Violence spread from that beginning throughout southwestern Minnesota. When it ended, it left 350 white persons killed and produced a racially charged frenzy in the white population of the Upper Midwest.

The president in Washington, preoccupied with Civil War events, made the mistake of sending General John Pope, the defeated general from Second Bull Run, to command the troops who would quell the outbreak. Arriving in Minnesota on September 16, General Pope felt he knew enough already on September 17 to write:

> The horrible massacres of women and children and the outrageous abuse of female prisoners, still alive, call for punishment beyond human power to inflict. There will be no peace in this region by virtue of treaties and Indian faith. It is my purpose to utterly exterminate the Sioux if I have the power to do so and even if it requires a campaign lasting the whole of next year. Destroy everything belonging to them and force them out to the plains, unless, as I suggest, you can capture them. They are to be treated as maniacs or wild beasts, and by no means as people with whom treaties or compromises can be made.

The rebellion was quelled, and a military commission sentenced 303 Sioux warriors to be executed for killings and "outrages," by which the commission meant rapes.

Lincoln brought to his dealings with this matter, as his pidgin English address to the chiefs would suggest, no sophisticated understanding of the American Indian and certainly no late twentieth-century sympathy for "Native Americans." What he did have, though, was not only a basic charity but also an inclination to be very careful in the presence of passionate "malice"—to pause, to check, to seek out the particular facts, not to be carried along in a rush of passion. In a crucial action in this event, he promptly directed the angry authorities in Minnesota to execute *no one* without further word, and he ordered that the complete records of the trial be sent to him.

General Pope, a Minnesota senator, and the Minnesota governor all told him that the people of the state were so infuriated that if the Sioux were not all executed legally, they would be killed illegally. A representative letter from Minnesota argued:

> [W]e kill the wolfes that prey on our sheep . . . Shall we not kill those savages who not only kill our sheep, but kill & steal all our stock, murder & rape our mothers, wives & daughters, depopulate counties, burn towns, & turn thousands of acres of hay & wheat, oats & corn out to destruction? The voice of this people calls for vengeance . . . Not only does justice require the blood of these savages, but vengeance will have it—the people of this State . . . are so exasperated against the Indians that if the authorities do not hang them, they will. This is a settled purpose.

But Lincoln resisted all that. He did have a voice telling him a different story: Bishop Whipple. In addition, the politician William P. Dole, whom Lincoln had appointed commissioner of Indian affairs (not because he knew anything about Indian affairs but as a political reward), also turned out to have a certain sympathy for the Indians. Dole and Bishop Whipple were lonely dissenting voices in the angry chorus calling for the execution of the entire group of 303 Sioux, but Lincoln listened to them. Learning from his judge advocate general that presidential powers could not be delegated, he personally—in the midst of Civil War pressures and woes—went through the records, one by one, of the convicted Sioux and sorted out those who were guilty of the serious crimes.

He was shocked by what he found in the trial transcripts, but not in the way the angry Minnesota population was shocked. The governor of the state, a man named Henry Sibley, who had himself become wealthy and therefore politically prominent by fraudulent dealings with the Sioux, had determined that the number of executions "will be sufficiently great to satisfy the longings of the most blood thirsty." The "trials" had become shorter and shorter, averaging less than fifteen minutes each. "The lack of evidence against the accused was manifest. Indians who honestly admitted their involvement in battles had condemned themselves. Hearsay evidence and a denial of the process and counsel were characteristic of General Sibley's trial proceedings." The leading scholarly article on this affair reports that forty-two Indians were "tried" in a single day.

Among the most shocking features was a conspicuous betrayal. Indians who had peaceably surrendered, having been told they would be safe, were then convicted on the slimmest basis; if one admitted to firing a gun, that was enough for a sentence of death. Lincoln worked through the transcripts for a month, sorting out those who were guilty of serious crimes. The number kept shrinking. To his surprise, he found only 2 who were clearly guilty of rape, and only 39—out of the 303 condemned by the military—who were guilty of killing innocent farmers. One of these was later exonerated, so that finally only 38 were to be executed by the president's order. David Herbert Donald presents the touching picture of Lincoln conscientiously going over each individual case, and then, when he had sorted out the 39, carefully writing out in his own hand the names—"Te-he-hdo-ne-cha; Tazoo alias Plan-doo-ta"—and telling the telegraph operator to be particularly careful because a slight error with these unfamiliar names might lead to the execution of the wrong man.

On the day after Christmas 1862 the 38 Sioux were hanged in Mankato, Minnesota. On the one hand, that was the largest mass execution in American history, and it was carried out under the administration of Abraham Lincoln. On the other hand, there were 265 Sioux who would have been hanged but were still alive because the conscientious president stopped the process and went through the cases one by one.

There was much resentment in Minnesota against his radical reduction in the number of condemned men—against, in effect, his multiple pardons. In the 1864 election Republicans did less well than before in Minnesota. A Minnesota senator, and a former governor, said that Lincoln would have had a larger majority in Minnesota if he had hanged more. Lincoln responded: "I could not afford to hang men for votes."

A modern interpretation might argue, as the scholar Carol Chomsky does, that the Indians in this case—the Dakota—should have been treated not as criminals but as prisoners of war in a contest between sovereign treaty-bound nations. But that perspective was not available to Lincoln or anyone else in the nineteenth-century American setting; even Bishop Whipple did not reach that understanding.

Lincoln did not make many of the just and humane changes in Indian policy that we may now, looking back, wish he had done. He did not reform the corrupt Indian system, although he did at one point endorse that reform. He did not oppose the sometimes cruel policy of Indian "removal," which often meant forced displacement of Indians from their ancient lands so the prosperity-seeking pale faces could take over. In fact, part of the settlement with angry Minnesota whites who wanted many more hangings was the removal of the Sioux from Minnesota and, just for good measure, the removal also of the Winnebago, who had done nothing but occupy land that white men wanted.

The chief scholar dealing with Lincoln and the Indians, in the illumination of twentieth-century enlightenment, David Nichols, criticizes Lincoln for not doing more. Although Nichols acknowledges that "Lincoln was clearly more humanitarian toward Indians than most of the main military and political figures of his time," he then writes:

> While Lincoln was a cautious reformer, that does not completely answer the question as to whether his Indian policies support his traditional image as a humanitarian. One might point to what happened to Indian people following Lincoln's interventions in both Kansas and Minnesota. While his attention was elsewhere the Kansas refugees suffered. Lincoln's armies killed more Indians than he pardoned in Minnesota. While he pardoned a large number, he still executed thirty-eight men on superficial evidence and permitted even more to die in miserable prison conditions and under forced removal.

Hans Trefousse responds to Nichols that "[Lincoln's] commutation of the sentences of the Indian prisoners, no matter what their fate afterward, was an act of courage and compassion as well as of justice. The political risks were great; yet Lincoln did not really hesitate."

And for all the limitations evident to another age, that unhesitating "act of courage and compassion as well as of justice" toward utterly distant strangers whom most of his peers wanted to hang surely is enough to contradict Herndon.

Bishop Whipple, moreover, did report, about a meeting he had with Lincoln toward the end of the war, that Lincoln promised: "If I live, this accursed system shall be reformed." But he did not live, and it was not reformed.

CHAPTER SEVENTEEN

Must I Shoot a Simple Soldier Boy?

A NEW ARMY

THE LITTLE ARMY of 17,000 professionals with which the United States began the war was suddenly swollen by an enormous influx of civilians, first of 75,000 volunteers, signing on for ninety days in the first flush of idealistic zeal; then by the enlargement of the numbers and lengthening of the service already that first summer; and then, as the war ground on, by conscripts drawn by the coercion of state power in the hundreds of thousands. These farm boys and small-town men, and raw civilians from the growing cities, would not under ordinary circumstances have had any connection at all with war and the military life. It was the nation's first experience of a modern popular army drawn from the whole people. A handful of professional soldiers had to fashion a giant army out of these thousands who were not soldiers, helped, or hindered, by the politicians appointed to army commands. In the four years of war about two million men served, and more than a hundred thousand went before courts-martial for some offense. The greater number of offenses, to be sure, were minor, but also many resulted in severe punishment, including being shot to death.

This transformed army inherited a military code of conduct that reflected the disciplining severities of a long European professional military tradition—including summary execution by firing squad for serious dereliction, as the military tradition, with its insistent rigidity, defined it. All capital cases were supposed to come to the president; for most of the war that was the law. But it is clear that not all of them did.

If one had never heard the Lincoln legend and encountered only Lincoln the tenacious war leader, one might believe that he would allow the military justice system to function according to this tradition without any intrusion. Lincoln, as we have seen throughout this book, had two sides, one of which was the realistic and resolute war leader who persisted after

327

multiple defeats; who pressed his generals to take the battle to the enemy; who insisted that the objective was the destruction of Lee's army and not the capture of territory; who said that breath alone kills no rebels; who remarked that he regretted that war did not admit of holy days; who asked with rhetorical sarcasm whether he was to fight with elder stalks filled with rose water. This statesman-commander could take his losses, even after a destructive defeat like Fredericksburg. *That* Lincoln, the thoroughly realistic analyst of the larger scene and the long-range objective, might have accepted the hard-line argument of many of his generals and some civilians—that severe punishments, including executions, were necessary to the discipline of the armies. Or at least he might have left the issue untouched by executive intervention.

But that was not the side of Lincoln that prevailed. When a wife or a congressman told him about a soldier about to be shot, he sent a telegram and stopped it. When he sat with the papers from a court-martial ordering a soldier to be shot, again and again he said no.

THE SLEEPING SENTINEL

THE MOST FAMOUS of his military pardons came in 1861, before anyone had had much experience with the grim realities of the whole people's war. This case was to have a gaudy afterlife as a treacly poem and as a legend, but for all the legendary improvements, it turns out that the bare bones of the story are true.

William Scott was a volunteer in that first wave, a private in the Third Vermont Volunteers, which was part of the Army of the Potomac that McClellan whipped into shape around Washington after Bull Run. Private Scott, while on sentry duty at Chain Bridge, fell asleep. The generals and the court-martial apparently decided to impress upon these new soldiers the seriousness of what they were about and, as prescribed by received military law, sentenced Scott to be shot dead by a firing squad.

Shocked Vermonters who were in Washington protested to the president. A friend of Scott's mother, Mrs. Horatio King, the wife of the postmaster in Buchanan's cabinet, wrote him a letter, which had some of the flavor of the poem that would appear in 1863.

> Allow me to address you—You in your high position, in whom the power of life, or, death in this case is vested.—I come before you—I implore you—almost on bended knee, I implore you, to interpose and by your

pardon save the life of him who by military law is doomed to die an igno-
minious death, tomorrow.

Mrs. King made a sharp distinction between a professional army and
the army of which young Scott was a part—a distinction that would be
important to Lincoln later, in his exercise of clemency:

> I am aware that the most exemplary discipline in our army should be
> observed,—and, that, the most rigid punishment for real crime should be
> enforced. And were this, a foreign army, with life long hireling soldiers—
> trained to do their masters bidding, be it right, or be it wrong, my voice
> should not be heard in their behalf—But, Sir, the case is so different.

Young Scott was no lifelong hireling soldier. Mrs. King cited Lincoln's
own call for volunteers:

> You call for help—you call on our common country to come to the res-
> cue, and save this glorious Union from that destruction into which its
> foes would plunge it. How nobly—how bravely it has responded to that
> call—and among the rest is William Scott of company H, 3 Vermont
> Volunteers. Inspired with love of Country—his soul fired with purest
> patriotism—young and ardent—Sacrificing home and all its cherished
> endearments—burning with intense desire to meet the foe in deadly
> combat—

Private Scott's offense had an explanation:

> He comes to Washington—full of noble—brave resolve—And he has
> never changed! Noble and brave still! Is it so? Then why, condemned to
> die?—Unused to Camp life—unused to military discipline—the exhaus-
> tion of the climate (new to him)—the exhaustion of military discipline
> (new to him) and the enfeebling effects of temporary illness—all con-
> spired this ruin—Exhausted nature could endure no more, and obeying
> its own dictates, sought relief in momentary sleep—Sir:—It was not vol-
> untary!—And shall he die?—Shall this brave patriot this son of New
> England—of our Common Country—who has given his life for its
> defense—shall he die before his heaven sent mission be accomplished? It
> may be said, the discipline of the Army requires it? No, Sir, I think I
> know enough of human nature, to know, that, the whole volunteer army

will bless you . . . and that every one will double their diligence as duty requires—

The legend that would grow out of this event would have a more melodramatic rescue, but what did happen, apparently, was that Lincoln—who would demonstrate over time that he agreed with many of Mrs. King's points but had not yet had much practice intervening in military justice— would request General McClellan to pardon Scott. The pardon warrant was signed by McClellan. Maybe Lincoln and Mary rode out to Camp Advance and talked to McClellan about it; we do know they took a drive that day. McClellan wrote to his wife on September 8, the day before Scott was to have been executed, that "Mr. Lincoln came this morning to ask me to pardon a man I had ordered to be shot, suggesting that I could give as a reason . . . that it was by request of the 'lady president.' "

The sentimental poem that would be produced by a government clerk in 1863—after Lincoln and the country had had much more experience with his role as the pardoner of soldiers—would have a more wonderful intervention: the president himself roaring up in his coach, at the last minute, as the "fatal volley" is about to sound, with a pardon in his hand:

> *Then suddenly was heard the noise of steeds and wheels approach,*
> *—And, rolling through a cloud of dust, appeared a stately coach.*
> *On, past the guards, and through the field, its rapid course was bent,*
> *Till, halting, 'mid the lines was seen the nation's President!**

However his pardon was effected, William Scott, the sleeping sentry from Vermont, did return to his company and did then fulfill his legendary role by dying bravely on April 16, 1862, in an attack by Vermont volunteers at the battle of Lee's Mills, before Yorktown, in an early stage of the Peninsula Campaign. As the grapevine passed this story through the country and the army, Scott was said to have actually addressed dying words to the president who had pardoned him. The poem had the dying William Scott bless the president:

> *While yet his voice grew tremulous, and death bedimmed his eye—*
> *He called his comrades to attest, he had not feared to die!*

---

*The complete poem—"The Sleeping Sentinel" by Francis De Haes Janvier—can be found on the Civil War poetry Web site: http://www.civilwarpoetry.org.

And, in his last expiring breath, a prayer to heaven was sent—
That God, with His unfailing grace, would bless our President!

The poem, recited by a noted elocutionist, first in the executive mansion and then in the Senate chambers, in 1863, to audiences that included President and Mrs. Lincoln, would be printed as a little pamphlet along with Portia's speech from *The Merchant of Venice* and would pass on into myth.

LEARNING ABOUT MILITARY JUSTICE

IN THE FIRST WINTER and second spring of the war, before any such poems had been written, Lincoln's preliminary ventures into the rapidly expanding military justice system had a certain understandable tentativeness. He would ask the army's chief lawyer, a West Point graduate and longtime army man with the resonant American name of John Fitzgerald Lee, what he could do and how he should do it. In Major Lee one can detect a certain wariness about interference by the new civilian group over in the executive mansion, and on Lincoln's side a developing conviction that he should exercise responsibility. In response to a presidential comment on one case Judge Advocate Lee remarked: "The President's suggestion as to the construction to be . . . put upon the finding is in accordance with legal logic . . . but it is not according to the rule and usage of courts martial." Although the case "would be bad pleading in a court of common law," it "is good in a court martial." Lincoln was learning the difference between military law and the law to which he was accustomed in the civil courts of Illinois; one can imagine him formulating the wisecrack of a later century that military justice is to justice as military music is to music.

In another early pardon—April 10, 1862—Lincoln wrote pointedly to General George G. Meade: "What possible injury can this lad work upon the cause of this great Union? I say let him go."

In July 1862 Congress created a new office of Judge Advocate General, and Postmaster General Montgomery Blair passed on to Lincoln a letter saying that the old-line army hoped that Major Lee would be appointed to that office. But on September 3, 1862, Lincoln appointed a civilian lawyer and politician named Joseph Holt, whose education had been not at West Point and not in the army but in Kentucky politics.*

---

*On September 4, 1862, John F. Lee resigned from the army. Lee had been the Judge Advocate; Holt in the new post would be the Judge Advocate *General.*

Holt, a former Democrat from Kentucky, was the Union-supporting member of Buchanan's cabinet who, as the outgoing secretary of war, had handed Lincoln the fateful message from Major Anderson and the officers at Fort Sumter. As judge advocate general, Holt would play a leading role in dealing with Copperheads; after Lincoln's assassination he would be in charge of the investigation and first trial of the conspirators. But before he was called upon to perform those more widely known services, he dealt every day with the expanding flow of capital cases coming from the courts-martial. He made recommendations to Lincoln and carried out the president's decisions even when he disagreed with them, as he often did.

In a representative case in the fall of 1862, a court-martial meeting in Helena, Arkansas, had fastened on one Private Conrad Zachringer of Company A, Twelfth Missouri Volunteers, an imposing series of grim formal classifications of his multiple alleged offenses. Private Zachringer, according to the record, "caused, and excited mutiny by taking hold of First Lieutenant Mittman, then officer of the day, by the throat" (thereby violating the Seventh Article of War) and "did strike First Lieutenant Engelmann, and throwed [sic] him on the ground" (thereby violating the Ninth Article of War) and "did refuse to obey" and "did resist and strike" (thereby violating the Twenty-seventh Article of War). Therefore, despite his plea "that he was drunk and knew nothing of them," he had been found guilty on all charges and sentenced to be shot dead.

No, said Lincoln, on October 25, 1862; *don't shoot him dead.** Lincoln perceived that, despite all the elaborate paraphernalia of military law, the offense amounted to a drunken binge, and on October 25 he ordered an enormous reduction in Zachringer's punishment from death to a year's imprisonment and a dishonorable discharge.

THESE CASES CAME BY THE HUNDREDS

WITH THE ENLARGEMENT of the war, these cases would grow in number. Joseph Holt himself, in an interview with John Nicolay after the war, described the sessions that would eventually result:

> The President would call me over to go over them [capital cases from courts-martial] with him—occupying hours at a time. He was free and

---

*For the pardon cases in the text and notes for this chapter we cite only the date. They all may be found in *CW*.

communicative in his criticism and comment on them, and his true nature showed itself in these interviews ... In a great army like ours these cases came by the hundreds.

Those hundreds of courts-martial would order some private (as it almost always was) to be shot for "desertion" (as it most often was) or for "cowardice and absence without leave" or for "mutiny" or for "violence to a superior officer" or for "disobedience and insubordination" or for "striking and using threatening language toward his superior officer" or for "willful disobedience of orders" or for "sleeping on post." And Lincoln would, again and again, grant a reprieve, a commutation, a pardon—he would stop the execution. Holt described Lincoln's response: "He shrank with evident pain from even the idea of shedding human blood . . . all these many sentences impressed him as nothing short of 'wholesale butchery.' In every case he always leaned to the side of mercy. His constant desire was to save life."

Often before a case came through military channels, it would be brought to the president by a distressed father, or a congressman, or friends at home, and he would send a telegram ordering that the execution be suspended and the papers sent to him. He would then look into the papers for extenuation, which often he would find, and he would instruct Holt to issue a pardon or commutation.

One realizes how important it was that they now had the telegraph. Sometimes the telegram would be sent on the day before a scheduled execution or even on the day of a scheduled execution, so that the last-minute, hairsbreadth aspect of the anecdotes of folklore had a certain chilling truth.

Fairly often Lincoln's telegraphed clemency would exhibit an unsettling doubt about the soldier's name, or the sentence, or the scheduled time of the execution, reminding the reader that this grim business was taking place in the chaos of a gigantic, disorganized nineteenth-century war. More chilling still are those telegrams in which there appears a troublesome phrase like "suspend the execution if it is not already done." In at least four cases printed by the editors of *The Collected Works,* we read the melancholy message that Lincoln's attempted clemency came too late.

FINDING SOME REASON

IN NICOLAY'S 1875 interview Holt reproduced an argument he himself made (like the arguments of many generals and some hard-boiled civilians) in behalf of the executions:

I used to try and argue the necessity of . . . executing these sentences. I said to him, if you punish desertion and misbehavior by death, these men will feel that they are placed between two dangers and of the two they will choose the least. They will say to themselves, there is the battle in front where they may be killed, it is true, but from which they have a good chance to escape alive; while they will know that if they fly to the rear their cowardice will be punished by certain death.

But Lincoln, as Holt remembered his response, was no more persuaded by Holt than he would be when similar arguments were made by the many military officers:

Yes, your reasons are all very good, but I don't think I can do it. I don't believe it will make a man any better to shoot him, while if we keep him alive, we may at least get some work out of him.

And then, as Holt quoted the dead president through the mists of memory, Lincoln mentioned a category that was to become a part of his legend, the "leg case"—a soldier with a brave heart but with cowardly legs when the battle begins; "a man who honestly meant to do his duty but who was overcome by a physical fear greater than his will."

On his way overseas in World War I, Captain Harry S. Truman of the 129th Field Artillery from Missouri, a reader of books about Lincoln (despite his Missouri-bred mother's disapproval), would write to his girl-friend Bess Wallace back home that he hoped he would not prove to be one of the leg cases.

Lincoln also quickly made it a principle not to allow the execution of the very young. He said in a wire to General Meade: "I am unwilling for any boy under eighteen to be shot" (October 8, 1863). The father of the boy in that case "affirms that he is yet under sixteen." Again and again Lincoln would stop the execution of a "boy" or a "lad" who was seventeen, sixteen, fifteen, "very young."

Lincoln would regularly adduce—sometimes in combination with youth—"insanity," "unsoundness of mind," or "other debilitating ailments," or say that a soldier was "so diseased as to be unfit for Military duty." A different kind of extenuation, also usually in combination with others, was the hardship and poverty of the family. "[The mother] says she is destitute."

A few pardons refer to misunderstandings on the part of those (of German background, usually) who did not fully comprehend what was said to them either by a mustering official or by an officer. Problems arose about recruiting and mustering youngsters, as is indicated by this terse message to Holt on February 10, 1864:

Boy discharged and mustering officer rebuked.

A. Lincoln

Here is a typical inquiry by the president, sent on November 3, 1863, to General Meade, that reveals a quite Lincolnian basis for clemency: "Samuel Wellers, private in Co. B 49th. Penn Vols. writes that he is to be shot for desertion on the 6th. Inst. His own story is rather a bad one, and yet he tells it so frankly, that I am some what interested in him."* Then he asked, in hope, about this frank storyteller: "Has he been a good soldier, except the desertion?" And of course: "About how old is he?"

SHOVELING FLEAS AND SHOOTING DESERTERS

DESERTION AND ABSENCE without leave would become an enormous problem in the Union armies, as in the Confederate armies, and the problem would increase as the war expanded and the casualty lists became longer, and as the draft brought in soldiers with backgrounds and motivations different from those of the first waves of volunteers. Lincoln certainly knew the problem that desertions presented; trying to move McClellan's Army of the Potomac from one place to another, he had said, was like "shoveling fleas." Article 20 of the military code, passed in 1806, prescribed for desertion "death, or such other punishment as by sentence of court-martial, shall be inflicted"—and required that the sentence of death be approved by the president. That set up a tug-of-war between commanders of armies, many of whom wanted to use executions to stop desertions, and the commander in chief, who kept pardoning the convicted soldiers. A general and a court-martial (composed of officers), eager to achieve an instructively terrifying result, might look only at the fact of a soldier's absence; but Lincoln, often appealed to by touching letters and visits,

---

*This is not the only time that telling one's story well had an effect on the lover of good storytelling, Abraham Lincoln. On July 1, 1864, he issued an order for the release of a Confederate prisoner that read: "This man being so well vouched, and talking so much better than any other I have heard, let him take the oath . . . and be discharged."

looked at the larger story. Why was the soldier absent? Some reasons did
not merit sympathy: some soldiers, for example, joined the Union army in
order to be sent south and then took the opportunity to desert and enlist in
the Confederate army. Sometimes bounty jumpers enlisted, collected a
bounty for enlistment, then deserted and reenlisted in order to collect a
second (or third, or more) bounty. Lincoln did not pardon them.

But many more of the convicted deserters had much more sympathetic
stories, and Lincoln listened to them. Particularly as the war ground on, the
hardships of war, weariness, and discouragement increased. Lack of shoes
and clothing; lack of supplies, food, and arms; illness and disease; rain,
cold, and mud in the winter; and battle losses all took their toll. Concern
for their families and lack of pay often sent men home to tend to their obligations there. Further, many recruits in this mainly civilian army knew
virtually nothing of military law or their obligations under it. Soldiers frequently left one command and joined another, not realizing they were
deserting. Some never received their enlistment bounty and therefore
assumed they had not obligated themselves to serve. The foreign-born and
the illiterate often had not even been able to read what they were signing
on to. Even in the case of bounty jumpers, the money paid was an entice-
ment for desertion and reenlistment, a kind of entrapment, to which poor
and ignorant recruits were particularly susceptible. Other deserters were
encouraged by civilians to desert, in many cases so that civilian recruiters
could collect fees for enlistment of substitutes, or out of lack of sympathy
with the war—the situation Lincoln would excoriate in a famous public
letter.

TOMORROW IS BUTCHER DAY

OFTEN THE General Court-Martial Orders commanded the death of the
offending soldier with the explicit grisly phrase that he be "shot to death
with musketry." It was necessary to specify shot to *death* because sometimes the first volley would not kill the condemned. Because the executions
were intended to have a powerful deterrent effect, they were carried out in
full view of the company, which was commanded to watch and then to
march by the corpse.

As the executions increased, a place and a day would be set aside: "A
gallows and a shooting-ground were provided in each corps and scarcely a
Friday passed during the winter of 1863–64 that some wretched deserter
did not suffer the death penalty in the Army of the Potomac." That army
was often close enough that Lincoln could hear the shots. John Eaton

reported him saying, upon hearing the sound of rifles from across the Potomac, "This is the day when they shoot deserters." He went on to make a comment that would have stunned a number of his generals, given that they strongly believed the opposite: "I am wondering whether I have used the pardoning power as much as I ought."

That Lincoln was repelled by the execution of young privates for the reasons that the courts-martial gave is evident in his use of the metaphor of butchery. Holt in his interview with Nicolay, quoted above, said that Lincoln regarded the executions as "wholesale butchery." Not long after Lincoln's assassination, Leonard Swett, Lincoln's longtime friend and associate, told Herndon of an occasion when Lincoln dismissed him: "Get out of the way, Swett; to morrow is butcher-day, and I must go through these papers and see if I cannot find some excuse to let these poor fellows off." Lincoln said in explanation of one of his pardons (January 7, 1864): "I did this, not on any merit in the case, but because I am trying to evade the butchering business lately."

Leonard Swett's description of his visit to Lincoln on the day before butcher day is an account much like others: "The pile of papers he had were the records of Courts Martial of men who on the following day were to be shot. He was not examining the Records to see whether the evidence sustained the findings. He was purposely in search of occasions to evade the law in favor of life."

DISCRIMINATING MERCY

To be sure, Lincoln did not give every soldier a pardon or reprieve. In the letter to Herndon we have already quoted, Swett said this:

> He [Lincoln] had very great kindness of heart. His mind was full of tender sensibilities; he was extremely humane, yet while these attributes were fully developed in his character and unless intercepted by his judgment controlled him, they never did control him contrary to his judgments. He would strain a point to be kind, but he never strained to breaking. Most men of much kindly feeling are controlled by this sentiment against their judgment, or rather that sentiment beclouds their Judgment. It was never so with him. He would be just as kind and generous as his judgment would let him be—no more.

By the official count, 272 Union soldiers were executed by the U.S. Army, 141 of them for desertion. Thomas Lowry, who with Beverly Lowry has gone through an enormous number of Union army courts-martial in the National Archives, has discovered that executions were far more numerous than the official numbers specify. Many of them were not brought to Lincoln's attention, despite the law. But then Lincoln did not pardon every accused person for whom an appeal came to his desk. His mercy, although generous, was discriminating. He did not pardon any soldier found guilty of rape. He did not pardon a soldier, however tearful his wife's plea, who deserted three times and was incorrigible. Writing to Nicolay about the long July 18, 1863, session with a hundred cases, in which Lincoln seized on any excuse for mercy, Hay added: "He was only merciless in cases where meanness or cruelty were shown."

THE COURT-MARTIAL GRINDSTONE:
I DO WANT TO BE CONSIDERATE OF EVERY CASE

LINCOLN SAID to John Eaton, "I would not relax the discipline of the army, but I do want to be considerate of every case." By 1864 he would be sitting there with Holt and Nicolay or Hay, in sessions as long as six hours, going through as many as a hundred records of courts-martial.

In early 1864 the painter Francis Carpenter, the artist who did the famous painting *First Reading of the Emancipation Proclamation of President Lincoln,* worked on his painting in the Lincoln executive mansion and was able therefore to produce a valuable little book with the subtitle *Six Months at the White House.* Hearing Lincoln respond to repeated appeals for clemency, Carpenter wrote:

> I shall never cease to regret that an additional private secretary could not
> have been appointed, whose exclusive duty it should have been to look
> after and keep a record of all cases appealing to executive clemency. It
> would have afforded full employment for one man, at least; and such a
> volume would now be beyond price.

It is a striking feature about Lincoln's pardons that there were so many of them, and that he took the time to consider them, as much as he could, in the chaos of wartime, case by case. On July 19, 1863, John Hay would write to Nicolay, who was back in Illinois visiting, "I am in a state of entire collapse after yesterday's work. I ran the Tycoon through one hundred Court martials! a steady sitting of six hours!" Nine days later he would write, "It would do you good to see how I daily hold the Tycoon's nose to the Court Martial grindstone."

It was not as though the president had nothing else to do. July 1863 was a huge moment in the history of the war. July 4 had brought the enormously heartening good news of the victory at Gettysburg, and soon thereafter it was reported that Grant had at last taken Vicksburg on the Mississippi. Gettysburg and Vicksburg created a brief moment of triumph and hope for Lincoln and the Union: it seemed that the war might soon be over. But then General Meade, not following his advantage, allowed Lee to take his army back across the Potomac. And on July 11, the Saturday a week before the steady sitting with the courts-martial, New York City exploded in the riot against the draft. Before long, as noted, it turned into a race riot and lasted throughout the week, finally being quelled only on Friday, July 17. And so, still watching and prodding Meade, and still dealing with the riots against the draft, on a hot mid-July Saturday in Washington the president sat down with Joseph Holt and John Hay and scrupulously went through a hundred courts-martial. This case. That case. Another case. One by one. It was on this occasion, on July 18, that he wrote one of his most quoted pardons, of Private Michael Delany, Company K, First Colorado Cavalry, who had been sentenced to be shot for desertion: "Let him fight instead of being shot."

By 1864 these heroic sessions would be frequent and tended to come in clusters. Joseph Holt would bring huge stacks of courts-martial over to the executive mansion, at a time he could arrange with the president.* The president would summon him with stacks already accumulated in a pigeonhole in his desk and, sitting usually with Nicolay or Hay, would work them through, "occupying hours at a time," Holt would remember later. On February 9, 1864, Lincoln reviewed 63 court-martial cases, with "routine endorsements" of "pardon, approval, remission, or commutation of sentence." On February 10 he reviewed 32 cases. (After a long morning reviewing court-martial cases, Lincoln learned that his private stables had caught fire and were burning down. The president leaped over the hedge in an unsuccessful attempt to rescue the horses, among them his late son Willie's pony. He was afterward found weeping in the East Room, watching the burning stables.) On February 11, Holt and Lincoln considered 46 cases (thus 139 cases in three days); on February 15, 48 cases; on April 14, 67 cases; on so on through ten other such heavy days in 1864 and early 1865.

*For example, on April 13, 1863, Holt made an appointment to consider court-martial cases on the following day; on April 25 a presidential message to Holt said it would be impossible to take up court-martial cases that day; one infers much juggling to find the time to consider 48 cases; 67 cases; 72 cases.

In February 1864 the Union army was defeated in a bloody battle at Olustee, with almost nineteen hundred federal casualties; the president issued an order for half a million more soldiers; he met with a Southern commission to discuss possibilities for peace; he spoke with a Northern delegation to discuss a constitutional amendment abolishing slavery—and he spent three long sessions, on the ninth, tenth, and fifteenth, dealing with court-martial cases.

In April 1864 news of the disastrous Red River Campaign arrived from Arkansas, and of the Fort Pillow Massacre from Tennessee. General Grant, newly promoted to commander, was preparing the Army of Northern Virginia for its big push in the Wilderness Campaign. And the president had four long sessions with court-martial cases.

A POLITICIAN'S MERCY

MANY CRITICIZED Lincoln's tenderheartedness, but almost no one on the Union side denied that it was real—on the contrary, the prevailing criticism was that it was all too real. But there was one Union man who, long after the war, flatly rejected the folklore picture of the merciful Lincoln. By his sheer rarity he would come to be often quoted. This was Donn Piatt, a reporter and writer who served as an officer in the Union army. Looking back in the 1880s, he wrote that he doubted that Lincoln had "a kind, forgiving nature." The popular belief in Lincoln's mercy, Piatt would write, is "erroneous . . . His good-natured manner misled the common mind."

He was not alone in having difficulty assimilating the apparently disparate elements of Lincoln's makeup and conduct—the resolute commander pressing to destroy Lee's armies on the one hand and the tenderhearted leader on the other. But Piatt resolved the problem by starting with a stereotype of what "great leaders" had to be and then imposing that a priori stereotype on Lincoln. One of his peculiar statements was that "successful leaders in history" are "oily, elastic" on the outside but "angular, hard" in inner purpose—and Lincoln must have been like that too.

He made a quite revealing further observation: "As for his steady refusal to sanction the death penalty in cases of desertion, there was far more policy than kind feeling in this course. To assert the contrary is to detract from Lincoln's force of character as well as intellect."

This last sentence gives away Piatt's worldview: he saw it as a sign of an intellectual and moral defect to act out of "kind feeling" toward deserting soldiers—so, being a great leader, Lincoln must not have done so. There is a kind of cynic who cannot discern, or cannot admit that he does discern, moral characteristics that extend beyond his own outlook. One is reminded of the saying that when a pickpocket looks at a saint, what he sees are his pockets.

Piatt was surely wrong to deny that Lincoln was genuinely merciful. The evidence to the contrary is overwhelming. It includes the sheer number of Lincoln's acts of clemency, the testimony of many observers, and the accounts of many who asked him for pardons. Many words from Lincoln's own hand would be difficult to explain if his humane sense were not genuine and primary. His remark that he wanted to be out of the "butchering business" is not a metaphor that a calmly hard-boiled politician would have come up with.

YOU PARDON HIM, AND THE ARMY
IS WITHOUT DISCIPLINE

A PARTICULARLY pointed statement of the alleged result of Lincoln's tenderheartedness was attributed perhaps surprisingly, or perhaps not surprisingly, to the most radical member of his cabinet, Treasury Secretary Salmon Chase: "Such kindness to the criminal [meaning the pardons] is cruelty to the army, for it encourages the bad to leave the brave and patriotic unsupported."

If civilian officials—including Lincoln's close associates Chase, Welles, Bates, and Stanton—had reservations about his (as they thought) overdone kindness, how much more would it be true of the leaders of vast armies?

General Daniel Tyler said, for a characteristic example, that whereas Confederate general Braxton Bragg shot his deserters, "if we attempt to shoot a deserter, you pardon him and our army is without discipline." Colonel Theodore Lyman, on the staff of the Army of the Potomac in General Meade's day, complained not to Lincoln but privately, "All this [great outrages in the rear] proceeds from one thing—the uncertainty of the death penalty through the false merciful policy of the President."

The colorful scamp General Benjamin Butler, an actor in such varied roles in so many different acts of the Civil War, joined in this one: "President Lincoln, I pray you not to interfere with the courts-martial of the army. You will destroy all discipline among our soldiers."

Most of the writing about Lincoln since his apotheosis has treated his pardons of soldiers favorably, indeed as an important part of his myth—but not all biographers do. William Barton, writing in the 1920s, put it harshly and suggested that Lincoln may have been fooled:

> Lincoln had little time to investigate and it is to be feared that in some cases the alleged widow had rented the black clothes for the occasion, and had help in inventing the fiction about her family. Lincoln was very easily imposed upon . . . In the long run it had been better for the discipline of the army if he had kept his hands off.

WAR LOOKS BUT TO THE FRONTAGE

THE ARGUMENT against what Lincoln was doing as it might be stated in the exigency of war was put with distinctive force by the American novelist of the Civil War generation Herman Melville in his short, posthumously discovered novel *Billy Budd*. Writing years later and placing his story not in the American Civil War but on a British man-of-war at sea in the Napoleonic Wars, Melville has a ship captain, "Starry" Vere, to most readers a sympathetic character, make the argument that Billy must hang for striking a superior officer, even though Billy did not mean to strike him, let alone to kill him, had a most strong provocation, and in the eyes of heaven (as Vere knows and says) would be totally innocent. But, says Captain Vere, doing his hard duty, "Budd's intent or not intent is nothing to the purpose" in this wartime shipboard situation: "War looks but to the frontage, the appearance. And the mutiny act, war's child, takes after the father."

Generals Sherman and Butler and Dix might have said that that reasoning applied in Civil War cases: these "men" (whom Lincoln often called "boys," and who often were really boys) had left their post, slept on sentry duty, run at gunfire, or gone home in despair—that is, committed a punishable offense—and the uniform code of military justice looked but to the frontage, to the deed itself and no more, and had to condemn them to be executed. One did not ask how old the soldier was, or whether the mustering officer deceived him, or whether he was having trouble with his girlfriend back home, or even what his intent or reason or motive or excuse was. One must look solely at the overt act (these generals believed)—because this was war. Is your heart moved? Even so is mine, says Vere. "But let not warm hearts betray heads that should be cool." The critics thought Lincoln's heart had betrayed his head, which should have been cool; Vere goes on to a point the critics of Lincoln repeatedly suggested: "[W]ill an upright judge allow himself off the bench to be waylaid by some tender kinswoman of the accused seeking to touch him with her tearful plea"?

PEOPLE WON'T STAND IT, AND THEY OUGHT NOT STAND IT

WILLIAM TECUMSEH SHERMAN produced, as one might expect, the most grimly utilitarian argument for execution, in a letter to Judge Advocate General Holt in April 1864: "[F]orty or fifty executions now would in the next twelve months save ten thousand lives."

Lincoln certainly was not going to agree with that proposition. Forty or fifty executions now! How carefully would each be considered on its individual merits if the commanding general had the collective purpose of setting examples? When Lincoln was asked in 1862 why, with thousands of absentees from the armies, the death penalty for desertion was not enforced, he answered, "Because you cannot order men shot by the dozens and twenties. People won't stand it, and they ought not stand it." It is significant that he gave not only the practical political reason—people won't stand it—but also the moral one: they *ought* not to stand it.

As the American Civil War was fought with military tactics outdated by the rifle and the new weaponry, so Lincoln may have had the moral instinct that traditional military punishments were outdated in the age of the people's army. For the professional military men, the relation of the army to the civilian population was not a matter of immediate consideration. But the president had to have that civilian connection in mind all the time—it would affect the role of volunteering, acceptance of conscription, avoidance of uproars like the July 1863 antidraft riots in New York, and how the Union army was regarded.

Lincoln may have questioned whether shooting deserters dead was as efficacious in stopping desertions as some in the military believed or as the professional army tradition held. A politician with insight into human complexity may perceive that advocates of the most drastic punishments regularly overestimate both the deterrent effect of their threatened use and the exemplary effect of actually carrying them out.

One of the most widely read and appreciated presentations of Lincoln's role as "The Pardoner" would be a chapter by that name in the massive twentieth-century biography by Carl Sandburg. Given the warmly positive flavor of the book and particularly that chapter, one is startled to read this paragraph, which simply takes for granted the claimed efficacy of the shootings:

> To what extent did the President's frequent pardons interfere with army discipline? Chauncey M. Depew was to answer by quoting General Sherman. "How did you carry out the sentences of your court-martials and escape Lincoln's pardons?" Depew asked. Sherman answered, "I shot them first!" Whatever the irregular or illegal device used by Sherman in this respect, it was probably also used by Grant, Thomas, Sheridan and every other commander who won campaigns and battles.

Sandburg did not know this about these generals; he made a sweeping assumption. It does not appear that all the most successful generals executed soldiers without approval by the president, as Sherman may well have done;* some of the most vociferous critics of Lincoln's practice were conspicuously unsuccessful political generals like Butler. In the letter to Herndon by Leonard Swett written on January 17, 1866, Swett quotes Lincoln interrupting the discussion of Swett's request for a pardon by saying, reflectively, "Grant never executed a man did he? . . . I have been watching that thing." It was not quite true that Grant never executed a man, but it is significant that Lincoln should think so: that the general he regarded as the most successful of all militarily should not require the grim discipline of formulaic executions.

THE OFFICERS' CLUB

THE JUSTICE OF Lincoln's pardons to young enlisted soldiers is supported by the fact that officers were never executed. Did officers never do the deeds that presented a mortal danger to the troops?

Officers made the arrests; officers preferred charges; commanding officers established the courts-martial. Officers staffed the courts-martial, by the appointment of the commander; the commander then accepted or rejected the court's order and put it into effect. Executions were often ordered—*he shall be shot to death with musketry*—but never of officers.

Thomas Lowry and Beverly Lowry, going through an enormous number of Union army courts-martial in the National Archives, find no officers:

---

*Sherman was garrulous, spraying ideas in many directions, and he was also a quick-shot moralist, needing to articulate moral reasons for what he would do.

"Hundreds of Union soldiers were shot by firing squads. If a Union officer stood before a firing squad, we have not seen the record."

Officers could resign; privates could not resign. For severe offenses officers were cashiered, drummed out of office, or dishonorably discharged— painful, often life-damaging punishments no doubt, but still not the same as being shot dead. One can find contrasting treatments of officers and men for essentially the same offense spread throughout the record.

Mark E. Neely, Jr., remarks in his article on "Clemency" in *The Abraham Lincoln Encyclopedia* that Lincoln was notably tougher on officers than on enlisted men: "Of fifty-nine convictions involving officers in the last half of 1863, fourteen were given more severe punishments by the president than by their courts-martial."

YOU ALL ASK ME FOR PARDONS

LINCOLN HIMSELF noted that many who in general criticized his leniency nevertheless made specific (perhaps embarrassed) requests for pardons for soldiers whom they personally knew or were connected to.

Gideon Welles, the secretary of the navy, criticized his chief's excessive leniency in his diary more than once, including this entry for Saturday, December 24, 1864: "Called on the president to commute the sentence of a person condemned to be hung. He at once assented. Is always disposed to mitigate punishment. Sometimes this is a weakness."

But we may note, significantly, that Welles here criticizes the president for doing what in this instance he, Welles, himself had just asked him to do.

Senator Henry Wilson tells another tale of a request for a particular pardon and of Lincoln's significant response:

> My officers tell me the good of the service demands the enforcement of the Law, but it makes my heart ache to have the poor boys shot. I will pardon him, and then you will all join in blaming me for it. You all censure me for granting pardons, and yet you all ask me to do so.

A GREAT MERCY TO A SIMPLE SOLDIER

THAT LINCOLN WAS acutely troubled by those butcher-day shootings of young deserters is indicated by a famous passage in one of his best state papers on another subject. In June 1863 he gathered together ideas he had jotted on scraps of paper and sat down to write a public letter responding to resolutions by an assembly of New York Union Democrats condemning the notorious arrest, and conviction, of a Northern opponent of the war, Clement Vallandigham, the Peace Democrat and Southern sympathizer from Ohio. When Vallandigham made deliberately provocative speeches against the war, General Burnside, commanding the military department of Ohio, had him arrested. Lincoln, who would not have initiated the arrest, had the problem that presented itself often, as we have seen, in his elevated position: what to do about a subordinate whose action he did not agree with. In this case he did not repudiate what Burnside had done but changed Vallandigham's punishment from imprisonment to the poetic justice of banishment behind Confederate lines, preventing his becoming a martyr. In answer to the protests against the arrest by New York Democrats, Lincoln wrote a strong public letter. Its best-known sentence ("Must I shoot a simple soldier boy . . .") is often quoted in isolation, but let us look at the paragraph in which that sentence appears.

> I understand the meeting, whose resolution I am considering, to be in favor of suppressing the Rebellion by military force—by armies. Long experience has shown that armies cannot be maintained unless desertions shall be punished by the severe penalty of death. The case requires, and the law and the Constitution sanction, this punishment.

It is by no means clear that Lincoln himself accepted the alleged necessity in the case of the soldiers in this people's army, but he gave a tidy summary of the position of many generals and others, stated for his own argumentative purposes in this context of a dispute about a different matter.

And now with those premises there comes a rhetorical challenge in the often-quoted sentence: "Must I shoot a simple-minded soldier boy who deserts, while I must not touch a hair of the wily agitator who induces him to desert?"

Suddenly Lincoln has shifted the focus from the boy, standing alone in his ruinous act, to his social context. And he goes on. Most simpleminded soldiers are not *directly* induced to desert by a wily agitator, so Lincoln makes a less direct connection:

> This is none the less injurious when effected by getting a father, or brother, or friend, into public meeting, and there working upon his feelings, till he is persuaded to write the soldier boy that he is fighting in a

bad cause, for a wicked administration of a contemptible government, too weak to arrest and punish him if he shall desert.

So now Lincoln's conclusion:

> I think that in such a case to silence that agitator, and save the boy is not only constitutional, but withal a great mercy.

The soldier boy is not (Lincoln argues) an isolated atom. He hears the voices in society—of agitators, of his friend, brother, father. They are at least as culpable as the soldier. And under the condition of rebellion and war—which is like a time of great sickness in a man's body—it is necessary to take restrictive measures that one would not take in times of health. It is constitutional, and it is just, to constrain Mr. Vallandigham at one point in the flow of public argument in order that this mercy be done at another: that the boy not be induced to desert and thus be saved from shooting.

THEY WOULD THINK THAT WE FLINCH

OPPONENTS of his leniency urged that any display of humanity or generosity would be misinterpreted as weakness or timidity. And further the corollary, *The beneficiaries will not appreciate your generosity. All they understand is brute power.* One of the letters Lincoln received at the time of the Sioux Massacres included this argument against his pardons:

> The Indians, if unpunished, will not give the Great Father as they term you, credit for magnanimity, or generosity; they will boast in their Wigwams, and as they dance around their war fires, decorated with the scalps of our hardy pioneers & their daughters & wives, & children, that we dared not punish them.

Butler, like some other generals, blamed his losses on the president, and when asked why victory took so long, he answered: "Pusillanimity and want of executive force in government." "Executive force" apparently meant, to Butler, the endorsement of executions.

In *Billy Budd* Captain Vere uses a variant of the word that Butler used; if Vere agreed with the tenderhearted officers not to hang Billy, then the conclusion of the men on board would be: "Your clement sentence they would account pusillanimous. They would think that we flinch."

Executives obviously do need to make decisions that cause someone harm. Avoiding such decisions is a fault. But is that the only blameworthy syndrome in our leaders? Is there not also a familiar pattern in the opposite direction? Don't leaders often exhibit a certain Machiavellian relish, a certain braggadocio about how "tough" they must be to make the "tough" decisions? And a considerable self-sympathy for the heavy "burden" of decisions that they must carry? And may they not justify their toughness by insisting that generosity will be misinterpreted, that all "they" understand is raw power? Which of the two self-indulging syndromes here suggested is the more common in leaders of states and armies and great institutions? May it not be that self-congratulation on one's toughness, and the inertia of the acceptance of received patterns, may lead to a certain cauterizing of the conscience? And so one may accept, and not only accept but insist on, those Fridays when the firing squad steps forward and shoots to death with musketry a row of scared and confused kids, who a few months ago were harmless civilians. And it then takes an outsider inclined to charity and armed with the power of the pardon to cut through that—to say, *Wait a minute; what are we doing?* And it may take a certain amount of that vaunted "toughness" in another mode to insist on issuing pardons in the face of military resistance.

Lincoln himself made statements that he pardoned some "boy" who was about to be shot to give himself the satisfaction of going to bed knowing he had saved a life; but it fits what we know of Lincoln to believe that he was operating not out of ungoverned emotion—sheer pity, without intelligent appraisal—and certainly not out of sheer self-regard, to give himself a little shot of self-satisfaction, but out of a moral conviction that rejected the radical disproportion of the sentence of death in the typical case. Looking at the case with the eyes of charity, he had found the sentence unjust.

Lincoln had been responding to cases as he saw them, one by one, and then developing a few principles of extenuation. But at the same time he was implicitly developing a larger general principle rejecting the death penalty in standard desertion cases. On March 10, 1863, he issued a proclamation granting a general amnesty to all soldiers then absent without leave. Hence all those absent without leave, treated as a category, whatever their individual case, could be in effect pardoned if they would report by April 1.

This proclamation also linked the deserter to others in society and used against *these others* arguments that his critics make against the deserting soldier. Lincoln again showed that he understood the problem of desertions:

And whereas evil disposed and disloyal persons at sundry places have enticed and procured soldiers to desert and absent themselves from their regiments, thereby weakening the strength of the armies and prolonging the war, giving aid and comfort to the enemy, and cruelly exposing the gallant and faithful soldiers remaining in the ranks to increased hardships and danger, I do therefore call upon all patriotic and faithful citizens to oppose and resist the aforementioned dangerous and treasonable crimes, and to aid in restoring to their regiments all soldiers absent without leave.

That episode led at least General Joseph Hooker to conclude that Lincoln had adopted a general deserter-pardoning principle. Hooker promptly forwarded the court-martial records of fifty-five soldiers who had been sentenced to be shot for desertion, recommending "pardon in view of the proclamation of March 10, 1863, pardoning all deserters who returned before April 1, 1863." So the president proceeded to write on the envelope containing these records: "Pardoned A. LINCOLN."

Presumably the beleaguered president wanted to group and combine these multitudinous cases, because there were getting to be so many of them that he was in danger of being overwhelmed. At the same time he was working out a more general moral rule for these cases, contradicting on this one point the severity of the military code.

Lincoln was no reformer, let alone revolutionary; he had a clear understanding of the necessary and worthy role of settled law and of government. He did not challenge the death penalty as such—indeed, he concurred in a number of executions—and he did not challenge the military code as such or in its entirety. But with respect to one particular matter, the charity informing his judgment would lead him to see that the strict application of that code should be resisted.

It has been suggested that Lincoln was not unaware of the advantages to himself, in his own political career, of being thought merciful. Perhaps so; but in the midst of the war, that was a two-edged sword. By far the most important consideration in his own political fortunes was for the Union army to win victories. To be thought unduly merciful, if the Union armies kept losing, would be to be thought weak, and to bear even more of the blame than he otherwise would for the defeats.

Of course Lincoln wanted the Union armies to be effective, more than anyone. In other contexts he could be relentless, in taking losses of life now to get the war won sooner, in dismissing generals who did not fight. But he was not in favor of having Union firing squads shoot scared Union youngsters in order, allegedly, to achieve victory, and he stuck to that view and acted on it.

Congress made its own entrance into this topic, amending the basic draft act, directing the president to issue the Proclamation Offering Pardon to Deserters, which he did, on March 11, 1865. The first part was a threat:

> [A]ll persons who have deserted the military or naval service of the United States who shall not return to said service, or report themselves to a Provost Marshal within sixty days after the proclamation hereinafter mentioned shall be deemed and taken to have voluntarily relinquished and forfeited their rights of citizenship.

But the second part, in Lincoln's own name, brought the law into accord with Lincoln's policy, now in its more benign version, "Let him fight instead of being shot":

> Now, therefore, be it known that I, Abraham Lincoln, President of the United States, do issue this my Proclamation, as required by said act, ordering and requiring all deserters to return to their proper posts, and I do hereby notify them that all deserters, who shall, within sixty days from the date of this proclamation, viz: on or before the tenth day of May 1865, return to service or report themselves to a Provost Marshal, shall be pardoned, on condition that they return to their regiments.

Having come to be convinced that military justice in this particular matter needed a redefinition, Lincoln gave a general order and saved the lives of many at one stroke.

On April 12, 1865, in the middle of a busy schedule, the president wrote on the court-martial papers of Private George Maynard, 46th New York Volunteers, who had been sentenced to death for desertion: "Let the Prisoner be pardoned and returned to his Regiment."

Two nights later the president himself was shot.

CHAPTER EIGHTEEN

A Hard War Without Hatred

Brigadier General P. G. T. Beauregard of the Confederate army addressed this ardent cry to the "good people" of three northern Virginia counties:

> A reckless and unprincipled tyrant has invaded your soil. Abraham Lincoln, regardless of all moral, legal, and constitutional restraints, has thrown his abolition hosts among you, who are murdering and imprisoning your citizens, confiscating and destroying your property, and committing other acts of violence and outrage too shocking and revolting to humanity to be enumerated. All rules of civilized warfare are abandoned . . . All that is dear to man, your honor, and that of your wives and daughters, your fortunes, and your lives, are involved in this momentous contest.

Had this reckless and unprincipled tyrant Abraham Lincoln indeed abandoned all rules of civilized warfare? It was perhaps a little premature for General Beauregard to say so, because he issued this outcry from Alexandria on June 5, 1861, before Lincoln and his "abolition hosts" had had an opportunity to conduct much warfare at all. The Union forces had withdrawn from Fort Sumter under shelling by Beauregard himself; had seen Harpers Ferry and Gosport Navy Yard taken over by Virginia troops and added to the collection of federal installations seized by seceding states; had managed after a struggle to get troops around and through Baltimore to protect the endangered capital; and in the person of Lincoln's friend Elmer Ellsworth had been shot dead trying to remove a Confederate flag flying in Alexandria itself.

A month and a half after Beauregard's utterance his commander Jefferson Davis issued another roar of anticipatory outrage:

[T]hey [the United States] . . . are waging an indiscriminate war . . . with a savage ferocity unknown to modern civilization. In this war, rapine is the rule: private residences, in peaceful rural retreats, are bombarded and burnt: Grain crops in the field are consumed by the torch.

Mankind will shudder to hear of the tales of outrages committed on defenceless females by soldiers of the United States now invading our homes.

Davis too was perhaps a little premature: he made this condemnation of "the outrages of a brutal soldiery" the day before the first major encounter, the battle of Bull Run.

The condemnation of the Union effort as an immoral war conducted by an immoral leader with immoral means was thus already in place before there had been any war, and it has continued full whistle in Lost Cause circles throughout American history ever since. During the war that condemnation served the political purpose of strangling any impulse toward re-union on the part of the rebel constituency; Jefferson Davis's speeches often include a description of the horrid deeds done by horrid people of the North, with whom one was embarrassed ever to have been connected and with whom one certainly would never want to be connected again. In the war's long aftermath the myth of Northern outrages would serve other political purposes: the memory of a glorious victory would provide the North with what Robert Penn Warren called a "treasury of virtue," but the legend of Yankee perfidy would provide the South a deposit of collective self-justification.*

One reason that belief that the Union's armies used immoral means seeped into public discourse after World War II was that many historians used the term "total war" to describe what the American Civil War became. Unwary readers may, understandably, infer that the totality includes— everything. And that that *everything* would include the deliberate targeting of civilians.

---

*Mark Grimsley explains why the Lost Cause indictment of the Union army soldiers as immoral and indiscriminately destructive continues to persist. The myth served a variety of agendas, both during the war and much later: in prolonging the rebellion; in assuaging the humiliation of defeat and Reconstruction; as a scapegoat for the South's economic devastation long after the war (even though much of the army's damage to infrastructure was repaired in just a few years); and finally as a prophetic illustration of the brutality of modern warfare in the coming century. See *The Hard Hand of War: Union Military Policy Toward Southern Civilians, 1861–1865* (New York: Cambridge University Press, 1995), pp. 219–22.

Surely the term "total war" is not useful, either for description or for moral appraisal. It is a twentieth-century term that even in its home century may blur important practical and moral distinctions; applied retroactively to a nineteenth-century war, even one as destructive and bloody as the American Civil War, it is a source of confusion, not of understanding. It must be a cardinal rule in fighting wars, in writing history, and in making moral judgments that one keep clearly in mind the distinctions that matter. Although property was appropriated and destroyed on a large scale, and there was guerrilla warfare in some areas, and specific atrocities, the American Civil War nevertheless, in the main, did not become a "total war." And the man at the head of the U.S. government was something very different from an unprincipled tyrant.

To say that the Civil War was not a "total war" is not to deny that it was an extremely destructive event. It took place in what had been "the least militarized of Western societies." Each side sent out "hastily assembled amateur armies" expecting a quick victory. But neither attained that early victory, and each enlarged its army and enlarged it again, until the South would assemble nearly 1 million men in arms, and the North 2 million, out of a total prewar national population of 32 million. Of these men, on the two sides, battle and disease would cause the deaths of 620,000—more than the number of Americans killed, it is commonly observed, in both world wars, Korea, and Vietnam combined.

Historian James McPherson has calculated:

If the same proportion of soldiers to the total American population were to be killed in a war fought today, the number of American war dead would be five million. Fully one-quarter of the white men of military age in the South lost their lives. And that ghastly toll does not include an unknown number of civilian deaths, nearly all in the South . . . Altogether nearly 4 percent of the Southern people, black and white, civilians and soldiers, died as a consequence of the war . . . The amount of property and resources destroyed in the Confederate States . . . has been estimated at two-thirds of all assessed wealth, including the market value of slaves.

It is important to remember that the commonly cited figure for soldiers' deaths in the Civil War—620,000—includes more who died from disease than from bullets. Historian John Keegan puts the round numbers at 200,000 dead in battle, 400,000 from disease or hardship. The American

Civil War was one of the last major wars in the Western world in which deaths of soldiers from disease exceeded deaths from battle, a point that, as we have seen, Lincoln recognized.*

For the most part the adversaries in the American Civil War did maintain the distinction between combatants and noncombatants; there was no systematic, deliberate targeting of civilians en masse by the U.S. armies, not even by Sherman. The absence of any equivalent of the firebombing of Tokyo, or the bombing of Dresden, Hamburg, London, Coventry, Hiroshima, or Nagasaki, was not the result simply of the absence of the airplanes or missiles to deliver such destruction; murderous attacks on civilians had certainly been perpetrated before such means were available for that purpose, and they have been carried out without them in terrible wars since.

In many wars the number of civilians killed has been larger than the number of soldiers; James McPherson notes that "[p]robably twice as many civilians as soldiers in Europe died as a direct or indirect result of the Napoleonic wars." This was not true in the American Civil War.

It was an immensely destructive war, as we have said; at the same time, there were limits and restraints in its conduct. The question for historians would be whether to underscore the destruction or the restraint. Mark Neely in 1991 asked, "Was the Civil War a total war?" and gave the answer no, emphasizing, with evidence, the restraint. Even though there were many particular misdeeds, he wrote, "Union and Confederate authorities were in substantial agreement about the laws of war, and they usually tried to stay within them." Historian Michael Fellman—who having written a book on the guerrilla warfare in Missouri, and a biography probing the tormented "war is hell" warrior William Tecumseh Sherman, surely knows the dark side of the American Civil War—denies that it can be described as a "total war":

> Unlike the combatants on both sides of the guerilla war, Sherman never intended in actual practice, nor would he permit, a level of destructive war that would erase the line between civilian and military enemies . . . He certainly had the military means to make total war—overwhelming force and no viable opposing army . . . but he held himself and his men back because of the shared cultural value system.

*To give the more exact official numbers, counting both sides and those who died of disease, 617,528 dead. In the U.S. Army 110,070 would be killed in action or would die from wounds; more than twice as many, or 249,498, would die from disease.

Mark Neely, returning to this topic in a Gettysburg lecture on atrocity and retaliation, gives evidence that the war did not necessarily become "harder" as it went on but rather that harsher attitudes and actions and more humane and restrained ones—including forgiveness—*contended* throughout the war:

> When all was said and done . . . the President and much of the society he directed to victory in the Civil War, came down on the side, not of retaliating for atrocities, but of avoiding atrocity . . . [T]he relative absence of atrocity from the history of the Civil War remains to this day one of its most remarkable qualities. It is wrong to think of the war's "destructive," "terrible," and "hard" qualities, vividly real though they certainly were, as the things that call out to us for historical explanation more than their opposite. What needs explanation and description now is the remarkable restraint of the people who had organized and mobilized such vastly powerful armies. And President Lincoln's role in retaining those traditional limits on war needs reaffirmation more than ever.

We want to reaffirm that role: to specify the ways in which Lincoln encouraged the warriors to observe traditional moral limits on warfare. But at the same time we need to note again Lincoln's role in widening and hardening the war (the "directed severity"), which increased the opportunity for, and pressure toward, unrestrained warfare and therefore increased the necessity and difficulty of that restraint.

It is in the combination of these two roles—as a resolute and aggressive leader of the nation's armed services to an essential victory, and as an interpreter of the war who mitigated its vengeful passions and brutal conduct—that Lincoln's moral distinction is to be found.

When it became his duty to suppress this giant rebellion, the peacefully inclined but profoundly dutiful civilian Abraham Lincoln expected that the task could be completed in a relatively short time with a relatively small force—relative, that is, to what actually happened. On the day after the fall of Sumter, as we have seen, he called into service 75,000 of the federalized state militia, whose term of service under the 1795 Militia Act was ninety days. Four years later he would say, surely correctly, that no one on either side had expected a war of the "magnitude" or "duration" that it would by then have attained. In the end more than two million men would have served under his ultimate command in the U.S. armies; the war would have lasted all of four years, with much more destruction than anyone foresaw.

Lincoln was known to have remarked on his own "aversion to bloodshed." Once he mused, "[D]oesn't it seem strange that I should be here—I, a man who couldn't cut a chicken's head off—with blood running all around me?" And yet, strange or not, there he was.

Lincoln's avowed purpose, put forth in his First Inaugural Address, was to fulfill his duty: to preserve the Union, to restore the authority of the United States against "a clear, flagrant, and gigantic case of Rebellion." When as president-elect out in Springfield he had read of the purported "secession" of South Carolina and six other states, and of their takeovers of forts, mints, customhouses, and other general facilities within their borders, his first instinct had been to write General in Chief Winfield Scott asking him to prepare a plan to *take back* those usurped federal facilities, and in his first draft of his inaugural he announced his intention to do that. Under the advice of his friend Browning and the counsels of prudence, as we have seen, he struck the announced intention to "repossess" the federal facilities and limited his immediate stated purpose to *holding* the facilities still in federal control—which meant Fort Pickens and, above all, Fort Sumter, whose symbolic importance became thereby intense. When the South Carolina forces fired upon the American flag and "reduced" the fort, Lincoln in his call for the militia felt freed now to propose the recovery of the purloined facilities, but at the same time he stated quite sharply the limited Union purposes:

> I deem it proper to say that the first service assigned to the forces hereby called forth will probably be to re-possess the forts, places, and property which have been seized from the Union; and in every event, the utmost care will be observed, consistently with the objects aforesaid, to avoid any devastation, any destruction of, or interference with, property, or any disturbance of peaceful citizens in any part of the country.

This "utmost care" passage would lead a distinguished historian to observe: "This was a national strategy of limited war—very limited, indeed scarcely a war at all, but a police action to quell a rather large riot."

Well before the stunning defeat at Bull Run, however, the president had become aware that this was going to be more than a police action to quell a riot. In his first annual message to Congress, on December 3, 1861, he made a statement that was often to be quoted about avoiding degeneration into "a violent and remorseless revolutionary struggle," and also about not resorting to "radical and extreme measures." But in this midst of these cautionary self-restrictions, he made a statement about using "all indispensable means" to preserve the Union. That statement was the true harbinger of the future, the core purpose he would state many other times and act upon until the rebellion was in fact quelled.

In the late winter and early spring of 1862, when there had been victories in the West and at sea, and when McClellan's mighty Army of the Potomac was preparing to fight its way up the peninsula to take Richmond, there was an optimistic expectation for a limited war and an early government victory. But the battle of Shiloh in Tennessee in early April began to change that expectation, and the nature of the war. A key figure, Ulysses S. Grant, wrote in his memoirs about that battle:

> Up to the battle of Shiloh I, as well as thousands of other citizens, believed that the rebellion against the Government would collapse suddenly and soon, if a decisive victory could be gained over any of its armies . . . But when Confederate armies were collected which not only attempted to hold a line farther south, from Memphis to Chattanooga, Knoxville and on to the Atlantic, but assumed the offensive and made such a gallant effort to regain what had been lost, then, indeed, I gave up all idea of saving the Union except by complete conquest.

Did Grant's civilian commander back in Washington, who had not yet met him, at this point believe in the necessity of "complete conquest"? Perhaps not yet. Grant went on to say about his policy after Shiloh:

> Up to that time it had been the policy of our army . . . to protect the property of the citizens whose territory was invaded, without regard to their sentiments, whether Union or Secession. After this, however, I regarded it as humane to both sides, to protect the persons of those found at their homes, but to consume everything that could be used to support or supply armies . . . Their destruction was accomplished without bloodshed and tended to the same result as the destruction of armies. I continued this policy to the close of the war . . . This policy I believe exercised a material influence in hastening the end.

Grant's most important subordinate, William Tecumseh Sherman—who would prove to be a key figure indeed in the policy of a harder war—had fought in border country with guerrilla warfare not unlike that in Missouri: "[Sherman's] experiences in Tennessee and Mississippi, where guerrillas sheltered by the civilian population wreaked havoc behind Union lines, convinced him that 'we are not only fighting hostile armies, but a hostile people, and must make [them] . . . feel the hard hand of war.' "

Had Lincoln come to his version of this conclusion? Perhaps not until the failure of McClellan before Richmond the following summer. In July 1862, when he realized that this rebellion against the United States was not going to be suppressed by the limited and conciliatory means recommended and pursued by McClellan, he made large decisions: an order that "contemplated authority to Commanders to subsist their troops in the hostile territory" and the preliminary emancipation proclamation. The "foraging" by Union armies—by Pope, Grant, Sheridan, and particularly Sherman—with results that represent one charge of unjust conduct by critics, thus had one root in an order presented to the cabinet by Lincoln himself.

Lincoln had the clarity of mind and the discipline of will to face difficulties rather than to deny that they existed or to avoid them or to postpone dealing with them. His letters in 1848–49 to his shiftless stepbrother, telling Johnston rather briskly to shape up and go to work where he was and not dream of some other place, are often cited as evidence of this Lincolnian trait—but then his whole life is. He was a person who confronted reality as it was.

"The year 1863 marked a significant watershed," writes historian Mark Grimsley, "because during that year one can see the emergence of large-scale destruction carried out, in fairly routine fashion, by large bodies of troops." That year also saw important Union victories at Gettysburg, Vicksburg, and Chattanooga, the first two neatly falling on July 4. Gettysburg stopped a second northern advance by Lee's army, but once again Lincoln was frustrated that the U.S. general, George Meade, did not follow up the victory with an attack upon the retreating rebel army. Lincoln seems always to have been urging his generals to attack.

The victory of Vicksburg, which had even greater practical importance, split the Confederacy and gave the Union control of the Father of Waters. The taking of Chattanooga in November split the Confederacy on an east-west line. But these successes did not lead to Confederate capitulation.

So the war went on into 1864, bringing the campaigns by Union armies that were at once the most destructive, the most often subject to moral condemnation, and the most important in achieving Union victory: Grant's holding the line "if it takes all summer," chewing and choking Lee's army in Virginia; Sherman's taking Atlanta and marching his army through

Georgia and the Carolinas; and Sheridan's following Jubal Early to the death, upsetting the "breadbasket of the Confederacy" and ending the use of the Shenandoah Valley as an attack route on Washington. These aggressive actions by the American army were all encouraged by the commander in chief.

Lincoln certainly was supporting Grant all the way through the battles in 1864. He had found a general whose drive for victory matched his own.

But some of that general's actions were surely vulnerable to criticism. Grant, a hero in March, when he had been named general in chief, in the spring of 1864 began to be called a "butcher," by among others Mary Lincoln.* Grant admitted that Cold Harbor had been a profound mistake. He would write in his memoirs: "I have always regretted that the last assault at Cold Harbor was ever made . . . no advantage whatever was gained to compensate for the heavy loss we sustained."

After the carnage at Cold Harbor Grant and Lee had a sad exchange about tending the wounded and collecting the dead on the bloody battlefield. While the bodies of the dead and dying and suffering lay on the blood-soaked field, the two West Point gentlemen sent polite notes back and forth about the possibility of a truce. They could not get it arranged until "forty-eight hours after [the correspondence] commenced . . . In the meantime all but two of the wounded had died."

Despite such grisly occurrences and severe losses, Lincoln supported Grant and urged him on. On June 15, after Grant sent Halleck a telegram about his movement from Cold Harbor, slipping his army across the James River, Lincoln wired Grant:

Have just read your despatch of 1 p.m. yesterday. I begin to see it. You will succeed. God bless you all. A. LINCOLN

Grant laid siege to Lee in Petersburg in mid-June. At the end of July there came the catastrophe of the Crater—an attempt to dig underneath the Confederate lines that literally exploded in the Union army's faces. "The effort was a tremendous failure. It cost us about four thousand men . . . all

---

*"In the first month of the 1864 campaign, from the Wilderness through Cold Harbor, the Army of the Potomac . . . suffered 55,000 casualties, not far from the total strength with which the rival Army of Northern Virginia began the month. In the process the Federals inflicted 32,000 casualties upon Lee's army." Russell F. Weigley, *The American Way of War* (New York: Macmillan, 1973), p. 144.

due to inefficiency on the part of the corps commanders and the incompetency of the division commander."

On August 3 Lincoln saw Grant's dispatch to Halleck:

> I want Sheridan put in command of all the troops in the field, with
> instructions to put himself South of the enemy, and follow him to the
> death. Wherever the enemy goes, let our troops go also.

Lincoln wired Grant:

> This, I think, is exactly right, as to how our forces should move . . .
> I repeat to you it will neither be done nor attempted unless you watch
> it every day, and hour, and force it.

And on August 17, having seen a wire from Grant to Halleck explaining that state militias, not his troops, should be called upon for duties in other places, because his troops should do what they were doing, Lincoln famously wired:

> I have seen your despatch expressing your unwillingness to break your
> hold where you are. Neither am I willing. Hold on with a bull-dog gripe,
> and chew & choke, as much as possible.

Did Lincoln also support the deeds of William Tecumseh Sherman, a man said by a North Carolina official, as recently as 1994, to have been "more evil than Ivan the Terrible or Genghis Khan"? Yes, fundamentally, he did. His relationship to Sherman was different from his relationship to Grant, but when he comprehended what Sherman was doing on his march through the Deep South, he endorsed it.

When he brought Grant east, made him general in chief, and met him for the first time, the two men hit it off. They were leaders who could discern the essential and keep a steady eye on it, and they respected that in each other. Sherman, on the other hand, had had some brief and (for Sherman at least) unsatisfactory encounters with Lincoln, and there was much less communication between them.

As Sherman became a commander in the West, he presented difficulties for Lincoln in his fierce contempt for the press, and particularly in his resistance to using black troops. History always produces ironies, and it is certainly one of them that the reelection of the man who would be cele-

brated as the Great Emancipator would depend heavily upon a victory—
the taking of Atlanta in September 1864—won by a commander who
surely deserves the twentieth-century epithet "racist."

Sherman marched eight hundred miles to Savannah and through the
Carolinas without any supply lines, feeding sixty thousand soldiers from
October to April. The amount of food and fodder, and the number of ani-
mals taken, were immense.*

Foraging—troops living off the land—was by no means new either to
European armies or to the Union armies (or to the Confederate). Having
his army march light and live off the land, cut off from a communication
link, was an essential element of Grant's successful Vicksburg campaign.

Soldiers on both sides had often stolen food, but on these marches
Sherman explicitly legalized foraging and the officers organized it. Small
foraging units made their way ahead of the army into the dangerous setting
of enemy country to bring food back. En route they had encounters with
the natives that range across the spectrum of human conduct from kindness to murder, providing each side with stories forever.

Sherman's army created much destruction wherever it went, including
deliberate destruction. The strategic purpose was to show the Southern
people that their government was hollow and could not protect them and
they should give up, but another motive, particularly in South Carolina,
was the kind of sheer revenge their commander in chief disavowed.

Joseph T. Glatthaar's careful account—written on the basis of many,
many letters and diaries and accounts by Sherman's soldiers—shows that
part of this vengeful element came from the fact that these veterans of three
or four years of war and of many battles had been kept away from homes,
wives, children, jobs; had seen their comrades killed; and had seen the war
go on far longer than anyone had expected. After Jubal Early burned down
Chambersburg, Pennsylvania, in July, Union soldiers would cite that event
as justification for their own acts of destruction. But the indictment of
Sherman's army was much broader than any specific incident. Sherman's

---

*"From Georgia alone they confiscated 6,871 mules and horses, 13,294 head of cattle,
10.4 million pounds of grain, and 10.7 million pounds of fodder as Georgia farmers un-
willingly contributed almost 6 million rations of beef, bread, coffee, and sugar to the Union
infantry and artillery. Statistics from the Carolinas campaign are much less complete, yet they
do indicate that foragers stripped the countryside of at least 7 million pounds of foodstuffs,
11.6 million pounds of corn, 83 million pounds of fodder, and 11,825 horses and mules."
Joseph T. Glatthaar, *The March to the Sea and Beyond: Sherman's Troops in the Savannah
and Carolinas Campaigns* (New York: New York University Press, 1985), p. 130.

soldiers, like Sherman himself, blamed the Confederacy for starting and then for continuing the war. Their reasons for burning the South Carolina capital, Columbia, are disputed: perhaps the departing rebels lit fires; perhaps the fires were accidental; certainly whiskey played a role. But Sherman had announced his intention not to be tender about public buildings, and a number of other South Carolina towns were torched by the Union army.

The record of evils committed in other wars, as well as the anticipations of Southern spokesmen, requires us to observe that in this war rape was not used as a systematic instrument of war, and apparently there were very few undisciplined individual instances either. Glatthaar reports that although one cannot know the precise number of rapes committed by Sherman's soldiers, only two rather dubious instances are reported in the diaries (in which soldiers frequently report something done by other soldiers of which they disapprove). And as Sherman biographer Michael Fellman observes, Sherman's men were often in a situation in which they could do pretty much whatever they wanted. Neely quotes an observer who wrote during the First World War: "Events . . . have made the vandalism of Sherman seem like discipline and order. The injury done by him seldom affected anything but property. There was no systematic cruelty in the treatment of noncombatants, and to the eternal glory of American soldiers be it recorded that insult and abuse toward women were practically unknown during the Civil War."

Once Sherman left Atlanta for the sea, he cut all communication. Nevertheless, when the general took Savannah, Lincoln sent him, on December 26, 1864, a characteristic letter:

> Many, many thanks for your Christmas-gift—the capture of Savannah.
>
> When you were about leaving Atlanta for the Atlantic coast, I was anxious, if not fearful; but feeling that you were the better judge, and remembering that "nothing risked, nothing gained" I did not interfere. Now, the undertaking being a success, the honor is all yours . . . it brings those who sat in darkness, to see a great light. But what next? I suppose it will be safer if I leave Gen. Grant and yourself to decide.
>
> Please make my grateful acknowledgments to your whole army, officers and men. Yours very truly A. LINCOLN.

In a letter to Grant on November 6, Sherman, describing the devastating effect on Southern morale of marching a well-appointed army right through the South, wrote this defining sentence: "This may not be war, but rather statesmanship." And it actually was "statesmanship," although not many Confederates would be likely to use that word for it. Grant's bloody attrition of Lee's army was a military strategy to bring the rebels to submit by the brutal directness of destroying their army. But now Sherman was employing an indirect strategy to compel submission, by destroying resources that could supply the army and—much more—by acting on the mind of the Southern people.

Sherman held that in Georgia his strategy had had its desired effect: "I know that this recent movement of mine through Georgia has had a wonderful effect in this respect. Thousands who had been deceived by their lying papers into the belief that we were being whipped all the time, realized the truth, and have no appetite for a repetition of the same experience."

CIVILIZED BELLIGERENTS

Lincoln was unusual among leaders of great wars, including other leaders and generals in his own war, in resolutely pressing for the "directed severity" of a hard war like that of Grant and Sherman, and at the same time disavowing malice toward the enemy or any desire for revenge.

If Lincoln was urging his generals to attack, if he supported "directed severity," and if in addition there were dubious episodes in the conduct of the armies for which he held ultimate responsibility, how then did he contribute to restraint in the conduct of the war?

First of all, by some explicit acts and statements. As we have seen, when Frémont out in Missouri in 1861 proposed a program of retaliatory execution of Confederate soldiers, Lincoln countermanded his order. He explained the practical reason, which presumably reinforced the moral reason: "[S]hould you shoot a man, according to the proclamation, the Confederates would very certainly shoot our best man in their hands in retaliation; and so, man for man, indefinitely."

Under intense pressure from the Confederate practice of reenslaving or summarily executing captured black soldiers in the Union army, Lincoln would issue an order of retaliation that required the corresponding execution of Confederate prisoners. But in the event he did not carry it out. He then would tell Frederick Douglass why, after all, he could not: killing an innocent soldier for other soldiers' deeds was not only wrong but would lead to a cycle of retaliation.

In his letter to James Conkling, Lincoln presented explicitly his own little nugget about the conduct of the war: "Civilized belligerents do all in their power to help themselves, or hurt the enemy, except a few things regarded as barbarous or cruel. Among the exceptions are the massacre of vanquished foes, and non-combatants, male and female."

Much of the moral restraint in the conduct of war on both sides came not from orders but from the habits and moral shaping of free men: as civilized belligerents, they were not (usually) going to indulge in murder, genocide, rape, torture, assassination (killing pickets), or massacre. The reason was not that their superiors told them not to but because these "thinking bayonets" had been morally shaped before their service in armies. Much of the restraint of the "civilized belligerents" was simply taken for granted. Lincoln, also a thinking bayonet, reflected and encouraged that civilized self-limitation.

But then in the midst of the war the Lincoln administration issued the famous General Order No. 100, "Lieber's Code," the first such code of conduct for armies in the Western world, an influence on such codes ever since and around the world.* Five thousand copies of this code of conduct were distributed to the armies, by Halleck's order. Lieber was a strong supporter of the Union, and critics of his code say his category of "military necessity" was large enough to drive a truckload of evils through; nevertheless it did provide a written, official, and widely circulated condemnation of many kinds of misconduct and atrocity. One example has, alas, not lost its pertinence: "Military necessity does not admit of cruelty—that is, the infliction of suffering for the sake of suffering or for revenge, nor of maiming or wounding except in flight, nor of torture to extort confessions." Halleck was more directly responsible than Lincoln for the development of the code by Lieber, but Lincoln did issue and endorse it.

AN UNMALICIOUS WARRIOR

WE MAY SURELY INFER, however, that Lincoln's influence on the conduct of the Union armies went beyond the implicit and explicit restraints on particular forbidden acts and included also, and most importantly, the moral implications, the human implications, of his own conduct and his own interpretation of the war, of the enemy, and of the war's meaning.

*Francis Lieber was a well-known German-born jurist and political philosopher who strongly supported the Union, even though he had taught before the war in South Carolina. During the war he taught at Columbia University in New York.

Although he was resolute and persistent in pressing the war to subdue the rebels' will—more so than many of his generals appeared to be—and although he did widen the war to that purpose in 1862 and continued to support what Sherman would call the "hard hand of war" (including Grant's bloody engagements in 1864 and Sherman's destructive marches), Lincoln nevertheless did *not* allow that "directed severity" to spill over into hatred, self-righteousness, or the desire for vengeance.

He gave uniquely eloquent expression to the underlying moral meaning of the war without turning it into a moralistic melodrama. Even as he widened the war, he did not deal in blame. He gave carefully stated reasons—not slogans—justifying his actions, displaying respect for the humanity of the enemy, for his own side, and for the society of mutual deliberation that was being protected and reborn. He explicitly avoided malice and hatred.

Lincoln in fact was a quite unusual war leader, mostly in what he did not say. He led one side in a bloody war not by arousing the aggressive tribalism, the assertive collective will, that war leaders often summon and that war publics often display, but by rather reasoning and eloquence. He gave careful arguments for his position, implying that he and his followers and their adversaries—their "dissatisfied countrymen"—were all part of a universal community of human reason. From his First Inaugural Address and his July 4 Message to Congress, through his great public letters to Corning and Conkling, through the succinct eloquence of his remarks at the Gettysburg cemetery, to the unique profundity of his Second Inaugural, and also in passages of his annual messages and in a stream of letters and papers, he gave reasoned arguments for the preservation of the United States of America. His arguments had to do not only with the continued existence of this one nation-state but also with the moral significance of that continuation to the history of the world.

He did not demean or demonize the enemy, as war leaders generally do. From that first post-Sumter Sunday afternoon in April 1861, when he dissented from the dismissive remarks others were making in his office about the South, through to the generosity of the Second Inaugural, he did not deal in disdain or contempt for the adversary.

Much of his distinction on this point, in other words, would rest in what he did *not* say, which another in his place would have said. One might compare his successor, Andrew Johnson, who dealt with the war as it was ending and erred successively in two directions. In the early stages of his presidency, he was fiercely unforgiving. Grant would write in his memoirs:

Mr. Johnson's course towards the South did engender bitterness of feeling. His denunciations of treason and his ever-ready remark, "Treason is a crime and must be made odious," was repeated to all those men of the South . . . He uttered his denunciations with great vehemence, and as they were accompanied with no assurances of safety, many Southerners were driven to a point almost beyond endurance.

One cannot find any equivalent vehemence in Lincoln's words.

Jefferson Davis's utterances, of which the passage quoted at the start of this chapter is a sample, were more characteristic of the condemnatory vehemence of leaders in the violent passions of war. Davis spoke of Lincoln as, among other things, "an ignorant usurper" and a despot; described the Union action as "barbarous," waging a war "for the gratification of the lust of power and of aggrandizement, for your conquest and your subjugation, with a malignant ferocity and with a disregard and a contempt of the usages of civilization, entirely unequalled in history." And much more.* Perhaps Davis had as his excuse for rhetorical bombardment the political problem of squelching any yearnings of his constituency to return to the Union— but Lincoln also had political problems maintaining support for a long and terrible war. Lincoln did not choose to demean the adversary as a means to this end. The word "barbarism" and its cognates, which figure large in the rhetoric of both sides of the Civil War—Charles Sumner used it in the title of a famous address—appear only once in all the words that Lincoln wrote as president, and that once in the quite specific context of the order of retaliation for the enslaving or shooting of captured black Union soldiers.

He did not deal in blame. In the midst of the hard decisions of the summer of 1862, as we have seen, when he was explaining that he would not surrender the game while leaving any available card unplayed, he was also writing that he was a patient man and was always willing to forgive on the Christian terms of repentance. At the same time that he was making plain

---

*One of the more interesting of Davis's condemnations of the Yankee enemy—the *Puritan* enemy—is this from a speech in the Mississippi capitol in 1862: "Our enemies are a traditionless and a homeless race; from the time of Cromwell to the present moment they have been disturbers of the peace of the world. Gathered together by Cromwell from the bogs and fens of the North of Ireland and of England, they commenced by disturbing the peace of their own country; they disturbed Holland, to which they fled, and they disturbed England on their return. They persecuted Catholics in England, and they hung Quakers and witches in America." Jefferson Davis, speech at Jackson, Mississippi, House Chamber, Mississippi Capitol, December 26, 1862.

that he was not going to fight only with elder-stalk squirts charged with rose water, he was also saying that what he dealt with was too vast for malice.

Perhaps the most interesting comparison would be with the moralist-warrior William Tecumseh Sherman. Suppose Sherman had been president during the Civil War—imagine what the presidential utterances *then* would have been.

When Sherman made his famous remark that "war is hell," extemporaneously, to a group of veterans fifteen years after the war, he apparently had in mind a repudiation not of all restraint but of all romanticizing of war. ("Its glory is all moonshine," one report has him saying.) But in another context, during the war itself, another oft-quoted line of his did indeed mean what the world has taken him to have meant. As he stood before Atlanta, Sherman had a remarkable exchange both with the young Confederate general John B. Hood and with the mayor and city councilmen of Atlanta. His demand that Atlanta be evacuated became an occasion for a discussion of morality in warfare. Sherman approximated his signature statement, this one also to be often quoted in the years to come: "You cannot qualify war in harsher terms than I will. War is cruelty and you cannot refine it, and those who brought war into our country deserve all the curses and maledictions a people can pour out." Lincoln did not say anything like that. Sherman went on:

> You might as well appeal against the thunderstorm as against these terrible hardships of war. They are inevitable, and the only way the people of Atlanta can hope once more to live in peace and quiet at home is to stop the war . . . The South began war by seizing forts, arsenals, mints, custom-houses, &c., long before Mr. Lincoln was installed and before the South had one jot or tittle of provocation.

Sherman's commander in chief in Washington might have said those things, but he did not; he did not continually emphasize the blame on the South for starting the war, in order then to provide the justification for the destruction that his armies wreaked. And moralist though he was, he did not indulge in the continual self-justification that Sherman did.

Although as much as anyone he saw giant moral issues in the war, Lincoln did not see evil concentrated exclusively on the other side or see his own side as altogether in the right; he recognized throughout his career the complicity of the North in the sin of slavery.

It requires a distinct moral and intellectual discipline to achieve the combination that Lincoln achieved as war leader: the ability to prosecute the war with persistent energy to subdue the will of the enemy, without indulging in the passionate simplifications that war engenders.

Lincoln's attitude toward the treatment of Confederate leaders will serve as a symbol of his larger outlook. A member of Lincoln's own cabinet, the comparatively moderate secretary of the navy Gideon Welles, certainly no "radical," wrote in his diary of June 1, 1864: "No traitor has been hung. I doubt of there will be, but an example should be made of some of their leaders, for present and for future good." But Lincoln did not believe in such executions after the war. He hoped the rebel leaders would escape; in any case, he did not propose their execution. When at the end of the war the subject came up—the war crimes of Confederate leaders, now in territory about to come into the control of Union forces—President Lincoln, according to Welles in his diary, said that he "was particularly desirous to avoid the shedding of blood, or any vindictiveness or punishment. No one need expect that he would take any part in hanging or killing these men, even the worst of them." His suggestion? "Frighten them out of the country . . . scare them off," Lincoln said, throwing up his hands, according to Welles, as if to scare sheep.

The decisions about what actually to do with the Confederate leaders would be made by others, after Lincoln was dead, but surely his influence played a role. While Lincoln was still alive, Grant handed Lee his sword and returned their horses to the Confederate officers at Appomattox. No high Confederate official, political or military, was executed, not even Jefferson Davis, who was released after two years in prison. No Southern generals were imprisoned, let alone executed. Temporary exile was the severest penalty any other Confederate official suffered.

Lincoln was quite explicit in disavowing vengeance. In the draft of a letter to Secretary of War Stanton in March 1864, the president said, "[The government] can properly have no motive of revenge, no purpose to punish merely for punishment's sake." On November 19, 1864, he wrote to General William Rosecrans: "I wish you to do nothing merely for revenge, but that what you may do shall be solely done with reference to the security of the future."

That is a particularly clear statement of Lincoln's position: do nothing "merely" for revenge, do whatever may be done "solely" for the security of the future. But what the security of the future required would be disputed. Lincoln would, once again, with respect to that *policy* point, recommend generosity, or the avoidance of harsh treatment. He wrote in his March 18, 1864, letter to Stanton: "While we must, by all available means, prevent the overthrow of the government, we should avoid planting and cultivating too many thorns in the bosom of society." That was a figure of speech he would use on other occasions. In response to a "serenade" (a friendly visit by citizens) on November 11, 1864—after the 1864 election—he said: "So long as I have been here I have not willingly planted a thorn in any man's bosom."

In the whole sweep of human history there cannot have been many war leaders—especially in civil wars, especially in wars on the giant scale of the American Civil War—who could make such a claim.

CHAPTER NINETEEN

Temptation in August

W HEN WE THINK NOW about the presidential election of 1864, we
know who won, and we have made the winner into a national monument. Therefore it is not easy for us to think our way back before that
election and to accept the idea that this monumental figure really might
have been defeated. But if we are to appreciate the temptations and decisions of August 1864, we must really imagine this: for a moment Lincoln
himself believed, with good reason, that he would lose. And that belief put
him in a tight moral squeeze.

AS DESPERATE FIGHTING AS THE
WORLD HAS EVER WITNESSED

LINCOLN WAS in deep political trouble in the summer of 1864 mainly
because of the appalling news from the battlefield. Abruptly reversing
the high hopes of early spring, the reports began in May to tell of failure,
stalemate, defeat, and, in June, carnage. The overarching design by the new
general in chief, U. S. Grant, to press the Confederate armies simultaneously at all points—much as Lincoln had wanted his generals to do all
along—when actually put into execution began to falter at almost all points.
Three politicians appointed to generalships who had ancillary roles all
demonstrated plainly the defects of political generals. Former Speaker of
the House Nathaniel Banks, out in the Department of the Gulf, "failed to
accomplish what he had been sent to do on the Red River, and eliminated
the use of forty thousand veterans whose cooperation in the grand campaign had been expected." In the Shenandoah Valley, from which Grant
expected good news, he was told instead: "[Franz] Sigel is in full retreat . . .
He will do nothing but run; never did anything else." Benjamin Butler
moved too slowly on Richmond with the Army of the James and got his

army bottled up between rivers, and "the enemy had corked the bottle and with a small force could hold the cork in its place."

But the most devastating reports would come from the focus of primary attention, the Army of the Potomac. With that ill-starred army Grant himself* engaged Robert E. Lee in relentless, brutal, and apparently endless battle for two bloody months, to no apparent gain, with a new level of casualties, in "as desperate fighting as the world has ever witnessed." In the battle of the Wilderness the armies fought for three inconclusive and terrible days (May 3–5) in the confusing thicket of underbrush and trees not far from the site of the battle of Chancellorsville. The war had gone on so long that multiple spots in Virginia had been fought over repeatedly. The Union forces in the Wilderness had a staggering seventeen thousand casualties. Instead of withdrawing, as past commanders of the Army of the Potomac would have done, Grant kept after Lee and fought a two-week series of gory battles at Spotsylvania Court House. The grisliest fighting was still to come. Grant pursued Lee to a desolate crossroads outside Richmond called Cold Harbor, where he ordered an attack on the entrenched Confederates. There were seven thousand Union casualties in less than an hour. In this battle some Union soldiers are reported to have pinned to their uniforms little notices of their names and addresses, in the expectation that they would be killed. If a full report of the concentrated killing at Cold Harbor on June 3 had reached the public in a timely fashion, the despair of the Northern public would have been even deeper than it was.

While Grant was sending troops into apparently futile killing fields in Virginia, Sherman was stymied in front of Atlanta and lost a difficult battle at Kennesaw Mountain. Shortly thereafter Confederate general Jubal Early brought despair of another kind to the Northern public: he made humiliating cavalry raids up into Maryland towns, and on July 11 he turned up right under the government's nose, in Silver Spring, on the outskirts of Washington, threatening the capital itself. If Oliver Wendell Holmes, a young officer on duty during the firing on Fort Stevens, really did say to the tall civilian president standing there observing the battle, "Get down, you damned fool," it was on July 12, during this raid.† At the end of July, Early

---

*Technically, General Meade still commanded the Army of the Potomac; Grant as general in chief made his headquarters with that army and directed strategy.

†Alas, Holmes apparently did not say it. Matthew Pinsker tells what historians find really happened at Fort Stevens on July 11 and 12 in *Lincoln's Sanctuary: Abraham Lincoln and the Soldiers' Home* (New York: Oxford University Press, 2003), pp. 136–42, especially p. 140.

produced another humiliation for the North: when the residents of Chambersburg, Pennsylvania, refused to come up with half a million dollars, he burned the city to the ground.

The almost unremitting bad news from the war, after three and a half years of exploded hopes and wrenching disappointments, brought an enormous yearning for peace and deeply eroded the political standing of the commander in chief.

The usual link between a war president's popularity and the progress of the war was tightened by this president's close identification with this particular war. He had appointed these generals and urged them on and backed them. He certainly knew, as well as anyone, the war's terrible costs. "[The war] has carried mourning to almost every home," he told the Great Central Sanitary Fair in Philadelphia on June 16, with his characteristic literary flair, "until it can almost be said 'the Heavens are hung in black.' " And yet in that same speech he gave a grimly determined answer to the universal question: When will this cruel war be over? He said, "We accepted this war for an object, a worthy object, and the war will end when that object is attained." He even went on to underscore that answer: "Under God, I hope it never will end until that time." "General Grant is reported to have said I am going through on this line if it takes all summer," Lincoln told the Philadelphia fairgoers. ". . . I say we are going through on this line if it takes three years more."

WE CAN NOT HAVE FREE GOVERNMENT
WITHOUT ELECTIONS

Looming over the carnage on the battlefield was the anticipation of the presidential election coming in November. The familiar line from Clausewitz of course works in reverse: armies also pursue their military ends by means of politics. The two means, politics and war, affect each other, especially in a war over issues internal to one nation. The coming election entered into the military calculations on both sides: even after his troops suffered horrendous losses, Grant would fight "on this line if it takes all summer," in part because withdrawing would hurt the administration politically; Lee, in spite of his horrendous losses and exhausted manpower reserves, fought on in the hope that the election would change the Union's commander and therefore its policy.

It is altogether to the credit both of Abraham Lincoln and of the United States that in the midst of this mighty scourge of war, and indeed at one of its most perilous moments, this election went forward as scheduled and proceeded without violence to an honest result. "I am struggling to maintain government, not to overthrow it," Lincoln said to another serenade, on October 19, 1864—that is, before the election. "We can not have free government without elections," he said afterward. "If the rebellion could force us to forgo, or postpone a national election, it might fairly claim to have already conquered and ruined us." Holding the election as scheduled, with all its strife, would do a great good. "It has demonstrated that a people's government can sustain a national election, in the midst of a great civil war. Until now it has not been known to the world that this was a possibility."

WHAT IS THE PRESIDENCY TO ME
IF I HAVE NO COUNTRY?

THE ELECTION would not be postponed—and neither would the deeply unpopular call for troops. On July 19 Grant wrote Lincoln that he should issue an immediate call for 300,000 troops; his esteem for his chief was boosted when he learned that Lincoln had the previous day issued a call not for 300,000 but for 500,000 troops. Moreover, the call planted some political dynamite in the president's own path to reelection; although it sought volunteers, the bottom of the barrel had been scraped, and in fact volunteers were going to be few. Lincoln's call also provided that "in every town, township, ward of a city, precinct or election district" in which volunteers had not filled the assigned quota, a draft for troops to serve one year should be held immediately after September 5. (In other words, at the worst possible time for the October and November elections.) Grant, Sherman, and Union soldiers in the field were much gratified by Lincoln's call, which would reinforce them and put devastating new pressure on the weakened rebel armies. But the call for troops, with the sting of a draft in its tail, was, to put it mildly, not welcomed by the Northern public or by Republican politicians, who urged the president to modify or postpone it. But he would not do it. "What is the presidency to me," Lincoln said to a protesting Ohio committee, "if I have no country?" Republican leaders in Indiana in particular pleaded with him to postpone the draft until after the election. He did what he could do to help in that difficult state, which had not provided, as other states had done, for soldiers to vote in the field; he wrote a letter to General Sherman in which he urged (but did not order) the general to let Indiana soldiers go home to vote. But he nevertheless flatly stated in that same letter that "the draft proceeds, notwithstanding its strong tendency to lose us the state." Mark Neely writes, "Lincoln's clear-

sighted unwillingness to allow partisan concerns to interfere with decisions critical to the army was an admirable trait crucial to winning a major
war in a democracy."

But however admirable in the large view, the draft was politically staggering in the short view. It was another element, alongside military stalemate and bloody casualty lists, that endangered Lincoln's reelection. The
revulsion at the war after three and a half years and after the shock of
defeats in the early summer was deep. The desire for peace was palpable,
ubiquitous, immense. The Copperheads—Peace Democrats—surged in
strength, and the yearning for peace affected all parties.* The great amor-
phous atmosphere of public opinion, filled with yearning and revulsion
and hope and frustration, can hold contradictions without reconciling
them, impossibilities without testing them against reality. The public
yearned deeply now for peace. At the same time much of the public wanted
badly to preserve or restore the Union. And out of these yearnings came
the illusion that somehow they could have both—the end of this awful war,
but also the country put back together. The shrewdest of rebels saw that it
was not their role to enlighten the Northern public that achieving "peace"
now would not bring reunion.

BLAMING BLACKS AND EMANCIPATION AND LINCOLN

AND IF PEACE was not to be, those who desired it had a familiar scapegoat: the black man. Hostility to emancipation was a noxious part of the
illusion that one could have peace with reunion. The Emancipation
Proclamation, and the recruitment of black soldiers, had found favor with a
significant part of the public, going beyond the older antislavery circles,
and also among generals and ordinary soldiers, as black soldiers fought
bravely at Port Hudson, Milliken's Bend, Fort Wagner, and other places. At

---

*"Motivated by a horror over the loss of life, both Republicans and Democrats moved into
the antiwar column . . . These recent converts were not ideologically driven hard-liners.
They did not use the same kind of rhetoric the Copperheads did . . . These newcomers simply wanted the bloodletting to end. Because they were people who responded to the head-
lines, they were particularly fickle. They gave the hard-liners tremendous force and influence
over the summer, but as soon as the Union fortunes turned, so did they—as the Democrats
would find out to their dismay." Jennifer L. Weber, "The Divided States of America: Dissent
in the Civil War North" (Ph.D. diss., Princeton University, 2003), p. 180, since published as
Copperheads: The Rise and Fall of Lincoln's Opponents in the North (New York: Oxford University Press, 2006).

the same time, however, the entrenched racial prejudice planted deep in the culture by 250 years of slavery persisted; it was pervasive in the North as well as the South, and much of the hostility was grounded in what would later come to be called "racism." It was there already; it was magnified by the frustration of stalemate, bloodshed, and defeat; and it was manipulated and exploited for political purposes. The Democratic Party campaign against Lincoln and the Republicans in 1864 would be the most explicitly and virulently racist campaign by a major party in American history.* In a repugnant hoax intended to heighten racist hostility to emancipation, two Democratic newspapermen would invent the word "miscegenation," pandering to fears of an alleged threat to white women by black males and of the mixture of "racial" lines in the population. In the setting of 1864 that theme was tied to the war: Lincoln was continuing the war in order to free slaves and bring about racial equality and amalgamation. The notion that Lincoln's insistence on freeing slaves was impeding the achievement of a peace with reunion was widespread, including among the War Democrats, whom Lincoln needed in order to be reelected.

OUR BLEEDING COUNTRY LONGS FOR PEACE

LINCOLN HAD to pay attention to peace illusions even though he knew they were illusions. The loquacious vibraphone Horace Greeley, whose itinerary through Civil War politics would resemble the homeward journey of a New Year's Eve reveler, was now on the side of negotiating peace. His was a voice Lincoln could not ignore, however much he might have liked to; Greeley edited the most widely read newspaper in the country and was a barometer of the feeling in Lincoln's own Republican constituency.

Greeley now claimed to know not only that Confederates in general yearned for peace but that they were ready to deal. He had a way of presumptuously reminding the president of conditions he certainly did not need to be reminded of: "I venture to remind you that our bleeding, bankrupt, almost dying country also longs for peace—shudders at the prospect of fresh conscriptions . . . and of new rivers of human blood. And a widespread conviction that the Government . . . [is] not anxious for Peace . . . is doing great harm."

---

*"The vulgarity of their tactics almost surpasses belief." James M. McPherson, *Battle Cry of Freedom: The Civil War Era* (New York: Oxford University Press, 1988), p. 789.

Greeley proposed that Lincoln investigate the peace proposals of some Confederate emissaries up in Niagara Falls in Canada. Lincoln responded by indicating that Greeley himself should do it: "I not only intend a sincere effort for peace, but I intend that you shall be a witness that it is made." Greeley had not bargained for that, and squirmed but could not get out of it. He found out that Lincoln was right—those Confederates had no authority or readiness to deal. In each of the illusionary projects for peace during that troubled summer, Lincoln assigned the chief proponent to be the chief operative to check it out—and then find it to be empty. Davis and the rebels would not accept any peace that did not grant them independence.

When he sent Greeley to Niagara Falls, Lincoln wrote out a statement "To Whom it may concern," stating that "any proposition which embraces . . . the restoration of the peace, the integrity of the whole Union, and the abandonment of slavery" will be "received and considered" by the executive.* It was the third item—"the abandonment of slavery"—that set hair on fire. It went further than Lincoln had gone before. Whatever shadows the Emancipation Proclamation had cast, it had had limits of geography and of status as a war measure; it was vulnerable to later decision. It did not indicate that the entire institution of slavery was to be uprooted and permanently destroyed. But now this phrase from Lincoln suggested that a permanent and complete end to slavery was a condition of peace. And Democrats seized upon the phrase as confirmation that Lincoln's position on slavery would prevent peace.

SOMEBODY OTHER THAN LINCOLN?

HERE WAS LINCOLN'S political plight: the Copperheads condemned him because he was conducting an abolitionist war, and the abolitionists condemned him because he wasn't. And the apparent bloody stalemate accentuated the negative on all sides.

Lincoln was by no means guaranteed the support of all Republicans; the Republican Party was a newly formed entity, without any prior experience with presidencies and administrations. Lincoln's term was the first time the party had held office. The party had suffered blows in the congressional election of 1862, after Lincoln's preliminary emancipation

---

*This little document, with the date July 18, 1864, was identified in the controversy that followed both by reference to Niagara and by the phrase "To Whom it may concern."

proclamation. When the party did better in the 1863 elections, the Radicals took credit. Mingled with the usual disgruntlements and the usual rival ambitions—*why should he be president instead of me?*—were heavy ideological components. That a president would serve two terms was not presumed. None of the eight presidents since Andrew Jackson had served two terms. Polk had indicated from the start that he would serve only the one term; Tyler, Fillmore, Pierce, and Buchanan had not been nominated by their own party for a second term. No sitting president had been renominated by his party since Van Buren in 1840; no sitting president had been reelected since Jackson in 1836.

The Republican Party comprised conservatives or "moderates" (like Lincoln's friends Orville Browning and David Davis, and perhaps Lincoln himself) and the more sharply etched and abundantly labeled group, most often called Radicals but also called Jacobins (by John Hay), Ultras or Unconditionals (by William Zornow), and Vindictives (by James Randall). In addition to these groups within the Republican Party, Lincoln needed the Democrats who supported the war; in the 1864 election his party would call itself the Union Party and nominate for vice president the Union-supporting Tennessee Democrat Andrew Johnson.

The Radicals, the most pungently ideological Republican group, were the chief source of proposed alternatives to Lincoln, beginning at least at the end of 1863, when in his annual message Lincoln proposed a generous amnesty for rebels, and continuing throughout the election year of 1864, even after the renomination of Lincoln in June in Baltimore. Of the various boomlets for alternatives to Lincoln, the ones that had the most support and persistence were for Salmon Chase and John C. Frémont. Salmon Chase was right on slavery and race but also righteous, and endlessly eager to be president, even as he served in Lincoln's cabinet. Chase had a long-cultivated cadre of supporters in the minions of the Treasury, and he coyly let others take initiatives toward his supplanting his chief. Two pamphlets circulating in February indicated that Lincoln could not and even should not be reelected and that Secretary Chase had exactly the qualities needed in a president. The effort boomeranged; in response to the second of these pamphlets (called the Pomeroy circular, from the name of the Kansas senator who sent it out), the legislature of Chase's home state, Ohio, declared for Lincoln. After Lincoln was renominated in Baltimore in June, Chase made another of his many threats to resign; Lincoln surprised him by accepting it. The incorrigible Chase thereupon hinted that he might now be willing to accept the *Democratic* nomination. As historian William

Zornow observes: "Chase apparently would not only swap horses but was willing to exchange streams as well."

Frémont, his military career long since over, had the support of Missouri German radicals and of leading abolitionists, going back to his effort at emancipation by military decree in August 1861. He was nominated as a third-party candidate by a convention in Cleveland that allowed anyone passing by on the street to enter, speak, and vote. When the *New York Herald* estimated finally that there were four hundred in attendance, Lincoln "at once asked for a Bible." When a Bible was brought in, he found 1 Samuel 22:2 and read aloud: "And everyone that was in distress, and every one that was in debt, and everyone that was discontented, gathered themselves unto him; and he became a captain over them; and there were with him about four hundred men."

Frémont's third-party candidacy—the party called "Radical Democracy"—continued as a threat to split the Lincoln vote throughout the month of August; he was not persuaded to withdraw until he finally did, under complicated and somewhat disputed circumstances, on September 22.

A DEEP LATENT SADNESS

IN THE SUMMER of 1864 the Lincolns were spending their nights, as they had done in the previous two summers, in the cooler surrounding of the Soldiers' Home, a facility for disabled veterans on the border of the district with Silver Spring, Maryland, that had come to function as the Camp David of its time.* "He never sleeps at the White House during the hot season," Walt Whitman had written the previous summer about Lincoln, "but has quarters at a healthy location some three miles north of the city, the Soldiers' home, a United States military establishment."

Lincoln would ride back and forth each morning and evening, and Whitman would see him go by. "I see the President almost every day, as I happen to live where he passes to or from his lodgings out of town." One August morning in 1863 Whitman had written: "I saw him this morning about 8½ coming in to business, riding on Vermont avenue, near L street. He always has a company of twenty-five or thirty cavalry . . . They say this guard was against his personal wish, but he let his counselors have

---

*Mary and Tad left at some point in August for the still cooler hills of New Hampshire. Through the key events to come, Lincoln was alone at the Soldiers' Home.

their way . . . Mr. Lincoln . . . looks about as ordinary in attire, &c., as the commonest man." Although Whitman and Lincoln never spoke, Lincoln seems to have come to expect this bearded stranger at Vermont and L Street: "We have got so that we exchange bows, and very cordial ones . . . They pass'd me once very close, and I saw the President in the face fully, as they were moving slowly, and his look, though abstracted, happen'd to be directed steadily in my eye. He bow'd and smiled." "Far beneath" Lincoln's smile Whitman discerned something else that artists and photographers did not catch—that it would have taken a great portrait painter to catch: "I see very plainly ABRAHAM LINCOLN'S dark brown face, with the deep-cut lines, the eyes, always to me with a deep latent sadness in the expression."

On Friday, August 5, 1864, Seward read to Lincoln the angry effusion by leading Republican Radicals in Congress, the so-called Wade-Davis Manifesto, attacking Lincoln for his pocket veto of the demanding reconstruction bill that Congress had passed that summer. The "manifesto" was said by Nicolay and Hay to be "the most vigorous attack that was ever directed against the President from his own party during his term." The document said the president in his reconstruction efforts "strides headlong toward . . . anarchy . . . If he wishes our support, he must confine himself to his executive duties—to obey and execute, not make the laws—to suppress by arms armed Rebellion, and leave political reorganization to Congress."

On August 10 Lincoln met with John Eaton, a sympathetic friend of black Americans who had been appointed by Grant to a key position dealing with freedmen in the Mississippi Valley. Eaton wanted to tell Lincoln about damaging regulations and treatment of "contrabands" in his care, and he found in the president a deep curiosity about the freedmen. On his way to Washington to see the president, Eaton had heard a lecture by Frederick Douglass, which included criticisms of Lincoln's performance. Lincoln had Eaton tell him what Douglass had said, and then had a proposal. "[T]he President of the United States and the greatest man of his time asked me," Eaton wrote, "with the curious modesty characteristic of him, if I thought Mr. Douglass could be induced to come to see him. I replied that I rather thought he could."

That's a scene: Lincoln, expecting to lose the election, making earnest queries about the life and condition of the freedmen—there would be more than one conversation with Eaton—and modestly asking whether the freedmen's greatest spokesman would be willing to meet with him.

On Friday, August 12, the astute New York Republican manager Thurlow Weed came to visit and generously shared the information that Lincoln's reelection was impossible.

On Tuesday, August 16, a former governor of Wisconsin, named Alexander Randall, who was now in Washington serving as assistant postmaster general, handed Lincoln a long letter written by the editor of the *Green Bay Advocate,* Charles D. Robinson, who announced his position forthrightly: "Mr President: I am a War Democrat, and the editor of a Democratic paper. I have sustained your Administration since its inauguration, because it is the legally constituted government—I have sustained its war policy, not because I endorsed it entire, but because it presented the only available method of putting down the rebellion." Robinson had taken "hard knocks" from his fellow Democrats who accused him of having been "abolitionized": "We replied that we regarded the freeing of the negroes as sound war policy, in that the depriving the South of its laborers weakened the strength of the Rebellion. That was a good argument, and was accepted by a great many men who would have listened to no other." Moral arguments passed them by. In fact, they felt much hostility to emancipation and black troops. But now Lincoln said his peace terms included "the abandonment of slavery." Robinson wrote: "This puts the whole war question on a new basis, and takes us War Democrats clear off our feet, leaving us no ground to stand upon."

The next day Lincoln took up his pencil and drafted a response, trying to work out what argument he could make to the Union supporters who were cool about, or hostile to, emancipation and black troops. He would later edit, tighten, and rewrite it in ink. The drafts included rigorous statements both of the moral and of the practical reasons for not betraying the black soldiers in the Union army. But Lincoln also wrote in these drafts a couple of dubious sentences that hinted at something else. The first sentence in the penciled draft reads:

> To me it seems plain that saying re-union and abandonment of slavery would be considered, if offered, is not saying that nothing else would be considered, if offered.

In the later draft in ink, Lincoln made it worse by adding the words "or less":

> To me it seems plain that saying re-union and abandonment of slavery would be considered, if offered, is not saying that nothing *else* or *less* would be ~~accepted~~ considered, if offered.

Something less than abandonment of slavery would be "accepted"—strike that—considered?

The suspicion that Lincoln might have momentarily gone wobbly on emancipation (or might have hinted that he might consider suggesting that he might go wobbly) is increased by a last line he added to the draft in ink:

> If Jefferson Davis wishes, for himself, or for the benefit of his friends at the North, to know what I would do if he were to offer peace and re-union, saying nothing about slavery, let him try me.

It must be added immediately that the point of these arguments was to bring the War Democrats to face the reality that Davis's insistence on dis-union, not Lincoln's on emancipation, prolonged the war; that the *body* of these drafts included rigorous statements of both the moral and the practical reasons not to betray the black soldiers in the Union army; and finally, most important, that no version of this letter was ever sent.

On Thursday, August 18, Lincoln had a with-friends-like-these conversation with his longtime accomplice Leonard Swett, who told Lincoln he could not be reelected and asked if he was going to withdraw.*

ON FRIDAY, August 19, at the executive mansion, in the context of these expectations of defeat, Lincoln had his second meeting with Frederick Douglass. This encounter was—not to put too small a frame on it—one of the signal meetings in American history, the great president meeting with the greatest black American at this crunch point in the national story, a defining moment for both men: as it would be seen in later years, icon meeting icon, worth examining in detail.

It was extraordinary in several obvious ways: first, that it happened at all (a president of a still slaveholding and widely racist republic meeting with a black man); second, that it came about through the president's initiative ("President Lincoln did me the honor," Douglass would write, "to invite me to the Executive Mansion for a conference on the situation"); third, that Lincoln seems from Eaton's report to have been diffident about issuing the invitation.

---

*Swett wrote to his wife, apparently on Monday, August 22, "Unless material changes can be wrought, Lincoln's election is beyond any possible hope. It is probably clean gone now." David E. Long, *The Jewel of Liberty: Abraham Lincoln's Re-election and the End of Slavery* (New York: Da Capo Press, 1994), pp. 193, 322n.

While Douglass was meeting with Lincoln, there came a fourth extraordinary feature: his secretary twice announced Governor William Buckingham of Connecticut, and Lincoln told him to tell Governor Buckingham to wait because he wanted to have a long talk "with my friend Frederick Douglass." Douglass himself observed that this last episode was probably the first time in the history of this republic when anything like that had happened—a white governor had been told to wait while the president talked to a black man. "We were long together and there was much said," Douglass would write in a letter eight weeks later.

IN HIS REPORT of the meeting to the abolitionist editor Theodore Tilton eight weeks after the event, by which time the political situation had altered radically, Douglass would remind Tilton of the situation that had then prevailed:

> The country was struck with one of those bewilderments which dethrone reason for the moment. Everybody was thinking and dreaming of peace, and the impression had gone abroad that the President's antislavery policy was about the only thing which prevented a peaceful settlement with the Rebels . . . men were ready for peace almost at any price. The President was pressed on every hand to modify his letter, "To whom it may concern."

That means he was pressed to modify the specific objective "the abandonment of slavery."

Now came another extraordinary feature of this meeting: the president asked the ex-slave for his political advice in this highly charged, subtly complicated, and immensely consequential political situation. Douglass wrote to Tilton: "How to meet this pressure he did me the honor to ask my opinion."

Lincoln showed Douglass the draft of the letter to Robinson, written, as Douglass would say, "with a view to meet the peace clamor raised against him." The first point it made was that no man or set of men authorized to speak for the Confederate government had ever submitted a proposition for peace to him. Hence the charge that he had in some way stood in the way of peace fell to the ground. He had always stood ready to listen to any such propositions.

That was presumably what Lincoln was trying to get across with his concluding let-him-try-me sentence in the draft. But the next point was much harder:

> [T]he charge that he had in his Niagara letter committed himself and the country to an abolition war rather than a war for the union, so that even if the latter could be attained by negotiation, the war would go on for Abolition.

The "Niagara letter" is another name for the "To Whom it May Concern" production; the point, to repeat, is its assertion that the abandonment of slavery is a requirement of peace. Douglass gave abolitionist Tilton the positive report about Lincoln's position that both of them would want: "The President did not propose to take back what he had said in his Niagara letter." But at the same time Douglass explained to his anti-Lincoln abolitionist friend Lincoln's intricate political dilemma:

> [He] wished to relieve the fears of his peace friends, by making it appear that the thing which they feared could not happen, and was wholly beyond his power. Even if I would, I could not carry on the war for the abolition of slavery. The country would not sustain such a war, and I could do nothing without the support of Congress. I could not make the abolition of slavery an absolute prior condition to the reestablishment of the Union.

That is certainly a peculiarly difficult argument to make: Although I hold the abandonment of slavery as a war aim, please be reassured that I cannot attain it, and therefore continue to support me.

Whether or not Douglass got Lincoln's attempted nuance exactly right, he certainly gave the right advice:

> Now the question he put to me was—Shall I send forth this letter—To which I answered—Certainly not. It would be given a broader meaning than you intend to convey; it would be taken as a complete surrender of your anti-slavery policy, and do you serious damage. In answer to your Copperhead accusers, your friends can make the argument of your want of power, but you cannot wisely say a word on that point.

In general Douglass was not as shrewd a political strategist as Lincoln, but in this case he surely was correct both on the practicalities and on the moralities. Lincoln *himself* could not write a letter in August 1864 like the letter he had written in August 1863 to an audience that was pro-Union and anti-emancipation, because the situation had changed. Now "the peace clamor" had been raised against Lincoln, who was in political trouble in an impending election, and he had included the abandonment of slavery in his conditions for peace. Close reasoning would be lost on the public. Whereas his August 1863 letter to James Conkling and the Springfield Unionists, a big success, had been seen to be pulling racists up to his Union standard, a letter to a similar body of opinion in August 1864 would be seen to be lowering his own standard down to that of the racist Unionists. *Don't do it,* advised Douglass.

Lincoln did not send the letter. Writing Tilton in October, Douglass said: "I have . . . feared that Mr. Lincoln would say something of the sort, but he has been perfectly silent on the point, and I think he will remain so."*

IN LATER YEARS Douglass would scarcely mention this inside-politics discussion of the Robinson draft in public; another, much bigger item was on the agenda. Lincoln had an astonishing project to propose.

Douglass described the background to Tilton: "The increasing opposition to the war, in the North, and the mad cry against it, because it was being made an abolition war, alarmed Mr. Lincoln, and made him apprehensive that a peace might be forced upon him which would leave still in slavery all who had not come within our lines." Lincoln had told Eaton what he now said "in a regretful tone" to Douglass, that the slaves are not coming "so rapidly and so numerously to us" as he had hoped. Douglass replied that "the slaveholders knew how to keep such things from their slaves, and probably very few knew of his proclamation."

"Well," Lincoln said, according to Douglass's report, "I want you to set about devising some means of making them acquainted with it, and for bringing them into our lines."

The president of the United States was proposing to this private citizen, an ex-slave, the most extraordinary of all the features of this extraordinary meeting: that they collaborate in a kind of government-sponsored

---

*The Buffalo Union League would ask Lincoln for a public letter in September, and Lincoln would attempt a draft, but although the situation had changed, he put it aside and did not finish it.

underground railroad that would get the word to slaves on plantations in the South and help them get behind Union lines.

That Lincoln made this remarkable proposal underlines two facts: one, that he did indeed expect to be defeated; and, two, that he did indeed, even in prospective defeat, want to do all he could to bring people out of slavery.

Douglass was impressed: "What he said on this day showed a deeper moral conviction against slavery than I had ever seen before in anything spoken or written by him."

Ten days later Douglass wrote Lincoln from Rochester saying he had conversed with "several trustworthy and Patriotic Colored men" about Lincoln's proposal. "All ... concur in the wisdom and benevolence of the Idea," he wrote, and then made a distinction, "and some of them think it practicable." Lincoln's proposal was to appoint a general agent. Let him then employ twenty or twenty-five good men, "having the cause at heart," empowered to visit the front nearest the most slaves, and in turn appoint sub-agents (paid "a sum not exceeding two dollars a day") who know the territory and could conduct "squads of slaves" safely within loyal lines.

The letter setting forth this astonishing program was dated August 29, which proved to be the beginning of the week in which the political world underwent a thorough reversal that would make this Douglass-Lincoln project moot.

On the evening of August 19, the busy day he had met with Douglass, Lincoln rode back out to Soldiers' Home and had a discussion with two Wisconsin politicians: Alexander W. Randall, who had handed him the Robinson letter, and a sometime judge named Joseph T. Mills. (William Dole, the commissioner of Indian affairs, joined the conversation late.) Mills wrote out such a thorough account of this meeting that the editors made an exception to their rule against such secondary accounts and included it in Lincoln's *Collected Works.**

Mills found Lincoln to be "not the pleasant joker I had expected" but an impressive mind. He managed to get down persisting Lincolnian affirmations:

1. First, Lincoln would insist, as he had throughout, that saving the Union was his *only* purpose. "My enemies say I am now carrying on this war for the sole purpose of abolition. It is & will be carried on so long as I am President for the sole purpose of restoring the Union."

*CW, 7:506–8.

2. But, second, emancipation was *essential* to that objective: "No human power can subdue this rebellion without using the Emancipation lever as I have done." "The slightest acquaintance with arithmetic will prove" the utterly practical necessity of employing emancipation, for the sole purpose of saving the Union. "Freedom has given us control of 200,000 able bodied men, born & raised on the southern soil. It will give us more yet. Just so much it has sub[t]racted from the strength of our enemies." "Abandon all the posts now possessed by black men surrender all these advantages to the enemy, & we would be compelled to abandon the war in 3 weeks."

3. And, third, having proclaimed emancipation and recruited blacks into the army, Lincoln now had both a *practical* and a *moral* obligation— a categorical duty—to the black soldiers: "There have been men who have proposed to me to return to slavery the black warriors of Port Hudson & Olustee to their masters to conciliate the South. I should be damned in time & in eternity for so doing." Port Hudson, fought in Louisiana in May 1863, had been one of the earliest battles in which black soldiers had acquitted themselves bravely; Olustee in Florida in February 1864 had been a more recent one. "The world shall know that I will keep my faith to friends & enemies, come what will."

Here is another example of the "chain of steel" moral resolve that runs through Lincoln's career, setting the moral boundaries to his usual weighing and balancing of consequences: "Let grass grow where it may . . . this must not be allowed . . . come what will."

On the following Tuesday, August 23, in the aftermath of all these events, a remarkable episode occurred in the cabinet meeting. Lincoln asked each member to sign, without reading, the cover of a folded paper.* Inside the fold was a brief handwritten statement from Lincoln that began (as would be learned when it was opened some months later) with the statement that it now seemed "exceedingly probable" that he would not be reelected. "You think I don't know I am going to be beaten," he was reported to have said, "but I do and unless some great change takes place badly beaten." The blind memorandum the cabinet had signed read in full:

---

*It was folded in such an intricate way that scholars in later years would have difficulty preserving it while unfolding it. *CW,* 7:514; see also the notes on that page.

This morning, as for some days past, it seems exceedingly probable that this Administration will not be re-elected. Then it will be my duty to so co-operate with the President elect, as to save the Union between the election and the inauguration; as he will have secured his election on such ground that he can not possibly save it afterwards. A. LINCOLN

Remarkably, Lincoln, the conscientious Union supporter, was specifying his duty in defeat—to save as much of the Union for as long as he could. And he made his cabinet witness to his intention. He expected to lose.

Meanwhile, on the day before that cabinet meeting, the Republican (or now, National Union) committee had met with fear and trembling in New York. According to the letter that the chairman, Henry Raymond, would write to Lincoln, Lincoln's "staunchest friends in every state" had said that "the tide is setting strongly against us." Congressman E. B. Washburne wrote that "were an election to be held now in Illinios we should be beaten. Mr. Cameron writes that Pennsylvania is against us. Governor Morton writes that nothing but the most strenuous efforts can carry Indiana. This state [New York] . . . would go 50,000 against us tomorrow." Raymond wrote in his long summary to Lincoln: "Nothing but the most resolute and decided action . . . can save the country from falling into hostile hands." One of the two great causes is "the fear . . . that we are not to have peace . . . under this administration until slavery is abandoned." The suspicion is "widely diffused that we can have peace with Union if we would."

These widespread illusions, said the top Republican leadership through Raymond's letter, could not be dispelled by reason or denunciation— a bold act was necessary. And they had a bold act to propose: Lincoln should appoint a commission to make a peace offer to Jefferson Davis, on the sole condition of "acknowledging the supremacy of the Constitution— all other questions to be settled in a convention of the people." The point was what was left out: no requirement as to slavery.

The committee, "in obvious depression and panic," then came to Washington three days later to promote its view, and Raymond would meet with Lincoln. The president in the meantime had drafted a letter that is the core evidence that he might have been tempted by their proposal. The letter was addressed to Raymond and, seeming to accept their proposal, told Raymond himself to carry it out. This "experimental" letter of August 24, as Nicolay and Hay call it, "thereafter slept undisturbed, in the envelope in which he placed it, for nearly a quarter of a century."

When however the long sleep of that letter was at last disturbed, some less inclined to give Lincoln the benefit of every doubt than were his two secretaries have wondered whether just for a moment, on August 24, when he drafted that letter, he allowed himself to consider the ploy Raymond and the committee proposed. One of the drawbacks of being not only president but also a monument among presidents is that every scribble you ever made on any scrap of paper that survives is not only kept and printed but seriously examined.

Lincoln's draft addressed to Raymond—written on August 24, 1864—said, "You will propose [to Jefferson Davis] . . . that upon the restoration of the Union and national authority, the war shall cease at once, all remaining questions to be left for adjustment by peaceful modes." The large "remaining question," of course, would be slavery.

Did Lincoln seriously entertain the possibility of doing this? As Raymond's letter had said, Jefferson Davis would certainly have turned down the proposal, and his doing so would have demonstrated to the bewitched and self-deceived public that it was not Lincoln's insistence on abandoning slavery that kept the war going but Davis's insistence on disunion. The Raymond committee's proposal would thus have been only a device to educate the public. Accepting it would not have meant abandoning emancipation, a proponent of Raymond's plan might say, but only floating the possibility in order to expose the real resistance to peace—the rebels' insistence on separation—and thus win the election. It would have been a piece of mild chicanery with that political object.

But if Lincoln thought about it on the twenty-fourth, he did not do it on the twenty-fifth.

On Thursday morning, August 25, Gideon Welles called on the president at about eleven o'clock and, in a way one cannot imagine happening in later administrations, floated right in: "I went in as usual unannounced, the waiter throwing open the door as I approached." Welles had blundered into an enormously important meeting, although he did not know it. "I found Messrs. Seward, Fessenden, and Stanton with Raymond, Chairman of the Executive National Committee in consultation with the President."

"The President," wrote the bemused Welles in his diary, "was making some statement as to a document of his" and kept on talking "as if there had been no addition to the company, and as if I had been expected and belonged there." We may surely infer that this was the draft that the president had written the day before, authorizing Raymond to try peace talks with Davis, and that this was the meeting with Raymond to discuss it.

"It was easy to perceive that Seward, Stanton, and Raymond were disconcerted by my appearance," Welles wrote. Fessenden, Chase's replacement as secretary of the treasury, got up and whispered in the president's ear. Someone politely asked Welles a question about naval matters—his home field—and after answering, Welles got the point and left the room and let them make their important decisions without him.

A memorandum by John Nicolay recorded what happened in that meeting. "The President and the stronger half of the cabinet, Seward, Stanton, and Fessenden, held a consultation with him [Raymond] and showed him that they had thoroughly considered and discussed the proposition of his letter of the twenty-second." And rejected it. After hearing their reasons, Raymond "readily concurred" that to send such a commission to Richmond "would be worse than losing the presidential contest—it would be ignominiously surrendering it in advance." The new birth of freedom had come to be so integral to the preservation of the Union that even suggesting abandoning emancipation would be surrendering.

Perhaps Lincoln's August 24 draft authorizing Raymond's project had been merely "experimental," as Nicolay and Hay say it was, "to facilitate examination and discussion of the question," and he never really intended to go forward with it. But if he did for the moment entertain the possibility—under the immense pressure of impending defeat and immense frustration with the popular illusion that his insistence on emancipation stood in the way of peace, and in response to an intervention he had to take seriously after all, by the committee of his party—then between the time he wrote the draft on August 24 and the eleven o'clock meeting on August 25, he saw that even hinting at setting aside emancipation as a political ploy would have been a catastrophic betrayal.

Whether or not Lincoln had been truly tempted, the fact is that he took no overt public action. He did not send the letter to Raymond; he did not authorize the commission to Richmond; he did not mail the letter to Robinson saying "Let him [Davis] try me." He did not take any public action that would indicate that he was willing to let go of emancipation as a requirement for peace.

In the long after years of Lincoln's legend, a distinguished professor at a great university, when he reached this point in the Lincoln story, would (so it is reported) apply to Lincoln himself the famous pronouncement of Lincoln's youthful hero Henry Clay, "I had rather be Right than be President." Lincoln himself would have been unlikely to use such a formulation. He believed that it was hugely important—not for reasons of ego or personal vindication but for the nation's good—that he be reelected, and the verdict of future wisdom would agree with him. The defeat of Lincoln in 1864 would have been catastrophic. Moreover, Clay's pronouncement has a touch of moral bragging that was not characteristic of Lincoln.* Although Lincoln on a number of occasions, including this one, would reach boundary-line firmness, he was a man for moral reasoning, not for moral posturing. About old Henry Clay: it is not clear that when he made his famous pronouncement, he really had the choice. Lincoln did have something like the choice. He was already a sitting president. He was facing an election that he seemed likely to lose but still might win. His party committee proposed a high-stakes gamble designed to keep him (and them) in office. Lincoln judged it to be morally repulsive and practically ineffective and said no.

Of course he did not make any self-praising public drama out of it. He did not announce that *some* advisers had proposed this *popular* course, but he had rejected it because it would be *wrong*. But he did decide it would be wrong.

NEW OCCASIONS TEACH NEW DUTIES

LINCOLN HAD proclaimed emancipation as a military necessity and therefore as his duty under his oath to preserve the Union. He had included in that proclamation the recruitment of black soldiers, an action of immense significance: it guaranteed a United States that could not be defined by race. Slaves poured into Union army camps. Freed slaves and free blacks volunteered for and were recruited into the Union armed services in numbers that reached 186,017 in the army and 10,000 in the navy. Having at first been reluctant to arm blacks, Lincoln now not only acquiesced in their arming but took initiatives to recruit black men into the Union army.

The Emancipation Proclamation would transform the war: already just two weeks after it was issued Lincoln could describe the rebel effort to the

---

*Clay uttered this famous phrase in the Senate on February 7, 1839, when warned that a speech he was about to give—ironically, a speech critical of abolitionists—would harm his presidential chances. Lincoln probably would have enjoyed, although not himself used, the best riff on Clay's pronouncement, the perennial twentieth-century socialist candidate Norman Thomas's comment: "Of course I would rather be right than be president, but I am quite willing at any time to be both." There might have been times when he would have affirmed the version of Harry Truman, soon after the moon, the sun, and all the stars dropped on him in 1945: "I would rather be *anything* than president."

workingmen of Manchester, England, as "the attempt to overthrow this government, which was built upon the foundation of human rights, and to substitute for it one which should rest exclusively on the basis of human slavery." The following November he could say at Gettysburg that the "honored dead" had given "the last full measure of devotion" in order not only to defend the old freedom but also that there be "a new birth of freedom."

These developments would reorder Lincoln's duties yet again. He now had acquired a giant obligation to the "whole family of man," to whom he had presented the American war as a contest between slavery and human rights, and to the American people as the occasion for that new birth. Ending slavery was of course a great desideratum not only for its primary victims but for all citizens and for the nation's moral meaning.

But Lincoln also now had acquired much more stringent duties to some specific human beings: to the already liberated slaves, to preserve their liberty; to those still in slavery, to bring them into the promised freedom; and above all to the black men who "with silent tongue, and clenched teeth, and steady eye, and well-poised bayonet" would help mankind on to the "great consummation." It bespoke the intensity of his felt obligation to those black warriors that he took the trouble to prod his imagination to produce that image. These were human beings who had acted in response to deeds he had done and words he had spoken. The resounding echo of the proclamation he had issued had encouraged the "contrabands" to flee their masters and swarm into Union army camps; the soldiers had joined the Union army as volunteers or as recruits in response ultimately to his initiatives as commander in chief. He had made promises: "And the promise being made, must be kept."

Lincoln had made statements of his duty to the free slaves and to the black Union soldiers that were as strict as anything he wrote about his duty to the Union or about any other obligation whatever.

It is true that Lincoln justified emancipation throughout in utterly practical terms. But those strictly practical justifications were nestled in a surrounding moral justification that would keep breaking through.

Here is what he argued, plainly enough, in the second Robinson draft (August 17, 1864):

> Take from us, and give to the enemy, the hundred and thirty, forty, or fifty thousand colored persons now serving us as soldiers, seamen, and laborers, and we can not longer maintain the contest. The party who could

elect a President on a War & Slavery Restoration platform, would, of necessity, lose the colored force; and that force being lost, would be as powerless to save the Union as to do any other impossible thing. It is not a question of sentiment or taste, but one of physical force, which may be measured, and estimated as horsepower, and steam power, are measured and estimated.

But preceding that stark physical calculation there was an appeal, still utterly practical, in which a certain moral appreciation of a black man's position was interwoven—he wrote "And rightfully too" and used the strong moral word "betray":

> As matter of policy, to announce such a purpose [to abandon emancipation], would ruin the Union cause itself. All recruiting of colored men would instantly cease, and all colored men now in our service, would instantly desert us. And rightfully too. Why should they give their lives for us, with full notice of our purpose to betray them?

And preceding that appeal—we are working backward through his draft—initiating the whole argument, he had made a forthright argument in unabashed moral terms. He had begun by quoting the paragraph from his letter the year before to the Springfield Unionists about the promise that must be kept. He then wrote a paragraph of earnest moral reasoning that implied all that a moral theorist might expound in explaining the element of trust in the making and keeping of promises:

> I am sure you will not, on due reflection, say that the promise being made, must be broken at the first opportunity. I am sure you would not desire me to say, or to leave an inference, that I am ready, whenever convenient, to join in re-enslaving those who shall have served us in consideration of our promise. As matter of morals, could such treachery by any possibility, escape the curses of Heaven, or of any good man?

In the other autumn 1864 draft that would not be sent, the mid-September effort requested by people in Buffalo, he repeated his argument that no administration could retain the service of black Americans with the express or implied understanding that "upon the first convenient occasion they are to be re-enslaved," and then he would add: "It can not be, and it ought not to be." A certain satirical exaggeration suggests the moral absurdity ("upon the first convenient occasion"), and then explicit moral affirmations keep abruptly breaking through: "and rightly so . . . and *ought* not to be."

Lincoln, the writer and the moral man, significantly kept coming up with phrases that were not only forceful but also freshly minted. Any return of these men to slavery would be treachery and betrayal; it could not "escape the curses of Heaven, or any of good man"; he would be "damned in time and eternity" if he did any such thing. Plainly when there was any suggestion that black Union soldiers be reenslaved, Lincoln heard Duty, the stern daughter of the voice of God, shouting in his ear.

He felt the whiplash of the absolute also with respect to the reenslaving of anyone freed by the Emancipation Proclamation: that would have been a cruel and astounding breach of faith. These were quite specific and personal moral claims, by human beings who had acted in response to specific actions of his own, and to whom he now had a particular categorical duty.

In his annual message for 1863, looking backward to the proclamation, Lincoln had mentioned the cruel breach of faith: "To now abandon them [the laws and proclamations about slavery] . . . would . . . be a cruel and an astounding breach of faith." He then added a strong personal pledge: "I may add at this point, that while I remain in my present position I shall not attempt to retract or modify the emancipation proclamation; nor shall I return to slavery any person who is free by the terms of that proclamation, or by any acts of Congress."

In these compositions of the late summer and early fall of 1864 Lincoln repeated himself, sometimes in almost the same words. In the first draft, in pencil, of the letter to Robinson, Lincoln put sharply his refusal personally to be the agent of any reenslavement:

> But if the rebels would only cease fighting & consent to reunion on condition that I would stipulate to aid them in re-enslaving the blacks, I could not do that . . . I never could be their agent to do it—For such a work, another would have to be found.

Then, in what would prove to be his last annual message, in December 1864, he made this pledge public:

> I repeat the declaration made a year ago, that "while I remain in my present position I shall not attempt to retract or modify the emancipation proclamation, nor shall I return to slavery any person who is free by the

terms of that proclamation, or by any Acts of Congress." If the people should, by whatever mode or means, make it any Executive duty to re-enslave such persons, another, and not I, must be their instrument to perform it.

Get somebody else, not me.

WHEN THE PINCH CAME, and it appeared that he would be defeated in the coming election if he did not drop emancipation as a war aim, he nevertheless refused to do it. One is reminded of the great moment in the best book by Lincoln's near contemporary and fellow humorist Mark Twain when Huck Finn confronts his great sin of helping the slave Jim escape, and then, considering his tie to Jim, says—"All right, then, I'll go to hell."

It is part of the power of Twain's satire that the world Huck grew up in causes him to reverse the formal moralities—he thinks he *ought* to return Jim to slavery, that helping him flee is *sinful*—but that because of the strength of his human connection he nevertheless gets the decision right. Lincoln's world had a more mixed moral teaching, but he got the decision right also: if they propose to reenslave anybody, "another, and not I, must be their instrument."

THE POLITICAL CLIMATE changed markedly with Sherman's capture of Atlanta at the start of September, reinforced by Sheridan's victory in the valley in midmonth. In November Lincoln was reelected rather handily. One may attribute his political victory to his generals' military victories, or one may broaden the lens and say Lincoln shaped, put in place, and supported the armies that won those victories, so that his reelection was not altogether a gift from Sherman and Sheridan.

Lincoln had insisted that Republicans insert in their platform for the 1864 election a plank supporting an amendment to the Constitution as the only certain way to ensure slavery's definite nationwide termination. He might have waited to press for the passage of an amendment until the convening of the more Republican Congress that was elected with him in 1864, but he made instead a significant choice that indicated his seriousness about ending slavery. He worked for the amendment's immediate passage by the sitting Congress; to wait would have postponed the glorious moment of freedom. Indeed, he worked harder for the passage of the slavery-ending Thirteenth Amendment than he had worked for any other piece of legislation in his presidency, even to the point of twisting arms and doling out projects, dangling offices in front of congressmen to help them make up their minds. During the effort to persuade the last few Democrats to switch votes in order to pass the Thirteenth Amendment, a devastating rumor circulated, ruinous to the chances of passage if believed, that Southern commissioners were headed for Washington to sue for peace. When the manager of the amendment effort appealed to the president, Honest Abe responded, on January 31, 1864, with this statement: "So far as I know there are no peace commissioners in the City, or likely to be in it." In fact, there were commissioners on the way to confer with him, not headed for "the City" but for Fort Monroe. Before they arrived, the peace rumor evaporated.

On the last day of January the amendment did receive, just barely, the required two-thirds vote. The *Congressional Globe* recorded the response when the Speaker announced the result:

> The announcement was received by the House and by the spectators with an outburst of enthusiasm. The members on the Republican side of the House instantly sprang up to their feet and, regardless of parliamentary rules, applauded with cheers and clapping of hands. The example was followed by male spectators in the galleries, which were crowded to excess, who waved their hats and cheered loud and long, while the ladies, hundreds of whom were present, rose in their seats and waved their handkerchiefs, participating in and adding to the general excitement and intense interest of the scene. This lasted for several minutes.

The ratification by the states followed rapidly during the next year, and slavery in the United States was abolished.

CHAPTER TWENTY

The Almighty Has His Own Purposes

M ARCH 4, 1865. Saturday. Still wartime, but nearing the end. A president of the United States to be inaugurated a second time. Cloudy, rainy, much like four years earlier. Procession up Pennsylvania Avenue. Crowds. Mud on skirts, mud on boots. In the procession, for the first time, black troops, members of a black lodge.

Four years ago "soldiers clad in all the panoply of war . . . aided greatly in keeping up the feelings of insecurity and danger that were so prevalent among the white residents of the city." This time "four companies of colored troops formed the military escort." One feature in the procession is "the colored troops and the Odd-Fellows, with their band of music."

Four years ago the *New York Times* reported "a dense mass of armed cavalrymen eight deep . . . drawn sabres . . . carbines clanking at their sides, . . . sharp-shooters stationed at every corner." This time there were "no soldiers, only a lot of civilians on horseback, with huge yellow scarfs over their shoulders."

Four years ago the new president, scarcely known in official Washington, had presented an appearance "full of life, of energy, of vivid aspiration." This time he had "a look of one on whom sorrow and care have done their worst."

Inside the Capitol an embarrassing scene was taking place. The president, the cabinet, and various ambassadors, governors, and dignitaries are assembled; the new vice president, exhausted from travel, ill, and fortified by too many whiskies, rambles, fumbles, brags, extemporizes, and goes on. And on. Much looking at the floor, throat clearing, eye rolling. The president says quietly to a marshal, "Don't let Johnson speak outside."

The presidential party moved out to the East Front of the Capitol, now with the great bronze statue of freedom (Genius of Liberty) at the top of the iron dome. Four years earlier, not yet elevated to her pedestal, she had waited with exquisite symbolic aptness spread flat upon the ground.

Now the symbolism was completed as Liberty herself stretched toward the heavens.

On March 4, 1861, Congress had just passed a proposed thirteenth amendment that would have *protected* slavery in the slave states; it had been beyond imagining that just four years later Congress would already have passed and sent to the states the Thirteenth Amendment *abolishing* slavery.

The tall, bearded president appeared on the platform. Cheers, flags, music. "Hail to the Chief." The Senate sergeant at arms quieted the crowd. On this occasion, as not four years earlier, the president took the oath before he delivered the address. Then the oath had been administered by the old secessionist Chief Justice Roger Taney; now the oath was administered by the newly appointed abolitionist Chief Justice Salmon Chase.

As he took the oath, the sun furnished another improbably punctual symbol, suddenly breaking through the clouds.

What would one say on this occasion? One would certainly refer to the first inauguration, four years earlier. The president began, sotto voce, with a contrast: "Fellow Countrymen: At this second appearing to take the oath of the presidential office, there is less occasion for an extended address than there was at the first."

So this time apparently he was not going to say much. A special correspondent to the *New York Times* had reported on the previous day that the address would be "very brief, and as a consequence the ceremony short." The Associated Press, mindful of its newspaper clients, had said that the address would probably be "no more than a column in length." No one standing in the mud, but now also in the sunlight, could have anticipated that they were about to hear the most remarkable speech ever given by an American president.

"Then [on the first occasion] a statement, somewhat in detail, of a course to be followed, seemed fitting and proper." Yes indeed, he had then, a long, long four years ago, made such a statement. But it had been more than that. It had been a strong argument to his "dissatisfied countrymen" against the course they were following—the course they had promptly followed after his election in November 1860. He founded his refutation in general principles of all national governments, which do not provide for their own termination ("secession is the essence of anarchy"), and in American history—the nation preceded the states and made them states.

. . .

BUT THAT extended address four years before had been more than a fundamental philosophical argument. It had also included a marked conciliatory pledge: "The government will not assail you, unless you first assail it ... You can have no conflict without being yourselves the aggressors." (In his own view he had then taken pains not only to keep that promise but also "to keep the case so free from the power of ingenious sophistry, as that the world should not be able to misunderstand it.")

So he had argued, powerfully and at length, on the first occasion, back on that day, only four years earlier by the calendar but an epoch away in memory and national experience.

He had closed that extended address at his first appearing with a newly composed paragraph of warmth and shared life and common history, appealing to "the mystic chords of memory" that would "swell the chorus of the Union, when are again touched, as surely they will be, by the better angels of our nature."

But they wouldn't be. No better angels had touched the mystic chords of memory in Charleston Harbor. There had been no swelling of the chorus of the Union in Montgomery, Alabama.

"Now, at the expiration of four years, during which public declarations have been constantly called forth on every point and phase of the great contest which still absorbs the attention and engrosses the energies of the nation, little that is new could be presented." Sherman marching through South Carolina, Columbia burning, Richmond threatened, Charleston occupied, Fort Fisher taken and Wilmington occupied, Grant closing in on Lee in Virginia, Sheridan defeating Early in the valley—little that is new could be presented?

"[P]ublic declarations had been constantly called forth on every point and phase." It was true that those four years had called forth a steady stream of messages of many kinds. But did that mean he should not speak now? Should he not now, on this second appearing, conclude the fundamental argument he had commenced at the first and clinch the rejection of secession, the vindication of the unbroken Union? Should he not now add the immense fact that the nation was rejecting slavery? Who would have believed on his first appearing that Maryland and Missouri would by this short time later have abolished slavery?

His own "public declarations" on that subject had been a key to that incredible transformation. Should he not now conclude the moral argument?

He was the leader of one side in a terrible civil war, after four years of killing that the other side—ignoring all his pleas, promises, arguments, and most explicit warnings—had brought about. That war still was not quite finished. These words were not those merely of an observer, or a philosopher in his closet, or a preacher in his pulpit, or a poet with his muse; they did not come from someone detached and reflective, surveying the scene from some point safely above and outside it. These words were the sober expression of a central combatant—of the top combatant—on one side in a fierce and bloody contest of the highest importance and the largest meaning for a whole nation (and also, as this president had claimed with particular eloquence at a dedication of a cemetery a year and a half earlier, for the world).

Suppose you had been in this president's shoes. You, who did not like guns or shooting or killing even animals in the hunt; you, a gentle civilian professional who had never personally done battle against any enemy fiercer than the mosquitoes in the Black Hawk War; who had been forced by your oath and your convictions and the persistent defiance of the rebels to send wave after wave of young men—and, for the first time in American history, conscripts torn away from the farm and the shop—to risk their lives, at Shiloh, Antietam, Fredericksburg, Gettysburg, Spotsylvania, Cold Harbor. You had had to do this, they had had to do this, the country had had to go through this, because of the persistently defiant—you might have said arrogant and willful—secessionists. So you, at your second inauguration, drawing near to the end of this terrible, destructive rebellion—with the end in sight now—might have allowed yourself just a hint of vindication, just an undercurrent of I-told-you-so, looking back to the warnings and pleadings of four years earlier, just a trace of condemnation for these opponents who had endeavored to rend the Union to defend human slavery, just a suggestion of triumph now that it appeared that they would not succeed, that the heroic efforts of the Union forces would after all save the nation. So you would have done in this president's place.

> The progress of our arms, upon which all else chiefly depends, is as well known to the public as to myself, and it is, I trust, reasonably satisfactory and encouraging to all. With high hope for the future, no prediction in regard to it is ventured.

"Reasonably satisfactory and encouraging"? "No prediction"? That is all he is going to say? Are there to be no anticipations of victory, no trumpets of triumph? Arkansas free, Louisiana free, Tennessee free, Maryland free, Missouri free, the Father of Waters flowing unvexed to the sea; the flag flying again over Fort Sumter, four terrible years, and now, at last, victory in sight, he is just going to say "reasonably satisfactory"?

Aren't war leaders supposed to predict victory, insist on the rightness of their cause, and rouse the troops to battle?

> On the occasion corresponding to this four years ago, all thoughts were anxiously directed to an impending civil war. All dreaded it—all sought to avert it.

All thoughts? *All* dreaded it? *All* sought to avert it? Does he mean to include Beauregard's batteries surrounding Charleston Harbor or those fire-eaters in Montgomery?

> While the inaugural address was being delivered from this place, devoted altogether to saving the Union without war, insurgent agents were in the city seeking to destroy it without war—seeking to dissolve the Union, and divide effects, by negotiation.

Even as he had spoken his pleas, warnings, careful arguments, and reassurances, they had been ignoring all that and seeking to destroy the Union.

> Both parties deprecated war; but one of them would make war rather than let the nation survive; and the other would accept war rather than let it perish. And the war came.

What sort of remarks are these going to be? "Both parties" deprecated war? One of those parties consisted of traitors who brought it on. He is the leader of the other side, the defenders of the United States.

"And the war came"?

That's the way he is now going to put it? The war just "came," like a thunderstorm or a flood? Or like a clash between two equivalent parties that he is viewing from outside and above?

Did he not remember his quite explicit contrast "on the occasion corresponding to this four years ago" between these "dissatisfied countrymen," who had taken no oath to destroy the Union, while he had "registered in Heaven" the most solemn oath to "preserve, protect, and defend" it?

And might he not remember that for all the mystic chords and better angels, he had still said in the penultimate paragraph, with unmistakable clarity, "In *your* hands, my dissatisfied countrymen, and not in *mine,* is the momentous issue of civil war."

And then there followed four years of this mighty scourge of war, which "carried mourning to almost every home, until it can almost be said 'the Heavens are hung in black.' " Those four years of killing were altogether caused by these "dissatisfied countrymen" (these traitors, these rebels), in whose hands the issue had rested.

But now this war leader, on the cusp of victory, after the deluge of destruction, is saying in memory and in summary only—"And the war came"?

THE ADDRESS that the president gave this second time—six weeks before his death, less than five weeks before the end of the war—was indeed short, only 703 words. It supplies a striking contrast, perhaps a corrective, to the thread of national self-congratulation that is woven into American history and usually featured in events of this kind. It would one day be carved, along with his even shorter address at Gettysburg, on a memorial behind a giant brooding statue of the president who spoke the words this day. The final paragraph—one long beautifully managed sentence, actually—began with a clause that would become as familiar as any comparable collection of words written by any citizen of his country. That last paragraph, and the familiar clause about malice toward none and charity for all, gained power from what came before—and it did not include any sounding of the trumpets of anticipated triumph in battle.

The speech was to be set in contrast not only to his own longer and more argumentative First Inaugural but also to most such speeches before or since. It contains virtually nothing about public policy or specific issues of the day, nor anything hortatory, celebratory, or self-congratulatory.

Near the end of a conflict, the apparent victor is usually not expected to demonstrate the evenhandedness that Lincoln displayed in his address. Max Weber, in "Politics as a Vocation," introduces his discussion of ethics and politics by dismissing the "quite trivial falsification" in which "ethics" is exploited as a means of "being in the right." He gives as one instance the way that "after a victorious war the victor in undignified self-righteousness claims, 'I have won because I was right.' " With Lincoln it was otherwise: "And the war came."

He did have an interpretation of the cause of the war. It did not, however, work out to a self-vindicating result.

> One eighth of the whole population were colored slaves, not distributed generally over the Union, but localized in the southern part of it. These slaves constituted a peculiar and powerful interest. All knew that this interest was, somehow, the cause of the war.

He thus states explicitly that slavery caused the war. There is no hint of those later interpretations that would question or complicate that point. But his statement of the point does not have the bane of self-righteousness. It has the generous imprecision represented by that marvelous "somehow": all knew that this interest (slavery) was "somehow" the cause of the war. Somehow it was.

"A peculiar and powerful interest": Lincoln had recognized, more than many antislavery leaders had done, what an immense economic interest American slavery was. "The property influences the mind," Lincoln said in New Haven in 1860. It was an "interest" in the North as well as the South: "We all use cotton and sugar," Lincoln said as president.

> To strengthen, perpetuate, and extend this interest was the object for which the insurgents would rend the Union, even by war; while the government claimed no right to do more than to restrict the territorial enlargement of it.

"Rend the Union" would not be the secessionist way of speaking, as in the earlier paragraphs the phrases "civil war," "insurgent agents," and "would make war rather than let the nation survive" would not be. These, and the phrase "the government claimed no right to do more than to restrict the territorial enlargement," may be faintly argumentative; at least they honestly preserve Lincoln's interpretation of what happened—but without moralizing it or making it absolute. That the "somehow" is the governing attitude of the speech is made explicit in the sentences that follow.

> Neither party expected for the war, the magnitude, or the duration, which it has already attained. Neither anticipated that the cause of the conflict might cease with, or even before, the conflict itself should cease. Each looked for an easier triumph, and a result less fundamental and astounding.

This president is not only admitting but insisting that every stage of this immensely destructive conflict had an unanticipated unfolding. He did not blame the South for the war or for its destructiveness: neither party expected this "terrible" destruction; neither party wanted it, nor is to bear exclusive blame for it. Neither party expected the ending of slavery. He does not reach back and claim retroactively a sweeping moral objective to vindicate the outcome now known, a "result" so "fundamental and astounding." Henry Adams, the son of the Adams who would be Lincoln's ambassador to England and the well-connected grandson and great-grandson of two of Lincoln's predecessors, would write in his *Education* forty years after the astonishing events of 1861: "Not one man in America wanted the civil war, or expected or intended it."

LINCOLN'S ADDRESS sets aside an emphasis now upon who was right and wrong in the first place, and explicitly refers to forces larger than the contending parties. Now he puts those points in religious terms:

> Both read the same Bible, and pray to the same God; and each invokes His aid against the other.

The outlook in these sentences is a long way from that of, say, "The Battle Hymn of the Republic," in which God is drafted to serve the Union cause. He has loosed the fateful lightning of His terrible swift sword by means of the Union armies. His truth is marching on, strictly on that side of the war.

Lincoln's sentences, by contrast, represent one of those thoughtful moments when there is no drumbeat of a battle hymn and no serpents to be crushed by anyone's heel. In such a moment the observer of the complex life of humankind, and the role of religious belief in it, notices the irony of the two sets of believers killing each other, each praying to the same God for victory over the other. In this unusual case the reflective observer is himself a central participant.

Now comes a sentence, almost an aside, about the "interest" that "somehow" caused the war:

> It may seem strange that any men should dare to ask a just God's assistance in wringing their bread from the sweat of other men's faces; but let us judge not that we be not judged.

The great twentieth-century religious thinker about politics Reinhold Niebuhr wrote that this passage "puts the relation of our moral commitments in history to our religious reservations about the partiality of our moral judgments more precisely than, I think, any statesman or theologian has put them." The moral commitment against slavery is expressed in the remark that it may seem strange that any men should dare to ask a just God's assistance in wringing their bread from the sweat of other men's faces. But that remark is quickly followed by the religious reservation "but let us judge not that we be not judged."

Lincoln had often before used the figure of speech about toil and sweat and bread—he seemed to particularly favor it, with its echo of the sentences in Genesis when Adam and Eve are sent out of Eden, as a way to express the moral wrong of slavery. And he linked it to a universal and perennial moral struggle between these two principles, right and wrong, throughout the world. In the last of his debates with Douglas in 1858, at Alton, on October 15, he had said:

> That is the real issue. That is the issue that will continue in this country when these poor tongues of Judge Douglas and myself shall be silent. It is the eternal struggle between these two principles—right and wrong— throughout the world. They are the two principles that have stood face to face from the beginning of time; and will ever continue to struggle. The one is the common right of humanity and the other is the divine right of kings. It is the same principle in whatever shape it develops itself. It is the same spirit that says "You work and toil and earn bread, and I'll eat it." [Loud applause.] No matter in what shape it comes, whether from the mouth of a king who seeks to bestride the people of his own nation and live by the fruit of their labor, or from one race of men as an apology for enslaving another race, it is the same tyrannical principle.

Lincoln's moral condemnation of slavery stood alongside, and was derived from and part of, his devotion to the Union. He was devoted to a United States of America that had as its moral essence a creed that finds human slavery a monstrous injustice.

Lincoln was a politician, not a social prophet. He articulated opposition to slavery at the point at which it became politically realistic to do so. He had reluctantly tolerated slavery in the states where it already existed, but only there, and insisted throughout on its profound wrongness. He proposed to contain it, as we might now say, and not to allow it to expand, by "popular sovereignty" or otherwise, and to put it "on the road to ultimate extinction." The blunt premise of his position was that slavery was a great evil: in that first strong condemnation in Peoria in 1854 he used the adjective "monstrous." Ten years later he would write: "If slavery isn't wrong, nothing is wrong." In the speech Lincoln came east to deliver at Cooper Union in February 1860, he put the explicit moral judgment against slavery—casting the issue in terms of the eternal warfare between right and wrong—in this way:

> If slavery is right all words, acts, laws, and constitutions against it are wrong, they cannot justly insist upon its extension—its enlargement. All they ask, we could readily grant, if we thought slavery right; all we ask, they could as readily grant, if they thought it wrong. Their thinking it right, and our thinking it wrong, is the precise fact upon which depends the whole controversy.

In that Cooper Union speech Lincoln rejected any "groping for some middle ground between the right and the wrong."

Lincoln sought, on the moral issue itself, no such middle ground. But even with forceful convictions he was able to add, in this different situation five years later, the "religious reservation" "but let us judge not that we be not judged." This paraphrase of the sentence from Matthew, from the collection of sayings that is called the Sermon on the Mount, had appeared in a different way in the Lincoln-Douglas debates. When Lincoln had insisted on the moral difference between the two sides, Stephen Douglas had responded with a reference to this familiar sentence. But Douglas in 1858 was saying (judgmentally) to Lincoln and his partisans— to his opponents—that *they* should not judge lest they be judged. Here seven years later Lincoln as wartime president is saying the same thing to his own followers—and to himself as well—that *we* are to "judge not."

This sentence, one would think, should never be used as defense, attack, or riposte but only as confession or self-criticism; otherwise the speaker himself is tripped by its meaning and falls into self-contradiction: to use this sentence against "judging" as a means of doing so.

> The prayers of both could not be answered; that of neither has been answered fully.

Lincoln completes the paragraph of compassionate evenhandedness with his observation about these two sets of believers in the same God: he now says that they cannot both have their prayers answered and that neither in fact has been answered fully—not those in the South who wanted its victory, with secession and slavery, nor those in the North who wanted the Union preserved painlessly.

The next sentence, freestanding in the text he read from, is perhaps the key sentence of the address. Here Lincoln sets the frame of the larger drama within which these human actors play their limited roles.

The Almighty has His own purposes.

Douglas Wilson has persuasively argued that a fragment from Lincoln's hand that his secretaries labeled "meditation on the divine will" and is generally dated at the summer or early fall of 1862 was probably written in 1864, in the philosophical run-up to the Second Inaugural, of which it is an anticipation. It fits with other productions from Lincoln's hand in the last year of the war that show him ruminating on a topic that the friends of his skeptical youth might not have thought he would be ruminating about: the will of God. Lincoln had long shown that even as he declined to accept the creedal claims of the Christian religion, joining no church and (while sitting with his wife in Presbyterian churches in Springfield and Washington) making no profession of faith, he nevertheless grasped the moral core of the Christian religion.

But now, buffeted by immense historical events, he meditated on a distinctly theological topic, the will of God in this fundamental and astounding conflict. And he reached radically different conclusions than war leaders who invoke the Almighty frequently reach—one might say almost the reverse. Certainly no one would have been surprised if the president of the United States, nearing the end of this bloody, religion-drenched war, had in his address claimed that the impending victory showed that God was on the side of the Union. But—astonishingly—he did not do that; he said something that almost contradicts it: the Almighty has His *own* purposes, beyond those of either side.

A logician might assume that Lincoln affirmed the Almighty's almighty purposes in order to relieve himself of responsibility for the carnage in which he was implicated, off-loading it onto an all-controlling Providence, or to make himself passive. But its effects were, rather, personal and national humility and self-criticism: while we act, responsible for our actions, with firmness in the right as God gives us to see it, we recognize that there are purposes beyond our own.

Lincoln himself, commenting afterward on the speech in a letter to

Thurlow Weed, remarked, "Men are not flattered to be told there has been a difference of purpose between the Almighty and them. To deny it [that is, this difference of purpose] however in this case," Lincoln went on to say in the short letter to Weed, "is to deny that there is a God governing the world."

Belief in a God governing the world can do much damage in politics, as no one in the twenty-first century needs to be reminded. One kind of damage is fanaticism, self-righteousness, uncompromising zeal, cruelty to infidels, masquerading as devotion to God. When the belief in an Absolute—in "the Almighty"—is put forward in the mingled relativities of human social conflict, the result can often be confusion and inhumanity. Lincoln's speech, to an unusual degree for a political document drenched in a biblical outlook, avoids these perils, in the way that is appropriate to the source: by enlarging the vision of the stage upon which the historical drama is played and turning its affirmations critically against his own side and himself rather than using them self-defensively against opponents. In his letter to Weed about his speech, this president went on to make this extraordinary statement: "It is a truth [that is, the truth that the Almighty has purposes different from those of human actors] which I thought needed to be told, and as whatever of humiliation there is in it falls most directly on myself I thought others might afford for me to tell it."

In the address, after affirming his truth about the Almighty's larger purposes, he breaks suddenly into a fierce biblical quotation that he applies to slavery and the war.

Woe unto the world because of offences! for it must needs be that offences come; but woe to that man by whom the offence cometh!

Lincoln quotes this passage (Matthew 18:7) from the King James Version. No modern biblical scholar was standing by to tell him that he would do better to use a different translation, that this passage, in the middle of the "woes," right after a well-known sentence condemning those who tempt little children, and right before a sentence about cutting off your hand if it "offends," probably does not mean what he takes it to mean. The word "offence," which he takes to mean a gross moral evil, is later translated as "temptations" or "stumbling blocks." That gives the sentence a different twist and may link it back to the "little ones" not to be tempted, woe to you if you do.

But Lincoln did not know all that. He found the sentence he wanted and—as has been known to happen with others quoting the Bible—made his own use of it. In his case it was very much in keeping with the spirit of a profound version of biblical religion. Indeed, this whole paragraph is a sudden bursting out of "prophetic" utterance, darker, less "rational" perhaps, than what goes before or follows (also more difficult and less often quoted).

If we shall suppose that American Slavery is one of those offences which, in the providence of God, must needs come, but which, having continued through His appointed time, He now wills to remove, and that He gives to both North and South, this terrible war, as the woe due to those by whom the offence came, shall we discern therein any departure from those divine attributes which the believers in a Living God always ascribe to Him?

Douglas Wilson writes that the "master rhetorical stroke of this masterly address is the way northern complicity in the offense of slavery is so smoothly and unobtrusively . . . presented."

He gives both North and South this terrible war as the woe due to those by whom the offense came.

Niebuhr says that Lincoln retained in this most biblically religious of presidential addresses still a trace of his youthful skepticism when he referred to "those divine attributes which the believers in a Living God always ascribe to Him" without specifically numbering himself among those believers. But the youthful skepticism certainly is not present in the rest of the paragraph, nor in the one that follows, which reverberates with the outlook of "believers in a Living God" in one of its most teeth-rattling forms. Perhaps something like Lincoln's youthful fatalism or determinism is contained in these sentences—but it has now taken on the shape of the Calvinistic providential history-arranging God, which is not the same as fatalism. It does make quite a difference, even if one believes that historical events are determined and are beyond the control of any human actor, whether or not one sees that determination done with a purpose by an agent with an active will, and with the "attributes" to which Lincoln refers, that "believers in a Living God" assign to Him. This speech by Lincoln certainly does see human history in that providentially ordered way: "in

the providence of God"; "His appointed time"; "He now wills to remove."
Many modern minds may not find it very appealing, may even find it
repugnant: this picture of a God by whose providence slavery "came," who
allowed it for an "appointed time," and who then removed it with terrible
war as a "woe" to the human participants. But though Lincoln had read
skeptics in his youth, he now confronted a depth of tragic complexity that
evoked the profoundest symbolic and imaginative expression in the culture by which he was surrounded.*

In some sense it "came" by "the providence of God." In another sense it
is the responsibility of both sides in the terrible war. "Woe to that man,"
says the King James Version of Matthew, "by whom the offence cometh!"
"That man" is not only the slave power, or the South. "Woe" has been sent
to North as well as South, the "woe" of the war:

> Fondly do we hope—fervently do we pray—that this mighty scourge of
> war may speedily pass away.

The astounding "magnitude" and "duration" of the war—the bloody
battles continuing on beyond anything he or anyone else expected—were
surely the provocation for his sober ruminations on the purposes of God.
Now after expressing the prayer for its speedy end, he suddenly produces,
as a great *nevertheless* a dark and powerful passage that is more like Dos-
toyevsky or Job than a straight-thinking American boy from the Hoosier
woods:

> Fondly do we hope—fervently do we pray—that this mighty scourge of
> war may speedily pass away. Yet, if God wills that it continue, until all the
> wealth piled by the bond-man's two hundred and fifty years of unre-
> quited toil shall be sunk, and until every drop of blood drawn with the
> lash, shall be paid by another drawn with the sword, as was said three
> thousand years ago, so still it must be said "the judgments of the Lord,
> are true and righteous altogether."

*Richard Carwardine, in his *Lincoln: A Life of Purpose and Power* (New York: Alfred A.
Knopf, 2006), has shown how important American Protestantism was as a political force that
supported Lincoln, the Republicans, and the attack on slavery. When one asks why Lincoln
chose this topic for this key address, then presumably that regular connection was a prime
answer. But on this topic he surely did not say what most in the churches might have
expected him to say.

Imagine the fierce passion and anguish in which this wartime president wrote that remarkable paragraph, with its grim imagining of a retribution in which the 250-year-old evil of American slavery is compensated by the destruction of every bit of wealth that slavery created, and further by all the killing in the war: a retribution, of course, against both sides, against the whole country, matching slavery's drops of blood on the one side with warfare's drops of blood on the other. It is a horrendous vision.

The passage implies, at the same time, not only a deep and simultaneous abomination of slavery and revulsion against the war but also the most somber determination to finish that war and end the great evil. Lincoln wrote many condemnations of slavery but none so stark as the moral condemnation implied here. Lincoln's Second Inaugural would in years to come often be shrunk, skimmed, and simplified, presented merely as a message of charity and healing. But it has at its core something much more profound: this stark invocation of the justice of God against slavery. The dramatic picture—drop of blood for drop of blood—sets up the affirmation at the end, the severe piety, some might say the perverse piety, of an acceptance of the whole terrible mixture, no matter what. Even if there should be so dreadful a bloodletting, still it must be said: the judgments of the Lord are true and righteous altogether.

Lincoln found this sentence in the King James Version of the Nineteenth Psalm, the familiar psalm that begins, "the Heavens declare the glory of God, and the firmament showeth his handiwork," and that ends with the stanza that is often used as a benediction: "may the words of my mouth, and the meditation of my heart, be acceptable in thy sight." We are told that this is one of the oldest of the Psalms; Lincoln may even have underestimated its age when he said "three thousand years ago." Ironically, it is rather a serene poem, praising the creator of the sky and the stars, who is the maker of the moral law within as well as the physical law that governs the heavens. From this tranquil ancient poem of wonder and of praise an American president more than three thousand years later took this one sentence to make a ringing statement in quite a different religious context: the mood of "no matter what," "nevertheless," and "even so," like that of Job. When Job's wife said to him after his multiple afflictions that he should "curse God and die," Job instead answered, "The Lord giveth and the Lord taketh away, blessed be the name of the Lord." But in that famous exchange, the adversity in the face of which Job makes his unshaken affirmation is a personal adversity; in Lincoln's great speech, the adversity is collective and in part prospective, and would be deserved: even if the war should continue until the blood drawn with the sword should be enough to pay for—to match—every drop drawn by the slave driver's lash, and to destroy all the wealth that slavery built—even if that should come—God is just. Buried in the skillful sermonic complexity of this unusual composition lies the most profound of all condemnations of American slavery.

In the complicated earlier sentence there was a rhetorical question— "shall we discern therein [that is, in the sending of the terrible war as a 'woe' to offense-givers] any departure from those divine attributes which the believers in a Living God always ascribe to Him?" The implied answer was no. One may be permitted to discern the struggle of the man writing this speech to give that answer in the face of the terrors of history—an abominable institution and an interminable war—with which his life had made him intimately acquainted. This paragraph contains the element of an act of will that marks religious faith, in this case the act of will of a strong person: nevertheless, despite all this "offence" and "woe," there is no "departure" from the "divine attributes." What are the "divine attributes"? The sentence at the end of the paragraph, appropriated from the psalm, gives the answer: "the judgments of the Lord are true and righteous altogether."

It was this passage in the Second Inaugural, even more than the final paragraph, that meant the most to Frederick Douglass; he could quote it from memory.

THE CONCLUSION of the address—the part of it that would come to be best known—should be read against the background of tremendous affirmation that has preceded it. It answers the question: What should we do?

> With malice toward none; with charity for all; with firmness in the right, as God gives us to see the right, let us strive on to finish the work we are in; to bind up the nation's wounds; to care for him who shall have borne the battle, and for his widow, and his orphan—to do all which may achieve and cherish a just, and a lasting peace, among ourselves, and with all nations.

"Malice," as we know, was the word Lincoln used often for the central human evil of ill will. We project our anger at the frustrations of the world onto other people. We wish others harm; we take satisfaction in their defeat; we nurse grudges and cultivate envy and hatred. And this human sea of envy and malice is multiplied in collective life. The individual power holder has his ego; the collective has its cruder ego. Behind the politician and statesman stands the flag-waving, slogan-making, sword-wielding tribal impulse of the collective. Therefore politics has intrinsic and peculiar moral dangers; therefore the combination represented by Lincoln's Second Inaugural has an intrinsic importance: an awareness of purposes larger than one's own, requiring therefore criticism and restraint toward oneself, and magnanimity—and absence of vindictiveness—toward opponents. "I shall do nothing in malice. What I deal with is too vast for malicious dealing."

with charity

"Charity" is the corrective for that human inclination to malice. It is the central term of the religion of which this address is (whatever its author's true state of belief may have been) so remarkable an expression.

The habit of charity—not achieved by human beings for often or for long or ever purely, even without the passions of warfare—depends upon what has gone before: the cleansing away of self-righteousness, with its secret links to cruelty, to ill will, and to malice; the avoidance of "judging" others (that is, setting oneself categorically in the place of superior righteousness); the recognition of the working purpose—"the Almighty has His own purposes"—beyond one's own; the affirmation even after the most terrible events that "the judgments of the Lord, are true and righteous altogether."

charity for *all*

"Charity" extended to one party to a political dispute may, if it affects the disposition of policy itself, be uncharitable, even unjust, to another party.*

Lincoln had to decide, as the tide of war turned in 1863, what to propose for that immense collection of human beings who had rejected and defied the earnest plea of the First Inaugural and taken up arms against their

---

*The notable early twentieth-century film *The Birth of a Nation,* with its fiercely antiblack plot celebrating the Ku Klux Klan, derived from the racist novel *The Clansman,* invokes Lincoln and the Second Inaugural at the end. See Merrill D. Peterson, *Lincoln in American Memory* (New York: Oxford University Press, 1994), p. 170. The implication is that charity, with no malice, was extended to the defeated white South, while black Americans were caricatured and demeaned, not only left out of this "charity" but deeply harmed by it.

government and "committed and are now guilty of treason against the United States." The possible role of the virtue of charity in this collective case was more complicated than in the instances of forgiveness to individuals, because it would have an effect, for good or ill, on the reshaping of an entire society—the new South—and because in that reshaping there was, alongside the soon-to-be-defeated Confederates, another claimant, asking for justice at least if not charity, the soon to be freedmen. An undue or overdone or inappropriate "charity" to the defeated white South might, in effect, deny elementary justice, let alone charity, to the former slaves. When groups have conflicting claims, and issues of power lie between them, a "charity" or "mercy" or "forgiveness" to one group may be unjust to another; "justice," which makes moral comparisons and asks about respective merit, must be the stand-in, in such a situation, at least in the first instance, for charity.

BUT IN LINCOLN'S address, we do not get to the widows and orphans right away, or to the binding up of wounds and the taking care of veterans. Instead there is first:

firmness in the right, as God gives us to see the right

Here is the moral affirmation again, with the important qualifying apposition ("as God gives us to see the right") that was characteristic of Lincoln. He had ended his Cooper Union speech, to great applause from the gathering of New York leaders, "Let us have faith that right makes might, and in that faith, let us, to the end, dare to do our duty as we understand it." Perhaps it crippled his peroration a little to end with the qualifying phrase "as we understand it," but it is to Lincoln's moral if not his rhetorical credit that he did it. It is characteristic and desirable that even in the very moment of a ringing affirmation of "right," he adds the grace note that implies that our own understanding of what is right is not the whole story.

Nevertheless: firmness in the right, which means at the least a United States in which human slavery has no place.

Now comes what is in fact the main clause of the long sentence:

let us strive on to finish the work we are in

Charity, yes, malice, no, but—finish the work. Bring the war to a successful conclusion, and follow the Emancipation Proclamation with an amendment ending slavery in the United States and bringing a new birth of freedom.

The whole larger, deeper vision does not obliterate but gives meaning to a central, merely human, but still "firm" purpose, done without fanaticism or self-congratulation or vindictiveness, but finished all the same.

And now comes the healing, the caring, the widows and orphans:

> to bind up the nation's wounds; to care for him who shall have borne the battle, and for his widow, and his orphan—to do all which may achieve and cherish a just, and a lasting peace, among ourselves, and with all nations.

This address does not have the tight structure of the Gettysburg Address, but after the furious paragraphs about the drops of blood and the righteous God, it has this coda of healing: no malice; act from charity, bind up the wounds, care for the bereaved and injured; achieve and "cherish" peace—a peace that is just—among ourselves and with all our fellow human beings on this troubled earth.

THE MAN WRITING this address took the occasion to make a lasting human achievement, an achievement at once political, historical, and literary. He wrote in the letter to Weed that he expected it "to wear as well as—perhaps better than—anything I have produced," even though it would not be immediately popular. He was right on both counts.

It takes on its extraordinary significance because the man who delivered it was no mere poet or essayist "composing for the anthologies" (as the late Justice Robert Jackson once wrote in an opinion from the bench), or even your ordinary president, but rather the nation's leader in a war that would "rend the Union." Nevertheless, despite all the accumulated reasons for Lincoln to be partisan, his speech resounds with a quiet acceptance of purposes beyond his own and an absence of vindictiveness that would be remarkable even if written by that solitary essayist in his chambers.

The address, as given by that man in that circumstance, combined active moral engagement with an explicit awareness of the larger drama within which that engagement played its role. That awareness, then, led to the rare humility and evenhandedness about the conflict, and to the attitude toward opponents for which the address is remembered. It is a supreme example—better perhaps than bullfighters—of "grace under pressure." The observation about the larger purposes together with the evenhanded references to "both sides" and "neither side," and especially then the repudiation of malice at the speech's end, give it its stature. Or, rather, that stature comes from the combination of these sentences and the moral engagements already described.

This larger awareness and self-criticism would not be so impressive were it not joined to the moral engagement that it qualifies. The serious recognition of the limitation of his own side and party is joined to his equally serious engagement in the moral issue: his determination, as a leader in battle and in moral struggle, to "finish the work we are in."

It is the entire combination, in its setting, that makes this address remarkable. To turn the combination around, the generosity, self-criticism, and perspective for which the address is justly renowned did not cloud the speaker's moral perception or diminish the executive force with which he pursued his purposes. The address, therefore, is a model not simply of charity and largeness of spirit but of these qualities held by an engaged, active, committed, embattled, and political human being.

A COMMENT by Frederick Douglass on Lincoln's Second Inaugural was destined to be quoted many times in the future. But Douglass also described other episodes of the day that indicate the reason he would want the whole address remembered—particularly the strong next-to-last paragraph about the bondsman's 250 years of unrequited toil, and the blood drawn with the lash, and the judgments of the Lord being true and righteous altogether.

Waiting with a black friend named Mrs. Dorsey for the inaugural ceremonies to begin, Douglass saw Lincoln, standing with Andrew Johnson, point out Douglass to the vice president. "The first expression to his [Johnson's] face, and which I think was the true index of his heart," wrote Douglass, "was bitter contempt and aversion . . . I turned to Mrs. Dorsey and said, 'whatever Andrew Johnson may be, he certainly is no friend of our race.' "* Douglass went on to say, "No stronger contrast between two men could well be presented than the one exhibited on this day between President Lincoln and Vice President Johnson."

---

*"There are moments in the lives of most men," wrote Douglass, "when the doors of their souls are open . . . and their true character may be read . . . I caught a glimpse of the real nature of this man, which all subsequent developments proved true." *Frederick Douglass: Autobiographies,* ed. Henry Louis Gates, Jr. (New York: Library of America, 1994), p. 802.

That evening at the executive mansion, another episode indicated the deep contradiction that would persist. When Douglass tried to attend the reception there, to give Lincoln his congratulations, policemen at the door, from long racist practices, rudely stopped him and tried to usher him away. It took Lincoln's own intervention to secure his admission.

These episodes suggest why Douglass would not want the "charity" that the Second Inaugural's last paragraph recommends to be separated from the stark picture of injustice that the penultimate paragraph recognizes. The monstrous injustice of slavery both fed upon and reinforced the further injustice of racial caste, which the abolition of slavery would not end. "Charity" should lead to justice but, if misapplied, can reinforce injustice. Charity to whom? Does nonvindictiveness mean a return to power of the slave state leaders who would subordinate freed black citizens? Does healing the nation's wounds mean reconciling the white North and the white South, leaving black citizens excluded? The United States at the end of the Civil War faced yet another perplexing moral-political conundrum: how to secure the equal place of the freed black citizens while without vindictiveness bringing the fractured nation back together. It was an exacting test that for a lost hundred years the nation would fail. Frederick Douglass would say in a memorial lecture six weeks after Lincoln's death: "Whosoever else have cause to mourn the loss of Abraham Lincoln, to the colored people of the country his death is an unspeakable calamity." It turned out to be an unspeakable calamity for the entire nation.

Douglass did manage, by sending an appeal to Lincoln himself, to break the racial barrier and to be admitted to the reception on the evening of the second inauguration. He would write this about what happened:

> Recognizing me, even before I reached him, [the President] exclaimed, so that all around could hear him, "Here comes my friend Douglass." Taking me by the hand, he said, "I am glad to see you. I saw you in the crowd to-day, listening to my inaugural address; how did you like it?"
>
> I said, "Mr. Lincoln, I must not detain you with my poor opinion, when there are thousands waiting to shake hands with you."
>
> "No, no," he said, "you must stop a little, Douglass; there is no man in the country whose opinion I value more than yours. I want to know what you think of it?"
>
> I replied, "Mr. Lincoln, that was a sacred effort."

Abraham Lincoln Among the Immortals

O N APRIL 11, 1865, speaking about a proposed Louisiana constitution, the president hoped that the "elective franchise" would be conferred on "the very intelligent [Negroes] . . . and those who serve our cause
as soldiers." The actor John Wilkes Booth had already been shocked by
the sight in Richmond, a week earlier, of newly freed slaves ecstatically welcoming the visiting president. Now Booth, hearing this presidential
speech, said, "That means nigger citizenship . . . That is the last speech he
will ever make."

On Friday, April 14, 1865, the president was sitting with his wife in a
box in the dress circle in Ford's Theater in Washington, watching a play
called *Our American Cousin.* At 10:13 p.m., when Booth the actor knew
audience laughter would muffle the sound, he opened the door of the state
box, drew his derringer, and shot Lincoln behind the left ear. Major Henry
Rathbone, who had accompanied the Lincolns, struggled with Booth;
Booth stabbed Rathbone, leaped from the box the eleven feet to the stage,
caught his foot in the drape, broke a bone in his leg, perhaps shouted "Sic
semper tyrannis," and fled out the back door of the theater to his waiting
horse. Lincoln, unconscious, paralyzed, and barely breathing, was carried
across the street to a private home and died the next morning, April 15, at
7:22 a.m.

The kings and queens and emperors and empresses, the counts and
countesses, the highnesses and the majesties and the excellencies, the
viceroy, the sultan, and the tycoon, who had just four short years earlier
suddenly become, officially, his great good friends, now suddenly found it
necessary to become, officially, his grief-stricken mourners.

If the world's rulers did not yet know quite what to make of this unlikely
American leader, they did know what to say about the shooting of a head
of state: this act was execrable, horrid, vile, cowardly, abhorrent, brutal,
deplorable, despicable, atrocious, criminal, and odious.

As was said in the English House of Lords, so it would be said in ruling circles everywhere: "I think that your lordships will agree with me that in modern times there has hardly been a crime committed so abhorrent to the feelings of every civilized person. [Hear, hear.]"

Lincoln's great and good friend Queen Victoria wrote a personal, private letter of condolence, in her own hand, as Parliament was informed, to Mrs. Lincoln, as one sorrowing widow to another. (Prince Albert had died in December 1861, not long after the *Trent* affair.)

But there was a bit of awkwardness, if truth be told, for the British aristocracy, which had never quite got over a first snobbish response to the uncouth provincial who had somehow come to be head of this runaway colony. The aristocracy had harbored a surprising sympathy for the Confederacy and a surprising disinclination to support emancipation. Some of the world's worst editorials against the Emancipation Proclamation had appeared in the London *Times*.

In the House of Commons Sir Gordon Grey began his address by saying that although English people held different opinions, "still I believe that the sympathies of the majority of the people of this country have been with the North." He was greeted with loud denials. (Cries of "No, no," "Hear, hear," and "Question, question.")

English aristocrats were caught abruptly in a double embarrassment by their own past disdain for Lincoln and their mixed attitude to the cause for which he was now suddenly a martyr, on the one side, and by the overwhelming grief of the English people, on the other.

It fell to the British foreign secretary Lord John Russell to speak in the House of Lords. First he referred to the Queen's letter:

> [H]er Majesty . . . has instructed me already to express to the government of the United States the shock which she felt at the intelligence of the great crime which has been committed. [Hear, hear.] Her majesty has also been pleased to write a private letter to Mrs. Lincoln [cheers] expressive of sympathy with that lady in her misfortune. [Cheers.]

But Lord Russell also had to say something about the victim, and as with many, what he had said in the past about Lincoln made it awkward. He had written back in early 1861 that "President Lincoln looming in the distance is a still greater peril than President Buchanan" and later that year that Lincoln was capable of "getting up war cries to help his declining popularity." But perhaps he had learned something in four years' experience. He said:

> President LINCOLN was a man who, though not conspicuous before his election, had since displayed a character of so much integrity, so much sincerity and straightforwardness, and at the same time of so much kindness, that if any one was able to alleviate the pain and animosities which prevailed during the period of civil war, I believe that ABRAHAM LINCOLN was that person. It was remarked of President LINCOLN that he always felt disinclined to adopt harsh measures, and I am told that the commanders of his armies often complained that when they had passed a sentence which they thought no more than just, the President was always disposed to temper its severity. Such a man this particular epoch requires. The conduct of the armies of the United States was intrusted to other hands, and on the commanders fell the responsibility of leading the armies in the field to victory. They had been successful against those they had to contend with, and the moment had come when, undoubtedly, the responsibilities of President LINCOLN were greatly increased by their success.

Lord Russell apparently never did get Lincoln right: he thought it was the commanders who had won the war; now in the aftermath of their victory Lincoln would have become useful because he was such a meek and lenient fellow.

> But, though it was not for him to lead the armies, it would have been his to temper the pride of victory, to assuage the misfortunes which his adversaries had experienced, and especially to show, as he was well qualified to show, that high respect for valor on the opposite side which has been so conspicuously displayed.

One might say to the British foreign secretary that a good deal of valor had been displayed also on the side of the legitimate government of the United States, which the British government should have supported unequivocally.

The English humor magazine *Punch* was another organ of the upper reaches of British society that had to do a quick repair of attitude. It had mocked Lincoln for years (his "length of shambling limb . . . his unkempt, bristling hair . . . his garb uncouth"). After the assassination, *Punch* published a poem by its editor that a later British biographer of Lincoln, Lord

Charnwood, would describe as having "embodied in verse of rare felicity the manly contrition of its editor for ignorant derision in past years."

> *Yes, he had lived to shame me for my sneer*
> *To lame my pencil, and confute my pen—*
> *To make me own this kind of prince's peer,*
> *The rail-splitter a true-born king of men.*

An American less willing to forget the ignorant derision would write a little poem responding to *Punch:*

> *What need hath he now of a tardy crown,*
> *His name from mocking jest and sneer to save*
> *When every ploughman turns his furrow down*
> *As soft as though it fell upon his grave.*

And that was the worldwide story: What need had he for the labored and qualified approbation of the excellencies when every plowman gave his heart?

Years later Nicolay and Hay would see it clearly:

> In fact it was among the common people of the entire civilized world that the most genuine and spontaneous manifestations of sorrow and appreciation were produced, and to this fact we attribute the sudden and solid foundation of Lincoln's fame . . . [T]he progress of opinion from the few to the many is slow . . . But in the case of Lincoln the many imposed their opinion all at once; he was canonized as he lay on his bier, by the irresistible decree of countless millions. The greater part of the aristocracy of England thought little of him but the burst of grief from the English people silenced in an instant every discordant voice.

"The irresistible decree of countless millions" came not only from the English people but from all the world.

"The burst of grief" was universal.

Argentina declared three days of mourning.

John Bigelow, the U.S. ambassador to France, reported that forty thousand French citizens subscribed to a memorial medal for presentation to Mrs. Lincoln, asking that she be told "that in this little box is the heart of France."

An American foreign service officer reported from Chile: "Strong men wandered about the streets weeping like children, and foreigners, unable even to speak our language, manifested a grief almost as deep as our own."

The governments of the world were required by their position to say some word of official condolence and graveside commendation, but there was no such requirement for the Working Class Improvement Association of Lisbon or the Students in the Faculty of Theology in Strasbourg or the Teachers of the Ragged School in Bristol or the Vestry of the Parish of Chelsea or the Cotton Brokers' Association of Liverpool.

Messages of sympathy and condolence poured into Washington and American embassies and consulates everywhere. Municipal governments by the hundreds tried to express their sympathy and grief, and sent the written result to an American representative. Lesser bodies did the same; several local boards of health around the world took time out from their work to have their say about the death of an American president.

Hundreds of worthy nongovernmental bodies did the same: antislavery societies to be sure, and church groups—many Wesleyan groups, vestries, evangelical alliances, and many other entities that would seem to have no connection to the great world of nations and governments. A surprising number of singing societies would add their voice to the worldwide lament.

One might not have thought that the Men's Gymnastic Union (Männer Turnverein) of the city of Berne, Switzerland, would pause before gymnastics one evening and join—all forty-four members—in an expression of sympathy and condolence to the United States of America on account of the assassination of President Lincoln. But they did.

And an immense number of unorganized citizens gathered together for the sole purpose of making a statement or individually composed letters at their desks. Grace W. Gray of Northampton, England, expressed her grief and her tribute by composing an acrostic with Lincoln's name, the "Abraham" part of which goes like this:

> *A nation—nor one only—mourns thy loss,*
> *Brave LINCOLN, and with voice unanimous*
> *Raise to thy deathless memory*
> *A dirge-like song of all thy noble deeds.*
> *High let it rise; and I, too, fain would add*
> *A loving tribute to thy priceless worth,*
> *More widely known since banished from the earth.*

The executive of the United Kingdom Alliance for the Legislative Suppression of the Liquor Traffic felt particularly keenly Lincoln's death "by the hand of a murderer moved by drink." (Booth had gone into a nearby saloon and had a brandy just before he mounted the theater's stairs to the president's box.) There were a large number of statements from temperance groups.

The State Department would eventually gather together an immense collection of these messages under the main title *Appendix to the Diplomatic Correspondence of 1865* but with a subtitle that told what it was really about: *The Assassination of Abraham Lincoln . . . Expressions of Condolence and Sympathy,* an enormous collection of statements sent to Washington or to an embassy from every imaginable sort of gathering, the first 837 pages of which came from outside the United States.

It would be called "one of the most interesting and deeply affecting books in the English language."

"It forms a large quarto of a thousand pages, and embraces the utterances of grief and regret from every country under the sun, in almost every language spoken by man."

Would one have thought that condolences for the death of an American president would come from the Grand Trunk R.R. Company at its semiannual meeting at a London tavern?

Something about this head of state evoked grief, mourning, and condolence from an unusually broad spectrum of humanity.

Would the company of free hunters of the city of St. Gall have taken the trouble to compose a message of condolence if the assassinated president had been James Buchanan?

Would the Polish refugees in Zurich have put their feelings on paper if the president killed across the Atlantic had been Franklin Pierce?

Would the local board of health in Luton, England, have paused in its business to compose and send a message of condolence to the American ambassador if the assassinated statesman had been Millard Fillmore?

Lincoln had captured the world's heart because of what he *was,* what he *stood for,* and what he *did.*

Those apparent disqualifications as he took office—his humble origins, and meager education, and limited experience in great affairs—turned around and became sterling qualifications to the ordinary folk of the world.

As a public meeting of the trading and working classes of Brighton, in Sussex, England, put it: "This meeting of working men sympathize the more deeply with the untimely death of Abraham Lincoln, as he was the first President elected from the working classes to the high position of ruler of one of the mightiest nations of the globe."

The members of the Fraternal Association of Artisans of Leghorn, Italy, sending sincere condolence and brotherly grief, said they were "aware that the valorous champion of the American Union was born an artisan, and that liberty made him great and powerful, not to oppress but to strengthen and ennoble an entire nation; for this they have loved him as though they had been his sons or brothers."

As the citizens of Acireale, Sicily, put it: "Abraham Lincoln was not yours only—he was also ours . . . a brother whose great mind and fearless conscience guided a people to union, and courageously uprooted slavery."

All the world knew that he had fought slavery.

Moving messages arrived from Haiti and Liberia, which had first been recognized by the Lincoln administration, and from the Gold Coast. The chargé d'affaires in Monrovia would say: "Much of that great flood of tears shed over this great sorrow will flow from the children of Africa." The president of Liberia would write that Lincoln's "virtues can never cease to be told so long as the republic of Liberia shall endure; so long as there survives a member of the negro race to tell of the chains that have been broken; of the griefs that have been allayed; of the broken hearts that have been bound up by him who, as it were a new creation, breathed life into four millions of that race whom he found oppressed and degraded."

An American in the legation in Vienna, after trying to describe "the consternation which the event has caused throughout the civilized world," especially in Europe, asked, "And if the inhabitants of foreign and distant lands are giving expressions to such deep and unaffected sentiments, what must be the emotions now sweeping over our own country?"

Seventeen hundred miles of mourners stood for hours, stood in the rain, lined the road, crowded the stations and the squares, in the most astonishing funeral in the nation's history.

The citizens of Pella, Iowa, said: "[W]e acknowledge in Abraham Lincoln the genuine embodiment of true democracy . . . not only in our beloved country, but also in the whole civilized world."

Or as it was put by José Santos Valenzuela, first vice president of the Workingmen of Santiago, Chile: "The memory of Abraham Lincoln will live in the heart of humanity so long as the current of the Potomac flows or the Andes endure."

NOTES

All quotations from Abraham Lincoln in this book, unless otherwise indicated, are drawn from *The Collected Works of Abraham Lincoln,* ed. Roy P. Basler, 11 vols. (New Brunswick, N.J.: Abraham Lincoln Association/Rutgers University Press, 1953). The documents are available online at http://quod.lib.umich.edu/l/lincoln/.

ABBREVIATIONS

AL Papers *The Abraham Lincoln Papers at the Library of Congress,* a collaborative project of the Library of Congress Manuscript Division and the Lincoln Studies Center at Knox College in Galesburg, Illinois. The collection includes incoming and outgoing correspondence and enclosures, drafts of speeches, and notes and printed material. Most of the twenty thousand items are from the 1850s through Lincoln's presidential years. The collection is available online at http://memory.loc.gov/ammem/malquery.html.

AP The Avalon Project at Yale Law School, *Documents in Law, History, and Diplomacy,* online at www.yale.edu/lawweb/avalon/federal/fed.htm.

CW *The Collected Works of Abraham Lincoln,* ed. Roy P. Basler, 11 vols. (New Brunswick, N.J.: Abraham Lincoln Association, Rutgers University Press, 1953), online at http://quod.lib.umich.edu/l/lincoln/.

N&H John G. Nicolay and John Hay, *Abraham Lincoln: A History,* 10 vols. (New York: Century, 1917).

OR United States War Department, *The War of the Rebellion: A Compilation of the Official Records of the Union and Confederate Armies,* 3 vols. (Washington, D.C.: Government Printing Office, 1880–1901), online at http://cdl.library.cornell.edu/moa/browse.monographs/waro.html.

ORN United States Naval War Records Office, *Official Records of the Union and Confederate Navies in the War of the Rebellion,* 30 vols. (Washington, D.C.: Government Printing Office, 1894–1922), online at http://cdl.library.cornell.edu/moa/browse.monographs/ofre.html

INTRODUCTION. HONEST ABE AMONG THE RULERS

4 the quite unlikely equal and "friend": Lincoln addressed at least one letter to these great and good friends: His Majesty the Tycoon of Japan; Her Majesty Isabel II; His Highness Mohammed Said Pacha, Viceroy of Egypt and its Dependencies; Alexander II, Emperor and Autocrat of all the Russias; His Majesty Dom Luiz I, King of Portugal; His Majesty Somdetch Phra Paramendr Maha Mongut, King of Siam; His Majesty William I, King of Prussia; His Royal Highness Frederick, Grand Duke of Baden; His Royal Majesty Francis Joseph I, Emperor of Austria; His Excellency Señor Don José M. Acha, Constitutional President of the Republic of Bolivia; His Excellency Señor Don Francisco Solano López, President of the Republic of Paraguay; His Excellency Señor Don Bartolomé Mitre, President of the Argentine Republic; His Excellency The Marshal Don Miguel San Roman, Constitutional President of the Republic of Peru; His Excellency Señor Don Jesús Jiménez, President of the Republic of Costa Rica; His Majesty Leopold, King of the Belgians; His Majesty Frederick VII, King of Denmark; His Majesty Christian IX, King of Denmark; His Majesty Kamehameha V, King of the Hawaiian Island; His Excellency General Don José Maria Medina, President of the Republic of Honduras; His Majesty Charles XV, King of Sweden and Norway; Señor Don Atanasio Cruz Aguirre, President of the Oriental Republic of Uruguay; and His Imperial Majesty Napoleon III, Emperor of the French. Lincoln's letters to these great and good friends, which can be found in *The Collected Works,* communicated about such matters as the marriage of a niece; the birth of a prince to a well-beloved daughter-in-law; the decease of a royal nephew; the demise of a late king and the recipient's recent accession to the throne; the death of a cousin, accompanied by deep sympathy as well as sincere and hearty congratulations upon accession to the throne; the death of a brother, conveying profound sorrow and also pleasure at the intelligence of the recipient's constitutional succession to the throne; the birth of a prince; the birth of a son; the elevation by constitutional forms to the presidency; the decease of the wife of a royal's well-beloved cousin; the happy birth of a princess to a beloved daughter-in-law; an elevation to the presidency; the death of a justly lamented parent; and the birth and baptism of an infant.

CHAPTER ONE. A SOLEMN OATH REGISTERED IN HEAVEN

7 "good and well disciplined men": Major Anderson in *OR,* ser. 1, vol. 1, p. 197.

7 "strange, penniless, uneducated": *CW,* 1:320. Lincoln was describing, on March 26, 1843, how astonished older citizens of Menard County would be to hear he was a candidate of the aristocracy, given that they saw him in the way the well-worn quotation describes.

8 "What a happy conception": From Buchanan's March 4, 1857, inaugural address, in *The Works of James Buchanan: Comprising His Speeches, State Papers, and Private Correspondence,* ed. Bassett Moore, 10 vols. (Philadelphia: J. B. Lippincott, 1910), 10:105.

9 take and hold the hat: David Herbert Donald, in *Lincoln* (New York: Simon & Schuster, 1995), flatly accepts Douglas's hat-holding and gives sources (p. 283); Benjamin Thomas, in *Abraham Lincoln: A Biography* (1952; repr. New York: Modern Library,

1968), accepts it too but allows that it has been questioned (pp. 245–46). Reinhard Luthin, in *The Real Abraham Lincoln* (Englewood Cliffs, N.J.: Prentice-Hall, 1960), rather mocks the whole matter (p. 261).

10   "a rope of sand": James Buchanan said that "the Confederacy is a rope of sand" in his fourth annual message, December 3, 1860, *Works of James Buchanan*, 2:12; the entire address is on pp. 7–43.

10   "As a specimen of absurdity": John G. Nicolay, *The Outbreak of Rebellion* (New York: Da Capo Press, 1995), pp. 19–20.

11   Frederick Douglass's response to the whole address: Frederick Douglass wrote in his magazine about Lincoln's inaugural:

> Making all allowances for circumstances, we must declare the address to be but little better than our worst fears, and vastly below what we had fondly hoped it might be . . . Mr. Lincoln opens his address by announcing his complete loyalty to slavery in the slave States and quotes from the Chicago platform a resolution affirming the rights of property in slaves, in the slave States . . . [H]e also denies having the least *"inclination"* to interfere with slavery in the States. This denial of all feeling against slavery, at such a time and in such circumstances, is wholly discreditable to the head and heart of Mr. Lincoln. Aside from the inhuman coldness of the sentiment, it was a weak and inappropriate utterance to such an audience, since it could neither appease nor check the wild fury of the rebel Slave Power . . . It was, therefore, weak, uncalled for and useless for Mr. Lincoln to begin his Inaugural Address by thus at the outset prostrating himself before the foul and withering curse of slavery . . . The occasion was one for honest rebuke, not for palliations and apologies . . . Some thought we had in Lincoln the nerve and decision of an Oliver Cromwell; but the result shows that we merely have a continuation of the Pierces and the Buchanans, and that the Republican President bends the knee to slavery as readily as any of his infamous predecessors.

Frederick Douglass, "The Inaugural Address," *Douglass' Monthly* (April 1861).

12   "[He] shows conclusively": Seward's witty comment is quoted from Frederic Bancroft, *The Life of William Seward*, 2 vols. (New York: Harper & Brothers, 1900), 2:3.

13   "The courteous old gentleman": Michael Burlingame, ed., *At Lincoln's Side: John Hay's Civil War Correspondence and Selected Writings* (Carbondale: Southern Illinois University Press, 2000), p. 119. He goes on to say: "Lincoln listened with that weary, introverted look of his, not answering, and the next day, when I recalled the conversation, admitted he had not heard a word of it. Through every chamber of his heart and brain were resounding those solemn strains of long-suffering warning which he that day addressed to the South: 'With you, not with me, rests the awful issue. Shall it be peace or the sword?' " Lincoln had not in fact said this line, which Hay is remembering from the draft—it was "solemn" issue, not "awful"—and it was cut in the editing in the Willard.

13   "[W]hile the battery on the brow of the hill": *N&H*, 3:344.

14   "in a room upstairs over a store": William H. Herndon and Jesse W. Weik, *Herndon's Life of Lincoln* (1942; repr. New York: Da Capo Press, 1983), p. 386.

14   "It follows from these views": *CW*, 4:253. The First Edition and Revisions of the First Inaugural Address—Lincoln's draft and changes, quoted here and on later pages—can be found in *CW*, 4:249–62.

15   Mississippi's declaration: *AP*.

15 The proclamation by the Texas convention: Ibid.

16 "SIR: I herewith demand": Colonel John Cunningham, December 30, 1860, *OR,* ser. 1, vol. 1, p. 7.

17 "SIR: I am constrained to comply": F. C. Humphreys, December 30, 1860, ibid.

18 "The public interest": *N&H,* 3:371.

19 As Joshua Shenk has observed: Joshua Shenk, *Lincoln's Melancholy: How Depression Challenged a President and Fueled His Greatness* (Boston: Houghton Mifflin, 2005), p. 179.

20 "little better than our worst fears": Douglass, "Inaugural Address."

20 "This, then, was the much vaunted 'firm' policy": David M. Potter, *Lincoln and His Party in the Secession Crisis* (Baton Rouge: Louisiana State University Press, 1995), p. 329.

21 "This commentary certainly highlights": Harry V. Jaffa, *A New Birth of Freedom* (Lanham, Md.: Rowman & Littlefield, 2000), p. 273.

21 "That draft . . . was a no-nonsense document": Donald, *Lincoln,* p. 283.

21 "an imperfectly blended mixture of opposites": Ibid.

21 Donald quotes the ending challenge to the South: Ibid., pp. 283–84.

22 "will be construed as a threat": Orville Browning to AL, February 17, 1861, *AL Papers.*

23 "Mr. Douglas said": "The New Administration," *New York Times,* March 5, 1861, p. 1 (ProQuest Historical Newspapers).

25 "let grass grow where it may": This quotation was reported by Lucius E. Chittenden, who was at the meeting; Michael Burlingame, *The Inner World of Abraham Lincoln* (Urbana: University of Illinois Press, 1994), p. 199.

27 "outstanding precedent": Edward S. Corwin, *The President: Office and Powers* (New York: New York University Press, 1984), p. 64.

28 He did not continually invoke: A newspaper report of the remarks he made when as president-elect he was speaking to a gathering of German citizens in Cincinnati. The *Cincinnati Daily Commercial,* in one of two varying newspaper accounts, has him using the familiar and vulnerable utilitarian slogan "The greatest good of the greatest number." This was on February 12, his birthday, in 1861:

> Mr. Chairman, I hold that while man exists, it is his duty to improve not only his own condition, but to assist in ameliorating mankind; and therefore, without entering upon the details of the question, I will simply say, that I am for those means which will give the greatest good to the greatest number.

The familiar slogan is vulnerable to logical criticism because it has two superlatives that may conflict; but joined with the other familiar utilitarian slogan—"Everyone to count as one, none to count as more than one"—it did great good in the world because its universalism encouraged *reform,* a moral challenge to existing injustices. Although Lincoln certainly was a moral agent who calculated consequences, he nevertheless had too much shaping by *duties* to be strictly a utilitarian.

30 "At a dark period of the war": John Hay, in Burlingame, *At Lincoln's Side,* p. 126.

CHAPTER TWO.
ACT WELL YOUR PART, THERE ALL THE HONOR LIES

31   "on the whole with great success": *CW*, 4:252. The notes show the changes Lincoln made.

32   President Polk, whom some would name as the best: "When his four years in the president's office were completed, James K. Polk would have added to the United States the huge state of Texas, . . . the American piece of 'Oregon,' which included today's states of Oregon and Washington; the territory that is now the states of California, Nevada, and Utah, most of New Mexico and Arizona, and parts of what have become Wyoming and Colorado. If the test of presidential greatness should be sheer *acreage,* then James K. Polk would rank very high indeed." William Lee Miller, *Lincoln's Virtues: An Ethical Biography* (New York: Alfred A. Knopf, 2002), p. 483.

36   Hamilton argued strongly for "unity": Federalist 79, *AP*.

36   "Have republics in practice": Federalist 6, *AP*, p. 59.

36   "a rough farmer": David Herbert Donald, *Charles Sumner,* 2 vols. (New York: Da Capo Press, 1996), 2:18.

36   When Senator Charles Sumner: Ibid., 2:383.

37   "could not get rid of his misgivings": Ibid.

37   "I must . . . affirm": This statement by Charles Francis Adams came in a mitigating context, with a mitigating introduction. Adams was speaking in 1873 to the two houses of the legislature of New York, in honor of the late William Seward. He introduced his remark by saying:

> Let me not be misunderstood as desiring to say a word in a spirit of derogation from the memory of Abraham Lincoln. He afterward proved himself before the world a pure, brave, capable and honest man, faithful to his arduous task, and laying down his life at last for his country's safety. At the same time, it is the duty of history, in dealing with all human actions, to do strict justice in discriminating between persons, and by no means to award to one honors that clearly belong to another.

The other of course is Seward. Adams, observing events strictly from a diplomatic post in London, communicating primarily with Seward, and perhaps a bit of a snob to start with, thought the worthy accomplishments of the Lincoln administration were largely the work of Seward. The passage appears in Adams's *Address on the Life, Character, and Services of William Henry Seward* (Albany, N.Y.: Weed, Parsons, & Co., 1873), pp. 48–49, and is quoted in William E. Barton, *The Life of Abraham Lincoln,* 2 vols. (Indianapolis: Bobbs-Merrill, 1925), 2:18.

39   "that he had done nothing to make any human being": Douglas L. Wilson and Rodney O. Davis, eds., *Herndon's Informants: Letters, Interviews, and Statements About Abraham Lincoln* (Urbana: University of Illinois Press, 1998), p. 197.

39   "He reminded me of the conversation": Ibid.

39   "Despite the stature which Abraham Lincoln afterward assumed": David M. Potter, *Lincoln and His Party in the Secession Crisis* (Baton Rouge: Louisiana State University Press, 1995), p. 315. Then Potter wrote—as I say, with a certain exasperation:

This fact may seem too obvious to justify notice, and, indeed, it would be, were it not for the fact that the Lincoln legend has obscured the shortcomings of the man, and has glossed over the periods of his life during which he groped and blundered. Consequently the picture of Lincoln coming east from Springfield with his misgivings and his misconceptions is lost. Instead, there is a picture of a man following the well-marked path of destiny to abolish slavery, to console Mrs. Bixby, to reach maximum at Gettysburg, to give his life in the cause of Union, and, finally, to belong to the ages.

40 Given the power of the Lincoln legend: I wrote in *Lincoln's Virtues* (p. xiii) a warning that applies double strength to *President* Lincoln, that the myth can have a perverse effect on true appreciation:

> If his instant and constant wonderfulness is stipulated in advance, taken for granted from the outset, and woven into the national memory as a universally accepted fact, then his actual moral achievements are discounted. Exaggerated preliminary expectations that he was a spectacularly virtuous man may diminish our appreciation of the ways in which he may actually have become one.

42 He was not exactly a "child of nature": On September 30, 1859, as a rising politician, Lincoln spoke to the Wisconsin State Agricultural Society—the state fair, in other words—in Milwaukee. He made no reference at all to his own farming and made it clear that he was not a farmer: "I suppose it is not expected of me to impart to you much specific information on Agriculture. You have no reason to believe, and do not believe, that I possess it—if that were what you seek in this address, any one of your own number, or class, would be more able to furnish it."

42 "I once remarked to him": Wilson and Davis, *Herndon's Informants*, p. 499.

42 He had energetically and sometimes eloquently presented: Stephen Skowronek, *The Politics Presidents Make* (Cambridge, Mass.: Harvard University Press, 1993), p. 205. Also included is a good articulation of the core message of the Republicans.

45 "He alone can do good": Josef Pieper, *The Four Cardinal Virtues* (New York: Harcourt, Brace, 1954), p. 10.

45 "It is necessary for the prudent man": Ibid.

46 "The President's programme": John Maynard Keynes, *Essays and Sketches in Biography* (New York: Meridian Books, 1956), pp. 266–67.

47 "[I]t must be remembered": *N&H*, 3:443.

CHAPTER THREE. ON MASTERING THE SITUATION: THE DRAMA OF SUMTER

This chapter relies more than the notes may reveal on the books most often cited on the Sumter crisis: Richard N. Current, *Lincoln and the First Shot* (Philadelphia: J. B. Lippincott, 1963), and Kenneth M. Stampp, *And the War Came: The North and the Secession Crisis, 1860–1861* (Baton Rouge: Louisiana State University Press, 1950).

49 "The first thing that was handed to me": T. C. Pease and James G. Randall, eds., *The Diary of Orville Hickman Browning*, 2 vols. (Springfield: Illinois State Historical Library, 1925–33), 1:476.

49 "twenty thousand good and well disciplined men": Joseph Holt and Winfield Scott to Abraham Lincoln, March 5, 1861, *AL Papers*.

49 The limitations of the available force: *N&H*, 4:65.

49 "the northern press": U. S. Grant, *Personal Memoirs of U.S. Grant* (New York: Library of America, 1990), p. 206.

50 "of a most important and unexpected character": Holt and Scott to Lincoln, March 5, 1861, *AL Papers*.

50 "Browning, of all the trials I have had": Note headed "July 3, 1861," in John Nicolay file, *AL Papers*.

51 "all the troubles and anxieties of his life": Pease and Randall, *Diary of Orville Hickman Browning*, 1:476.

52 "By nine o'clock that night": John G. Nicolay, *The Outbreak of Rebellion* (New York: Da Capo Press, 1995), p. 29.

53 "was besieged from morning till night": Washington correspondence, *Cincinnati Gazette,* March 21, 1861 (courtesy of Michael Burlingame).

54 "When Major Anderson first threw himself into Fort Sumter": Holt and Scott to Lincoln, March 5, 1861, *AL Papers*.

55 "on reflection": July 4, 1861, Message to Congress, *CW,* 4:423. The phrase "at the request of the executive" in the manuscript was replaced by "on reflection" in first proof.

56 "came reluctantly, but decidedly": July 4, 1861, Message to Congress, *CW,* 4:424.

56 pungent detail about the dwindling supplies: Winfield Scott to AL, March 11, 1861, *AL Papers*.

57 "I am directed by the President": *CW,* 4:280.

58 "Sir, I desire that an expedition": *CW,* 4:301.

59 "That night Lincoln's eyes": *N&H,* 3:395.

60 "himself conceived the idea": Orville Browning's diary (pp. 26, 46), quoted in Current, *First Shot,* p. 181.

61 "The U.S. government has directed me": G. V. Fox to Governor Pickens and Captain Jackson, in Robert Means Thompson and Richard Wainwright, eds., *Confidential Correspondence of Gustavus Vasa Fox: Assistant Secretary of the Navy, 1861–1865,* 2 vols. (New York: Naval History Society, 1920), 1:18; and also in Current, *First Shot,* pp. 99–100.

61 changed "but starving" to "and hungry": *CW,* 4:425.

62 "your flag flying": *CW,* 4:321.

63 "not only to keep the latter promise good": *CW,* 4:425.

63 "The tables were now completely turned": Charles W. Ramsdell, "Lincoln and Fort Sumter," *Journal of Southern History 3* (August 1937), p. 281.

64 "Sir—you will proceed directly": The last clause in Lincoln's message is a little awkward. Perhaps he should have broken the sentence and started over, composing a new sentence to say what was surely plain enough—that the Union would certainly feel free to "throw in" forces should the rebels attack the fort.

64 "But to allow the provisioning": Ramsdell, "Lincoln and Sumter," p. 282.

65 "Nor could they be sure": Ibid.

66 "Biographers of Davis and historians of the Confederacy": Current, *First Shot,* p. 201.

66   "[I]t is unnecessary, it puts us in the wrong": Ramsdell, "Lincoln and Sumter," p. 283, from Pleasant A. Stovall, *Robert Toombs: Statesman, Speaker, Soldier, Sage* (New York: Cassell, 1892), p. 226. Toombs is further quoted as having said, "[A]t this time it is suicide, murder, and will lose us every friend at the North. You will wantonly strike a hornet's nest which extends from mountains to ocean, and legions, now quiet, will swarm out and sting us to death." Michael Burlingame will quote in his forthcoming biography a letter from a South Carolinian living in New York who wrote Davis similar good advice, with a similarly accurate prediction of the Northern response.

66   "Of course Lincoln was aware": J. G. Randall and David Herbert Donald, *The Civil War and Reconstruction*, 2nd ed. (Boston: Heath, 1961), p. 175.

67   He had said that the principle of secession: "[W]hy may not any portion of a new confederacy . . . arbitrarily secede again, precisely as portions of the present Union now claim to secede from it. All who cherish disunion sentiments, are now being educated to the exact temper of doing this. Is there such perfect identity of interests among the States to compose a new Union, as to produce harmony only?" First Inaugural Address, March 4, 1861, *CW*, 4:268.

67   "Under no circumstances": *OR*, ser. 1, vol. 1, p. 289.

67   The Confederate authorities in Montgomery: Indeed, it appears from letters that Davis wrote to his commander at Fort Pickens that he may have made the decision to fire a first shot even before Robert Chew arrived in Charleston with Lincoln's message. Historian Grady McWhiny, in "The Confederacy's First Shot," *Civil War History* 14 (1968), has brought forward exchanges Davis and Confederate secretary of war Walker had with General Braxton Bragg, Beauregard's equivalent at Fort Pickens. A long letter written April 3, received by Bragg on April 6, explored what Bragg should do. In the most interesting sentence, Davis wrote: "There would be an advantage in so placing them that an attack by them would be a necessity, but when we are ready to relieve our territory and jurisdiction of the presence of a foreign garrison that advantage is overbalanced by other considerations." McWhiny says that this letter "indicates that Davis was willing to start a war. He would have liked to do precisely what Ramsdell claimed Lincoln had done—maneuver the enemy into firing the first shot—but the Confederate President considered such a scheme, in his own words, 'overbalanced by other considerations.' "

      Bragg explained the practical difficulties concerning an attack on Fort Pickens; a Confederate attack was not made—a first shot in Florida—only because the general in charge judged it not to be practically sound. McWhiny writes in conclusion:

> He [Davis] encouraged Bragg to capture Fort Pickens, but when Bragg insisted that the only possible way to take Pickens was by a reckless assault which might become an embarrassing failure, Davis shifted his attention to Sumter and directed Beauregard to open fire. Thus war came at Fort Sumter only because the Confederates were neither subtle enough nor strong enough to begin it at Fort Pickens.

67   "I have the honor to acknowledge" (April 11): *OR*, ser. 1, vol. 1, p. 15.

68   "By authority of Brigadier-General Beauregard": *OR*, ser. 1, vol. 1, p. 14.

68   "I have the honor to acknowledge" (April 13): *OR*, ser. 1, vol. 1, p. 15.

70   "You and I both anticipated": *CW*, 4:351.

70   "Was this statement merely intended to soothe": Ramsdell, "Lincoln and Sumter,"
      p. 285.

70   "He himself conceived the idea": Pease and Randall, *Diary of Orville Hickman
      Browning*, 1:476.

70   "It completes the evidence": Ramsdell, "Lincoln and Sumter," p. 288.

70   "When he finally gave the order": *N&H*, 4:62.

CHAPTER FOUR. ON *NOT* MASTERING THE SITUATION:
THE COMEDY OF THE *POWHATAN*

Major participants left accounts of this episode. Much of the story can be found in the letters
to and from Gustavus Fox in *Confidential Correspondence of Gustavus Vasa Fox: Assistant
Secretary of the Navy, 1861–1865*, ed. Robert Means Thompson and Richard Wainwright,
2 vols. (New York: Naval History Society, 1920), 1:15–41, which prints the letters about
both the Sumter and the Pickens-*Powhatan* expeditions, which from Fox's point of view
were woven together. Gideon Welles offers perhaps the most detailed account of the
Powhatan affair. Of particular value in writing this chapter was the first volume of his *Diary
of Gideon Welles* (Boston: Houghton Mifflin, 1911), pp. 3–69. He dealt with these expeditions again in two articles he wrote almost a decade afterward: "Fort Sumter," *Galaxy* 10, no.
5 (November 1870), pp. 613–28, and "Fort Pickens," *Galaxy* 11, no. 1 (January 1871), pp.
92–108. John Niven's biography, *Gideon Welles: Lincoln's Secretary of the Navy* (New York:
Oxford University Press, 1973), was another helpful resource. Montgomery Meigs's interpretation of the event is taken from diary excerpts that were published in "General M. C.
Meigs on the Conduct of the Civil War," *American Historical Review* 26, no. 2 (January
1921). Admiral Porter told his anecdotes from the *Powhatan* episode in a book written many
years after the event: David D. Porter, *Incidents and Anecdotes of the Civil War* (New York: D.
Appleton & Co., 1885).

73   "We are at the end": Seward to Lincoln, April 1, 1861, *AL Papers*.

73   One way to do that: Seward preceded his proposal of a foreign war with this state-
      ment of his "system": "I am aware that my views are singular, and perhaps not suffi-
      ciently explained. My system is built upon this idea as a ruling one, namely that we
      must change the question before the Public from one upon Slavery, or about Slavery
      for a question upon Union or Disunion. In other words, from what would be regarded
      as a Party question to one of Patriotism or Union. The occupation or evacuation of
      Fort Sumter . . . is so regarded. Witness, the temper manifested by the Republicans in
      the Free States, and even by Union men in the South. I would therefore terminate it as
      a safe means for changing the issue. I deem it fortunate that the last Administration
      created the necessity." April 1, 1861, *CW*, 4:317–18.

73   "I said 'The power confided to me' ": *CW*, 4:316.

75   "I would call in Captain M. C. Meigs": Seward to Lincoln, March 29, 1861, *AL
      Papers*.

75   "ought to see some of the younger officers": *ORN*, 4:104.

75   When Lincoln asked Meigs: *N&H*, 3:395.

76 Seward insisted that the Pickens expedition must be kept secret: David Porter— Admiral Porter as he became—published twenty years after the war this account of the meeting with Lincoln, with suspiciously precise quotations from the participants:

> When we arrived at the White House, Mr. Lincoln—who seemed to be aware of our errand—opened the conversation. "Tell me," said he, "how we can prevent Fort Pickens from falling into the hands of the rebels ... Pensacola would be a very important place for the Southerners, and if they once get possession of Pickens, and fortify it, we have no navy to take it from them."
>
> "Mr. President," said I, "there is a queer state of things existing in the Navy Department at this time. Mr. Welles is surrounded by officers and clerks, some of whom are disloyal at heart, and if the orders for this expedition should emanate from the Secretary of the Navy, and pass through all the department red tape, the news would be at once flashed over the wires, and Fort Pickens would be lost for ever. But if you will issue all the orders from the Executive Mansion, and let me proceed to New York with them, I will guarantee their prompt execution to the letter."
>
> "But," said the President, "is not this a most irregular mode of proceeding?"
>
> "Certainly," I replied, "but the necessity of the case justifies it."
>
> "You are commander-in-chief of the army and navy," said Mr. Seward to the President, "and this is a case where it is necessary to issue direct orders without passing them through intermediaries.

Porter, *Incidents,* pp. 14–15.

76 "Hard at work all day": Meigs's diary, as cited at the head of this chapter.

77 The most remarkable of these letters: We learn from Welles in his *Galaxy* article on Fort Pickens that the body of the letter was in Meigs's handwriting, and the long postscript was in that of David Porter. The postscript asked Welles to give Captain Barron all possible help in mastering the detail of the Navy Department. One must remember that in these days loyalties had yet to be clarified—before April 14–15 and the fall of Sumter and the call of the militia, before April 22 and the great exodus of rebels from the government. Porter's plugging of Barron suggests that Foote was right to be wary of Porter's moving in navy circles, where there were secessionist sentiments. Barron was a Virginian who was an influential navy man in Washington, a "navy diplomat," who would soon join the Confederate navy. In a perfect irony, in an August 1861 encounter at Hatteras Inlet, he would be the first Confederate naval officer captured by Union forces, the naval component of which would be led by Commodore Silas Stringham. Barron would not have been a good appointment as head of the Bureau of Detail of the United States Navy.

77 "[R]aising his head from the table": Welles, *Diary,* p. 17.

77 An embarrassed Lincoln told Welles: Welles's biographer John Niven suggests that Lincoln was not altogether candid with Welles, telling him that he had not read the flurry of orders that he signed when Seward brought them to him that day (orders to Foote, Mercer, and especially Porter that set this bollixed event in motion). Niven argues that the orders are short, the longest only forty-two words, and that a trained lawyer could get the gist of them at a glance and know what he was signing. I answer that at least the document rearranging naval personnel, the one Welles would bring to him indignantly that very evening, was longer than forty-two words and not easy to

"gist" even if one knew what it was all about, which Lincoln didn't. Surely he did sign that one without comprehending it—and when he did comprehend it, he immediately repudiated it. On the other hand, can we not assume that Lincoln *did* know that he was setting in motion an expedition to succor Fort Pickens, signing orders rapidly to make that happen, with Meigs whom he had met and liked in the key position? It is just that he did not read the orders closely enough to register the names *Powhatan* and Mercer when they came around again.

78 "[f]it out the *Powhatan*": Welles, "Fort Sumter."

79 "Delay the *Powhatan*": Roll 82, M625, Navy Records, National Archives.

79 "I am with Captain Meigs": *ORN,* 4:111.

80 "off Charleston bar": Simon Cameron to G. V. Fox, in Thompson and Wainwright, *Confidential Correspondence,* 1:23–25.

80 "On seeing us": Welles, *Diary,* p. 24.

81 "Seward, tense and tired": Niven, *Welles,* p. 335.

82 "Give the *Powhatan* to Mercer": William Seward to D. D. Porter, *ORN,* 4:112.

83 "[H]eavy guns were heard": Gustavus V. Fox to Gideon Welles, from a report regarding the expedition under his command for the relief of Fort Sumter, *ORN,* 4:249–50.

84 "I . . . proceeded to Fort Sumter": John P. Gillis to Gideon Welles, *ORN,* 4:251–52.

85 "[W]hen the arrow has sped": *OR,* ser. 1, vol. 1, p. 369.

85 "I do not think I have deserved this treatment": G. V. Fox, in Thompson and Wainwright, *Confidential Correspondence,* 1:33. Fox's report, written on April 17, with a pencil on the *Baltic,* is on pp. 31–36. It ends: "As for our expedition, somebody's influence made it ridiculous."

86 "Early in April 1861": Gustavus V. Fox to John G. Nicolay, February 22, 1865, *AL Papers.*

86 Nicolay had to answer: John G. Nicolay to Gustavus V. Fox, February 24, 1865, *AL Papers.*

87 "He took upon himself": Welles, *Diary,* p. 25.

87 "I sincerely regret": Lincoln to G. V. Fox, *ORN,* 4:251.

88 According to Welles: Welles, *Diary,* 1:25.

88 Lincoln not only held no grudge against Meigs: To the proposal that Meigs should be promoted to the important post of quartermaster general (the top supply man for the whole army), Secretary of War Cameron that first summer wrote a terse message to the president telling him that a Colonel Thomas was the oldest in point of service in the Quartermaster Corps—obviously reflecting a departmental preference for the senior Thomas over the younger Meigs. Lincoln then wrote to General Winfield Scott:

Executive Mansion

June 5, 1861

My dear Sir

Doubtless you begin to understand how disagreeable it is to me to do a thing arbitrarily, when it is unsatisfactory to others associated with me.

I very much wish to appoint Col. Meigs Quarter-Master General; and yet Gen. Cameron does not quite consent. I have come to know Col. Meigs quite well for a short acquaintance, and, so far as I am capable of judging I do not know one who combines the qualities of masculine intellect, learning and experience of the right sort, and physical power of labor and endurance so well as he . . .

You will lay me under one more obligation, if you can and will use your influence to remove Gen. Cameron's objection. I scarcely need tell you I have nothing personal in this, having never seen or heard of Col. Meigs, until the end of last March.

Your obt. Servt

A. Lincoln

90 "For a daring and dangerous enterprise": Lincoln to G. V. Fox, in Thompson and Wainwright, *Confidential Correspondence,* p. 44.

CHAPTER FIVE. DAYS OF CHOICES: TWO APRIL SUNDAYS

91 "policy which the federal executive is to pursue": *CW,* 4:329–30; also see Richmond Virginia Convention, April, 8, 1861, *AL Papers.*

92 "It is with deep regret": *CW,* 4:330.

94 "drafted by himself": *N&H,* 4:77.

94 "that the loyal states had suffered": *N&H,* 4:78.

94 invigorating shot of clarified resolve: B. H. Liddell Hart called it "that vast human sigh of relief" and remarked in 1929 that it was "one of the most recurrent phenomena in history, marking the outset of every great conflict down to 1914." One could continue the story to 1939 in Europe, 1941 in the United States, and beyond. See Charles Royster, "Fort Sumter: At Last the War," in G. Boritt, ed., *Why the Civil War Came* (New York: Oxford University Press, 1996).

95 "While discussing the proclamation": *N&H,* 4:79.

98 "You, gentlemen, come here": James G. Randall, *Lincoln the President* (New York: Da Capo Press, 1977), vol. 1, pt. 2, p. 365. All citations from Randall's *Lincoln* are to this edition, which reproduces the original four-volume work published in 1945 by Dodd, Mead & Company. The Da Capo edition is divided into two volumes, each consisting of two parts. All notes herein are from Volume 1, *Springfield to Gettysburg.*

100 "The President, at once": Mayor Brown Report, *N&H,* 4:124.

102 "a clear, flagrant, and gigantic case": Letter to Erastus Corning and others, June 12, 1863, *CW,* 6:264.

102 "in exceedingly narrow terms": Don E. Fehrenbacher, *Lincoln in Text and Context* (Stanford, Calif.: Stanford University Press, 1987), p. 122.

102 "I there upon summoned my constitutional advisers": *CW,* 5:241; Lincoln's May 26, 1862, message to the House, quoted throughout this section, is found on pp. 240–43.

104 "Slavery was killed years ago": Francis B. Carpenter, *The Inner Life of Abraham Lincoln: Six Months at the White House* (1866; repr. Lincoln: University of Nebraska Press, 1995), pp. 72–74.

105 "General Scott received him kindly": *N&H,* 4:103–4.

105 "proved false to the hand which had pampered them": July 4, 1861, Message to Congress, *CW.*

105 There were significant defections: Allan Nevins, *The War for the Union,* 4 vols. (New York: Charles Scribner's Sons, 1959–71), 1:108.

105   "When I took charge of the Navy Department": Gideon Welles, *Diary of Gideon Welles,* 3 vols. (Boston: Houghton Mifflin, 1911), 1:19.

106   "Any amount of feverish rumors": Hay's diary entry for April 21, 1861, in Michael Burlingame and John R. Turner Ettlinger, eds., *Inside Lincoln's White House: The Complete Civil War Diary of John Hay* (Carbondale: Southern Illinois University Press, 1997), p. 6.

107   "Day after day prediction failed": *N&H,* 4:151.

107   "I don't believe there is any North": John Hay's diary entry for April 24, 1861, in Burlingame and Ettlinger, *Inside,* p. 11.

107   "Why *don't* they come?": *N&H,* 4:152.

107   Washington in those April days: Randall, *Lincoln the President,* vol. 1, pt. 1, p. 363.

107   Scott had chosen: Nevins, *War for the Union,* 1:79.

107   "[T]he national capital": Ibid. Nevins does not say where he learned that the defenders of the capital were flat-chested.

108   "a man who couldn't cut a chicken's head off": William C. Davis, *Lincoln's Men* (New York: Simon & Schuster, 2000), p. 177.

108   "Allow the President to invade": Lincoln to Herndon, February 15, 1848, *CW,* 1:451.

109   "attempt to divide and destroy": July 4, 1861, Message to Congress, *CW.*

109   "Those who were in the federal capital": *N&H,* 4:156.

CHAPTER SIX. REALISM RIGHT AT THE BORDER

110   If all three of these slave states: James M. McPherson, *Battle Cry of Freedom: The Civil War Era* (New York: Oxford University Press, 1988), p. 284.

111   "In the four Border States": Ibid.

112   The historian William Freehling has remarked: William W. Freehling, *The South vs. the South: How Anti-Confederate Southerners Shaped the Course of the Civil War* (New York: Oxford University Press, 2001), p. 57.

112   "In 1860, slaves accounted": Ibid., p. 50.

112   The opposition to Yankee invaders: "A week into the Civil War, with so many different types of borderites aching to consider the war an anti-American mistake, the mistake invaded Baltimore. The city's motley mob trampled all over the mistake and then with Yankee troops gone from center city, went back to trading with the North." Ibid.

113   "sent an imploring request": Michael Burlingame and John R. Turner Ettlinger, eds., *Inside Lincoln's White House: The Complete Civil War Diary of John Hay* (Carbondale: Southern Illinois University Press, 1997), p. 12.

113   "The question has been submitted": Lincoln to Winfield Scott, April 25, 1861, *CW,* 4:344.

114   "They called Benjamin Butler a Beast": Freehling, *South vs. South,* p. 51.

114   "the state . . . be spared the evils": *CW,* 4:356.

115   The poem was written: Jean Baker, *The Politics of Continuity* (Baltimore: Johns Hopkins University Press, 1973), p. 69. Baker tells about the poem and the song, written by "Baltimore-born James Ryder Randall after the Baltimore riot in April 1861 while he was teaching at a Louisiana College."

116   "Gen'l: After full consultation": Stephen W. Sears, ed., *The Civil War Papers of*

George B. McClellan: Selected Correspondence, 1860–1865 (New York: Da Capo Press, 1992), p. 99.

117   "the activities of the army": Baker, *Politics,* pp. 71–72.

117   "Maryland was made to seem": *CW,* 5:49.

118   "Which Virginia?": Allan Nevins, *The War for the Union,* 4 vols. (New York: Charles Scribner's Sons, 1959), 1:138. After the Virginia convention voted a secession ordinance on April 17, former senator James Mason traveled to Maryland to talk to the legislature of the sister state about joining the rebellion.

118   East Virginia in 1860: John G. Nicolay, *The Outbreak of Rebellion* (New York: Da Capo Press, 1995), p. 138.

119   Wheeling, a river city: McPherson, *Battle Cry,* p. 298.

119   "The right of revolution can be exercised": Nicolay, *Outbreak,* p. 139.

119   the minute that secession was proposed: Edward Conrad Smith, *The Borderland in the Civil War* (New York: Macmillan, 1927), p. 202. The official returns have been lost, and there were charges of intimidation in opposite directions on both sides of the mountains. When the Virginia secession ordinance was submitted to a vote of the people on May 23, the citizens in the twelve counties farthest north and west, in stark contrast to those back east, voted against it ten to one.

119   A rump legislature: Randall, who objects to much in the making of West Virginia, more than once notes the injustice that the makers of the new state attached to the previous forty-eight counties the two counties (Jefferson and Berkeley) farthest east, which compose the peculiarly shaped Eastern Panhandle, when the population of those counties was "almost universal" in adhering to old Virginia and to secession. J. G. Randall and David Herbert Donald, *The Civil War and Reconstruction,* 2nd ed. (Boston: Heath, 1961), pp. 239, 242. There may be a thoroughly realistic Union explanation: adding those two counties to West Virginia meant that the entire route of the Baltimore and Ohio Railroad was in Union-controlled territory.

120   "Pierpoint": The spelling of the governor's name varies not only according to whether there is an "i" in the second syllable (*point* instead of *pont*) but also whether the "e" and the "i" are reversed in the first. The governor's messages to Lincoln are signed "Peirpoint," which evoked what may be a faint glint of humor in the notes to Lincoln's *Collected Works,* perhaps the only humor in the eight volumes that does not come from Lincoln's own hand. The note on page 511 of volume 4 on a letter from the governor reads: "The letter is signed 'F. H. Peirpont,' and this spelling is followed throughout the present work rather than 'Pierpoint' or 'Pierpont' on the assumption that the governor is entitled to spell his name as he chooses, other considerations notwithstanding." But then a scholar who had dealings with the governor's daughter spelled it "Pierpont," claiming "he himself adopted that spelling in later life." See Smith, *Borderland,* pp. 214, 215. One can find three, possibly four, spellings spread across the materials about the first days of West Virginia. One should note, however, that Peir-Pier-point-pont was never governor of West Virginia but only of the state of Virginia as Restored, with the capital first in Wheeling and then in Alexandria.

120   by the end of 1861 had raised many more troops: Smith, *Borderland,* p. 217.

121   "We all know—everybody knows": *N&H,* 6:309.

121 "It is said that the admission of West-Virginia is secession": When he read through the cabinet opinions, he made marginal corrections that *narrowed* the issue. When Chase mentioned states "formed" within the boundaries of an old state, Lincoln noted that to "admit" is not to "form." In other words, the question that came to the Congress and now to the president was only whether to *admit* an *already formed* state. And then when both Chase and Seward mentioned the consent by "the state" to this action, he put in the margin the correction that the Constitution specifies that the consent shall be by the *legislature,* which, interpreting what he is thinking, we may say, is more specific than "the state." And he is picking these nits because he has his own answers to the objections to the legislature of "restored" Virginia. Writing this out on the last day of 1862, one would think with some haste, on the day before the huge event of his Emancipation Proclamation, he gave his opinion on the statehood bill:

> The consent of the Legislature of Virginia is constitutionally necessary to the bill for the admission of West-Virginia becoming a law. A body claiming to be such Legislature has given its consent. We can not well deny that it is such, unless we do so upon the outside knowledge that the body was chosen at elections, in which a majority of the qualified voters of Virginia did not participate. But it is a universal practice in the popular elections . . . to give no legal consideration whatever to those who do not choose to vote.

The nonvoters in this case are not just undutiful citizens; they are opponents of the government:

> [T]hey were not merely neglectful of their rights under, and duty to, this government, but were also engaged in open rebellion against it . . . Can this government stand, if it indulges constitutional constructions by which men in open rebellion against it, are to be accounted, man for man, the equals of those who maintain their loyalty to it?

122 "Kentucky will furnish no troops": *OR,* ser. 3, vol. 1, p. 70.

122 "A public meeting of leading citizens": *N&H,* 4:228.

124 "I should have dispatched": *OR,* ser. 1, vol. 4, p. 185.

124 "I had information": Ibid.

124 "[T]he people of Kentucky": *OR,* ser. 1, vol. 1, pp. 185–86.

125 "General Polk has been ordered": *OR,* ser. 1, vol. 4, p. 189.

125 "General Polk: the necessity justifies the action": *OR,* ser. 1, vol. 4, p. 181.

125 "Governor Harris and others": *OR,* ser. 1, vol. 4, p. 188.

125 "Kentucky has been invaded": Smith, *Borderland,* p. 301.

128 Lincoln responded by sending: The exchange between Frémont and Lincoln can be found in *CW,* 4:506, 517. See the notes.

129 "I was so assured": Lincoln to Orville Browning, September 22, 1861, *CW,* 4:532.

129 Lincoln took comfort: The objection to his order to Frémont that most surprised Lincoln came from his old friend Orville Browning, now (since his appointment in June to succeed Stephen Douglas) senator from Illinois. Browning was by no means one of the shrill whistles of radicalism; on the contrary—on most issues at most times he was

more conservative than Lincoln. But here he was, endorsing Frémont's order as a good move, approved by all loyal citizens of the West and Northwest. Lincoln took time to write a careful letter to Browning setting forth his argument against Frémont's order. One part of what he wrote had to do with constitutional propriety, and since just one year later Lincoln would himself emancipate slaves by proclamation, we may postpone that section of the letter for later treatment. But the gravamen of the letter had to do with political effect and with Kentucky, implicitly with timing. This is the letter in which he wrote that "to lose Kentucky is nearly the same as to lose the whole game." But the Union did not lose Kentucky.

130 "the cause of the Union [in Kentucky]": Smith, *Borderland,* p. 293.

130 "Fortunately for the national government": Ibid., p. 294.

131 "each party WITHIN": Lincoln address at Peoria, October 16, 1854.

132 "While anti-slavery men were the first to organize migration": David Potter, *The Impending Crisis* (New York: Harper Torchbooks, 1976), p. 200.

132 a short, intense, no-nonsense Connecticut Yankee: General Nathaniel Lyon, in the view of his supporters the "Savior of Missouri," came from Connecticut, went to West Point, and fought in Mexico; up to that point he supported the Democrats. But then he was assigned to Fort Riley in Kansas, under invasion by Missouri bushwhackers, and switched his politics to become a strong antisecession Republican. Jim Lane also came to Kansas as a Democrat and switched under the impact of border attacks.

133 "Sir: The President of the United States directs": *OR,* ser. 1, vol. 1, p. 675.

134 On May 29 Blair handed Harney: *OR,* ser. 1, vol. 3, p. 381. A certain confusion about command had prevailed through April and May. The official records in a footnote at one point say, with quite uncharacteristic inexactitude, "[Harney] had relinquished command April 23 pursuant to orders of April 21, and Captain Nathaniel Lyon, second U.S. Infantry, seems to have exercised command during General Harney's absence." Very rarely does one read, in the official records of the American armed forces, the puzzled inexactitude that an officer "seems to have exercised command." After May 29 Lyon, now lifted up as a brigadier general of the volunteers, undoubtedly exercised command.

136 "Lincoln's policies were fairly successful": William E. Gienapp, "Abraham Lincoln and the Border States," *Journal of the Abraham Lincoln Association* 13 (1992), p. 46.

136 "When questioned about military repression": Mark E. Neely, Jr., *The Fate of Liberty: Abraham Lincoln and Civil Liberties* (New York: Oxford University Press, 1991), pp. 49–50.

136 "With the matters of removing": Lincoln to Gen. John M. Schofield, October 1, 1863, *CW,* 6:492.

137 "Tonight, Mother": Clark Clifford, *Counsel to the President—a Memoir* (New York: Random House, 1991), p. 73.

138 Missouri had a toxic mixture: Freehling, *South vs. South,* p. 55: "No Civil War area endured worse terrorizing. Some afflicted Missourians blamed the disorder on the indiscreet Lyon . . . but take away the tempestuous Connecticut Yankee and no becalmed Missouri would have emerged." And even more certainly, it would not have emerged just from altering the decisions of a harried president to support Lyon.

138 Broad historical treatments: William Gienapp, in "Border States," notes and objects to this misleading feature of Civil War surveys.

CHAPTER SEVEN. THE MORAL MEANING OF THE UNION AND THE WAR

The Message to the Special Session on July 4, 1861, which has a central place in this chapter, is found in *CW,* 4:421–41. The notes are important to show changes as Lincoln wrote it. Douglas Wilson's *Lincoln's Sword* (New York: Alfred A. Knopf, 2006) gives an illuminating discussion of its composition.

140   "I consider the central idea": Michael Burlingame and John R. Turner Ettlinger, eds., *Inside Lincoln's White House: The Complete Civil War Diary of John Hay* (Carbondale: Southern Illinois University Press, 1997), p. 20.

140   "he [Lincoln] remarked that the real question involved": Michael Burlingame, ed., *With Lincoln in the White House: Letters, Memoranda, and Other Writings of John G. Nicolay, 1860–1865* (Carbondale: Southern Illinois University Press, 2000), p. 41.

141   "He is engaged in constant thought": Burlingame and Ettlinger, *Inside,* p. 20.

141   "perfunctory manner": James G. Randall, *Lincoln the President* (New York: Da Capo Press, 1977), vol. 1, pt. 1, p. 383.

142   "an exalted commentary on fundamentals": Ibid., vol. 1, pt. 1, p. 381.

146   "a sweeping practical negation": John G. Nicolay, *The Outbreak of Rebellion* (New York: Da Capo Press, 1995), p. 41.

147   "sugar-coated": These quotations are also from Lincoln's July 4, 1861, Message to Congress, *CW.*

148   "merely asserted a right": Jefferson Davis's Inagural Address, February 18, 1861, *AP.*

148   If the rebels claimed to have: John Hay, in his diary for May 8, 1861, reported a conversation about Jefferson Davis's "manifesto" presented to the Confederate Congress that ignored "all mention of the right of revolution" and confined his defense of his position "to the reserved right of a state to secede." Hay commented that Davis thereby impeded his "claim upon the recognition of the world." Nations that would recognize new governments that have a de facto existence by virtue of a revolution would *not* recognize one that claimed existence on the basis of "the constitution of the government against which it rebels." That would seem to be an *internal* dispute, a matter of conflicting interpretations with which no outside power should interfere. Hay wrote that Davis was anxious to satisfy the "restless consciences" of the border states, where, he implies, the sugarcoating of constitutional legitimacy was particularly important.

148   "Any people anywhere": Abraham Lincoln, "Speech in United States House of Representatives: The War with Mexico," January 12, 1848, *AL Papers.*

150   "My paramount object in this struggle": One can argue that the significance of Lincoln's letter to Greeley in its own time was almost exactly the opposite to its meaning in a modern seminar. That he would save the Union with slavery was not news—that would have been taken for granted, even expected, in a time when slavery still existed. That he would, on his own executive decision, abolish slavery, if doing so would save the Union—that was the news. And when he wrote the letter to Greeley, he had the preliminary emancipation proclamation in his desk.

151   "the one for empire": John M. Taylor, *William Henry Seward: Lincoln's Right Hand* (Washington, D.C.: Brassey's, 1991), p. 176.

152 "an *even* start": Douglas Wilson, *Lincoln's Sword* (New York: Alfred A. Knopf, 2006), p. 98.

153 "I happen temporarily to occupy": He made a similar statement to yet another Ohio regiment on August 31.

153 When he was elected—they revolted: South Carolina's declaration of the causes for its secession, with its many echoes of the Declaration of Independence, named the election of Lincoln as one such cause. It then went on to condemn voting by blacks in some northern states:

> This sectional combination for the submersion of the Constitution, has been aided in some of the States by elevating to citizenship, persons who, by the supreme law of the land, are incapable of becoming citizens; and their votes have been used to inaugurate a new policy, hostile to the South, and destructive of its beliefs and safety.
>
> On the 4th day of March next, this party will take possession of the Government. It has announced that the South shall be excluded from the common territory, that the judicial tribunals shall be made sectional, and that a war must be waged against slavery until it shall cease throughout the United States.
>
> The guaranties of the Constitution will then no longer exist; the equal rights of the States will be lost. The slaveholding States will no longer have the power of self-government, or self-protection, and the Federal Government will have become their enemy.

"Declaration of the Immediate Causes Which Induce and Justify the Secession of South Carolina from the Federal Union," December 24, 1860, *AP*.

CHAPTER EIGHT. BULL RUN AND OTHER DEFEATS: LINCOLN'S RESOLVE

155 "inexpressibly bitter": John G. Nicolay, *The Outbreak of Rebellion* (New York: Da Capo Press, 1995), p. 208.

155 "The solemn midnight March": Michael Burlingame, ed., *Lincoln's Journalist* (Carbondale: Southern Illinois University Press, 1998), pp. 75–76.

156 "a confused mob": *OR*, ser. 1, vol. 2, p. 316.

156 "Firing more in the distance": One can follow the wires Lincoln received in Manassas Virginia Telegraph, July 21, 1861 (Dispatches), *AL Papers*.

156 "We passed Bull Run": *OR*, ser. 1, vol. 2, p. 316.

157 "The men having thrown away": Ibid.

157 "He listened in silence": *N&H*, 4:353.

157 "General McDowell's army": *OR*, ser. 1, vol. 2, p. 747.

158 "it is to be hoped": Burlingame, *Lincoln's Journalist*, p. 76.

158 The novice in the executive mansion: Lincoln would be criticized for the breakdown of discipline because in his July 4 Message to Congress he placed the "unanimous firmness" of common soldiers and sailors—"to the last man, so far as known"—in invidious contrast to the large numbers of officers and had "proved false to the hand which had pampered them"; he even pictured the common soldier as successfully resisting those "whose commands, but an hour before, they obeyed." Critics sug-

gested that the president implied that only the common soldier could be trusted and "his officer was a leader not entitled to confidence." But it is difficult to believe that a short passage in the middle of a long presidential document could have had any such effect on the actual battlefield.

159   "You are green": Quoted often in biographies and histories. See, for example, James M. McPherson, *Battle Cry of Freedom: The Civil War Era* (New York: Oxford University Press, 1988), p. 336, with citations.

159   "A Commander-in-Chief": James A. Rawley, *Turning Points of the Civil War,* 2nd ed. (Lincoln: University of Nebraska Press, 1989), p. 54.

159   "An old soldier feels safe": *OR,* ser. 1, vol. 2, p. 334.

160   "On the eve of the battle": *OR,* ser. 1, vol. 2, p. 325.

160   "Many of the volunteers": *OR,* ser. 1, vol. 2, p. 316.

161   "the largest citizens' army": Rawley, *Turning Points,* p. 58.

162   "THE NATION'S WAR CRY": Harry J. Maihafer, *War of Words: Abraham Lincoln and the Civil War Press* (Washington, D.C.: Brassey's, 2001), p. 42.

163   "[I]t is certain that the talk": Walt Whitman, *Specimen Days* (Boston: David R. Godine, 1971), chap. 20, online at www.bartleby.com/229/1020.html.

163   "All the forenoon": Burlingame, *Lincoln's Journalist,* p. 78.

164   And so began a sleepless night: Nicolay and Hay do not report any expression of distress on Lincoln's part but twenty-eight years later an assistant to the Indiana Republican who had been appointed superintendent of public printing, John D. Defrees, sent Nicolay a report saying that he had often heard his boss tell about finding Lincoln pacing the floor on the day after the Bull Run defeat, saying, "John, if hell is not any more than this, it has no terror for me." *AL Papers.*

165   "[W]hatever returns": Whitman, *Specimen Days,* chap. 21. Whitman wrote about the battle itself: "All battles, and their results, are far more matters of accident than is generally thought; but this was throughout a casualty, a chance. Each side supposed it had won, till the last moment. One had, in point of fact, just the same right to be routed as the other. By a fiction, or series of fictions, the national forces at the last moment exploded in a panic and fled from the field."

CHAPTER NINE. ON HOLDING McCLELLAN'S HORSE

169   "least militarized": John Keegan, *A History of Warfare* (New York: Alfred A. Knopf, 1994), p. 356.

171   He became proud of the men: Defenders of McClellan, in the long future of endless debates about the Civil War, could even claim that the army with which Grant would finally defeat Lee, in 1864–65, was the army that McClellan had shaped back in 1861–62.

171   "I almost think": Stephen W. Sears, ed., *The Civil War Papers of George B. McClellan: Selected Correspondence, 1860–1865* (New York: Da Capo Press, 1992), p. 70.

171   "You are aware": Bruce Catton, *Terrible Swift Sword* (New York: Pocket Books, 1967), p. 77.

171   "Who would have thought": Sears, *Papers of McClellan,* pp. 70–71.

171   "perfect imbecile": Scott was a "perfect imbecile" who "understands nothing, appreciates nothing, and is ever in my way" (August 8); "the great obstacle . . . either a trai-

tor or incompetent" (August 9—the previous day either "dotard or a traitor"); "the most dangerous antagonist I have" (August 15). All from various letters in Sears, *Papers of McClellan*.

172　"who has treated me with distinguished kindness and courtesy": Winfield Scott to Simon Cameron, October 31, 1861. *N&H*, 4:465.

172　"I can do it all": Michael Burlingame and John R. Turner Ettlinger, eds., *Inside Lincoln's White House: The Complete Civil War Diary of John Hay* (Carbondale: Southern Illinois University Press, 1997), p. 30.

172　"the most stupid idiot": "[T]he cowardice of the Presdt, the vileness of Seward, & the rascality of Cameron—Welles is an old woman—Bates an old fool" (October 31, 1861). All from various letters in Sears, *Papers of McClellan*. One historian has interpreted McClellan's defect, in the categories of modern psychology, as "paranoid personality disorder." The description includes: "individuals who suffer from this affliction interpret actions of other people as deliberately threatening or demeaning. They ponder innocuous and insignificant remarks and find hidden, unintended meanings that affront them . . . Mistrust rests at the core." Joseph Glatthaar, *Partners in Command: Relationships Between Leaders in the Civil War* (New York: Simon & Schuster, 1993), p. 237.

172　"my enemies are crushed": McClellan to his wife, September 7, 1862, Sears, *Papers of McClellan*, p. 438.

173　Shortly after McClellan was made general in chief: Burlingame and Turner, *Inside*, p. 32.

173　"Never mind": Ibid., p. 289.

174　"the enemy probably have": Sears, *Papers of McClellan*, p. 100.

174　In fact, the peak strength: Although later inflations of the opposing armies would be supported by intelligence, usually mistaken, from Allan Pinkerton—an acquaintance of McClellan from his railroad days—this initial mistake was all his own. The president and the secretary of war had no independent source of information with which to contradict McClellan's estimates. In anticipation of a problem not unknown in the superpower days to come, McClellan could get "intelligence" to tell him what he wanted to hear.

174　"With the figures for his own forces": Kenneth P. Williams, *Lincoln Finds a General: A Military Study of the Civil War*, 5 vols. (New York: Macmillan, 1949), 1:124.

174　"The normal sick": Ibid., 1:130.

174　This mathematical wizardry: McClellan's legerdemain with numbers was implicated in the hottest point of dispute with Lincoln, both at the time and among historians looking back. Departing for the peninsula, he promised to leave sufficient troops to protect Washington, but he manipulated the numbers and effectively left Washington undefended. When Lincoln discovered what McClellan had done, he held back McDowell's first corps to be kept in front of Washington to protect the capital instead of allowing it to go to the peninsula. McClellan was indignant. When he was the commander defending Washington, that defense was the absolute top priority; when he wasn't, it wasn't.

174　"The president told me": James G. Randall, ed., *The Diary of Orville Hickman Browning*, 2 vols. (Springfield: Illinois State Historical Library, 1925), 1:563.

175　"such an overwhelming strength": Sears, *Papers of McClellan*, p. 75.

176 One distinguished military historian: T. Harry Williams, *Lincoln and His Generals* (New York: Alfred A. Knopf, 1952), pp. 65–68.

176 "A Massachusetts officer noted": Catton, *Sword*, pp. 416–17.

177 "Soldiers of the Army of the Potomac!": Sears, *Papers of McClellan*, p. 211.

177 "promenade": Margaret Leech, *Reveille in Washington, 1860–1865* (New York: Harper & Brothers, 1941), p. 133.

178 "He liked siege warfare": Williams, *Lincoln and Generals*, p. 90.

178 "indefinite procrastination": The whole telegram from Lincoln is: "Your call for Parrot guns from Washington alarms me—chiefly because it argues indefinite procrastination. Is anything to be done?" May 1, 1861, *CW*, 5:203.

179 "It is characteristic of him": *N&H*, 5:414–15.

179 One can count in Lincoln's *Collected Works*: Sears counts fifty-three, apparently starting or ending some day different from my pick. In any case, there was a large number of messages, including, as Sears remarks, "some of the most masterful Lincoln ever wrote."

179 "By delay the enemy": Lincoln's quotation comes from his excellent letter of April 9. The authority is the English general Colin Ballard, the title of whose book tells the story: *Military Genius of Abraham Lincoln;* quoted in Williams, *Lincoln Finds a General,* 1:166.

180 McClellan's long telegram to Stanton: *OR*, ser. 1, vol. 11 (pt. I), p. 61. The telegram was sent at 12:20 a.m. June 28. Lincoln responded later that day.

181 "The time has come": Sears, *Papers of McClellan*, p. 344.

181 "This . . . War . . . should be conducted": McClellan to Lincoln, July 7, 1862, ibid., pp. 344–45.

183 "had General McClellan willed it": Stephen W. Sears, *George B. McClellan: The Young Napoleon* (New York: Ticknor & Fields, 1988), p. 253.

183 "it really seemed to him": Burlingame and Ettlinger, *Inside*, p. 37.

183 "Mr. Lincoln certainly had the defects": *N&H*, 6:28–29.

184 "for my sake": Sears, *Papers of McClellan*, p. 427.

184 "There was a more . . . desponding feeling": Gideon Welles, *Diary of Gideon Welles,* 3 vols. (Boston: Houghton Mifflin, 1911), 1:105.

185 "Again I have been called upon": Sears, *Papers of McClellan*, p. 435.

185 "I have all the plans": In McClellan's enthusiasm about finding Lee's order he added, in the War Department telegram, "my respects to Mrs. Lincoln. Received most enthusiastically by the ladies. Will send you trophies." Military historian Kenneth Williams writes that when Lincoln received this telegram, "on the critical morning of September 14, it is safe to assume that he did not hurry to Mrs. Lincoln to present his general's regards, or send a messenger to Mrs. McClellan with the thrilling news that her husband had been well received by the ladies of Frederick. Nor did he probably give much thought to the promised trophies." Williams, *Lincoln Finds a General*, 1:170–71.

185 For McClellan to take advantage: Sears's description is most telling. "He [McClellan] reacted as he had before Richmond in June: realizing it was now his decisions that would decide the fate of the nation, and borne down by the added responsibility, he became more sensitive to risk than ever." Sears, *Young Napoleon*, pp. 283–84.

185 "[I]t is to be hoped": Williams, *Lincoln Finds a General*, 1:371.

185 "our victory [is] complete": McClellan to Halleck and to Mary Ellen McClellan, both on September 19, 1862. Sears, *Papers of McClellan*, pp. 469–70.

186 "firm steady and honest support": Ibid., p. 493.

186 "We are about to be photographed": Quoted under the front picture in Stephen W. Sears, "Lincoln and McClellan," in Gabor Boritt, ed., *Lincoln's Generals* (Urbana: University of Illinois Press, 1988), p. 2.

187 From a hilltop he and his friends saw: *N&H*, 6:175.

187 That order was issued: "I am instructed to telegraph you as follows: The President directs that you cross the Potomac and give battle to the enemy or drive him south. Your army must move now while the roads are good." *OR*, ser. 1, vol. 19 (pt. II), p. 72.

187 "The dispatch opened a thirty-day war": Sears, *Young Napoleon*, p. 332.

188 "I have just read your dispatch": Lincoln's telegram and McClellan's response can be found in *CW*, 5:474 (with the note) and *OR*, ser. 1, vol. 19 (pt. II), p. 485. The "three day dustup"—the exchange of telegrams between Lincoln and McClellan about the tired horses—continues in *OR*, ser. 1, vol. 19 (pt. II), pp. 490–91. The last exchange—about filling up the regiments—is in *OR*, ser. 1, vol. 19 (pt. II), pp. 497–98.

190 "I began to fear": Quoted in Burlingame and Ettlinger, *Inside*, p. 232.

190 "tried long enough": Lincoln to Francis Blair, in Sears, *Young Napoleon*, p. 338.

191 "an exceptionally unforgiving boss": Eliot A. Cohen, *Supreme Command: Soldiers, Statesmen, and Leadership in Wartime* (New York: Free Press, 2002), p. 21. In support of his contention that Lincoln was an "unforgiving" boss, Cohen lists the sequence of commanders of the Army of the Potomac and their brief months of service. But one cannot accept the complex history of that sequence in a suddenly created army in an expanding war fought by an unmilitary people—each change with its particular reason—as evidence that Lincoln was "ruthless" or "unforgiving." The case of McClellan certainly argues the opposite.

191 "Well . . . put yourself in my place": Helen Nicolay, *Personal Traits of Abraham Lincoln* (New York: Century, 1912), p. 255.

192 "[T]he most compelling reason": Catton, *Sword*, p. 421.

CHAPTER TEN. THE *TRENT* AND A DECENT RESPECT
FOR THE OPINIONS OF MANKIND

194 "Probably no two men in the entire South": Charles Francis Adams, "The *Trent* Affair," *American Historical Review* 17, no. 3 (1912), p. 541.

195 "an affront to the British flag": Earl Russell, quoted in Bruce Catton, *Terrible Swift Sword* (New York: Pocket Books, 1967), p. 104.

195 It was even rumored: Ibid.

196 "the utter absence of any acquaintance with the subject": David Herbert Donald, *Charles Sumner*, 2 vols. (New York: Da Capo Press, 1996), 2:18.

199 "This paper is for your own guidance": Seward's draft, with Lincoln's changes, is printed in *N&H*, 4:270–75.

201 "there will be no war": Donald, *Sumner*, 2:36.

201 "The President's usual cool judgment": *N&H*, 5:25.

201 "a well-known writer": We learn from James Randall that the writer was a historian named Benson J. Lossing, who "participated in an interview" with Lincoln and who wrote *A Pictorial History of the Civil War*. Randall's account is in James G. Randall,

Lincoln the President (New York: Da Capo Press, 1977), vol. 1, pt. 2, p. 41. Nicolay and Hay's use of the quotation is in *N&H,* 5:25.

201 "The United States did not have": Adams, "*Trent* Affair," p. 544.

201 "We must stick to American principles": *N&H,* 5:25–26.

202 "intended no affront": Lincoln's draft response to the *Trent* affair is in *CW,* 5:62–64.

202 "two wars on his hands": Randall, *Lincoln the President,* vol. 1, pt. 1, p. 41, quoting a letter from R. M. Mason to Amos Lawrence.

204 "What a magnificent move": Adams, "*Trent* Affair," p. 558.

205 "Though Lincoln's part": Randall, *Lincoln the President,* vol. 1, pt. 2, p. 50.

205 "the original mistake": *N&H,* 6:49.

206 "The vessel was English": *N&H,* 6:55.

206 "In reviewing this long correspondence": *N&H,* 6:51.

207 "grasped the main facts": Colin Ballard quotes another authority who says, "[M]ilitary genius shows itself first in character, and, second, in the application of the grand principles of war." And then he continues: "The *application* of grand principles—not the mere knowledge of them . . . like the poet, the strategist is born, not made, and Lincoln had the character of a born strategist. He could not apply the grand principles because he had never had an opportunity to study them; but instinctively he grasped the main facts and gave them their proper value. It is undeniable that a knowledge of the technical side of war would have been of use to him; it would have helped him to pick up the threads more quickly and surely; it would have enabled him to detect the weak points in his own forces. But theoretical knowledge is like a powerful drug, of great worth in the hands of a wise man but a deadly poison when misapplied. . . . The mules of Frederick the Great went through twenty campaigns but still remained mules.' There have been other mules since the days of Frederick, but Abraham Lincoln was not one of them." Colin R. Ballard, *The Military Genius of Abraham Lincoln* (Cleveland: World, 1952), pp. 8–9.

208 "[I]t remains one of the unsolved mysteries": Mark E. Neely, Jr., *The Last Best Hope of Earth: Abraham Lincoln and the Promise of America* (Cambridge, Mass.: Harvard University Press, 1993), p. 114.

208 "how unhesitatingly we all use cotton and sugar": Lincoln's annual message, December 1, 1862, *CW,* 5:531–32.

208 "The American Civil War was becoming": Catton, *Sword,* p. 377.

208 "Jefferson Davis and other leaders": Gladstone's "notorious speech" at Newcastle is quoted and discussed in Randall, *Lincoln the President,* vol. 1, pt. 2, pp. 342–43.

209 A series of "remarkable meetings": Randall, *Lincoln the President,* vol. 1, pt. 2, p. 177.

209 "Lincoln himself began a campaign": David Herbert Donald, *Lincoln* (New York: Simon & Schuster, 1995), p. 415.

209 "I know and deeply deplore": Abraham Lincoln to the Workingmen of Manchester, England, January 19, 1863, in *CW,* 6:63–65.

210 "the family of Christian and civilized nations": Lincoln's draft is printed in *CW,* 6:176–77, with a valuable note.

211 "I can not believe that civilization": John Bright, extract from speech [copy in Lincoln's hand], December 18, 1862, *AL Papers.*

CHAPTER ELEVEN. TOO VAST FOR MALICIOUS DEALING

212 called the president an "idiot": Stephen W. Sears, ed., *The Civil War Papers of George B. McClellan: Selected Correspondence, 1860–1865* (New York: Da Capo Press, 1992), pp. 85, 106, 135.

212 he was "concealed": Ibid., p. 113.

213 "imbecility": Stanton wrote of "the painful imbecility of Lincoln" (to John Dix in New York, June 11, 1860) and stated that "the imbecility of the administration culminated in the catastrophe" of Bull Run (to ex-President Buchanan in retirement in Pennsylvania).

213 "While men are striving nobly": Benjamin P. Thomas and Harold M. Hyman, eds., *Stanton: The Life and Times of Lincoln's Secretary of War* (New York: Alfred A. Knopf, 1962), p. 170.

213 "[B]ecause Lincoln was a great man": Ibid., p. 381.

213 "[T]he good of the country": Sears, *Papers of McClellan*, p. 515.

214 "had been profoundly concerned at the present state of affairs": Salmon P. Chase, *Inside Lincoln's Cabinet: The Civil War Diaries of Salmon P. Chase*, ed. David Herbert Donald (New York: Longmans, Green, 1954), p. 95.

215 "contemplated authority to Commanders": Ibid.

215 "[i]n an orderly manner": *OR*, ser. 1, vol. 11 (pt. III), pp. 362–63. The order was issued by Stanton for the president.

215 "directly the reverse instructions": George B. McClellan to his wife, August 8, 1862, in Sears, *Papers of McClellan*, p. 388.

215 "should be conducted up on the highest principles": *OR*, ser. 1, vol. 11 (pt. III), p. 364.

215 "When forced to choose": Harry S. Stout, *Upon the Altar of the Nation: A Moral History of the American Civil War* (New York: Viking, 2006), p. 138.

217 "If the same battle were to be fought": This oft-quoted and sometimes-disputed comment by Stoddard appears and is discussed in Michael Burlingame, ed., *Dispatches from Lincoln's White House* (Lincoln: University of Nebraska Press, 2002), p. xv.

220 Republican congressman Schuyler Colfax: Colfax felt he might have been passed over for a cabinet post because he not only had held out for Seward against Lincoln at the 1860 Republican convention but, back in 1858, had committed the far worse sin, in the eyes of Illinois Republicans, of joining in the suggestion by easterners that it might be all right to drop their opposition to Senator Stephen Douglas. If you were Douglas's designated Republican opponent, that surely did not seem to be a good idea. So did Lincoln now take the opportunity to get his own back by passing over Colfax? President Lincoln, with the weight of a nation abruptly dropped on his shoulders, nevertheless took time to write to Colfax to insist that this was not so.

220 "You have more of that feeling": Michael Burlingame and John R. Turner Ettlinger, eds., *Inside Lincoln's White House: The Complete Civil War Diary of John Hay* (Carbondale: Southern Illinois University Press, 1997), pp. 244–55.

220 "rather the mildest cussing": Ibid., p. 100.

226 "What would you do in my position?"; "I am in no boastful mood": Abraham Lincoln to Cuthbert Bullitt, July 28, 1862, *CW*, 5:344–46.

227 "I am a patient man": Lincoln to Reverdy Johnson, July 26, 1862, *CW*, 5:343.

227 "Lincoln had demonstrated from the start": Mark E. Neely, Jr., *The Last Best Hope of Earth: Abraham Lincoln and the Promise of America* (Cambridge, Mass.: Harvard University Press, 1993), pp. 74–75.

227 "[e]xecutive skill and vigor are rare qualities": "The President is the best of us, but he needs constant and assiduous cooperation." William H. Seward to Frances A. Seward, June 5, 1861, in Doris Kearns Goodwin, *Team of Rivals: The Political Genius of Abraham Lincoln* (New York: Simon & Schuster, 2005), p. 590.

228 "It is due to the President to say": W. Seward to F. Seward, March 17, 1861, ibid., p. 575. One of the great backstories of the early days of the war, well told in Goodwin's *Team of Rivals,* is Seward's growing appreciation of Lincoln.

228 "the vast and long-enduring consequences": Lincoln to Rev. Alexander Reed, February 22, 1863, *CW,* 6:114.

A SECOND INTRODUCTION.
LINCOLN'S NATION AMONG THE NATIONS

233 "expectations that the peculiar institution would wither away": "During the years preceding the Civil War, slavery, and the Southern economy that was based on it, seemed to be thriving as never before, and expectations that the peculiar institution would wither away had themselves largely withered away. On the eve of the war, it seemed as if Southern slavery would survive for a long time." Peter Kolchin, *American Slavery, 1619–1877* (New York: Hill & Wang, 1993), pp. 98–99.

CHAPTER TWELVE. I FELT IT MY DUTY TO REFUSE

I wrote this chapter before I knew that Ron Soodalter was at work on the Gordon case. When C-SPAN carried a presentation I made of this chapter, I met him and also Karen Needles, an archivist working on the Gordon case, who generously helped me. Soodalter's book, *Hanging Captain Gordon: The Life and Trial of an American Slave Trader* (New York: Atria Books, 2006), gives an excellent account of Gordon and his case in the setting of the terrible history of the slave trade. He graciously read this chapter and improved it but is not to be blamed for errors that remain.

236 "I have sometimes told him": Francis B. Carpenter, *The Inner Life of Abraham Lincoln: Six Months at the White House* (1866; repr. Lincoln: University of Nebraska Press, 1995), pp. 68–69.

236 "Clemency invoked by": Record Group 204, Stack Area 230, Row 40, Compartment 27, Shelf 2, "Docket of Pardon Cases 1853–1923," vol. 3 of 81, PI-87 Entry 7, *AL Papers.*

236 "he was met by his wife": Ron Soodalter, in *Hanging Captain Gordon,* includes several indications of the devotion of the Gordons (for example, on pp. 216–17) and sympathetic pictures of the troubles of Elizabeth Gordon.

236 a woman named Rhoda White: When Lincoln's son Willie was ill with the typhoid fever from which he would die, Rhoda White would write to the president: "I would not intrude upon the sanctity of your sick room and upon your hours of grief but for the sake of Mercy, and for the sake of an afflicted Mother and wife who are bowed

down with sorrow and look to God and to you to lift the heavy burden they are suffering under." Rhoda White to Abraham Lincoln, February 17, 1862, *AL Papers*.

237　The accused's neighbors in Portland: Petitions to the President of the United States (two), from Portland, Maine, dated December 1861, 1861 Executive Clemency files, Record A, p. 391, *AL Papers*.

237　"His wife, an interesting woman": Rhoda E. White to Abraham Lincoln, February 17, 1862, *AL Papers*.

237　"I have felt it to be my duty": Stay of Execution for Nathaniel Gordon, February 4, 1862, *AL Papers*.

238　"Thus, the thing is hid away": *CW*, 2:274.

238　"the first action against the trade": Warren S. Howard, *American Slavers and the Federal Law* (Berkeley: University of California Press, 1963), p. 3.

239　And that almost unanimous act: Ibid., p. 26.

239　"Indeed, for all the talk": Peter Kolchin, *American Slavery, 1619–1877* (New York: Hill & Wang, 1993), p. 63.

239　"S. Carolina and Georgia were inflexible": Madison's letter to Jefferson about the Constitutional Convention, including his remark about the inflexibility of South Carolina and Georgia, was dated October 24, 1787, and is printed in Robert A. Rutland and W. M. E. Rachal, eds., *The Papers of James Madison,* 17 vols. (Chicago: University of Chicago Press, 1977), 10:206–19.

239　"It is as though the Framers": Don E. Fehrenbacher, *Slavery, Law, and Politics: The Dred Scott Case in Historical Perspective* (New York: Oxford University Press, 1981), p. 15.

240　"Twenty years will produce": Max Ferrand, ed., *The Records of the Federal Convention of 1787,* 4 vols. (New Haven: Yale University Press, 1966), 2:415.

240　Those few slavers who were caught: I count six full pardons in the list of criminal prosecutions under the slave trade acts from 1837 to 1862 in Howard's *American Slavers* appendix (pp. 224–35). None of these, of course, was a capital case.

240　"At the Constitutional Convention": Fehrenbacher, *Slavery, Law,* p. 15.

241　"It has been estimated": Soodalter, *Hanging,* pp. 21–22.

241　"I got them by barter": Quoted in James A. Rawley, *Turning Points of the Civil War,* 2nd ed. (Lincoln: University of Nebraska Press, 1989), p. 54, and Soodalter, *Hanging,* p. 1.

241　"In 1781, running short of water": Soodalter tells about this outrage in *Hanging,* p. 21.

242　Henry Wise, a leading Virginia politician: Howard, *American Slavers,* pp. 11–12.

243　And the states' rights interpretation: W. E. B. DuBois, *The Suppression of the African Slave Trade to the United States of America, 1638–1870* (1896; repr. Baton Rouge: Louisiana State University Press, 1969), pp. 188–91.

243　"lying on their right sides": Howard, *American Slavers,* p. 194.

244　"thinks it a pity": Ibid., pp. 195–96.

246　"you are soon to pass": Stuart Lutz, "Lincoln Let Him Hang," *Civil War Times,* March 1998, p. 37.

246　"For more than forty years": This quote and those that follow are from Dean's letter in Gilbert Dean to Abraham Lincoln, February 18, 1862, *AL Papers*.

246 "Captain Nathaniel Gordon is under sentence": Edward Dicey, *Spectator of America* (Chicago: Quadrangle Books, 1971), p. 59.

248 "[Y]ou have amongst you": *CW*, 2:264.

248 "If it is a *sacred* right": *CW*, 2:267.

249 "prolongs the time": Edward Bates to Abraham Lincoln, February 19, 1862, *AL Papers.*

249 "whereas, it has seemed to me probable": Stay of Execution, *CW*, 5:128–29.

250 The authorities moved the execution: Dicey, *Spectator*, pp. 59–60.

251 "It is a subject of gratulation": *CW*, 5:46–47.

253 "It was held in a rented room": Howard, *American Slavers*, p. 63.

CHAPTER THIRTEEN. IN GIVING FREEDOM TO THE SLAVE,
WE ASSURE FREEDOM TO THE FREE

255 That conviction ran so deep that even the Anti-Slavery Society: "We fully and unanimously recognize the sovereignty of each State, to legislate exclusively on the subject of the slavery which is tolerated within its limits; we concede that Congress, under the present national compact, has no right to interfere with any of the slave States, in relation to this momentous subject: But we maintain that Congress has a right, and is solemnly bound, to suppress the domestic slave trade between the several States, and to abolish slavery in those portions of our territory which the Constitution has placed under its exclusive jurisdiction." American Anti-Slavery Society, "Declaration of Sentiments" (1833), in Louis Ruchames, ed., *The Abolitionists: A Collection of Their Writings* (New York: G. P. Putnam's Sons, 1963), p. 78.

255 the cabinet members all affirmed it: Secretary Welles, expressing his surprise when Lincoln mentioned his proclamation in mid-July, wrote, "Every member of the Cabinet . . . including the President, considered it a local, domestic question appertaining to the states respectively." Gideon Welles, *Diary of Gideon Welles*, 3 vols. (Boston: Houghton Mifflin, 1911), 1:71.

256 "a drop of the creature": Phillips in his letter to his wife, Ann, probably botched Lincoln's story; he was not a man well attuned to Lincoln's humorous style. He had Lincoln saying the antislavery ingredient was "unbeknownst" to *Congress*, but of course the point of the story is that the recipient of the drink really *wants*, without being able to admit it, the secret dollop, and that was *Lincoln* wanting the unadmitted antislavery feature in the message. Lincoln used this anecdote on other occasions to illustrate other points. In *Memoirs of William T. Sherman*, 2 vols. (New York: Appleton & Co., 1887), 2:320, Lincoln tells it to suggest that Jefferson Davis be allowed to escape, unbeknownst to Lincoln; in *Personal Memoirs of U. S. Grant*, 2 vols. (New York: Charles L. Webster & Co., 1886), 2:533, it is an Irishman who has taken the pledge, and the point is allowing Governor Smith of Virginia and a few others to leave the country, unbeknownst to Lincoln; and in the memoirs of an abolitionist, *Autobiography: Memories and Experiences of Moncure Daniel Conway*, 2 vols. (Boston: Houghton Mifflin, 1904), 1:345–46, a "thirsty soul in Maine" is the subject and the point is similar to that told by Wendell Phillips—some antislavery action slipped into policy, unbeknownst to the policy makers.

256   "You say you will not fight to free negroes": Lincoln's great letter to Conkling and the people in Springfield has the date August 26, 1863, and is found in *CW*, 6:406–10.

257   "Here is the first indication": Mark E. Neely, Jr., *The Last Best Hope of Earth: Abraham Lincoln and the Promise of America* (Cambridge, Mass.: Harvard University Press, 1993), p. 102.

259   There was a bit of history: On May 26, 1836, the House of Representatives was voting on a set of resolutions dealing with a recent pesky influx of petitions against slavery in the District. The first resolution was simply the axiomatic statement, taken for granted by everybody, even including the new abolitionists, that the Constitution did not allow Congress to interfere with slavery in the states. It was expected that House members would routinely vote aye. But when the clerk called the roll, the very first to vote, a crotchety and balding seventy-year-old sitting in the front row, began arguing (to shouts of "Order! Order!") that if allowed five minutes he could prove the resolution "false and utterly untrue." John Quincy Adams was not allowed to make his point on that occasion, but he did so later in connection with a discussion of the Seminole War: "From the instant you slave-holding states become the theater of war ... the war powers of Congress extend to the interference with slavery in every way it can be interfered with." Five years later, in 1841, a much troubled congressman expressed "his astonishment and horror at what had fallen from the gentleman from Massachusetts," as he understood it, that a servile war would mean the end of the Constitution. Not at all, explained Adams—he had pointed out how the Constitution could then be *preserved* by using its war power for universal emancipation. This explanation did not end the congressman's astonishment and horror.

Adams's shocking claim had found this horrifying power, in wartime, in Congress, because Congress declared war, raised armies, appropriated funds, and passed laws. But Lincoln had claimed to act, in the emergency of 1861, as executive and commander in chief, on the basis of his war power. And with the migration of the war power to the presidency came that astonishing power that Adams had shocked Congress with: as a war measure, out of military necessity, to free slaves.

In his old age Adams had as a young follower in Massachusetts, Charles Sumner. On April 12, 1861, learning that the president would hold and provision Fort Sumter, Senator Charles Sumner called on the new president and told him what he had learned from John Quincy Adams: "Then the war power will be in motion, and with it great consequences." When the Confederates attacked and reduced the fort, Sumner told Lincoln: "Under the war power the right had come to him to emancipate the slaves." David Donald, *Charles Sumner* (New York: Da Capo Press, 1920); part 1, *Charles Sumner and the Coming of the Civil War*, p. 17, and part 2, *Charles Sumner and the Rights of Man*, p. 388. Sumner telling Lincoln what he had learned from Adams is the very last line in the earlier book.

260   "Bishop Fowler in his noted lecture": William E. Barton, *The Life of Abraham Lincoln*, 2 vols. (Indianapolis: Bobbs-Merrill, 1925), 2:390. Ward had recently sent Lincoln, an admirer, a copy of his new collection.

260   Chase in his diary: Salmon P. Chase, *Inside Lincoln's Cabinet: The Civil War Diaries of Salmon P. Chase*, ed. David Herbert Donald (New York: Longmans, Green, 1954), p. 149.

260 "hesitating a little": This presidential hesitation appears in parentheses in Chase's diary entry. Ibid., p. 150.

261 "perhaps the greatest document": Don E. Fehrenbacher, quoted in Douglas L. Wilson, *Lincoln's Sword* (New York: Alfred A. Knopf, 2006), p. 105.

264 "Abraham Lincoln's Emancipation Proclamation constituted": Ibid., p. 141.

266 "Freeing the slaves and saving the Union": Phillip S. Paludan, *The Presidency of Abraham Lincoln* (Lawrence: University of Kansas Press, 1994), p. xv.

267 "recognizes": Chase, *Inside*, p. 151.

267 "He [Lincoln] will appeal to the black blood of the African": London *Times*, October 7, 1982, quoted in John Hope Franklin, *The Emancipation Proclamation* (New York: Doubleday, 1963), p. 73.

268 "Few Confederate editors": Ibid.

268 "Wherever Negroes were": Ibid., p. 93.

268 "However deficient in majesty or grandeur": Ira Berlin et al., *Slaves No More: Three Essays on Emancipation and the Civil War* (Cambridge: Cambridge University Press, 1992), pp. 49–50.

CHAPTER FOURTEEN.
THE PROMPT VINDICATION OF HIS HONOR

The materials for Doctor Wright's case are found in Dr. D. M. Wright (Citizen) file #MM-631, Entry 15, Court Martial Case Files, Record Group 153, Records of the Judge Advocate General (Army), in the National Archives and Records Administration, Washington, D.C. Almost all of the material in this chapter comes from that file; it includes the record of his trial, the transcript of his own fateful address in self-defense; the materials submitted in his defense—the letters from fellow citizens; Judge Advocate General Holt's summary of the case and his recommendation; and President Lincoln's handwritten decision.

274 President Lincoln himself had been present: Chester D. Bradley, "President Lincoln's Campaign Against the Merrimac," *Journal of the Illinois State Historical Society* 51 (Spring 1958), p. 77; William E. Baringer, "On Enemy Soil: President Lincoln's Norfolk Campaign," *Abraham Lincoln Quarterly* 7 (March 1952), pp. 8–10.

276 "human beings of an inferior race": Jefferson Davis's response to the Emancipation Proclamation can be found in, among many other sources, *Harper's Weekly*, January 31, 1863. Davis's clause about the execrable *massacre* that the proclamation would bring forth is sometimes misquoted.

279 "definitely stood a step above no law": Mark E. Neely, Jr., *The Fate of Liberty: Abraham Lincoln and Civil Liberties* (New York: Oxford University Press, 1991), p. 166.

279 "Trials by military commission were all recorded": Ibid., p. 162.

284 "their quantity was limited enough": Ibid., p. 166.

284 "But when Lincoln defied Holt's advice": Ibid.

284 "his excellency A. Lincoln": Lemuel J. Bowden to Abraham Lincoln, July 31, 1863, *AL Papers*. Wright's other lawyer, L. H. Chandler, addressed a letter to Lincoln the following day, also held in the Library of Congress collection.

285 The petitions that poured into the White House: The petitions from the citizens of

Norfolk, and an accompanying letter from Wright's lawyers, are dated, respectively, October 17 and 21, 1863, *AL Papers.*

285 a plea she would later write: The letter from Wright's wife, "Mrs. P. M. Wright to Mrs. Stone," is dated October 19, 1863, *AL Papers.*

286 proposed another "alienist," one John P. Gray: *CW,* 6:437–38.

287 "[B]eing satisfied that no proper question remained open": Lincoln's approval of Wright's sentence is in *CW,* 6:505, and *OR,* ser. 2, vol. 6, p. 360.

287 "It would be useless": Lincoln's note declining to see "Mrs. Dr. Wright" is in *CW,* 6:522.

CHAPTER FIFTEEN.
AND THE PROMISE BEING MADE, MUST BE KEPT

289 Some slaves did work: William W. Freehling, *The South vs. the South: How Anti-Confederate Southerners Shaped the Course of the Civil War* (New York: Oxford University Press, 2001), pp. 90–91.

290 Jamaica had ten blacks for every one white: Peter Kolchin, *American Slavery, 1619–1877* (New York: Hill & Wang, 1993), p. 100.

290 "A geographical line has been drawn": "Declaration of the Immediate Causes Which Induce and Justify the Secession of South Carolina from the Federal Union," December 24, 1860, *AP.*

290 "chosen their leader": Charles B. Dew, *Apostles of Disunion: Southern Secession Commissioners and the Causes of the Civil War* (Charlottesville: University Press of Virginia, 2001), p. 48.

291 "[M]ost slaves learned": Ira Berlin et al., *Slaves No More: Three Essays on Emancipation and the Civil War* (Cambridge: Cambridge University Press, 1992), p. 11.

291 "The moment the Union army moved into slave territory": W. E. B. DuBois, *Black Reconstruction in America, 1860–1880* (Philadelphia: Albert Saifer, 1935), pp. 62–63.

292 Racism led to some horror stories: Bruce Catton quotes a white woman working with refugees as saying, "The barbarities from our soldiers are unparalleled." Catton, *Never Call Retreat* (1965; repr. New York: Pocket Books, 1967), pp. 116–17.

292 It is reported: DuBois, *Reconstruction,* p. 60.

292 "passing quickly through": Butler wrote to Governor Hicks:

> I have understood . . . that some apprehensions were entertained of an insurrection of the negro population of this neighborhood. I am anxious to convince all classes of persons that the forces under my command are not here in any way to interfere with, or countenance any interference with, the laws of the State. I am therefore ready to co-operate with your excellency in suppressing, most promptly and effectively, any insurrection against the laws of Maryland. I beg, therefore, that you announce publicly that any portion of the forces under my command is at your excellency's disposal to act immediately for the preservation and quietness of the peace of this community.

OR, ser. 1, vol. 2, pp. 589–90, 593.

Butler corrected an "ill-advised designation" of men under his command. In insistent italics he said: *"They are not Northern troops; they are part of the whole militia of the United States, obeying the call of the President." OR,* ser. 1, vol. 2, p. 590.

292   "It has been represented": *OR,* ser. 2, vol. 1, p. 778.

293   slavery and martial law: Hunter's claim that martial law and slavery are incompatible
       has sometimes provoked amused dismissal by historians, but perhaps it was not as
       far-fetched as it sounds. In Hunter's view it reflected the theory that had been devel-
       oped in abolitionist circles: that slavery could exist only by specific positive local
       ("municipal") enactments and ceased to exist whenever and wherever those enact-
       ments did not apply—as in waters beyond state jurisdictions, as in the territories, and
       now as under U.S. martial law supplanting the laws of Carolina and Georgia. That
       American abolitionist theory reflected a ruling by an English judge, Lord Mansfield,
       in a famous case in 1772, *Somerset v. Stewart,* "that slavery is so odious that nothing
       can be suffered to support it but positive law."

       By this theory abolitionists had, while recognizing perforce the claims of states
       under the American federal system, squeezed the legitimacy of slavery down to its
       smallest application. They took Southerners' continual claim that slavery was strictly
       a *state* matter and applied it back against them: slavery was *strictly* a state matter.
       Under the universal moral order that the American Constitution reflected, all human
       beings were by nature free; slavery could exist only where states made specific posi-
       tive law enacting it, and it became illegitimate immediately outside the jurisdiction of
       that "municipal" law. Slaves—*property* in Kentucky under state law—abruptly
       become *men* when they escaped into Ohio. Or revolted on shipboard on the high
       seas. Or were taken into a federal territory. (Hence the Dred Scott decision was
       invalid.) Abolitionists had employed this theory, in the decades before the war, to
       shrink slavery's legal base and challenge it on all sides—to the horror, to be sure, of its
       defenders. Now here was a general applying that theory under Union army occupa-
       tion: the "municipal" law of South Carolina, Georgia, and North Carolina now no
       longer applied, under the martial law of the army of the United States, and therefore
       all "slaves" abruptly reverted to their natural status, which was freedom.

294   "I reply that no regiment": Edward A. Miller, Jr., *Lincoln's Abolitionist General: The
       Biography of David Hunter* (Columbia: University of South Carolina Press, 1997),
       p. 106.

294   A Kentucky colleague: Ibid.

295   "altogether void": Allen C. Guelzo, *Lincoln's Emancipation Proclamation: The End
       of Slavery in America* (New York: Simon & Schuster, 2004), p. 74.

295   "Lincoln repudiated": Miller, *Abolitionist General,* p. 102.

296   "a mass of data": Benjamin Quarles, *Lincoln and the Negro* (1962; repr. New York: Da
       Capo Press, 1991), p. 22.

296   But in another case, embarrassing to his admirers: Ibid., pp. 22–24.

296   "I never was in a meeting": Ibid., p. 15.

297   "a black's dream of freedom": William W. Freehling, "Absurd Issues: Colonization as
       a Test Case," in *The Reintegration of American History* (New York: Oxford Univer-
       sity Press, 1994), p. 146.

297   Even the great opponent: Ibid., p. 147.

297   "nadir": Freehling, *South vs. South,* pp. 108, 109.

298   sheer impossibility of the numbers: At an earlier stage of the colonization movement,
       the famous Quaker poet John Greenleaf Whittier, a committed "immediatist" aboli-
       tionist, produced this sardonic calculation of colonization's success:

Let facts speak. The Colonization Society was organized in 1817. It has two hundred and eighteen auxiliary societies. The legislatures of fourteen states have recommended it. Contributions have poured into its treasury from every quarter of the United States. Addresses in its favor have been heard from all our pulpits. It has been in operation sixteen years. During this period nearly one million human beings have died in slavery, and the number of slaves have increased more than half a million, or in round numbers, 550,000.

The Colonization Society has been busily engaged all this while in conveying slaves to Africa; in other words, abolishing slavery. In this very charitable occupation it has carried away of manumitted slaves: 613.

Balance against the society: 549,387.

Freehling argues provocatively, in "Absurd Issues," that the numbers were nevertheless not impossible—or rather perhaps that supporters, and apprehensive Deep South slaveholders, could plausibly *believe* that colonization was possible, given the many movements of peoples across oceans and continents and out from under problems.

298 "The practical thing": Lincoln's address on colonization is in *CW*, 5:370–75.

299 "always the careful politician": Michael Vorenberg, "Abraham Lincoln and the Politics of Black Colonization," *Journal of the Abraham Lincoln Association* 14, no. 2 (Summer 1993), pp. 25, 24.

301 "Despite the resistance": Joseph Glatthaar, *Forged in Battle: The Civil War Alliance of Black Soldiers and White Officers* (Baton Rouge: Louisiana State University Press, 1990), p. 10.

301 "at one time had over 123,000 soldiers": Ibid.

302 the words that U. S. Grant had used in a letter: Grant wrote to Lincoln on August 23, 1863 (*AL Papers*):

I have given the subject of arming the negro my hearty support. This, with the emancipation of the negro, is the heavyest blow yet given the Confederacy. Gen. Thomas is now with me and you may rely on it I will give him all the aid in my power. I would do this whether the arming the negro seemed to me a wise policy or not, because it is an order that I am bound to obey and do not feel that in my position I have a right to question any policy of the Government. In this particular instance there is no objection however to my expressing an honest conviction. That is, by arming the negro we have added a powerful ally. They will make good soldiers and taking them from the enemy weaken him in the same proportion they strengthen us.

302 Douglas Wilson, in his illuminating discussion: Douglas L. Wilson, *Lincoln's Sword* (New York: Alfred A. Knopf, 2006), p. 186.

305 "I need not say that at the time"; "I entered the room": *Frederick Douglass: Autobiographies,* ed. Henry Louis Gates, Jr. (New York: Library of America, 1994), pp. 785–86.

306 "considering the conditions": Quoted by John Eaton, cited in Thomas F. Schwartz, ed., *"For a Vast Future Also": Essays from the Journal of the Abraham Lincoln Association* (New York: Fordham University Press, 1999), p. 77n86.

306 "In all my interviews": Quarles, *Lincoln and Negro,* p. 204. This "entire freedom

from popular prejudice" seems to have applied not just to Douglass or to other black eminences (Sojourner Truth had a memorable meeting with him) but to his dealings with all black persons, including servants. Quarles also wrote: "In his person-to-person relationships with Negroes, Lincoln was characteristically kind and considerate. He did favors for Negroes, favors that could bring him no political advantage or private gain."

307   "We ought never to be inconvenienced": James M. McPherson, *Battle Cry of Freedom: The Civil War Era* (New York: Oxford University Press, 1988), p. 793.

309   "It is now quite certain": Lincoln's note to the cabinet on the Fort Pillow massacre is in *CW*, 7:328. See the extensive note on the next page.

CHAPTER SIXTEEN. THE BENIGN PREROGATIVE
TO PARDON UNFORTUNATE GUILT

315   "This is indeed": William Blackstone, *Commentaries on the Laws of England: A Facsimile of the First Edition of 1765–1769* (Chicago: University of Chicago Press, 1979), online at http://presspubs.uchicago.edu/founders/documents/a2_2_1s17.html and at *AP*.

315   "In democracies this power of pardon": "Whenever the nation see him personally engaged, it is only in works of legislature, magnificence, or compassion. To him therefore the people look up as the fountain of nothing but bounty and grace; and these repeated acts of goodness, coming immediately from his own hand, endear the sovereign to his subjects, and . . . root in their hearts that filial affection, and personal loyalty, which are the sure establishment of a prince." Ibid.

316   "The criminal code of every country": Federalist 74, March 25, 1788, *AP*.

317   a mere one hundred dollars: "Order Annulling Sentence of Benjamin G. and Franklin W. Smith," March 18, 1865, *CW*, 8:364.

317   Lincoln pardoned more than three hundred "nonmilitary" offenders: P. S. Ruckman, Jr., and David Kincaid, "Inside Lincoln's Clemency Decision Making," *Presidential Studies Quarterly* 29 (Winter 1999), pp. 84–99, is a study of 331 warrants from Lincoln clemency cases in the civil courts. An older study is J. T. Dorris, "President Lincoln's Clemency," *Journal of the Illinois State Historical Society* 20 (January 1928). There is additional material in Dorris's much later book, *Pardon and Amnesty Under Lincoln and Johnson* (1953; repr. Westport, Conn.: Greenwood Press, 1977). There is a helpful article on clemency in Mark E. Neely, Jr., *The Abraham Lincoln Encyclopedia* (New York: McGraw-Hill, 1982), p. 60.

317   The largest single episode: The excellent leading article on this event, Carol Chomsky, "The United States–Dakota War Trials: A Study in Military Injustice," *Stanford Law Review* 43, no. 1 (November 1990), explains that the episode involved the Dakota, who are part of the Sioux nation, and refers to them by that name; most treatments have called them Sioux.

318   "Mr. Lincoln was tender hearted": William H. Herndon, quoted in Richard N. Current, *The Lincoln Nobody Knows* (New York: McGraw-Hill, 1958), p. 181.

318   "Lincoln was a man of deep sympathy": William E. Barton, *The Life of Abraham Lincoln*, 2 vols. (Indianapolis: Bobbs-Merrill, 1925), 2:249.

319   he saved the life of an old Indian: Two accounts of this incident can be found in the

memories of "informants" who knew Lincoln, interviewed by Herndon: Douglas L. Wilson and Rodney O. Davis, eds., *Herndon's Informants: Letters, Interviews, and Statements About Abraham Lincoln* (Urbana: University of Illinois Press, 1998), William G. Greene mentions the incident twice (pp. 19 and 390); Royal Clary's version is on pp. 372–73.

320   A presidential audience he held on March 27, 1863, in the "big wigwam": The Washington *Daily Morning Chronicle*'s account of Lincoln's meeting with the Indian chiefs is published as "Speech to Indian Chiefs," March 27, 1863, *CW*, 6:151–52.

321   the irony of the president making this claim: David Herbert Donald, in *Lincoln* (New York: Simon & Schuster 1995), p. 393, writes that "the irony was unintentional." Mark E. Neely, Jr., in *The Last Best Hope of Earth* (Cambridge, Mass.: Harvard University Press, 1993), p. 150, says that Lincoln spoke "without conscious irony." And David Nichols, in an article that summarizes much of his book, "Lincoln and the Indians," in Gabor Boritt, ed., *The Historian's Lincoln* (Urbana: University of Illinois Press, 1988), makes a much more earnest comment: "Considering the bloodiness of the white Civil War in 1863, this was a remarkably ethnocentric statement" (p. 166).

322   "A nation which sowed robbery would reap a harvest of blood": In his memoir, *Light and Shadows of a Long Episcopate: Being Reminiscences and Recollections of the Right Reverend Henry B. Whipple, Bishop of Minnesota* (1902), Whipple claims to have repeated this phrase many times publicly. Excerpts of his writings about the Indians are online at the Dakota Conflict Trials Web site: www.law.umkc.edu/faculty/projects/ftrials/dakota/Light&Shadows.html.

323   "all the rights and all the justice": Senator William Pitt Fessenden, quoted in David A. Nichols, *Lincoln and the Indians: Civil War Policy and Politics* (Columbia: University of Missouri Press, 1978), p. 189.

323   "[S]o far as I am concerned": Quoted ibid., p. 77. Carol Chomsky, in "War Trials," attributes this statement to a trader named Andrew Myrick, later one of the first casualties of the war, whose body was found with his mouth stuffed with grass (p. 17).

323   "The horrible massacres": General John Pope, quoted in Chomsky, "War Trials," p. 23, and partially in Nichols, "Lincoln and the Indians," p. 87.

323   a military commission sentenced 303 Sioux warriors: According to Chomsky, "War Trials," by the last day of the trials, November 3, the commission had tried 392 Dakota (p. 27).

324   "[W]e kill the wolfes": Thaddeus Williams, M.D. to Abraham Lincoln, November 22, 1862, *AL Papers*. This is a long, bloodthirsty letter, full of lurid details.

324   Learning from his judge advocate general: Lincoln wrote to Holt inquiring about the procedure for pardoning the Sioux and received this response: "I do not understand the precise form in which the question, referred to in your not[e] of this morning presents itself. If it be on an application to pardon the indians condemned, or a part of them, I am quite sure that the power cannot be delegated, and that the designation of the individuals, which its exercise involves, must necessarily be made by yourself." Joseph Holt to Abraham Lincoln, December 1, 1862, *AL Papers*.

324   "will be sufficiently great to satisfy": Henry Sibley, quoted in Nichols, *Lincoln and the Indians,* p. 98.

325   "The lack of evidence": Ibid., p. 100.

325   forty-two Indians were "tried": Chomsky, "War Trials," p. 27.

325   David Herbert Donald presents: Donald, *Lincoln,* pp. 392–95.

325   "I could not afford to hang men for votes": Nichols writes: "The President noted [to Ramsey] that he carried Minnesota only by seven thousand votes compared to ten thousand in 1860. Ramsey replied 'that if he had hung more Indians, we should have given him his old majority.' Lincoln failed to appreciate the humor of the remark. 'I could not afford to hang men for votes,' he said." Nichols, *Lincoln and the Indians,* p. 118; quoting the November 23, 1864, diary entry of Minnesota senator Alexander Ramsey, in Roll 39, vol. 36, Ramsey Papers, in the Abraham Lincoln Collection of the Blue Earth Historical Society.

326   "Lincoln was clearly more humanitarian": Nichols, "Lincoln and the Indians," p. 166.

326   "[Lincoln's] commutation of the sentences": Hans Trefousse, quoted ibid., p. 172.

326   "If I live": This quotation, found in William C. Harris, *Lincoln's Last Months* (Cambridge, Mass.: Harvard University Press, 2004), p. 171, is taken from Whipple's "My Life Among the Indians," *North American Review* 150 (April 1890), p. 438. Harris writes: "As the troubles on the Plains multiplied late in the Civil War, Lincoln signaled, at least to one visitor, that he intended to take a more active role in Indian matters. Henry B. Whipple, the Protestant Episcopal bishop of Minnesota and a missionary among the Indians, spoke to him at this time about the mistreatment of the western Indians. Moved by Whipple's account, the president promised, according to the bishop, 'if I live, this accursed system shall be reformed.' "

CHAPTER SEVENTEEN.
MUST I SHOOT A SIMPLE SOLDIER BOY?

327   more than a hundred thousand went before courts-martial: William C. Davis, *Lincoln's Men* (New York: Simon & Schuster, 2000), p. 167.

327   All capital cases: Carol Chomsky, "The United States–Dakota War Trials: A Study in Military Injustice," *Stanford Law Review* 43, no. 1 (November 1990), pp. 13, 26. Article of War 65 provided that, in time of peace, sentences involving loss of life could not be executed until laid before the president for his approval. Act of April 10, 1806, ch. 20, §1, art. 65, 2 Stat. 359, 367. By Act of December 24, 1861, Congress provided that, in time of war, approval was necessary only from the general commanding the army in the field or colonel commanding a separate department. Ch. 3, 12 Stat. 330. In July 1862, however, Congress specified that no sentence of death should be carried out until approved by the president. Act of July 17, 1862, ch. 201, §5, 12 Stat. 597, 598.

328   "Allow me to address you": Anne C. King to Abraham Lincoln, September 8, 1861, *AL Papers.*

330   McClellan wrote to his wife: George B. McClellan, *McClellan's Own Story* (1887; repr. Digital Scanning, 1998), p. 91.

331   He would ask the army's chief lawyer: In December 1861 he would ask, "Will the Judge Advocate please say what are Gen. Benham's rights in the case?" In January 1862 he would ask Major Lee, "Will the Judge Advocate please tell me whether anything, & what I ought to do in this case?" and in February, "Would it be proper for me to order a Court Martial, as within requested?" In July he wrote: "Please examine

once more, the case of Lieutenant Colonel Francis B O'Keefe, and tell me what I, as President, can lawfully do, if anything." In March 1862 he would write: "I wish to grant a pardon in this case, and will be obliged to the Judge Advocate of the Army, if he will inform me as to the way in which it is to be done." "I wish to grant the suspension within requested," Lincoln wrote in another March case. "Will the Judge Advocate please carry it into effect."

331 "The President's suggestion as to the construction": This note can be found in Lee's endorsement of a court-martial file. George A. Rowley, Monday, July 7, 1862 (General Court Martial; endorsed by Abraham Lincoln and John F. Lee), *AL Papers.*

331 But on September 3, 1862: Benjamin S. Roberts to Montgomery Blair, July 19, 1862 (Judge Advocate; endorsed by Blair), *AL Papers.*

332 Holt, a former Democrat: Elizabeth Leonard, *Lincoln's Avengers: Justice, Revenge, and Reunion After the Civil War* (New York: W. W. Norton, 2004), describes Holt's career.

332 "The President would call me over": Nicolay's October 29, 1875, conversation with Holt, mentioned throughout this chapter, can be found in Michael Burlingame, ed., *An Oral History of Abraham Lincoln: John G. Nicolay's Interviews and Essays* (Carbondale: Southern Illinois University Press, 1996), p. 69.

333 "He shrank with evident pain": Ibid.

333 He would then look into the papers: "Let execution of William H. Ogden be suspended until further order from me" (November 12, 1863). "Suspend execution in case of Adolphus Morse, Seventy-sixth New York, deserter, and send record to me" (November 25, 1863). "Let the execution of John A. Welch, under sentence to be shot for desertion to-morrow, be suspended until further order from here" (December 10, 1863). "Suspend execution of the death sentence of James Whelan [Wheelan], One hundred and sixteenth Pennsylvania Volunteers, until further orders and forward record for examination" (March 2, 1864). "Suspend execution of sentence of death in case of Solomon Spiegel 9th Michigan cavalry until further orders, and forward record of trial for examination" (January 12, 1865).

333 More chilling still: On May 14, 1864, he wrote, "If Thomas Dorerty, or Welch, is to be executed to-day, and it is not already done, suspend it till further order." In another case Lincoln noted on the envelope of a capital case, "These papers reached me at 1 PM June 6th 1863," apparently recording the hour for reference, in relation to an impending execution. Fortunately, in that case, they arrived in time.

333 In at least four cases: See Lincoln's messages on June 25, 1863, to Major General Slocum; on October 29, 1863, to General Meade (two soldiers already shot); and on January 6, 1865, to Grant; all in *CW.*

334 "I am unwilling for any boy under eighteen to be shot": "Despite issuance of War Department orders as early as August 1861 forbidding acceptance without parental consent of minors under eighteen and an unqualified barring of them the next year, thousands of boys seventeen years and younger found their way into the ranks." Bell Irvin Wiley, *The Life of Billy Yank: The Common Soldier of the Union* (Garden City, N.Y.: Doubleday, 1952), p. 298.

336 Because the executions were intended: For an account of the executions, see ibid., p. 19.

336 "A gallows and a shooting-ground": Ella Lonn, *Desertion During the Civil War* (New York: Century, 1928), p. 181.

337 "This is the day": John Eaton, *Grant, Lincoln, and the Freedmen: Reminiscences of the Civil War* (London: Longmans, Green, 1907), p. 180.

337 "Get out of the way"; "The pile of papers": Leonard Swett to William Henry Herndon, January 17, 1866, in Douglas L. Wilson and Rodney O. Davis, eds., *Herndon's Informants: Letters, Interviews, and Statements About Abraham Lincoln* (Urbana: University of Illinois Press, 1998), p. 166. Swett revised this letter in 1887.

337 "He [Lincoln] had very great kindness of heart": Ibid.

338 He did not pardon any soldier: Of the 272 Union soldiers executed during the Civil War, 22 were found guilty of rape. Robert I. Alotta, *Civil War Justice: Union Army Executions Under Lincoln* (Shippensburg, Penn.: White Mane, 1989), p. 30. Alotta notes that Lincoln "provided clemency for all types of military offenders, except rapists" (p. 31).

338 "He was only merciless": Michael Burlingame and John R. Turner Ettlinger, eds., *Inside Lincoln's White House: The Complete Civil War Diary of John Hay* (Carbondale: Southern Illinois University Press, 1997), p. 64.

338 "I would not relax the discipline": Don E. Fehrenbacher and Virginia Fehrenbacher, *Recollected Words of Abraham Lincoln* (Stanford, Calif.: Stanford University Press, 1996), p. 148.

338 "I shall never cease to regret": Francis B. Carpenter, *The Inner Life of Abraham Lincoln: Six Months at the White House* (1866; repr. Lincoln: University of Nebraska Press, 1995), p. 43. Carpenter himself gave a sample of the president's pardoning, featuring not only a wife and tears but also a baby. An old White House retainer named Daniel told the mother after Lincoln had granted a pardon to her husband: "Madam, it was the baby that did it."

338 "I am in a state of entire collapse": Michael Burlingame, ed., *At Lincoln's Side: John Hay's Civil War Correspondence and Selected Writings* (Carbondale: Southern Illinois University Press, 2000), pp. 45, 46.

339 "occupying hours at a time": Ibid., p. 69.

339 ten other such heavy days: By 1864 Holt would come over to the executive mansion with so many proposed pardons that years later the sheer numbers and sheer repetition would create a problem for the valiant editors of Lincoln's *Collected Works*.

In the early wartime volumes, for 1860–61 and 1861–62 and 1862–63 (as in the years before the presidency), those editors would print almost every scrap they could find that came from Abraham Lincoln's hand, including utterly routine messages and five-, four-, three-, and even two-word "endorsements" that Lincoln had scribbled on an envelope. These brief jottings (for example, "All right"—November 7, 1861; "Come here"—August 15, 1862; "What news?"—several times; "None at all"—June 28, 1862 (to Seward, giving his own answer to the same question) were to be part of his "works." (My favorite is "Profoundly laid by"—June 2, 1862—of course, this one is a joke, about the outrageous impossibility of the proposal inside the envelope.) But for the period after the war intensified, when pardon cases came in by the dozens, the editors' scrupulously conscientious thoroughness seems to have collapsed under the weight of all the pardons.

Thus, for February 9, 1864, *The Collected Works* prints one brief pardon message to Joseph Holt—because it refers to a case to which there are other references—and then in the accompanying note reports that "this is only one of 63 court martial cases reviewed by Lincoln on this date." "Sentences in other cases," the note goes on to say, "were approved, remitted, commuted, or pardons were ordered" in "routine endorsements." Almost nothing, up to that point, had been regarded as too routine to be printed. But then for the next day, February 10, in appendix 2 one learns that Holt brought 32 cases, and for February 11, 1864, in the text itself the editors print three messages that have some distinguishing feature, then add a note that on this day, in addition to these three, Lincoln reviewed 43 more (thus 139 cases in three days!), the others again "routine endorsements" of "pardon, approval, remission, or commutation of sentence." Either in the text or appendix 2 one finds that on February 15, Holt and Lincoln considered 48 cases; on April 14, 67 cases; April 21, 72 cases; April 26, 51 cases; April 27, 36 cases; July 8, 35 cases; July 9, 31 cases; August 9, 10 cases; August 16, 7 cases; August 17, 15 cases. Then in 1865, on January 23, 45 cases; and on January 25, 30 cases.

That is 606 cases that the editors of *The Collected Works* simply count, without reproducing any name or word from Lincoln, in just these fifteen concentrated heavy days. In addition, as noted, for the date March 31, 1863 (approximately), appendix 2 of *The Collected Works* mentions the 55 cases of soldiers sentenced to be shot for desertion by Hooker. That is 661 (606 plus 55) cases, without names given, that Lincoln had brought to him in great batches, according to *The Collected Works*.

Because according to the editors these numbers, except for the 55 from Hooker, include *approvals* (of the sentences) as well as pardons, remissions, and commutations, we cannot know quite how many of the latter three kinds of decisions (the instances of clemency) these counts include, but surely they are much the larger part. We also cannot know, except in those 55 cases, how many were capital cases, but they were a high percentage of the cases that came to the president.

Whatever the exact number of courts-martial of Union soldiers considered for all offenses and all punishments and outcomes, or of (the smaller but crucial category) capital sentences pardoned, the numbers are already higher than had been thought. Ida Tarbell, the great muckraker-turned-Lincoln-biographer early in the twentieth century, made a count and could find at that time telegrams and other messages representing 275 of these military pardons, reprieves, and stays of execution in the two years from March 1863 until the end of the war. Basler and company, working forty years later with more resources as a team with a formal role, found many more than that. Looking at *The Collected Works,* dealing just with the one category of instances in which the president stopped by his pardon, commutation, or stay of execution the shooting of a Union soldier; and excluding acts of clemency for Union soldiers and officers for offenses with a lesser punishment (the officers characteristically were sentenced not to be shot but to be dismissed); and excluding Confederate spies and citizens accused of treason, many of whom were sentenced to be hanged; and being careful not to count any soldier twice (or three times!) even though there were two or more messages about him, I count in the text 186 soldiers whose names I could give, whom Lincoln saved from shooting (perhaps in rare cases with the stays of execution only temporarily), and 9 more in the material the editors added in appendix 2.

By the late 1990s Dr. Thomas Lowry and Beverly Lowry, researchers diligently working away in the difficult and misfiled records in the National Archives, found 570

Lincoln pardons of men condemned by courts-martial that are not recorded by name in *The Collected Works.* Those pardons, and the further pardons the Lowrys may yet find, may or may not have been included in those piles of papers Holt brought over to Lincoln on the days courts-martial were considered, which the editors of *The Collected Works* just reported by number. The records have not been as easy to deal with as those in the civil cases because, as Dr. Lowry puts it, the Civil War was not fought for the benefit of later researchers.

340   "erroneous": Donn Piatt, *Men Who Saved the Union* (New York: Belford, Clarke & Co., 1887), pp. 36, 37. Piatt's chapter on Lincoln was later included in, and is often cited from, Allen Thorndike Rice's collection *Reminiscences of Abraham Lincoln by Distinguished Men of His Time* (New York: Harper & Brothers, 1909), pp. 343–66.

340   "successful leaders in history": Piatt, *Men Who Saved the Union,* p. 36.

340   "As for his steady refusal": Ibid., p. 37.

341   Piatt was surely wrong to deny: The most astonishing of Piatt's comments on Lincoln cannot be matched anywhere in the vast literature by those who supported Lincoln. It was this: "Lincoln could hate with an intensity known only to strong natures, and when just retribution demanded it he could punish with an iron will no appeals for pity could move." Ibid., p. 56. To cite but one more of his uniquely peculiar remarks, Piatt also had a view of, and a chapter on, Stanton, wherein he wrote that the president "is weak and timid and the indomitable will, intellect, and energy of Mr. Stanton controls him."

341   "Such kindness to the criminal": Salmon Chase, quoted ibid., p. 37.

341   "if we attempt to shoot"; "All this [great outrages]": General Daniel Tyler and Colonel Theodore Lyman, quoted in Richard N. Current, *The Lincoln Nobody Knows* (New York: McGraw-Hill,1958), p. 169.

341   "President Lincoln, I pray you not to interfere": Benjamin Butler, quoted ibid., p. 166.

342   "Lincoln had little time to investigate": William E. Barton, *The Life of Abraham Lincoln,* 2 vols. (Indianapolis: Bobbs-Merrill, 1925), 1:249–50.

343   "[F]orty or fifty executions now": William Tecumseh Sherman, quoted in Jonathan Truman Dorris, *President Lincoln's Clemency* (Springfield: Illinois State Historical Society, 1928), p. 551.

343   "Because you cannot order men shot by the dozens": Ella Lonn, *Desertion During the Civil War* (New York: Century, 1928), p. 223.

344   "To what extent": Carl Sandburg, *Abraham Lincoln: The Prairie Years and the War Years* (New York: Harcourt, Brace, 1954), p. 592.

345   "Hundreds of Union soldiers were shot": Thomas P. Lowry, *Don't Shoot That Boy! Abraham Lincoln and Military Justice* (Mason City, Iowa: Savas, 1999), p. 263.

345   One can find contrasting treatments: The contrasting treatment of officers and men was sharply exhibited to Lincoln on successive days in June 1863. On June 23 he dealt with the case of a Private James G. Lyon, Fifth Vermont Volunteers, who was found guilty of "cowardice and absence without leave"—and sentenced to be *shot.* On the next day, June 24, he dealt with the case of Captain William P. Eagan of the Twenty-third Kentucky Volunteers, who had also been found guilty of "cowardice"— and was sentenced only to dishonorable dismissal. Lincoln commuted the sentence of

Private Lyon to imprisonment at hard labor during the war but upheld the dismissal of Captain Eagan. In the case of a West Point graduate named John Benson Williams, a first lieutenant of the Third Infantry, who was dismissed from the service for "deserting his company in the presence of the enemy," Lincoln wrote to Stanton: "I decline to interfere in behalf of Lieut. Williams" (April 11, 1863). On July 18 and July 20, 1863, respectively, the president dealt with the separate cases of Lieutenant Alpheus Scott of the Sixth Iowa Cavalry, and Major Joseph Gilmer of the Eighteenth Pennsylvania Cavalry, both of whom were found guilty of "drunkenness"—and sentenced to dismissal. Lincoln, who had drastically mitigated the punishment of Private Zachringer, upheld the punishment of the two officers.

345 "Of fifty-nine convictions": Mark E. Neely, Jr., *The Abraham Lincoln Encyclopedia* (New York: McGraw-Hill, 1982), p. 61.

345 "My officers tell me": Henry Wilson, in Fehrenbacher and Fehrenbacher, *Recollected Words*, p. 498.

346 "Must I shoot"; "I understand the meeting": Abraham Lincoln to E. Corning and others, June 12, 1863, *CW*, 6:260–69.

347 "The Indians, if unpunished": Thaddeus Williams M.D. to Lincoln, November 22, 1862, *AL Papers.*

347 "Pusillanimity and want of executive force": Ben Butler, quoted in Current, *Lincoln Nobody Knows*, p. 169.

CHAPTER EIGHTEEN. A HARD WAR WITHOUT HATRED

351 "A reckless and unprincipled tyrant": *OR*, ser. 1, vol. 2, p. 907.

352 "[T]hey [the United States] . . . are waging": Jefferson Davis, Message to Congress, July 20, 1861, in Mark E. Neely, Jr., "Was the Civil War a Total War?" *Civil War History* 50, no. 4 (December 2004), pp. 434–58, quoting *Message of the President* (Richmond, Va.: Ritchie & Dunnavant, 1861), pp. 3–4.

353 "the least militarized"; "hastily assembled": John Keegan, *A History of Warfare* (New York: Alfred A. Knopf, 1994), p. 355.

353 prewar national population of 32 million: Ibid.

353 "If the same proportion": James M. McPherson, "From Limited War to Total War in America," in Stig Förster and Jörg Nagler, eds., *On the Road to Total War: The American Civil War and the German Wars of Unification, 1861–1871* (Washington, D.C.: German Historical Institute and Cambridge University Press, 1997), p. 295.

353 Historian John Keegan puts the round numbers: Keegan, *Warfare*, pp. 360–61.

354 "[p]robably twice as many civilians as soldiers": James M. McPherson, *Battle Cry of Freedom: The Civil War Era* (New York: Oxford University Press, 1988), p. 619n.

354 "Union and Confederate authorities were in substantial agreement": Neely, "Was the Civil War a Total War?" p. 443.

354 "Unlike the combatants": Michael Fellman, "At the Nihilist Edge," in Förster and Nagler, *Road to Total War*, pp. 535–36.

355 "When all was said and done": Mark E. Neely, Jr., "Retaliation: The Problem of Atrocity in the American Civil War," Forty-first Annual Robert Fortenbaugh Memorial Lecture, Gettysburg College, pp. 28–30.

356 "aversion to bloodshed": Lincoln is quoted as saying, with respect to his clemency: "I

reckon there never was a man raised in the country, on a farm, where they are always butchering cattle and hogs and think nothing of it, that ever grew up with such an aversion to bloodshed as I have and yet I've had more questions of life and death to settle in four years than all the men who ever sat in this chair put together." Interview with Henry P. H. Bromwell in the *Denver Tribune,* May 18, 1879, reprinted in the *New York Times,* May 27, 1879; see Don E. Fehrenbacher and Virginia Fehrenbacher, *Recollected Words of Abraham Lincoln* (Stanford, Calif.: Stanford University Press, 1996), pp. 40–41.

356　"[D]oesn't it seem strange": William C. Davis, *Lincoln's Men* (New York: Touchstone, 1999), p. 177, quoting Democratic congressman Daniel Voorhees in Fehrenbacher and Fehrenbacher, *Recollected Words,* p. 458.

356　"I deem it proper": Proclamation Calling Militia and Convening Congress, April 15, 1861, *CW,* 4:332.

356　"This was a national strategy of limited war": James McPherson, "Lincoln and the Strategy of Unconditional Surrender," in Gabor Boritt, ed., *Lincoln the War President* (New York: Oxford University Press, 1992), p. 75.

357　"Up to the battle of Shiloh": Ulysses S. Grant, *Memoirs and Selected Letters* (New York: Library of America, 1990), p. 246.

357　"Up to that time it had been the policy": Ibid., pp. 246–47.

357　"[Sherman's] experiences in Tennessee": McPherson, "Lincoln and Unconditional Surrender," p. 79.

358　"contemplated authority to Commanders": Salmon P. Chase, *Inside Lincoln's Cabinet: The Civil War Diaries of Salmon P. Chase,* ed. David Herbert Donald (New York: Longmans, Green, 1954), p. 95.

358　"The year 1863 marked a significant watershed": Mark Grimsley, *The Hard Hand of War: Union Military Policy Toward Southern Civilians, 1861–1865* (Cambridge: Cambridge University Press, 1995), p. 143.

359　"I have always regretted": Grant, *Memoirs,* p. 588.

359　"forty-eight hours after": Ibid., pp. 585–88. William S. McFeely's *Grant: A Biography* (New York: W. W. Norton, 1982) presents what he called the "inexcusable behavior" of Grant and Lee with particular force: "Union soldiers, who had charged, lay where they had fallen wounded, moaning in the blistering sun. Their brothers watched their torment, unable to retrieve them because of Confederate sharpshooters. After two days, on June 5, Grant sent one of Meade's aides across the lines with a letter suggesting that firing cease while litter bearers went out on the field. Lee insisted that 'a flag of truce be sent, as is customary.' The next morning, June 6, Grant wrote Lee that at noon men with stretchers and white flags would go out for the wounded, but again Lee insisted that he could 'accede with propriety' only to a request made under flag of truce: 'I have directed that any parties you may send out be turned back.' Grant, that afternoon, reminded Lee that 'wounded men are now suffering from want of attention' and agreed to a formal two-hour truce. Lee replied that it was too late to accomplish this by daylight, but agreed to a break between 8:00 p.m. and 10:00 p.m. that evening. The letter was received by Grant after 10:45 p.m., and it was not until late the next morning, June 7, that Grant wrote and informed Lee of the missed opportunity. Lee then proposed, and Grant accepted, a second truce, which took place that evening. For days, as commanders stupidly corresponded, untended men had lain in agony dying" (pp. 171–73).

359 "The effort was a tremendous failure": Grant, *Memoirs*, p. 613.

360 "more evil than Ivan the Terrible": North Carolina secretary of cultural resources, in the *Raleigh News Observer*, quoted in Grimsley, *Hard Hand*, p. 1.

361 Joseph T. Glatthaar's careful account: Joseph T. Glatthaar, *The March to the Sea and Beyond: Sherman's Troops in the Savannah and Carolinas Campaigns* (New York: New York University Press, 1985).

362 "Events . . . have made the vandalism of Sherman": Gameliel Bradford, *Union Portraits* (Boston: Houghton Mifflin, 1916), p. 155n; quoted in Neely, "Was the Civil War a Total War?," p. 445.

363 "This may not be war": W. T. Sherman to U. S. Grant, November 6, 1864, *OR*, ser. 1, vol. 39 (pt. III), p. 660.

363 "I know that this recent movement": W. T. Sherman to H. Halleck, December 21, 1864, *OR*, ser. 1, vol. 44, p. 799.

363 "[S]hould you shoot a man": Lincoln to John C. Frémont, September 2, 1861, *CW*, 4:566.

364 "Civilized belligerents": Lincoln to James C. Conkling, August 26, 1863, *CW*, 6:408.

364 "Military necessity": General Order No. 100, "Instructions for the Government of Armies of the United States in the Field," *OR*, ser. 2, vol. 5, p. 672. Francis Lieber's code does include glimpses of philosophical or ethical statements about war. He says: "Men who take up arms against one another in public war do not cease on this account to be moral beings, responsible to one another and to God" (p. 150); and "Peace is their normal condition; war is the exception. The ultimate object of war is a renewed state of peace"; but nonetheless, "The more vigorously wars are pursued the better it is for humanity. Sharp wars are brief" (p. 151). Lieber's document also comprises more basic instructions for the administration of war; it establishes the treatment of prisoners of war and private citizens, the management of enemy land and private property, protection for flags of truce, and other sorts of provisions one might expect to find in a military code.

366 "Mr. Johnson's course": Grant, *Memoirs*, p. 751. Very soon Andrew Johnson switched—already on the next page of Grant's *Memoirs:* in "a complete revolution of sentiment," as the issue of black suffrage arose, he favored the white South.

366 "an ignorant usurper": Jefferson Davis, speech at Richmond, Virginia, Spotswood Hotel, June 1, 1861, *The Papers of Jefferson Davis,* 11 vols. (to date), edited at Rice University and available online at http://jeffersondavis.rice.edu.

366 "barbarous": Davis to the Congress of the Confederate States, Richmond, Va., November 18, 1861, and elsewhere, ibid.

366 "for the gratification of the lust": Speech at Jackson, Mississippi, House Chamber, Mississippi Capitol, December 26, 1862, ibid.

367 "Its glory is all moonshine": Sherman, quoted in Keegan, *Warfare,* p. 6.

368 "No traitor has been hung"; "was particularly desirous to avoid": Gideon Welles, *Diary of Gideon Welles,* 3 vols. (Boston: Houghton Mifflin, 1911), 2:43.

CHAPTER NINETEEN. TEMPTATION IN AUGUST

The treatment of Lincoln's August 1864 tribulations I have drawn on most is David E. Long, *The Jewel of Liberty: Abraham Lincoln's Re-election and the End of Slavery* (New York: Da Capo Press, 1994). I have also used Matthew Pinsker's excellent book about Soldiers' Home, *Lincoln's Sanctuary: Abraham Lincoln and the Soldiers' Home* (New York: Oxford University Press, 2003), which examines with sensitivity parts of Lincoln's life that happened there, including events in this month. The two books about the 1864 election are William Frank Zornow's *Lincoln and the Party Divided* (Westport, Conn.: Greenwood Press, 1954), and John C. Waugh, *Reelecting Lincoln: The Battle for the 1864 Presidency* (New York: Crown, 1997).

370 "failed to accomplish what he had been sent to do": U. S. Grant, *Personal Memoirs of U. S. Grant* (New York: Library of America, 1990), p. 489. Gideon Welles reported in his diary entry for May 9, 1864, that Lincoln said he had at first rather "cousined up" to Banks as a general but more recently had come to think he had erred in doing so. He expressed his disappointment rather incongruously by quoting lines from the romantic Irish melodist Thomas Moore that in their original setting express the disappointment not of a president about his general but of a young maiden about her lover:

> *Oh! ever thus, from childhood's hour,*
> *I've seen my fondest hopes decay . . .*

Gideon Welles, *Diary of Gideon Welles,* 3 vols. (Boston: Houghton Mifflin, 1911), 2:26.

370 "[Franz] Sigel is in full retreat": Grant, *Memoirs,* p. 489.

371 "the enemy had corked the bottle": Ibid., pp. 493–94.

371 "as desperate fighting as the world has ever witnessed": Ibid., p. 512.

371 If a full report of the concentrated killing: Long, *Jewel of Liberty,* explains and discusses the holding back by some mixture of accident and design of the devastating news about the casualties at Cold Harbor. The accidents included a telegraphic breakdown and the absence of the reporters from critical newspapers, some to cover the Republican convention in Baltimore; the design included something approaching a cover-up by Grant and Stanton. "Grant's initial release, if not an outright fabrication, was a serious distortion of the truth" (pp. 201–4).

373 "in every town, township, ward of a city": Proclamation Calling for 500,000 Volunteers, July 18, 1864, *CW,* 4:449.

373 "What is the presidency to me": Benjamin P. Thomas, *Abraham Lincoln* (New York: Modern Library, 1968), p. 448.

373 "Lincoln's clear-sighted unwillingness": Mark E. Neely, Jr., *The Last Best Hope of Earth: Abraham Lincoln and the Promise of America* (Cambridge, Mass.: Harvard University Press, 1993), p. 90.

375   "I venture to remind you": Horace Greeley to Lincoln, Negotiations at Niagara Falls, July 7, 1864, *AL Papers.*

378   "Chase apparently would not only swap horses": Zornow, *Party Divided,* p. 108.

378   "at once asked for a Bible": David Homer Bates, *Lincoln in the Telegraph Office* (Lincoln: University of Nebraska Press, 1995), pp. 194–95.

378   "He never sleeps at the White House": This and the Whitman quotes that follow are all from *Specimen Days* in *Prose Works* (Philadelphia: David McKay, 1892); published October 2000 by Bartleby.com.

379   "the most vigorous attack": *N&H,* 9:125.

379   "[T]he President of the United States and the greatest man of his time": John Eaton, *Grant, Lincoln, and the Freedmen: Reminiscences of the Civil War* (New York: Longmans, Green, 1907), p. 175.

380   "Mr President: I am a War Democrat": Charles D. Robinson to Abraham Lincoln, August 7, 1864, *AL Papers.*

380   The next day Lincoln took up his pencil: Lincoln to Charles D. Robinson, August 17, 1864, *CW.* The second draft of this letter, in ink, is undated in *CW.*

381   "President Lincoln did me the honor": *Frederick Douglass: Autobiographies,* ed. Henry Louis Gates, Jr. (New York: Library of America, 1994), p. 795.

382   "We were long together": Frederick Douglass to Theodore Tilton, October 15, 1864, in *The Life and Writings of Frederick Douglass,* ed. Philip S. Foner, 5 vols. (New York: International Publishers, 1952), 3:422–24.

385   Ten days later Douglass wrote Lincoln: Douglass to Lincoln, August 29, 1864, *AL Papers.*

386   "You think I don't know I am going to be beaten": Zornow, *Party Divided,* p. 112.

387   "staunchest friends in every state": Henry J. Raymond to Lincoln, August 22, 1864, quoted in *N&H,* 9:218.

387   "Nothing but the most resolute and decided action": Ibid.

387   "experimental": *N&H,* 9:220.

388   "I went in as usual unannounced": Welles, *Diary,* 2:119–20.

389   "The President and the stronger half of the cabinet": *N&H,* 9:221.

389   "to facilitate examination and discussion of the question": *N&H,* 9:220.

392   "upon the first convenient occasion": Lincoln to Isaac Schermerhorn, September 12, 1864, *AL Papers.*

395   "The announcement was received": *Congressional Globe,* January 31, 1865, p. 531.

CHAPTER TWENTY. THE ALMIGHTY HAS HIS OWN PURPOSES

396   March 4, 1865: The quotations comparing the Second Inaugural with the First are from the *New York Times* articles "Inauguration Day," March 6, 1861, p. 1, and "Washington," March 12, 1865, p. 5. The description of Lincoln on the two occasions is drawn from John Hay's description of the two life masks by Leonard Volk made in 1860 and in 1865, published in an 1890 *Century* magazine article, "Life in the White House in the time of Lincoln." One account of the vice president's "disgraceful" behavior, that of Colonel John W. Forney, is quoted in a *New York Times* article printed years afterward, on September 10, 1871 (p. 3). Salmon Chase describes the sun's sudden appearance at the inauguration in a letter written to Mrs. Lincoln on

the same day, March 4, 1865, which can be found in the Robert Todd Lincoln Collection at *AL Papers*. The moment is also accounted for in Noah Brooks's *Washington in Lincoln's Time* (New York: Century, 1895), p. 74. The names of states that were now free—Arkansas free, Louisiana free, etc.—are chapter titles in vol. 8 of *N&H*.

401 "quite trivial falsification": Max Weber, "Politics as a Vocation," in H. H. Gerth and C. Wright Mills, eds., *From Max Weber: Essays in Sociology* (New York: Oxford University Press, 1958), pp. 77–156.

403 "Not one man in America": Henry Adams, *The Education of Henry Adams* (New York: Library of America, 1983), p. 809.

403 "puts the relation of our moral commitments": Reinhold Niebuhr, "The Religion of Abraham Lincoln," *Christian Century* 82 (February 10, 1965), p. 173.

405 "If slavery is right": Address at Cooper Institute, New York City, February 27, 1860.

408 "master rhetorical stroke": Douglas L. Wilson, *Lincoln's Sword* (New York: Alfred A. Knopf, 2006), p. 272.

415 "The first expression": *Frederick Douglass: Autobiographies*, ed. Henry Louis Gates (New York: Library of America, 1994), p. 802.

416 "Recognizing me, even before I reached him": Ibid., p. 804.

A CONCLUSION. ABRAHAM LINCOLN AMONG THE IMMORTALS

The quotations expressing condolences from around the world come from the U.S. State Department document "The Assassination of Abraham Lincoln . . . and the Attempted Assassination of William H. Seward, Secretary of State, and Frederick W. Seward, Assistant Secretary, on the Evening of the 14th of April, 1865. Expressions of Condolence and Sympathy Inspired by These Events" (Washington, D.C.: Government Printing Office, 1867). Also available online at www.hti.umich.edu/cgi/t/text/text-idx?c=moa;idno=ACK9017. Quotations from the Houses of Parliament come from the London *Times* for May 1, 1865, reprinted in that collection.

417 "That means nigger citizenship": Lewis Paine (aka Powell) heard Booth say this. Paine told Thomas T. Eckert, who testified about it in House Report, 7, 40th Cong., 1st sess. (1867), p. 674.

418 "President Lincoln looming in the distance": James G. Randall, *Lincoln the President*, 2 vols. (New York: Da Capo Press, 1977), vol. 1, pt. 2, p. 32.

420 "embodied in verse of rare felicity": Lord Charnwood, *Abraham Lincoln* (New York: Pocket Books, 1939), p. 493.

420 "Yes, he had lived": This is the stanza most often quoted. It appears, along with one more stanza, in *N&H* and is quoted in Merrill D. Peterson, *Lincoln in American Memory* (New York: Oxford University Press, 1994). But *Punch*'s full poem, which appeared in the issue for May 6, 1865, and is printed in full on pp. 540–41 in the State Department's collection, has nineteen stanzas and many more words of contrition and appreciation, worthy of quotation.

420 "What need hath he now": Peterson, *Memory*, p. 25.

420 "In fact it was among the common people": *N&H*, 10:345–46.

422 "one of the most interesting": Quoted in Peterson, *Memory*, p. 26.

422 "It forms a large quarto": *N&H*, 10:346.

ACKNOWLEDGMENTS

My strongest personal debts for this book, except for the supreme obligation indicated by the dedication, are to Lou Cannon, the noted journalist and Reagan biographer, who once again in the midst of his own writing projects gave every chapter the benefit of his superior editorial judgment; to Michael Burlingame, the scholar who has all of Lincoln at his finger-tips and is endlessly generous in giving help to the rest of us; to William Freehling, the much-honored historian of the prewar South, who miraculously appeared in Charlottesville and miraculously arrived at Lincoln in his own work just in time to encourage me on this book with lunches, chapter readings, editorial criticism, and wise counsel; and to Alexis Luckey, an experienced writer and editor working for a master's degree, who brought judgment and insight as well as the skills of a research assistant to the making of this book. After a year assisting me at the Miller Center and a stint teaching in Japan, she generously agreed to come back again in the last throes of this book, and solved the mysteries of formatting.

I have once again a strong institutional debt to the Miller Center of Public Affairs at the University of Virginia. That excellent center provided—as on three previous books—a con-genial place to work, a computer link, a most helpful library connection, stimulating events and surroundings, and gatherings at which my chapters could be discussed. The former director of the Center, Philip Zelikow, gave this particular project his vigorous endorsement, and the new director, former Virginia governor Gerald Baliles, went out of his way to show support as well. The Miller Center staff has been uniformly helpful and encouraging. The former communications director, Margaret Edwards, read chapters, organized a discussion, and continued to support this book after she had left the Center to pursue her own projects. Chief of staff Robin Kuzen, with a picture of Lincoln on her office wall, has been a staunch supporter of this book and of its predecessor, as well as of their author through the years of their production.

The Miller Center draws especially able students. I have been privileged to have the assistance, in successive years, through this two-book Lincoln project, of Ashley McDonald, who was present at the creation; Jason Baker; Jonathan Riehl from the Law School, for two years; Brooke Caroline Greene; and finally and most importantly for this book Alexis Luckey.

Professor Sid Millkis, an expert on presidential greatness, gave advice and criticism of my effort to deal with this greatest of presidents; his colleague Martha Derthick, not only a political scientist but also a discriminating editor, gave me the benefit of close readings of some parts of this book.

Living in Charlottesville has the immense advantage that people you want to see not only visit but sometimes also stay, as in the case of the providential appearance of William Freehling mentioned above. A friend from my youth, Thomas C. Sorensen, after a career in government and foreign affairs and then in investment banking, moved on his retirement from London to Charlottesville, and we had seven years of conversation—including considering what I was going to write about Lincoln—before his death in 1997. William F. May, the eminent religious ethicist, a friend for fifty years, moved on his retirement from Dallas to Charlottesville. I remember Bill May giving a characteristically penetrating critique of my first venture into the Lincoln field, an essay on the Second Inaugural, thirty years ago; we renewed our conversation, and Bill and Beverly May gave essential support to the author in finishing this book.

I wish also to thank the Roasted Bean Coffee Group, meeting every morning on the Charlottesville mall, for their continuous encouragement throughout the writing of this book.

The world of Lincoln studies has been welcoming and accommodating. Since I came into the Lincoln world, two Lincoln organizations have taken me into the official machinery: the Abraham Lincoln Institute, which sponsors the annual Lincoln Symposium at the National Archives in Washington, D.C., and the Lincoln Studies Center at Knox College, whose codirector, Douglas Wilson, gave encouragement once again on this book, as on its predecessor. Through the symposium I met Jennifer Weber, the emerging scholar who had just read *Lincoln's Virtues* and, in the midst of work on her own book on the Copperheads, and of a move to her first academic post, generously read chapters of this book, to its great benefit.

Others who have given some specific incidental help or particular encouragement at some stage of my Lincoln project include Michael Greco, John Sellars, Clifton McCleskey, Joseph Fornieri, Fred Martin, Jr., Gary Gallagher, Merrill Peterson, Doris Kearns Goodwin, Michael Holt, Harold Holzer, Thomas Swartz, Kim Bauer, Linwood Holton, Ed Ayers, Ron Soodalter, Karen Needles, Michael Musick, Thomas P. Lowry. I thank them all, and others who have helped this undertaking as well.

My agent, Henry Dunow, set this book on course. Jane Garrett, my editor at Knopf, supported it from the start and gave it her incisive criticism. Leslie Levine, at Knopf's New York office, was cheerfully helpful in many ways. My greatest debt is indicated by the dedication.

INDEX

Page numbers beginning with 425 refer to endnotes.

473